January 7–10, 2018
Sanibel Island, FL, USA

I0047351

Association for Computing Machinery

Advancing Computing as a Science & Profession

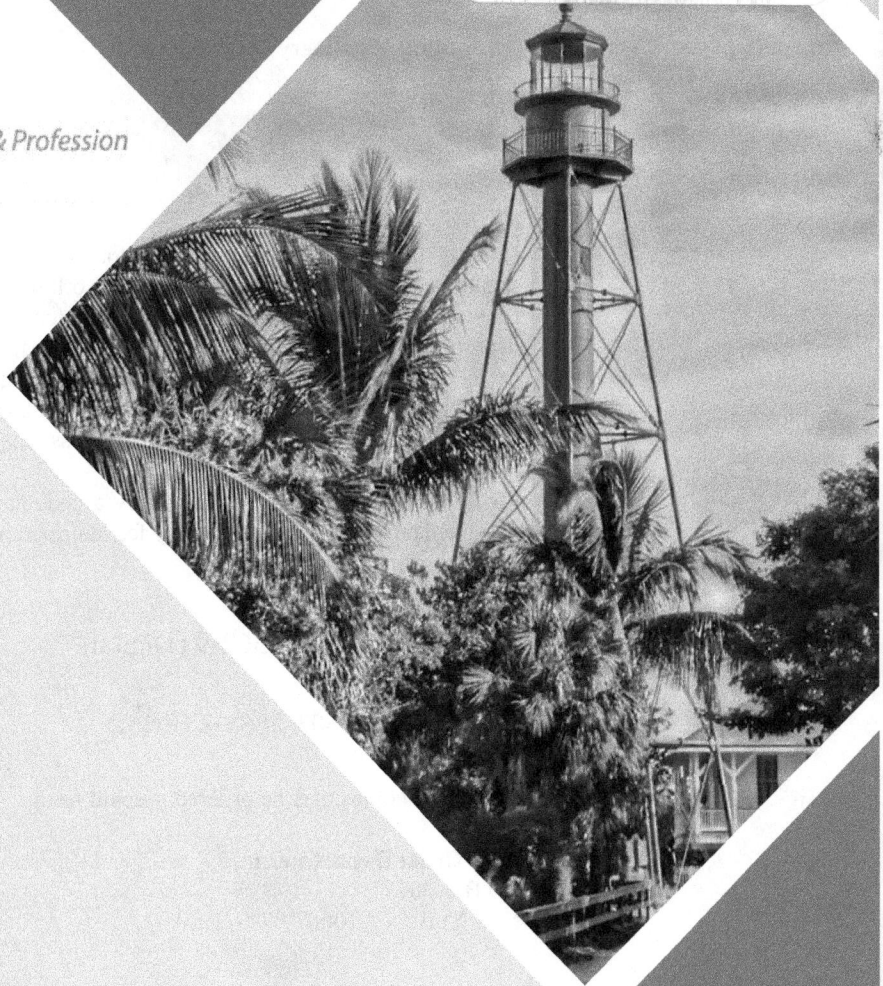

GROUP 2018

Proceedings of the 2018 ACM Conference on
Supporting Groupwork

Sponsored by:
ACM SIGCHI
Supported by:
Microsoft Research & NSF

**Association for
Computing Machinery**

Advancing Computing as a Science & Profession

The Association for Computing Machinery
2 Penn Plaza, Suite 701
New York, New York 10121-0701

ISBN: 978-1-4503-5562-9 (Digital)

ISBN: 978-1-4503-5868-2 (Print)

Additional copies may be ordered prepaid from:

ACM Order Department
PO Box 30777
New York, NY 10087-0777, USA

Phone: 1-800-342-6626 (USA and Canada)
+1-212-626-0500 (Global)
Fax: +1-212-944-1318
E-mail: acmhelp@acm.org
Hours of Operation: 8:30 am – 4:30 pm ET

Welcome from the Chairs

We are excited to welcome back the Group community to Sanibel Island for the 2018 ACM Conference on Supporting Group Work!

2018 marks a memorable anniversary for the Group conference, which evolved from the ACM conference series on Office Information Systems (1982-1990), then Organizational Computing Systems (1991-1995), and finally, the International Conference on Supporting Group Work (1997-present). This year, the community meets for the 20th time to discuss and debate technical, social, and organizational features of collaboration and cooperation. What began with a focus on the office context evolved with the appearance of lower-cost, versatile networked systems to understand how groups work in a variety of contexts and conditions.

Today, the Group conference series is a premier venue for research on Computer-Supported Cooperative Work, Human-Computer Interaction, Computer-Supported Collaborative Learning and Socio-Technical Studies. The conference integrates work in social science, computer science, engineering, design, values, and other diverse topics related to group work, broadly conceptualized. Group 2018 continues the tradition of being truly international and interdisciplinary in both organizational structure as well as participants.

Our diversity is reflected in the broad methodological and topical coverage of submissions to our program of research papers, working papers, design fictions, posters and demos, workshops, and the doctoral colloquium. 22 out of 94 submissions were accepted to the peer-reviewed papers track and Group 2018 also includes presentation of 4 design fictions, 4 working papers, 16 posters, 2 demos, 3 workshops, and 5 works by doctoral colloquium participants. In addition, GROUP 2018 continues with the initiative of providing authors of recent publications in 'The Journal of CSCW' (JCSCW) the opportunity to present their paper to the community; 3 JCSCW papers have been selected this year.

Every year, the Group conference is a collaborative effort among volunteers from around the globe. We thank each of the steering committee, chairs, organizers, reviewers, and submitters, all of whom helped make the 2018 conference an intellectually innovative and community-oriented event where ideas can grow.

General Co-Chairs	*Papers Co-Chairs*
Andrea Forte	**Claudia Müller**
Michael Prilla	**Lionel P. Robert**
Adriana Vivacqua	

Table of Contents

Paper Session: Crowdsourcing and Funding
Session Chair: Yun Huang *(Syracuse University)*

Paper Session: Metadata, Sensemaking and Depersonalization
Session Chair: Aaron Halfaker *(Wikimedia Foundation)*

Paper Session: Peer Production and Co-Creation
Session Chair: Brian McInnis *(Cornell University)*

Keynote Talk
Session Chair: Andrea Forte *(Drexel University)*

Poster Session
Session Chair: Pamela Wisniewski *(University of Central Florida)*

Paper Session: Social Media and Wellbeing
Session Chair: Michael Prilla *(Clausthal University of Technology)*

Paper Session: Digital Media & Policy Engagement

Session Chair: Casey Fiesler *(University of Colorado Boulder)*

Workshop Session

Session Chair: Thomas Ludwig *(University of Siegen)*

Doctoral Consortium

Session Chair: David W. McDonald *(University of Washington)*

Panel Session

Session Chair: Michael Muller *(IBM Research AI)*

Demonstrations

Session Chair: Birgit Krogstie *(NTNU)*

GROUP 2018 Conference Organization

General Chairs:	Andrea Forte *(Drexel University, USA)*
	Michael Prilla *(Clausthal University of Technology, Germany)*
	Adriana Vivacqua *(Universidade Federal do Rio de Janeiro, Brazil)*
Program Chairs:	Claudia Müller *(University of Siegen, Germany)*
	Lionel P. Robert Jr. *(University of Michigan, USA)*
Design Fictions Chairs:	Nora O Murchú *(University of Limerick, Ireland)*
	Bonnie Nardi *(University of California, Irvine, USA)*
Working Papers Chairs:	Lars Rune Christensen *(IT University of Copenhagen, Denmark)*
	Jacki O'Neill *(Microsoft Research India, India)*
Posters Chairs:	Birgit Krogstie *(Norwegian University of Science and Technology, Norway)*
	Pamela Wisniewski *(University of Central Florida, USA)*
Workshops Chairs:	Libby Hemphill *(University of Michigan, USA)*
	Thomas Ludwig *(University of Siegen, Germany)*
Doctoral Consortium Chair:	David McDonald *(University of Washington, USA)*
Student Volunteer Chairs:	Konstantin Aal *(University of Siegen, Germany)*
	Marina Kogan *(University of Colorado Boulder, USA)*
Proceedings Chair:	Aparecido Fabiano Pinatti de Carvalho *(University of Siegen, Germany)*
Local Arrangements Chair:	Sean Goggins *(University of Missouri, USA)*
Publicity Chairs:	Casey Fiesler *(University of Colorado Boulder, USA)*
	Telmo Menezes *(Centre Marc Bloch Berlin, Germany)*
Treasurer & Registration Chair:	Stephen Hayne *(Colorado State University, USA)*
Webmaster:	David Gurzick *(Hood College, USA)*
Steering Committee Chair:	Pernille Bjørn *(University Copenhagen, Denmark)*
Steering Committee:	Mark Ackerman *(University of Michigan, USA)*
	Sean Goggins *(University of Missouri, USA)*
	Tom Gross *(University of Bamberg, Germany)*
	Stephen Hayne *(Colorado State, USA)*
	Kori Inkpen *(Microsoft Research, USA)*
	Wayne Lutters *(UMBC, USA)*
	Michael Müller *(IBM Research, USA)*
	Aleksandra Sarcevic *(Drexel University, USA)*
	Hilda Tellioglu *(TU Wien, Austria)*

Program Committee: Mark Ackerman *(University of Michigan, USA)*
Valerie Bartelt *(University of Denver, USA)*
Pernille Bjorn *(University of Copenhagen, Denmark)*
Jeanette Blomberg *(IBM Almaden Research Center, USA)*
Claus Bossen *(Aarhus University, Denmark)*
Nina Boulus-Rodje *(University of Copenhagen, Denmark)*
Erin Brady *(Indiana University - Purdue University Indianapolis, USA)*
Alissa Centivany *(Western University, USA)*
Yung-Ju (Stanley) Chang *(National Chiao Tung University, Taiwan)*
Yunan Chen *(University of California, Irvine, USA)*
Luigina Ciolfi *(Sheffield Hallam University, UK)*
Gregorio Convertino *(Informatica Corporation, USA)*
Dan Cosley *(Cornell University, USA)*
Tawanna Dillahunt *(University of Michigan, USA)*
Xianghua (Sharon) Ding *(Fudan University, China)*
Gunnar Ellingsen *(UiT - The Arctic University of Norway, Norway)*
Ingrid M Erickson *(Syracuse University, USA)*
Rosta Farzan *(University of Pittsburgh, USA)*
Casey Lynn Fiesler *(University of Colorado, Boulder, USA)*
Laura Forlano *(Illinois Institute of Technology, USA)*
Susan Fussell *(Cornell University, USA)*
Sukeshini Grandhi *(Eastern Connecticut State University, USA)*
Erik Grönvall *(IT University Copenhagen, Denmark)*
Tom Gross *(University of Bamberg, Germany)*
David Gurzick *(Hood College, USA)*
Carl Gutwin *(University of Saskatchewan, Canada)*
Aaron Halfaker *(Wikimedia Foundation, USA)*
Stephen Hayne *(Colorado State University, USA)*
Libby Hemphill *(Illinois Institute of Technology, USA)*
Shuyuan Ho *(Florida State University, USA)*
Yun Huang *(Syracuse University, USA)*
Kori Inkpen *(Microsoft Research, USA)*
Tomoo Inoue *(UTsukuba, Japan)*
Josh Introne *(Michigan State University, USA)*
Michal Jacovi *(IBM Research – Haifa, Israel)*
Nassim Jafarinaimi *(Georgia Institute of Technology, USA)*
Isa Jahnke *(University of Missouri, USA)*
Mohammad Jarrahi *(University of North Carolina, USA)*
Jeremiah Johnson *(Purdue University, USA)*
Michael Koch *(Bundeswehr University Munich, Germany)*
Airi Lampinen *(Mobile Life Center, Sweden)*
Myriam Lewkowicz *(Troyes University of Technology, France)*
Joseph Lindley *(Lancaster University, UK)*
Tun Lu *(Fudan University, China)*

Program Committee (continued):

Alex Wilkie, Goldsmiths *(University of London, UK)*
Susan Winter *(University of Maryland, USA)*
Pamela J. Wisniewski *(University of Central Florida, USA)*
Volker Wulf *(University of Siegen, Germany)*
Naomi Yamashita *(NTT, Japan)*
Xi Jessie Yang *(University of Michigan, USA)*
Sangseok You *(Syracuse University, USA)*

GROUP 2018 Sponsor & Supporters

Sponsor:

Supporters:

Pay-per-Question: Towards Targeted Q&A with Payments

Steve T.K. Jan, Chun Wang
Computer Science
Virginia Tech
Blacksburg, VA, USA, 24060
{tekang, wchun}@vt.edu

Qing Zhang
School of Education
Virginia Tech
Blacksburg, VA, USA, 24060
qingz@vt.edu

Gang Wang
Computer Science
Virginia Tech
Blacksburg, VA, USA, 24060
gangwang@vt.edu

ABSTRACT

Online question and answer (Q&A) services are facing key challenges to motivate domain experts to provide quick and high-quality answers. Recent systems seek to engage real-world experts by allowing them to set a price on their answers. This leads to a "targeted" Q&A model where users to ask questions to a target expert by paying the price. In this paper, we perform a case study on two emerging targeted Q&A systems Fenda (China) and Whale (US) to understand how monetary incentives affect user behavior. By analyzing a large dataset of 220K questions (worth 1 million USD), we find that payments indeed enable quick answers from experts, but also drive certain users to game the system for profits. In addition, this model requires users (experts) to proactively adjust their price to make profits. People who are unwilling to lower their prices are likely to hurt their income and engagement over time.

ACM Classification Keywords

H.5.0 Information Interfaces and Presentation (e.g. HCI): Miscellaneous; J.4 Computer Applications: Social and Behavioral Sciences

Author Keywords

Online Q&A Service; Crowdsourcing; Payments

INTRODUCTION

The success of online question and answer (Q&A) services depends on the active participation of users, particularly domain experts. With highly engaging experts, services like Quora and StackOverflow attract hundreds of millions of visitors worldwide [47]. However, for most Q&A systems, domain experts are answering questions *voluntarily* for free. As the question volume going up, it becomes difficult to draw experts' attention to a particular question, let alone getting answers on-demand [34].

To motivate domain experts, one possible direction is to introduce monetary incentives [10]. Recently, a payment-based Q&A service called *Fenda* [4] is rising quickly in China.

Fenda is a social network app that connects users to well-known domain experts and celebrities to ask questions with payments. Launched in May 2016, Fenda quickly gained 10 million registered users, 500K paid questions, and 2 million US dollar revenue in the first 2 months [44]. The success of Fenda has created a new wave of payment-based Q&A services in China (Zhihu, DeDao, Weibo QA) and the U.S. (Whale, Campfire.fm, Yam).

Fenda focuses on verified, real-world domain experts, which is different from earlier payment-based Q&A services driven by an anonymous crowd (*e.g.*, Google Answers, ChaCha [2, 11, 19]). More specifically, Fenda uses a *targeted model* where users ask questions to a target expert by paying the question fee set by the expert. This model seeks to better engage and motivate experts. In addition, Fenda is the first system that explicitly rewards people for asking good questions. After a question is answered, other users in the network need to pay a small amount ($0.14) to access to the answer. This "listening fee" will be split evenly between the question asker and the answerer (Figure 1). A good question may attract enough listeners to compensate the initial question fee.

In this paper, we seek to understand the effectiveness of the targeted Q&A model and the impact of monetary incentives to the Q&A system. By performing a case study on Fenda and a U.S.-based system Whale [42], we explore the answers to a list of key questions: How does the question price affect the answering speed? What is the potential problematic user behavior caused by the monetary incentives? Whether and how could the pricing behavior predict user income and engagement level? These questions are critical for payment-based Q&A design, and Fenda and Whale provide a unique opportunity to study them.

For our analysis, we collected a large dataset of 88,540 users and 212,082 answers from Fenda (2 months in 2016), and 1,419 users and 9,199 answers from Whale (6 months in 2016–2017), involving over 1 million dollar transactions. Our analysis makes three key findings:

- *First*, using the new incentive model, both Fenda and Whale successfully attract a small group of high-profile experts who make significant contributions to the community. Fenda experts count for 0.5% of the user population, but have contributed a quarter of all answers and nearly half of the revenue.

- *Second*, the incentive model has a mixed impact on user behavior. Monetary incentive enables quick answers (average delay 10–23 hours) and motivates users to ask good questions. However, we find a small number of manipulative users who either aggressively ask questions to make money from listeners, or collude/collaborate to improve their perceived popularity.

- *Third*, we find that different pricing strategies of users (question answerers) can affect their own engagement level. Users who proactively adjust their price are more likely to increase income and engagement level. However, certain celebrities are unwilling to lower their price, which in turn hurts their income and social engagement.

To the best of our knowledge, this is the first empirical study on payment-based, targeted Q&A services. Our study provides practical guidelines for other arising payment-based Q&A services (Zhihu, DeDao, Campfire.fm, Yam) and reveals key implications for future online Q&A system design. We believe this is a first step towards understanding the economy of community-based knowledge sharing.

RELATED WORK

Online Question Answering. In recent years, researchers have studied online Q&A services from various aspects [33]. Early studies have focused on identifying domain experts [26, 8] and routing user questions to the right experts [20, 27, 39]. Other works focused on assessing the quality of existing questions and answers [36, 29, 45, 30, 37, 1, 9, 35] and detecting low quality (or even abusive) content [16]. Finally, researchers also studied Q&A activities in online social networks [25, 7]. As the sizes of Q&A systems rapidly grow, it becomes challenging to engage with experts for timely and high-quality answers [34].

Crowdsourcing vs. Targeted Q&A. As shown in Table 1, most Q&A systems rely on crowdsourcing where any users in the community can answer the question. Fenda and Whale adopt a targeted Q&A model where users can ask questions to a target expert with payments. In this targeted Q&A model, it is the answerer (*e.g.*, the expert) who has the upper hand to set the price for their answers. This differs Fenda and Whale from the earlier crowdsourcing Q&A services (*e.g.*, Google Answers [2], and Mahalo [11]), and the broader crowdsourcing marketplace (*e.g.*, Mechanical Turk) [17]. In those crowdsourcing marketplaces, monetary incentive could affect the work quality and/or the response time [15, 23, 14, 46].

User Motivations in Q&A Services. Prior works have summarized three main user motivations to answer questions online: "intrinsic", "social" and "extrinsic" [13]. Intrinsic motivation refers to the psychic reward (*e.g.*, enjoyment) that users gain through helping others [48, 24]. Social factors refer to the benefits of social interactions, *e.g.*, gaining respect and enhancing reputation. Intrinsic and social factors are critical incentives for non-payment based Q&A services [13]. Extrinsic factors refer to money and virtual rewards (*e.g.*, badges and credit points) [24, 6].

Monetary incentive is an extrinsic factor implemented in payment-based Q&A services such as Google Answers, Mahalo, ChaCha and Jisiklog [2, 11, 19, 18]. These systems

Service	Q&A Model	Fee?	Mobile?	Content
Fenda	Targeted	Y	Y	Text/Audio
Whale	Targeted	Y	Y	Text/Video
Jisiklog	Crowdsource	Y	Y	Text
ChaCha	Crowdsource	Y	Y	Text
Google Answer	Crowdsource	Y	N	Text
Mahalo Answer	Crowdsource	Y	N	Text
Naver Q&A	Crowdsource	N	N	Text
Quora	Crowdsource	N	N	Text
Yahoo Answer	Crowdsource	N	N	Text
StackOverflow	Crowdsource	N	N	Text

Table 1. Fenda/Whale vs. other Q&A services.

(most are defunct) are driven by an anonymous crowd instead of a social network that engages real-world experts. Users are primarily driven by financial incentives without a strong sense of community [19, 10]. This is concerning since research shows monetary incentive plays an important role in getting users started, but it is the social factors that contribute to the persistent participation [28].

Researchers have studied the impact of monetary incentives but the conclusions vary. Some researchers find that monetary incentives improve the answer quality [9] and the response rate [49]. Others suggest that payments merely reduce the response delay but have no significant impact on the answer quality [2, 12, 11]. Studies also show that payment-based Q&A can reduce low-quality questions since users are more selective regarding what to ask [10, 11].

Mobile Q&A. Mobile Q&A services leverage the ubiquitous mobile devices to enable user-friendly Q&A experience [18, 19]. Systems like ChaCha and Jisiklog allow users to interact with an online crowd via text messages. Fenda and Whale are also mobile-only Q&A services (their web interfaces are read-only). The questions in Fenda and Whale are still written in text, but the answers are recorded vide/audio messages.

RESEARCH QUESTIONS AND METHOD

Systems like Fenda and Whale are leading the way to socially engage with real-world experts for question answering. The introduction of monetary incentives makes user interactions even more complex. If not carefully designed, monetary incentives can lead the systems down to the wrong path with users chasing financial profits and losing engagement in the long run. In this paper, we use Fenda as the primary platform to investigate how monetary incentives impact the user behavior and engagement. We include Whale (a younger and smaller system) for comparison and validation purposes.

We choose Fenda and Whale for two main reasons. First, Fenda and Whale represent the first targeted Q&A model with a unique incentive model to motivate both question askers and respondents. Second, the system (Fenda in particular) has received an initial success with a significant volume of data and revenue flow. We aim to understand the reasons behind their success and potential problems moving forward, which will benefit future Q&A system design.

Background of Fenda. Fenda is a payment-based Q&A app in China, which connects users in a Twitter-like social network. Launched in May 2016, Fenda quickly gained 10

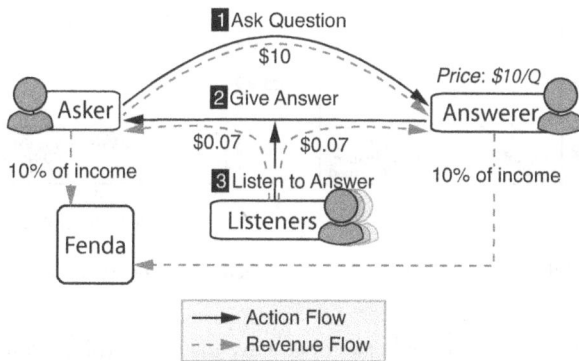

Figure 1. Fenda's Q&A workflow and revenue flow: a user can ask another user a question by making the payment. Any other users who want to listen to the answer need to pay a small amount ($0.14) which will be split evenly between the asker and the answerer. Fenda takes 10% commission fee.

million registered users and over 2 million US dollars' worth of questions answers in the first two months [44].

As shown in Figure 1, Fenda has a unique monetary incentive model to reward both question askers and answerers. A user (asker) can ask another user (answerer) a question by paying the price set by the answerer. The answerer then responds over the phone by recording a 1-minute audio message. If the answerer doesn't respond within 48 hours, the payment will be refunded. Any other user on Fenda can listen to the answer by paying a fixed amount of 1 Chinese Yuan ($0.14), and it will be split evenly between the asker and answerer. A good question may attract enough listeners to compensate the initial cost for the asker. Users set the price for their answers and can change the price anytime. Fenda charges 10% of the money made by a user.

There are two types of users on Fenda: verified real-world experts (*e.g.*, doctors, entrepreneurs, movie stars) and normal users. There is an *expert list* that contains all the experts that have been verified and categorized by the Fenda administrators. Users can browse questions from the social news feed or from the public stream of popular answers (a small sample). To promote user engagement, Fenda selects 2-4 answers daily on the public stream for free-listening for a limited time.

Background of Whale. Whale is a highly similar system launched in the US in September 2016. By analyzing the Whale's app (as of June 2017), we noticed a few differences: First, Whale users record video (instead of audio) as their answers. Second, Whale has free questions and paid questions. For paid questions, Whale takes a higher cut (20%) from the question fee. Third, listeners use the virtual currency "whale coins" to watch the paid answers. Users can receive a few *free coins* from the platform by logging-in each day, or purchase *paid coins* in bulks ($0.29 – $0.32 per coin). Only when a listener uses *paid* coins to unlock a question will the asker and answerer receive the extra payment ($0.099 each).

Our Questions. In the following, we use Fenda and Whale as the platform to analyze how monetary incentives impact

Service	#Questions	#Users	#Askers	#Answerers
Fenda	212,082	88,540	85,510	15,529
Whale	9,199	1,419	1,371	656

Table 2. Summary of Fenda and Whale dataset.

user behavior and their engagement-level. We seek to answer the following key questions.

- First, as an expert-driven Q&A system, to what extent does the system rely on experts to generate content and particularly revenue?

- Second, how does the monetary incentive affect the question answering process? Does money truly enable on-demand answers from experts? Do monetary incentives encourage users to game the system for profits?

- Third, in this targeted Q&A model, how do users set and dynamically adjust the price of their answers? How does the pricing strategy affect their income and engagement-level over time?

DATA COLLECTION

We start by collecting a large dataset from Fenda and Whale through their mobile APIs. Our data collection focused on user profiles, which contained a full list of historical questions answered by the user. Data collect has a few challenges. First, there is no centralized list to crawl all registered users. Second, a user's follower list is not public (only the total number is visible). To these ends, we started our crawling from the expert list. For each expert, we collected their answered questions and the askers of those questions. Then we collected the askers' profiles to get their answered question list and extract new askers. We repeated this process until no new users appeared. In this way, we collected a large set of active users who asked or answered at least one question[1].

We collected data from Fenda in July 2016. The dataset contains 88,540 user profiles and 212,082 question-answer pairs ranging from May 12 to July 27, 2016. Each question is characterized by the asker's userID, question text, a timestamp, question price, and the number of listeners. Each answer is characterized by the answerer's userID, a length of the audio and a timestamp. UserIDs in our dataset have been fully anonymized. We briefly estimated the coverage of the Fenda dataset. Fenda announced that they had 500,000 answers as of June 27, 2016 [44]. Up to the same date, our dataset covers 155,716 answers (about 31%). For Whale, we collected 1,419 user profiles and 9,199 question-answer pairs (1114 paid questions and 8085 free questions) from September 7, 2016 to March 8, 2017. It is difficult to estimate the coverage of the Whale dataset since there is no public statistics about Whale's user base. Table 2 shows a summary of our data.

ENGAGING WITH DOMAIN EXPERTS

We first explore the roles and impact of domain experts in the system. More specifically, we examine the contributions of domain experts to the community in terms of generating content and driving financial revenue.

[1]Our study has received IRB approval: protocol # 16-1143.

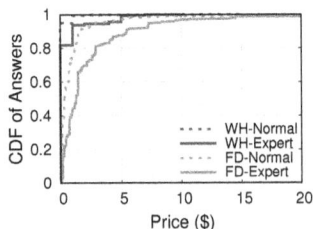

Figure 2. Price of each answer.

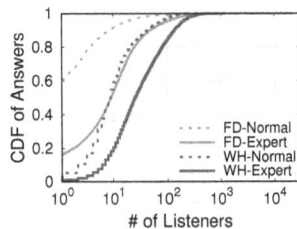

Figure 3. # of Listeners per answer.

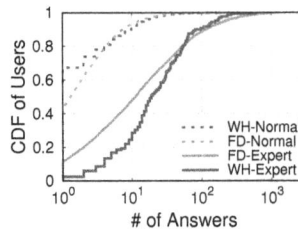

Figure 4. # of Answers per answerer.

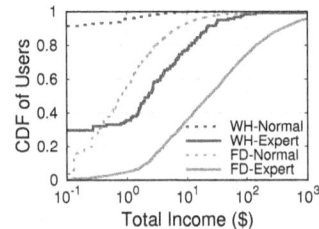

Figure 5. Income per answerer.

Fenda			Whale		
Category	Income	Experts	Category	Income	Experts
Health	$123K	204	Startups	$1.9K	63
Career	$81K	222	Tech	$1.8K	61
Business	$81K	108	Entertain.	$877	2
Relation.	$73K	90	Snapchat	$869	1
Movies	$52K	84	Motorcycle	$869	1
Entertain.	$52K	51	Marketing	$471	20
Academia	$49K	64	Design	$383	15
Media	$45K	138	Travel	$203	18
Real Estate	$43K	28	Fitness	$191	19
Education	$39K	174	Finance	$141	8

Table 3. Top 10 expert categories based on total income.

Fenda maintains a list of verified experts and celebrities. As of the time of data collection, there were 4370 verified experts classified into 44 categories by Fenda administrators. We refer these 4,370 users as *experts* and the rest 84,170 users as *normal users*. Whale has a similar expert list (118 experts), and we refer the rest 1301 Whale users as normal users.

Money. Experts play an important role in driving revenue. In total, the questions in the Fenda dataset were worth $1,169,994[2] Experts' answers generated $1,106,561, counting for a dominating 95% of total revenue in our dataset. To gauge experts' contribution in the context of the entire network, we again performed an estimation: Fenda reached 2 million revenues as of June 27 in 2016 [44]. Up to this same date (June 27), expert answers in our dataset have attracted $909,876, counting for a significant 45% of the 2 million revenue. Figure 2 and Figure 3 show that, on average, experts charge higher ($2.9 vs. $1.0) and draw more listeners (27 vs. 5) than normal users. Individually, experts also make more money than normal users as shown in Figure 5.

On Fenda, a small group of experts (5%) made more than $1000. The highest earning is $33,130 by Sicong Wang, a businessman and the son of a Chinese billionaire. He answered 31 questions related to gossip and investment. He charged $500 for each of his answers, which drew 9484 listeners ($664 extra earning) per answer on average.

On Whale, experts are also the major contributors to the revenue flow. The total collected questions on Whale worth $2,309 and experts contributed to $2,028 (89%). Compared with Fenda (FD), Whale (WH) users earned significantly less money (Figure 5). A possible reason, as shown in Figure 2, is that most users (more than 80%) provide answers for free.

---

[2]We convert Chinese Yuan to US dollar based on $1 = 6.9 Yuan.

Experts of different categories have distinct earning patterns. Table 3 shows the top 10 categories ranked by the total earnings per category. In Fenda, the most popular experts are related to professional consulting. The top category is `health`, followed by `career`, `business`, and `relationship`. In the `health` category, many experts are real-world physicians and pediatricians. They give Fenda users medical advice on various (non-life-threatening) issues such as headache and flu with the expense of several dollars. Other popular categories such as `movies` contain questions to celebrities about gossip. Whale, on the other hand, has fewer experts. The highest earning experts are related to `startups` and `technology`.

Question Answering. The small group of experts have contributed to a significant portion of the answers. Out of the 212K answers in the Fenda dataset, 171K (81%) are from experts. Using this dataset, we can briefly estimate the experts' contribution in the context of the entire network. On June 27 of 2016, Fenda officially announced total 500K answers and 10 million users [44]. Up to the same date, our dataset shows the 4,370 experts (0.44% of the population) have contributed 122K answers (24.4% of total answers). As shown in Figure 4, experts have answered significantly more questions than normal users. Whale (WH) has a similar situation where 118 experts (8% of users) have contributed 4,967 answers (54% of answers).

Engagement. Finally, we quickly examine whether users are more engaged on Fenda and Whale, compared to non-payment based services (*e.g.*, StackOverflow). We use the mean value of the number of answers per day per user as a proxy for engagement (e). On Fenda, the value is 0.51 for experts and 0.006 for normal users. One Whale, the value is 0.23 for experts and 0.02 for normal users. As a comparison, StackOverflow's e value is 0.01 [22]. This indicates that experts are more engaged on Fenda and Whale.

IMPACT OF MONETARY INCENTIVES

So far we show that Fenda and Whale are highly dependent on domain experts' contribution. Then the question is how to motivate experts to deliver timely and high-quality answers. In this section, we perform extensive analysis on the monetary incentive model to understand its impact on user behavior. Noticeably, Fenda and Whale use money to reward both question answerers and askers. Below, we first analyze *answerers* to understand whether payments lead to on-demand responses. Then we focus on *askers* analyzing whether and how users make money by asking the right questions. Finally, we seek

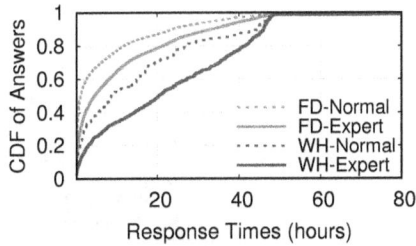

Figure 6. Response time of answers.

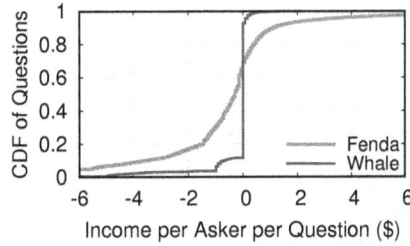

Figure 7. Income of askers per question.

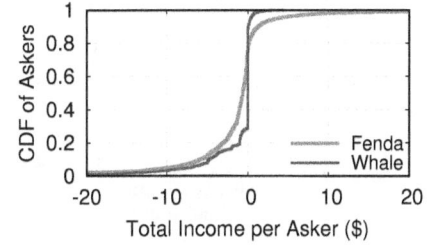

Figure 8. Total income of askers.

Pearson Correlation	Fenda	Whale
# Followers v.s. Answer Price	0.53*	0.30*
Avg. # Listeners v.s. Answer Price	0.65*	0.08*
# Questions Answered v.s. Answer Price	0.04*	0.14*
Avg. Response Time v.s. Answer Price	0.01	-0.07

Table 4. Pearson correlation between a user's answer price and key behavior metrics. * indicates significant correlation with $p < 0.05$.

Service Name	Avg. Resp. Time (hr)	Payment Based?	Crowdsourcing or Targeted?
Yahoo Answers	8.25	N	Crowdsourcing
Fenda	10.4	Y	Targeted
Whale	23.6	Y	Targeted
Google Answers	36.9	Y	Crowdsourcing
Stack Overflow	58.0	N	Crowdsourcing

Table 5. Average response time of the first answer (in hours). We compare Fenda and Whale with different Q&A sites including Yahoo Answers [43], Google Answers [3] and StackOverflow [22].

to identify *abnormal users* who aggressively or strategically game the system for profits.

Answerers

To motivate users (particularly domain experts), both Fenda and Whale allow users to determine the price for their answers. In the following, we investigate how money affects the way users answer questions. Particularly, we examine if monetary incentives truly enable on-demand quick answers.

Setting the Answer Price.   To understand how users set a price for their answers, we calculate the Pearson correlation [32] between a user's price and different behavior metrics. In Table 4, we observe that the price has positive and significant correlations with the number of followers, listeners, and answered questions. A possible explanation is that users with many followers and listeners are real-world celebrities who have the confidence to set a higher price. The higher price may also motivate them to answer more questions. Note that these are correlation results, which do not reflect causality.

Surprisingly, there is no significant correlation between price and response time (for both Fenda and Whale). This is different from existing results on crowdsourcing markets, where an asker can use a higher payment to collect answers more quickly [15, 23, 11].

Answering On-demand?   We further examine the response time to see if monetary incentives truly enable answering questions on-demand. As shown in Figure 6, answers arrive fast on Fenda: 33% of answers arrived within an hour and 85% arrived within a day. Note that there is a clear cut-off

at 48 hours. This is the time when un-answered questions will be refunded, which motivates users to answer questions quickly. After 48 hours, users can still answer those questions for free. We find that only 0.7% of the answers arrived after the deadline, but we cannot estimate how many questions remain unanswered due to the lack of related data. Despite the high price charged by experts, experts respond slower than normal users.

The result for Whale is very similar. Figure 6 shows that for *paid* questions, 50%–70% of answers arrived within a day and normal users respond faster than experts. Comparing to Fenda, Whale has a slightly longer delay possibly because recording a video incurs more overhead than recording a voice message.

We then compare Fenda and Whale with other Q&A systems in Table 5. The response delay in Fenda and Whale is shorter than that of Google Answers and StackOverflow, but longer than that of Yahoo Answers. As payment-based systems, Fenda/Whale beats Google Answers probably because Fenda/Whale only asks for a short audio/video, while Google Answers require lengthy text. Compared to Yahoo Answers, we believe it is the crowdsourcing factor (*i.e.*, a large number of potential answerers) that plays the role. Systems like Yahoo Answers crowdsource questions to a whole community where anyone could deliver the answer. Instead, Fenda/Whale's question is targeted to a single user. The answerer is likely to answer the question within 48 hours in order to get paid, but is not motivated to answer quicker since there is no competition.

Askers

Fenda and Whale implement the first monetary incentive model to reward users for asking good questions. More specifically, once a user's question gets answered, this user (the question asker) can earn a small amount of money from people who want to listen to the answer. This model, if executed as designed, should motivate users to contribute high-quality questions for the community.

Can Askers Make Money?   For each question, the question asker's income is half of listeners' payments, with Fenda's commission fee and initial question fee deducted. As shown in Figure 7, out of all questions, 40% have successfully attracted enough listeners to return a positive profit to the asker. For individual askers, Figure 8 shows 40% of them have a positive total income. This demonstrates a good chance of making profits by asking good questions on Fenda. However, for Whale, the vast majority of askers did not earn money. Part of the reason is most people only ask free questions. More

Behavior	Fenda			Whale		
Metric	Askers $\$>0$	Askers $\$\leq0$	p	Askers $\$>0$	Askers $\$\leq0$	p
Avg. Followers	2155.5	3758.5	*	750.2	790.0	
Avg. Listeners	55.2	16.9	*	28.3	38.1	*
Avg. Price	1.58	4.58	*	0.0	0.3	*
Avg. Questions	3.99	1.86	*	5.4	6.6	

Table 6. Two sample t-test compares the behavior metrics for askers with positive income and those with negative income. * indicates the differences between the two types of askers are significant with $p < 0.05$.

importantly, Whale gives away free coins every day to motivate users to login. If a listener uses free coins (instead of paid coins), the asker will not receive any money.

How Do Askers Make Money?　To understand why certain users make money (and others don't), we compare askers who have positive income with those with negative income in Table 6. Specifically, we examine to whom they ask questions (*i.e.*, the number followers and listeners of the answerer), average question price, and total questions asked. A two-sample t-Test [32] shows the significance of the differences between the two groups of askers.

On Fenda, users of positive income are more likely send questions to people who have more listeners and charge less. The counter-intuitive result is the *number of followers*: asking people with more followers is more likely to lose money. Our explanation is the inherent correlation between a user's number of followers and her answer price — famous people would charge higher and the money from listeners cannot cover the initial cost. Askers with a higher income often asked more questions. Again, correlation does not reflect causality: it is possible that the positive income motivates users to ask more questions, or people who asked more questions get more experienced in earning money.

It is hard to interpret the Whale results in Table 6 since only a very small of fraction of askers have a positive income (Figure 8). Noticeably, askers with positive income exclusively ask free questions (average price = 0).

Abnormal Users

Next, we examine suspicious users in the Q&A system who seek to game the system for financial profits.

Bounty Hunters.　For certain users, financial gain is the primary reason to participate in payment based Q&A systems as shown in prior works [19, 11]. On Fenda and Whale, users can make a profit not only by answering questions, but also by asking good questions. Below, we analyze askers who aggressively ask questions to gain profits (referred as "bounty hunters").

To identify potential bounty hunters in Fenda, we examine outliers in Figure 9, which is a scatter plot for the number of questions a user asked versus the ratio of questions to experts. We find clear outliers at the right side (*e.g.*, users with >100 questions). They asked way more questions than average, and exclusively interact with experts (ratio of expert questions is close to 1). The most extreme example is a user who asked more than 1300 questions in two months, with 95% of ques-

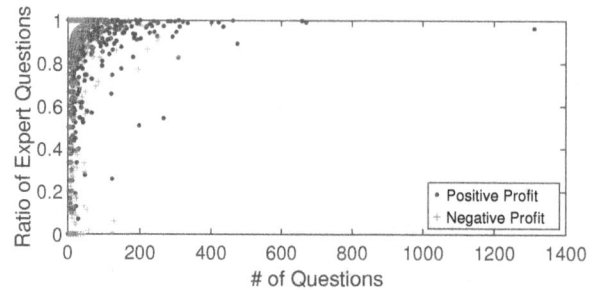

Figure 9. Total # of questions of each asker vs. the ratio of questions to experts in Fenda. Blue dots (red crosses) represent askers with positive (negative) total income.

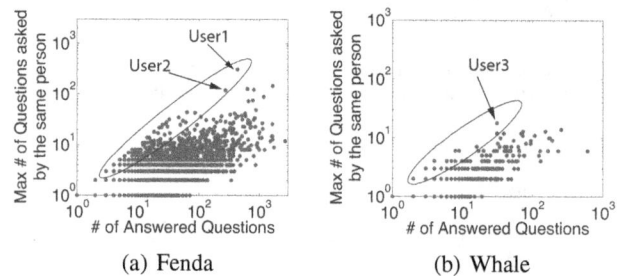

(a) Fenda　　　　　　(b) Whale

Figure 10. Total # of questions of each answerer vs. Maximum # of questions asked by the same person. Dots in the circled area are likely the collusive users.

tions to experts. This user earned \$194.20, which is much higher than the average income of askers (-\$1.95).

To further examine these outliers, we select askers who asked more than 100 questions. This gives us 111 users who count for 0.13% of askers but aggressively asked 11% of the questions. These users carefully target experts who charge a lower price (\$0.80 per answer) but still draw significant listeners (15.5 per answer). The rest of the experts on average charge \$2.49 and draw 23.0 listeners per answer.

We performed the same analysis on Whale and did not find such outlier users because most askers did not make a positive profit (Figure 8).

Collusive/Collaborative Users.　In addition, there are some users who work collaboratively together to make money. For example, an asker can collude with an answerer by asking many questions (with an extremely low price) to create the illusion that the answerer is very popular. Then both the asker and the answerer can make money from the listeners of these questions. This is similar to "Sybil attacks" where multiple fake accounts are controlled by the same attacker to manipulate a social network system [40].

To identify collaborative users, we focus on answerers whose questions are primarily asked by the same user. Figure 10 shows a scatter plot for the number of questions a user answered versus the maximum number of these questions asked by the same person. Users that are close to the diagonal are suspicious. For example, *user1* answered 435 questions and 309 (71%) were asked by the same asker. We notice that this asker did not ask any other users any questions. The questions between these two users charge $0.16 each, which is much lower than *user1*'s other questions ($0.25 on average). By using a lower price for collusion, the two users can minimize their loss — the 10% commission fee to Fenda. In this way, *user1* earned $689.9 in total and this asker also earned $244 from the listeners. The second example *user2* follows the same pattern.

Figure 10(b) shows the result of Whale. The example user (user3) answered 31 questions, 18 of which were from the same asker. This asker only asked these 18 questions and all 18 questions were free of charge. This is likely an attempt to boost user3's popularity.

Discussion. Our analysis shows that monetary incentives did foster questionable behavior. On the positive side, these users (bounty hunters or collaborative users) are actually working hard to come up with interesting questions in order to earn money from listeners. On the negative side, such behavior has a disruptive impact on the marketplace. For example, bounty hunters are injecting a large volume of questions to experts. The large volume of questions would act as spam to experts, blocking other users' chance to get the experts' attention. The collusive/collaborative behavior creates a fake perception of popularity, which could mislead listeners to making the wrong spending and make it unfair for honest experts.

DYNAMIC PRICING AND USER ENGAGEMENT
Fenda and Whale allow users to set the price for their answers. How users set this price may affect their financial income and their interaction with other users. In this section, we turn to the *dynamic* aspect to analyze how users adjust their answer prices over time and how different pricing strategies affect their engagement level. Understanding this question is critical since keeping users (particularly experts) engaged is the key to building a sustainable Q&A service.

In the following, we first identify common pricing strategies by applying unsupervised clustering on users' traces of price change. Then we analyze the identified clusters to understand what type of users they represent, and how their engagement-level changes over time.

Identifying Distinct Pricing Strategies
To characterize users' dynamic price change, we construct a list of features to group users with similar patterns.

Key Features.   For each user, we model their price change as a sequence of events. Given user i, our dataset contains the complete list of her answers and the price for each answer. We use P_i to denote user i's price sequence $P_i = [p_{i,1}, p_{i,2}, ..., p_{i,N_i}]$ where N_i is the total number of answers of user i. A price change event happens when $p_{i,j-1} \neq p_{i,j}$ for any $j \in [2, N_i]$. We denote the price change sequence as $C_i = [c_{i,1}, c_{i,2}, ... c_{i,M_i}]$ where M_i is a number of times for price change and $c_{i,j}$ is a price change event (price-up, price-down, or same-price).

Table 7 list our 9 features: the overall frequency of price change (*i.e.*, $\frac{M_i}{N_i}$), a frequency for price-up and price-down, and the frequency difference between price-up and down. In addition, we consider the average price change magnitude

id	Feature Name	Feature Description
1	Price Change Freq.	# of price change / # answers
2	Price Up Freq.	# price up / # answers
3	Price Down Freq.	# price down / # answers
4	Price Up - Down	(# price up - # price down) / # answers
5	Price Up Magnitude	Average percentage of price increase
6	Price Down Magnitude	Average percentage of price decrease
7	Consecut. Same Price	Max # consecutive same price / # answers
8	Consecut, Price Up	Max # consecutive price up / # answers
9	Consecut. Price Down	Max # consecutive price down / # answers

Table 7. A list of features for price change dynamics.

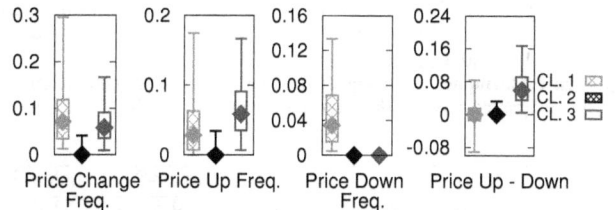

Figure 11. The distribution of top 4 features for the 3 clusters in Fenda. We depict each distribution with box plot quantiles (5%, 25%, 50%, 75%, 95%).

for price-up and price-down events. Finally, we consider the maximum number of consecutive events of same-price, price-up and price-down in the sequence.

User Clustering.   Based on these features, we then cluster similar users into groups. First, we compute the pair-wise Euclidean distance between users based on their feature vectors. This produces a fully connected similarity graph [41] where each node is a user and edges are weighted by distance. Then, we apply hierarchical clustering algorithm [5] to detect groups of users with similar price change patterns. We choose hierarchical clustering for two reasons: 1) It does not pre-define the number of clusters. 2) It is deterministic and the clustering result does not depend on the initial seeding.

To determine the number of clusters, we use *modularity*, a well-known metric to measure clustering quality [5]. High modularity means users are more densely connected within each cluster than to the rest of the users. We choose the number of clusters that yields the highest modularity.

Data.   For this analysis, we only consider users who have answered enough questions. Otherwise, discussing their dynamic price change would be less meaningful. We heuristically set the threshold as 10 (we have tested 5 questions and the conclusion is consistent). On Fenda, this filtering produces 2094 users who have answered 171,322 questions (85% of all questions). On Whale, however, only 68 users meet the criteria. The following clustering analysis will focus on Fenda. The results of Whale are omitted due to the small number of qualified users.

Clustering Results
Our method produces 3 clusters for Fenda (modularity 0.59). To understand the pricing strategy of each cluster, we plot their feature value distributions in Figure 11. Due to space limitation, we plot 4 (out of 9) most distinguishing features that have the largest variance among the 3 clusters selected by Chi-Squared statistic [32].

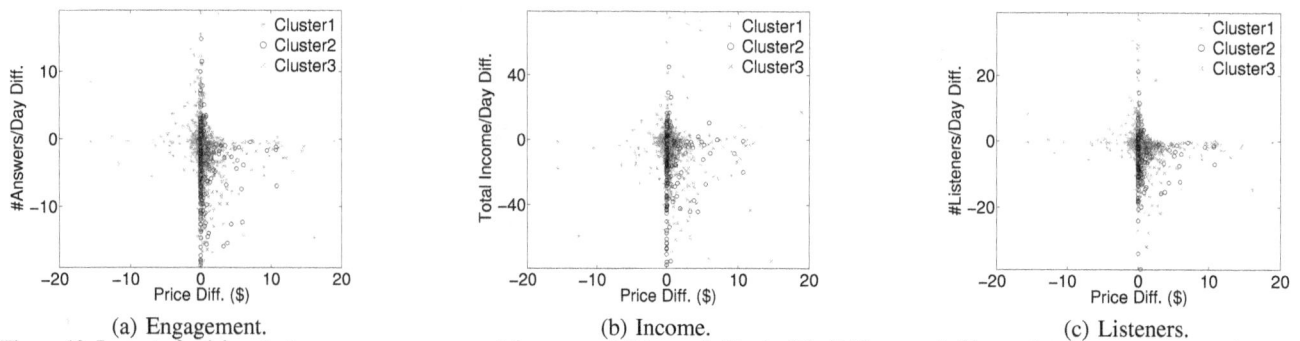

(a) Engagement.   (b) Income.   (c) Listeners.

Figure 12. Impact of pricing strategy on user engagement, income, and listeners in Fenda. We divide a user's lifespan into two even parts, and compute the difference between the later half and the first half. A positive value indicates an upward trend.

Metrics	Cluster-1	Cluster-2	Cluster-3
Avg. #Followers	627.6	749.5	951.4
Avg. #Listeners	16.6	27.0	25.9
Avg. Price ($)	1.7	2.4	2.6
Avg. #Questions	106.5	68.8	71.4

Table 8. User statistics of the identified clusters.

- **Cluster-1 (33%):** *Frequent price up and down.* 687 users (76% are experts) who have a high price change frequency. Price up and down are almost equally frequent.

- **Cluster-2 (43%):** *Rarely changing price.* 908 users (76% are experts) who rarely change their price.

- **Cluster-3 (24%):** *Frequent price up.* 499 users (74% are experts) who increase price frequently but rarely lower their price.

We find that the 3 types of pricing patterns on Fenda correspond to users of different popularity. As shown in Table 8, cluster 1 represents the least popular answerers, who have the least followers and listeners but answered more questions. These users constantly adjust their price (primarily dropping the price), possibly to test the market. Cluster 3 represents the most popular experts and celebrities. They charge higher than others and keep increasing the price. Cluster 2 stands between cluster 1 and 3 in terms of popularity, and its users rarely change the price. The results indicate that popular users on Fenda have the luxury to keep increasing the price while less popular users need to carefully adjust the price to survive in the market.

Impact on User Engagement

Next, we analyze how price adjustments affect a user's engagement level over time. Price is a key parameter within users' control, and adjusting price is a way to test their answers' value in the market.

Figure 12(a) shows the interplay between price change and engagement level over time for 3 identified clusters on Fenda. We quantify engagement-level using number of answers per day. To measure changes over time, we divide a user's lifespan (time between her first and last answer in our dataset) into two even parts. Then we compute the differences for average price and engagement-level between the later half and first

half. In a similar way, we also measure the changes in income (Figure 12(b)) and listeners (Figure 12(c)), which represent the strength of monetary and social incentives

We observe different patterns: for cluster 2 and 3, more users are located in the lower right corner than upper right, indicating a decrease of engagement, income and number of listeners. A possible explanation is that there is a mismatch between the answer's price and its value, but users did not make the right adjustments. In contrast, we find a significant number of users in cluster 1 located in the upper left corner. By lowering their price, these users get to answer more questions, and receive more money and listeners over time. We validate the statistical significance of the results by calculating the Pearson correlation [32] between the price change (x) and behavior metrics (y) for all three clusters in Figure 12. We find 8/9 of the correlations are significant ($p < 0.05$) except for cluster1's income/day metric.

Our result suggests that users need to set their price carefully to match their market value. This requires proactive price adjustments and lowering their price when necessary. Right now, highly popular users on Fenda (*e.g.*, cluster 3) are less motivated or unwilling to lower their price, which in turn hurts their income and engagement level over time.

DISCUSSION

Next, we discuss the key implications of our results to future Q&A system design.

Answering On Demand. Fenda and Whale adopt a targeted Q&A model where experts set a price for their answer. This model is suitable for targeted questions (users know who to ask), but can have a longer delay compared to crowdsourcing (where anyone can be a potential answerer). Fenda and Whale achieve faster responses than most Q&A services, but are still not as fast as the crowdsourcing based Yahoo Answers. Recently, Fenda added a new crowdsourcing channel for "medical" and "legal" questions. This channel is customer-driven: users post their questions with a cash reward, and any experts can give their answers to compete for the reward. We did a quick crawling on the crowdsourcing channel and obtained 1344 questions. We find their average response time is 4.38 hours, which is even faster than the 8.25 hours of Yahoo Answers.

Rewarding Good Questions. Fenda and Whale are the first systems that reward users financially for asking good questions. This leads to a mixed effect. On the positive side, users are motivated to ask good questions that attract broad interests. 40% of the questions on Fenda received enough listeners to cover the asker's cost. On the negative side, this model motivates a small number of users to game the system for profits. We find "bounty hunters" who aggressively ask questions to low-priced experts, and collaborative/collusive users who work together to manipulate their perceived popularity. Manipulators mainly introduce unfairness, but they still need to come up with good questions to attract listeners.

Bootstrapping for New Users. In this targeted Q&A model, a well-known expert has the key advantage to receive questions. As a result, the top 5% answerers get about 90% of the total profits in Fenda. For new comers or less known users, they receive much fewer questions. To help users to bootstrap popularity, Fenda recently introduced a system update, which allows users to set their answers "free-for-listening" for 30 minutes after posting. Whale also recently (on June 26, 2017) opened up all the questions and answers for free to encourage user participation.

Q&A Communication Channels. Fenda and Whale allow users to directly record their answers in audio/video, to avoid the inconvenience of typing text on the phone. In the context of education and communication, audio and video are also more effective than text to enhance the social bounding between communicators [21, 31], which seem to be the natural choices for mobile Q&A systems. To make online Q&A even more interactive, another possible direction is to use live streaming channel such as Periscope and Facebook Live [38]. The common challenge for audio and video communication is that answerers need to react to the questions on the fly, which makes it difficult for them to give longer and more in-depth answers. Future research can examine the proper communication channels (text, audio, video) for different Q&A contexts.

Fenda vs. Whale. Finally, we want to briefly discuss the differences between Fenda and Whale. Although these two sites are similar by design, Fenda's has been more successful so far with a significantly larger user base and more content. Other than cultural differences (China vs. U.S.), one possible factor is Fenda has been taking advantage of China's largest social network WeChat. First, users can directly signup in Fenda using their WeChat accounts, which helps users to directly locate their friends. Second, Fenda's payment is made by "WeChat pay", a mobile payment service already integrated with WeChat account. The social network effect may have helped Fenda to quickly gain a wide adoption. A similar effect has been observed in Periscope, which has successfully bootstrapped through Twitter [38].

LIMITATIONS

Our study has a few limitations. First, our study only focuses on two services: Fenda and Whale. A broader comparison with other payment-based Q&A services can help to further generalize our results. Second, our dataset is not perfect. The crawler produces a dataset with a complete list of experts but an incomplete list of normal users. We argue that most of the missing users are likely lurkers (or inactive users) who are less influential in the community. We also used Fenda's official numbers to justify parts of our results. Third, much of our analysis is based on correlation analysis, which is a simple and powerful tool to examine the interplay of different factors in a given system. However, correlation analysis has limitations to capture more complex system dynamics (*e.g.*, revealing causality). Future work will consider using tools such as time series analysis to study the causal relationship.

CONCLUSION

In this paper, we discuss lessons learned from the first targeted, payment-based Q&A systems. By analyzing a large empirical dataset, we reveal the benefits of applying monetary incentives to Q&A systems (fast response, high-quality questions) as well as potential concerns (bounty hunters and over time engagement). As more payment-based Q&A systems arise (Campfire.fm, DeDao, Zhihu Live), our research results can help system designers to make more informed design choices.

ACKNOWLEDGMENTS

The authors want to thank the anonymous reviewers for their helpful comments. This work is supported by NSF grant CNS-1717028. Any opinions, findings, and conclusions or recommendations expressed in this material are those of the authors and do not necessarily reflect the views of any funding agencies.

REFERENCES

1. Lada A Adamic, Jun Zhang, Eytan Bakshy, and Mark S Ackerman. 2008. Knowledge sharing and yahoo answers: everyone knows something. In *Proc. of WWW*.

2. Yan Chen, Tech-Hua Ho, and Yong-Mi Kim. 2010. Knowledge market design: A field experiment at Google Answers. *Journal of Public Economic Theory* 12, 4 (2010), 641–664.

3. Benjamin Edelman. 2011. Earnings And Ratings At Google Answers. *Economic Inquiry* 50, 2 (2011), 309–320.

4. Fenda. 2017. (2017). `http://fd.zaih.com/fenda`.

5. Santo Fortunato. 2010. Community detection in graphs. *Physics Reports* 486 (2010), 75 – 174.

6. Scott Grant and Buddy Betts. 2013. Encouraging user behaviour with achievements: an empirical study. In *Proc. of MSR*.

7. Rebecca Gray, Nicole B. Ellison, Jessica Vitak, and Cliff Lampe. 2013. Who Wants to Know?: Question-asking and Answering Practices Among Facebook Users. In *Proc. of CSCW*.

8. Benjamin V. Hanrahan, Gregorio Convertino, and Les Nelson. 2012. Modeling Problem Difficulty and Expertise in Stackoverflow. In *Proc. of CSCW*.

9. F Maxwell Harper, Daphne Raban, Sheizaf Rafaeli, and Joseph A Konstan. 2008. Predictors of answer quality in online Q&A sites. In *Proc. of CHI*.

10. Gary Hsieh and Scott Counts. 2009. mimir: A market-based real-time question and answer service. In *Proc. of CHI*.

11. Gary Hsieh, Robert E Kraut, and Scott E Hudson. 2010. Why pay?: exploring how financial incentives are used for question & answer. In *Proc. of CHI*.

12. Grace YoungJoo Jeon, Yong-Mi Kim, and Yan Chen. 2010. Re-examining price as a predictor of answer quality in an online Q&A site. In *Proc. of CHI*.

13. Xiao-Ling Jin, Zhongyun Zhou, Matthew KO Lee, and Christy MK Cheung. 2013. Why users keep answering questions in online question answering communities: A theoretical and empirical investigation. *IJIM* 33, 1 (2013), 93–104.

14. Manas Joglekar, Hector Garcia-Molina, and Aditya G. Parameswaran. 2013. Evaluating the Crowd with Confidence. In *Proc. of SIGKDD*.

15. Aikaterini Katmada, Anna Satsiou, and Ioannis Kompatsiaris. 2016. Incentive mechanisms for crowdsourcing platforms. In *Proc. of INSCI*.

16. Imrul Kayes, Nicolas Kourtellis, Daniele Quercia, Adriana Iamnitchi, and Francesco Bonchi. 2015. The Social World of Content Abusers in Community Question Answering. In *Proc. of WWW*.

17. Aniket Kittur, H. Chi, and Bongwon Suh. 2008. Crowdsourcing user studies with Mechanical Turk. In *Proc. of CHI*.

18. Uichin Lee, Hyanghong Kang, Eunhee Yi, Mun Yi, and Jussi Kantola. 2012. Understanding mobile Q&A usage: an exploratory study. In *Proc. of CHI*.

19. Uichin Lee, Jihyoung Kim, Eunhee Yi, Juyup Sung, and Mario Gerla. 2013. Analyzing crowd workers in mobile pay-for-answer q&a. In *Proc. of CHI*.

20. Baichuan Li and Irwin King. 2010. Routing questions to appropriate answerers in community question answering services. In *Proc. of CIKM*.

21. Tom Lunt and John Curran. 2010. Are you listening please? The advantages of electronic audio feedback compared to written feedback. *Assessment & Evaluation in Higher Education* 35, 7 (2010), 759–769.

22. Lena Mamykina, Bella Manoim, Manas Mittal, George Hripcsak, and Björn Hartmann. 2011. Design lessons from the fastest Q&A site in the west. In *Proc. of CHI*.

23. Winter Mason and Duncan J Watts. 2010. Financial incentives and the performance of crowds. *ACM SigKDD Explorations Newsletter* 11, 2 (2010), 100–108.

24. Kevin Kyung Nam, Mark S Ackerman, and Lada A Adamic. 2009. Questions in, knowledge in?: a study of naver's question answering community. In *Proc. of CHI*.

25. Jeffrey Nichols, Michelle Zhou, Huahai Yang, Jeon-Hyung Kang, and Xiao Hua Sun. 2013. Analyzing the Quality of Information Solicited from Targeted Strangers on Social Media. In *Proc. of CSCW*.

26. Aditya Pal, Shuo Chang, and Joseph A. Konstan. 2012. Evolution of Experts in Question Answering Communities. In *Proc. of ICWSM*.

27. Aditya Pal, Fei Wang, Michelle X. Zhou, Jeffrey Nichols, and Barton A. Smith. 2013. Question routing to user communities. In *Proc. of CIKM*.

28. Daphne Ruth Raban. 2008. The incentive structure in an online information market. *Journal of the American Society for Information Science and Technology* 59, 14 (2008), 2284–2295.

29. Sujith Ravi, Bo Pang, Vibhor Rastogi, and Ravi Kumar. 2014. Great Question! Question Quality in Community Q&A. In *Proc. of ICWSM*.

30. Chirag Shah and Jefferey Pomerantz. 2010. Evaluating and predicting answer quality in community QA. In *Proc. of SIGIR*.

31. Lauren E. Sherman, Minas Michikyan, and Patricia M. Greenfield. 2013. The effects of text, audio, video, and in-person communication on bonding between friends. *Cyberpsychology* 7, 2 (2013).

32. David J. Sheskin. 2007. *Handbook of Parametric and Nonparametric Statistical Procedures*.

33. Ivan Srba and Maria Bielikova. 2016a. A Comprehensive Survey and Classification of Approaches for Community Question Answering. *ACM TWeb* 10, 3 (2016), 18:1–18:63.

34. I. Srba and M. Bielikova. 2016b. Why is Stack Overflow Failing? Preserving Sustainability in Community Question Answering. *IEEE Software* 33, 4 (2016), 80–89.

35. Qi Su, Dmitry Pavlov, Jyh-Herng Chow, and Wendell C. Baker. 2007. Internet-scale Collection of Human-reviewed Data. In *Proc. of WWW*.

36. Yla Tausczik, Ping Wang, and Joohee Choi. 2017. Which Size Matters? Effects of Crowd Size on Solution Quality in Big Data Q&A Communities. In *Proc. of ICWSM*.

37. Qiongjie Tian, Peng Zhang, and Baoxin Li. 2013. Towards Predicting the Best Answers in Community-based Question-Answering Services. In *Proc. of ICWSM*.

38. Bolun Wang, Xinyi Zhang, Gang Wang, Haitao Zheng, and Ben Y. Zhao. 2016b. Anatomy of a Personalized Livestreaming System. In *Proc. of IMC*.

39. Gang Wang, Konark Gill, Manish Mohanlal, Haitao Zheng, and Ben Y. Zhao. 2013a. Wisdom in the Social Crowd: an Analysis of Quora. In *Proc. of WWW*.

40. Gang Wang, Tristan Konolige, Christo Wilson, Xiao Wang, Haitao Zheng, and Ben Y. Zhao. 2013b. You are How You Click: Clickstream Analysis for Sybil Detection. In *Proc. of USENIX Security*.

41. Gang Wang, Xinyi Zhang, Shiliang Tang, Haitao Zheng, and Ben Y. Zhao. 2016a. Unsupervised Clickstream Clustering For User Behavior Analysis. In *Proc. of CHI*.

42. Whale. 2016. (2016). `https://techcrunch.com/2016/10/31/justin-kan-launches-video-qa-app-whale/`.

43. Dan Wu and Daqing He. 2014. Comparing IPL2 and Yahoo! Answers: A Case Study of Digital Reference and Community Based Question Answering. In *Proc. of IConf*.

44. Li Xuanmin. 2016. Putting a price on knowledge. `http://www.globaltimes.cn/content/997510.shtml`. (August 2016).

45. Yuan Yao, Hanghang Tong, Feng Xu, and Jian Lu. 2014. Predicting Long-term Impact of CQA Posts: A Comprehensive Viewpoint. In *Proc. of KDD*.

46. Teng Ye, Sangseok You, and Lionel P. Robert. 2017. When Does More Money Work? Examining the Role of Perceived Fairness in Pay on the Performance Quality of Crowdworkers. In *Proc. of ICWSM*.

47. Ken Yeung. 2016. Quora now has 100 million monthly visitors, up from 80 million in January. VentureBeat. (March 2016).

48. Jie Yu, Zhenhui Jiang, and Hock Chuan Chan. 2007. Knowledge Contribution in Problem Solving Virtual Communities: The Mediating Role of Individual Motivations. In *Proc. of SIGMIS CPR*.

49. Haiyi Zhu, Sauvik Das, Yiqun Cao, Shuang Yu, Aniket Kittur, and Robert Kraut. 2016. A Market in Your Social Network: The Effects of Extrinsic Rewards on Friendsourcing and Relationships. In *Proc. of CHI*.

Enabling Uneven Task Difficulty in Micro-Task Crowdsourcing

Yu Jiang, Yuling Sun, Jing Yang, Xin Lin, Liang He

Department of Computer Science and Technology
East China Normal University
Shanghai 200062, China

Shanghai Key Laboratory of Multidimensional
Information Processing
East China Normal University
Shanghai 200241,China

yjiang@ica.stc.sh.cn; {ylsun, jyang, xlin, lhe}@cs.ecnu.edu.cn

ABSTRACT

In micro-task crowdsourcing markets such as Amazon's Mechanical Turk, how to obtain high quality result without exceeding the limited budgets is one main challenge. The existing theory and practice of crowdsourcing suggests that *uneven task difficulty* plays a crucial role to task quality. Yet, it lacks a clear identifying method to task difficulty, which hinders effective and efficient execution of micro-task crowdsourcing. This paper explores the notion of *task difficulty* and its influence to crowdsourcing, and presents a difficulty-based crowdsourcing method to optimize the crowdsourcing process. We firstly identify task difficulty feature based on a local estimation method in the real crowdsourcing context, followed by proposing an optimization method to improve the accuracy of results, while reducing the overall cost. We conduct a series of experimental studies to evaluate our method, which show that our difficulty-based crowdsourcing method can accurately identify the task difficulty feature, improve the quality of task performance and reduce the cost significantly, and thus demonstrate the effectiveness of task difficulty as task modeling property.

Author Keywords

Micro tasks; crowdsourcing; task feature; task difficulty; assignment; context; quality; budget.

ACM Classification Keywords

H.5.m. Information interfaces and presentation (e.g., HCI): Miscellaneous.

INTRODUCTION

In CSCW and related fields, crowdsourcing provides a scalable and efficient way to outsource large volumes of relatively simple jobs, like image labelling, object recognition, video tagging, text translation, etc. [1, 14, 32,

33], to an "undefined, generally large group of people in the form of an open call" [7]. Many general-purpose crowdsourcing markets are created, e.g. AMT, CrowdFlower, Freelancer, Ali Crowdsourcing, etc. Such "micro-task" markets typically involve users to self-select and complete short HITs (Human Intelligence Tasks, which need short time, ranging from a few seconds to a few minutes, to finish) for monetary gain or just for fun [15]. Despite the successes and the perceived promise of these markets [15, 18, 29], however, would-be employers face a serious practical challenge: they need *efficient budget allocation* with *accuracy guarantees* (the payment for one task is very cheap – usually less than 10 cents, but the huge amounts of tasks dramatically increase the cost).

Given this challenge, the literatures have provided rich evidences and explanations to the significant influence of *uneven task difficulty* to task quality and various difficulty-based task assignment methods are proposed [5, 11, 23, 31]. As Shaw *et al.* point out, the crowd result mainly depends on the task difficulty [26]. For the more efficient mechanism of micro-task crowdsourcing, it is crucial to better understand the influence of task difficulty to the effectiveness and accuracy of crowdsourcing work. Meanwhile, a more human-centered perspective, *i.e.*, taking the uneven human factors (*e.g.* worker situation [8, 22], location [12, 16], reliability [21] etc.) as a kind of uneven task difficulty factor, is also proposed for a better collaborative crowdsourcing.

Despite the growing understanding and attention of *task difficulty*, however, most existing methods are based on the known or computable task difficulty factors. Yet, due to the open-calling form of crowdsourcing, task difficulty in crowdsourcing is a kind of context-sensitive characteristic [2, 10, 13, 16, 17, 21, 25, 34, 36], *i.e.*, not only task itself, but also context and human factors, such as unpredictable workers [34], workers' educational background [36], reliability [21], etc., as well as crowdsourcing platform [25] and interaction mechanism [2, 10], shape the task difficulty together. As Tamilin *et al.* and Whitehill *et al.* insightfully put it, context is an essential element in crowdsourcing system [30], which affects the level of difficulty [35]. Hence, it is almost impossible to identify the specific task difficulty in advance, which challenges most existing methods. Currently, little pay sufficient and explicit attention to explore how to identify and quantify this *uneven task difficulty*, especially in the real crowdsourcing context, which becomes to be one crucial challenge in micro task markets (**Challenge 1**).

Moreover, for the purpose of accuracy guarantees, a usual method is assigning multiple workers to one task in order to reduce uncertainty, as a single answer might be unreliable. Then, much research attention has gone into investigating how to aggregate the answers [9, 27, 28, 35]. This dominant approach, however, has been increasingly attacked as suffering an obvious higher cost [22], and unavailability sometimes for increasing task accuracy [23]. How to find an efficient trade-off between the cost and result accuracy is another significant challenge in micro-task markets (**Challenge 2**).

The study we present in this paper aims at addressing these challenges from a more practical insight. Our goal is to improve the crowdsourcing efficiency by enabling the uneven task difficulty. For challenge 1, our first research question follows:

RQ1: how to identify and quantify task difficulty in the real crowdsourcing context?

After identifying task difficulty, an effective task assignment is needed for challenge 2. Here, we express the second research questions as the following two sub-questions:

RQ2-1: how to assign micro tasks based on task difficulty?

RQ2-2: how to find an efficient trade-off between the cost of task allocation and the accuracy of the result?

Our Contributions
For these research questions, we present *Crowdsourcing Based on task Difficulty feature (CBD)*, a technological solution for collaborative micro-task crowdsourcing. More specifically, compared to previous works, our method focuses on the role of *uneven task difficulty* – the difficulty for the users to correctly execute the tasks under the real crowdsourcing context, and formalizes it based on the specific context. Because of this, *CBD* can be applied to various micro-task crowdsourcing processes without limits to platforms and task types in practical contexts. To the best of our knowledge, this is the first attempt to link task difficult with context. Our main contributions are as follows.

Firstly, instead of an assumed scenario with known task difficulty in advance, we propose a *local estimation method* to identify and formalize the value of task difficulty in the real crowdsourcing context. We firstly divide task set based on the intrinsic features and select the appropriate samples based on a *Minimum Coverage Algorithm (MC)*. We then crowd them in the real crowdsourcing context for obtaining an approximate but effective and real task difficulty value. The feature that divides task set with the largest

differentiation of difficulty is identified as the most effective task difficulty feature.

Secondly, based on task difficulty, we propose a difficulty-based optimization for task assignment, which can achieve an efficient trade-off between the cost and result accuracy. We group the overall tasks into several subgroups based on the identified difficulty feature, and consider different assignment strategies for subgroups with different level of difficulty, *i.e.*, assigning a little few crowds to the subgroups with very low or high difficulty value for a lower cost, due to the less obvious improvement even by more crowds, and assigning a little more crowds to the subgroups with difficulty value in a relatively moderate range for a higher quality. Based on these strategies, we get the optimal assignment for each subgroup.

Thirdly, during the crowdsourcing process, we propose a *Half-Majority Voting method (HMV)* to automatically optimize the budget, *i.e.*, we stop the crowdsourcing process for one task if more than half workers provide the same answers. Because in such a case, more workers cannot change the result any more, but generate higher cost.

Finally, we evaluate the effectiveness and applicability of our method through crowdsourcing three different datasets in both experimental environment and real crowdsourcing platform. Experimental results show that our *CBD* method achieves a significant improvement in crowdsourcing performance in both theory and practical. Specifically, 1) our method can identify the most effective task difficulty feature in the real crowdsourcing context; 2) we achieve an optimal assignment, which improves the result accuracy under the limit budget; 3) the dynamically budget optimizing process can further reduce the actual cost under guaranteeing task quality. Interestingly, 4) our method break the limitation of crowd size in generic majority vote method based on uniform assignment strategy, which makes it more widely applicable to different crowdsourcing context.

RELATED WORK
Micro-task crowdsourcing markets are becoming more and more popular for both academic and commercial use. The current approaches of improving task quality mainly focus on how to assign tasks (e.g. [4, 6, 31]), and how to aggregate answers into the higher quality one [9, 27, 28, 35].

While different algorithms and perspectives are explored, these researches share a similarity – instead of the equal attitude to tasks and workers, they all draw more attentions to the uneven features, including uneven human factors [2, 10, 13, 16, 17, 21, 25, 34, 36], uneven task features [5, 23, 31], etc., and their influences to crowdsourcing. Chen et al., for example, investigate budget assignment strategy based on the age of workers [4]. Similarly, Li et al. put forward the weighted majority voting method based on the reliability of workers [19]. These works illustrate the important of uneven features in crowdsourcing. As Kazai *et al.* and Shaw *et al.* put it, it is necessary to better understand the task difficulty and use them to support better crowdsourcing [17, 26].

In spite of high attentions to these uneven properties in crowdsourcing, existing approaches have faced plenty of challenges in both theory and practice. On the one hand, many of them do not work very well in achieving the effective trade-off between task qualities and cost, *i.e.*, many pay attention to one of them and neglect another one [23, 31]. For instance, many assign more workers to one task for increasing task accuracy, which follows the higher cost and unavailability sometimes [22, 23, 35]. Ipeirotis *et al.* propose a method for evaluating worker quality that simultaneously measured the difficulty of individual tasks with all the labels provide by worker [9]. [35] describes an approach for estimating task difficulty but without considering the overall payment of crowdsourcing. On the other hand, while many studies explore different uneven features during crowdsourcing, they face a general challenge – feasibility. That is, their approaches usually based on the known or computable uneven factors [3, 8, 12, 13, 16, 21, 31], e.g., the known task difficulty level [31], known human factors [13, 16], or computable human ability [3, 9]. It is, however, almost impossible to get a known task difficulty in practical context in advance due to the context-sensitive characteristic, which challenges most existing methods.

Relevant of our work is CrowdBudget [31], which allocates different number of workers for each task under a limit budget, with considering the known difficulty level of task. However, they do not provide an effective method to identify the task difficulty. Similarly, Mozafari et al. consider grouping the tasks based on features and assign different number of workers to each task but without consideration of the overall cost of crowd [23]. An effective method of identifying the uneven task difficulty based on the real crowdsourcing context and a difficulty-based task assignment for the crowdsourcing is necessary.

UNEVEN TASK DIFFICULTY
In this section, we will introduce what is *uneven task difficulty*, and how to define and identify it. For the better understanding, we use a case study to explain our method. We take crowdsourcing image annotation tasks as a typical scenario, and randomly select 624 images from CMU Facial Expression (the same task set with [23]) with three features – *person*, *pose* and *eyes*. We crowd these tasks to 275 workers for emotion labeling (9 workers for each) and calculate the accuracy of each task. Table 1 shows the results. From this case study, we draw the following findings.

a) There is an underlying *uneven task difficulty* for every task. Table 1-left shows the results of 5 images, with the accuracy ranging from 0 (all false) to 1 (all correct) (Acc is the accuracy). The different accuracies indicate that these tasks are different in difficulty for users' executing.

b) The task difficulty is shaped not just by task itself, but also the crowdsourcing context. It is effective only in the real context. Inspired by Mozafari et al.'s work [23], we group the whole tasks into different subgroups based on three features – *person* (with Glickman, choon, kk49 etc.), *pose* (with Left, Straight, Right and up) and *eyes* (with Open and Sun), and conduct a statistical analysis to the accuracy of different subgroups. Table 1-right shows the result of subgroups based on *person* and *pose*. While we conduct the same study based on the same database with Mozafari et al.'s work, we can see obvious difference between our studies (see the content marked with gray in table 1). The different crowdsourcing context between our studies – might be workers' language skill, or platform, shapes the different results. Moreover, it, apparently, is impossible to identify every factors of affecting task difficulty in advance.

c) Similar to Mozafari et al.'s work, we also support that assigning tasks to different numbers of crowd based on different subgroups would be effective to optimize results. While Mozafari et al.'s work uses a random feature to group and assign the tasks, our result show that there is an obvious difference in average accuracy among different feature-based grouping methods (see table 1-right which comparing the results of *person*-based grouping and *pose*-based grouping, A_Acc is the average of accuracy). This difference in accuracy can be explained that, the subgroups in *person*-based grouping have more levels of difficulty, which leads to more different accuracy (ranging from 0.31 to 0.73). Therefore, if we can identify the most differentiated grouping methods (here is *person*-based), get these different difficulty levels of subgroups, and assign the crowdsourcing process based on difficulty, it will be more effective to improve result accuracy and reduce the cost.

Based on these findings, we reconsider our key research questions and propose the following definitions.

Definition 1. *Task difficulty feature* Θ_t is defined as one of the inherent features in task set T, which generates the most differentiated subgroups in task difficulty in the real crowdsourcing context and influences the accuracy of crowdsourcing work most (*person* in this case). For solving **RQ1**, we need to identify this most influential feature Θ_t. And we can use some clustering methods as group feature when the task set T is lack of feature.

1 – happy Acc: 0	2 – angry Acc: 0.333	3 – sad Acc: 0.556	4 – neutral Acc: 0.778	5 – happy Acc: 1

person	A_Acc	pose	Acc_[23]	A_Acc
glickman	0.73	*Left*	0.63	0.50
choon	0.60	*Straight*	0.62	0.49
kk49	0.36	*Right*	0.60	0.49
karyadi	0.31	*up*	0.48	0.38

Table 1 Labelling result of 5 images from CMU Facial Expression (left) and different subgroups (right)

Definition 2. *Crowdsourcing budget B and actual cost B^*.* For T, consisting of N tasks, we employ V workers to execute one task with the pay of A per each (the total budget of one task is $V * A$), then budget B can be calculated as $B = N * V * A$ (N and A are both constants). In generic crowdsourcing strategy, each task is assigned the same number v_0 of users to execute, and the actual cost B^* equals to B.

Definition 3. *The error rate Ω.* For a task set T, Ω is the ratio of the number of error tasks to N. The traditional methods usually reduce Ω through increasing the worker number v_0 of each task, which results a rapid increase of B [34]. Consequently, for **RQ2**, we need to explore how to optimize v_0 based on task difficulty feature Θ_t, and generate an efficient trade-off between the crowdsourcing cost (the less overall actual cost B^* compared to budget B), and the accuracy of the result (the minimum error rate Ω).

CROWDSOURCING BASED ON TASK DIFFICULTY FEATURE (CBD)

Overview of our method

To solve these two research questions, a *Crowdsourcing method Based on task Difficulty* (*CBD*) is proposed, which consists of two main steps. Compared to the generic uniform assignment strategy, which crowds the tasks evenly to n workers (figure 1-i), our *CBD* method (figure 1-ii) will firstly group and select the appropriate samples. We then crowd them to the real crowdsourcing context to identify the effective difficulty feature (figure 1-ii-left, how to find difficulty). Secondly, we group the whole tasks and optimize the assignment process based on the difficulty feature (figure 1-ii-right, how to use difficulty). In our study, for ease of presentation, we choose the binary task classification (task with two options) to describe our method. But our method can apply to arbitrary classifiers (with different formulas to quantify the accuracy). Moreover, we assume that workers are independent of each other and not malicious (*i.e.* they do not provide wrong answers on purpose). Because each micro-task can be completed in short time, our approach also does not consider the the parallel issue [20]. In the next two sessions, we will introduce our *CBD* method in details.

Measuring and Identifying Task Difficulty Feature (RQ-1)

Due to context-sensitive characteristic of crowdsourcing, it is hard to calculate task difficulty value in advance. Hence, our method identifies task difficulty feature Θ_t by using a local optimal estimation method in real crowdsourcing context to ensure the availability. The process of identifying task difficulty feature are a) grouping task set T into different subgroups based on intrinsic features, b) selecting the appropriate samples based on a minimum cover algorithm, and c) identifying the task difficulty feature Θ_t with the maximum differentiation. The details are as follows.

a) Grouping Task Set

For task set T with n features $\{\Theta_1, \Theta_2, ..., \Theta_n\}$, we group T into several subgroups by *these* features. Each feature Θ_i divides the T into m_i subgroups G_{Θ_i} (if the intrinsic task features support grouping enough). $G_{\Theta_i} = \left\{g_{\Theta_i}^1, g_{\Theta_i}^2, ..., g_{\Theta_i}^{m_i}\right\}$ states the whole subgroups of task set T divided by feature Θ_i. $n_{\Theta_i}^l$ is the task number of each subgroup $g_{\Theta_i}^l$, and $N_{\Theta_i} = \left\{n_{\Theta_i}^1, n_{\Theta_i}^2, ..., n_{\Theta_i}^{m_i}\right\}$ for all the subgroups. For task set T consisting of N tasks, for each $\Theta_i, \sum_{l=1}^{m_i} n_{\Theta_i}^l = N$. If the intrinsic feature is very few, or cannot support the effective grouping, we will normalize the feature value via the common 0-1 or z-score standardized methods firstly, and then employ unsupervised clustering algorithms, like K-means or DBSCAN, to group the task set T.

b) Selecting the Appropriate Samples Based on a Minimum Coverage Algorithm

After grouping task set T, we select the appropriate samples from each subgroup, and use the local estimating method to identify the task difficulty feature. Assuming task set T has n grouping methods based on features $\{\Theta_1, \Theta_2, ..., \Theta_n\}$ and the group set is $G_{Set} = \left\{G_{\Theta_1}, G_{\Theta_2}, ..., G_{\Theta_n}\right\}$. Each G_{Θ_i} includes m_i subgroups, and $m_{cnt} = \{m_1, m_2, ..., m_n\}$. We need to randomly select K tasks as samples, which cover all subgroups in G_{Set} and include not less than k_0 tasks in each subgroup (k_0 is the minimum amount of samples for ensuring the estimating accuracy). In general, the amount K could be quantified as $\sum_{l=1}^n m_l * k_0$. For instance, there are two grouping methods G_1 and G_2 in one task set (red line and blue line respectively in figure 1-iii), with $m_1 = 3$ and $m_2 = 2$. While $k_0 = 2$, $K = (3 + 2) * 2 = 10$ in theory.

The process of executing samples, however, also consume the budget. So, the *appropriate* samples should be as small as possible, while cover all subgroups simultaneously. Considering one task might belong to several subgroups, as the red rectangles labelled in figure 1-iii belong to both G_1 and G_2, and also cover all subgroups, a coverage approach based on greedy algorithm is employed to select the appropriate samples with $min(K)$, which considers the tasks within more subgroups as the first choice of samples. Then, the amount K reduces to 6. We symbolize the error rate of sample tasks as Ω', which can be calculated as the ratio of the number of error sample tasks to the sample size K, and the cost of executing samples as B'.

c) Identifying Task Difficulty Feature

In this process, we calculate the accuracy of each sample in subgroup $g_{\Theta_i}^l$ and the difficulty differentiation of G_{Θ_i}. Then, the feature Θ_i with the maximum differentiation is approximately identified as task difficulty feature Θ_t.

We firstly calculate the accuracy of sample j in subgroup $g_{\Theta_i}^l$, noted as acc_j, $acc_j = N_{right}/N$, in which N_{right} is the

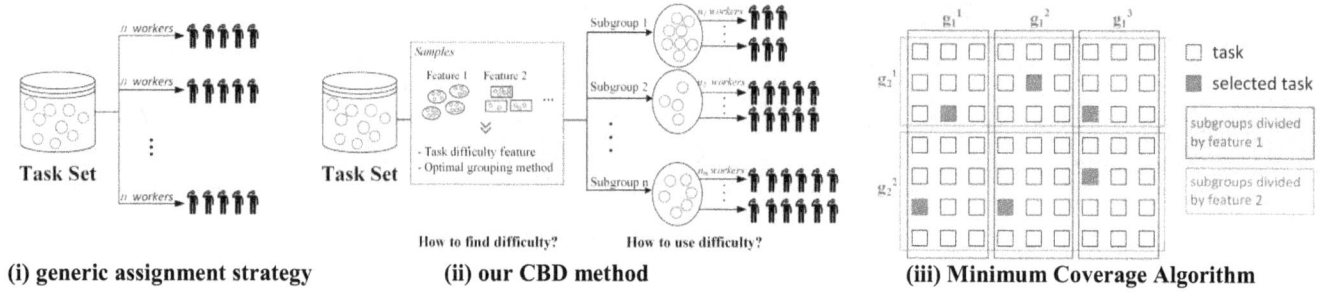

(i) generic assignment strategy   (ii) our CBD method   (iii) Minimum Coverage Algorithm

Figure 1   Our methods

size of workers who provide correct answers, and N is the size of overall workers who execute the sample j. Then, we use formula (1) to calculate the average probability that one task in subgroup $g_{\Theta_i}^l$ is executed correctly, where $n'^l_{\Theta_i}$ is the size of samples for subgroup $g_{\Theta_i}^l$, and $\sum_{l=1}^{m_i} n'^l_{\Theta_i} = K$. This average probability is used to represent the difficulty value of the subgroup $g_{\Theta_i}^l$,

$$p_{g_{\Theta_i}^l} = \sum_{j=1}^{n'^l_{\Theta_i}} acc_j / n'^l_{\Theta_i} \tag{1}$$

We then use formula (2), a weighted variance method, to calculate the differentiation α of different grouping G_{Θ_i}.

$$\alpha = \frac{\sum_{l=1}^{m_i}(x_l - \bar{x})^2 \cdot n^{*l}_{\Theta_i}}{\sum_{l=1}^{m_i} n^{*l}_{\Theta_i}} \tag{2}$$

Here, $n^{*l}_{\Theta_i} = n^l_{\Theta_i} - n'^l_{\Theta_i}$ is the remaining task numbers of subgroup $g_{\Theta_i}^l$, x_l is equal to $p_{g_{\Theta_i}^l}$, and $\bar{x} = \sum_{l=1}^{m_i} x_l \cdot n^{*l}_{\Theta_i} / \sum_{l=1}^{m_i} n^{*l}_{\Theta_i}$. We select the task feature Θ_i with $\max(\alpha)$ as the local optimal approximate value of task difficulty feature Θ_t, and G_{Θ_t} as the optimal grouping.

After identifying task difficulty feature Θ_t and optimal grouping G_{Θ_t}, we propose a method to optimize the task assignment strategy for solving RQ2 as follows.

Task Assignment Based on Difficulty Feature (RQ2-1)
Based on different difficulty levels, we propose the following three assignment principles.

-   For subgroups with low difficulty level (e.g. it includes many pictures like pic5 in Table 1), $p_{g_{\Theta_t}^l}$ will be very high. What more workers leads to might not be the higher accuracy, but higher cost. So we assign relatively small amounts of workers to execute.

-   Similarly, for subgroups with high difficulty level (e.g. it includes many pictures like pic1 in Table 1), $p_{g_{\Theta_t}^l}$ will be very low. In this case, we also assign relatively small amounts of workers for the lower cost.

-   For subgroups with difficulty level in a relatively moderate range, we will assign more workers for the higher accuracy based on assignment strategy provided by *CBD* method.

Due to the binary task classification, the probability $p_{g_{\Theta_t}^l}$ — one task in subgroup $g_{\Theta_t}^l$ is executed correctly, is consistent with Bernoulli distribution. When we assign n workers for one task, the probability P of this task be executed correctly, follows binomial distribution $L \sim b(x, n, p)$, where x is the correct times among n workers, $b(x, n, p) = C_n^x p^x (1 - p)^{n-x}$ and $C_n^x = n!/(x! (n - x)!)$. Then, we have formula (3) to calculate the probability that one task in subgroup $g_{\Theta_t}^m$ is executed correctly by v crowds.

$$P_{g_{\Theta_t}^l}^v = \sum_{r=0}^{(v-1)/2} C_v^r \cdot p_{g_{\Theta_t}^l}^{v-r} (1 - p_{g_{\Theta_t}^l})^r \tag{3}$$

Where v is the worker amount of each task, $p_{g_{\Theta_t}^l}$ is the estimating probability based on the samples that one task in subgroup $g_{\Theta_t}^l$ can be executed correctly (calculated by formula (1)). Formula (3) also verifies our proposed assignment principles, that the more crowds to the task with very high or very low difficulty cannot greatly improve the probability that this task is executed correctly. For example, when $p_{g_{\Theta_t}^l} < 0.5$, $P_{g_{\Theta_t}^l}^v$ will decrease with increasing of v.

With the purpose of getting the optimal assignment strategy for high accuracy of results, we formalize the error rate firstly and employ integer linear program to optimize the assignment process by minimizing the error rate. We have formula (4) to calculate estimating error rate $\Omega^*(B)$ of remaining tasks in T, and formula (5) to calculate the error rate Ω of task set T under limit budget B.

$$\Omega^*(B) = \frac{\sum_{g \in G_{\Theta_t}} \sum_{v=1}^{v^{max}} x_{gv}(1 - P_g^v) \cdot n_g}{\sum_{g \in G_{\Theta_t}} n_g} \tag{4}$$

$$\Omega(B) = \frac{\Omega'(B) * K + \Omega^*(B) * (N - K)}{N} \tag{5}$$

Here, the N, K and $\Omega'(B)$ are constants. For minimizing error rate $\Omega(B)$ under limit budget B, we determine a set of $V_{\Theta_t} = \{v_{g_{\Theta_t}^1}, v_{g_{\Theta_t}^2}, ..., v_{g_{\Theta_t}^m}\}$ with the following constraints:

$$\forall g \in G_{\Theta_t}, \sum_{v=1}^{v^{max}} x_{gv} = 1 \tag{6}$$

$$\sum_{g \in G_{\Theta_t}} \sum_{v=1}^{v^{max}} x_{gv} \cdot v \cdot n_g \cdot A \leq B - B' \tag{7}$$

In which, the value of binary indicator x_{gv} is 1 if the task in subgroup g are assigned to v workers to execute, v^{max} is the max worker number for one task, A is the payment for one execution, and n_g is the remaining task amount of subgroup g, $\sum_{g \in G_{\Theta_t}} n_g = N - K$. K is the number of samples. B is the overall budget, and B' is the cost of executing the samples.

We use integer linear program to calculate x_{gv} and get the optimal assignment strategy $V_{\Theta_t} = \{v_{g_{\Theta_t}^1}, v_{g_{\Theta_t}^2}, ..., v_{g_{\Theta_t}^{m_t}}\}$ for the task grouping $G_{\Theta_t} = \left\{g_{\Theta_t}^1, g_{\Theta_t}^2, ..., g_{\Theta_t}^{m_t}\right\}$ based on task difficulty feature Θ_t, and the budget after optimization can be calculated as $B_o = \sum_{g \in G_{\Theta_t}} v_g * n_g * A + B'$.

Optimizing Budget Based on Difficulty Feature (RQ2-2)
During the crowdsourcing process, we use majority voting to aggregate answers, and choose the result selected by more than half of v crowds as the best result of one task. That is to say, for a task, which is assigned to v workers, if there is a result selected by $\lceil v/2 \rceil$ workers, we can identify this result as the best result. In this case, more workers cannot change the result any more, but generate higher cost until all v workers finish the task. So, considering the requirement of lower actual cost B^*, we propose a *Half-Majority Voting method (HMV)*, that is, when an alternative result is selected by $\lceil v/2 \rceil$ workers, we will stop this task immediately. The actual worker numbers of this task $v_{HM} \geq \lceil v/2 \rceil$ (table 2) and the actual overall cost is $B^* = \sum v_{HM} \cdot A + B'$.

Name	W1	W2	W3	W4	W5	Result	HMV
Task1(v=5)	1	1	1	\	\	1	3
Task2(v=5)	0	0	1	0	\	0	4
Task3(v=5)	0	1	1	0	0	0	5
Task4(v=3)	1	1	\			1	2

Table 2 Examples of HM method

* Task 1(V=5) states assigning 5 workers for task 1 based on the above-mentioned assignment method, Wn states different workers. Result states the best result of one task, and HMV states the final worker number based on our HMV method.

So shown in Table 2, for task1 and task2, the optimal scheme based on the above-mentioned method is $v = 5$. During the executing process, however, 3 workers for task 1 and 4 workers for task 2 have already generated the best result. Similarly, for task 4, comparing to the optimal scheme ($v = 3$), *HMV* method can reduce the worker number to 2, which further leads to the decrease of overall cost without reducing the crowd accuracy.

EVALUATION AND EXPERIMENTAL STUDY
During the experiments, we involve a large population of workers to accomplish these micro-tasks in both laboratory context and the real online (non-lab) crowdsourcing context and compare our method with uniform assignment strategy (UMV). Considering the uncontrollable and uncertainty of crowdsourcing, we repeat each experiment 5 times and use the average data as reported results.

Experimental Setup and Task Set
Image annotation and sentiment analysis are two representative tasks in micro task markets. They are difficult for computers, but crowdsourcing makes it easy to recruit a crowd of people to perform. In our experiments, we select these two classical tasks to evaluate the effectiveness of our *CBD* method in real micro-task crowdsourcing markets. We choose three different task sets for better verifying the universality, versatility, and effectiveness of our method, with the following details.

CMU Facial Expression Dataset[1]. This dataset consists of 640 black and white face images of people taking with varying *pose* (straight, left, right, and up), *expression* (neutral, happy, sad, and angry), *eyes* (open and sun), and *person* (20 different people). We randomly select 310 images from this dataset, and crowd them for facial expressions with *happy* (1) and *angry* (0).

Twitter Dataset. This dataset is from an online corpus[2], which consists of millions of tweets with extra information about publishing date and publisher. It provides truth labels for tweets with equal numbers of positive- and negative-sentiment. In our experiments, we randomly select 996 English tweets from this online corpus, and identify four features, including *"word number"*, *"punt number"*, *"publish date"* and *"publisher"*. We crowd them for sentiment analysis with *positive* (1) and *negative* (0).

Weibo dataset. This dataset is the testing data from COAE 2014 (Chinese Opinion Analysis Evaluation) competition[3], which consists of 4688 Chinese Weibo texts. It also provides truth labels for Weibos with equal numbers of positive- and negative-sentiment. In our experiments, we select all 4688 Weibos and count *"word number"* and *"punt number"* as the intrinsic features. We crowd them for sentiment analysis with *positive* (1) and *negative* (0).

Overview of the Results
Overall, comparing with UMV, our *CBD* method works better in both laboratory environment and the real (non-lab) environment. It identifies task difficulty feature, improves task accuracy and reduces the cost effectively. Specifically, (i) our experiments prove that the difficulty feature of crowdsourcing micro tasks is context-sensitive, and is hard to identify the specific value of difficulty in advance, which challenges the effectiveness of these proposed algorithms. Comparing with them, our method identifies the task difficulty feature and estimate the difficulty value in real crowdsourcing context, which improve its feasibility and accuracy. (ii) Our difficulty-based assignment method is proved effective in finding a trade-off between the overall cost and the accuracy of results. The experimental results show that, comparing with the generic UMV algorithm, our method can improve task accuracy effectively under limit

---

[1] http://kdd.ics.uci.edu/databases/faces/faces.data.html

[2] http://twittersentiment.appspot.com/

[3] http://www.liip.cn/ccir2014/index.html

cost. (iii) Comparing with [23], we add the dynamically optimizing process based on the proposed difficulty-based assignment, which further reduces the cost under guaranteeing the task accuracy. The experimental results prove this point. And (iv) surprisingly, while the generic uniform assignment strategy has been widely challenged due to its limitation to crowd size, our experimental results prove that our method breaks this limitation effectively, and is more widely applicable to different crowdsourcing context. In the next sections, we will describe the experimental studies we conducted and the results in details.

Study 1: Crowdsourcing CMU Dataset in Laboratory Environment

We firstly evaluate the effectiveness of our method through an experiment in the lab. We randomly select 310 tasks from CMU dataset, invite 10 independent and not malicious participants from our school with different professional background to collaboratively label the facial expression of 310 pictures with *HAPPY* (1) and *ANGARY* (0).

Step 1. According to our method, we firstly group these pictures into different subgroups based on three inherent features – *pose* with 4 subgroups, *eyes* with 2 subgroups, and *person* with 20 subgroups.

Step 2. For identifying the difficulty feature Θ_t, we then select the appropriate K samples based on the proposed minimum coverage algorithm and crowd them to estimate Θ_t. K tasks need cover all 26 subgroups and include not less than k_0 tasks in each subgroup.

As for k_0, comparing with [23, 24], which randomly select $k_0 = 2$ as the sample size of each subgroup, in our study, for more accuracy and academic rigor, we conduct an extra work to analysis the influence of sample size k_0 to crowdsourcing results. We randomly select 600 labelling tasks from Weibo dataset, and group them into 3 subgroups based on *"punt number"* feature. We crowd these tasks to 5 workers and get the overall accuracy value of each subgroup, with accuracy of 0.73, 0.86, 0.93 respectively.

We then randomly select samples with the various sample size k_0 ranging from 1 to 40, and repeats 10 times per each k_0 to calculate the variance and average of accuracy. Figure 2-i shows the result of variance, in which X-axis is the sample size (k_0) and Y-axis is the accuracy variance of 10 randomized trials. Figure 2-ii shows the accuracy average results of 10 randomized trials, while the horizontal line states the overall accuracy value of each subgroup.

From figure 2, we can find that, when sample size $k_0 >= 5$, the accuracy of samples is tending towards stability as the variance of 10 randomized trials is no less than 0.02. And the value also tends to the accuracy value in overall subgroups as the difference between them is less than 0.1. Similar results appear in several other datasets. So, we suggest 5 is the minimum value of k_0.

Hence, considering the size of CMU dataset, we set $k_0 = 5$ as the minimum task amount in each subgroup, and the sample size K is 100

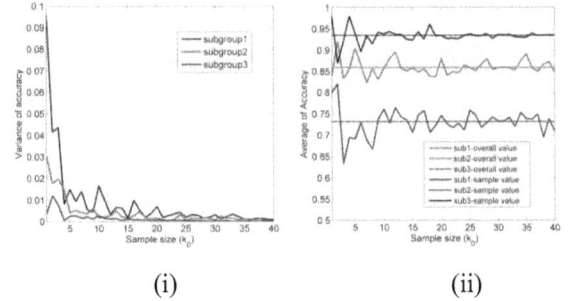

(i)　　　　　　(ii)

Figure 2 The results of 10 randomized trials (2-i is the accuracy variance of 10 randomized trials, and 2-ii is the average accuracy of each subgroup)

Step 3. We then crowd these 100 sample tasks to uniform $v_0 = 3$ participants. We have formula (1) to calculate average probability $p_{g_{\Theta_i}^m}$ that one task in subgroup $g_{\Theta_t}^l$ is correctly executed, as well as formula (2) to calculate the differentiation α of three grouping methods, with the result of α(person)=0.0237, α(pose)=0.0055 and α(eyes)=0.0003. The "*person*" feature has max(α). We identify it as the task difficulty feature Θ_t, and the grouping G_{person} is the optimal grouping in CMU dataset.

Step 4. For the remaining 210 tasks, we then group them into 20 subgroups based on the difficulty features – "*Person*", and use our *CBD* method to calculate the optimal assignment of each subgroup. Note that the overall budget B is linearly dependent with the overall execution times. Therefore, to better understand, we use the uniform assignment crowd number v based on generic UMV to state the overall budget B in the next experiment description. And the x-axis in following figures states the normalized budget. The maximum number of workers for each subgroup is $v_{max} =9$. Table 4 shows part of the results of our optimal assignment (CBD) for each subgroup ($v = 4$), with a distinct difference comparing with UMV.

Subgroup	UMV	CBD	Subgroup	UMV	CBD
an2i	4	3	*kawamura*	4	1
at33	4	5	*kk49*	4	7
boland	4	1	*megak*	4	7
glickman	4	1	*sz24*	4	3
karyadi	4	7	*tammo*	4	7

Table 4 Task assignments based on different methods

Figure 3 shows the comparison results from the accuracy and cost respectively between UMV and our method. Particularly, if there are an equal number of votes for both options of one task, we believe the task get the wrong result. We conduct the evaluation process in both theory and practical. Due to the uncontrollability and uncertainty of crowdsourcing, there is a little difference between the theoretical and practical results (see figure 3-i), but the overall trend is consistent and a noticeable improvement of our method, including improving the task accuracy and reducing the real payment, can be seen in both cases. Specifically, while UMV method is widely challenged by the bad results when the crowd number is even (which also be seen in our experimental results), our method effectively breaks this limit. Figure 3-ii prove the effectiveness of our method in reducing the real cost. In general, our *CBD* method increases the accuracy by up to 10.9% (when budget is 2) and reduces the real payment ranging from 14% (when budget is 2) to 25.5% (when budget is 9) in situations with different budget. As we set the maximum allocate size of user is 9, so the accuracy improvement decline when the budget close to 9.

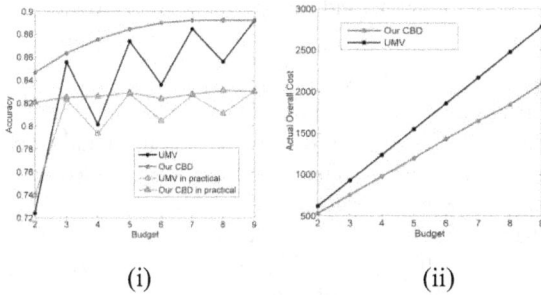

(i)   (ii)

Figure 3 The experimental results of CMU dataset. (i) is the accuracy result and (ii) is the actual overall cost result.

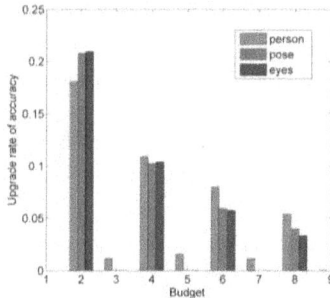

Figure 4 The upgrade rate of accuracy in different feature-based grouping

Step 5. In addition, for the purpose of validating the effectiveness of our method in identifying task difficulty features, *i.e.*, whether the "*person*" feature is indeed the exact difficulty feature – influencing the accuracy result most, we also group the CMU dataset based on the other two features –"*pose*" and "*eyes*", and use our method to crowdsource them. Figure 4 shows the accuracy results based on three features, in which x-axis states the normalized budget and y-axis states the upgrade rate of accuracy compared to UMV,

$$upgrade\ rate = \frac{Accuracy(CBD) - Accuracy(UMV)}{Accuracy(UMV)}$$

Figure 4, on the one hand, provides further evidence that our method provides better performance in crowdsourcing micro tasks comparing with the generic UMV algorithm, especially in the case of even crowd size. On the other hand,

it also proves that, in most cases with different normalized budget, the *person* based crowdsourcing process (red part in figure4) achieves the best performance, compared to the processes based on the other two features, which proves that the "*person*" feature is indeed the optimal difficulty feature in CMU dataset.

At present, the effectiveness of our method is proved in the laboratory environment. For the better evaluation, we also conduct a series of experiments based on Ali Crowdsourcing platform and prove the effectiveness of our method in real (non-lab) crowdsourcing environment.

Study 2: Crowdsourcing Weibo Dataset in Ali Crowdsourcing Platform

For Weibo task set with 4688 tasks, because all texts are described in Chinese and relatively easy for crowds in Ali crowdsourcing platform (most crowds in Ali crowdsourcing platform are Chinese), no restrictive qualification of crowd is defined for participating. The relatively easy characteristic of tasks also makes it difficult to group all tasks by the intrinsic features – "*text length*" and "*punt number*", and identify the task difficulty feature effectively. So we use K-means and DBSCAN clustering algorithm to extra group task set (with 4 subgroups). Then, we get six grouping – grouping based on text length (*Length*), grouping based on punt number (*Punt*), DBSCAN based on z-score normalization (*DBSCAN-z*), DBSCAN based on 0-1 normalization (*DBSCAN-01*), k-means based on z-score normalization (*kmeans-z*), and k-means based on 0-1 normalization (*kmeans-01*). Considering the limit of budget and the size of task set, we set $k_0 = 20$ and select $K = 134$ sample based on the minimum coverage algorithm to identify the task difficulty feature. We crowd the sample to estimate task accuracy. After calculating the differentiation of every group in accuracy, we identify *DBSCAN-01* as the task difficulty feature and then group the remaining tasks based on *DBSCAN-01*, and optimize the assignment process based on our *CBD*. In total, there are 1020 crowds taking part in our tasks and the results are shows in figure 5-i (accuracy comparison result) and 5-ii (cost comparison result).

Study 3: Crowdsourcing Twitter Dataset in Ali Crowdsourcing Platform

The 996 Twitter tasks, by contrast, are a little more difficult due to the English description. So we require college degree and above as the restrictive qualification of crowds. For grouping, there are several features in task set, including *word number*, *punt number*, *publish date*, *publisher* and so on. Due to too many numbers of *publishers*, we use *word number* (with 4 subgroups), *punt number* (with 4 subgroups), and *publish date* (with 7 subgroups) as the grouping methods, and set $k_0 = 10$ as the subgroup size in samples. We then and select $K = 70$ samples based on the minimum coverage algorithm and crowd them. Based on the results, we identify *word number* as the difficulty feature. After optimizing the task assignment and cost, 154 crowds take part in this task set and get the result shown as figure 5-iii and figure 5-iv, with the results of accuracy and payment comparison in both theoretical and practical situations respectively.

As shown in figure 5, due to the uncontrollable and uncertainty of crowdsourcing process, some deviations appear between the theoretical and the practical results, but the CBD-based results are generally better than the UMV-based results in both task sets. Separately, our method improves the task accuracy up to 9.8% (figure 5-i, when the budget is 2) and reduce the overall payment up to 41.6% (budget = 9) (figure 5-ii) in Weibo dataset. And for Twitter dataset, the task accuracy based on our CBD method can improve up to 38% (budget = 2) and the overall payment reduces up to 25.7% (budget = 7).

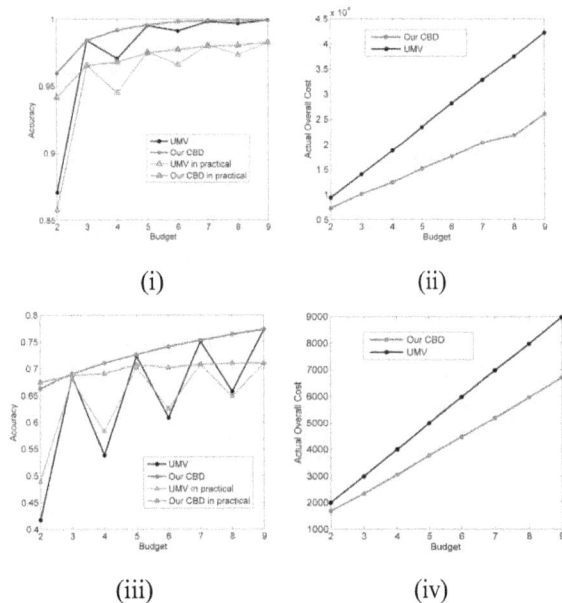

(i)   (ii)

(iii)   (iv)

Figure 5   The results of crowdsourcing Weibo and Twitter dataset in Ali crowdsourcing platform. (i) and (ii) are the accuracy and cost results of crowdsourcing Weibo tasks, and (iii) and (iv) are the accuracy and cost comparison results of crowdsourcing Twitter tasks.

In summary, the results shown in figure 3, 4, and 5 provide rich evidences that our *CBD* method perform better than the generic UMV, not only in the laboratory environment (Fig. 3, 4), but also in the non-lab crowdsourcing platform (Fig. 5).

CONCLUSION AND FUTURE WORK

In this paper, we studied the effect of uneven task difficulty to crowdsourcing and proposed a crowdsourcing method based on task difficulty *(CBD)*, by enabling the uneven difficulty feature of tasks. To broaden its applicability to different task classifications and crowdsourcing platforms, we identified the effective task difficulty in the real crowdsourcing context and optimized the assignment process for the efficient trade-off between the cost and the result accuracy. We conducted a series of experiments based on three datasets to evaluate its effectiveness. Our results, in both laboratory environment and the real (non-lab)

environment, show that our method makes substantially improvement in crowdsourcing performance both theoretically and practically.

Finally, as crowdsourcing becomes an integral component of many systems, we believe that the effective trade-off between cost and result accuracy, will prove to be immensely useful in micro-task crowdsourcing markets. This paper is a first step towards understanding the definition of difficulty as well as its influence in crowdsourcing. Actually, we have to stress that our method is rooted based on the assumption that all workers are independent and no malicious, we do not take into consideration of the difference of human factors. We hope to provide further understanding and analysis to these uneven human factors and their influences to crowdsourcing in the future work.

ACKNOWLEDGMENTS

We thank all viewers who provided the thoughtful and constructive comments on this paper. The third author is the corresponding author. This research was funded by the National Key Technology Support Program (No.2015BAH12F01), the National Natural Science foundation of China (No. 61773167, No. 61702191), and the Open Research Fund of Shanghai Key Laboratory of Multidimensional Information Processing, East China Normal University. The computation is performed in the Supercomputer Center of ECNU.

REFERENCES

1. Yukino Baba and Hisashi Kashima. 2013. Statistical quality estimation for general crowdsourcing tasks. In *Proc. KDD 2013*, 554-562. http://dx.doi.org/10.1145/2487575. 2487600.

2. Cynthia Breazeal, et al. 2013. Crowdsourcing human-robot interaction: New methods and system evaluation in a public environment. *Journal of Human-Robot Interaction 2*, 1: 82-111.

3. Caleb Chen Cao, Jieying She, Yongxin Tong and Lei Chen 2012. Whom to ask?: jury selection for decision making tasks on micro-blog services. *Proc. VLDB Endow.* 5, 11 (July 2012), 1495-1506. http://dx.doi.org/10.14778/2350229.2350264

4. Xi Chen, Lin Qihang, et al. 2013. Optimistic knowledge gradient policy for optimal budget allocation in crowdsourcing. In *ICML 2013*, 64-72.

5. Martin Davtyan, Eickhoff Carsten, and Hofmann Thomas. 2015. Exploiting Document Content for Efficient Aggregation of Crowdsourcing Votes. In *Proc. CIKM 2015*, 783-790. http://dx.doi.org/10.1145/2806416.2806460

6. Chien-Ju Ho, Jabbari Shahin, and W. Vaughan Jennifer. 2013. Adaptive task assignment for crowdsourced classification. In *Proc. ICML 2013*, 534-542.

7. Jeff Howe. 2006. The rise of crowdsourcing. *Wired magazine* 14, 6: 1-4.

8. Kazushi Ikeda, and Keiichiro Hoashi. 2017. Crowdsourcing GO: Effect of Worker Situation on Mobile Crowdsourcing Performance. In *Proc. CHI 2017*, 1142-1153. https://doi.org/10.1145/3025453.3025917

9. Panagiotis G Ipeirotis, Provost Foster, and Wang Jing. 2010. Quality management on Amazon Mechanical Turk. In *Proc. HCOMP 2010*, 64-67. https://doi.org/10.1145/1837885.1837906.

10. Ayush Jain, et al. 2017. Understanding workers, developing effective tasks, and enhancing marketplace dynamics: a study of a large crowdsourcing marketplace. *Proc. VLDB Endow* 10, 7 (March 2017), 829-840. https://doi.org/10.14778/3067421.3067431.

11. Huan Jiang, and Matsubara Shigeo. 2012. Improving Crowdsourcing Efficiency Based on Division Strategy. In *Proc. WI-IAT 2012*, 2: 425-429. http://dx.doi.org/10.1109/WI-IAT.2012.86

12. Oliver P. John, P. Naumann Laura, and J. Soto Christopher. 2008. Paradigm shift to the integrative big five trait taxonomy. *Handbook of personality: Theory and research* 3:114-158.

13. Sanjay Kairam, and Heer Jeffrey. 2016. Parting Crowds: Characterizing Divergent Interpretations in Crowdsourced Annotation Tasks. In *Proc. CSCW 2016*, 1637-1648. https://doi.org/10.1145/2818048.2820016

14. David R. Karger, Oh Sewoong, and Shah Devavrat. 2011. Iterative learning for reliable crowdsourcing systems. In *NIPS 2011*, 1953-1961

15. Nicolas Kaufmann, Schulze Thimo, and Veit Daniel. 2011. More than fun and money. Worker Motivation in Crowdsourcing-A Study on Mechanical Turk. In *AMCIS 2011*, 11:1-11.

16. Gabriella Kazai, Kamps Jaap, and Milic-Frayling Natasa. 2012. The face of quality in crowdsourcing relevance labels: demographics, personality and labeling accuracy. In *Proc. CIKM 2012*, 2583-2586. http://dx.doi.org/10.1145/2396761.2398697

17. Gabriella Kazai, Kamps Jaap, and Milic-Frayling Natasa. 2013. An analysis of human factors and label accuracy in crowdsourcing relevance judgments. *Information retrieval* 16, 2: 138-178.

18. Aniket Kittur, H. Chi Ed, and Suh Bongwo. 2008. Crowdsourcing user studies with Mechanical Turk. In *Proc. CHI 2008*, 453-456. https://doi.org/10.1145/1357054.1357127

19. Hongwei Li, and Bin Yu. 2014. Error rate bounds and iterative weighted majority voting for crowdsourcing. *arXiv preprint arXiv* 1411: 4086.

20. Greg Little, et al. 2010. TurKit: human computation algorithms on mechanical turk. In *Proc. UIST 2010*, 57-66. https://doi.org/10.1145/1866029.1866040

21. David Martin, et al. 2001. A database of human segmented natural images and its application to evaluating segmentation algorithms and measuring ecological statistics. In *ICCV 2001*, 2: 416-423.

22. Kaixiang Mo, Zhong Erheng, and Yang Qiang. 2013. Cross-task crowdsourcing. In *Proc. KDD 2013*, 677-685. http://dx.doi.org/10.1145/2487575.248759

23. Barzan Mozafari, et al.2014. Scaling up crowd-sourcing to very large datasets: a case for active learning. *Proc. VLDB Endow* 8, 2, 125-136. http://dx.doi.org/10.14778/2735471.2735474

24. Barzan Mozafari, et al. 2012. Active Learning for Crowd-Sourced Databases. *Computer Science*.

25. Vaibhav Rajan, et al. 2013. Crowdcontrol: An online learning approach for optimal task scheduling in a dynamic crowd platform. *Proc. ICML Workshop 2013*, 2.

26. Aaron D. Shaw, J. Horton John and L. Chen Daniel. 2011. Designing incentives for inexpert human raters. In *Proc. CSCW 2011*, 275-284. https://doi.org/10.1145/1958824.1958865

27. Edwin Simpson, et al. 2011. Bayesian combination of multiple, imperfect classifiers.

28. Rion Snow, et al. 2008. Cheap and fast---but is it good?: evaluating non-expert annotations for natural language tasks. In *Proc. EMNLP 2008*, 254-263.

29. Alexander Sorokin, and Forsyth David. 2008. Utility data annotation with amazon mechanical turk. In *CVPRW 2008*, 1-8.

30. Andrei Tamilin, et al. 2012. Context-aware mobile crowdsourcing. In *Proc. UbiComp 2012*, 717-720. http://dx.doi.org/10.1145/2370216.2370373

31. Long Tran-Thanh, et al. 2013. Efficient budget allocation with accuracy guarantees for crowdsourcing classification tasks. In *Proc. AAMAS 2013*, 901-908.

32. Sudheendra Vijayanarasimhan, and Grauman Kristen. 2011. Cost-sensitive active visual category learning. *International Journal of Computer Vision* 91, 1: 24-44.

33. Carl Vondrick, Donadl Patterson, and Deva Ramanan. 2013. Efficiently scaling up crowdsourced video annotation. *International Journal of Computer Vision* 101, 1: 184-204.

34. Jeroen Vuurens, Arjen P. de Vries, and Carsten Eickhoff. 2011. How much spam can you take? an analysis of crowdsourcing results to increase accuracy. In *Proc. CIR 2011*, 21-26.

35. Jacob Whitehill, et al. 2009. Whose vote should count more: Optimal integration of labels from labelers of unknown expertise. In *Advances in neural information processing systems* 2009, 2035-2043.

36. Bei Yu, et al. 2013. Crowdsourcing participatory evaluation of medical pictograms using Amazon Mechanical Turk. *Journal of medical Internet research* 15, 6.

Growth in Social Network Connectedness among Different Roles in Organizational Crowdfunding

Michael Muller*, Tanushree Mitra**, and Werner Geyer*
* IBM Research, Cambridge MA USA 02142
** Virginia Tech, Blacksburg VA USA 24061
{michael_muller, werner.geyer}@us.ibm.com, tmitra@vt.edu

ABSTRACT
When employees participate in organizational crowdfunding, they seek partial funding from their existing social networks. Among proposers of projects, teams with larger social networks tend to be more successful in reaching their funding goals. However, little is known about the consequences of participation on employees' social networks, during and after the crowdfunding campaign. In a study of activity logs and social networks from a very large-scale organizational crowdfunding campaign, we found that people in different crowdfunding roles experienced different degrees of growth in their social networks, during and after the crowdfunding campaign, as compared with baseline non-participants. These findings contribute to previous work on the strongly social nature of crowdfunding. Organizations can use these results to increase the density of their internal social networks. Employees can use these results to strategize their participation in workplace social networks and in organizational innovation.

Author Keywords
CSCW; Crowdfunding; Social network; Degree centrality.

ACM Classification Keywords
H.5.3. Group and organizational interfaces/CSCW.

INTRODUCTION AND RELATED WORK
Crowdfunding is an inherently collaborative approach to innovation [5]. At an Internet crowdfunding site, a Proposer publishes a proposal for a project, and the project cannot succeed unless it is funded by a group of Investors ("backers") [6], who each contribute relatively small amounts of the needed support as a form of micro-funding [18]. Proposers and Investors use the mediation of a crowdfunding site to engage in asynchronous collaboration, leading to success for a subset of the projects that are fully invested by "the crowd" of Investors [10, 11, 19].

GROUP '18, January 7–10, 2018, Sanibel Island, FL, USA
© 2018 Copyright is held by the owner/author(s). Publication rights licensed to ACM.
ACM 978-1-4503-5562-9/18/01...$15.00
https://doi.org/10.1145/3148330.3148335

Organizations may conduct an internal form of crowdfunding [19, 22]. In most projects, an executive allocates a spending budget to each participant (Investor). Investors spend the organization's money, rather than their own. Because the members of an organization are known, it is possible to combine datasets to understand some of the underlying dynamics, such as the role of attributes-in-common for supporting one anothers' innovations [20] and the importance of pre-existing social ties in gaining funding for one's project [21]. The mediating role of social ties has also been studied in multiple Internet crowdfunding sites [10, 14, 17, 18, 26]. For other factors that contribute to crowdfunding success, see [16, 25]. More broadly, social ties have been shown to be important in other types of innovative work in organizations [1, 2, 3, 7, 12, 23].

All of these studies used social networks as predictor variables. However, little is known about the reverse relationship – i.e., the influence of crowdfunding on each participant's social network. In this paper, we ask whether participants in crowdfunding experience a growth in their social networks. Based on [18, 21], we might expect that successful project-proposers activate their existing social networks in order to recruit investments into their projects. However, it is also possible that proposers might contact colleagues previously unknown to them, to expand their influence and their ability to recruit funds. We examine the growth of the social networks of the project proposers, and also of people in other roles in the crowdfunding campaign.

ORGANIZATIONAL SETTING AND PLATFORM

Organizational Crowdfunding Campaign
The crowdfunding campaign took place in a large software company, IBM, which is known for large-scale internal innovation practices []. Employees were invited to propose projects and/or to self-nominate as Investors, in a company-wide technology initiative ultimately involving over 100,000 employees and several million dollars of support. The goal was to jump-start IBM into a new business and technology domain. In practice, only projects with a relatively high degree of funding received approval to proceed.

Following the model of RocketHub (www.rockethub.com), a proposer could recruit people to work on the proposal team. People in these roles of TeamLead and TeamMember collaborated to publish a project proposal on a purpose-built internal crowdfunding Intranet site [19, 20], and their names were featured prominently in the crowdfunding proposal [21].

Role	n	Attributes	Necessary for crowdfunding
TeamLead	2357	Leadership+ Initiative	Necessary
TeamMember	12,622	Initiative	Necessary
Investor	101,294	Resources	Necessary
Commenter	654	Engaged in discussion	
Liker	535	Visible support	
Follower	3735	Measurable interest	
NonParticipant	256,038	Not engaged	(control)

Table 1. Relative prominence of roles in organizational crowdfunding.

Of course, crowdfunding cannot happen without Investors (backers). Each Investor received a budget of $2000 to spend on other people's proposals. The internal crowdfunding website followed conventional social media practices, allowing people to comment on a proposal, follow a proposal, and like a proposal.

Organizational Social Ties
IBM maintains an internal social networking system (SNS), similar to [4, 9]. The SNS records bilateral "friending" relationships. We used these data to compute each employee's personal network.

HYPOTHESIS DEVELOPMENT
Previous research has shown that crowdfunding proposers activate their social networks to seek investors [10, 14, 17, 18, 21]. However, on the Internet, there is no reliable way to estimate the size of an individual's personal social network (egonet – i.e., the number of bilateral friending relationships with that individual), because people may have different IDs on each of many social network sites (SNSs). By contrast, in the IBM Intranet, each employee was identified with an invariant, unique ID, and there was exactly one SNS, through which employees could form bilateral friendship relationships. We used the historical database of these friendship relationships as an index of each employee's egonet at particular moments in time.

Each employee was free to participate, or to decline, in the crowdfunding campaign, and s/he was free to choose which role or roles to engage in. Previous research has shown little effect of hierarchical organizational structures on such self-selection [21]. For analytic purposes, we constructed an ordinal ordering of crowdfunding roles, based on the degree of effort or engagement of each role in crowdfunding activities (see Table 1). We propose that TeamLeads put in the most effort, are most engaged, and have a greater career stake in crowdfunding, than the other roles. We propose that TeamMembers are similar to TeamLeads, but engage in less leadership. Next are Investors, who self-select to read proposals, and eventually allocate their funds. We propose that Commenters are the next most engaged, because they contribute public text to the website (note that some

comments may have been made via email, and thus the number of Commenters is likely an underestimate). Following Commenters are Likers, who change the data in the website through binary operations of liking selected projects. Followers track the project. The last row of Table 1 is non-participants, whom we treat as a control group.

For employees who participated in more than one role, we assigned that employee to the *highest* role in which s/he acted, according to Table 1. Thus, a person who Liked one project and served as TeamMember in another project, would be assigned to the role of TeamMember in Table 1. 99% of the combinations of roles involved Investors. This voluntary sorting of employees into roles became a major predictor variable in our analyses.

Based on the importance of social ties for crowdfunding success [10, 14, 17, 18, 21], we anticipated that people who were more socially active would self-select into more prominent roles in organizational crowdfunding. The first three roles in Table 1 are necessary for crowdfunding to take place – i.e., TeamLeads who organize a proposal team, Team-Members who do diverse types of work to create a proposal [10], and Investors who fund specific proposals. We reasoned that people with more social connections might be more inclined to take on one of these prominent roles. We predict:

H1a. TeamLeads will have larger egonets than other roles.

H1b. TeamMembers will have larger egonets than other roles (except for TeamLeads).

H1c. Investors will have larger egonets than other roles (except the TeamLead and TeamMember roles).

Over time, we anticipated that employees in more prominent roles would come into contact with a greater number of other employees. They would be more visible than other employees, and they would be more likely to interact with other employees – especially during the duration of the crowdfunding campaign. On this basis, we predict:

H2a. TeamLeads will experience greater egonet-gains than other roles.

H2b. TeamMembers will experience greater egonet-gains than other roles (except for TeamLeads).

H2c. Investors will experience greater egonet-gains than other roles (except for TeamLeads and TeamMembers).

We expect that participation in crowdfunding will contribute to growth in an employee's individual social network, which we measure via the metric of egonet size (a simple transform of degree centrality). Further, we expect that people in more active roles in Table 1 will experience more growth in their individual social networks, in the order specified in the table.

However, we know that *all* employees' individual social networks tend to grow slowly over time. Therefore, we evaluate each of these hypotheses against a control group of non-participants.

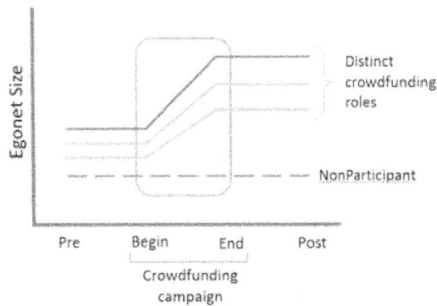

Figure 1. Idealized prediction: People who participate in crowdfunding will self-select into crowdfunding roles according to their antecedent social activity, and will grow their social networks in relation to their self-selected roles.

Figure 1 shows summary predictions. For **H1**, we predict that the size of each employee's *pre-crowdfunding* egonet will influence the role that the employee self-selects during the crowdfunding campaign ("Pre" and "Begin" in Figure 1). For **H2**, we predict that the amount of *growth* in each employee's egonet will be influenced by the crowdfunding role that they self-select (from "Begin" to "End" in Figure 1).

METHOD

Crowdfunding Data

We obtained the activity logs from the database of the Intranet crowdfunding site. This log allowed us to identify each action by each employee, including their participation in a crowdfunding team, investments, comments, following, and liking each proposal. Using these data, we created a list of TeamLead and TeamMembers for each project.

The activity logs allowed us to recover all actions by each employee who visited the crowdfunding site. Following the coding protocol described in the previous section, we assigned each employee to the highest or most engaged role in which they acted, per Table 1.

The historical SNS "friending" data allowed us to construct each employee's egonet at specific moments-in-time. Friending data were bitwise records that, on a particular date, a friending relationship existed, or did not. (We could not assess tie-strength; IBM policy is that emails and chats of employees are private, and are not available for analysis.)

Timeframe and Timeline

The crowdfunding campaign occurred over a period of 74 days, from 2016-02-20 to 2016-05-04. We were interested to compare the size of each person's egonet on the first of those dates ("Begin," in Figures 1 and 2), and on the last of those dates ("End"). To understand the network context and dynamics more completely, we sampled back in time to 74 days before the beginning of the crowdfunding campaign, i.e., 2015-12-08 ("Pre"), and we sampled forward in time to 74 days after the end of the crowdfunding campaign, i.e., 2016-07-19 ("Post"). We constructed each employee's social network at those dates, and we computed her/his egonet size for each of those dates.

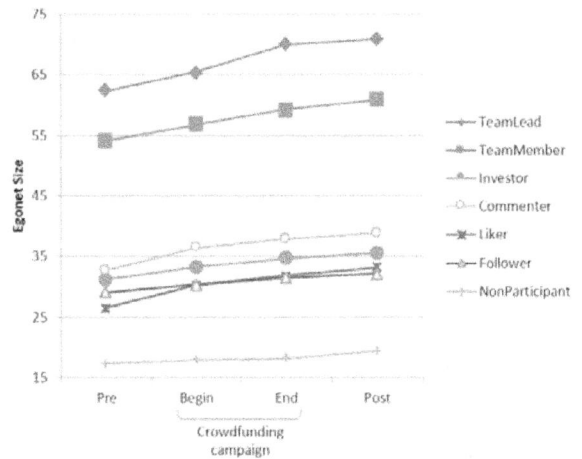

Figure 2. Growth of egonet for each role, at equally-spaced 74-day periods. Vertical axis is degree centrality (egonet size). Filled markers correspond to the most engaged roles (the top three rows of Table 1.

RESULTS

For **H1**, we predicted that people with larger personal networks would be more likely to take prominent roles in organizational crowdfunding. For **H2**, we predicted that people in more engaged roles (per Table 1) would experience greater growth in their personal networks, as they contacted people to seek expertise or funding for their projects.

Self-Selection into Crowdfunding Roles. Using General Linear Model software (GLM), we compared degree centrality among the different roles of Table 1 for each of the periods Pre and Before, and for their mean across those two periods (Figure 2). GLM allows detailed comparisons of curvilinear trends, such as quadratic trends. All analyses led to the same conclusions. We describe the results for the mean of Pre and Before.

The egonet sizes among the seven roles in Table 1 differed significantly ($F_{6,377228}$=676.967, p<.001). The LSD test showed that, as predicted by **H1a**, TeamLeads had significantly larger initial egonets than all other roles (p<.001 for all comparisons). As predicted by **H1b**, TeamMembers had significantly larger initial egonets than all other roles except for TeamLeads (p<.001 for all comparisons).

However, we were surprised that this pattern did not continue for Investors, as predicted by **H1c**. Investors' initial egonet sizes were of course less than that of TeamLeads and TeamMembers (as reported in the previous paragraph). However, Investors showed no significant differences with any of the other roles, except the NonParticipants (p<.001).

People who self-select into the role of Investor are no more socially connected than any other non-team participant in organizational crowdfunding. Based on [10], we hypothesize that TeamLeads and TeamMembers pursue necessarily social activities to promote their projects. By contrast, Investors may make more solitary decisions about how to allocate their company-assigned investment budgets.

Effect	Statistic	p <
Role	$F_{6,377228} = 724.789$	.001
Timeline	$F_{3,377228} = 789.178$	.001
Linear	$F_{1,377228} = 977.540$	.001
Quadratic	$F_{1,377228} = 130.378$	.001
Cubic	$F_{1,377228} = 0.398$	n.s.
Role * Timeline	$F_{18,1131684} = 471.838$	.001
Linear	$F_{1,1131684} = 587.165$	.001
Quadratic	$F_{1,1131684} = 60.271$	.001
Cubic	$F_{1,1131684} = 28.837$	.001

Table 2. Outcomes from repeated measures analysis.

Finally, we tested the generality of these results by removing the NonParticipants from the analyses. All of the effects reported above were unchanged, except trivially that the difference between TeamLeads and TeamMembers was slightly less significant than in the previous analysis (p<.002).

Personal Network Growth through Participation. The preceding analyses were conducted with data from before the crowdfunding campaign – i.e., the Pre and Begin datapoints in Figure 2. The results tell us that initial egonet size (proportional to degree centrality) may influence how people choose to participate in crowdfunding, and what role they may select in crowdfunding. We now turn to the outcomes of crowdfunding, analyzing the growth of people's egonets through their different roles.

Using a repeated-measures design, we analyzed the patterns of egonet growth across the four time-intervals of Figure 2. Table 2 summarizes the findings. Unsurprisingly, the roles differed significantly, and there were significant differences over time. In general, egonet size increased significantly over time (linear trend over the four time-periods), but decelerated after the end of the crowdfunding campaign (quadratic trend over the four-time-periods).[1]

Interactions of role by time-period were also significant. The linear trend was significantly steeper for TeamLead (**H2a**) and TeamMembers (**H2b**). The gradual deceleration also varied across roles, with a smaller deceleration for roles other than TeamLead and TeamMembers. Finally, there was a small but significant cubic trend across time-periods that varied across roles, possibly driven by the relatively ogival shapes of the trends for TeamLeads, TeamMember, and Investor, as contrasted with the more linear trends for Commenters and Followers.

Thus, **H2a** (greatest gains for TeamLeads) and **H2b** (TeamMembers) were supported. As with the initial, pre-crowdfunding results of **H1c**, **H2c** (Investors) was not supported. These results are consistent with the results of **H1a** and **H2a**, suggesting that TeamLeads and

TeamMembers work socially to promote their projects, while Investors make more private decisions.

DISCUSSION AND CONCLUSION

These results add a new facet to what is known of the highly social nature of crowdfunding. Hui et al. showed ethnographically that creating a crowdfunding proposal involves teamwork and even community effort among project proposers [10]. Mollick [18] and Muller et al. [21] showed that social ties were important predictors of crowdfunding success. Now, with this note, we show that social ties (egonets) are also affected by crowdfunding participation.

Taken together with [18, 20, 21], these results suggest a strong indirect relationship between social-connectedness and crowdfunding success. Stronger social ties have been argued to be important for trust in distributed teams [15], online communities [24], and institutional success [13]. Organizations can use these results to "tune" both their internal crowdfunding campaigns and their aggregate social networks, expanding their employees' strategic patterns of self-directed egonet growth.

Employees can use these results to strategize their self-selected role(s) in organizational crowdfunding, and perhaps in Internet crowdfunding as well. Using these results, an individual can ask, "Should I expand my social network, before engaging as TeamLead or TeamMember"? (**H1**). If other employees' egonet sizes were made visible to a TeamLead, s/he might be able to make more strategic decisions about whom to invite to join the proposal team (**H1**). If an employee wishes to increase their social network, they might use crowdfunding participation as part of their strategy (**H2**).

Limitations

The data in this paper come from a single large company, and we studied only one version of organizational crowdfunding. Therefore, these results may or may not generalize to Internet crowdfunding. However, the patterns of social ties as contributors to crowdfunding success appear to be broadly similar between the Internet [10, 18] and Intranet [21]. Therefore, we hope that these results will be useful to other researchers, who may wish to pursue questions that we could not examine, such as effects of homophily and reciprocity, and more macro-scale network configurations and reconfigurations during crowdfunding. We also note that the Intranet configuration, while not fully comparable to Internet crowdfunding, allows to test hypotheses about relations to individuals' social networks, that are difficult or impossible to test on the Internet.

REFERENCES

1. Ajay Agrawal, Christian Catalini, and Avi Goldfarb. 2015. Crowdfunding: Geography, social networks, and

---

[1] We tested for violations of the assumption of equal variances, using Mauchly test of sphericity. Variances were significantly different, so we examined three corrections: Greenhouse-Geisser, Hyynh-Feldt, and Lower-bound. After these corrections, all F-tests remained significant at p<.001.

the timing of investment decisions. *J. Econ. & Mgmt. Strategy 24*(2), 253-274.

2. Mohammad Y. Allaho, and Wang-Chien Lee. 2013. Analyzing the social ties and structure of contributors in open source software community. *Proc. ASONAM 2013*, 56-60.

3. Ana P. Appel, Victor F. Cavalcante, Marcos R. Viera, Vagner F. de Santana, Rogerio A. de Paula, and Steven K. Tsukamoto. 2014. Building socially connected teams to accomplish complex tasks. *Proc. SNAKDD 2014*, Article 8.

4. Joan DiMicco, David R. Millen, Werner Geyer, Casey Dugan, Beth Brownholtz, and Michael Muller. 2008. Motivations for social networking at work. *Proc. CSCW 2008*, 711-720.

5. Elizabeth M. Gerber, Michael Muller, Rick Wash, Elizabeth F. Churchill, Lilly Irani, and Amanda Williams. 2014. Crowdfunding: An emerging field of research. *CHI 2014 Extended Abstracts*, 1093-1098.

6. Michael D. Greenberg, Julie Hui, and Elizabeth M. Gerber. 2013. Crowdfunding: A resource exchange perspective. *CHI 2013 Extended Abstracts*, 883-888.

7. Junghil Hahn, Jae Yun Moon, and Chen Zhang. 2008. Emergence of new project teams from open source software developer networks: Impact of prior collaboration ties. *Info Sys. Rsrch. 19*(3), 369-391.

8. Mary Helander, Rick Lawrence, Yan Liu, Claudia Perlich, Chandan Reddy, and Saharan Rosset. 2007. Looking for great ideas: Analyzing the innovation jam. *Proc. WebKDD/SNA-KDA 2007*, 66-73.

9. Lester Holtzblatt, Jill Drury, Daniel Weiss, Laurie Damianos, and Donna Cuomo. 2012. Evaluation of the uses and benefits of a social business platform. *CHI EA 2012*, 721-736.

10. Julie Hui, Elizabeth M. Gerber, and Darren Gergle. 2014a. Understanding and leveraging social networks for crowdfunding: Opportunities and challenges. *Proc. DIS 2014*, 677-680.

11. Julie Hui, Michael D. Greenberg, and Elizabeth M. Gerber. 2014b. Understanding the role of community in crowdfunding work. *Proc CSCW 2014*, 62-74.

12. Julia Kotlarsky, and Ilan Oshri. 2005. Social ties, knowledge sharing and successful collaboration in globally distributed development projects. *European J. Info Sys. 14*, 37-48.

13. Franz Lehner and Nora Fteimi. 2013. Organize, socialize, benefit: How social media applications impact enterprise success and performance. *Proc. I-Know 2013*, art. 26.

14. Chun-Ta Lu, Sihong Xie, Xiangnan Kong, and Philip A. Yu. 2014. Inferring the impacts of social media on crowdfunding. *Proc. WSDM 2014*, 573-582.

15. Suzanne P. Mikawa, Sharon K. Cunnington, and Scott A. Gaskins. 2009. Removing barriers to trust in distributed teams: Understanding cultural differences and strengthening social ties. *Proc IWIC 2009*, 273-276.

16. Tanushree Mitra and Eric Gilbert. 2014. The language that gets people to give: Phrases that predict success in Kickstarter. *Proc. CSCW 2014*, 49-61.

17. Alexey Moisseyev. 2013. Effect of social media on crowdfunding project results. M.A. thesis, University of Nebraska, Lincoln NB USA.

18. Ethan R. Mollick. 2012. The dynamics of crowd-funding: Determinants of success and failure. *Social Science Research Network Working Paper Series*, 2012.

19. Michael Muller, Werner Geyer, Todd Soule, Steven Daniels, and Li-Te Cheng. 2013. Crowdfunding inside the enterprise: Employee-initiatives for innovation and collaboration. *Proc. CHI 2013*, 503-512.

20. Michael Muller, Werner Geyer, Todd Soule, and John Wafer. 2014. Geographical and organizational distances in enterprise crowdfunding. *Proc. CSCW 2014*, 778-789.

21. Michael Muller, Mary Keough, John Wafer, Werner Geyer, Alberto Alvarez Saez, David Leip, and Cara Viktorov. 2016. Social ties in organizational crowdfunding: Benefits of team-authored proposals. *Proc. CSCW 2016*, 1246-1259.

22. Mizuki Sakamoto and Tatsuo Nakajima. 2013. Micro-crowdfunding: Achieving a sustainable society through economic and social incentives in micro-level crowdfunding. *Proc. MUM 2013*, Article 29.

23. Leif Singer, Norbert Seyff, and Samuel A. Fricker. 2011. Online social networks as a catalyst for software and IT innovation. *Proc. SSE 2011*, 1-5.

24. Chuan-Hoo Tan, Juliana Sutanto, and Bernard C.Y. Tan. 2015. Empirical investigation of relational social capital in a virtual community for website programming. *ACM SIGMIS Database 46*(2), 43-60.

25. Anbang Xu, Xiao Yang, Rao Huaming, Wai-Tat Fu, Shih-Wen Huang, and Brian P. Bailey. 2014. Show me the money! An analysis of project updates during crowdfunding campaigns. *Proc CHI 2014*, 591-600.

26. Haichao Zheng, Dahui Li, Jing Wu, and Yun Xu. 2014. The role of multidimensional social capital in crowdfunding: A comparative study in China and US. *Info. & Mgmt. 51*(4), 488-496.

Reflektor: An Exploration of Collaborative Music Playlist Creation for Social Context

Jared S. Bauer
University of Washington
Seattle, WA USA
jaredsb@uw.edu

Aubury L. Jellenek
University of Washington
Seattle, WA USA
jellea@uw.edu

Julie A. Kientz
University of Washington
Seattle, WA USA
jkientz@uw.edu

ABSTRACT

Music is intrinsically linked to our social lives. As more music becomes available through streaming services, deciding what music is appropriate for social events becomes increasingly challenging and nuanced. While prior work has considered the social role of music and the creation of music playlists for user contexts, how individuals utilize music to create social contexts is an area that has largely gone unexplored. To investigate this topic, we created and evaluated a prototype music recommender system called Reflektor. Reflektor interactively visualizes users' chat conversations to generate music playlists. Our analysis of user conversations with Reflektor uncovered distinct strategies participants use to create the ambiance and conduct for social contexts. Our findings help to illuminate mismatches in the way metadata and recommendation systems align with user strategies to create social context. We elaborate on these strategies and discuss design implications for future collaborative music recommender systems.

Author Keywords

Contextual music recommendations; group displays; collaborative playlist creation; mood boards; natural language processing.

ACM Classification Keywords

H.5.m. Information interfaces and presentation (e.g., HCI): Miscellaneous;

INTRODUCTION

Music is fundamental to the social lives of people around the world [8]. Whether it is Pomp and Circumstance played at a graduation ceremony, hymns sung by a congregation, or pop hits enjoyed by friends at a club, music is often present when people interact socially. In fact, researchers have argued that improvements to the portability, availability, and reproducibility of music has transformed its role in everyday life from cognitive and emotional to primarily social [20]. But music is not merely a component of social occasions; music also helps to establish the ambiance and conduct that is expected. Mu-

sic's role in structuring social interaction has been studied extensively by ethnomusicologists who argue music acts as a "*framework for the organization of social agency, a framework for how people perceive (consciously or subconsciously) potential avenues of conduct*" [10:17]. Music's ability to structure social conduct extends beyond the individual; music acts as a medium through which individuals create social context [9].

One of the key challenges faced when designing music recommender systems is determining how social context should be viewed. HCI research has defined context as the information that can be used to characterize the situation of an entity [12,13] or more recently, as an emergent property of individuals' interaction [14]. While these views are useful ways to characterize context, they focus more on the situation an individual is engaged in and less on how an individual imposes meaning on a given situation. The role of meaning and meaning-making has become an increasingly important consideration in system design [21,38]. Because of the personal relationship individuals have with music, how music is utilized to create social context is worth critical reflection. Social context in HCI has been defined as individuals' social norms and cultural models, as well as the interaction between cultural models in a situation [28]. This definition of social context emphasizes the relationship between the meaning an individual brings to a context and the meaning that emerges from interaction between this meaning and the context. While this model, like other theoretical approaches, has been noted for challenges that it can create when designers try to apply it to a given problem space [34], it does help to illustrate how users' understanding of their context influences their experience and conduct of that context. This emphasis on the individuals' meaning and its relationship to their context aligns with ethnographic work that suggests music is fundamental to structuring social conduct [8,11].

While music is clearly important for social context, researchers have not directly explored the design of recommender systems to accommodate music's role in creating social context. Instead, researchers have explored how components of user context can be leveraged to create music recommendations [2,3,29], systems to select music socially [24,31,40], or how music is shared and experienced socially [5,8,23,26,42]. Building upon prior work examining recommender systems, our research explores how groups utilize music to create social context. To explore this topic, we designed a prototype recommender system called "Reflektor" (Figure 1). Reflektor utilizes natural language processing techniques on user chat conversations to surface and visualize key ideas. This creates opportunities for users to negotiate the meaning of the ideas and their fit with the evolving notion for the social context.

While much of this work focuses on the design of Reflektor, we do not feel that the Reflektor, as a system, is the main contribution of this work. Instead, Reflektor is best viewed as a prototype whose construction and evaluation was a useful tool to highlight some of the mismatches that occur between how recommender systems operate, the metadata on which they rely, and the strategies that users employ while discussing music. Our evaluation of Reflektor provides insight into participant strategies to achieve mutual understanding around music recommendations for social context. These insights illuminate opportunities for designers of music recommendation systems and other context-aware systems where social context is a key consideration.

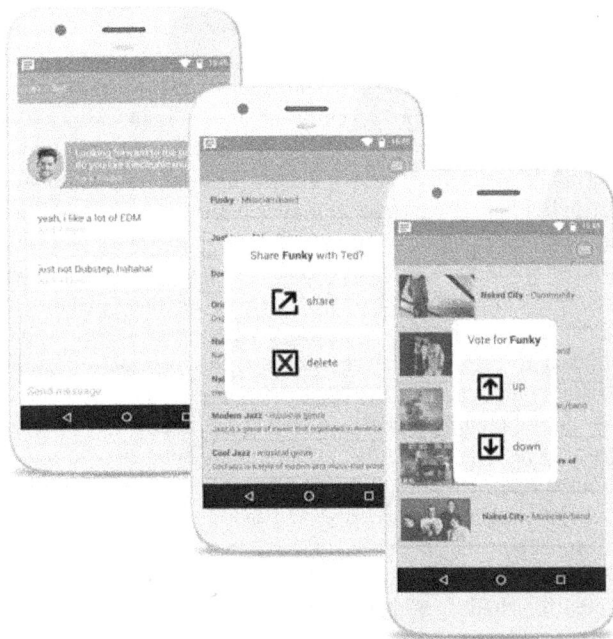

Figure 1: Reflektor application interface

RELATED WORK

Considerable research in the field of HCI has sought to determine what music should be played for social contexts. Prior work in this area can be largely organized as: research into how music is shared and experienced socially, the design of systems that automatically detect and create playlists for user contexts, and the design of interfaces to facilitate democratic music selection. We discuss each of these foci below.

The social role of music has also been studied in work that considers music in sharing and collaboration. Brown et al.'s [5] study of music highlighted the role of sharing as a social practice and explored alternatives to illegal file sharing services. Voida's work on practices of music sharing importantly illustrates the role of impression management through music [42]. Sease & McDonald's research on home media collections [36] contributed to Voida's work by revealing the role that intimacy and proximity play in how music is used in impression management. More recent studies of how music is used in social activities provide insights into interactions surrounding music. This includes a transition away from a focus on physical media and an emphasis on social media platforms that accommodate sharing [26]. This focus on shared listening experiences was further developed through the use of a technological probe, Pocketsong [23]. Their work highlighted design challenges for negotiating self-expression, co-listening, and developing cultural capital through mobile music applications interface design. Our work contributes to these studies by providing insights into how individuals establish and utilize the relevance of music for a social context

Research has also focused on the design of systems that detect and create playlists for groups of users automatically. One of the earliest examples was MusicFX [29], a group based recommender system that created playlists for gym members based on overlap in their music preferences. MusicFX determined what users were present from their ID badges when users entered the gym. One limitation of MusicFX is that it required participants to manually state their music preferences to use the system. Building off that work, Flytrap [7] logged the users listening history to automate the processes of determining listener preferences. The system then used ID badges to determine user copresence in a lab setting and combined user listening history with rules on music compatibility to determine what music should be played. Prior work has also shown that determining user emotion can be helpful in creating music recommendations for individuals [22]. MoodMusic [2] extended this idea to collocated groups by using audio signal processing to determine the group member's mood and then selecting songs appropriate for that mood based on the music's metadata and the group member's listening history.

In addition to work that seeks to determine group music preferences automatically, additional work has explored how group music preferences can be selected democratically. One early example is Jukola [31], which was deployed at a club and provided mobile devices for users to vote with to determine which songs would be played. UbiRockMachine also provides music for groups in public spaces based on mutual taste [24].

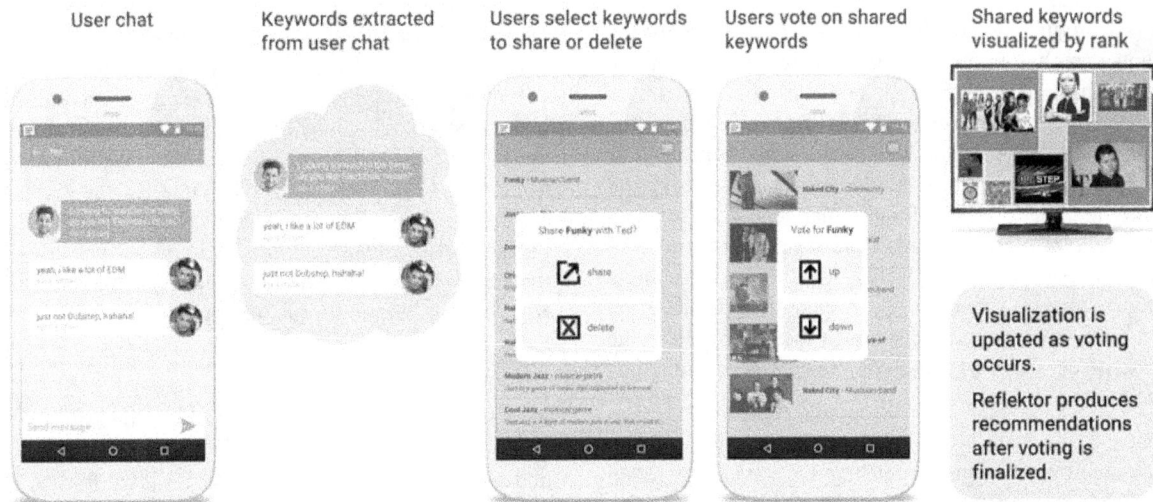

User chat

Keywords extracted
from user chat

Users select keywords
to share or delete

Users vote on shared
keywords

Shared keywords
visualized by rank

Visualization is
updated as voting
occurs.

Reflektor produces
recommendations
after voting is
finalized.

Figure 2: Overview of the components of Reflektor.

Unlike Jukola, UbiRockMachine also acted as a platform for unsigned musicians to share their work and gather feedback on their music. PartyVote [40] tried to address issues with users engaging in undemocratic behavior with group music recommendation systems by visualizing user influence on the recommendations. Sørensen, & Lagerl's work on MEET [39] explored multi-user and multi-device influence on music selection. Their work highlighted challenges with the feedback provided to users and the influence the environment has on collaboration. Our work contributes to prior work that aimed to automatically or democratically determine music playlists for groups by providing a new technique to accommodate this process. Furthermore, our work provides insight into how individuals establish mutual understanding around the relevance of music for a social context.

REFLEKTOR RESEARCH, DESIGN, AND DEVELOPMENT

In this section, we discuss the research, design, and development of Reflektor (see Figure 2). Our work on Reflektor was part of a larger year-long study of how individuals interact with intelligent agents. While much of that work is out of the scope of this paper, our research did motivate our primary interaction model for Reflektor. Our primary model of interaction is that intelligent agents, such as Amazon's Alexa (https://developer.amazon.com/alexa) and Apple's Siri (https://www.apple.com/ios/siri/), are more likely to be situated in our environments and expected to understand and respond to our environments without having to be explicitly asked to respond. This model of interaction aligns with prior work on implicit interaction through context [35] rather than explicit modes of interaction with intelligent agents [4]. As such, we sought to design a system that would enable users to interact with each other rather than directly with the technology. As intelligent agents become more prevalent in our daily life, we imagine a variety of scenarios of use for implicit models of interaction that could facilitate collaboration. For the purposes of this study we focused on a system that would

infer and respond to group conversations and select music suitable for the context being discussed.

Reflektor System Design

After identifying a model of interaction that we hoped to facilitate, we began exploring design opportunities. To accommodate the multifaceted preferences of groups, we aimed to provide an interface that could represent a variety of criteria used to produce recommendations. This also suggested an interface that is transparent and modifiable. After extensive ideation, we were drawn to mood boards as a design metaphor. Mood boards are often a collection of images or words and can be utilized to convey an overall design concept [30]. Mood boards represent an idea in a multifaceted way and can be used for framing and aligning views [27]. Because of these properties, we felt mood boards presented a useful mechanism for allowing groups to represent meaning.

With mood boards as an organizing design metaphor for how interfaces could reflect users' multifaceted views, the research team developed an interactive prototype of the interface using Processing (https://processing.org/). After exploring several options to facilitate the creation of the mood boards, including scraping user's social media for images or keywords, we determined that parsing chat conversations was ideal to explore how individuals utilize music to create social context. We opted to focus on user chat conversations because language is such a rich resource for contextual meaning-making [18]. It also allowed us to clearly scope the context to the user's conversation. At this point, we felt that the concept for the system began to unify: a music recommender system that allowed groups to discuss music and passively visualize, or reflect, the systems understanding of the conversation. Ultimately, it was this vision that led us to the name Reflektor.

Reflektor System Development

Reflektor operates as one system but has three distinct components (see Figure 2). The first is the *chat client* where the participants can chat with one another, share, and vote on the keywords from their conversation. The second component is a *server* where a text parsing module determines the keywords and phrases based on the users' conversation. The server uses those keywords to produce the visualization and music recommendations. The final component is an *interactive visualization* of the keywords from the participants' conversation. The participants interacted with the system using a smartphone running the chat client, and the visualization appeared on a wall-mounted display in the room where the study took place. Each of these components is explained in detail below.

Chat Client

The chat client is implemented using the JavaScript open source runtime environment node.js (https://nodejs.org). The application used web sockets to instantiate a chat environment for the users. In addition to operating as a chat client, the application also allows users to *share* and *vote* on the words or phrases from their conversation (see Figure 1). While users chat, the server suggests keywords or phrases that it determines to be important to the conversation. These words appear as a list in the Share page (the process by which the server determines what words or phrases are significant is discussed in the Server section below). Users are then able to share or delete the suggested words depending on whether they feel the phrases are important components of their conversation. Once shared, the words appear in both users' Vote page, thereby allowing the other participant to vote the phrase up or down. The system is thus a two-step process of collaboratively determining the content of the visualization and consequently what music is suggested.

Server

To ensure that the application surfaced portions of the conversation with social importance, we used a two-step filtering process. While users chat, each message is parsed and analyzed by the server for keywords and phrases. In the first step of the filtering, the server uses text frequency inverse document frequency (TF/IDF) to select keywords from the users' conversation. The server uses the NPS Chat Corpus from the Natural Language Tool Kit (NLTK) (http://www.nltk.org/) as a basis for the TF/IDF algorithm. The NPS Chat Corpus consists of 10,567 posts from of approximately 500,000 posts gathered from various online chat services in accordance with their terms of service. Therefore, making it a valuable corpus of common English language words. We determined a threshold for the words and phrases the system chose by processing posts from online music forums. The second step filtered phrases that passed the TF/IDF algorithm threshold using social media. This enabled us to surface socially significant phrases. For each word or phrase that passed the TF/IDF threshold, Reflektor searched the Facebook API for corresponding Facebook Pages. Searching for a corresponding Facebook Page was crucial because the TF/IDF algorithm can only tell if a word or phrase is common or uncommon relative to a corpus. If a Facebook Page exists for a word or phrase, that means it was intentionally created by a Facebook user and therefore it is more likely to hold some social importance instead of just being an uncommon phrase or expression. To illustrate the point, in the sentence: "The new Kanye West album is great" the TF/IDF value for the bigram "Kanye West" is likely equal to the bigram "West album" or "new Kanye," since each of those bigrams is a phrase that is unlikely to appear in a chat corpus. However, the Facebook API will return a page with numerous Likes for Kanye West but not for the other phrases.

To determine which pages to include for this method of social filtering, we used pages with a number of "Likes" greater than 100. The Page Like threshold was determined by iteratively processing conversations from online music forums and adjusting the number of Likes until we felt the right balance of results was achieved. During our calibration of the TF/IDF and Page Like threshold, we found some page categories—such as Shopping/retail, Business service, and Pet supplies—returned consistently unhelpful results and chose to omit them. To disambiguate homonyms, the metadata returned from the Facebook API for the keyword or phrase is shown in the users' Share page. The metadata included the page description and Facebook page category. For some words or phrases, multiple results are returned. In this situation, each result is shown in the Share page and the users can choose the phrase for the category they are discussing.

Interactive Visualization

After a word or phrase is shared by a user, it then appears in the system's visualization. We created the visualization using JavaScript and a jQuery plugin called freewall (https://github.com/kombai/freewall). During the study, the visualization was displayed at full screen on a 60" wall-mounted monitor (see Figure 3). Reflektor visualizes phrases in two different ways: as a mood board or as a word cloud. The content of the visualization will update dynamically as users share and vote on phrases.

Figure 3: Room layout for the study showing an example mood board generated by the application on the wall monitor.

To select images for the mood board visualization, Reflektor uses the Google Search API. The search included both the phrase and the category from the corresponding Facebook page in the search string. We initially created the mood board visualization using the images from the Facebook page itself, but while piloting the system, we found the quality of the images to be inconsistent. After further pilot testing, we felt that using the Google API produced the best mood boards in terms of consistent quality of images for the phrases.

To encourage transparency of how the items in the visualization influence the music being selected, we chose to make the size of the items change relative to the number of votes the phrase received. After being shared, the phrases begin with a default size equal to approximately 10% of the display. When voted on, the image size doubles to approximately 20% for two votes and 40% for three votes. If a phrase has zero votes, it is removed from the visualization. The text of the word cloud increases in size in the same manner as the images in the mood board.

SYSTEM EVALUATION

We conducted an evaluation of Reflektor with 10 sets of dyads, for a total of 20 participants. We recruited participants through online discussion boards and with paper flyers. We randomly assigned participants to each dyad. Their ages ranged from 18 to 28 with an average age of 21.6. Eight participants identified as female and the remaining 12 identified as male. We compensated participants with a $20 gift card for their time. The study was conducted in a conference room on a university campus with a table in the center and a 60" monitor on the wall (see Figure 3).

Our research objective was to explore how individuals utilize music to create social contexts. To encourage participants to engage in conversations that would elaborate on this relationship, we intentionally recruited individuals that were unacquainted prior to the study. Because the participants were unacquainted, they did not have a shared understanding of each other's views on the contextual relevance of music and therefore needed to establish it through their conversation. This approach draws on Garfinkel's work studying essential features of common understanding, which sought to elicit "seen but unnoticed features of common discourse" [17:227]. While this approach to recruiting likely reduces the ecological validity of this work, we feel that it encouraged participants to be explicit about their views on the relationship between context and music and therefore provide more specific insights about the strategies participants use to create shared understanding.

During the study, we instructed participants to use the chat client to discuss two hypothetical events and the music they would like to play at each event: a "quiet evening with friends" and a "party." We instructed them to discuss anything they felt was relevant to organizing each of those events. The order for the event they discussed was counter balanced along with the order for the visualization used.

Each study session lasted approximately 90 minutes and included two rounds of the participants using the chat client to discuss music for each condition. The lab session began with the research staff demonstrating Reflektor to the participants. Between the conversations, the participants rated songs for the condition discussed and were asked about their experience. After the second round of chatting, we conducted a longer interview. We video recorded each study session and logged the participants' chat conversation along with phrases they shared, deleted, and voted on.

Creating Recommendations

To evaluate the quality of recommendations produced by the system, we created two sets consisting of five songs for both scenarios the participants discussed. To create the sets of songs we used two techniques: the first technique used a similarity ranking and the second used the system to conduct text parsing on the participant conversations. In the remainder of the paper we will refer to the techniques as *similar* and *text parsing* respectively. Prior to the study, we emailed each participant a spreadsheet and instructed them to list ten songs that—to quote from the instructions included in the spreadsheet—"you would want played during a quiet evening with friends" and ten songs "you would want played at a party with friends." We drew upon this data to generate a set of similar songs. For each dyad, we used the API of Last.fm (http://www.last.fm/api). Last.fm is a social music service with millions of active users, which logs their listening history and make it publicly available. We utilized their API to search for music similar to the songs both participants provided. Last.fm's "Track.getSimilar()" function returns the most similar songs as determined from their extensive listening history of its entire user base. Tracks returned from the API were ranked to produce a list that represented the most similar songs for both participants based on pre-study musical preferences.

To generate the songs for the text parsing condition, we searched the Last.fm API for songs tagged with the key words voted on by the participants. The process of creating the recommendations was run once at the end of each of the participants' conversations. The songs were weighted by the number of participant votes. When the page for a phrase had the category "musician or band" we queried the Last.fm API for the top 10 tags for the musician and incorporated those tags into the song queries. The songs were then ranked and normalized by the number of tags. This allowed us to explore how musicians were used in the conversation, instead of allowing the participants to simply list musicians to generate recommendations.

Chat Log Analysis

The two lead researchers coded the chat logs of the participants' conversations. The participants' chat conversations lasted approximately fifteen minutes per condition. On average, each conversation had 72 lines of dialog (σ=21.5) and a mean word count of 438 words (σ=110.7). The themes presented in this paper emerged from the iterative coding and refinement of the participants' chat conversations. The authors refined and developed these themes by reviewing the videotaped interviews conducted with the participants during each study session. These codes were further developed by drawing on the sociological research presented by DeNora in *Music in Everyday Life* [10], which explores the social and personal role that music plays in people's lives. Between one and three codes were used on each section of the participants' conversation. To ensure that the codes were applied consistently, the authors independently coded the first two interviews and compared the results to determine how consistently the codes were applied. The authors then iterated and refined codes that were applied inconsistently and reviewed sections of the conversations where variation in codes were found. After revising the codes, the authors then coded one additional interview and compared the consistency with which the codes were applied. After the second round of coding, the raters achieved agreement in >70% of the codes they applied to the transcripts. The authors then applied the codes to the remaining chat logs independently (Table 1).

FINDINGS

We have organized the findings into two sections: the first section discusses our analysis of the participants' chat logs and the themes that emerged in the strategies the participants used to ground their views on music and context. The second section presents the participants' ratings of the recommended music and their views on the associated visualization. All names used in this paper are anonymous identifiers given to participants during the lab study.

Code	Definition
Elicit modes of conduct	Music suggests and elicits associated modes of conduct.
Organize social interaction	Music acts as an affordance for social interaction.
Emotional modulation and constitution	Music is used to encourage desired emotional states.
Promote concentration	Music is used to create an environment that promotes concentration.
Create space for intimacy	Music enables the possibility of intimate behavior.
Secondary significance	Music suggests connotations of additional aesthetic.
Sonic properties	Musical properties, such as tempo and rhythm, contribute to an environment that enables modes of interaction.

Table 1 Summary of codes and their definitions from the analysis of chat transcripts.

Understanding Views on Music and Context

As mentioned above, the participants were unacquainted prior to the study. We intentionally recruited unacquainted participants so that they would have to establish what constituted the two conditions of the study—a party or a quiet evening with friends. In this sense, the participants were required to make the common sense understanding visible, surface background understanding, and then incorporate their understanding into their evolving discussion about the context and appropriate music for that context.

We saw participants develop common understanding in a variety of ways. In general terms, this process consisted of one of the participants specifying what the context should consist of, or what music would be appropriate for that context. Then, participants determined if that suggestion was aligned with the evolving notion of the current context. To accomplish this, the participants often utilized one of three criteria, discussed below: *sonic properties* of the music, *interaction styles* associated with the context of the event, or what *location* enables similar forms of interaction.

Sonic Properties of Music and Their Fit for Context

Discussing what music would be appropriate for the two contexts necessitated that the participants unpack their language to ensure the other participant understood what they were proposing. This was the case in all participant conversations as they tried to determine what constituted a quiet evening with friends, or "a chill party" as it was often described. In the example below from Interview 2, we can see the two participants discuss what the language means and subsequently how the meaning of the words might correspond to what music is appropriate.

> Bonnie: *cool. so what do you do at chill parties?*
> Brian: *Music, drink, conversation...*
> Bonnie: *alright. so we probs want music that's easy to talk over*
> Brian: *What constitutes chill for you? Slow tempo, repetitive, acoustic...?*

We can see this conversation starts off as a discussion of the activities for the party, but then quickly Brian tries to match the word "chill" to sonic properties of the music. This invites Bonnie to provide more details on what chill means to her.

> Bonnie: *music that's easy to talk over*
> Bonnie: *oh um*
> Bonnie: *probably beats that aren't too hard*
> Bonnie: *not too many wubs lol*
> Bonnie: *you?*

Bonnie again discusses chill in terms of activities that the music would permit, specifically something that accommodates talking. Brian does not respond, thereby not validating her suggestion, so she further elaborates on her initial response by describing the music in terms of properties of the music. Instead of defining chill, she decides to negate things that are not chill. She does this by referencing "beats that aren't too hard" as being inappropriate features of chill music. She then goes on to elaborate that "wubs"—an expression used to describe the bass modulation commonly used in dubstep music—would be uncharacteristic of chill music. The approach that Bonnie applies is characteristic of *generators* in category theory [25:12]. Bonnie is establishing the idea of what music is part of her category of chill music by defining a rule that can be applied to music to "generate" the members of that category. Her formulation is:

Music without hard beats – "wubs" = chill music

This strategy is a lighthearted attempt to characterize the idea of chill, but it is specific enough that Brian seems to understand what she means and proceeds to prompt her to continue establishing what music should be played at their chill party.

Using Activity to Establish Contextually Appropriate Music
In every chat conversation, the participants discussed what activities they planned to engage in for the given context. This was the most common way that the interaction of the context was framed by the participants. This frequently occurred when participants discussed dancing and what music they felt would be appropriate for and encourage dancing. However, we also saw it extend beyond the direct influence that music has structuring physical interaction to activities that draw on music's cultural significance to establish ambiance. This process is illustrated in the chat dialogue from Interview 4 when the participants discussed the context of a quiet evening with friends. The first few lines of the conversation consisted primarily of the participants making sure they are connected, but once it is clear they are both connected, Dave states:

Dave: *I like jazz and crooners.*

After eight more lines of the participants discussing games, the following conversation begins in which they try to establish music that corresponds to the game-playing activity that was suggested.

Dan: *jazz huh?*

Dan: *oh I'id say poker. how could you even play blackjack with friends lol*

Dave: *Poker is fun. Bring some chips and cards.*

Dan: *but let's get a playlist with a lot of jazz piano*

Dan: *yeah yeah will do*

Dave: *Herbie Hancock*

Dan: *do you know if Sarah is coming? She's cute.*

Dave: *She might be. I dunno.*

Dan: *how about Thelonious Monk or Art Tatum?*

Dan: *my brother plays sax so always sends me stuff to listen to*

Dave: *Monk might be a bit on the strange side. Same with Tatum. But I would say Tatum or Monk.*

Dave: *What about Miles Davis? not piano but he is pretty good.*

Dave: *Frank Sinatra?*

Dan: *ok well specifics aren't super important. we can mix in Sinatra or Ella Fitzgerald too*

Dan: *the important thing is what are we going to be drinking*

Dave: *Whiskey or wine. Both go well with Jazz and Sinatra I feel.*

From this portion of the participants' conversation, we can see them trying to match styles of music with activities in which they hope to engage. This begins with card playing but quickly evolves into a more holistic context when Dan asks if Sarah is coming to their quiet evening with friends. Because these participants did not know each other, this was evidently an imaginary person and the idea of getting to talk with a person that he thought was "cute" was used as a suggestion for a form of interaction that they hoped to establish—namely flirting. In all, the participants outline card playing, flirting, and drinking as being appropriate modes of interaction. This portion of their conversation illustrates how the activities establish and contribute to the criterion of what is appropriate for the context that extends beyond the sonic properties of the music. Presumably one could play card games to any type of music. But, for the context that they hope to establish where drinking wine, whiskey, and cocktails while people play cards and flirt, jazz music is viewed by the participants as being appropriate because it is presumably viewed as being more sophisticated. This example illuminates the interplay between activity and music for creating social context.

Location as an Indication of Music Type
Another strategy participants employed to establish understanding was utilizing physical locations as indicators of what music could be defined as appropriate for the context. In Interview 9, participants had little overlap in their musical tastes and therefore struggled to determine what chill music would be appropriate. After some discussion of the music, Ira began to suggest various clubs to establish common understanding.

Ian: *but there is electronic music that is pretty chill too*

Ira: *same era as Fleetwood Mac*

Ian: *I might wanna check it*

Ian: *the blues I mean*

Ira: *yeah:[a local club] specialize s in that stuff*

Ira: *gimme some electronic recommendations*

Ian: *yeah like [a local club]. I went to a few clubs [downtown] and they play stuff that is like that*

In this example, we can see Ian suggest electronic music, but rather than establish the type of electronic music he would like by suggesting an artist, Ira contributes to the idea of electronic music by associating it with a popular local club. Ira then asks Ian to make some suggestions to which Ian also provides downtown clubs to establish mutual understanding. This technique seems to be effective in helping them further refine what music would be most appropriate because it causes them to refine the idea of electronic music.

By using the club as a stand-in for a type of electronic music, participants use metonymy to a valuable way to reference the relevant ambiance and music. Metonymy is a principle by which a well-understood or easy-to-perceive aspect of something and use it to stand either for the object as a whole for some other aspect or part of it [25:77]. An example of metonymy is the entire movie industry in the United States being referred to as "Hollywood." By referencing the club, Ira easily alludes to the music played there and its ambience.

Recommendations and Visual Representation

Now that we have discussed how participants established what music would be appropriate for the different contexts, we will discuss the music that was recommended to participants and the impact of the visualizations on the participants' ratings.

After the participants chatted for each condition, their conversation was used to generate a playlist of five songs using the text parsing technique described in the section Creating Recommendations. These songs were combined with the five similar songs generated for the participants prior to the study. The lists of text parsed and similar songs were then combined into one randomly ordered playlist, which participants rated on a Likert scale from 1 to 5 based on 1) how much they enjoyed the songs, 2) how appropriate the songs were based on what they had discussed, and 3) how familiar they were with the songs.

In our analysis of their ratings, we used R [33] and lme4 [1] to perform a linear mixed effects analysis of the relationship between the visualization type, recommendation technique, and the participants' ratings of the music for *appropriateness*, *familiarity*, and *enjoyment* of the music. As fixed effects, we entered visualization type (mood board or word cloud), recommender type (text parsing or similarity ranking), scenario, and order into the model. As random effects, we included intercepts for participants and participant dyads. Visual inspection of the residual plots did not reveal any obvious deviation from homoscedasticity or normality for the *enjoyment* and *appropriateness* dependent variables. The *familiarity* ratings were largely bi-modal with modes at both 1 and 5 ratings. P-values were obtained by likelihood ratio tests of the full model with the effect in question against a model without the effect. Our analysis found that neither the visualization nor the recommendation type had a significant effect on participants' ratings for any of the dependent measures. A likelihood ratio test for interaction also showed no significant effect on participants' ratings for any dependent measure.

Visual Representation and Mutual Understanding

The statistical analysis did not demonstrate that the visualization type had a significant influence on the participant's perceived quality of the recommendations. However, in six sessions, the participants expressed sentiment that the mood board provided a useful way to contextualize the recommendations and insights into what music would or would not be appropriate to suggest.

"If I saw just this and had no knowledge of the conversation I probably wouldn't suggest Beethoven or Miles David, but I might suggest Bruce Springsteen or Tom Petty." (Dave, Interview 4)

At times when the other participant was unfamiliar with a musician suggested by the other participant, the mood board helped provide insight into what a musician or band might be like.

"No I hadn't heard of [the band]. The mood board helped me see who it was. Because we were talking about mellow music, so that could be... That's something we could play at a mellow party" (Eve, Interviews 5)

However, participants were sometimes confused when the system selected a homonym for the phrase that was selected. For example, displaying a house after the participants had discussed the house music genre. The system sought to disambiguate homonyms by using the Facebook category as part of the search string when searching for the images to populate the mood board. However, when the incorrect images were selected and images with meanings that differed from the intended sentiment were displayed, participants felt that the mood board was less useful than the word cloud.

"I would say that the photographs are a little more confusing, because of their association with the word. So, there are like two levels of association we need to make." (Ira, Interview 9)

Based on comments of this type, the mood board was helpful when the images were understood by both participants or when it seemed consistent with the ambiance. However, when an image was unclear, it was more confusing to the participants than the phrase in the word cloud.

From Conversation to Recommendation

We were encouraged that, from the participants' brief conversation, Reflektor produced recommendations they rated as equally enjoyable, appropriate, and familiar to music from the Last.FM API. To further explore the differences in how the recommendation technique operates, we analyzed how the text parsing algorithm created recommendations and how this differed from traditional techniques.

One of the key differences in how the system operates, compared to a traditional recommender system, is by emphasizing how individuals utilize music in the creation of shared social context. To encourage the notion that the context was social, we drew on the Facebook API to provide a form of social filtering of key words and phrases. However, they were not always terms that could be easily associated with musical choices. This meant that the strategies that participants found useful to create understanding with the other participant did not always result in improved music recommendations.

To illustrate how these strategies influenced what music was recommended, we return to the participants' conversation in the section Understanding Views on Music and Context. In

Interview 4, we saw participants use activities to establish common understanding. The participants discussed card games, which appeared in their visualization (see Figure 4) and ultimately factored into their music recommendations. However, only seven songs on Last.fm are tagged with the phrase "card games" which led to none of these songs being chosen for their playlists. Similarly, in Interview 2, the participants' chat conversation had a total of 409 words. Of these 409 words, twenty-one words or phrases were eventually shared by the participants—meaning that these twenty-one phrases appeared in the visualization and were used to produce the music recommendations. Interestingly, despite Bonnie's vivid description of what chill meant to her, none of those terms appeared in the visualization and therefore were not used to create the playlists. While her phrase "wubs" did have associated tags on Last.fm, there were no Facebook Pages returned by the initial query so her description went unaccounted for.

The participants from Interview 9 who used clubs to denote which music was appropriate had a total of twenty-two unique shared phrases from their conversation. After inspecting the results of the suggested terms, we found that clubs mentioned did have associated Facebook Pages but did not have associated metadata in the Last.fm API. Unfortunately, this resulted in a loss of a rich way to explain contextualized music. From each of these strategies, we can see the same result: a mismatch between how context is understood and a lack of metadata available to support the participant's strategy.

Figure 4: Mood board from Interview 4.

DISCUSSION

Based on our findings from the evaluation, we will now discuss the key insights and their implications for the design of context-aware music recommendation systems. Our discussion begins with the strategies participants utilized while creating understanding around music for social context and how music recommendation systems can be designed to accommodate these strategies. We then discuss the mismatches revealed in the way existing metadata and recommendation systems align with user strategies to create social context.

Strategies for Achieving Mutual Understanding

Our findings suggest that to achieve mutual understanding about music for social context, participants utilized three strategies: 1) the sonic properties of music, 2) the activities associated with the social interaction or activity they hoped to encourage, and 3) the location where this ambiance or mode of interaction is prevalent. These three strategies were used in concert with suggesting musicians directly and therefore offer opportunities for designers of music recommendation systems to augment how recommendations are created for social context.

Discussing the sonic properties of music was a common strategy utilized by participants throughout the interviews. Prior recommender systems have allowed users to create recommendations based on musical features such as tempo [16,19], but we did not see participants use this language extensively when discussing music. In fact, only one participant seemed to be interested in engaging in a discussion of music using the formal language from music theory. Participants drew on more common language to describe the music, such as Bonnie's use of the phrase "wubs." As was mentioned in the findings, her method for describing music also leveraged the use of *generators* in the descriptions of music. We imagine this approach could allow for a more flexible method of describing the sonic properties of music for users without extensive knowledge of music. Using common language has been explored for movie recommendations [41], and through commercial services such as APM Music (https://www.apmmusic.com/); a digital music production company whose extensive track library can be accessed online. Allowing for more flexible forms of expression with this metadata than current systems afford offers additional opportunities for recommender system design.

The participants also leveraged activity while discussing social context. Using activity to create music recommendations has been explored in prior work, but has primarily focused on matching sonic properties to physical activity such as dancing [6] or exercising [32]. While dancing was a large topic of conversation in the interviews, music was clearly key in structuring activities where the participants emphasized the cultural connotations of the music instead of the sonic properties alone. In DeNora's work exploring the role of music in everyday life, she refers to "scenes" that are constructed by drawing on music as a cultural material [10:123]. This includes the connotations that the music suggests. Participants clearly hoped to establish specific scenes and used activity in conjunction with music as a resource in the creation of those scenes. This provides opportunities to explore activity and cultural connotations, instead of mapping physical activity to the sonic properties of music. Because music is so highly personal, a generalized dataset of cultural significance would be impractical to create. However, the extensive body of work on personal informatics and lived experience [15] could be leveraged to create personally significant music recommendations for social contexts. This creates opportunities for designers to explore how users can create associations between their music and the activities in which they engage. We emphasize that this should allow the user to determine the scope of the activity and its relationship to the music rather than relying on automatic detection and inference. The critical step for designers is emphasizing the personal nature of music and its relationship to users' contexts.

Participants' use of metonymy to describe music that would be appropriate suggested additional opportunities for design. While systems such as [3,29,37] have leveraged location as a mechanism for improving music recommendations, their focus has been on the songs played at the location. Instead, our findings suggested that participants hoped to use the location as a resource in meaning making. The design of future recommender systems could emphasize the ambiance of the location over the music at the location as a resource in creating recommendations for social context. Additionally, the interface should enable users to personalize their relationship with their location and what that location means to the user.

Mismatches Between Recommender Systems and user Strategies to Create Social Context

When participants discussed music for social contexts, their goal was not to find specific songs per se, but rather to find music that enables, or at least does not inhibit, modes of interaction. Unfortunately, recommender systems generally emphasize similarity in music—based on features of the songs or user listening histories—instead of similarity in the modes of interaction the music enables. We feel it is important that social music recommenders provide an overview of how songs fit modes of interaction. In fact, we have seen a trend toward this in how music playlists are organized on music streaming services. Examples of this include playlists entitled "Gaming," "Focus," and "Sleep". How these methods of organization extend to other modes of social interaction is an underexplored area and offers opportunities for research in recommender systems and interface design that seek to capture the nuanced relationship between the users' views of music's role in creating context.

Orienting toward how users interact with music and away from the music itself is further supported by the strategies used by participants for discovering music. In every interview, we observed participants suggesting musicians as a strategy to ground the conversation. In the instances where the band was unfamiliar to the other participant, this effectively ended the conversation. While this could lead to the design implication that recommenders should incorporate an easier form of previewing music, we instead feel that it reveals a limitation of how recommenders normally operate. By relying on similarity in the music without the user behavior to contextualize the music, recommender system designers rely on familiarity with musicians to encourage

discovery. By leveraging methods for grounding conversations, designers can provide recommendations better suited for the group context without having to rely on the specifics of the musicians being recommended.

LIMITATIONS
One limitation of this study arose from focusing on how music is communicated. We choose to focus on communication because language is such a rich resource in meaning making. By focusing on communication, we were given insight into how individuals communicated what music was appropriate for a given context. By limiting the interaction of the participants to just computer mediated communication, we encouraged the participants to unpack their views in a way that may not have been as necessary with a richer mode of interaction. However, because we relied on chat-conversations over a short duration of time, we limited behavior that would occur in real world setting and therefore the ecological validity of the findings. An additional limitation of this study came from recruiting individuals that did not know each other. The aim again was to require participants to elaborate their views on what music would be appropriate for different contexts; if participants had a personal relationship, the relevance of the music was more likely to be established and therefore not need explicit elaboration. However, by recruiting unfamiliar dyads, we likely missed out on more natural forms of interaction that would occur among friends or acquaintances. Despite these limitations, we feel that the findings provide useful insights into the process and practices of group context-specific music recommendations.

CONCLUSION
In this paper, we presented a study with a music recommender prototype called Reflector, which we used to explore how users utilize music in the creation of shared social context. Our study and analysis of the participants' conversations while using Reflektor revealed the importance of establishing mutual understanding when determining context-specific music. To accomplish this, participants drew on the sonic properties of the music, the modes of interaction that the music enabled and the locations where the music is prevalent. When designing recommender systems to accommodate social context, our findings suggest designers should focus on strategies used to create mutual understanding and how this will correspond to metadata. By identifying these practices as being key to creating socially situated music recommendations, this work provides useful insights into a previously underexplored area of context-aware recommendation research.

ACKNOWLEDGMENTS
We would like to thank the study participants who participated in this research. We also acknowledge Intel's generous gift funding for this research. All research was reviewed and approved by the University of Washington's Human Subjects Division.

REFERENCES

1. Douglas Bates, Martin Mächler, Ben Bolker, and Steve Walker. 2014. Fitting Linear Mixed-Effects Models using lme4. *submitted to Journal of Statistical Software* 67, 1: 51. http://doi.org/10.18637/jss.v067.i01

2. Jared S. Bauer, Alex Jansen, and Jesse Cirimele. 2011. MoodMusic: A Method for Cooperative, Generative Music Playlist Creation. In *Proceedings of the 24th annual ACM symposium adjunct on User interface software and technology - UIST '11 Adjunct*, 85. http://doi.org/10.1145/2046396.2046435

3. Stephan Baumann, Björn Jung, Arianna Bassoli, and Martin Wisniowski. 2007. BluetunA: let your neighbour know what music you like. *Proceedings of ACM CHI 2007 Conference on Human Factors in Computing Systems* 2: 1941–1946. http://doi.org/10.1145/1240866.1240929

4. Timothy W. Bickmore and Justine Cassell. 2005. Social Dialogue with Embodied Conversational Agents. 23–54.

5. Barry Brown, Abigail J. Sellen, and Erik Geelhoed. 2001. Music Sharing as a Computer Supported Collaborative Application. In *Proceedings of Ecscw 2001*, 179–198.

6. Dave Cliff. 2006. hpDJ: An automated DJ with floorshow feedback. In *Consuming Music Together*, Kenton O'Hara and Barry Brown (eds.). Dordrecht, The Netherlands, 241–264. http://doi.org/10.1007/1-4020-4097-0_12

7. Andrew Crossen, Jay Budzik, and Kristian J. Hammond. 2002. Flytrap: intelligent group music recommendation. *Proceedings of the 7th international conference on Intelligent user interfaces - IUI '02*: 184. http://doi.org/10.1145/502716.502748

8. Jane W. Davidson. 2004. Music as Social behavior. In *Empirical Musicology: Aims, Methods, Prospects*, Eric Clarke and Nicholas Cook (eds.). Oxford University Press, New York, New York, USA, 57–76. http://doi.org/10.1093/acprof:oso/9780195167498.003.0004

9. Tia Denora. 1999. Music as a technology of the self. *Poetics* 27, 1: 31–56. http://doi.org/10.1016/S0304-422X(99)00017-0

10. Tia DeNora. 2000. *Music in everyday life*. Cambridge University Press.

11. Tia DeNora. 2005. Music and Social Experience. In *The Blackwell Companion to the Sociology of Culture, Blackwell* (Jacobs M,), Mark D. Jacobs and Nancy Weiss Hanrahan (eds.). Blackwell Publishing Ltd., Malden, MA, 147–159.

12. Anind K. Dey. 2001. Understanding and using context. *Personal and ubiquitous computing*: 4–7. http://doi.org/10.1007/s007790170019

13. Anind K. Dey and Gregory D. Abowd. 2000. Towards a better understanding of context and context-awareness. In *CHI 2000 workshop on the what, who, where, when, and how of context-awareness*, 1–6.

14. Paul Dourish. 2004. What we talk about when we talk about context. *Personal and Ubiquitous Computing* 8, 1: 19–30. http://doi.org/10.1007/s00779-003-0253-8

15. Daniel A Epstein, An Ping, James Fogarty, Sean A Munson, Computer Science, and Human Centered Design. 2015. A Lived Informatics Model of Personal Informatics. In *UbiComp '15*, 731–742. http://doi.org/10.1145/2750858.2804250

16. Yazhong Feng, Yueting Zhuang, and Yunhe Pan. 2003. Popular music retrieval by detecting mood. In *Proceedings of the 26th annual international ACM SIGIR conference on Research and development in informaion retrieval - SIGIR '03*, 375. http://doi.org/10.1145/860500.860508

17. Harold Garfinkel. 1964. Studies of the Routine Grounds of Everyday Activities. *Social Problems* 11, 3: 225–250.

18. Charles Goodwin and Marjorie Harness Goodwin. 1992. Assessments and the construction of context. In *Rethinking Context: Language as an Interactive Phenomenon*. 147–189. http://doi.org/10.2307/2074658

19. Byeong Jun Han, Seungmin Rho, Sanghoon Jun, and Eenjun Hwang. 2010. Music emotion classification and context-based music recommendation. *Multimedia Tools and Applications* 47, 3: 433–460. http://doi.org/10.1007/s11042-009-0332-6

20. David J. Hargreaves and Adrian C. North. 1999. The Functions of Music in Everyday Life: Redefining the Social in Music Psychology. *Psychology of Music* 27: 71–83. http://doi.org/10.1177/0305735699271007

21. Steve Harrison, Deborah Tatar, and Phoebe Sengers. 2007. The three paradigms of HCI. In *alt.CHI*.

22. Jennifer Healey, Rosalind W. Picard, and Frank Dabek. 1998. A New Affect-Perceiving Interface and Its Application to Personalized Music Selection. In *In Workshop on Perceptual User Interfaces,(San Francisco)*.

23. David S Kirk, Abigail Durrant, Gavin Wood, Tuck Wah Leong, Peter Wright, and Newcastle Tyne. 2016. Understanding the Sociality of Experience in Mobile Music Listening with Pocketsong. In *DIS 2016*, 50–61. http://doi.org/10.1145/2901790.2901874

24. Hannu Kukka and Rodolfo Patino. 2009. UbiRockMachine: A Multimodal Music Voting Service for Shared Urban Spaces. In *Proceedings of the 8th International Conference on Mobile and Ubiquitous Multimedia - MUM 09*, 1–8. http://doi.org/10.1145/1658550.1658559

25. George Lakoff. 1987. *Women, Fire, and Dangerous Things: What Categories Reveal about the Mind.* The University of Chicago Press.

26. Tuck W. Leong and Peter C. Wright. 2013. Revisiting social practices surrounding music. In *Proceedings of the SIGCHI Conference on Human Factors in Computing Systems - CHI '13*, 951. http://doi.org/10.1145/2470654.2466122

27. Andrés Lucero. 2012. Framing, aligning, paradoxing, abstracting, and directing. In *Proceedings of the Designing Interactive Systems Conference on - DIS '12*, 438. http://doi.org/10.1145/2317956.2318021

28. Giuseppe Mantovani. 1996. Social context in HCI: A new framework for mental models, cooperation, and communication. *Cognitive Science* 20: 237–269. http://doi.org/10.1016/S0364-0213(99)80007-X

29. Joseph F. E. McCarthy and Theodore D. Anagnost. 1998. MUSICFX: an arbiter of group preferences for computer supported collaborative workouts. In *CSCW '1998 Proceedings of the 1998 ACM conference on Computer supported cooperative work*, 348.

30. Deana McDonagh and Howard Denton. 2005. Exploring the degree to which individual students share a common perception of specific mood boards: observations relating to teaching, learning and team-based design. *Design Studies* 26, 1: 35–53. http://doi.org/10.1016/j.destud.2004.05.008

31. Kenton O'Hara, Matthew Lipson, Marcel Jansen, Axel Unger, Huw Jeffries, and Peter Macer. 2004. Jukola: Democratic Music Choice in a Public Space. In *Proceedings of the 2004 conference on Designing interactive systems processes, practices, methods, and techniques - DIS '04*, 145. http://doi.org/10.1145/1013115.1013136

32. Nuria Oliver and Fernando Flores-Mangas. 2006. MPTrain: a mobile, music and physiology-based personal trainer. *Proceedings of the 8th conference on Human-computer interaction with mobile devices and services* Helsinki,: 21–28. http://doi.org/10.1145/1152215.1152221

33. R Core Team. 2012. *R: A language and environment for statistical computing.* Vienna, Austria.

34. Yvonne Rogers. 2004. New theoretical approaches for human-computer interaction. *Annual Review of Information Science and Technology* 38, 1: 87–143.

35. Albrecht Schmidt. 2000. Implicit human computer interaction through context. *Personal Technologies* 4, 2–3: 191–199. http://doi.org/10.1007/BF01324126

36. Robin Sease and David W. McDonald. 2009. Musical fingerprints: Collaboration around home media collections. *Proceedings of the ACM 2009 international conference on Supporting group work*: 331–340. http://doi.org/10.1145/1531674.1531724

37. Jan Seeburger, Marcus Foth, and Dian Tjondronegoro. 2012. The sound of music: sharing song selections between collocated strangers in public urban places. In *Proceedings of the 11th International Conference on Mobile and Ubiquitous Multimedia - MUM '12*, 1. http://doi.org/10.1145/2406367.2406409

38. Abigail J. Sellen, Yvonne Rogers, Richard Harper, and Tom Rodden. 2009. Reflecting human values in the digital age. *Communications of the ACM* 52, 3: 58. http://doi.org/10.1145/1467247.1467265

39. Henrik Sørensen and Selma Lagerl. 2012. The Interaction Space of a Multi-Device , Multi-User Music Experience. In *NordiCHI '12 Proceedings of the 7th Nordic Conference on Human-Computer Interaction: Making Sense Through Design Pages 504-513*, 504–513. http://doi.org/10.1145/2399016.2399094

40. David Sprague, Fuqu Wu, and Melanie Tory. 2008. Music selection using the PartyVote democratic jukebox. In *Proceedings of the working conference on Advanced visual interfaces - AVI '08*, 433. http://doi.org/10.1145/1385569.1385652

41. Jesse Vig, Shilad Sen, and John Riedl. 2012. The Tag Genome: Encoding Community Knowledge to Support Novel Interaction. *ACM Transactions on Interactive Intelligent Systems* 2, 3: 1–44. http://doi.org/10.1145/2362394.2362395

42. Amy Voida, Rebecca E. Grinter, Nicolas Ducheneaut, W Keith Edwards, and Mark W. Newman. 2005. Listening in: practices surrounding iTunes music sharing. In *Proceedings of the 2005 Annual Conference on Human Factors in Computing Systems - CHI '05*. http://doi.org/10.1145/1054972.1054999

Modeling User Intrinsic Characteristic on Social Media for Identity Linkage

Xianqi Yu
Shandong University
Jinan, China
xqyu1993@126.com

Yuqing Sun
Shandong University
Jinan, China
sun_yuqing@sdu.edu.cn

Elisa Bertino
Purdue University
West Lafayette, USA
bertino@cs.purdue.edu

Xin Li
Shandong University
Jinan, China
lx@sdu.edu.cn

ABSTRACT

Most users on social media have intrinsic characteristics, such as interests and political views, that can be exploited to identify and track them. It raises privacy and identity issues in online communities. In this paper we investigate the problem of user identity linkage on two behavior datasets collected from different experiments. Specifically, we focus on user linkage based on users' interaction behaviors with respect to content topics. We propose an embedding method to model a topic as a vector in a latent space so as to interpret its deep semantics. Then a user is modeled as a vector based on his or her interactions with topics. The embedding representations of topics are learned by optimizing the joint-objective: the compatibility between topics with similar semantics, the discriminative abilities of topics to distinguish identities, and the consistency of the same user's characteristics from two datasets. The effectiveness of our method is verified on real-life datasets and the results show that it outperforms related methods.

ACM Classification Keywords

J.4 Social and Behavioral sciences

Author Keywords

Social Media; Privacy Issue; Identity Linkage; Intrinsic Characteristic; Embedding Method.

INTRODUCTION

The User Identity Linkage (UIL) problem refers to the problem of recognizing that two user identities from two different data sources actually refer to the same individual in real life [25]. The problem has recently attracted an increasing amount of attention from both academia and industry. It is a special concern of social communities because of privacy issues. It is also of critical importance for service providers to have deeper understanding of their customers from multiple perspectives so as to profile users on social media for better promotions or services.

In this paper, we focus on a setting in which we are given user behaviors collected during two time periods on the same social media platform. It is a common setting in UIL approaches that link identities via behavior data [8, 9, 27, 29]. It is assumed that, in the first period, user identities are known and in the second period their identities are anonymized [22]. For example, user identities might be changed to anonymous after applying some identity management system for protecting against identity linkage attack [10]. A user's web behavior may refer to browsing a piece of news on CNN, rating a film on MovieLens, or answering a question on Quora. Generally, such behaviors are relevant to some topics. For example, a user answered the question *How to evaluate Donald J. Trump be elected the 45th president of the United States* on Quora, and topics of this behavior can be tags *Political* and *President Election* marked on the question. We regard these interactive activities between users and related topics as *interactions* and denote a user behavior as a set of topics here afterwards. Our goal is to answer whether users can be identified only by their interactions with topics. Since the above settings are widely available in practice, this work would provide meaningful results for many related applications.

The identification of users based on their topic interactions requires addressing two challenges. One is the dynamic evolution of popular topics. We collected some statistics on topic frequency among all user behaviors in two time periods and obtained two probability distributions over topics. Figure 1(a) shows the difference between two probability distributions. The X-axis represents topics and the Y-axis represents the changing ratio of topic proportion, which is calculated as their difference divided by the average of topic proportion in two periods. The red line can be seen as a reference for the case in which the popularity of topic does not change between two pe-

GROUP 2018, January 7–10, 2018, Sanibel Island, FL, USA
Copyright © 2018 Association of Computing Machinery.
ACM ISBN 978-1-4503-5562-9/18/01 ...$15.00.
http://dx.doi.org/10.1145/3148330.3148340

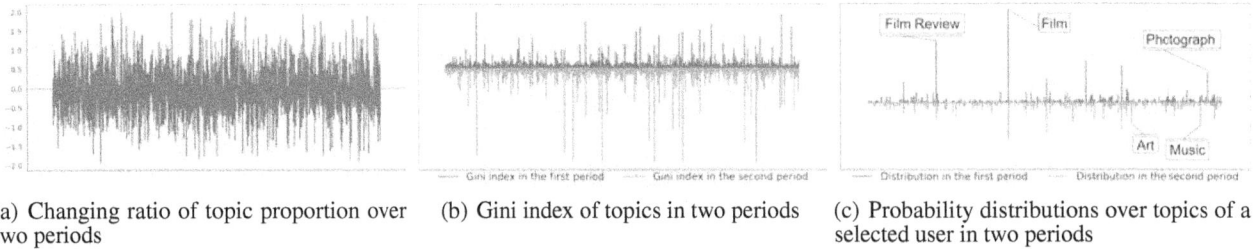

(a) Changing ratio of topic proportion over two periods

(b) Gini index of topics in two periods

(c) Probability distributions over topics of a selected user in two periods

Figure 1. The data are collected from Zhihu website which consist of users' behavior data in a whole year period. Figure(a) shows the changing ratio of topic proportion in two periods. Figure(b) shows the Gini index of topics in two periods. Figure(c) shows, for a randomly selected user, two probability distributions over his or her interested topics in two periods.

riods. The results show that most topics have obvious changes, either in an increasing trend or in a decreasing trend. Thus it is clear that popular topics vary a lot in different periods. As our problem is to distinguish user identities based on their behaviors, we also evaluate the discriminative abilities of topics. Considering the fact that many users pay almost the same attentions on some specific topics, it is difficult to distinguish them against these topics. However, if a topic is of concern to only a few users, this topic would be helpful to identify them. So we adopt Gini index to evaluate the discriminative abilities of topics, which is calculated as $1 - \sum_{i=1}^{m} p_i^2$, where p_i denotes the probability of the ith topic. It is often used as a measure of the impurity of data [12]. Figure 1(b) shows the Gini indexes of topics in two periods, where the X-axis represents topic and the Y-axis represents the Gini index. The higher Gini index, the higher the discriminative ability of the topic. In the figure, the upper half is the Gini index in the first period and the lower half is for the second period. The great difference between the two periods indicates that for each topic, the discriminative ability on user identities has changed over time.

Another observation is the change of topics of interest for each user. As shown in Figure 1(c), for a randomly selected user, the probability distributions over topics are quite different in two different periods, as shown by the difference between the blue and orange line in the figure. For example, the peak topics that this user has interacted with in the first period are *film review, film, photograph* etc., while in the second period, they changed to *art, music,* etc, which are marked in the figure. It is easy to understand that the statistics over topics in two periods are quite different and thus two identities cannot be linked by the similarity on the statistics over topics of interests.

To address the above challenges, this paper introduces the concept of user intrinsic characteristic so as to identify the inner motivations implied in user behaviors. Consider the example in Figure 1(c). Note that, although the topics of interest for the user seem different, it does not mean that the user's interests have changed. From the point of view of an art lover, the characteristics of this user remain the same in these behaviors. Thus our approach is to investigate the implicit semantics of topics by embedding each topic as a vector in a latent space and model users' intrinsic characteristics based on their interactions with topics. A topic representation is denoted by a d-dimensional vector, which can be learned from the training data. A user vector is the statistics on topics and

then is mapped to the same latent space as topics. In order to learn the embedding representations of both topics and user characteristics, we apply a joint-objective optimization. The first optimization objective is to maximize the compatibility between topics with similar semantics and their discriminative ability with respect to identity recognition. We define the semantic relevance between a pair of topics as their compatibility. Topics co-occurring in a behavior share a higher compatibility score, and thus their representations should be close in the latent space. The discriminating abilities of topics reflect the differences of user interactions on topics. We take the correlation between topics as a regularization in vector compatibility learning. The second optimization objective is to maximize the consistency of two characteristics in different time periods for each seed user, which reflects the fact that the intrinsic characteristics of an individual often remain stable over time. Then we adopt the learned embedding vectors to solve the task of identity linkage. We conduct experiments on two real-life datasets, and the results show that our method outperform related methods.

The rest of the paper is organized as follows. Section 2 discusses related works. Sections 3 and 4 present the formal definition of the UIL problem and the model of user intrinsic characteristics, respectively. We discuss in Section 5 the learning process of embedding representations. Section 6 presents the experimental results and Section 7 concludes the paper.

RELATED WORKS

Privacy & Identity Issues in Online Communities

The privacy and identity issues in online communities have attracted an increasingly amount of attention after the emergence of de-anonymization techniques, which match users in an anonymous dataset to real individuals. In recent years, organizations release more and more datasets in online communities for problem solving, such as business promotion or epidemic diseases prediction. These datasets contain many sensitive individual information, such as health histories or transactions. Although these datasets are anonymized by some techniques such as k-anonymization [6], recent research has shown that an adversary can use auxiliary information to de-anonymize users' records from the correlated and publicly available datasets [23, 24]. Narayanan et al. first introduced this problem [23], and used film reviews in IMDB as auxiliary information to successfully re-identify a number of specific users in anonymous Netflix data via comparing user activities in the two datasets. They also proposed a de-anonymization algorithm on user relation networks, which is able to effectively re-identify users in the anonymized graphs with only a few auxiliary information [24]. All these methods are based on the the presence of overlapping information between the anonymous and auxiliary datasets. Unlike such work, this paper focuses on the setting in which users' data are collected from two non-overlapping time periods. A different way of thinking to model users' intrinsic characteristics is presented to conduct de-anonymization.

Behavior Based Identity Linkage

Behavior based identity linkage is becoming a promising problem in the field of social computing in recent years. Many papers report results of analyses based on statistic methods to address this problem. Zang et al. performed a study on a nationwide call-data record dataset, and demonstrated that the most frequently visited locations can act as quasi-identifiers to re-identify users [29]. Gambs et al. introduced a Markov model to analyze the temporal evolution of the mobility patterns of the users [8, 9]. These data are all relevant to user mobile intelligent devices and reflect users' physical movements or real contacts. Comparatively, in our problem, user behaviors on social media are more noisy and random, which make the above methods inapplicable to our setting. Unnikrishnan et al. proposed a statistical method for matching user identity based on browsing history [22, 27]. They preprocess item data as categorical types and model user behavior as the statistics on these categories, where each user is formalized as a distinguished probability distribution pattern. The assumption behind such an approach is that each dimension of a random vector is independent from the others and each behavior follows an independent and identical distribution. However, in practice, such assumption does not always hold. For example, suppose that on a news there are the following topics: *Presidential Election*, *Trump* and *Political*. These topics are regarded as categorical data in the probability distribution but they are semantically related. Moreover, the behavior of reading a news about *Presidential Election* is probably followed by the behavior of reading a news about *Trump's Speech*, which is not an independent and identical distributed trial. Understanding semantics of people's behaviors on social media sites is a complex task, requiring a series of systematic studies. Bakhshi et al. examine the relationship between social signals and the emotional valence of users' reviews on the online recommendation community Yelp [2]. Some methods in collaborative recommendation systems model users' preference on the Web as a latent semantic vector by matrix factorization [4, 15]. Similar to this idea of finding latent factor, we model users' intrinsic characteristics in a latent vector space. Compared to these works, we learn the latent representations of users by a quite different objective function.

User Linkage Across Social Media Platforms

A lot of research has focused on the problem user linkage across social networks, which are highly related to our work. In social networks, information about user attributes and user relation network can be used to link user identity across different social platforms. Some researchers have demonstrated that

Table 1. Notations in this paper

SYMBOL	DESCRIPTION
u	user
U	set of users
T	set of topics
t_i	the ith topic in T
B_u	behavior sequence of user u
$\mathbf{b}_i$	the ith behavior in B_u
$\mathbb{B}$	set of behavior sequences of all users
$\mathbf{d}_u$	probability distribution over topics for user u
$\mathbf{v}_i$	embedding representation of topic t_i
$\mathbf{V}$	embedding matrix of topics in T
$\mathbf{p}_u$	intrinsic characteristic vector for user u
e	event of topic co-occurrence
c	normalization parameter for soft-max probability function
θ	parameters to be learned, including $\mathbf{V}$ and c
λ	weight parameter of regularization term
γ	preference parameter in joint objective optimization function

it is possible to recognize user identities by the structure of their social networks. Korula and Lattanzi introduced a many-to-many mapping algorithm based on the degrees of unmapped users and the number of common neighbors with the help of anchor users [16]. Bartunov et al. proposed an approach based on the conditional random fields called Joint Link-Attribute (JLA) [3], which considered both profile attributes and network properties. Liu et at. proposed a heterogeneous behavior modeling method [18]. They combined user attributes, topic distribution (obtained by LDA [5], which is a generative probabilistic model for collections of discrete data such as text corpora) and graph topology, and other information, and learn the mapping function by a multi-objective optimization to match user accounts from different social networks. Although these approaches show that jointly using user attributes and network structure can lead to better performance, such information is often unavailable in many online communities. So they are not appropriate for solving our problem. Amitay et al. studied the problem of author detection over a collection of blog pages originating from different sources and written to serve different online functions [1]. They proposed a compress based method to solve the problem. Different from focusing on the User Generated Content(UGC), we want to show how much the topics in users' web behaviors can reveal their identities. We propose an embedding method which focuses on interpreting the semantics of user behaviors. Then we are able to model users' intrinsic characteristics and identify users.

PROBLEM DEFINITION

Let U denote the user set in a given setting. For any user $u \in U$, his or her behaviors on social media are given as a sequence of topic interactions. Let $T = \{t_1, t_2, ..., t_{|T|}\}$ represent the set of all topics on a platform. The behavior sequence of u is denoted as $B_u = [\mathbf{b}_1, ..., \mathbf{b}_{|B_u|}]$, where each behavior $\mathbf{b}_i$ is a vector of size $|T|$, $\mathbf{b}_i \in \{0, 1\}^{|T|}$. For each behavior $\mathbf{b}_i$, $\mathbf{b}_i(k) = 1$

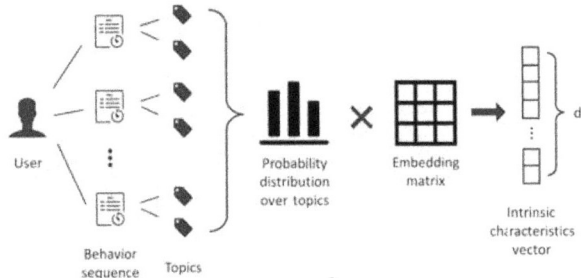

Figure 2. Modeling user intrinsic characteristic based on topic embedding

indicates that $\mathbf{b}_i$ interacts with topic t_k; And $\mathbf{b}_i(k) = 0$ otherwise. Let $\mathbb{B}_1 = \{B_1, B_2, ..., B_{|\mathbb{B}_1|}\}$ and $\mathbb{B}_2 = \{B_1, B_2, ..., B_{|\mathbb{B}_2|}\}$ denote two sets of behavior sequences collected from two separate time periods. We summarize the notations used in this paper in Table 1. The UIL problem is defined as follows.

Definition 1. **User Identity Linkage (UIL)**: Given a set of users U, and their behavior sequences from two time periods: the identity-labeled $\mathbb{B}_1$ and the anonymized $\mathbb{B}_2$, the UIL problem is to label behavior sequences in $\mathbb{B}_2$ with user identities in $\mathbb{B}_1$.

INTRINSIC CHARACTERISTIC MODELING

From the above discussion, we can see the challenges to UIL are topic popularity evolution and variations of the similar topics. To solve these challenges, we propose a topic embedding based user intrinsic characteristics model as illustrated in Figure 2. The model includes two parts: learning topic representation in latent space according to a joint-objective optimization and modeling user intrinsic characteristic against behavior related topics. Based on the intrinsic characteristics, we then verify user identity mapping relationships based on user vectors in the latent space.

To model user intrinsic characteristics, we first learn user behaviors by statistics over topics. For a user's behavior sequence B_u, let $\mathbf{d}_u \in R^{|T|}$ denote the probability distribution over topics, where the kth element of $\mathbf{d}_u$ is given by:

$$\mathbf{d}_u(k) = \frac{\sum_{i=1}^{|B_u|} \mathbf{b}_i(k)}{\sum_{i=1}^{|B_u|} \sum_{j=1}^{|T|} \mathbf{b}_i(j)} \quad , k = 1, 2, ..., |T|. \quad (1)$$

To interpret the semantics of topics, we embed them into a latent space. Each topic is represented as a d-dimensional vector representing some intrinsic characteristics. Let matrix $\mathbf{V} \in R^{|T| \times d}$ denote the embedding representations of topics,

$$\mathbf{V} = \begin{bmatrix} \mathbf{v}_1^\top \\ \mathbf{v}_2^\top \\ \vdots \\ \mathbf{v}_{|T|}^\top \end{bmatrix} \quad (2)$$

where $\mathbf{v}_i$ is the embedding representation of topic t_i. Then a user's intrinsic characteristic is modeled as a linear transformation of the topic distribution $\mathbf{d}_u$, namely $\mathbf{p}_u = \mathbf{V} \cdot \mathbf{d}_u$. Here the topic embedding matrix $\mathbf{V}$ is called the transformation matrix. Modeling user intrinsic characteristic has two benefits.

From the perspective of a single user, it helps in finding the common semantics in the dynamics of the topics of interest to the user and so to keep the consistency of one's traces in different time periods. From the global perspective, it helps interpreting the semantics of a newly emerged topic. Besides, since many topics are created by users, they might be noisy and sparse. The embedding method can reduce the dimension of topic space in user behaviors.

Based on the topic vectors, the UIL problem can be solved by three steps: 1)To model the intrinsic characteristics of each user behavior sequence in both $\mathbb{B}_1$ and $\mathbb{B}_2$; 2) To quantify the similarity between two user vectors $\mathbf{p}_u$ from $\mathbb{B}_1$ and $\mathbf{p}'_u$ from $\mathbb{B}_2$; 3) For a target anonymized user $\mathbf{p}'_u$, to use the nearest neighbor method to find the top k similar users in $\mathbb{B}_1$. There are many candidate distance functions, such as Euclidean distance and Cosine distance. We would discuss in details which is appropriate for the UIL problem in the experiments section .

EMBEDDING LEARNING

In this section, we first discuss the joint-objective of the topic embedding learning process and then present the learning algorithm.

Joint-Objective

The embedding representations are learned by jointly optimizing two objectives. The first objective is to maximize the compatibility between topics. This is motivated by the fact that topics associated with the same content are often related. For example, on the Q&A website Quora, a user answered the question *How to learn deep learning*. The tags marked by users on the question are regarded as topics, such as *Machine Learning* and *Deep Learning*. Although they are different words, they are actually highly related with respect to semantics. That is, topics co-occurring in a behavior always have high compatibility. Consequently, their embedding representations should be close in the latent space. So we introduce the compatibility score between a pair of topics as their semantic relevance.

The co-occurrence of topics t_i and t_j is defined as an event e_{ij}. The compatibility score of e_{ij} is given by:

$$S_\theta(e_{ij}) = \mathbf{v}_i \cdot \mathbf{v}_j \quad (3)$$

where $\theta = \{\mathbf{V}\}$ denotes the set of model parameters.

When we consider the topic compatibility with respect to semantics, at the same time, we also take into account the discriminating ability on identity linkage, that is, how much a pair of topics contribute in distinguishing identities. We thus introduce the correlation coefficient between two topics as an adjustment parameter, which is learned from the statistics on these topics against all user behaviors. There are many correlation function candidates. For example, the Pearson correlation coefficient (PCC)[1] can be chosen as a measure, which is the linear correlation between two variables and ranges from -1 to 1, where value 1 indicates they are totally positive linearly correlated, and value -1 indicates they are totally negative linearly correlated. Let PCC_{ij} denote the PCC of topic t_i and t_j.

---

[1] https://en.wikipedia.org/wiki/Pearson_correlation_coefficient

We refine the compatibility score between topics t_i and t_j as:

$$S_\theta(e_{ij}) = \frac{\mathbf{v}_i \cdot \mathbf{v}_j}{\sigma\left(\text{PCC}_{ij}\right)} \quad (4)$$

where $\sigma(x) = \frac{1}{1+\exp(-x)}$. The introduction of the sigmoid function $\sigma(x)$ is to prevent the denominator from being zero.

Here is an example to illustrate why PPC is helpful for the discriminative ability of a pair of topics. Consider the pair of topics *Dota* and *LOL*, two popular computer games of the same type. They are occasionally mentioned together for comparison and discussion purposes. But in a more general case, they appear independently. Based on general knowledge about the game field, a *Dota* game player seldom plays game *LOL*, and vice versa. If we learn their representations only by their co-occurrences, they would be very close to each other and it would be difficult to distinguish two types of players. Since these two topics share a low PCC, by using the correlation parameter, their compatibility score can also reach a high value without their representations being too close.

Let $\mathbf{E}$ be the set of events, namely all topic pairs, $|\mathbf{E}| = \frac{|T|(|T|-1)}{2}$. We adopt the soft-max function to model the occurrence probability of such an event.

$$P_\theta(e) = \frac{\exp(S_\theta(e))}{\sum_{x \in \mathbf{E}} \exp(S_\theta(x))} \quad (5)$$

Let E_p denote the event dataset of all pair-wise topic co-occurrences extracted from the training data. The loss function of topic compatibility is defined as follows:

$$J_T(\theta) = -\sum_{e \in E_p} \log P_\theta(e) \quad (6)$$

The second objective is to maximize the consistency of the intrinsic characteristics of the same user. Recall the notions of user behavior sequences in two periods, $B_u \in \mathbb{B}_1$ and $B'_u \in \mathbb{B}_2$, respectively. For any two sequences B_u and B'_u belonging to the same user u, the corresponding latent vectors are $\mathbf{p}_u$ and $\mathbf{p}'_u$. Let $\text{Dist}(\mathbf{p}_u, \mathbf{p}'_u) = -\mathbf{p}_u \cdot \mathbf{p}'_u$ evaluates the distance between them. Given a set of seed users labeled in both periods, denoted as $U_{\text{seed}} \subset U$, and B_u and B'_u from two periods belonging to the same user $u \in U_{\text{seed}}$, our goal is to maximize the consistency of the same user and the difference between different users. The objective function for minimization is defined as follows:

$$J_C(\theta) = \sum_{u \in U_{\text{seed}}, v \in U, u \neq v} \left(\text{Dist}(\mathbf{p}_u, \mathbf{p}'_u) - \text{Dist}(\mathbf{p}_u, \mathbf{p}'_v) \right) \quad (7)$$

We transform the function into the form of hinge loss and add a regularization term:

$$J_C(\theta) = \sum_{u \in U_{\text{seed}}, v \in U, u \neq v} \left(\max(0, \text{Dist}(\mathbf{p}_u, \mathbf{p}'_u) - \text{Dist}(\mathbf{p}_u, \mathbf{p}'_v) + \varepsilon) \right) + \lambda ||\mathbf{V}||_2^2 \quad (8)$$

Based on the above two objectives, we formulate the learning process of topic embedding as a joint-objective optimization.

We model the objective function as a linear combination of the above two objectives

$$J_U(\theta) = \gamma \cdot J_T(\theta) + (1 - \gamma) \cdot J_C(\theta) \quad (9)$$

where $\gamma \in [0, 1]$ is a preference parameter. The optimal solution of parameters is

$$\theta^* = \arg\min_\theta J_U(\theta) \quad (10)$$

Since the size of $\mathbf{E}$ in Equation 5 is $\frac{|T|(|T|-1)}{2}$, calculating the normalization part is quite time consuming. To address this challenge, we use the Noise Contrastive Estimation (NCE) [11] to estimate the parameters in our objective function. NCE provides a principle for unnormalized statistical models, which has been applied in estimating language models, word embedding, and anomaly detection [7, 20, 21]. NCE considers the normalization constant as an additional parameter of the model. We first consider the normalization constant as a parameter c. The probability in Equation 5 is thus re-written as:

$$P_\theta(e) = \exp(S_{\theta_0}(e) + c) \quad (11)$$

where $\theta = \{\theta_0, c\}$ represents the new parameters to be learned. In NCE, artificially generated noise data is added to the training data, and both parameters in probability density function and normalization constant can be estimated by discriminating the original data and noise data. The artificial noise distribution, denoted by $P_n(e)$, is the probability of an event e to be a noise sample. For each observed event e, we sample k noise samples $\{e'\}$ according to P_n. As for the chosen of P_n, it can be some factorized distribution on the event space, which can be specified uniformly or computed by counting frequency of topics in dataset. In this paper we use the strategy of counting frequency as it has been reported to be better [7]. We use $D = 1$ to indicate the event e in the observed data set $\mathbf{E}$ and $D = 0$ to indicate an event from the noise sample. The posterior probability is:

$$P(D = 1 | e, \theta) = \frac{P_\theta(e)}{P_\theta(e) + kP_n(e)}$$
$$= \sigma\left(\log P_\theta(e) - \log kP_n(e) \right) \quad (12)$$

$$P(D = 0 | e, \theta) = \frac{kP_n(e)}{P_\theta(e) + kP_n(e)}$$
$$= 1 - \sigma\left(\log P_\theta(e) - \log kP_n(e) \right) \quad (13)$$

where $\sigma(x) = \frac{1}{1+\exp(-x)}$ is the sigmoid function. Now we fit the model by maximizing the expectation of log-posterior probability over the mixture of observed samples and noise samples. The expectation is formulated as follows:

$$E_{P_\theta}[\log P(D = 1|e, \theta)] +$$
$$kE_{P_n}[\log P(D = 0|e, \theta)]$$
$$= E_{P_\theta}\left[\log \sigma\left(\log P_\theta(e) - \log kP_n(e)\right)\right] + \qquad (14)$$
$$kE_{P_n}\left[\log\left(1 - \sigma\left(\log P_\theta(e) - \log kP_n(e)\right)\right)\right]$$

Then the loss function of an event and its noise samples is formulated as:

$$J_T(\theta) = -\log\sigma\left(\log P_\theta(e) - \log kP_n(e)\right) -$$
$$\sum_{e'}\log\left(1 - \sigma\left(\log P_\theta(e') - \log kP_n(e')\right)\right) \qquad (15)$$

The gradient function for $\mathbf{V}$ in $J_T(\theta)$ is

$$\frac{\partial J_T(\theta)}{\partial \mathbf{V}} = \left[\sigma\left(\log P_\theta(e) - \log kP_n(e)\right) - 1\right]\frac{\partial S_\theta(e)}{\partial \mathbf{V}}$$
$$+ \sum_{e'}\left[\sigma\left(\log P_\theta(e') - \log kP_n(e')\right)\right]\frac{\partial S_\theta(e')}{\partial \mathbf{V}} \qquad (16)$$

Since the gradient function for c is similar to $\mathbf{V}$, for presentation simplification, we do not present it in this paper. The gradient function for another objective function $J_C(\theta)$ is formulated as follows:

$$\frac{\partial J_C(\theta)}{\partial \mathbf{V}} = \sum_{u \in U_{\text{seed}}, v \in U, u \neq v}\left[\mathbf{d}_u(\mathbf{d}_u'^\top - \mathbf{d}_v'^\top) + (\mathbf{d}_u' - \mathbf{d}_v')\mathbf{d}_u^\top\right]\mathbf{V} \qquad (17)$$

Algorithm 1: Adam SGD Algorithm

1 **Require:** α: Stepsize
2 **Require:** $\beta_1, \beta_2 \in [0, 1)$: Exponential decay rates for the moment estimates
3 **Require:** $f(\theta)$: Stochastic objective function with parameters θ
4 **Require:** θ_0: Initial parameter vector
5 $m_0 \leftarrow 0$, $v_0 \leftarrow 0$, $t \leftarrow 0$
6 **while** θ_t *not converged* **do**
7     $t \leftarrow t + 1$
8     $g_t \leftarrow \nabla_\theta f_t(\theta_{t-1})$(Get gradients w.r.t stochastic objective at timestep t)
9     $m_t \leftarrow \beta_1 \cdot m_{t-1} + (1 - \beta_1) \cdot g_t$
10    $v_t \leftarrow \beta_2 \cdot v_{t-1} + (1 - \beta_2) \cdot g_t^2$
11    $\widehat{m}_t \leftarrow m_t/(1 - \beta_1^t)$
12    $\widehat{v}_t \leftarrow v_t/(1 - \beta_2^t)$
13    $\theta_t \leftarrow \theta_{t-1} - \alpha \cdot \widehat{m}_t/(\sqrt{\widehat{v}_t} + \varepsilon)$
14 **end**
15 **return** θ_t (Resulting parameters)

Learning Algorithm

In our approach, we adopt the Stochastic Gradient Decent (SGD) method for learning the parameters. To speed up the learning procedure, we propose a weighted joint-objective optimization algorithm based on Adam [14].

The Adam algorithm has been shown to work well in practice and to favorably compare to other adaptive learning methods. To make this paper self-contained, we present the Adam steps in Algorithm 1. Our algorithm is summarized in Algorithm 2. In each iteration, for efficient computation, we randomly select an objective to update parameters $\mathbf{V}$ based on γ. And we sample a mini-batch of topic co-occurrences for objective J_T and sample a user from seed user set for objective J_C. All parameters in Adam, except for $\mathbf{V}$, are independent from each other in the optimization process of the two objectives.

Algorithm 2: Adam based Joint-objective SGD Algorithm

Input: Size of mini-batch n; Preference weight γ; Training samples of topic co-occurrences $\mathbf{E}$; Users set U and seed user set U_{seed}
Output: Embedding matrix V
1 Initialize V randomly
2 **while** $J_U(\theta)$ *not convergenced* **do**
3     $x = random(0, 1)$ //generate a real number $x \in [0, 1)$
4   **if** $x < \gamma$ **then**
5   Sample n topic co-occurrence events e and $k * n$ noise events e' randomly
6   Select $J_T(\theta)$ as objective function, perform an iteration in Adam to update $\mathbf{V}$
7   **end**
8   **else**
9   Sample a user u_i randomly
10   Select $J_C(\theta)$ as the objective function, perform an iteration in Adam to update $\mathbf{V}$
11   **end**
12 **end**
13 **return** V

EXPERIMENTS

Datasets

We use two real datasets, *MovieLens* and *Zhihu*, to experimentally evaluate the proposed method. The statistics of the two datasets are listed in Table 2. Details are given below.

MovieLens Dataset. The *MovieLens 20M* dataset released by Grouplens [13] contains user rating and free-text tagging activities on *MovieLens*, a popular movie recommendation platform. It contains data created by 138493 users between January 09, 1995 and March 31, 2015. Since most users do not keep active across 20 years, we select a part of the dataset which is created from April 2009 to March 2015, in which enough active users exist during this period. Users' ratings on movies are considered as user behavior records. Each pair of movie and tag is associated with a relevance score ranging from 0 to 1, using the Tag Genome approach [28]. Considering the semantic correlation between tags and a movie, only tags with relevance scores larger than 0.7 are selected as topics on this movie. To evaluate our method for solving the UIL problem, we partition the selected dataset into two parts according to time period: the first part $\mathbb{B}_1$ covers ratings from April 2009

Table 2. Statistics of Experiment Datasets

Datasets	# users	# topics	# events	# records
Zhihu	1,861	2,590	2,710,804	2,935,482
MovieLens	1,857	1,100	2,396,979	831,106

to April 2012, and second part $\mathbb{B}_2$ covers ratings from April 2012 to April 2015.

Zhihu Dataset. *Zhihu* is a Chinese Q&A website where questions are created, answered, edited and organized by the platform audience. We crawled user behavior records of around 8,000 users from October 2015 to September 2016, such as answering questions, voting up answers, etc. The tags marked on questions are selected as topics. The dataset is also partitioned into two parts: the first part $\mathbb{B}_1$ covers behaviors from October 2015 to March 2016, and second part $\mathbb{B}_2$ covers behavior data made from April 2016 to September 2016.

Evaluation Metrics and Distance Metrics

For the UIL problem, a widely adopted evaluation metric is to calculate the top-k similar candidates for a target user and verify whether the true identity is within the results. In our setting, for each user $u \in \mathbb{B}_2$, we calculate its distances with users in $\mathbb{B}_1$ and rank them in an ascending order. The index function $hit(u)$ is used to verify whether user u is correctly mapped to the same identity in $\mathbb{B}_1$ within the top-k users. $hit(u) = 1$ indicates that u has been correctly linked, $hit(u) = 0$ otherwise. Let U_{test} denote the set of test users, the accuracy for identity linkage is defined as follows:

$$acc = \frac{\sum_{u \in U_{test}} hit(u)}{|U_{test}|} \tag{18}$$

There are many candidate distance functions. Considering the semantics of user vectors, we adopt the Cosine distance and Euclidean distance in most experiments. Since some comparison methods adopt the probability distribution as user vectors, we also adopt the balanced KL divergence as the distance metrics in this method. For example, Naini et al. adopt the balanced KL divergence for user matching problem. It performs well in their statistics method [22, 27]. For justification purpose, we adopt their best results for comparison. However, this metric is not suitable for the intrinsic characteristic vectors that we use in our approach. So this metric is only used in the comparison methods.

Another evaluation strategy is matching all users simultaneously, which can be seen as the problem of minimum-weight perfect matching on a bipartite graph. We do not choose this strategy for two reasons. One is the complexity of the problem. The well-known Hungarian algorithm can solve the perfect matching problem with complexity $O(n^3)$ [17] where n represents the number of users. As n increases, the computation cost becomes high. Another reason is that the *exact matching* definition is not common in practice.

Comparison methods and settings

We compare the following state-of-art methods for UIL.

Statistics. In this method, the probability distribution over topics is seen as a user characteristic vector [22, 27], which is directly applied to the distance between users.

NMF. We also consider the topic model NMF [26], because it is similar to our method from the point of view of discovering latent characteristics. We define hyper-topic (or latent factor) as a higher level generalization among topics. We use the user-topic probability distribution matrix as the input of NMF. NMF outputs the relevance between user and hyper-topics, which is used as the user vectors for identity linkage.

E-T (Embedding with Topic compatibility). This method is a specific form of our proposed method which learns the embedding using only the objective of topic compatibility and ability to distinguish users, namely γ is equal to 1.

E-C (Embedding with Characteristic consistency). This method is the second form of our proposed method which learns the embedding using only the objective of user intrinsic characteristic consistency. It means that γ is set to 0.

E-TC (Embedding with Topic compatibility and Characteristic consistency). This is the general form of our proposed method, which learns the embedding using a joint-objective optimization.

The dimension of the latent space in our methods and the numbers of hyper-topics in NMF are set to 50. All parameters to be learned are initialized randomly. For each observed topic co-occurrence, we draw one negative sample. To speed up the computation of the stochastic gradient descent, we set a mini-batch of 1024 for sampling topic co-occurrence events. For the experiments on the *Zhihu* dataset, we set a behavior threshold of 100, which means we choose users who have more than 100 behavior records in both periods. We explore how this threshold influences identity linkage in the experiments. We also filter out topics that occur less than 200 times. Other parameters are set as follows: $\varepsilon = 10^{-1}, \gamma = 0.5, \lambda = 0$. In *MovieLens* dataset, we set behavior threshold to be 50 and $\varepsilon = 10^{-2}, \gamma = 0.1, \lambda = 10^{-5}$. We adopt a 5-fold cross-validation in our experiments.

Results for Identity Linkage

We first verify the accuracy of our methods and other comparison methods. The results, reported in Table 3, show that method **E-TC** largely outperforms other methods. On top-1 identity linkage, the accuracy of **E-TC** reaches nearly 50% in *Zhihu* dataset and nearly 13% in *MovieLens* dataset, respectively, which is 12% and 6% higher than the method NMF. On top-5 and top-10 linkage, the accuracy of method **E-TC** outperforms on both datasets. Furthermore, in the *MovieLens* dataset, an increasing k enhances the accuracy of method **E-TC** compared with the other methods. This good performance shows that although the learned characteristics of users can not guarantee an exactly identity matching, they are able to provide good approximations for recognizing a user.

When we use only a single objective to learn the embedding, namely methods **E-T** or **E-C**, the accuracy is still higher than the accuracy of baseline methods on both datasets. It is interesting to notice that in the *Zhihu* dataset under the Cosine

Table 3. Accuracy of Identity Linkage Compared with Different Methods

Distance Metric	top-1			top-5			top-10		
	cos	Euc	KL	cos	Euc	KL	cos	Euc	KL
Zhihu Dataset									
Statistics	0.366	0.302	0.354	0.528	0.435	0.493	0.586	0.489	0.564
NMF	0.379	0.344		0.576	0.520		0.651	0.584	
E-T	0.419	0.441		0.603	0.623		0.672	0.695	
E-C	0.372	0.372		0.607	0.602		0.693	0.687	
E-TC	**0.497**	**0.469**		**0.695**	**0.664**		**0.762**	**0.730**	
MovieLens Dataset									
Statistics	0.059	0.055	0.043	0.162	0.142	0.113	0.229	0.209	0.153
NMF	0.065	0.058		0.156	0.143		0.248	0.219	
E-T	0.090	0.088		0.210	0.208		0.280	0.277	
E-C	0.104	0.100		0.246	0.237		0.336	0.322	
E-TC	**0.129**	**0.126**		**0.279**	**0.270**		**0.366**	**0.355**	

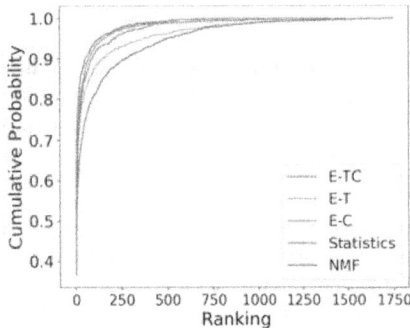

(a) CDF of ranking in Zhihu

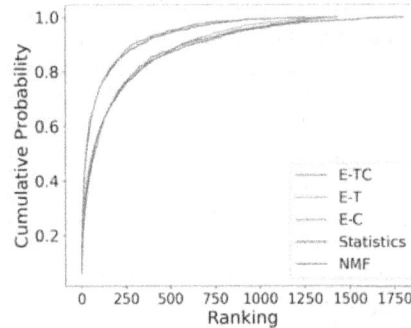

(b) CDF of ranking in MovieLens

Figure 3. The CDF of ranking of users with themselves in different methods. The X-axis corresponds to the ranking of true identity linkage. The Y-axis represents the cumulative distribution of users, which means the proportion of users whose ranking is less than the value in x-axis. Both figures indicate that introducing seed users (E-TC, E-C) improves the learning of the embedded user behavior semantics.

distance, method **E-T** outperforms **E-C** in the case of top-1 linkage. But as k increases, method **E-C** gradually outperforms **E-T**. Such a result indicates that the objective of topic compatibility is quite helpful when performing accurate identity linkage, and the objective of characteristic consistency makes a user's trace more identical from the global perspective.

When comparing different distance metrics, there is no obvious difference between Cosine and Euclidean distances. In most cases, the Cosine distance performs slightly better than the Euclidean distance except in the *Zhihu* dataset by method **E-T**. So we adopt the Cosine distance metric in the rest of the experiments.

Although our methods can not exactly link every user identity, they do reduce the difficulty in recognizing a specific user from a large user set. To have a clear explanation of such a result, for each anonymized user $u \in \mathbb{B}_2$, we calculate the distance between u and every user $v \in \mathbb{B}_1$, and count the ranking of his or her true identity. The smaller the ranking, the better the linkage performance. Figure 3 shows the Cumulative Distribution Function(CDF) curve on the rankings for the whole test dataset. We can see that, in both datasets, method **E-**

TC performs the best, shown as the fast rising curve, followed tightly by method **E-C**. Such results show that the introducing seed users provides more background knowledge; thus the embedding method can learn more comprehensive semantics from user behaviors. Since method **E-T** does not introduce such background knowledge, it performs worse than the other two.

Influence of Parameters and Settings

We first analyze the preference parameter γ, which is the trade-off term for two learning objectives. Figure 4(a) shows the performance for different values of γ on the *Zhihu* dataset, where $\gamma = 0$ indicates using only the characteristic consistency objective, and $\gamma = 1$ indicates using only the topic compatibility objective. We can see that when γ is around 0.3-0.4, our method performs best. Figure 4(d) shows the performance for different values of γ in the *MovieLens* dataset. Our method performs best when $\gamma = 0.1$. Such results show that, in the *MovieLens* dataset, tags are not so semantically relevant as in the *Zhihu* dataset. Consequently, the results show the small importance of topic compatibility in optimization.

Then we analyze the impact of the embedding dimension parameter d. As a comparison, we choose the same dimension

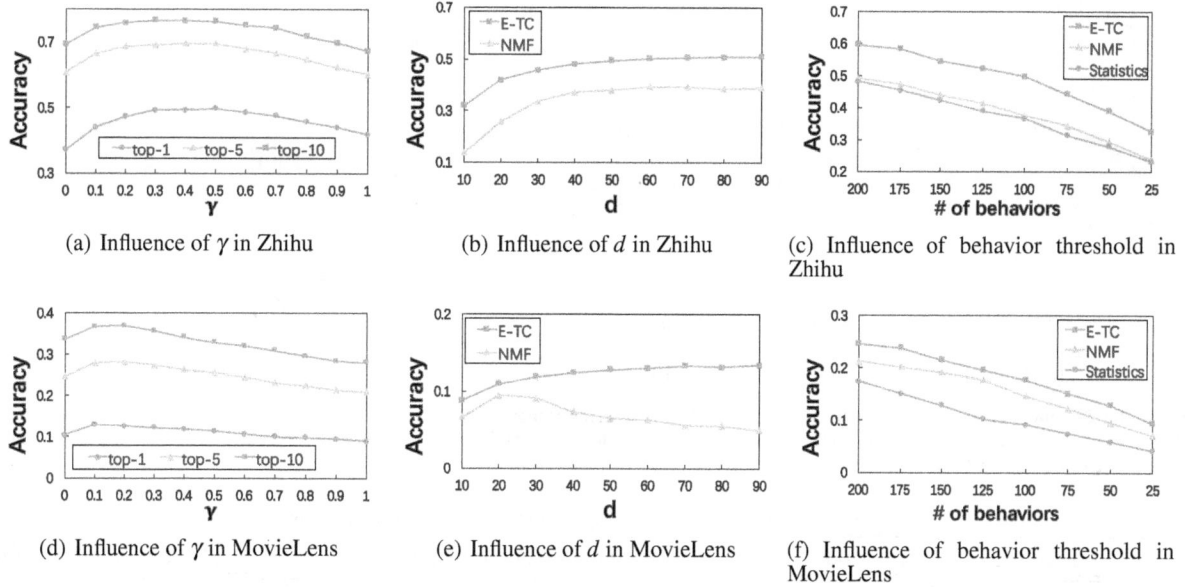

(a) Influence of γ in Zhihu

(b) Influence of d in Zhihu

(c) Influence of behavior threshold in Zhihu

(d) Influence of γ in MovieLens

(e) Influence of d in MovieLens

(f) Influence of behavior threshold in MovieLens

Figure 4. Influence of parameters and settings and comparison with other methods on two datasets. Figure (a)(d) show the performance with respect to γ. Figure (b)(e) show the performance with respect to d. Figure (c)(f) show the performance with respect to behavior threshold. The optimal value that leads to the best performance is dependent on the dataset for all parameters. Our method E-TC outperforms the other methods consistently.

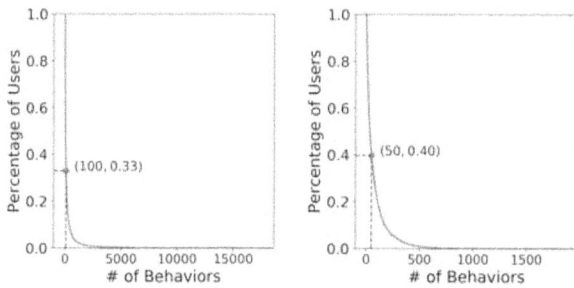

(a) # of behaviors in Zhihu   (b) # of behaviors in MovieLens

Figure 5. Statistics on user behavior quantity. X-axis represents the number of behaviors, and Y-axis represents the proportion of users whose number of behaviors is higher than a given threshold in both periods. We can see that users in both datasets follow a long-tail distribution. The selected behavior threshold in this paper is marked by the red point.

Table 4. Selected topics in three themes

Theme	Topics
Game	Overwatch, LOL, Dota2, Hearthstone Dota, MOBA, Clash of Clans, Steam Minecraft, iOS Game, Game Design
Movie	Hongkong film, micro film, Douban film Chinese film, American film, horror film Japanese film, film, Hollywood film Korea film, science fiction film
Programming Language	c/c++, JavaScript, JAVA, Python PHP, C#, Node.js, C

as the number of hyper-topics in method NMF. Figures 4(b) and 4(e) show the performance with respect to d in the two datasets. We can see that in the *Zhihu* dataset, the accuracy increases fast for both methods when d is less than 50 and becomes stable after d reaches 50. In the *MovieLens* dataset for method **E-TC**, the accuracy increases fast when d is smaller than 40. But for method NMF, the peak accuracy is at about $d = 20$. Since a larger d means more computation, in practice, we should take into account both accuracy and computation cost. In most of the experiments reported this paper, we choose d as 50 and 40 for the two datasets.

We also analyze how the number of user behaviors influences identity linkage. Figures 5(a) and 5(b) show the statistics about the number of behaviors in the two datasets, where the X-axis represents the number of behaviors, and the Y-axis represents the proportion of users whose number of behaviors is higher

than a given threshold in both periods. We can see that the number of user behaviors in both datasets follow a long-tail distribution. A large amount of users have only a small amount of behaviors. We conduct our experiments on different settings for the behavior threshold; the results are shown in Figures 4(c) and 4(f). As the behavior threshold decreases, the accuracy decreases since a large amount of users with a small amount of behaviors are taken into account. This makes it difficult to learn user intrinsic characteristics from a small quantity of behaviors. However, our method **E-TC** outperforms the other methods consistently.

Understanding Semantics of Topic Embedding

To provide more understandable results for other applications, we evaluate the semantics of embedding from two perspectives: topic relevance and user intrinsic characteristics. To give an intuitive view on the meanings of topic embedding, we first use the t-Distributed Stochastic Neighbor Embedding (t-SNE) technique [19] to find 2d coordinates of the original

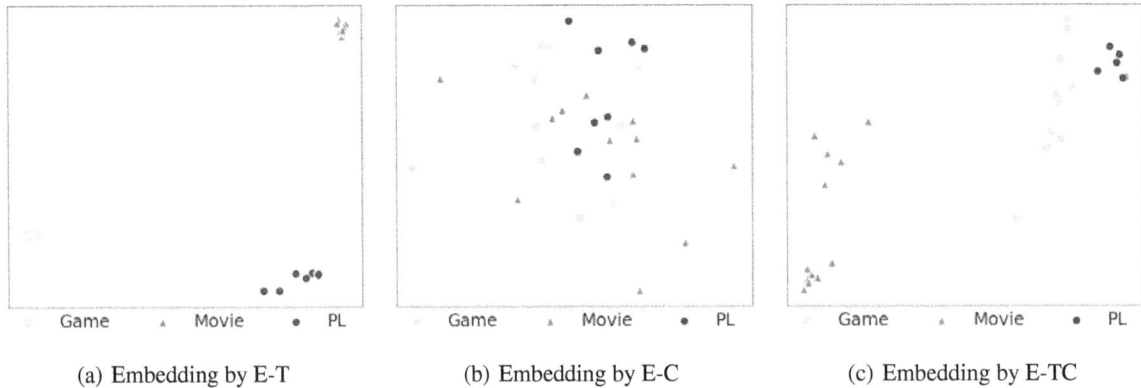

| (a) Embedding by E-T | (b) Embedding by E-C | (c) Embedding by E-TC |

Figure 6. The 2d coordinates representations of the embedding of selected topics for three methods. Topics selected from the theme of *Game*, *Movie* and *Programming Language* are labeled by yellow square, green triangle, purple solid circle, respectively. We can see that the results of dimensionality reduction of three methods are quite different.

Table 5. Top 10 topics concerned by three users in two time periods

	In the first time period	In the second time period	Ranking promotion
User 1	Living, Internet, History **Artificial Intelligence**, Society Experience, **Deep Learning** Google, Computer, Baidu	Internet, **Math**, Health Alibaba, Technology Didi Travel(online hailed car) Law, History,Google, Travel O2O	1200
User 2	Living, Literature, Experience Psychology, Film, Novel Interpersonal communication **Programmer**, society,survey question	**Python, Program**, Living Medical Science, Health, **Programmer Crawler(Computer Networks)** Life, Life history, Internet	912
User 3	Living, Psychology, Experience Homosexual, Variety Show, **Art Photograph**, Mentality, Film survey question	**Design, Japan, Living Drawing, Art, Graphic Design** Psychology, **Photoshop Photograph**, Film	652

topic embedding in the *Zhihu* dataset. t-SNE is a technique for dimensionality reduction particularly well suited for the visualization of high-dimensional datasets. We select topics from 3 themes, which are *Game, Movie* and *Programming Language(PL)*, respectively. The details of selected topics are reported in Table 4. We color topics according to their themes. We expect points in the same color to be clustered together, and each point is be distinguished from others.

Figure 6(a) shows the embedding learned by method **E-T**. We can see that the majority of topics in the same theme are clustered quite closely. There are clear boundaries between clusters of different themes. But topics in the same theme cannot be distinguished from each other. The reason is that in method **E-T** we learn semantics of topics based on their compatibilities, which is modeled based on the co-occurrences of topics. Our objective is to let the embedding of co-occurred topics be as close as possible. However, each topic has its own semantic which cannot be completely the same with similar topics. Using only the information of topic co-occurrence seems not enough to learn topic semantics comprehensively. Figure 6(b) shows the topic embedding learned by **E-C**. We can see that topics are roughly clustered together without clear boundaries between them. The reason is that method

E-C considers user characteristic consistency. The topics of interest to the same user are learned to be close in their vectors. Since this method uses the seed users rather than the platform population, it may lead to showing irrelevant topics to be close due to some users' occasional activities.

The semantics learned by **E-TC** overcomes the shortcomings of methods **E-T** and **E-C**. Figure 6(c) shows the topic embedding learned by **E-TC**. We can see that topics in the same theme are clustered together and the boundaries between clusters are obvious. It is worth noting that clusters for *Game* and *Programming Language* are closer than the cluster *movie* in method **E-TC**. Such a result reflects the fact that the background knowledge about seed users reveals that programmers are more likely to enjoy games, which is not shown by results obtained by method **E-T**.

Then we try to understand how the semantics solve UIL compared to other method. We analyze the representative users who are well recognized with great ranking promotion by our method than the Statistics method. We choose three such users from the *Zhihu* dataset and list the top-10 topics of interest for each one in Table 5. Although some common topics such as *Living, Experience, Life* and *Internet* are the same, most

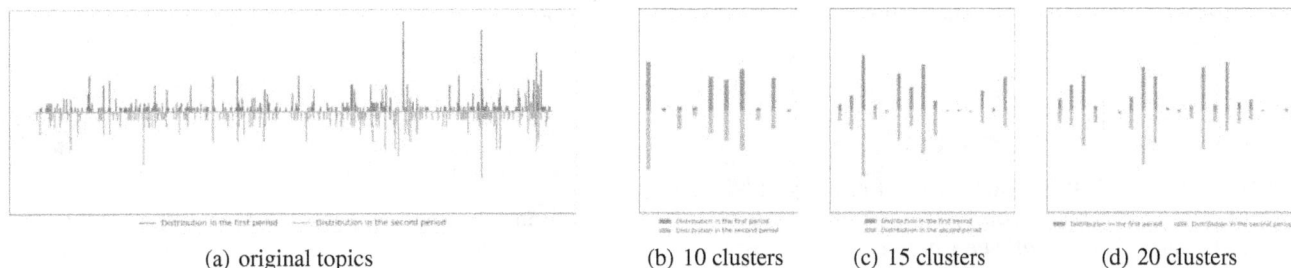

| (a) original topics | (b) 10 clusters | (c) 15 clusters | (d) 20 clusters |

Figure 7. A user's behaviors in two time periods are described in four forms of probability distributions over: (a) original topics; (b) 10 clusters; (c) 15 clusters; and (d) 20 clusters. The blue line denotes the first period, the orange line denotes the second period, and the clusters are classified based on learned topic embedding representations.

topics of interest for the same user in the two periods vary a lot. That is why the Statistics method cannot recognize them correctly. But we can catch some intrinsic characteristics from the semantic related topics (highlighted by colors in the table). For example, the first user is probably employed in an Internet company according to the topics in red, and the blue topics show his/her interests in the domain of artificial intelligence. The second user is probably a network programmer according to the topics colored in blue. For the third user, the blue topics indicate that he or she is a graphic designer, and red topics indicate the interests in psychology.

To further understand how the semantics of embedding help recognize a user, we compare a user's behavior pattern in different modes. First, we cluster all topics into k classes based on their embedding representations and then represent each user as the probability distributions over these classes. An example is given in Table 7. For the above first user, his or her behaviors are modeled as the probability distributions over topics and clusters, for $k = 10$, $k = 15$ and $k = 20$, respectively. The results show that the variants on user's topics of interest between two periods have been highly reduced under the learned embedding representation, and they are similarly consistent on different k settings. As we expected, it indicates that the embedding method learned the consistent intrinsic characteristics implied in user behaviors.

CONCLUSION
In this paper, we solve the problem of user identity linkage on social media by discovering user intrinsic characteristics. We propose an embedding method to understand the semantics of topics related to user behaviors. The embedding representations of topics are learned by a joint-objective optimization, which tries to maximize the topic compatibility, discriminating ability, and characteristic consistency of the seed user. Experimental results on two real social media datasets show that our method outperforms other related methods. We also analyze the semantics of embedding representations from both topic view and user behavior perspective. The effectiveness of our method highlights the privacy and identity issues in online communities. It reminds users to harness their behaviors to avoid being de-anonymized. From another perspective, for online service providers, they should provide more protection on users' private information.

As for future work, we plan to investigate the identity linkage problem on different social media platforms. Since users may have different interests and behave differently on different platforms, understanding topics from different sources and embedding them into the same latent space will be more complex and challenging. Another interesting direction is the selection of seed users. As we discussed in the paper, seed users allows us to introduce background knowledge that helps better understand the intrinsic characteristics of users. We would like to investigate how to select seed users to improve the performance under a given computation and seeding budget.

ACKNOWLEDGMENTS
We would like to thank Gong Hao from Fudan University, Shaoqing Wang from Shandong University for many helpful discussions. This work is supported by the National Natural Science Foundation of China (91646119), Shandong Provincial Natural Science Foundation under Grant No. ZR2014FM014, the Key Research and Development Program of Shandong Province (2014GGX101046, 2015GGX106002, 2017GGX10114), the Special Program on Independent Innovation & Achievements Transformation of Shandong Province (2014ZZCX03301) and SAICT Expert Program.

REFERENCES
1. Einat Amitay, Sivan Yogev, and Elad Yom-Tov. 2007. Serial sharers: Detecting split identities of Web authors. In *Proceedings of the SIGIR 2007 International Workshop on Plagiarism Analysis, Authorship Identification, and Near-Duplicate Detection PAN 2007, Amsterdam, Netherlands, July 27, 2007.*

2. Saeideh Bakhshi, Partha Kanuparthy, and David A. Shamma. 2015. Understanding Online Reviews: Funny, Cool or Useful?. In *Proceedings of the 18th ACM Conference on Computer Supported Cooperative Work & Social Computing.* ACM, New York, NY, USA, 1270–1276.

3. Sergey Bartunov, Anton Korshunov, Seung-Taek Park, Wonho Ryu, and Hyungdong Lee. 2012. Joint link-attribute user identity resolution in online social networks. In *Proceedings of the 6th International Conference on Knowledge Discovery and Data Mining, Workshop on Social Network Mining and Analysis. ACM.*

4. Mikhail Belkin and Partha Niyogi. 2002. Laplacian eigenmaps and spectral techniques for embedding and

clustering. In *Advances in neural information processing systems*. 585–591.

5. David M Blei, Andrew Y Ng, and Michael I Jordan. 2003. Latent dirichlet allocation. *Journal of machine Learning research* 3, Jan (2003), 993–1022.

6. Ji-Won Byun, Ashish Kamra, Elisa Bertino, and Ninghui Li. 2007. Efficient k-anonymization using clustering techniques. In *International Conference on Database Systems for Advanced Applications*. Springer, 188–200.

7. Ting Chen, Lu-An Tang, Yizhou Sun, Zhengzhang Chen, and Kai Zhang. 2016. Entity embedding-based anomaly detection for heterogeneous categorical events. In *Proceedings of the Twenty-Fifth International Joint Conference on Artificial Intelligence*.

8. Yoni De Mulder, George Danezis, Lejla Batina, and Bart Preneel. 2008. Identification via location-profiling in GSM networks. In *Proceedings of the 7th ACM workshop on Privacy in the electronic society*. ACM, 23–32.

9. Sebastien Gambs, Marc-Olivier Killijian, and Miguel Nunez del Prado Cortez. 2014. De-anonymization attack on geolocated data. *J. Comput. System Sci.* 80, 8 (2014), 1597–1614.

10. Hasini Gunasinghe and Elisa Bertino. 2016. RahasNym: Pseudonymous Identity Management System for Protecting against Linkability. In *Collaboration and Internet Computing (CIC), 2016 IEEE 2nd International Conference on*. IEEE, 74–85.

11. Michael Gutmann and Aapo Hyvärinen. 2010. Noise-contrastive estimation: A new estimation principle for unnormalized statistical models.. In *AISTATS*, Vol. 1. 6.

12. Jiawei Han, Jian Pei, and Micheline Kamber. 2011. *Data mining: concepts and techniques*. Elsevier.

13. F Maxwell Harper and Joseph A Konstan. 2016. The movielens datasets: History and context. *ACM Transactions on Interactive Intelligent Systems (TiiS)* 5, 4 (2016), 19.

14. Diederik Kingma and Jimmy Ba. 2015. Adam: A method for stochastic optimization. In *3rd International Conference on Learning Representations*.

15. Yehuda Koren, Robert Bell, and Chris Volinsky. 2009. Matrix factorization techniques for recommender systems. *Computer* 42, 8 (2009).

16. Nitish Korula and Silvio Lattanzi. 2014. An efficient reconciliation algorithm for social networks. *Proceedings of the VLDB Endowment* 7, 5 (2014), 377–388.

17. Harold W Kuhn. 2010. The hungarian method for the assignment problem. *50 Years of Integer Programming 1958-2008* (2010), 29–47.

18. Siyuan Liu, Shuhui Wang, and Feida Zhu. 2015. Structured Learning from Heterogeneous Behavior for Social Identity Linkage. *IEEE Transactions on Knowledge and Data Engineering* 27, 7 (2015), 2005–2019.

19. Laurens van der Maaten and Geoffrey Hinton. 2008. Visualizing data using t-SNE. *Journal of Machine Learning Research* 9, Nov (2008), 2579–2605.

20. Tomas Mikolov, Kai Chen, Greg Corrado, and Jeffrey Dean. 2013a. Efficient estimation of word representations in vector space. In *1st International Conference on Learning Representations*.

21. Tomas Mikolov, Ilya Sutskever, Kai Chen, Greg S Corrado, and Jeff Dean. 2013b. Distributed representations of words and phrases and their compositionality. In *Advances in neural information processing systems*. 3111–3119.

22. Farid M Naini, Jayakrishnan Unnikrishnan, Patrick Thiran, and Martin Vetterli. 2016. Where you are is who you are: User identification by matching statistics. *IEEE Transactions on Information Forensics and Security* 11, 2 (2016), 358–372.

23. Arvind Narayanan and Vitaly Shmatikov. 2008. Robust de-anonymization of large sparse datasets. In *2008 IEEE Symposium on Security and Privacy (sp 2008)*. IEEE, 111–125.

24. Arvind Narayanan and Vitaly Shmatikov. 2009. De-anonymizing social networks. In *2009 30th IEEE symposium on security and privacy*. IEEE, 173–187.

25. Olga Peled, Michael Fire, Lior Rokach, and Yuval Elovici. 2013. Entity matching in online social networks. In *Social Computing (SocialCom), 2013 International Conference on*. IEEE, 339–344.

26. Keith Stevens, Philip Kegelmeyer, David Andrzejewski, and David Buttler. 2012. Exploring topic coherence over many models and many topics. In *Proceedings of the 2012 Joint Conference on Empirical Methods in Natural Language Processing and Computational Natural Language Learning*. Association for Computational Linguistics, 952–961.

27. Jayakrishnan Unnikrishnan and Farid Movahedi Naini. 2013. De-anonymizing private data by matching statistics. In *Communication, Control, and Computing (Allerton), 2013 51st Annual Allerton Conference on*. IEEE, 1616–1623.

28. Jesse Vig, Shilad Sen, and John Riedl. 2012. The tag genome: Encoding community knowledge to support novel interaction. *ACM Transactions on Interactive Intelligent Systems (TiiS)* 2, 3 (2012), 13.

29. Hui Zang and Jean Bolot. 2011. Anonymization of location data does not work: A large-scale measurement study. In *Proceedings of the 17th annual international conference on Mobile computing and networking*. ACM, 145–156.

Optimizing User Experience through Implicit Content-aware Network Service in the Home Environment

Haixiang Yang, Xiaoliang Wang, Cam-Tu Nguyen, Sanglu Lu
National Key Laboratory for Novel Software Technology
Nanjing University
waxili@nju.edu.cn, ncamtu@gmail.com, sanglu@nju.edu.cn

ABSTRACT

There has always been a gap between Internet Service Providers (ISPs) and end users when considering the performance of network-based application. On one hand, ISPs keep raising the investment on infrastructures to speed up the data transportation. On the other hand, users are not satisfied with the perceived quality of experience (QoE). This happens mainly due to the inflexible network flow management, where only the function of rate limiting is provided for home users in the shared network environment. In this paper, we focus on the optimization of users experience by customizing bandwidth allocation for user specified preferences while maintaining high bandwidth utilization. We introduce implicit content-aware bandwidth allocation to minimize the involvement of users on complicated network setting. By leveraging the technique of software-defined networking (SDN), a prototype of content-aware traffic scheduling, *Conan*, is developed to verify the effectiveness of our design. Experiments show that *Conan* can reduce the average task completion time of interactive applications by 30-40%. During heavy traffic load, *Conan* can ensure stable bandwidth for each video streaming flow and greatly reduce the average stall duration.

ACM Classification Keywords

H.5.m. Information Interfaces and Presentation (e.g. HCI): Miscellaneous; C.2.m Computer-Communication Networks: Miscellaneous

Author Keywords

Quality of experience; Home networking

INTRODUCTION

In home network, Internet Service Providers (ISPs) measure the performance based on the bandwidth allocated to each customer. On the other hand, however, customers' consideration is more subjective, that the service performance is mainly judged by the response time of applications, the quality of display, the useability of network management, etc.[15]. There is a gap between the quality of service (QoS) metric of service providers and the quality of experience (QoE) from users

GROUP 2018, January 7–10, 2018, Sanibel Island, FL, USA
Copyright © 2018 Association for Computing Machinery.
ACM ISBN 978-1-4503-5562-9/18/01 ...$15.00.
http://dx.doi.org/10.1145/3148330.3148339

[11]. Therefore, despite the speed of network infrastructure is increasing, users are still suffering from poor QoE.

Current home networking configuration may continue to be problematic for many householders. First, some users lack of the skill of the complex network management. Therefore, they count on the application to passively adjust its service based on the network status in real time, such as the technique of dynamic adaptive video streaming [33]. As a consequence, these users will suffer from the bad quality of service when they have competing Internet demands. The situation is becoming worse with the increased use of Internet-capable devices (e.g., pad, web camera) and the raise of bandwidth intensive applications (e.g., VR, game streaming).

Second, the simple rate limiting at local access point may not work in a shared network environment. Through extensive measurement in the campus network (see Sect. 3) and reviewing the recent study in home network [27], the access link is most often the bottleneck. This happens due to the statistical multiplexing of bandwidth in the over-subscription access network, where users' traffics are not absolutely isolated. Therefore, it is not sufficient to count on the strategies only deployed in the home gateway to assure user's expectations of contextual quality.

In this paper, we present a design called *Conan* intended to address the problem from the viewpoint of network maintainer. Based on the data collected from local network, *Conan* identifies user's expectation by classifying the traffic into three categories most correlated to users' QoE, i.e., interactive traffic, online video streaming and background traffic. We balance different QoE objectives through automatic content-aware flow scheduling to minimize the involvement of home users. A joint optimization framework in home network and local access network (LAN) is proposed to improve end users' quality of experience. To make the system scalable to a large amount of flows, *Conan* introduces a distributed design by assigning the time-consuming traffic identification at home gateways and adopts the technique of software defined networking (SDN) to fast deploy such new service.

To evaluate the system, a prototype was implemented in commercial routers running OpenWrt [16]. We evaluated *Conan* on a small-scale testbed with two laboratory networks connected by a commercial Gigabit Ethernet switch. In the experiments, users found that *Conan* reduces the average task completion time of small flows by 30-40%. Moreover, during heavy traffic load, *Conan* can reduce the average latency of interactive traffic, and also reduce the average stall duration of online videos streaming by up to 90%.

The rest of the paper is organized as follows. We begin by revealing the traffic characteristic in home network, based on which we explain the interface and system design. We then describe the optimization for both interactive traffic and online video streaming. Finally, we present the implementation and performance evaluation. In summary, the contributions of this paper are threefold:

- We propose a content-aware access network flow scheduling system, *Conan*. The system leverages the technique of SDN, which provides an interface for end users, to apply resource in the access network. In conjunction with the functions of rate-limiting and flow-identification at home gateways, the SDN controller allocates bandwidth for different applications in order to satisfy users' QoE requests. Specifically, the functions integrated in the decentralized home gateways mitigate the problem of disruption and performance bottleneck at the centralized controller.

- Optimization is introduced for specific traffic based on its QoE metrics. For HTTP streaming video, a self-adaption bandwidth tuning algorithm is introduced to provide the minimum stable bandwidth. With regard to the slow traffic recognition or encryption traffics, we adopt the multiple-level feedback queue based approach to guarantee that the small flows, which are usually delay sensitive, are served with higher priority.

- Experimental results on our prototype verify the feasibility of our design, which is useful to reduce the latency of interactive traffic while achieve high QoE of HTTP video streaming.

RELATED WORK

Researchers in CSCW and HCI have taken interest in understanding and optimization of user experience in domestic network. Since 2000s, researchers have noticed the issue of network complexity and how householders might come to manage it for themselves (see [8, 10] and the reference therein). Grinter *et al.* [10] pointed out that one of the key issues in the domestic network is the development of networking facilities that do not require advanced networking knowledge. From a user driven perspective, usability plays a central role in domestic network. The works on home network bandwidth through phone-based technical support or remote problem diagnosis suggested the need for more tools that give consumers advance control over their broadband connections [19, 6]. New techniques have been proposed recently to diagnose network and networked application misconfiguration using shared knowledge from other homes [1].

With the rapid growth of residential broadband connections, the availability of home network has driven new Internet-centric applications, such as online gaming, IPTV, online video streaming, etc. On the application layer, many efforts have devoted to design the adaptive logic on specific applications to mitigate the impact of unstable network [29, 3]. For example, the technique of dynamic adaptive video streaming

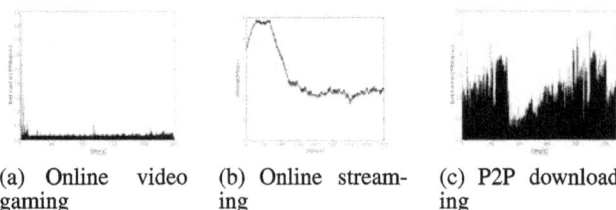

(a) Online video gaming   (b) Online streaming   (c) P2P downloading

Figure 1. Illustration of user's traffic flows

[33] was applied to proactively adjusts the bitrate level according to the current network status. It is notable, however, that the application layer approaches may cause poor fairness and stability when multiple traffics compete for the bottleneck bandwidth [24]. QoE-centric service delivery may continue to be problematic for stakeholders (Internet Service Providers, Content Service Providers, and customers).

In the network system community, great efforts have devoted to optimize bandwidth allocation at local gateway by introducing the priority-based flow scheduling [14, 28] or category-based bandwidth isolation [23] for traffic flows of different applications. Dynamic Quality of Service (QoS) have been adopted in the latest smart routers, like NET-GEAE Nighthawk router [1]. Dynamic QoS automatically prioritizes bandwidth to latency sensitive applications e.g., online gaming and video streaming by recognizing application and device information as well as bandwitdh needs. Dynamic QoS will also ensure that lower priority applications, e.g. file downloads will never get completely stopped. However, through extensive measurement in the campus network (see Sect. 3) and reviewing the recent study in home network [27], the access link is most often the bottleneck. This happens due to the statistical multiplexing of bandwidth in the over-subscription access network, i.e., users are not absolutely isolated. Therefore, it is not sufficient to rely on the strategies only deployed in the home gateway to assure user's expectations of contextual quality. On the other hand, a growing body of works attempt to provide user interface to interact with the network infrastructure [18, 6, 11, 5]. For example, the contextual home router [5] engaged users to explicitly point out their expectations through a web interface, which includes application priority, bandwidth allocation to applications and devices, etc. However, as mentioned in [18, 6, 19], due to the unfamiliarity of networking terminology, it is hard for the householders to verbally describe the detailed information about an intended ideal state.

Consequently, we aim at improving the user experience with network-based applications by dynamically adapting the limited bandwidth of a home network according to automatically detected traffic contents. Instead of providing interface for customers to explicitly specify their requests, we provide implicit service by determining the fraction of bandwidth according to the historical information. In what follows, we introduce the character of domestic network traffic and analyze user's preferences.

---

[1]https://kb.netgear.com/25617

PRELIMINARY

Based on the literature and observation in traffic data, we first classify the traffic based on the protocol and traffic properties and then define design goals for improving user's perceptive.

Protocol Characteristics

Despite a variety of applications are concerned, it is notable that HTTP over TCP protocol has become the dominant transport mechanism. There are several reasons for this phenomenon: 1) HTTP enables content providers to seamlessly bypass middleboxes, e.g. IDS. 2) Content service provider can easily deploy their service without the need of customer modification. 3) Content providers could implement better application-layer resilience using multiple existing servers [13]. Therefore, we mainly focus on the HTTP based services.

Traffic Characteristics

Generally, users are more sensitive to two kinds of applications, the interactive service, e.g., online gaming or web browsing and the online video streaming [32, 23, 28]. Interactive service is sensitive to network latency but the bandwidth requirement of such applications is usually small, as shown in Fig.1(a) where the bitrate of online gaming is usually less than 0.2 Mbps. In contrast, video streaming usually needs a stable average bitrate requirement to guarantee the transmission before deadline. Otherwise, user will experience stalling during the service session. An online video loading from Youtube is shown in Fig.1(b). We can observe that the bitrate is high at the beginning and slows down later. This characteristic directly motivates our flow scheduling solution for online video to improve QoE. Finally, the background traffic is usually generated due to system or software upgrades or P2P services. There is no strict time requirement for this kind of applications but they would introduce burst traffic (1-2 Mbps) as shown in Fig.1(c).

Previous investigations in home network have shown that the proportion of 15-20% downlink traffic is interactive traffic. Video streaming is a large proportion of 25-65% downstream traffic [10, 22, 15, 31]. We also review the traffic in one campus of our university. In the campus, students live in the dorm, which forms a small society. Rate limiting for one user account is 2 Mbps. The traffic distribution are shown in Fig.2. We can see that around 19% of traffic is web browsing, and 3.85% of traffic is VoIP. The HTTP online video traffic is 35.13%.

Furthermore, we analyze the student preferences based on the campus bulletin board system (BBS)[2], where users (students, age 18-35) can report the problem when using the campus network. We summarize the reports which have appeared multiple times (>10 times) during the last 6 months (2017.3-2017.9).

- The gap do exists between users and network maintainers. The college students complained they can not understand the networking terminologies, or even the figures provided

[2] http://bbs.nju.edu.cn/board?board=M_NIC

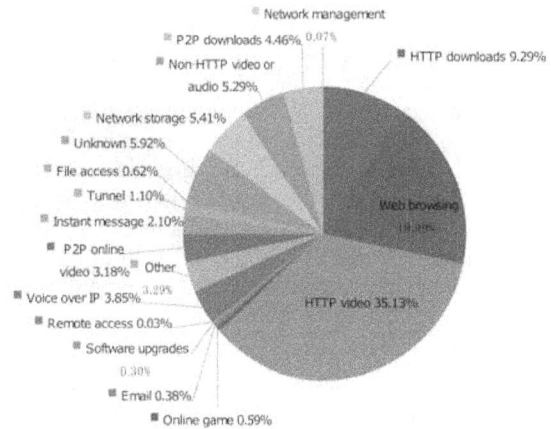

Figure 2. Traffic distribution in one campus of our university

by the network monitoring tools. Users prefer the solution instead of explanation.

- Since the P2P downloading or software update which runs on multiple threads will consume large bandwidth resource, users support the decision to confine the bandwidth usage of certain applications in campus network. Users would like to take the suggestion to run bandwidth consuming applications at non-working hours, or reduce the number of running networked tasks, e.g. video streaming.

- A lot of reports about the 'failed connection to a certain website'. However, this issue happens mainly due to the miss operation of the user or port failure of the switch.

- Users would like to compare the slow campus network service with the cellular network data service, which is much faster to access the online gaming or video providers during the rush hours (e.g. 19:00-23:00).

- The main source of irritation came from the slow web services and stalling of video services during the rush hour.

We explain the last item by an example which also demystifies the limitation of flow scheduling at local gateway of home network. Suppose that there are two users in one local access network. The downstream throughput of the access network is 10 Mbps, and each subscriber applied 6 Mbps bandwidth due to statistical multiplexing. The oversubscription ratio is 1.2:1. Assume that user A has an application of online video, which requires a minimum speed of 5 Mbps. At the same time, both user A and user B run P2P file downloading. Generally, the P2P service can lead to a high bandwidth consumption. Video streaming service will receive less than 5 Mbps rate which can not meet its bandwidth requirement. If user A limits the transmission of the P2P application at local gateway, which aims to improve the QoS of video streaming service, he can not get benefit from this operation because the P2P application of user B will obtain the released bandwidth from user A. As a result, user B achieves 6 Mbps and user A has 4 Mbps for video service. Consequently, user A may have even worse experience after the operation at his local home gateway.

Design Goals

QoE is the term which is used to describe how it is satisfied by subscribers to the provided service quality. The operation of QoE-oriented transportation for home users is based on the following considerations: 1) users' perspective is highly related to the contextual service; 2) users care more about the current applications they are using; 3) users may have personal preference like P2P downloading is more important than other applications; and 4) it is very difficult to measure user behaviors on an operational network [25], complicated measurement may slow down the networking service and result in poor user experience.

Based on the observation, we describe below how our QoE-centric design address above issues:

- Online traffic is roughly classified into three categories based on the time-sensitivity: *the interactive traffic, the online streaming traffic, and the background traffic.*

- The interactive traffic such as online gaming, web browsing is highly sensitive to delay and thus are always first served. The online streaming traffic requires to deliver within certain time periods.

- The unstable transmission rate may cause stalling and network congestion and thus we need to provide the minimum bandwidth guarantee based on the utilization function of video streaming. Despite the background traffic does not have strict time requirements, it can not be starving due to the high priority traffic.

- A proper queuing management mechanism is necessary, and a proportion of bandwidth is allocated to each type of traffics. We explore to satisfy the preferences of most users. By default, our system can determine the fraction of bandwidth according to the historical information.

- The minimum bandwidth of each user is guaranteed by inherently using the rate limiting approach in current domestic network, which is the Service Level Agreement (SLA) that prevails between a ISP and a customer.

Challenges

The proposed framework requires to tackle several challenges:

(1) How to identify the expectation of single user on network behaviors? Users show different preferences towards services associated with different devices, environment, etc. The subjective evaluation of a single user may also vary from time to time. A straightforward design is to provide interface for customers to explicitly present his/her request. However, most home users lack technical expertise to manage the network traffic between the Internet and home networks [6, 19]. With regard to the complex network setting, the involvement of user on networking management may also affect the QoE.

(2) How to deploy such a flexible flow scheduling in access network? The current practice on ISPs network only provide credit-based rate limiting to isolate bandwidth among users [4]. It is hard to deploy customized network management in LAN. We can not simply leverage priority queues provided

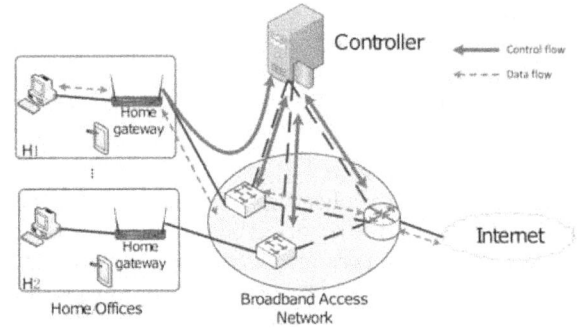

Figure 3. Illustration of system architecture

by existing commodity switch. With regard to the limited number of priority queues.

(3) How to make the system scalable to many users and millions of flows? With the popularity of mobile computing, the number of devices as well as rich media services are significantly increasing in local network. For network layer traffic identification, it will be a huge burden for the core routers, which work at the choke point of access network, to do the context-aware packet classification. Specifically, with the consideration of security and user privacy, the encryption services, e.g., HTTPS-based applications, can make the network function fail to work. This introduces a new research challenge for QoE guarantee in our design.

To address the above problems, our design balance different QoE objectives through automatic content-aware flow scheduling to minimize the involvement of home users. This operation is based on the observation that users are capable of actively adjust bandwidth allocation if they have any special requirement. For example, user can change video bitrate when using different devices (e.g., 1080p for desktop, 480p on Pad) as long as our work can guarantee the stable bandwidth of the video streaming.

We adopt the software defined networking (SDN) to fast deploy new services. SDN provides a programmable, logically centralized abstraction of network control, through which we can deploy fine-grained bandwidth allocation for applications in specified categorizes. Different from the operation that delegate application identification to an SDN controller [23], we perform the scalable appropriate application identification and QoS configuration for downstream traffic at the decentralized home gateway.

SYSTEM DESIGN

Architecture

We introduce *Conan*, a system that enables content-aware flow scheduling using SDN. *Conan* implements a combination of priority based scheduling and dynamic bandwidth allocation to meet the transportation requirement of applications. Specifically we seek to develop a scalable distributed implementation that run applications identification at each home gateway since the resource allocation at LAN is not sensitive to the identification delay, as shown in Fig. 3. Considering a new downstream traffic flow, it first passes through

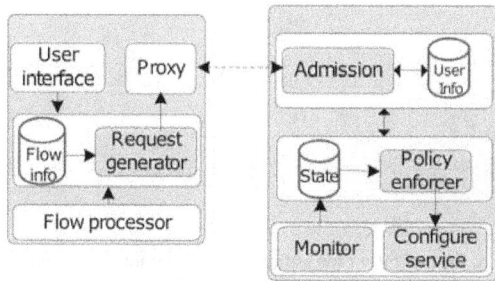

Figure 4. System overview

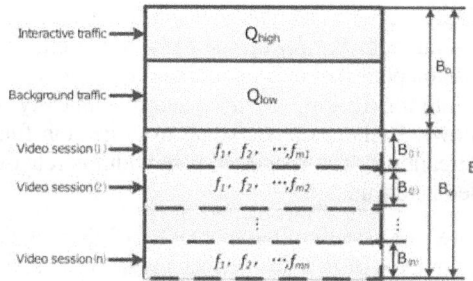

Figure 5. Buffer management and bandwidth pre-allocation

the access network. The content identification is then enabled when the flow comes to home gateway. If this flow is associated to a QoE sensitive application, the corresponding request is uploaded from home gateway to the access network controller and a policy rule is installed at routers of LAN for the remaining packets of this flow.

Fig.4 illustrates the system architecture of *Conan*. *Conan* consists of two components: (1) the *broker* hosting at the home gateway that identifies flows belonging to applications and sends the corresponding bandwidth requests to the controller; (2) the *centralized controller* of the access network receives requests, manages network resource and performs flow scheduling for downstream traffic. The home gateway communicates with controller through RESTful APIs (northbound APIs in SDN).

Broker

As illustrated in Fig.4, when a downstream flow arrives at home gateway, the *flow processor* extracts the flow information, such as transmitted bytes, TCP port, etc., and identifies the categories of applications through packet inspection. Then, it updates the database of flow information and notifies the *request generator* to send a policy request to controller according to the registered rules. For example, suppose that a rule for video streaming over HTTP is registered in *request generator*: when a new video streaming over HTTP is discovered then notify the *request generator*. In this case, when *flow processor* discovers a new flow of video streaming over HTTP, the *flow processor* will send the notification. Once notified, the *request generator* generates a request and sends it to controller through *proxy*. The request is associated with applications. An example of requests for video streaming is explained in Section 6. The *user interface* module enables ISP manager to install new policies required by users. Notice that the interface is not open to the customers directly due to the security consideration. But customers can upload their self-defined requests to ISP and ISP can deploy the corresponding policy rules after policy checking.

Controller

Once a request arrives at the controller, *admission* module would check the legality, including whether it is from a legal account and whether the requested bandwidth is beyond the maximum available bandwidth. If the request is illegal, it is rejected. Otherwise, the request is sent to the *policy enforcer*. The *policy enforcer* performs two operations: (1)

Solving conflicts. When a conflict happens, e.g., the total required bandwidth is larger than the available bandwidth, we will select the largest subset of requests such that the maximum number of users are satisfied. The left requests will be rejected. (2) Enforcing policy rules. Given the accepted requirements, the *policy enforcer* deploys the policy rules for routers in LAN through *Configure services*. An example of *policy enforcer* designed for video streaming is explained in Session 6. The *monitor* collects network information from routers and stores them in *state* database.

It is notable that the home gateway mentioned in this paper is different from the home router bought by users. The gateway is the nearest router/switch configured by the ISPs behind the information point, or the "home router" provided by the ISPs. Therefore, the ISP is entitled to deploy new functions on the gateway. User's self-configured home router is actually plugged in the LAN port of the gateway to provide network coverage for multiple devices, e.g., PC, mobiles. In addition, we leverage the function of rate limiting in current access network to ensure that the traffic of one user will not exceed the assigned bitrate according to the contract between users and ISPs.

Buffer Management and Bandwidth Allocation

The down-link bandwidth B is divided for traffic of different categories. The proportion of assigned bandwidth is based on the historical information as that shown in Fig. 2. Besides, since traffic varies at both time and space, the adaptive bandwidth management is flexible where the bandwidth allocation can change over time to fully utilize the LAN resource.

Fig. 5 shows the bandwidth allocation in our design. The overall bandwidth B is divided into two parts B_o and B_v, where $B = B_o + B_v$. Interactive traffic and background traffic will share bandwidth of B_o. All packets belonging to the interactive flows are tagged with highest priority at home gateway. Therefore, they are assigned to the highest priority queue and get served first. Due to the small size of interactive flows, they are batched to get the low latency transmission to avoid high overhead of proactive scheduling. The background traffic is assigned to low priority queue. We can leverage the network scheduler by applying a proper queuing principle, such as Priority queue or Weighted Fair Queue (WFQ), to provide QoS guarantee for two kinds of traffics.

All the online video sessions share the bandwidth B_v, which are isolated from traffics of other categories. When an explicit request comes from broker, controller would reserve a proper bandwidth $B_{(i)}$ for this new video session. During the transmission period of this video session, the *policy module* is responsible for tracking the trace and dynamically adjusting the bandwidth allocated according to utilization function of video streaming. The requested bandwidth is released when the video is terminated.

Therefore, the rate limiting approach of IPS provides bandwidth guarantee of B. The interface given to users, in form of a fraction-bar, can determine the value of B_v and B_o respectively. Users can actively adjust bandwidth allocation through either the interface of fraction-bar for multiple applications on multiple devices, or manually set the quality of a specific application on current device.

OPTIMIZATION FOR INTERACTIVE APPLICATIONS

Flow Scheduling

Our design is based on the following consideration: 1) Most interactive flows like online gaming are very short [2]; 2) Most irritation is associated with small flows [15]; 3) Users' perception is mainly determined by the application they are using. Therefore, instead of directly identifying the content of (encrypted) traffics, we classify the traffic based on flow size. To this end, we introduce Multi-Level Feedback Queue (MLFQ) to automatically schedule flows of different sizes which are correlated to the content of applications. Unlabeled flow is always put to highest priority queue. MLFQ mimics the approach of shortest flow first. Flows gradually demoted from higher priority queues to lower priority queue based on the bytes they have sent. As most web searching or interactive flows are very short [2], we can determine a proper demoted threshold to ensure that low latency transmission requirement of short flows will not be affected by bandwidth-sensitive applications which have relatively long flows.

OPTIMIZATION FOR VIDEO STREAMING

Video-on-demand (VoD) has become one of the most popular Internet services today. From a QoE perspective, end user quality perception in online video service is mainly determined by initial delay and stalling during watching [12]. Bad network environment may cause long waiting time and high stalling frequency for videos online.

An instance of *request generator* for video streaming is shown in Fig.6(a). There are three kinds of requests: *create_session*, *add_flow*, *release_session*. They are used for creating a new video session and allocating bandwidth, adding a new flow to an existing video session and releasing bandwidth respectively. When a new video flow is discovered by *flow processor*, if this new video flow belongs to an existing video session, it is added to the existing video session using *add_flow*. Otherwise, the *session manager* creates a new session and add the flow to the new session. When a video session terminates, *session manager* notifies the controller to release bandwidth using *release_session*.

Fig.6(b) shows an instance of *policy enforcer*. It provides minimum bandwidth for video streaming. The session database is used to store configuration settings, such as htb queue [17] or allocated bandwidth. When *create_session*

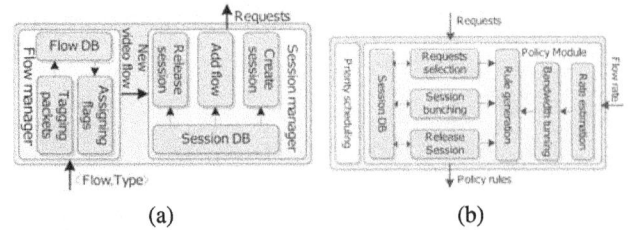

(a)   (b)

Figure 6. Optimization for online video streaming (a) *Request generator* at broker (b) *Policy enforcer* at the controller.

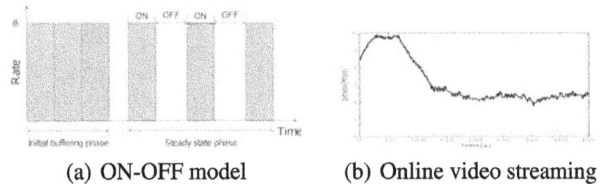

(a) ON-OFF model   (b) Online video streaming

Figure 7. Illustration of the characteristics of video streaming

requests arrive, the *requests selection* module handles the bandwidth conflict as aforementioned. It assigns bandwidth to each accepted request, generates a Session_ID and assigns queues. When an *add_flow* request arrives, the *session_bunching* module reads configuration of the session from database and schedule the new flow to share bandwidth. When a *release_session* request comes, both the queue assigned to the session and the bandwidth allocated are released. The procedure for *bandwidth tuning* is explained as follows.

Characteristics of Video Streaming

We first identify the characteristics of bandwidth requirement when playing video on Internet. Online video streaming is usually based on HTTP protocol, such as MPEG dynamic adaptive streaming over HTTP (MPEG-DASH), Apple HTTP Live Streaming (HLS), or Adobe Dynamic HTTP Streaming (HDS). In a typical streaming session, the video content is transferred in two phases: an *initial buffering phase* and a *steady state phase*, as illustrated in Fig. 7(a). At the initial buffering period, the playback buffer of video player is empty at the beginning, and the player fills it up as fast as possible to shorten the initial delay. The transfer rate is only capped by the end-to-end available bandwidth.

When a sufficient amount of video segments are available in the playback buffer, the player starts to play video and it comes to the steady state phase. In the steady state phase, the downloading rate is determined by the ON-OFF cycle [20]. At ON state, the player downloads video segments until the playback buffer becomes full. Then downloading stays in the OFF state until buffer size becomes low. Thus, the average downloading rate in steady state phase is lower than the initial buffering phase. See Fig.7(b), an example of Youtube video streaming shows the bitrate variation in two phases.

Based on this observation, we propose a flow scheduling approach to serving HTTP video streaming in *Conan*. The objective is to provide a stable network environment to improve users' QoE. The key is an incremental mechanism to tune the minimum allocated bandwidth. At the beginning, sufficient

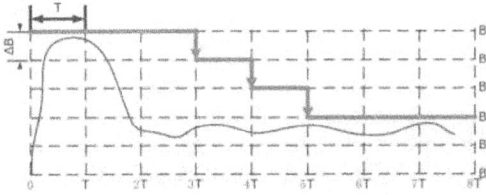

Figure 8. An example of bandwidth tuning procedure

bandwidth is provided at the initial buffering phase. When coming to the steady state phase, the bandwidth is decreased correspondingly. Notice that during the steady state phase, the provided bandwidth can be small but stable which will shorten the period of stalling and improve the bandwidth utilization.

Flow Rate Estimation

From the ON-OFF model[3], we can derive that the ideal situation for bandwidth allocation is that there is no OFF period such that the channel would never go to idle and all bandwidth is used by video streaming. In this ideal situation, the minimum bandwidth for a video is $B_{min} = S/T_{duration}$, where $T_{duration}$ is the duration of each segment, which means that the play rate is just exactly equal to the download rate. This ideal solution is not practical because of variable bitrate and lack of application layer information. Considering the observations and analysis, we propose to estimate the required bandwidth using flow rate. During initial buffering period, we would overestimate average bit rate. However it does not matter, as higher minimum bandwidth would not degrade video quality. Bandwidth tuning would decrease the gap.

Bandwidth Tuning

We propose to dynamically reduce the bandwidth to match flow rate requirement. A Delta(Δ) incremental approach is applied since it is suitable to our scenario and simple to be deployed. As shown in Fig. 8, first of all, the available bandwidth is divided into k segments with the interval of ΔB. The segments are denoted by $B_0, ..., B_{k-1}$ respectively, where $B_i < B_j \ \forall i < j \in [0, k-1]$. When a new video streaming request arrives, the maximum bandwidth B_{k-1} is assigned to it. Every T seconds, the bandwidth tuning procedure is triggered. Each time the bandwidth can be reduced by ΔB, which prevents the bandwidth being set as a small value due to rate underestimation.

Fig. 8 shows an example of bandwidth tuning. At the beginning, the maximum bandwidth is assigned to flow to shorten the initial buffering time. Since time slot $3T$, because the estimated rate is smaller than the threshold, the bandwidth is reduced by ΔB every time. At time slot $5T$, the allocated bandwidth is close to the traffic rate and thus becomes stable. And the allocated bandwidth will be released when the transmission is over.

EVALUATION

Implementation

We implemented *Conan* controller based on Ryu [21], an open source controller written in Python. *Broker* runs on

---

[3]Despite the ON-OFF Model is not universal, our bandwidth tuning algorithm can be easily extend to other scenarios.

OpenWrt [16], a Linux distribution for embedded devices. A deep packet inspection tool, nDPI [7], is deployed for flow identification. For example, video streaming is identified by inspecting the MIME in HTTP headers. Other approaches for HTTPs flow identification can refer to the tools introduced in [26, 35].

In our experiment, the topology is the same to that shown in Fig.3. Two TP-LINK TL-WDR4310 home routers connect to access network. Three devices (2 switches and 1 border router) in broadband access network are emulated through bridges of OpenVSwitch [17] in a software router. The border router connects to a server, which generates both video streaming flows and background traffic. Video streaming flows are generated by Nimble streamer[30]. The background traffic consists of 20 TCP connections generated by iPerf. The bandwidth between the server and the border router is capped by 30 Mbps using Linux TC tools.

Priority in Open vSwitch: As strict priority queues are not supported in Open vSwitch, we simulated priority queues using linux-HTB queues supported by Open vSwitch. Linux-HTB is a token-based scheduling mechanism. Queues with higher HTB priority are prioritized to get the shared tokens. We let interactive flows and background flows share the bandwidth of size $B_o = 0.5 \times B$. The interactive flow queue is assigned a higher HTB priority value while the default queue is assigned a lower value. So the queue for interactive flows can get tokens to get served first. Besides, the queue for interactive flows has short length to promise low queue-latency.

Bandwidth Guarantee: We leverage Open vSwitch HTB queues to provide bandwidth guarantee, as meter tables are not supported on Open vSwitch by now. A certain number of equal priority HTB queues are proactively created on each port via OVSDB protocol by the controller when the system starts up, in order to avoid high overheads introduced by frequently creating and deleting queues [9]. When a video QoS request arrives, the controller picks up one queue and forwards packets to the queue after setting it properly. During the bandwidth tuning, we leverage OVSDB to reconfigure queues. Due to the low frequency of adjustments, the overhead of reconfigurations is acceptable.

The complete source code is available at https://github.com/njunetsys/sdn_access_network

Experimental Setting

The interactive traffic is generated by multiple ICMP pings to represent many short-term flows. The video file is encoded by H.264/MPEG-4 AVC codec with resolution 240p, 360p, 480p and 720p respectively. *Nimble streamer*[30] is employed to generate video streaming over HLS and MPEG-DASH protocol through transmuxing MP4 files. Each chunk size is 10 seconds by default. The client player is Bitmovin for HLS and is Dash.js for MPEG-DASH. Background network load is generated through multiple TCP flows by Iperf.

In *Conan*, there are several parameters, T, β, B_{min}, B_{max}, and ΔB. T is the interval of bandwidth tuning, which is closely related to network burden of collecting network information and scheduling, $T = 60s$ in our testbed. β is designed to

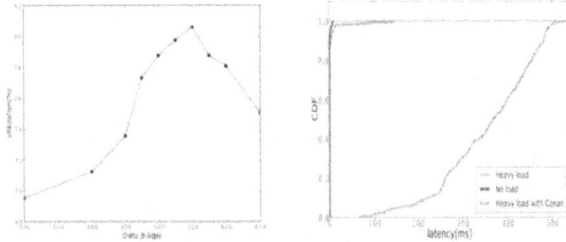

Figure 9. Bandwidth utilization varies with ΔB ($\beta = 0.9$ and $T = 60s$)

Figure 10. Latency of interactive flows under different network condtion.

avoid lacking bandwidth for VBR, which is closely related to the variation of bitrate, $\beta = 0.9$ in our simulation. B_{min} and B_{max} determine the bounds of the bandwidth of a video stream that can be guaranteed. These two parameters are closely related to the video bitrate distribution on the Internet. According to the recommendations from Youtube[34], we set $B_{min} = 500kbps$ and $B_{max} = 4000kbps$. ΔB is the parameter related to the bandwidth utilization. At the beginning, bandwidth allocated is usually higher than flow rate, so a larger ΔB would help to decrease to required minimum bandwidth faster. However, larger ΔB can also waste bandwidth after the bandwidth allocated matches the flow rate. Thus, we should carefully choose a ΔB, which can reach a high utilization of bandwidth as well as fast convergence to the flow rate. Fig. 9 shows that the utilization reaches more than 78% when ΔB is between 500kbps and 600kbps. We thus choose 500kbps as the value of ΔB.

Latency of interactive flows

Results of latency for the interactive flow on various network conditions are shown in Fig. 10. We can see that under heavy load condition, the latency measured by RTT between two hosts varies a lot using best-effort fair-share transport service. More than 70% packets experience more than 300 ms latency and the largest latency is 500 ms in our three-hop testbed network. In contrast, *Conan* significantly reduces the latency. More than 80% packets experience neglectable latency as in the scenario with no extra load. Little proportion of packets experiences more than 100 ms latency because that we did not use real pure priority queues due to the lack of support in Open vSwitch.

Table 1. Quantitative QoE index for video streaming using HLS.

Protocol	SF	AVQ	ASD	AQV
HLS only	3	1.97	5.247	70
HLS with *Conan*	0	3.96	0	6

Table 2. Quantitative QoE index for video streaming using MPEG-DASH.

Protocol	SF	AVQ	ASD	AQV
DASH only	34	2.28	5.71	223
DASH with *Conan*	2	3.86	0.65	38

QoE metrics of video streaming

To measure the performance of *Conan* on video streaming, we conduct our experiments on two popular segment-based video streaming protocols, HLS and MPEG-DASH. We measure the three QoE metrics as explained below. After that, we

show the video buffer length and the bandwidth allocation which microscopically explains the effectiveness of *Conan*.

Before explaining the metric for video streaming, we first introduce a non-descending function $q(\cdot) : \mathbb{R} \to \mathbb{N}$, which maps the selected bitrate R_k to the video quality perceived by user $q(R_k)$ [33]. Here, we define that $q(R_k) = i$, where i is the index of all available bitrate in the ascending order.

- *Average Video Quality (AVQ)* $\frac{1}{K} \sum_{k=1}^{K} q(R_k)$, where K is the number of consecutive video segments during a video, R_k is the bitrate of the k-th segment, $q(\cdot) : R \to \mathbb{N}$ is a non-descending function which maps the selected bitrate R_k to the video quality perceived by user [33]. This metric tracks the average video quality. Higher average video quality leads to higher QoE.

- *Average Quality Variations (AQV)* tracks the magnitude of the variations in the quality during a video session which equals to $\frac{1}{K-1} \sum_{k=1}^{K-1} |q(R_{k+1}) - q(R_k)|$. AQV is negatively correlated with QoE.

- *Stall Frequency (SF)* measures the stall times in a unit time interval.

- *Average Stall Duration (ASD)* measures the average duration of all the stalls in a unit time interval.

Overall QoE: We play a video of 1369.47 seconds via HLS and MPEG-DASH respectively. Table 1 shows the results of HLS. For average video quality (AVQ), the scores for HLS and HLS with *Conan* are about 1.97 and 3.96, respectively. The video quality value varies from 1 (240p) to 4 (720p). The detailed video quality distribution is shown in Fig.11(a)(b). When *Conan* is enabled, over 97% duration of this video is 720p. In contrast, without *Conan*, more than 70% duration of the video is below 480p, and only 11% is 720p, resulting in a lower score of average video quality. For Stall Frequency (SF), without *Conan* we see 3 stalls and stall interval of 5.247s on average, which makes user suffer from stalling of 15 seconds long. In contrast, no stall is observed when *Conan* is enabled. Besides, the average quality variants (AQV) is reduced about 90%. Similar observations can be found in Table 2 and Fig. 11(c)(d) for MPEG-DASH.

Buffer length: Fig.12 shows the playback buffer length. Under the heavy background traffic, the buffer length varies a lot for HLS when *Conan* is disabled. The buffer becomes empty and video stall happens at the time of 200s. When *Conan* is enabled, the variance is greatly reduced and no stall happens. Even with heavy background, the buffer length using *Conan* is close to the one with no background traffic. For DASH-MPEG, both playback buffer length fluctuate strongly, because Dash.js, is buffer-based adaptive algorithm by ignoring the change of available bandwidth. Stall happens frequently there. For DASH with *Conan* enabled, the playback buffer length is higher on average.

Bandwidth: Fig.13 shows the bandwidth allocation during transmission. As we mentioned in the previous section, the higher bandwidth allocation at the beginning guarantees higher flow rate, which leads to short initial buffering time shown

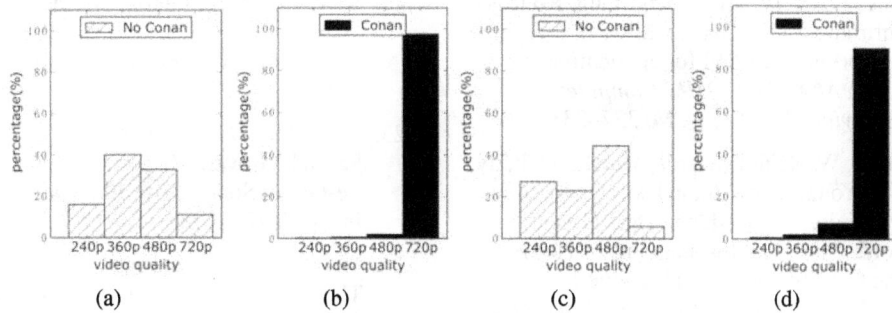

Figure 11. Distribution of adopted video quality (a) HLS *Conan* off, (b) HLS *Conan* on, (a) MPEG-DASH *Conan* off, (d) MPEG-DASH *Conan* on

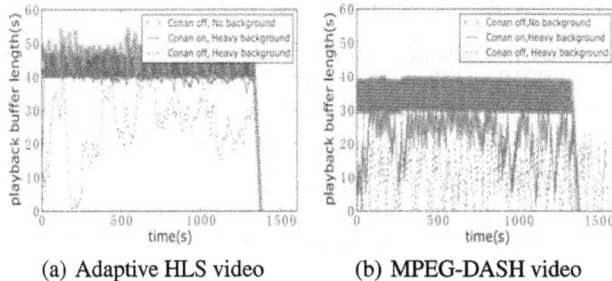

(a) Adaptive HLS video   (b) MPEG-DASH video

Figure 12. Playback buffer length

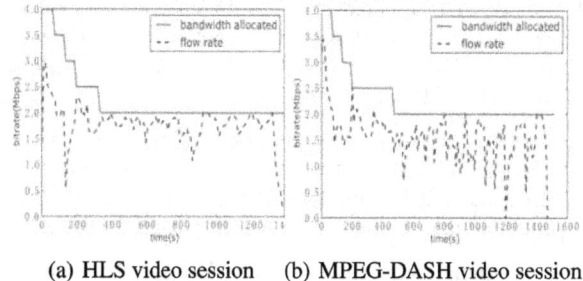

(a) HLS video session   (b) MPEG-DASH video session

Figure 13. Bandwidth allocated and flow rate

in Fig.12. After the initial time, the bandwidth allocation gradually reduces and converges to the flow rate. The gap between flow rate and bandwidth allocated becomes small after the initial time, and thus improves bandwidth utilization. The saved bandwidth can be used by other traffics. For example, the bandwidth sharing policy of linux-HTB guarantees that the spare bandwidth is filled by other traffic.

CONCLUSION
This paper presents a new framework to enable joint optimization for customized bandwidth allocation at LAN and flow scheduling at home network. The framework allows not only content-aware flow scheduling for different users but performance optimization for specific application, while maintaining high utilization of local access network. It is a scalable design by deploying automatic application identification at home gateway. A prototype *Conan* of the framework is deployed to verify the effectiveness of our design. Our testbed experiments show that *Conan* can reduce the average task completion time of interactive applications with small flows by 30-40%.

Acknowledgment
This work was partially supported by National Key R&D Program of China 2017YFB1001800; NSFC Grants No. 61370028; The Collaborative Innovation Center of Novel Software Technology and Industrialization;

REFERENCES
1. Bhavish Agarwal, Ranjita Bhagwan, Tathagata Das, Siddharth Eswaran, Venkata N Padmanabhan, and Geoffrey M Voelker. 2009. NetPrints: Diagnosing Home Network Misconfigurations Using Shared Knowledge.. In *NSDI*, Vol. 9. 349–364.

2. Mohammad Al-Fares, Khaled Elmeleegy, Benjamin Reed, and Igor Gashinsky. 2011. Overclocking the Yahoo!: CDN for faster web page loads. In *ACM SIGCOMM conference on Internet measurement conference*. ACM.

3. Athula Balachandran, Vyas Sekar, Aditya Akella, Srinivasan Seshan, Ion Stoica, and Hui Zhang. 2013. Developing a Predictive Model of Quality of Experience for Internet Video. *SIGCOMM Computer Communication Review* 43, 4 (Aug. 2013), 339–350.

4. Steven Bauer, David Clark, and William Lehr. 2011. Powerboost. In *2nd ACM SIGCOMM workshop on Home networks*. ACM.

5. Ilker Nadi Bozkurt and Theophilus Benson. 2016. Contextual Router: Advancing Experience Oriented Networking to the Home. In *SOSR*. ACM.

6. Marshini Chetty, David Haslem, Andrew Baird, Ugochi Ofoha, Bethany Sumner, and Rebecca Grinter. 2011. Why is My Internet Slow? Making Network Speeds Visible. In *SIGCHI Conference on Human Factors in Computing Systems (CHI)*. ACM, New York, NY, USA, 1889–1898. DOI:
http://dx.doi.org/10.1145/1978942.1979217

7. Luca Deri, Mario Martinelli, Tomasz Bujlow, and Alfredo Cardigliano. 2014. nDPI: Open-source high-speed deep packet inspection. In *IEEE Wireless Communications and Mobile Computing Conference (IWCMC)*.

8. W. Keith Edwards and Rebecca E. Grinter. 2001. At Home with Ubiquitous Computing: Seven Challenges. In *International Conference on Ubiquitous Computing*. 256–272.

9. Andrew D Ferguson, Arjun Guha, Chen Liang, Rodrigo Fonseca, and Shriram Krishnamurthi. 2013. Participatory networking: An API for application control of SDNs. In *ACM SIGCOMM Computer Communication Review*, Vol. 43. ACM, 327–338.

10. Rebecca E. Grinter, W. Keith Edwards, Marshini Chetty, Erika S. Poole, Ja-Young Sung, Jeonghwa Yang, Andy Crabtree, Peter Tolmie, Tom Rodden, Chris Greenhalgh, and Steve Benford. 2009. The Ins and Outs of Home Networking: The Case for Useful and Usable Domestic Networking. *ACM Trans. Computer-Human Interaction (TOCHI)* 16, 2, Article 8 (June 2009), 28 pages.

11. Hassan Habibi Gharakheili, Arun Vishwanath, and Vijay Sivaraman. 2016. Perspectives on Net Neutrality and Internet Fast-Lanes. *SIGCOMM Comput. Commun. Rev.* 46, 1 (Jan. 2016), 64–69.

12. Tobias Hoßfeld, Sebastian Egger, Raimund Schatz, Markus Fiedler, Kathrin Masuch, and Charlott Lorentzen. 2012. Initial delay vs. interruptions: between the devil and the deep blue sea. In *QoMEX*. IEEE.

13. Hongqiang Harry Liu, Ye Wang, Yang Richard Yang, Hao Wang, and Chen Tian. 2012. Optimizing Cost and Performance for Content Multihoming. In *SIGCOMM Conference on Applications, Technologies, Architectures, and Protocols for Computer Communication*. ACM.

14. Jake Martin and Nick Feamster. 2012. User-driven dynamic traffic prioritization for home networks. In *ACM SIGCOMM workshop on Measurements up the stack*. ACM.

15. J Scott Miller, Amit Mondal, Rahul Potharaju, Peter A Dinda, and Aleksandar Kuzmanovic. 2011. Understanding end-user perception of network problems. In *SIGCOMM workshop on Measurements up the stack (W-MUST)*. ACM.

16. OpenWrt-Wireless Freedom. 2016. openWRT. https://openwrt.org/. (2016).

17. OVS. 2015. Open vSwitch. (2015). http://openvswitch.org/.

18. Erika Shehan Poole, Marshini Chetty, Rebecca E. Grinter, and W. Keith Edwards. 2008. More Than Meets the Eye: Transforming the User Experience of Home Network Management. In *ACM Conference on Designing Interactive Systems (DIS)*.

19. Erika Shehan Poole, W. Keith Edwards, and Lawrence Jarvis. 2009. The Home Network As a Socio-Technical System: Understanding the Challenges of Remote Home Network Problem Diagnosis. *Comput. Supported Coop. Work (CSCW)* 18, 2-3 (June 2009), 277–299.

20. Ashwin Rao, Arnaud Legout, Yeonsup Lim, Don Towsley, Chadi Barakat, and Walid Dabbous. 2011. Network characteristics of video streaming traffic. In *CoNEXT*. ACM.

21. Ryu. 2013. Ryu SDN Controller. http://osrg.github.io/ryu/. (2013).

22. Sandvine. 2016. Global internet phenomena report. https://www.sandvine.com/trends/global-Internet-phenomena/. (2016).

23. M Said Seddiki, Muhammad Shahbaz, Sean Donovan, Sarthak Grover, Miseon Park, Nick Feamster, and Ye-Qiong Song. 2014. FlowQoS: QoS for the rest of us. In *HotSDN*. ACM.

24. Michael Seufert, Sebastian Egger, Martin Slanina, Thomas Zinner, Tobias Hobfeld, and Phuoc Tran-Gia. 2015. A survey on quality of experience of HTTP adaptive streaming. *IEEE Communications Surveys & Tutorials* 17, 1 (2015), 469–492.

25. Junaid Shaikh, Markus Fiedler, and Denis Collange. 2010. Quality of Experience from user and network perspectives. *annals of telecommunications-annales des telecommunications* 65, 1-2 (2010), 47–57.

26. Justine Sherry, Chang Lan, Raluca Ada Popa, and Sylvia Ratnasamy. 2015. Blindbox: Deep packet inspection over encrypted traffic. In *SIGCOMM*. ACM.

27. Renata Teixeira Sriknath Sundaresan, Nick Feamster. 2016. Home Network or Access Link? Locating Last-mile Downstream Throughput Bottlenecks. In *Passive and Active Network Measurement (PAM)*. Springer.

28. Florian Wamser, Thomas Zinner, Lukas Iffländer, and Phuoc Tran-Gia. 2014. Demonstrating the prospects of dynamic application-aware networking in a home environment. In *SIGCOMM*. ACM.

29. Xiao Sophia Wang, Aruna Balasubramanian, Arvind Krishnamurthy, and David Wetherall. 2013. Demystifying page load performance with WProf. In *NSDI*.

30. WMSPanel. 2016. Nimble Streamer. https://wmspanel.com/nimble. (2016).

31. Kuai Xu, Feng Wang, Lin Gu, Jianhua Gao, and Yaohui Jin. 2014. Characterizing Home Network Traffic: An Inside View. *Personal Ubiquitous Computing* 18, 4 (April 2014), 967–975.

32. Yiannis Yiakoumis, Sachin Katti, Te-Yuan Huang, Nick McKeown, Kok-Kiong Yap, and Ramesh Johari. 2012. Putting home users in charge of their network. In *ACM Conference on Ubiquitous Computing*. ACM.

33. Xiaoqi Yin, Abhishek Jindal, Vyas Sekar, and Bruno Sinopoli. 2015. A Control-Theoretic Approach for Dynamic Adaptive Video Streaming over HTTP. In *SIGCOMM*. ACM.

34. Youtube. 2017. Live encoder settings, bitrates and resolutions. https://support.google.com/youtube/answer/2853702?hl=en. (2017).

35. S. Zander, T. Nguyen, and G. Armitage. 2005. Self-learning IP traffic classification based on statistical flow characteristics. In *Passive and Active Network Measurement (PAM)*. Springer.

Collaboration Success Factors in an Online Music Community

Fabio Calefato   **Giuseppe Iaffaldano**   **Filippo Lanubile**

University of Bari, Italy

{fabio.calefato, giuseppe.iaffaldano, filippo.lanubile}@uniba.it

ABSTRACT

Online communities have been able to develop large, open-source software (OSS) projects like Linux and Firefox throughout the successful collaborations carried out by their members over the Internet. However, online communities also involve creative arts domains such as animation, video games, and music. Despite their growing popularity, the factors that lead to successful collaborations in these communities are not entirely understood.

In this paper, we present a study on creative collaboration in a music community where authors write songs together by 'overdubbing', that is, by mixing a new track with an existing audio recording. We analyzed the relationship between song- and author-related measures and the likelihood of a song being overdubbed. We found that recent songs, as well as songs with many reactions, are more likely to be overdubbed; authors with a high status in the community and a recognizable identity write songs that the community tends to build upon.

Author Keywords

Creative collaboration; music composition; overdub; remix; reuse; online community; social computing; open source.

ACM Classification Keywords

H.5.3. Information interfaces and presentation (e.g., HCI): Group and Organizational Interfaces – *collaborative computing, computer-supported cooperative work.*

INTRODUCTION

By almost exclusively relying on computer-mediated communication, participants in online communities have been able to develop large, open-source software (OSS) projects like Linux and Firefox. Besides, online communities also involve other kinds of peer productions [2] such as creative collaborations in domains like animation, video games, and music.

Despite the growing popularity of online communities, the

GROUP '18, January 7–10, 2018, Sanibel Island, FL, USA
© 2018 Association for Computing Machinery.
ACM ISBN 978-1-4503-5562-9/18/01 $15.00
https://doi.org/10.1145/3148330.3148346

factors that lead to the success of collaborations between members are not entirely understood [19]. For instance, we ignore whether success factors are domain dependent [15]. Previous research in OSS communities has established that successful collaborations between developers depend on both social and technical factors [8,10,21]. Also in the case of online creative arts communities, Luther et al. [14,15] found that participants' social reputation is key to the successful completion of collaborative animation efforts. Burke and Settles [3] found that users, especially newcomers, who engage in social features and one-to-one collaborations perform their songwriting goals better than those who are non-social. Other studies, instead, focused on factors that lead members of arts communities to select specific creative artifacts shared by others for reworking and recombining them into something new [5,13,20].

To further our understanding of the factors influencing the success of online creative collaborations and how they transfer across domains, we designed a study on Songtree,[1] an online community for collaborative music creation. We focused on the creative action of *overdubbing,* whereby exactly one new track is mixed with an existing audio recording (e.g., recording voice over an instrumental song), thus allowing a song to 'grow.' We analyzed the relationship between song- and author-related measures (e.g., likes, followers) and the 'success' of a song, represented by whether it is overdubbed or not. We found that recent songs, as well as songs with many reactions, are more likely to be further extended. Furthermore, authors with a high status in the community and a recognizable profile write songs that the community tends to build upon. These findings provide evidence that there are: (i) success factors specific to creative communities; (ii) common factors that are key to successful collaboration in both OSS projects and online creative arts communities.

SONGTREE

Born in late 2011 as a spin-off of the n-Track Software, Songtree is both an app, providing an all-in-one solution for recording songs, and an online creative music community, where artists collaborate to the creation of musical tracks. As of December 2016, the community counted about 26K registered users, of which ~5,300 are authors who uploaded over 26,000 songs.

---

[1] http://songtr.ee

Songtree allows any user to extend (namely, *overdub*) any publicly shared song in the community without permission. Songtree leverages the metaphor of a growing tree to represent and keep track of the collaborative creation of music tracks (see Figure 1). A new song is the root of the tree (the topmost node). For each song derived from it, a new branch is created and added to the song tree. Thus, over time, the tree of a song gradually grows as new overdubs are posted, each derived from any of the songs in the tree.

Several social-networking features are available in Songtree, including the ability to follow other musicians, as well as to like and bookmark songs. Analogously to Stack Overflow, Songtree also uses badges [4], which are earned by members through their activity within the community. There are three badge categories: *new songs*, *overdubs*, and *overdubs received*. Badges in these categories can be earned, respectively, by uploading new own songs, overdubbing other songs, or being overdubbed by others. Unlike Stack Overflow, however, earning badges does not unlock privileges (e.g., moderation). Instead, badges in Songtree act as a proxy measure of artists' reputation within the community, measured by the quantity and quality of the content created therein.

Finally, user profile pages (see Figure 2) list authors' personal information, biography, pictures, links to uploaded songs and followers, and statistics of their activity.

COLLABORATION IN ONLINE COMMUNITIES

In this section, we review the literature on creative communities, focusing specifically on arts and OSS communities. For each work, we highlight the type of collaboration studied, the definition of a successful collaboration, and the relevant success factors identified.

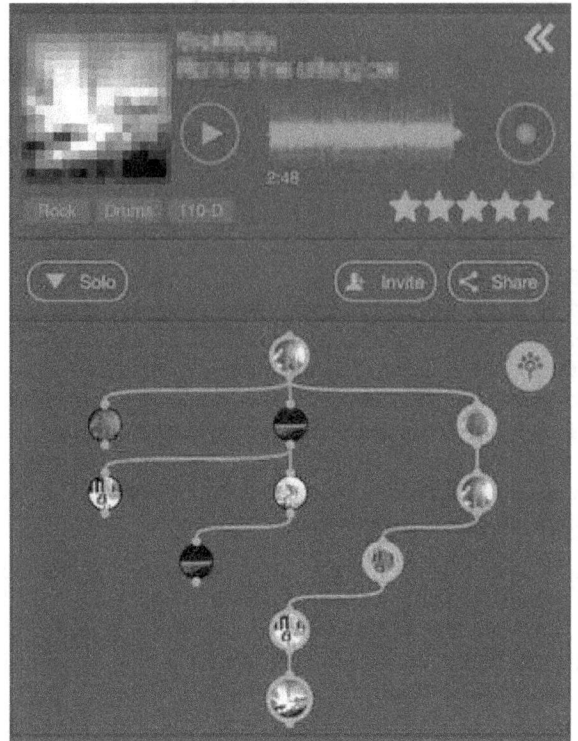

Figure 1. The tree of a song (topmost node) with branches generated by the overdubs received.

Online Creative Arts Communities

Collaboration in creative arts communities typically happens in the form of *reuse*, that is, the generation of derivative content through the reworking and recombination of existing member contributions [5,13]. In music communities, reuse is mostly referred to as *remix*, where it indicates "a reinterpretation of a pre-existing song" [18].

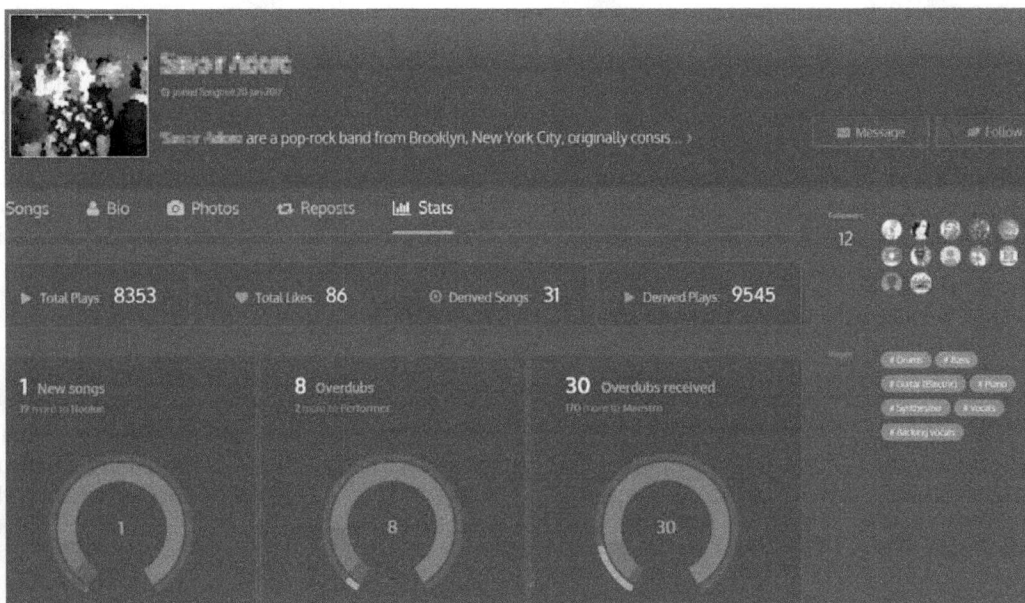

Figure 2. The stats available in the profile page of an artist in Songtree.

Nevertheless, the term remix has now become commonplace in creative contexts other than music to refer, for example, to reusing video animations [13] and 3D-printable content [20].

Cheliotis et al. [5] studied the likelihood of songs being remixed in the ccMixter music community. They fit a logistic regression model and observed that the positive antecedents of remixes are the following: remixes 'closer' to their parent songs (i.e., *degree of derivativity*), being an author with a history of remixes received (i.e., *fecundity*), and having a high level of commitment and contribution to the community (i.e., *social embeddedness*).

Hill and Monroy-Hernández [13] performed a study on Scratch, an online community where amateur creators combine images, music, and sound to obtain Adobe Flash-like video animations. The results of their logistic regression analysis show that the likelihood of engendering derivative works is related to work complexity, prominence of authors, and work cumulativeness. In particular, the result about cumulativeness (i.e., remixes themselves are reused more than *de novo* content) is in direct contrast with the finding by Cheliotis et al. [5] on the degree of derivativity (i.e., the 'newer' the content, the higher the likelihood of remix).

Stanko [20] investigated why some 3D-printable objects in the Thingiverse community are more generative than others. They found that the remixing likelihood is positively related to the interaction with other community members and the availability of content whose reuse would foster desired learning.

The review of prior work on remixing, especially in the music context, highlights commonalities and differences with overdubbing. Both remixes and overdubs leverage existing content to build something new. However, while remixing is 'derivative' by nature, overdubbing is 'additive,' since it implies adding a new track to an existing recording.

A few prior studies have investigated collaboration success factors in creative arts communities. Luther at al. [14,15] examined the role of leadership and other success factors in Newgrounds, a collaborative animation community. Specifically, they analyzed a dataset comprising completed (i.e., successful) and incomplete/abandoned (i.e., unsuccessful) animations created collaboratively by up to 10 co-authors. Successful collaborations are then hosted on the website, and the number of views and likes received contribute to building up authors' reputation within the community. Through a mix of qualitative and quantitative analysis, Luther at al. found that the collaborations more likely to succeed are those initiated by experienced 'leaders,' already well-known to the community, who are also inclined to communicate frequently; in addition, the quality of the idea for the animation initially presented is also positively associated with the chance of success.

Settles and Dow [19] analyzed FAWM, a hub for songwriters who meet online annually on February and collaborate to the creation of an entire album of 14 songs written in 28 days. They developed a logistic regression model on longitudinal data collected from four FAWM events (2009-2012) to predict whether any pair of songwriters would start and successfully complete a collaboration or not. Their findings, further corroborated by a survey administered to FAWM members, showed that prior interactions (i.e., exchange of direct messages) and slight differences in status are key factors in pairing, and that the perception of balanced efforts from both parties is the factor that contributes the most to the completion of such collaborations.

Overall, the review of prior work on creative arts communities highlights the existence of both content- and author-related success factors, suggesting the need for conducting the analysis of successful collaboration in Songtree on the same two levels, i.e., *songs* and *authors*.

Open-Source Software Communities

There has been a substantial amount of previous research on the factors affecting success in collaboration within OSS communities, where success is defined in terms of the acceptance of external code contributions (e.g., patches, pull requests) to project repositories. Baysal et al. [1] found that only about a half of the submitted pull requests to the Chrome and Firefox projects made it into the repository; Gousios et al. [9] found that about 80% of the ~170k pull requests analyzed in their study on GitHub were merged.

Regarding the factors that influence the acceptance of contributions, previous research found them to be both social and technical in nature [11,21]. Weißgerber et al. [22] analyzed successful collaboration in the form of the patch submission process in two OSS projects and found that small patches (i.e., affecting a few lines of codes and files) have significantly higher chances of being successfully merged. Yet, with the raise of 'transparent' social coding platforms such as Bitbucket and GitHub, integrators have started to make inferences about the quality of contributions not only by looking at their technical quality but also using developers' track record (e.g., history of previous contributions accepted) and reputation (e.g., number of stars and followers in GitHub) as auxiliary indicators [6,16]. Ducheneaut [7] found that contributions coming from submitters who are known to the core development team have higher chances of being accepted, as core developers also use the record of interactions as signals for judging the quality of proposed changes.

Tsay et al. [21] conducted a study where they developed a regression model to examine the association of several social and technical factors with the likelihood of accepting pull requests in GitHub projects. They found that submitters' reputation and their social distance from the code development team (i.e., track record) is surprisingly more relevant to the contribution acceptance than technical factors (e.g., the inclusion of test cases). Finally, Gousios et al. [9] consistently found in another study on GitHub that only ~13% of the pull requests reviewed were rejected for purely technical reasons.

Finally, Luther et al. [15] contrasted success factors identified in a creative community of animations (Newgrounds) to those reported in OSS literature. They reported frequent communication and project leader's experience and reputation as common factors. Our work aims at furthering this comparison.

HYPOTHESES

Previous work on OSS and creative arts communities suggests several potential factors, both social and technical, which may influence the success of collaboration in Songtree. In the following, we discuss a set of hypotheses, designed on two different levels of analysis, i.e., songs and authors. These hypotheses, built upon prior work, have also been revised during a couple of sessions conducted with Songtree administrators.

Song-related hypotheses

Community members show appreciation towards songs by liking and bookmarking them, and, of course, by playing them. Songs receiving a high amount of reactions from the community may also be showcased in Songtree under the *Popular* section of the website. As such, the visibility gained by being featured in the *Popular* section may further increase their chances to be overdubbed.

H1: Songs that generate a high amount of reactions are more likely to be overdubbed.

Besides, to favorite the serendipitous discovery of new artists and songs, the Songtree website also features a *Latest* section where newly uploaded contributions are promoted for also gaining visibility. Therefore, we expect that recent songs have more odds to be overdubbed.

H2: More recently uploaded songs are more likely to be overdubbed.

The main purpose of Songtree is to help musicians write songs collaboratively through overdubs. The more overdubs a song receives, the closer it gets to be considered 'finished.' Songtree even allows musicians to tag their songs as complete, to indicate that they do not intend to work on them anymore (albeit overdubbing may remain allowed). This speculation is in line with the finding by Cheliotis et al. [5] about the inverse relationship between a song's degree of derivativity and the chance of being overdubbed. Thus, we expect that these consolidated, more mature songs receive fewer overdubs than the others.

H3: More mature songs are less likely to be overdubbed.

Author-related hypotheses

Hill and Monroy-Hernández [13] and Cheliotis et al. [4] found that authors' prominence and their social embeddedness in the community increase the likelihood of

remix. Therefore, we expect that the same applies also to Songtree.

H4: Songs by authors with a high status in the community are more likely to be overdubbed.

Previous research on collaboration in OSS communities has found that the identity of the submitters is a very significant factor when it comes to assessing the quality of contributions [12]. Besides, Luther et al. [14,15] found that being able to browse members' history of contributions increases the chance of successful collaboration. Songtree allows artists to maintain their profile page where they upload their avatar pictures, provide a bio, share stage photos, thus creating a personal space that reflects their identity. Some members may perceive that the effort put into curating their personal space may reflect the same attention put into creating their music. As such, we hypothesize that Songtree members are more inclined to overdub songs by fellow authors who are more easily recognized.

H5: Songs by authors with a recognizable profile are more likely to be overdubbed.

EMPIRICAL STUDY

To test the hypotheses defined earlier, we built a dataset from the entire data dump of Songtree, including data from November 2011 to December 2016. Using this dataset, we fit a logistic regression model that associates both social and technical features measured in Songtree with the likelihood of a song being overdubbed. The study approach follows a similar research by Tsay et al. [21], who previously investigated the factors influencing the likelihood of pull requests acceptance in GitHub projects.

In the rest of this section, we provide a detailed description of the dataset and the measures extracted.

Dataset

We built a dataset consisting of authors, songs, and song trees. Information was gathered from the entire data dump of Songtree performed in December 2016.

As initial preprocessing steps, we first removed all the songs uploaded prior to March 2015, i.e., before the song's catalog and community reached a mass large enough to not require administrators' participation anymore. Then, we filtered out all the new songs uploaded in the last 27 days. Instead, overdubs were only accounted for when they derived songs outside such time window; otherwise, they were also ditched. The 27-day threshold corresponds to the 90th percentile of the overdub time intervals between the upload of a song and that of its first overdub. In other words, 90% of the songs in our rather sparse dataset receive their first overdub within 27 days since their upload. This step was necessary to avoid censoring issues and ensure that all the selected songs have had sufficient time to receive at least one overdub. We further discuss this preprocessing step in the Limitations section.

	Original dump*	Final dataset**
Users	26,727	-
Authors	5,306	3,790
Administrators	9	-
Songs	26,055	16,998
New songs	15,826	10,595
Contest songs	136	-
Closed songs	39	-
Hidden songs	5,063	-
Orphan songs	207	-
Self-overdubs	3,843	-
Overdubs	10,229	6,403
Remixes	52	-

*as of Dec. 2016; ** Mar. 2105 – Nov. 2016

Table 1. A comparison of data in the Songtree dump and the final dataset (rows in grey are filtered out).

A breakdown of the data dump is reported in Table 1. As of December 2016, the community counted about 26,000 members, of which ~5,300 (20%) are authors who had recorded and shared at least one on Songtree. Overall, over 26,000 songs had been upload to Songtree, of which ~15,000 new songs and ~10,000 overdubs.

To build the final dataset, we further preprocessed the dump and excluded the content matching the following criteria:

- *Non-authors* – community members who have not recorded and shared any song on Songtree. They are excluded because they have gained no reputation as authors.

- *Administrators* – accounts registered by the members of the Songtree development team. We opted for excluding administrators' accounts and the content shared by them (e.g., contest songs) to avoid altering our findings on how the Songtree community behave when collaborating.

- *Closed songs* – songs that, as per author's setting, either cannot be overdubbed or are marked as finished. Hence, they are excluded because, respectively, they disable or discourage overdubbing. Note that these are just leaf nodes. Instead, the song trees they belong to are retained.

- *Hidden songs* – songs that, as per author's setting, are not publicly listed and can be found and overdubbed only if the author shares a link with others. These songs are used by authors who want their music to remain private or keep the collaboration restricted to their inner circle.

- *Orphan songs* – songs that belong to no song tree and overdubs derived from no parent songs.

- *Self-overdubs* – any child song derived from a parent song recorded by the same author. They are excluded because they do not represent meaningful cases of collaborative songwriting.

- *Remixes* – songs that only add effects or alter frequencies through the equalizer. They are excluded because they do not help their authors earn badges or improve their status.

- *Contest songs* – songs uploaded by the Songtree team to start contests with prizes awarded to the best overdubs.

At the end of the preprocessing stage, we ended up with a final dataset consisting of 16,998 songs (10,595 new songs + 6,403 overdubs), and 3,790 authors.

Measures

From the final dataset built, we defined several measures to inform our analysis (see Table 2). Since the outcome measure for our statistical model is whether a song has been overdubbed, we define overdubbed as a dichotomous, yes/no variable.

To draw causal conclusions, all the measures detailed next are calculated prior to the event '*song has received the first overdub.*' As an example, consider a song S from our dataset. First, in case that S has been overdubbed, we retrieve the time T_S when it received the first overdub. Then, all the measures are calculated at the instant before T_S (e.g., we compute the number of likes received by S *before* S was first overdubbed). We can safely ignore any subsequent overdub of S because we conduct a logistic regression and our outcome variable is binary (i.e., S has received 0 overdubs vs. S has received 1+ overdubs). For songs that received no overdubs, instead, we retrieve the timestamp of the last event recorded in the entire dump and, hence, we apply no time-based measurement.

In the following, the measures are described accordingly to the two levels of analysis, that is, songs and authors.

Song-level measures

For our song-related measures, we capture various dimensions as well as signals expressed by community members in form of likes and plays. These measures are presented in the following, grouped by hypothesis/main factor.

H1 – Reactions

#likes_received – A numeric variable that counts how many times the song has been liked by someone in Songtree.

#bookmarks_received – A numeric variable that counts how many times the song has been bookmarked by someone in Songtree.

#times_played – A counter of the number of times that a song has been played in Songtree.

	Measure	Type	Description	Hypothesis
	overdubbed	nominal	Whether the song has received any overdubs or not. Values: {*Yes, No*}	-
Song level	#likes_received	ratio	No. of likes that the song received by Songtree members.	H1
	#bookmarks_received	ratio	The number of times that the song has been bookmarked.	
	#times_played	ratio	No. of times the song was played in Songtree.	
	overdub_time_interval	interval	Time difference (in minutes) between the respective upload times on Songtree of an overdub (if any) and its parent song.	H2
	song_depth	ratio	The distance in number of nodes from the root song that started the song tree. It is 0 for root songs.	H3
Author level	#followers	ratio	No. of users following author's activities on Songtree.	H4
	songtree_ranking	ratio	$\dfrac{\#followers + \#user\_likes + \#user\_plays + \#derived\_plays}{\#shared\_songs}$	
	new_songs_badge	ordinal	Badge gained by uploading new songs. Values: {*None, Rookie, Songwriter, Composer*}	
	overdubs_badge	ordinal	Badge gained by overdubbing other authors' songs Values: {*None, Performer, Top performer, Virtuoso*}	
	overdubs_received_badge	ordinal	Badge awarded when enough overdubs are recorded an authors' songs. Values: {*None, Songsmith, Band leader, Maestro*}	
	has_avatar	nominal	Whether the author has uploaded a profile picture or not. Values: {*Yes, No*}	H5

Table 2. Measures defined for the study, grouped by level of analysis and hypothesis.

H2 – Recent Songs

overdub_time_interval – A variable measuring (in seconds) the time interval between the upload of an overdub and that of the parent song from which it was derived.

H3 – Mature Songs

song_depth – A continuous variable measuring the length of the path to its root. A root song (i.e., a new song) has depth 0.

Author-level measures
Regarding the author-related measures, we capture various signals and dimensions of identity, social status, and productivity within the community.

H4 – Status in Community

#followers – A numerical variable that counts the number of followers of an author.

songtree_ranking – A *coolness* index, updated on a weekly basis and used by Songtree administrators to rank the community authors. It is computed per author as follows:

$$\frac{\#followers + \#user\_likes + \#user\_plays + \#derived\_plays}{\#shared\_songs}$$

where #followers is the same measure defined earlier, #user_likes is the cumulative number of likes received by all the songs by the author, #user_plays is the cumulative number of times that all the songs by the author have been played, #derived_plays is the cumulative number of times that all the songs derived from the author's songs have been played, and #shared_songs is the number of tracks shared by the author on Songtree.

new_songs_badges – Depending on the number of new songs uploaded, users unlock badges that reflect their level of productivity. This ordinal variable is defined in the set {*None, Rookie, Songwriter, Composer*}. The *Rookie* badge is unlocked by uploading at least 20 new songs. The *Songwriter* badge is unlocked by uploading at least 50 new songs. The last one, *Composer*, is unlocked by uploading at least 320 new songs.

overdubs_badges – Depending on the number of overdubs uploaded, users unlock badges that reflect their attitude towards contributing to others' songs. This ordinal variable is defined in the set {*None, Performer, Top performer, Virtuoso*}. The *Performer* badge is unlocked by uploading at least 10 overdubs. The *Top performer* badge is unlocked by uploading at least 40 overdubs. The last one, *Virtuoso*, is unlocked by uploading at least 200 new songs.

overdubs_received_badges – Depending on the number of overdubs received by their own songs, users unlock badges that reflect the extent to which their songs attract external contributions from other authors in Songtree. This ordinal variable is defined in the set {*Songsmith, Band leader, Maestro*}. The *Songsmith* badge is unlocked by uploading at least 10 overdubs. The *Band leader* badge is unlocked by uploading at least 40 overdubs. The last one, *Virtuoso*, is unlocked by uploading at least 200 new songs.

H5 – Recognizable Profile

has_avatar – A dichotomous variable indicating whether the author has uploaded a personal picture to customize the profile image.

RESULTS

In the following, we examine our hypotheses and how each measure (i.e., predictor variable) is associated with our dependent variable that models a successful collaboration, i.e., whether a song has been overdubbed.

Using these measures, we created a model that predicts the likelihood of a song being overdubbed (see Table 3). Specifically, we fit a multi-level mixed-effects logistic regression model to our data. We choose a logistic regression approach to predict better our binary outcome variable. The multi-level approach accounts for the two layers of the dataset, with the variable *song* nested under *author*. Finally, in the mixed-effect model, all measures are *fixed effects* except for the author, which is represented as a *random effect* term; this allows us to capture author-to-author variability in the response variable (overdubbed), that is, some authors write songs that are more likable or leave more room for collaboration than others.

To perform the logistic regression, we used the lme4 R package, which accounts for cross-classification of data, as authors appear in multiple song trees in our dataset. To ensure normality, each of the continuous variables in the model was log-transformed and standardized, such that the mean of each measure is 0 and the standard deviation is 1. Furthermore, we checked our dataset for multicollinearity problems [7]. We first computed the correlation matrix for the predictors and found that #followers and the three badges-related measures (i.e., new_songs_badge, overdubs_badge, overdubs_received_badge), as well as times_played and songtree_ranking, have strong pairwise correlations (i.e., ≥ 0.7). Therefore, to fix the multicollinearity, we retained the times_played and #followers measures while discarding the others. Then, after fitting the model, we checked again for collinearity using the Variance Inflation Factor (VIF) and found no value larger than 4.

In Table 3, we report the results of the logistic model. All predictors are important, that is, statistically significant at 1% level (p < 0.01) or smaller, as obtained from Wald test. Given the large size of our dataset, however, we report and discuss predictor contributions in terms of odds ratio, which is an unstandardized effect size statistic that tells the direction and the strength of the relationship between predictors and the odds that a song is overdubbed, i.e., the increase or decrease of the odds of 'success' occurring per 'unit' of the measure. We remind the reader that an odds ratio close to 1 means that exposure to property A (i.e., one of the considered predictors) does not affect the odds of a song being overdubbed. An odds ratio far smaller than 1 is instead significantly associated with lower odds. Conversely, an odds ratio much larger than 1 means that there are higher odds for a song to be overdubbed with exposure to predictor A.

Finally, to evaluate the fit, in Table 3 we report *AIC* and R^2 for the statistical model developed [17]. Regarding R^2, we used the MuMIn package in R to computed both the marginal (R_m^2) and conditional (R_c^2) version: the former describes the proportion of variance explained by fixed effects alone, whereas the latter combines fixed and random effects together. Results show that our model fits the data very well, as it explains 95% of the variability of the data ($R_c^2 = 0.95$).

H1 – Songs that generate a high amount of reactions are more likely to be overdubbed

To test our first hypothesis, we examined the association between the probability of a song to receive an overdub and

	Factor	Measure (predictor)	Odds Ratio
		(Intercept)	0.068
Song level	Reactions (H1)	#likes_received	1.176**
		#bookmarks_received	**2.116***
	Recent Songs (H2)	overdub_time_interval	**0.002***
	Mature Songs (H3)	song_depth	**0.557***
Author level	Status in Community (H4)	#followers	0.817***
		songtree_ranking	**9.479***
	Recognizable Profile (H5)	has_avatar (default: false)	**3.114***
		AIC	3925
		R_m^2	0.94
		R_c^2	0.95

Table 3. The logistic mixed-effects model for the likelihood of song overdubbing (sig.: ** p<0.01, *** p<0.001). Predictors with large effect sizes are shown in bold.

the number of times that the song has been liked and bookmarked.

From the odds ratios reported in Table 3, we observe that while the association of the likelihood of a song being overdubbed with the measure #likes_received (1.176) is negligible, the #bookmarks_received predictor is positively and strongly associated with the likelihood of the song to be overdubbed (2.116).

Therefore, we found strong support for H1.

H2 – More recently uploaded songs are more likely to be overdubbed

We tested H2 by measuring the time interval between the upload of an overdub and the upload of its parent song.

From the results reported in Table 3, we observe that the measure of overdub_time_interval is one of the strongest predictors in our model (0.002). Specifically, the small odds ratio for this predictor indicates that time is strongly and negatively associated with the odds of a song being overdubbed (i.e., the longer since the upload of the song, the smaller the chances to be overdubbed).

Therefore, we found strong support for our hypothesis H2.

H3 – More mature songs are less likely to be overdubbed.

We tested H3 by measuring the distance of a song from the root of its song tree. We found the measure song_depth to be strongly and negatively correlated with the likelihood of the song to be overdubbed (0.557).

Hence, also H3 is supported.

H4 – Songs by authors with a high status in the community are more likely to be overdubbed

To test H4, we look at the author-level predictors in our statistical model (see Table 3).

Specifically, while the effect of #followers is negligible (0.817), the songtree_ranking predictor is positively and very strongly associated with the likelihood of highly-ranked author's songs being overdubbed (9.479).

Therefore, we found support for our hypothesis that the higher the authors' status in Songtree, the higher the odds of their songs to be overdubbed.

H5 – Songs by authors with a recognizable profile are more likely to be overdubbed

We tested H5 by examining the association of the dichotomous predictors has_avatar with the likelihood of songs to be overdubbed. We found that the predictor is strongly and positively associated with the outcome variable (3.114).

Therefore, we found strong support for our fifth hypothesis, according to which songs by authors whose profile is easily recognized are more likely to be overdubbed.

DISCUSSION

In this section, we summarize the results, discuss them in terms of prior research, and show the implications for the Songtree community and developers.

Popular Songs

The results for our first hypothesis H1 show that 'popular' songs, i.e., songs that generate larger amounts of reactions in terms of bookmarks have significantly higher chances to be overdubbed.

Regarding OSS communities, this lack of evidence is explained by the nature of code contributions, as there are no 'popular' pull requests or patches. In fact, in their analysis of pull request acceptance in GitHub, Tsay et al. [21] discuss the effect of popularity at the project level, using the number of stars and collaborators as proxies. This finding complements those previous studies performed on other creative arts communities, such as Newgrounds [14,15] and FAWM [3,19], who did not evaluate the popularity of creative artifacts as a predictor of future successful collaborations. In this regard, Songtree is already leveraging these features, as it promotes popular songs in a dedicated section of its landing page.

Recent and Mature Songs

Regarding H2, we found very strong evidence that the longer since the upload of a song, the less its chance to be overdubbed. The cause of this strong effect arguably depends on how Songtree provides recommendations to its members, that is, by suggesting recent songs, usually uploaded in about the last two days. Given the incidence of the time factor in the current implementation of the recommender system, introducing some randomness or other factors would favorite the discovery of 'older' songs.

Regarding H3, we found that more mature songs, i.e., songs created towards the end of a long collaboration process, are less likely to be overdubbed. In fact, the predictor that measures the depth of a song in its tree is significantly and negatively associated with the likelihood of being overdubbed. This finding confirms the results reported by Cheliotis et al. [5] on the degree of derivativity. A related finding is also reported by Hill and Monroy-Hernández [13] who found that older remixes, comparable to mature songs close to completion, are reused less because believed to be more complex. Our finding is particularly relevant to musicians seeking to increase the number of overdubs received by their songs. To this end, they should either start new songs or overdub less mature songs so that others still have enough 'room' to build upon their own work.

Status and Profile of Authors

The results our study provide support for our hypothesis H4 that songs by authors who have gained a higher status in the Songtree community are more likely to be overdubbed. This finding is consistent with previous results from previous studies on arts communities [5,13–15]. Currently, Songtree shows a rank (updated weekly) of top artists in a dedicated section of the website. To further leverage the effect of author prominence in the community, the visibility of other status signals might be increased, for example, by showing next to the author's name also the number of followers and other counters, which are now only accessible by visiting the profile page.

Furthermore, we also provide support for hypothesis H5, according to which songs by authors easily recognized by their profile picture are overdubbed more. Surprisingly, Stanko [20] found that promoting artists and songs on the front page of Thingiverse community website had no impact on the likelihood of remixing. Still, our finding confirms the evidence provided by an earlier study on OSS communities, which found that the identity of pull request submitters is a very significant factor when it comes to assessing the quality of contributions [12]. Albeit not entirely novel, our finding is particularly relevant to the Songtree community because it is another actionable success factor among those identified in the study. As such, authors looking for increasing their visibility in the community should select their avatar picture carefully and leverage other platform features that may make their identity easier to recognize.

Overall, given the results of hypotheses H4 and H5, our study provides new evidence that the status and the identity of community members are consistently used as proxies of artifact quality regardless of the domain, whether technical (as in OSS communities) or artistic (as in music communities).

Causal relationships
One of the main contributions of this observational study is the certainty about the direction of causality for the predictors used to build the statistical model and the outcome variable.

In fact, because all the values have been computed prior to each event '*song is overdubbed*,' the predictors are inherently robust to reverse causality. As such, we can make inferences about the underlying causal relationships uncovered by our study and state that the increase in the likelihood of song overdubbing is the result of the occurrence of any of the events and song properties described earlier.

Limitations
The main limitation of this work concerns the generalizability of our findings. We cannot affirm that Songtree is representative of all online music communities, nor we are certain that our findings would transfer to other types of online creative arts communities. We intend to address this limitation by replicating the study on other music communities, as well as on creative arts communities of a different genre.

Regarding the findings on the derivability of recent and mature songs (H2), we acknowledge the risk that the strength of the related predictors in the regression model is due to the recommender system adopted to feed the list of *Recent* and *Popular* songs on Songtree's website. Future replications on other communities will help us overcome also this threat.

As for dataset construction, we chose to exclude all the songs uploaded in the last 27 days to ensure that all the songs in the dataset had had sufficient time to be overdubbed at least once. Of course, the older a song, the more overdubs it may have received. Therefore, rather than considering the number of received overdubs, we consistently chose to build a logistic regression model that predicts the likelihood of a song being overdubbed (i.e., 1+ times) or not. Future works involving the development of linear regression models to predict the number of overdubs will require a finer approach with longitudinal analysis.

Another limitation concerns the validity of the construct defined to assess the extent to which authors are recognizable in Songtree. While we acknowledge that using only a dichotomous variable (i.e., has_avatar) to model an entire author's identity may appear simplistic, we underline that the having a customized profile picture is one of the strongest predictors in the developed statistical model.

Cheliotis et al. operationalized the prominence of authors in the community using a bow-tie analysis [5]. Instead, we relied on Songtree's own metric of commitment. In our future extension, we aim to leverage clique analysis for a finer-grain evaluation of author status as an overdub factor.

Previous research has found that communication has a positive relationship with remixing [19,20]. In our future work, we will extend our explanatory model to include message exchange.

Finally, we acknowledge that the lack of qualitative analysis (e.g., questionnaires) does not allow us to triangulate data and gather a better understanding of our findings. We intend to overcome this limitation in a future extension of the study.

CONCLUSION
In this paper, we examined the factors that influence the songwriting collaboration within the Songtree music community. Specifically, we created a statistical model to analyze the relationship between song- and author-related measures and the likelihood of songs being overdubbed (i.e., completed thanks to other musicians).

We found that recent songs, as well as songs with many reactions, are more likely to be derived. These success factors related to the popularity of artifacts are specific to online creative arts communities. Furthermore, authors with a high status in the community and a recognizable identity write songs that continue to be evolved by the community. Comparing to similar results in OSS communities, we have evidence that people-related factors are also key to successful contribution in OSS projects. Our findings are also useful to inform the administrators of creative arts communities about aligning their policies with the signals that members are already using to discover songs and collaborate.

As future work, we intend to improve our statistical model by including new predictors. For example, we intend to study the effect of messages exchanged by authors and their polarity. In addition, author status within Songtree can also be assessed through social network analysis measures, such as degree centrality, calculated from the collaboration and communication networks. Furthermore, as we acquire further snapshots of Songtree's database, we intend to conduct a longitudinal study to uncover new success factors, regarding, in particular, the retention and loyalty of community members over time.

ACKNOWLEDGMENTS

We are grateful to Songtree for opening their data for research purposes.

REFERENCES

1. O. Baysal, R. Holmes, and M.W. Godfrey. 2012. Mining usage data and development artifacts. In *IEEE Int'l Working Conf. on Mining Software Repositories* (MSR '12), 98–107.

2. Y. Benkler. 2007. *The wealth of networks: How social production transforms markets and freedom*. Yale University Press, New Haven, CT, USA.

3. M. Burke and B. Settles. 2011. Plugged in to the community. In *Proc. of the 5th Int'l Conf. on Communities and Technologies* (C&T '11).

4. F. Calefato, F. Lanubile, M.C. Marasciulo, and N. Novielli. 2015. Mining successful answers in stack overflow. In *IEEE Int'l Working Conf. on Mining Software Repositories*, 430–433.

5. G. Cheliotis, N. Hu, J. Yew, and J. Huang. 2014. The Antecedents of Remix. In *Proc. of the 17th ACM Conf. on Computer Supported Cooperative Work* (CSCW '14), 1011–1022.

6. L. Dabbish, C. Stuart, J. Tsay, and J. Herbsleb. 2012. Social Coding in GitHub: Transparency and Collaboration in an Open Software Repository. *Proc. of the ACM 2012 Conf. on Computer Supported Cooperative Work*: 1277–1286.

7. N. Ducheneaut. 2005. Socialization in an open source software community: A socio-technical analysis. *Computer Supported Cooperative Work: CSCW: An Int'l Journal* 14, 4: 323–368.

8. G. Gousios, M. Pinzger, and A. van Deursen. 2014. An exploratory study of the pull-based software development model. In *Proc. of the 36th Int'l Conf. on Software Engineering - ICSE 2014*.

9. G. Gousios, M. Pinzger, and A. van Deursen. 2014. An Exploratory Study of the Pull-based Software Development Model. In *Proc. of the 36th Int'l Conf. on Software Engineering*, 345–355.

10. G. Gousios, M.-A. Storey, and A. Bacchelli. 2016. Work practices and challenges in pull-based development: The contributor's perspective. In *Proc. of the 38th Int'l Conf. on Software Engineering - ICSE '16*.

11. G. Gousios, M.-A. Storey, and A. Bacchelli. 2016. Work Practices and Challenges in Pull-Based Development: The Contributor's Perspective. In *Proc. of the 38th Int'l Conf. on Software Engineering - ICSE '16*, 285–296.

12. G. Gousios, A. Zaidman, M.-A. Storey, and A. van Deursen. 2015. Work Practices and Challenges in Pull-Based Development: The Integrator's Perspective. In *2015 IEEE/ACM 37th IEEE Int'l Conf. on Software Engineering*.

13. B.M. Hill and A. Monroy-Hernández. 2012. The Remixing Dilemma. *American Behavioral Scientist* 57, 5: 643–663.

14. K. Luther and A. Bruckman. 2008. Leadership and success factors in online creative collaboration. In *IEEE Potentials* (CSCW '08), 27–32.

15. K. Luther, K. Caine, K. Ziegler, and A. Bruckman. 2010. Why it works (when it works). In *Proc. of the 16th ACM Int'l Conf. on Supporting group work* (GROUP '10).

16. J. Marlow, L. Dabbish, and J. Herbsleb. 2013. Impression Formation in Online Peer Production : Activity Traces and Personal Profiles in GitHub. *16th ACM Conf. on Computer Supported Cooperative Work*: 117–128.

17. S. Müller, J.L. Scealy, and A.H. Welsh. 2013. Model Selection in Linear Mixed Models. *Statistical Science* 28, 2: 135–167.

18. E. Navas. 2012. *Remix Theory: The Aesthetics of Sampling*.

19. B. Settles and S. Dow. 2013. Let's get together. In *Proc. of the SIGCHI Conf. on Human Factors in Computing Systems - CHI '13* (CHI '13), 2009.

20. M.A. Stanko. 2016. Toward a Theory of Remixing in Online Innovation Communities. *Information Systems Research* 27, 4: 773–791.

21. J. Tsay, L. Dabbish, and J. Herbsleb. 2014. Influence of social and technical factors for evaluating contribution in GitHub. In *36th Int'l Conf. on Software Engineering*, 356–366.

22. P. Weißgerber, D. Neu, and S. Diehl. 2008. Small patches get in! In *Proc. of the 2008 Int'l workshop on Mining software repositories* (MSR '08), 67.

Geographic Biases are 'Born, not Made': Exploring Contributors' Spatiotemporal Behavior in OpenStreetMap

Jacob Thebault-Spieker
University of Minnesota
thebault@cs.umn.edu

Brent Hecht
Northwestern University
bhecht@northwestern.edu

Loren Terveen
University of Minnesota
terveen@cs.umn.edu

ABSTRACT

The evolution of contributor behavior in peer production communities over time has been a subject of substantial interest in the social computing community. In this paper, we extend this literature to the geographic domain, exploring contribution behavior in OpenStreetMap using a *spatiotemporal* lens. In doing so, we observe a geographic version of a "born, not made" phenomenon: throughout their lifespans, contributors are relatively consistent in the places and types of places that they edit. We show how these "born, not made" trends may help explain the urban and socioeconomic coverage biases that have been observed in OpenStreetMap. We also discuss how our findings can help point towards solutions to these biases.

Author Keywords

Peer production; coverage biases; OpenStreetMap; geographic human-computer interaction.

ACM CLASSIFICATION KEYWORDS

H.5.3. Group and Organization Interfaces: Computer-supported cooperative work;

INTRODUCTION

Peer production has been very successful as a model of content production [3]. For instance, the peer produced Wikipedia is consistently the fifth most-visited website globally [1] and OpenStreetMap – the "Wikipedia of maps" [8] – provides map data to Craigslist, Apple Maps, and others [43]. Large peer produced datasets even play an essential role as training data for many AI systems (e.g. [11,27]).

Contributor choice is a fundamental characteristic of peer production: contributor choice differentiates peer production from other forms of crowdwork [3] and may even be necessary for the success of the peer production content generation model [3]. Indeed, the ethos of contributor autonomy is so foundational in peer production that, for instance, the introductory documentation of OpenStreetMap, states that "anybody can enter anything she wishes" [29].

Because of the importance of peer produced content and the role of contributor autonomy in producing that content, researchers have long sought to understand and model contributor focus in various peer production contexts (e.g. [6,14,31,33]). One common thread in this research involves studying how contributor focus evolves over the lifespan of a contributor (e.g. [2,31]). In other words, this research examines contributor focus through a *temporal* lens.

While a temporal lens is sufficient to understand contributor evolution in many peer production contexts, in *geographic peer production* – e.g. contributing to OpenStreetMap and editing geotagged Wikipedia articles – a purely temporal lens cannot detect another critical type of potential focus evolution: that which unfolds spatially. For instance, while it is useful to know that an OpenStreetMap contributor is increasing her/his contribution rate, it is also important to understand *where* and in *which types of places* the user is contributing, and *how this changes over time*. Among other applications, such knowledge can provide critical insight into the troubling coverage biases that have been observed in peer produced geographic datasets (e.g. on socioeconomic and urban/rural lines [13,20,37]).

In this research, we extend the literature on temporal focus evolution to geographic peer production with an exploratory analysis that examines contributor focus with a *spatiotemporal* lens. Our work uses OpenStreetMap – the world's largest peer produced geographic dataset – as a case study and centers around two basic research questions adapted from the temporal literature [31]. First, we ask:

(RQ1) How does contributors' geographic focus change over time?

To address this question, we operationalize four geographic contribution metrics and explore if and how they change over time. Overall, our results suggest that contributors are broadly consistent in their geographic editing behavior over the course of their contribution lifespan, although there are some deviations from this trend. Further, the consistency is of a particular nature: people tend to consistently edit in relatively specific geographic areas.

These results recall the findings of one well-known GROUP paper that examined contributor focus with a temporal lens, finding that Wikipedia power editors have different editing behavior than other users from day one of their editing career, i.e. that power editors are "born, not made" [31]. In our study, we observed this "born, not made" dynamic in a very different peer production context: the geographic editing behavior of OpenStreetMap editors (although we observe a somewhat softer version of the dynamic).

Our spatiotemporal approach also advances understanding of mechanisms behind a second (and concerning) trend that has been observed in the literature: geographic biases in peer production. In the face of peer production's immense success – which is predicated on the idea that "anyone can enter anything she wishes" – recent research shows that urban and wealthy areas receive better geographic coverage than rural and less wealthy areas [20,26]. While prior work characterizes these biases, few have studied their root causes. Thus, our second research question asks:

(RQ2) Can the spatiotemporal evolution of contributors' focus help to explain systemic coverage biases?

Our exploratory results suggest that most contributors are "born" urban-focused and wealthier-focused and stay that way. In other words, for most editors, the proportions of edits in rural and poor areas are consistent and consistently low across contribution lifespans. We also find that the few editors who do consistently focus in rural and poorer regions tend to have lower survival rates, exiting OpenStreetMap sooner than their urban- and wealthier-focused counterparts

Our study makes four primary contributions:

- We explore the geographic contribution behavior of OpenStreetMap editors over time and observe that most editors exhibit similar behavior across their entire contribution lifespans. Thus, for many people, we find evidence that *geographic editing behavior is "born, not made".*

- We show how this consistent contribution behavior applies also to the types of regions people edit. In other words, we find some evidence that *geographic biases also are "born, not made".*

- These *focus biases are amplified by a survival bias* – people who focus in rural and high-poverty areas tend to contribute for shorter periods of time.

- While we did observe a *small group of people who focus primarily in rural or high-poverty areas*, they *produce only a small portion of OpenStreetMap content.*

RELATED WORK
Our work here builds primarily on prior work in three areas: (1) peer production contributors' geographic contribution behavior, (2) temporal evolution of contributor behavior, and (3) geographic biases in peer production. Below we situate our work relative to each of these areas.

Contributors' Geographic Patterns
The literature examining contributor geographic patterns falls broadly into two categories: *where* contributors focus and the *geographic ranges* of contributors' work. Our research extends these two categories of prior work by considering the evolution of these types of geographic trends

over time. Below, we describe each category in more detail and put each in the context of our work.

Where Contributors Focus
Several different studies have sought to understand and characterize the geographic focus of contributors to peer production platforms. For instance, Panciera et al. [30] examined geographic trends in the Cyclopath platform, an early bicycling-centered community. In particular, they found that "Cyclopaths" (defined as the top 5% of contributors) had geographically constrained contribution regions, even within the relatively small area in which Cyclopath operated. Zielstra et al. [40] described the geographic extents of 13 OpenStreetMap contributors and show a method of characterizing which contributions are a part of a contributors' 'home location', and which are not. They found that the contribution ranges of these 13 people do not generally exceed approximately 50 square kilometers. Lieberman et al. [25] conducted a similar study, exploring the geographic extent of Wikipedia editors' contributions.

Geographic Ranges of Contribution
Hecht and Gergle [16] compared different 'spatial content production models' for generating volunteered geographic information [9] and found that Flickr contributions tended to be much closer to a contributors' 'home location' than was the case with Wikipedia. Hardy et al. [15] considered geographic contribution as a *spatial interaction* process, using an exponential distance decay model for each language edition. They found that anonymous edits to geotagged Wikipedia articles decay exponentially as the contribution location gets further form a contributor's 'home'. We return to this idea of *spatial interaction* in the Discussion section.

Temporal Evolution of Contributor Behavior
Whereas the work described above focused on geographic behavior, others have focused on the evolution of non-geographic peer production contributor behavior *over time.* In one of the seminal studies in this space, Priedhorsky et al. [33] took a temporal approach to understanding how value is created in Wikipedia and by whom. Panciera et al. [31] built on this paper with a study of 'Wikipedian' lifecycles and found that 'Wikipedians' (the term they use to describe those who contribute most of the Wikipedia content) *begin* contributing at a high level and maintain this trend over time, resulting in distinctive differences in contribution behavior between different classes of users. In other words, "Wikipedians are born, not made" [31]. As noted above, this work strongly informs our study. One of the key takeaways of our work is that this finding, which describes temporal contribution levels in Wikipedia, also applies to spatiotemporal contribution behavior in OpenStreetMap. Panciera's work also inspired the methodologies in this paper: as described below, the spatiotemporal contributor class-specific analyses are a direct analogue to the temporal analyses done in Panciera et al.

Other work uses temporal evolution as a way to characterize the status of a geographic region (versus focusing on contributors and their behavior). One example of such a study is work by Gröchenig et al [12], who computationally estimated the 'completeness' of twelve urban areas, based on identifying three temporal stages ('start', 'growth', and 'saturation'), and modeling the development of a region through these stages.

More recently, others have begun to explore what roles contributors play in peer production communities, and how that changes over time. Arazy et al. [2] described 'career paths' of Wikipedia editors. Rehrl et al. [36] took a similar approach, and considered the different roles that people have in OpenStreetMap. Dittus et al. [6] explored the activation of newcomers and reactivation of previously dormant contributors during disaster events on Humanitarian OpenStreetMap (HOT).

Our study here is deeply informed by the work of Panciera et al. [31], and the studies mentioned in the subsection above. Whereas prior work has focused on understanding geographic behavior *or* the temporal evolution of behavior, our study sits at the intersection. A spatiotemporal lens helps inform our understanding how contributors' geographic behavior evolves, and how this may impact the geographic variations seen in OpenStreetMap.

Geographic Biases in Peer Production

Geographic coverage biases in peer produced datasets have become a subject of relatively substantial research interest in recent years. For instance, Sen et al. [37] found that most content in some parts of the world (e.g. sub-Saharan Africa) is not produced by people from those parts of the world, but instead by Westerners. Other work shows that these biases manifest along two important human geography variables: the urban/rural divide, and socioeconomic status variation. As one example, Johnson et al. [20] found that the quality of Wikipedia and OpenStreetMap content is much greater in urban areas than in rural areas, a result that informs key analyses below. Haklay [13] found a similar result when considering socioeconomic status as well – the quality of OpenStreetMap data is much better in wealthier regions. Informed by these (and other 'geographic HCI' [18,21,26]) studies, we focus one of our research questions on these two specific dimensions (we discuss this in more detail below).

Prior work in this area has quantified and shown the existence of these geographic biases in peer produced datasets, but little work has been done to understand the mechanisms behind these biases. As mentioned above, our work takes a spatiotemporal approach, at the intersection between studies of temporal contributor behavior and those characterizing the geographic behavior of contributors. For this reason, our work is well-situated to shed light on how the temporal evolution of geographic behavior may (or may not) facilitate the geographic biases that others have found.

METHODS

To study the spatiotemporal evolution of contributors in OpenStreetMap, we needed to (1) develop our OpenStreetMap dataset, (2) define geographic variables of interest (i.e. the *'spatio'* in spatiotemporal), and (3) characterize these variables of interest over time (i.e. the *'temporal'*). We first provide a brief introduction to how contributions occur in OpenStreetMap and then discuss each of these three steps.

Introduction to Contribution in OpenStreetMap

Where Wikipedia editors help create articles, OpenStreetMap contributors help create a worldwide map (or, more formally, a worldwide spatial database). OSM contributions either add or annotate geographic entities, e.g. bus stops, roads, buildings or even logical collections of buildings like a university. Nodes (points) are the simplest geometric unit in OSM, and they may stand alone (e.g. a bus stop), or they may comprise other types of geometries, namely 'ways' (e.g. roads or buildings) and 'relations' (e.g. a university). Early in the life of OpenStreetMap, contributions depended heavily on "GPS traces" recorded as contributors moved about the world. However, it is now much more common to trace new entities from satellite imagery using a web-based tool [44].

Similar to Wikipedia, OpenStreetMap records a "version history" for each map entity. For instance, when the node for a bus stop is first created, it will be version 1. If the location is adjusted later, the version will be incremented to 2. If the bus stop is then annotated with the available bus lines, the version would be incremented again.

Dataset

Our dataset focuses on OpenStreetMap nodes (points) and consists of the full, versioned history of OpenStreetMap, through February 2014. Because ways and relations are made up of nodes, nodes define the underlying geometry of contributions. For this reason, we limit our analysis to OSM nodes (we discuss implications for ways and relations later).

We limit our study site to the continental United States so that we can take advantage of readily-available government census data published by the U.S. Census – a common practice in geographic human-computer interaction studies (e.g. [17,18,20,21,26,39]). Because a key contribution of this work is developing an understanding of urban-rural and socioeconomic biases, it was necessary to ensure that there would be "urbanness" and socioeconomic census variables for our study site. We discuss how our work may extend to other geographic contexts in our Discussion section below.

From the broad OSM dataset, we first extracted all nodes in the continental United States, including every version of every node. We then excluded nodes created in an automated manner (e.g. large imported road datasets and bot-created geometries) using the technique in Johnson et al. [20]. Since we were interested in spatiotemporal trends, we excluded nodes created by people with fewer than five contributions out of sparsity concerns that we discuss in more detail below. Finally, we used a standard reverse geocoding approach to associate each node with the United States county that contains it. In total, we considered more than 28 million (28,021,802) contributions by 23,329 contributors.

Because contribution rates are so skewed in peer produced datasets (i.e. power-law dynamics [31,33]) and informed by Panciera et al. [31], we organize our analysis around three classes of contributors, defined by the number of edits they made:

- *1%ers*: The 1% of contributors that produce the most content. In total, "*1%ers*" contribute 68% of all OpenStreetMap nodes.
- *9%ers:* The "middle" 9% of contributors, i.e. those between the *1%ers* and the *90%ers*. "*9%ers*" produce 27% of OpenStreetMap content;
- *90%ers:* The bottom 90% of contributors. They produce only 11% of OpenStreetMap content.

Note that the percentages above refer to statistics once contributors with fewer than five edits have been removed (these contributors made only 0.07% of edits in total).

Geographic Variables of Interest
We operationalize four geographic variables using our historical dataset of human-generated nodes in the United States. These variables were selected because they had one of two properties: (1) they (or close variants) had been employed in non-temporal characterizations of geographic contributor focus, or (2) they are metrics related to observed geographic biases in peer produced geographic data. Our first two variables meet the first property and describe the geometric characteristics of contributors: (1) their geographic ranges [40] and (2) where they focus [25]. Our second two variables meet the second property and capture the (1) urbanness [5,18,20,21,34] and (2) socioeconomic status [5,13,35,39] of where people contribute. Below, we detail each of our four variables in turn.

Geometric Variables
std_dist: *Standard distance* is a common point-pattern analysis metric of geographic dispersion. *std_dist* is analogous to a standard deviation; it represents the geometric spread of a set of points relative to the geometric center of the set. Specifically, a *std_dist* describes the radius of a circle around the mean center point. Like a standard deviation, 68% of the points fall within this circle.

For our analysis, we computed the *std_dist* for each contributor simply by finding the mean center point of their contributions and then computing their dispersion. Prior to making this calculation, we projected all data points into a 2D reference system using the Albers' Equal Area Conic projection.

plurality_focus: While our *std_dist* variable describes the spatial distributions of people's contributions, our *plurality_focus* variable describes the actual locations where people focus. Each contributor's *plurality_focus* county is simply the county in which a plurality of their contributions were made (i.e., the mode). Prior work in geographic HCI

[22] often uses this approach to attribute the "home region" of a contributor, but here we interpret "plurality county" more conservatively: we just take it as the region where a contributor has focused their contributions.

Human Geography Variables
Our next two variables focus on human geography and describe the *kinds of places* people contribute. In other words, while our first two variables describe the locations and geographic spread of contributions, the next two describe characteristics of the people who live in the contribution locations. Specifically, we define variables that describe the biases shown in prior literature: ruralness and poverty. Based on the county associated with each node, we label each contribution with: (1) a county urbanness class (from the National Center for Health Statistics' Urban-Rural Classification Scheme [28]), and (2) the percent of the county's population that is in poverty (from the US Census' American Community Survey [4]).

With these labels in place, we compute two variables for each contributor:

pct_rural: This variable describes the percent of a person's contributions that occurred in counties with urbanness classes 5 and 6 (the two nonmetropolitan classes in the classification scheme mentioned above). In Florida, for example, Miami-Dade County (where the city of Miami is located) is a 1 on this urbanness scale, whereas Monroe and Hamilton Counties (near the border with the state of Georgia, approximately halfway between the cities of Jacksonville and Tallahassee) are urbanness classes 5 and 6.

pct_high_poverty: This variable describes the percent of a person's contributions that occurred in 'high-poverty' counties, where at least 20% of the population is in poverty. We base this variable on the definition of 'high-poverty' provided by the United States Census American Community Survey [4]. For example, Webb County in Texas is a high-poverty county. Webb County is home to Laredo, Texas – one of the largest cities on the United States-Mexico border – and has an average per-capita income of approximately $10,000 (approximately $2,000 below the US poverty line in 2015).

Temporal Units of Analysis
Each of our four variables are a descriptive summary of the *geography* of contributors' focus, but they are not temporal. To understand how these geographic summaries *change*, we temporally group each person's contributions into quarters (Jan. 1 - Mar. 31st, April 1 - June 30, July 1 - Sept. 30, and Oct. 1 - Dec. 31). We selected three-month periods to ensure that (a) there would be sufficient data in each period, and (b) the temporal periods were granular enough to analyze the evolution of contributors' behaviors over time. For each *contributor-quarter*, we computed our four geographic variables. As we noted above, we excluded contributors with fewer than five contributions to avoid drawing conclusions from excessively small samples.

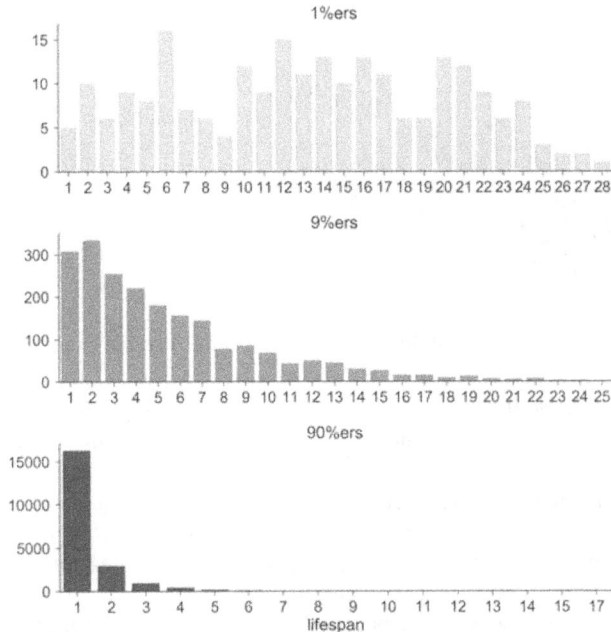

Figure 1: A histogram of contributors who participate for each number of quarters.

Figure 1 shows a histogram of the number of quarters that people participate in OpenStreetMap. Most people (71%) participate in only one quarter. These contributors are (a) predominantly *90%ers*, and (b) account for only about 4% of the total edits in our dataset. *1%ers* participate for a median of thirteen quarters, *9%ers* for a median of five quarters, and *90%ers* for a median of two quarters. We discuss the implications of these medians below.

RESULTS

We use our two main research questions to frame the presentation of our results. As we previewed, we generally find that most people are quite consistent throughout their contribution lifespans – contributors' geographic behavior tends to be 'born, not made'. Since this is exploratory work, we approach both research questions by identifying and characterizing the general trends in the data. We also highlight important deviations from those trends. We now discuss the results for each of our research questions in turn.

RQ1: How does contributors' geographic focus change over time?

The spatiotemporal trends in our *std_dist* and *plurality_focus* variables tell a relatively clear story: most contributors and contribution groups tend to have consistent geographic ranges and focus areas. In other words, most (though not all) contributors' geographic focus behavior is 'born, not made'. We now unpack these findings in more detail.

std_dist: Figure 2, which visualizes contributors' quarterly geographic ranges over time as defined by *std_dist,* shows a relatively clear trend: contributor groups have meaningfully distinct standard distances, and these distinctions are mostly consistent over time. Along the y-axis in Figure 2 – following the method used by Panciera et al. [31] – we plot the mean and 95% confidence interval in each quarter. We

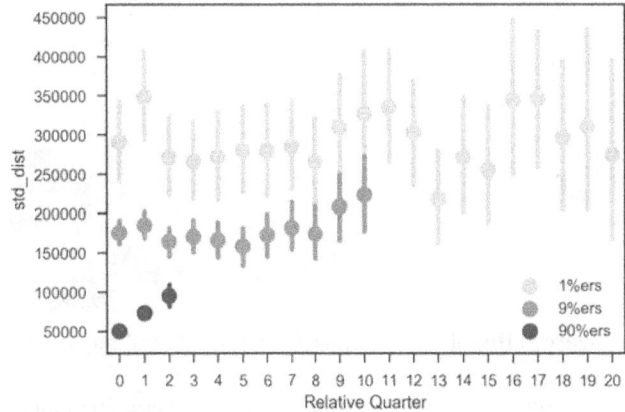

Figure 2: Mean *std_dist* over time, by user class. Error bars show 95% confidence intervals.

find that *1%ers'* and *9%ers'* average standard distances do not meaningfully vary over time. At first glance, Figure 2 may suggest that *1%ers* and *9%ers* increase their average *std_dist* over their lifespan. However, a closer inspection of the quarterly confidence intervals shows that these changes in means are not meaningfully different from one quarter to the next; the confidence intervals are highly overlapping. By contrast, we do see a meaningful uptick in *90%ers* standard distances as their lifespan increases. Note that this figure does not show quarters that exceed the 90th percentile of participation length, because the number of contributors becomes very small.

Although the 95% confidence interval ranges in Figure 2 look small and stable over time, we wanted to ensure that individual contributors do not substantially vary their *std_dist*s over time within their group ranges. The potential for this outcome is most salient for *1%ers* for two primary reasons: (1) *1%ers* contribute most of the content in OpenStreetMap so their geographic behavior has a substantial impact, and (2) in Figure 2, *1%ers* show the largest confidence interval ranges, conceivably allowing for more individual variation.

To address this question, we did a targeted analysis of *1%ers* to evaluate their consistency over time, the results of which are visible in Figure 3. The figure plots each individual *1%ers'* *std_dist* distribution, showing the median and interquartile range (IQR) of their *std_dist* in each quarter. The IQR is the distance between the 25th and 75th percentiles of a distribution, or the width of the middle 50% of *std_dist* values here. Individuals are ranked by IQR in increasing order along the x-axis. Critically, shorter lines (smaller IQRs) indicate a higher degree of 'born, not made' behavior with regard to standard distances

The large number of small grey bars on the left side of Figure 3 confirms that most 1%ers exhibit 'born, not made' *std_dist* patterns, i.e. their geographic ranges are largely consistent in every quarter. Figure 3 also reveals that the higher variance we see in Figure 2 is primarily the result of a minority of 1%ers who do not display 'born, not made' *std_dist* patterns.

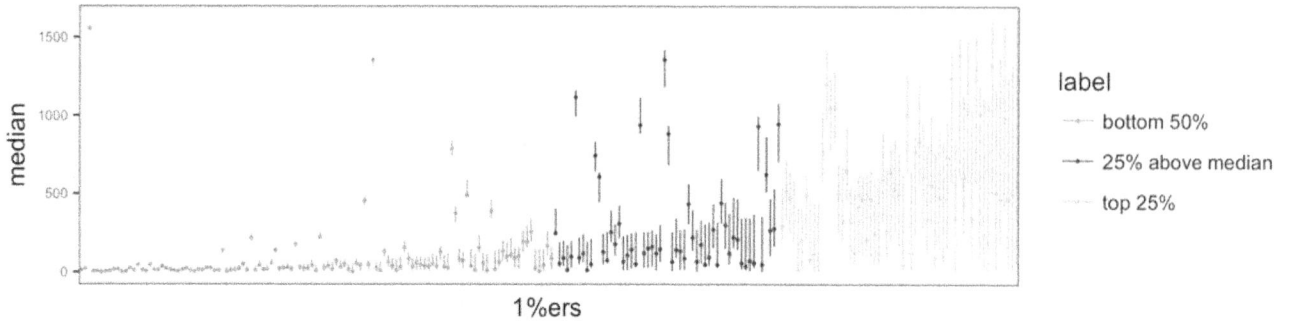

Figure 3: Distributions of each individual 1%ers' *std_dist*. Dots indicate medians, and lines indicate IQR (interquartile range).

This non-trivial minority exhibits different geographic range patterns across quarters.

It is important to note that the IQR values in Figure 3 do not appear to be strongly driven by the number of quarters in which a contributor participates. For instance, a 1%er's *std_dist* IQR and the number of quarters they participate are only weakly correlated (Pearson's r=0.2).

plurality_focus: While *std_dist* characterizes the geographic dispersion of contributor edits, it does not capture *where* contributors focus. For this, we use *plurality_focus*.

Figure 4 plots the median number of unique *plurality_focus* counties over time. Each solid line represents a user class, truncated at the 90th percentile of participation length. The dashed line shows what would occur if the median contributor had a new *plurality_focus* county every quarter.

Figure 4 makes one trend clear: while the median contributor does increase the number of counties in which they focus over time, this increase is gradual and substantially less than

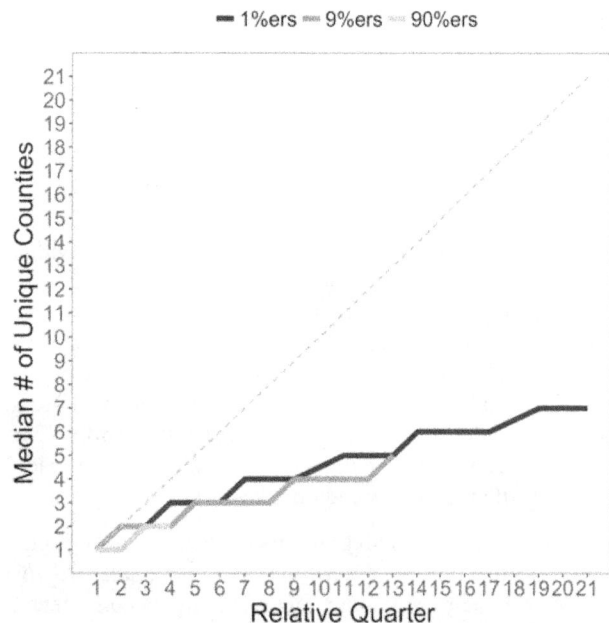

Figure 4: Plots the growth of unique *plurality_focus* counties over time. Each color is a different user class, and the dashed line represents a new *plurality_focus* county every quarter.

would be the case if the median contributor focused in new areas each quarter. Intuitively, the median contributor tends to be fairly consistent in where they focus, returning to the same few counties over time. For instance, the median 90%er participates for two quarters, but has a single *plurality_focus* county on average. The median *9%er* participates for five quarters, and this contributor has only three unique *plurality_focus* counties on average. Strikingly, the median 1%er participates for 13 quarters (more than 3 years), and on average has five unique *plurality_focus* counties.

RQ2: Can the spatiotemporal evolution of contributors' focus facilitate systemic coverage biases?
We now turn to our second research question, which. uses the *pct_rural* and *pct_high_poverty* variables to investigate patterns in geographic behavior concerning *kinds of places* (e.g. poor vs. rich) rather than specific places (i.e. individual counties). We highlight the general trends in these variables as well as impotant deviations from the trends.

Overall Trends
Figure 5 (*pct_rural*) shows the mean rate of contributions in counties classified as 5 or 6 on the National Center for Health Statistics urbanness scale. Figure 6 (*pct_high_poverty*) shows the mean rate of contributions in counties designated as 'high-poverty', according to the US Census. As before, these plots show the 90th percentile number of participation quarters. In both cases, the means of these distributions remain consistent across time for all three user classes, suggesting that most people consistently contribute a relatively small proportion of their edits in rural and poor counties. Even *1%ers*, who have the largest standard distance (and thus contribute across larger distances) make less than one fifth of their contributions in rural areas on average, and even fewer in high-poverty areas (and do so consistently across their lifespans).

As before, while the community-level trends are consistent over time, we also wanted to check whether these trends hold at the idividual level. We again focused on *1%ers,* who have the widest confidence intervals in Figures 5 and 6 and who contribute the most edits. Figures 7 and 8 confirm that the majority of *1%ers* tend to be quite individually consistent, having persistently low individual median *pct_rural* and *pct_high_poverty* values. The median *pct_rural* IQR is 0.11

and the median *pct_high_poverty* IQR is 0.02, both of which are quite small (on a scale from 0 to 1)[1]. Moreover, the small variation is centered on mostly urban and mostly-non-poor regions, as can be seen by the tendency of the grey lines on the left of Figures 7 and 8 to be at the bottom of the y-axis.

The results in Figures 7 and 8 indicate that there is a strong 'born, not made' signal in our *pct_high_poverty* and *pct_rural* variables. In other words, *geographic biases may* be *"born, not made"*. If contributors start by contributing the large mjaority of their content in urban areas, this trend typically will persist for their entire time in OpenStreetMap. Our *pct_high_poverty* variable shows the same result – most contributors (a) do not contribute much content in high-poverty areas, and (b) maintain this trend over time.

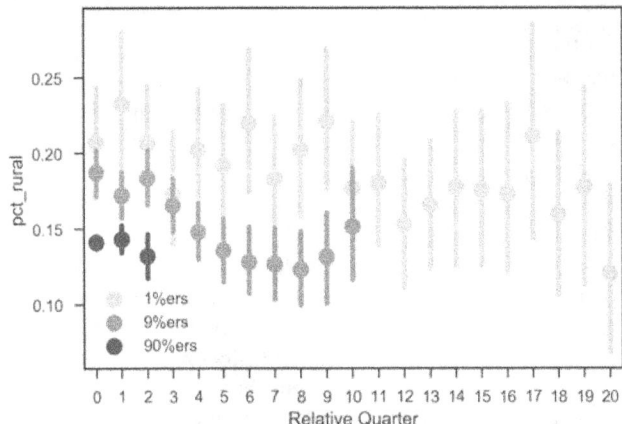

Figure 5: Mean *pct_rural* over time, by user class. Error bars show 95% confidence intervals.

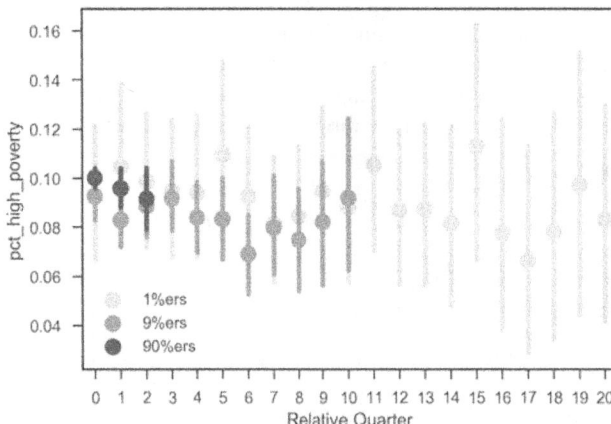

Figure 6: Mean *pct_high_poverty* over time, by user class. Error bars show 95% confidence intervals.

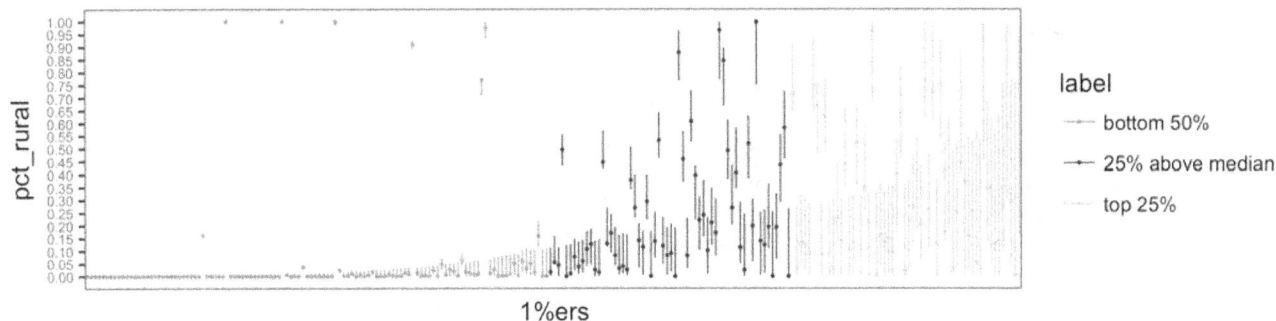

Figure 7: Distributions of each individual 1%ers' *pct_rural* values. The dot indicates the median, and the line indicates their interquartile range.

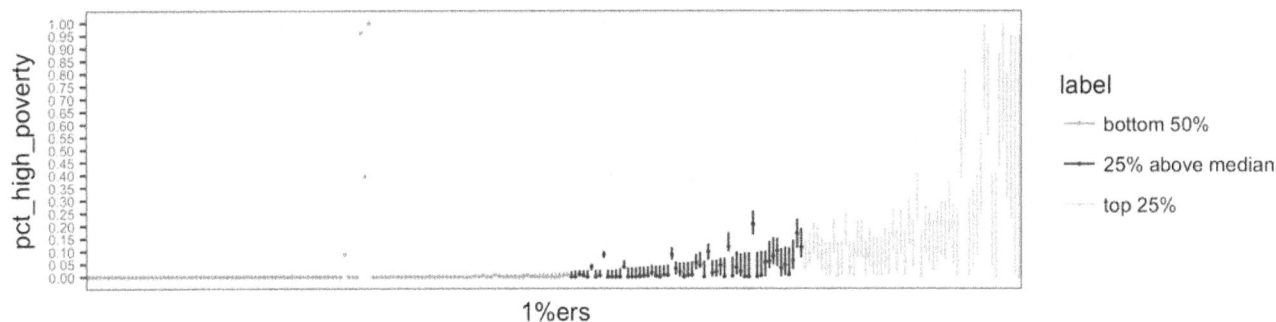

Figure 8: Distributions of each individual 1%ers' *pct_high_poverty* values. The dot indicates the median, and the line indicates their interquartile range.

[1] As was the case above with std_dist, we see very weak correlation between the number of quarters a 1%er spends in OpenStreetMap and their IQR (Pearson's $r = 0.09$ and 0.06 for *pct_rural* and *pct_high_poverty*, respectively).

Contextualizing pct_rural and pct_high_poverty values

To put our *pct_rural* and *pct_high_poverty* results into context, we now consider three dimensions against which to compare these results. Specifically we ask if the *pct_rural* and *pct_high_poverty* findings in Figures 5-8 are proportional to what would be expected given (1) the population of these counties, (2) the number of rural or high-poverty counties themselves, or (3) the number of contributors focusing in rural or high-poverty areas.

With regard to county population, according to the United States Census [28], nearly 15% of the US population lives in rural areas, and approximately 14% live in high-poverty areas. Comparing these numbers against Figures 5 and 6 suggests that the average rate of rural contribution is actually proportional to the population rate in these counties. However, this is not true for our *pct_high_poverty variable*. The average rate of contribution in high-poverty areas is approximately 10%, indicating that high-poverty counties are underrepresented across the board.

Another option to consider is whether these *pct_rural* or *pct_high_poverty* rates are proportional to the number of counties that are rural or high-poverty counties, i.e. maybe there are just fewer of these counties. 63% of counties are rural (have urbanness classes 5 or 6), and 24% of counties are high-poverty (at least 20% of their population is in poverty). Comparing these numbers to the median *pct_rural* or *pct_high_poverty* rates shown in Figures 5 and 6, the conclusion is clear: in terms of the number of counties, OSM contributors in all user classes are undercovering rural and high-poverty counties. While there may be fewer people in many of these counties, these counties still have road networks, natural features like lakes and rivers, and many other entities that are not directly correlated with population [19].and that typically are mapped in OpenStreetMap.

A third consideration is whether the number of contributors focusing in rural or high-poverty counties is proportoinal to the population of these regions. One important reason to consider this dimension is the effect it may have on content quality. Prior work has shown that people who focus near where they live produce more diverse [40], richer [20], and higher quality [7] content. Unfortunately, Figures 7 and 8 suggest concerning trends here too. As noted above, 15% of the US population live in rural areas, and 14% live in high-poverty areas. However, Figures 7 and suggest substantially fewer *1%ers* focus in rural or high-poverty areas – very few have medians near the top of the y-axis.

Thus far, our results suggest that most contributors – across all user classes – are consistent across time, and contribute in consistently urban and wealthier areas. Further still, rural and high-poverty areas are disproportionately undercovered in comparison to (a) the number of rural and high-poverty counties, and (b) the number of contributors who focus in these areas. Taken together, our results suggest that (a) where contributors focus, (b) the kinds of places they focus in, and

(c) the consistency with which this occurs all contribute to the geographic coverage biases shown in prior literature.

Additional Mechanisms of Bias

We noted above that *1%ers* participate for the longest period of time, which creates a secondary mechanism facilitating bias – longevity bias. Specifically, people who participate longer *contribute* longer and because of 'born, not made' trends, *contribute in the same places (and kinds of places) longer.*

While this trend is intuitive when comparing *1%ers* and *90%ers* (after all, *1%ers* produce most of the content), we wanted to understand how a longevity bias might facilitate socioeconomic and urbanness focus biases. Therefore, we split contributors into two groups, those who tend to be rural-focused (have a median *pct_rural* of at least 50%), and those who tend to be urban-focused (have a median *pct_rural* below 50%). We computed how long each contributor participated, and compared the urban-focused and rural-focused groups. Examining the means of these groups (urban-focused: 1.9 quarters, rural-focused: 1.65 quarters) suggests that urban-focused contributors participate longer, on average. Due to a skewed distribution, we conducted a Wilcoxon Rank-Sum Test which found significant differences between the two groups ($z=2.67$, $p < 0.01$). We ran the same analysis for our *pct_high_poverty* contributors. Again, the means (non-high-poverty focused: 1.9 quarters, high-poverty focused: 1.55 quarters) suggest that high-poverty focused contributors participate longer, on average. A Wilcoxon Rank-Sum Test also found significant differences between the two groups ($z=4.81$, $p < 0.001$).

While these findings are not causal – and future work should examine predictors of retention in OSM – they do potentially have implications for the evolution of bias in OSM. Specifically, these results suggest that the bias in where people focus is perpetuated by who remains a contributor. Most people, across all user classes, consistently contribute small amounts of content in rural and high-poverty areas over the course of their time in OSM. People who do focus in rural and high-poverty areas stop contributing earlier than people who focus in more urban, or wealthier areas. This finding potentially has important implications for improving coverage in rural and high-poverty areas, something to which we return in the Discussion section.

Deviations from Trend

Faced with results that suggest that most people consistently contribute in urban and non-high-poverty areas, we sought to better understand contributors who *do* primarily focus in rural and/or high-poverty areas and the contributions that they make. What we found aligns strongly with what is shown in Figures 7 and 8. The majority of rural and high-poverty content is not contributed by consistently rural or consistently high-poverty contributors. Figures 7 and 8 indicate that relatively few *1%ers* have high median *pct_rural* and *pct_high_poverty* values, and that many of those who do also tend to have wider IQRs, indicating that they are less consistent over time in terms of the types of places they edit than the median *1%er*.

To understand these rural and high-poverty focused contributors in more detail, we use the same metric as above: if a contributors' median *pct_rural* and median *pct_high_poverty* are at least 50%, we consider them rural-focused and high-poverty-focused, respectively.

Beginning with rural-focused contributors, we found that 3,126 people tend to contribute in rural areas, and as a group contribute less than 40% of content in rural areas. There are 27 rural-focused *1%ers* (those nearer the top of the Y axis in Figure 7), 315 rural-focused *9%ers*, and the rest (2,748) are *90%ers*. They account for 25%, 11%, and 2% of rural content, respectively (totaling 38% of rural content). Because *1%ers* contribute most of the content in OpenStreetMap, we have mapped the plurality focus counties for the seven most prolific rural-focused *1%ers* in Figure 9. We selected only the seven most prolific to aid in map legibility [41].

There are two primary trends in Figure 9: (1) people who contribute in national parks (and national forests), and (2) people who contribute regionally. With respect to the national parks, (a) prior studies have shown that vacation destinations are common locations for VGI contribution [32], and (b) very few people live in counties with national parks. What this suggests is that some of the participants who we termed rural-focused may instead be 'national park-focused', with national parks serving huge numbers of urban visitors. The second pattern in Figure 9 involves regional contributors. To take one example, consider the person contributing in northern Maine (in the upper northeast corner of Figure 9). This area is very sparsely populated, and yet a single, consistently rural 1%er contributes most their content, over multiple quarters, in those counties. Both groups have implications for recruitment in peer production communities, which we discuss further below.

Turning to high-poverty contributions (Figure 10), the trend we observed for rural areas is even more severe. We found that 2,014 people consistently contribute in high-poverty areas, and as a group contribute slightly more than one-fourth of the content in high-poverty areas. There are 11 high-poverty-focused *1%ers* (those nearer the top of the Y axis in Figure 8), 126 high-poverty-focused *9%ers*, and the rest (1,877) are *90%ers*. They contribute 16%, 8%, and 2% of high-poverty content, respectively (totaling 26% of high-poverty content). We have mapped the plurality focus counties for the seven most prolific high-poverty focused *1%ers* in Figure 10. We again selected only the seven most prolific to aid in map legibility.

The contributors in Figure 10 show similar trends to those in Figure 9: many of the counties shown contain national parks and forests and a few are contributors who contribute regionally. One example of the first trend is the large teal section in the southwestern section of the map (the area surrounding the Grand Canyon). The counties that contain the Grand Canyon also contain the Navajo Indian Reservation, one of the five most impoverished reservations in the United States [42]. This lends further credence to the idea that some contributors focus in natural parks, and it is likely that these contributors *are not* contributing in the very impoverished parts of this region. However, there are some contributors who are consistently focused in high-poverty areas. For example, consider Sierra County, New Mexico (reddish), also in the southwestern corner of the map. The person primarily contributing here *is* focused on high-poverty counties. Residents of Sierra County tend to be quite poor, with a median household income of $25,583, and a per-capita income of $16,667. Another example of a high-poverty area is the more northern county in Texas (pink, central southern section of the map) – Webb County, Texas. Webb County is home to Laredo, the third largest city on the Mexico-United States border. The median household income in Webb County is $28,100, and the per-capita income is $10,179. As before, both examples suggest implications for recruitment that we discuss below.

DISCUSSION

In this section, we step up a level and discuss the implications of our findings more broadly. This section follows the same structure as the results section. Specifically, we first discuss what our findings mean for our understanding of contributor behavior in peer production systems. Second, we discuss

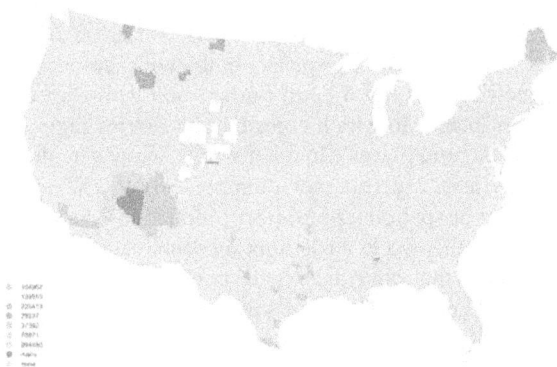

Figure 9: All counties for rural focused 1%ers.

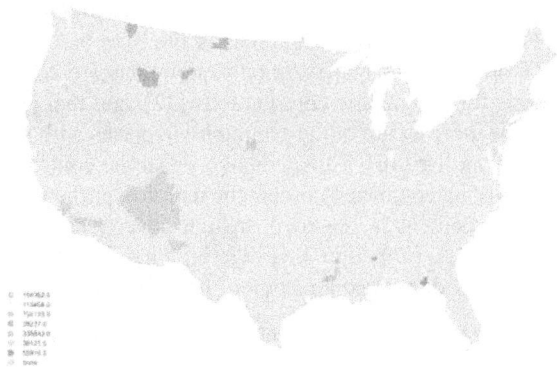

Figure 10: All counties for high poverty focused 1%ers.

what our findings suggest for the mitigation of urban and socioeconomic coverage biases in peer production systems.

Implications for Peer Production

Standard Distance and Spatial Interaction Behavior

Closely related to our *std_dist* variable is a concept from geography called *spatial interaction* [23,24,38], which is used to describe 'flow' between regions, e.g., of physical goods [23,24] or people [38]. This process often is modeled with gravity models and characterizes, e.g., the rate at which travel between regions changes as a function of distance and attributes of the regions. The 'cost of distance' aspect of these models is particularly relevant to our findings here.

We find that different classes of contributors (e.g. *1%ers* vs. *90%ers*) have consistently distinct sizes of geographic range, which presents an important opportunity for future work. Intuitively, these findings suggest that different contributor classes interact consistently differently across distance. Prior "GeoHCI" [17] work using gravity models has not accounted for contributor class, but doing so may provide for better understanding of the mechanisms behind spatial content production. This may also help support predictions about which areas would receive contributions if, for instance, a concerted recruiting effort were made in rural areas (as is discussed in more detail below).

Mitigating Coverage Biases

Our results suggest that 'born, not made' dynamics may naturally facilitate the creation of geographic coverage biases, which are in part enabled by who remains a contributor over time. We next reflect on how our results suggests mechanisms for reducing these biases.

Existing Consistently Rural or High-poverty Contributors

The first intuitive approach to mitigating biases is to examine those participants who *do* consistently focus in rural and high-poverty areas. After all, these participants are contributing a non-trivial amount of content in rural and high-poverty areas already. As noted above, our results suggest that there are two trends in where these rural-focused or high-poverty-focused *1%ers* contribute: national parks and regional areas.

National Parks: Leveraging existing contributors who focus in the counties that contain national parks and forests to address poverty or urban/rural bias is likely to be difficult. Prior work suggests that vacation destinations are common locations for geographic contributions [32], and that people tend to be more aware of the geography in places with which they are familiar [10]. Thus, it is likely that the contributors who focus in counties that contain national parks are not producing content in the rural or high-poverty sections of those counties (although investigating this hypothesis in detail is a good targeted direction of future work).

Regional Focus: The other group of rural- or high-poverty-focused *1%ers*, however, may be more promising. These contributors *already* are focusing their effort in rural or high-poverty areas. We see two implications for design here. The

first is simple: find ways to keep these contributors in the community! Our results suggest that the longevity of these contributors in OpenStreetMap is less than their peers, and targeting this issue would be one immediate and effective partial solution to coverage biases. Second, our results suggest that targeted recruitment of regionally-focused *1%ers* in low-coverage areas could be effective.

LIMITATIONS AND FUTURE WORK

In this work, we took an exploratory approach to understanding contributor behavior. Our results outline important specific hypotheses that should be investigated using more formal quantitative approaches (e.g. targeted hypothesis testing). Future work might also consider deeper qualitative approaches that would help shed light on *why* contributors choose to focus in the areas they do.

We limited this study to the contiguous United States, but examining different study sites would be valuable. For instance, it may be the coverage biases in different parts of the world (e.g. China [20]) are connected to different spatiotemporal focus patterns.

While the atomic unit of our study – the OpenStreetMap node – captures most editing behavior in OpenStreetMap, it does not capture all editing behavior, e.g. edits that added a tag to other OSM geometries (ways or relations). We also focused on human contributor behavior here and excluded automated edits. Future work should directly examine automation behavior in OpenStreetMap, as this may provide useful insight into mitigating coverage biases.

Both our *plurality_focus* and our *std_dist* metrics build a measure of central tendency (mode and mean center, respectively). We rely on *plurality_focus* because it is a common approach for this purpose, and makes no assumptions about the 'normality' of a distribution (analogous to using the mode vs. the mean). Future work should consider similarities and differences between these metrics, and alternative approaches to characterizing where people primarily focus their contributions (e.g. [22]).

CONCLUSION

In this paper, we performed the first examination of the spatiotemporal behavior of contributors to geographic peer production communities. We observed that contributors' spatiotemporal behavior is generally consistent throughout their contribution lifespans, both with respect to the geometric structure of contributions and with respect to the types of places to which contributions are made (e.g. urban places vs. rural places). In other words, we saw evidence that there is a strong (but not omnipresent) 'born, not made' tendency in spatiotemporal peer production behavior. More generally, this work sheds light on some of the mechanisms by which the coverage (and coverage biases) of peer produced geographic datasets may occur.

ACKNOWLEDGEMENTS

This research was supported by NSF grants IIS-1218826, IIS-1707296 and IIS-1707319.

REFERENCES

1. Alexa. 2010. wikipedia.org Traffic Statistics. Retrieved January 13, 2017 from http://www.alexa.com/siteinfo/wikipedia.org
2. Ofer Arazy, Hila Liifshitz-Assaf, Oded Nov, Johannes Daxenberger, Martina Balestra, and Coye Cheshire. 2017. On the "How" and "Why" of Emergent Role Behaviors in Wikipedia. In *Proceedings of the 2017 ACM Conference on Computer Supported Cooperative Work and Social Computing* (CSCW '17), 2039–2051. https://doi.org/10.1145/2998181.2998317
3. Yochai Benkler and others. 2016. Peer production and cooperation. *Handbook on the Economics of the Internet* 91.
4. US Census Bureau. American Community Survey (ACS). Retrieved July 4, 2017 from https://www.census.gov/programs-surveys/acs
5. Ashley Colley, Jacob Thebault-Spieker, Allen Yilun Lin, Donald Degraen, Benjamin Fischman, Jonna Häkkilä, Kate Kuehl, Valentina Nisi, Nuno Jardim Nunes, Nina Wenig, and others. 2017. The Geography of Pokémon GO: Beneficial and Problematic Effects on Places and Movement. In *Proceedings of the SIGCHI Conference on Human Factors in Computing Systems*.
6. Martin Dittus, Giovanni Quattrone, and Licia Capra. 2017. Mass Participation During Emergency Response: Event-centric Crowdsourcing in Humanitarian Mapping. In *Proceedings of the 2017 ACM Conference on Computer Supported Cooperative Work and Social Computing* (CSCW '17), 1290–1303. https://doi.org/10.1145/2998181.2998216
7. Melanie Eckle and João Porto de Albuquerque. 2015. Quality Assessment of Remote Mapping in OpenStreetMap for Disaster Management Purposes. In *ISCRAM*.
8. Killian Fox. 2012. OpenStreetMap: "It's the Wikipedia of maps." *The Guardian*. Retrieved October 25, 2016 from https://www.theguardian.com/theobserver/2012/feb/18/openstreetmap-world-map-radicals
9. Michael F Goodchild. 2007. Citizens as sensors: the world of volunteered geography. *GeoJournal* 69, 4: 211–221. https://doi.org/10.1007/s10708-007-9111-y
10. Peter Gould and Rodney White. 1986. *Mental Maps*. Routledge, London; New York.
11. Mark Graham, Matthew Zook, and Andrew Boulton. 2013. Augmented reality in urban places: contested content and the duplicity of code. *Transactions of the Institute of British Geographers* 38, 3: 464–479. https://doi.org/10.1111/j.1475-5661.2012.00539.x
12. Simon Gröchenig, Richard Brunauer, and Karl Rehrl. 2014. Estimating Completeness of VGI Datasets by Analyzing Community Activity Over Time Periods. 3–18. https://doi.org/10.1007/978-3-319-03611-3_1
13. Mordechai Haklay. 2010. How good is volunteered geographical information? A comparative study of OpenStreetMap and Ordnance Survey datasets. *Environment and Planning B: Planning and Design* 37, 4: 682–703. https://doi.org/10.1068/b35097
14. A Halfaker, Aaron Halfaker, J T Morgan, and J Riedl. 2013. The Rise and Decline of an Open Collaboration System: How Wikipedia's Reaction to Popularity Is Causing Its Decline. *American Behavioral Scientist* 57, 5: 664–688. https://doi.org/10.1177/0002764212469365
15. Darren Hardy, James Frew, and Michael F Goodchild. 2012. Volunteered geographic information production as a spatial process. *International Journal of Geographical Information Science* 26, 7: 1191–1212. https://doi.org/10.1080/13658816.2011.629618
16. Brent Hecht and Darren Gergle. 2010. On the "localness" of user-generated content. 229. https://doi.org/10.1145/1718918.1718962
17. Brent Hecht, Johannes Schöning, Muki Haklay, Licia Capra, Afra J Mashhadi, Loren Terveen, and Mei-Po Kwan. 2013. Geographic human-computer interaction. In *CHI '13 Extended Abstracts on Human Factors in Computing Systems*, 3163. https://doi.org/10.1145/2468356.2479637
18. Brent Hecht and Monica Stephens. 2014. A Tale of Cities: Urban Biases in Volunteered Geographic Information. In *Eighth International AAAI Conference on Weblogs and Social Media*. Retrieved October 20, 2016 from http://www.aaai.org/ocs/index.php/ICWSM/ICWSM14/paper/view/8114
19. Isaac Johnson and Brent Hecht. 2016. Structural Causes of Bias in Crowd-derived Geographic Information: Towards a Holistic Understanding. In *AAAI Spring Symposium on Observational Studies through Social Media and Other Human-Generated Content*.
20. Isaac L. Johnson, Yilun Lin, Toby Jia-Jun Li, Andrew Hall, Aaron Halfaker, Johannes Schöning, and Brent Hecht. 2016. Not at Home on the Range: Peer Production and the Urban/Rural Divide. 13–25. https://doi.org/10.1145/2858036.2858123
21. Isaac L. Johnson, Connor J McMahon, Johannes Schöning, and Brent Hecht. 2017. The Effect of Population and "Structural" Biases on Social Media-based Algorithms -- A Case Study in Geolocation Inference Across the Urban-Rural Spectrum. In *Proceedings of the 35th Annual ACM Conference on Human Factors in Computing Systems (CHI 2017)*. https://doi.org/http://dx.doi.org/10.1145/3025453.3026015
22. Isaac L. Johnson, Subhasree Sengupta, Johannes Schöning, and Brent Hecht. 2016. The Geography and Importance of Localness in Geotagged Social Media. 515–526. https://doi.org/10.1145/2858036.2858122
23. Won W. Koo and David Karemera. 1991. Determinants of World Wheat Trade Flows and Policy Analysis. *Canadian Journal of Agricultural Economics/Revue canadienne d'agroeconomie* 39, 3: 439–455. https://doi.org/10.1111/j.1744-7976.1991.tb03585.x

24. Won W. Koo, David Karemera, and Richard Taylor. 1994. A gravity model analysis of meat trade policies. *Agricultural Economics* 10, 1: 81–88. https://doi.org/10.1016/0169-5150(94)90042-6

25. Michael D Lieberman and Jimmy Lin. 2009. You Are Where You Edit: Locating Wikipedia Contributors through Edit Histories. In *ICWSM*.

26. Linna Li, Michael Goodchild, and Bo Xu. 2013. Spatial, temporal, and socioeconomic patterns in the use of Twitter and Flickr. *Cartography and Geographic Information Science* 40, 2: 61–77. https://doi.org/10.1080/15230406.2013.777139

27. Olena Medelyan, David Milne, Catherine Legg, and Ian H. Witten. 2009. Mining meaning from Wikipedia. *International Journal of Human-Computer Studies* 67, 9: 716–754. https://doi.org/10.1016/j.ijhcs.2009.05.004

28. NCHS. 2010. NCHS Urban-Rural Classification Scheme For Counties. Retrieved January 13, 2017 from https://www.cdc.gov/nchs/data_access/urban_rural.htm

29. OpenStreetMap. Good practice - OpenStreetMap Wiki. Retrieved October 24, 2016 from http://wiki.openstreetmap.org/wiki/Good_practice

30. Katherine Panciera. 2011. User lifecycles in cyclopath. In *the 2011 iConference*, 741–742. https://doi.org/10.1145/1940761.1940892

31. Katherine Panciera, Aaron Halfaker, and Loren Terveen. 2009. Wikipedians are born, not made. In *Proceedings of the ACM 2009 international conference*, 51. https://doi.org/10.1145/1531674.1531682

32. Adrian Popescu and Gregory Grefenstette. 2009. Deducing Trip Related Information from Flickr. In *Proceedings of the 18th International Conference on World Wide Web* (WWW '09), 1183–1184. https://doi.org/10.1145/1526709.1526919

33. Reid Priedhorsky, Jilin Chen, Shyong Tony K Lam, Katherine Panciera, Loren Terveen, and John Riedl. 2007. Creating, destroying, and restoring value in wikipedia. In *the 2007 international ACM conference*, 259. https://doi.org/10.1145/1316624.1316663

34. Giovanni Quattrone, Licia Capra, and Pasquale De Meo. 2015. There's No Such Thing As the Perfect Map: Quantifying Bias in Spatial Crowd-sourcing Datasets. In *Proceedings of the 18th ACM Conference on Computer Supported Cooperative Work & Social Computing* (CSCW '15), 1021–1032. https://doi.org/10.1145/2675133.2675235

35. Giovanni Quattrone, Davide Proserpio, Daniele Quercia, Licia Capra, and Mirco Musolesi. 2016. Who Benefits from the "Sharing" Economy of Airbnb? *arXiv:1602.02238 [physics]*. Retrieved February 25, 2016 from http://arxiv.org/abs/1602.02238

36. Karl Rehrl, Simon Gröechenig, Hartwig Hochmair, Sven Leitinger, Renate Steinmann, and Andreas Wagner. 2013. A Conceptual Model for Analyzing Contribution Patterns in the Context of VGI. In *Progress in Location-Based Services*, Jukka M. Krisp (ed.). Springer Berlin Heidelberg, Berlin, Heidelberg, 373–388. Retrieved July 1, 2017 from http://link.springer.com/10.1007/978-3-642-34203-5_21

37. Shilad W. Sen, Heather Ford, David R. Musicant, Mark Graham, Oliver S.B. Keyes, and Brent Hecht. 2015. Barriers to the Localness of Volunteered Geographic Information. In *Proceedings of the 33rd Annual ACM Conference on Human Factors in Computing Systems* (CHI '15), 197–206. https://doi.org/10.1145/2702123.2702170

38. Chris Smith, Daniele Quercia, and Licia Capra. 2013. Finger on the Pulse: Identifying Deprivation Using Transit Flow Analysis. In *Proceedings of the 2013 Conference on Computer Supported Cooperative Work* (CSCW '13), 683–692. https://doi.org/10.1145/2441776.2441852

39. Jacob Thebault-Spieker, Loren Terveen, and Brent Hecht. 2017. Towards a Geographic Understanding of the Sharing Economy: Systemic Biases in UberX and TaskRabbit. *ACM TOCHI*.

40. Dennis Zielstra, Hartwig H. Hochmair, Pascal Neis, and Francesco Tonini. 2014. Areal Delineation of Home Regions from Contribution and Editing Patterns in OpenStreetMap. *ISPRS International Journal of Geo-Information* 3, 4: 1211–1233. https://doi.org/10.3390/ijgi3041211

41. 2012. Cartographic guidelines for public health. Retrieved October 6, 2017 from https://stacks.cdc.gov/view/cdc/13359

42. 2017. Reservation poverty. *Wikipedia*. Retrieved July 4, 2017 from https://en.wikipedia.org/w/index.php?title=Reservation_poverty&oldid=776694412

43. Apple Maps | OpenStreetMap Blog. Retrieved July 4, 2017 from https://blog.openstreetmap.org/2012/10/02/apple-maps/

44. OpenStreetMap Statistics. Retrieved October 6, 2017 from http://www.openstreetmap.org/stats/data_stats.html

Information Fortification: An Online Citation Behavior

Andrea Forte, Nazanin Andalibi, Tim Gorichanaz,
Meen Chul Kim, Thomas Park
Drexel University
{aforte, na477, gorichanaz, mk3266}@drexel.edu
parkov@gmail.com

Aaron Halfaker
Wikimedia Foundation
ahalfaker@wikimedia.org

ABSTRACT

In this multi-method study, we examine citation activity on English-language Wikipedia to understand how information claims are supported in a non-scientific open collaboration context. We draw on three data sources—edit logs, interview data, and document analysis—to present an integrated interpretation of citation activity and found pervasive themes related to controversy and conflict. Based on this analysis, we present and discuss *information fortification* as a concept that explains online citation activity that arises from both naturally occurring and manufactured forms of controversy. This analysis challenges a workshop position paper from Group 2005 by Forte and Bruckman, which draws on Latour's sociology of science and citation to explain citation in Wikipedia with a focus on credibility seeking. We discuss how information fortification differs from theories of citation that have arisen from bibliometrics scholarship and are based on scientific citation practices.

Author Keywords

Citation, Bibliometics, Open Collaboration, Wikipedia

ACM Classification Keywords

H.5.m. Information interfaces and presentation (e.g., HCI): Miscellaneous

INTRODUCTION

When groups of people work together to create information, they must systematically document its veracity in a way that can be interpreted and assessed by others. In the sciences and humanities, this has traditionally been done via citation systems, using techniques like bibliographies and footnotes. Online, such citation practices have been adapted to the context of open collaboration, blogging, citizen journalism, and other activities where participants are not necessarily trained as scientists or academics.

Understanding online citation behaviors and tools is important first because it can strengthen scholarly citation analysis: Analyses of citation data generated in online contexts should not be uncritically informed by assumptions derived from historic scientific practice, but should incorporate an understanding of contemporary online practice. Second, it is important to understand these online behaviors because citation tools themselves can be designed to better suit the motivations and goals of participants in online projects.

In this paper, we examine the history of citation as a shared information practice and reexamine the act of citation in the context of open collaboration on English-language Wikipedia. We use analysis of citation-related edits on Wikipedia and interviews with Wikipedia editors to deconstruct the act of "citing" on the open web. We demonstrate how the tools and context of online participation create a new kind of citation data that challenge some traditional assumptions.

A BRIEF HISTORY OF CITATION TOOLS AND NORMS

The academic practice of citing written works dates back hundreds of years to the exchange of letters among Renaissance scholars, but much of the contemporary interest in citations is owing to a more recent technological renaissance that enabled citation analysis and visualization at unprecedented scale. The intricacies of citation networks have attracted journals full of primarily quantitative analyses of citation patterns and trends that reveal what topics and authors attract increasing, decreasing, or enduring scientific interest. Yet, the meaning of citation and the motivations of citers is not often examined in connection with the interlinked artifacts they produce. Why scientists cite and how they make sense of their own citations is a less-traveled empirical path.

Historian of science Alex Csiszar tracks the rise of the modern scientific publishing apparatus in 19th century Western Europe [6, 7]. Csiszar's account describes how scientific discourse through the early nineteenth century largely unfurled through ad hoc personal relationships, written letters and meetings that were punctuated by monographs [7]. During the 19th century, the proceedings of academic societies such as Britain's Royal Society came to be published in volumes [6]. As the emerging global scientific community sought political legitimacy, peer review was established in order to improve the public's view of science. Publication and citation became more clearly connected to prestige and stature in the scientific community as evidenced by use of publication count in *Philosophical Transactions* in order to determine fellowship in the Royal Society.

As Csiszar explained: "*these events were prompted by, and helped to consolidate, a monumental shift whereby scientists increasingly perceived the social and intellectual life of science to be lodged in the pages of the specialized scientific literature, and especially in the expansive terrain of the scientific periodical. This shift was qualitative, rather than quantitative, and it concerned the ascendancy of the journal as the primary media type for representing authoritative scientific knowledge*" [7, p. 400].

In the wake of this transformation, and particularly since literature came to be practically equated to knowledge, there grew a need to tame the unwieldy and ever-growing scientific literature. Tools like bibliographic artifacts and lists of references were developed as means of accessing knowledge. Following references became a way that scientists kept abreast of the knowledge in their fields [25].

In the 20th century, citations became a form of data and a kind of scientific enterprise in their own right. Not only did cited scientific material become more easily and broadly accessed, but the use of citations in the 20th century as data for both self-assessment and wayfinding in scientific disciplines helped engender new conceptions of science.

In *The Citation Process*, Blaise Cronin described how science was recast from a "storybook science" in which passions and predilections of the scientist were subordinate to the greater institutional imperatives of procedure and objective truth, to a more pragmatic view of science as a kind of game in which scientists jockey for visibility and recognition [5]. Similarly, Latour and Woolgar observed the role of citations in scientific practice as taking two forms: 1) as a tool that allows scientists to strengthen and defend knowledge claims and 2) as a currency, the accrual of which lends credibility to scientists and their work [17]. In Latour and Woolgar's work as in others, the academe is characterized as a marketplace of credibility, in which the value of having one's work cited is manifest in the award of grants, allocation of space, and other tangible benefits. Latour's description of knowledge construction [18] involves the gradual phasing out of citation as knowledge propositions pass from being regarded as tentative to being regarded as common knowledge in a process they describe as stylization, similar to Merton's notion of obliteration by incorporation (OBI), which was popularized by Garfield [11]. Simply, when a knowledge proposition is tentative, anyone who refers to the claim is required to make liberal use of citations to position and attribute it appropriately; however, if a proposition is accepted as fact, it eventually can be claimed without citation.

Henry Small, an early citation analysis specialist, was among the first to develop a theory of citation. For Small, citations are "concept symbols," not for the document being cited, but for the ideas therein [27]. In Small's framework, citations can be metonymical (having physically shared characteristics, e.g., quotes or the same words), or metaphorical (no obvious shared characteristics, e.g., turning some finding into a more general statement). Small considers metonymical citations to be "more faithful" to the originating idea. In either case, what is essential to citation for Small is a reference to ideas, and thus citations are not merely technical devices for making attributions, but rather they manifest the social process of idea exchange in the development of knowledge.

The functions of citation in facilitating idea exchange were explored by Moravcsik and Murugesan [23] who identified four dimensions of citation function, each representing two categories: 1. Conceptual or Operational, 2. Organic or Perfunctory, 3. Evolutionary or Juxtapositional, and 4. Confirmative or Negational. They further found that 36% of citations in physics papers were redundant, for example by supporting claims already made in other cited papers, and mainly served the purpose of keeping everyone happy and distributing credit over a larger number of people in the "game."

In the intervening decades, the "game" has changed radically—a proliferation of citation databases and rankings expanded the playing field. Proposals emerged for alternative metrics that circumvent some of the constraints and game-ability of traditional citation metrics [24]. Moreover, genres and practices of writing and publication have been altered by tools that support not only writing, and not only citation, but collaborative writing and citing at a massive scale. Among the foremost examples of transformation of publishing and writing practices is the open collaboration project, Wikipedia.

Citation Tools and Practices in Wikipedia

There exists a large literature that explains how, unlike many traditional models of information production that rely on expert gatekeepers and peer review processes, Wikipedia relies on an open, participatory model to maintain its quality [28] and coverage [16]. In this section, we will highlight features of Wikipedia's culture, policies and toolkit that characterize and influence the role of citation.

Wikipedia is built on the collaborative writing platform, MediaWiki. The platform started out with few distinctions from other early wikis like the original wikiwikiweb or usemodwiki but with a few modifications to serve the needs of an encyclopedia writing community. Features like edit logging, recent changes lists, discussion pages, and watchlists were quickly developed to allow the community to write together, come to consensus, and keep a watchful eye on the content to maintain its quality.

Citation tools were notably missing from early Mediawiki development efforts. Over the years, citation became a well-documented and central practice, yet Mediawiki was not designed to support the creation of reference data. Instead of being stored as objects in a database that can be linked with articles, citations are embedded in the text of each revision of each article using markup and are rendered as a bibliography when the article is displayed in a browser (See Figure 1).

As Wikipedia grew in scale and popularity, verification of claims quickly became a critical practice inscribed in policies like Wikipedia:Verifiability [32] and standards for identifying reliable sources [31]. Around 2006, about five years after its creation, the project entered a period of rapid content growth, during which commitments to quality were strengthened and policies (the official rules of Wikipedia) began to "calcify," which lead to formalization and automated enforcement of quality-related policies [12]. Yet the tools to support citation practices remained largely external to the infrastructure that support collaborative writing. Third-party tools like *ProveIt* [20] soon materialized to make citation simpler for editors and, eventually, support for citation was integrated into the Wikipedia visual editor via *RefToolBar* in 2010 and the tool *Citoid [30]*, which is still in beta testing for English Wikipedia as of this writing. Automated tools like *Citation bot* have also been deployed to automatically standardize and structure citations (User:Citation bot).

As the Wikipedia community evolved citation norms and tools to ensure quality, discussion of Wikipedian citation patterns and practices appeared in some research papers. Notably, Sundin used ethnographic methods to capture the conservatism of Wikipedia's citation policies in his description of knowledge stabilization in Swedish language Wikipedia articles [29]. In Sundin's words, Wikipedia authorship is a process of "recycling" knowledge from established publications in a process through which Wikipedia authors become "janitors" of what is known. Conversely, Ford et al. [8] suggested that, despite policies that state a preference for peer-reviewed, established sources, citations that appear in Wikipedia often include links to "alternative" news or primary sources; however, their analysis omitted references that did not include a URL, which may have excluded citations to preferred secondary and tertiary sources such as textbooks. In an earlier quantitative examination of Wikipedia citation edit histories, Chen and Roth described patterns of citation over time, observing that articles did not experience consistent attention to citations, but experienced periods of citation-related activity once they had matured; they also noted that experienced Wikipedians were more likely to add citations than novices [4].

Wikipedia articles and authors differ in terms of goals, tools, and practices from the academic publications and their authors who have informed so much of our understanding of citation practices. If our understanding of

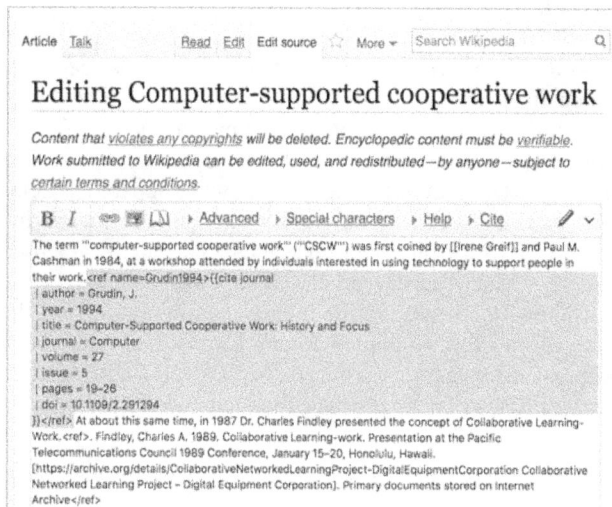

Figure 1: Example of reference syntax (highlighted) when editing a Wikipedia article.

citation is grounded in centuries-old traditions of academic—and specifically scientific—practice, can it be applied to understand the practices of people who contribute to online information sources like Wikipedia? In reviewing literature about traditional scientific citation practice, we saw that citation not only plays the role of justifying claims, but as a way of accruing and conferring credit in the scientific community. Is citation in Wikipedia embedded in a similar system of accountability and prestige? What motivates acts of citation in Wikipedia and how do editors make sense of their own citation practices? What roles do citations play in the online encyclopedia?

STUDY DESIGN AND METHODS

To answer these questions, we use a sociotechnical perspective and mixed methods approach to examine the interplay between tools, norms, and individual motivations as people adapted citation to meet the demands of open collaboration on English-language Wikipedia (All further references to "Wikipedia" are to the English language site unless otherwise noted).

First, we obtained all of the reference-related changes made to the Wikipedia articles through March 2015 using standard wiki markup tags. Using these data, we were able to examine citation-related editing activity over time. Second, we used Wikipedia citation data to identify Wikipedia editors who added citations to the site and recruited 9 Wikipedia editors who were prolific citers to participate in interviews about their practices. Third, we manually inspected revisions of thirty-five random articles to develop an artifact-based understanding of how citations are used in the development of articles. We explain how we obtained each of these data and the kind of analysis we conducted to understand different features of citation.

Reference Revision Data and Quantitative Analysis

To explore reference-related activity on Wikipedia and identify likely interviewees, we parsed all reference-related revisions to English language Wikipedia between 2001 and March 2015 that used the standard <ref> markup tag. From these data, we were able to ascertain which references were edited in a given revision, whether reference-related text was inserted or removed, and what username (or IP address) was associated with the revision. To understand citation activity at the article level, we compared articles that had undergone peer review as part of achieving Featured Article status as well as those that hadn't. Featured Articles, which appear on the Wikipedia main page, are considered to be among the highest quality articles on the site. We randomly sampled 50 articles that had never been nominated for featured article status, as well as 50 that had been chosen as featured articles and examined their citation activity over time.

Interview Data and Thematic Analysis

To understand the meaning and role of citation to the people doing the citing, three of the authors conducted 10 semi-structured interviews with Wikipedia editors using phone or Skype and, in one case, email. Using the reference revision dataset described above, we identified Wikipedia editors who had a record of prolific citation activity. Those whose email addresses were available publicly online or who had enabled email communication on Wikipedia were invited to participate. In all, we attempted to reach sixty-six people, although we do not know how many of these received our messages. The 10 individuals who were interviewed included 8 men and 2 women. All participants had logged thousands of citation-related edits, so it is unsurprising that all were experienced editors. Each recounted approximately ten years of editing experience.

As we conducted interviews, we discussed their content and continued recruitment until we reached data saturation, meaning all the interviewers reported hearing similar themes in each interview. Interview recordings were transcribed with the exception of one interview during which the recording failed and only interviewer notes were retained and one which was conducted via email by participant request. In the interviews, we started off by asking Wikipedians about how they got started editing Wikipedia and how their perceptions and contributions changed over time. Then we prompted them to review a few specific citations they had added in the recent past and asked them to share why they added that citation, as well as details about how they came across the article, and how they chose that particular citation. We also asked them about citation-related tools they use, citation habits outside of Wikipedia, personal and perceived rules about citations on Wikipedia and off, removing citations or having their citations removed, interactions with other Wikipedians and perceptions of others' citation behavior.

These interviews were semi-structured and retrospective, and the resulting data are subject to limitations such as fallible memories and uneven coverage of data points, depending on the idiosyncratic experiences of the interviewees.

Article Data and Document Analysis

We collected a sample of thirty-five Wikipedia articles and used an inductive approach based on holistic reading analysis techniques [21] to understand reference editing activity as a feature of the article. To collect this sample, we used the *random article* feature of Wikipedia. If *random article* returned an article without references, we discarded that article until thirty-five articles with references had been identified. Unsurprisingly, since only about 6,000 out of over 5.5 million English language articles have been featured articles (approximately 0.1%), none of the 35 randomly selected articles had been nominated for featured article status. The articles age averaged 7 years at the time of the analysis (max: 13; min: 2).

We reviewed the edit history of each of these articles with attention to reference-related changes as well as talk page content. The goal was to develop a holistic understanding of how Wikipedia articles evolve, inspired by Joseph Campbell's notion of the *monomyth*—a kind of general template that describes commonalities among myths [14]. Campbell explored the myths and folklore of diverse cultures and discerned recurring typical themes in human mythology. In this spirit, we sought to construct a narrative that characterizes the evolution of typical Wikipedia articles with respect to citation activity. Van Manen advocates a similar sort of anecdote construction for the conveying and understanding of possible, plausible experiences in phenomenology of practice [21].

Integrated Analysis

These methods seek to integrate social-scientific and humanistic approaches. There is some precedent for this in HCI research. For example, Blythe and Cairns conducted a qualitative social-science analysis (grounded theory) alongside a critical-hermeneutic analysis of the same dataset [3]. The grounded theory approach gave them a sense of what was going on macroscopically, and the hermeneutic approach allowed them to dig deeper into an apparent anomaly. The concept of defamiliarization is also an important humanistic feature of our work [2]. Defamiliarization is a matter of becoming naive toward a familiar phenomenon in attempt to uncover aspects of it that have been taken for granted. In our case, the authors sought to rediscover citation (an activity we practice ourselves regularly) in a new context with different goals and meanings.

As Bardzell and Bardzell argue, adopting social scientific and humanistic approaches in concert can further inquiry into aspects of life "*that are so hard to pin down adequately with any single method or mentality*" [1] (p. 57). In our work, we took a critical-thinking approach to integrating the findings from our various data, keeping in mind the epistemological commitments of each, in order to accomplish theoretical work.

In our findings and discussion sections, we use the term *sourcing* to refer to the act of substantiating a statement with a source, a *reference* to refer to the text that refers to the source, *referencing* to refer to the technical act of inserting the reference, and *citation* to refer to the activity as a whole. In revision history data, we have access to *references* and *referencing* acts. In document analysis we have access to both *references* and, to a limited extent, *sourcing* as we examine the citation activity in context. In interviews, we receive explanations of both *sourcing* and *referencing* activity.

FINDINGS

The data and analyses described above revealed different aspects of citation activity; in this section, we draw on all three data sources to present an integrated interpretation of citation on Wikipedia that is reinforced by each of our analyses. Each data type yielded different insights related to themes of controversy and conflict.

Contrary to Forte and Bruckman's insights in [10], citing in Wikipedia seems to bear only a tenuous connection to the marketplace of credibility described by Latour and Woolgar [17]. In fact, citation behavior on Wikipedia appears to be much more closely related to Latour and Woolgar's militaristic descriptions of citation.

In interviews and document analysis, we observed that citation activity is frequently an outgrowth of conflict, either due to *naturally arising controversy* that yield article improvement activity or as a result of review processes, which we cast here as a form of *manufactured controversy,* designed to generate debate and scrutiny to yield improvements. In the findings sections, we describe how natural and manufactured controversy give rise to citation activity in Wikipedia. In the discussion section, we use these findings to generate the concept of information fortification.

Natural Controversy

Our interviews and document analysis demonstrated how citation activity was often a result of shared norms and observation of policy, but this activity increased in the presence of real or perceived controversy that arose spontaneously as article co-editors worked and interacted.

In interviews with editors whose contributions to Wikipedia includes a large number of reference-related edits, we most often heard general explanations of citation activity that implicitly or explicitly invoked Wikipedia policy. Citation-related policies were summarized by one participant as encapsulating a defensive editing mindset: "*The basic idea is that everything that is disputable is most likely to be challenged and has to have a reference with a reliable source*" (P2). The same participant also explained that on Wikipedia, statements that might constitute common knowledge when writing in a "normal way" still require a verifiable source on Wikipedia:

> ...on Wikipedia you have to—if you take for example, a football player who was born in Leimen, usually on Wikipedia, you have to source this. But if everyone knows because the guy is very popular,

then you would not put any reference on this in, let's say, work or normal way, because it's widely known that he was born there and so, this is not something that is disputed (P2).

Another participant also explained that anything might be considered contentious:

> The rules strictly say that you only need to cite something if it's contentious, if someone is likely to bother you about it or disagree with it. But the reality is that you have to cite everything, because someone will decide that it's contentious... And it gets very weary, because I mean, many things, you'll know yourself, you don't need to cite them, they're just--people know they're true (P4).

When asked to describe the rationale for adding specific references, participants sometimes described local conditions such as whether a statement was likely to be challenged or removed. When asked to explain why they had added references in recent edits, one participant noted that it was "*because somebody had challenged what I'd put in, so I went back and added the citations as needed*" (P7). In another case, a participant explained that they had noticed a quotation (which had been added by another editor) had been removed from an article (by a second editor) because it was unsourced, so the participant (the third editor in this case) restored the content and inserted a reference to an appropriate source in order to protect the passage from deletion:

> Somebody—an history editor—deleted a quotation because it did not have a citation. So, I looked through and found the citation and found a better citation for his previous quote, so I changed two of his footnotes. I restored one. And I do the search, in this case, through Google Scholar. Google Scholar picks up the quotations real easy (P6).

Google Scholar came up repeatedly as an easy way to locate appropriate sources to support encyclopedic claims.

Our manual inspection of the reference-related edit histories of 35 articles revealed that historically many pages were created with no references. In fact, none of the 13 articles that were created before 2007 included references at the time they were created. The 13 articles created from 2007 to 2009 sometimes included references at inception. The remaining 9 articles created in 2010 and later all included references from the beginning. In the case of articles that were created without references, reference sections were often later created by a bot, and eventually populated by a human who, based on the interviews described above, did not want their edits or other content removed. Over the life of early articles, we noted that references were often inserted to support later-added material, but much of the original article content can remain unsubstantiated unless it is challenged.

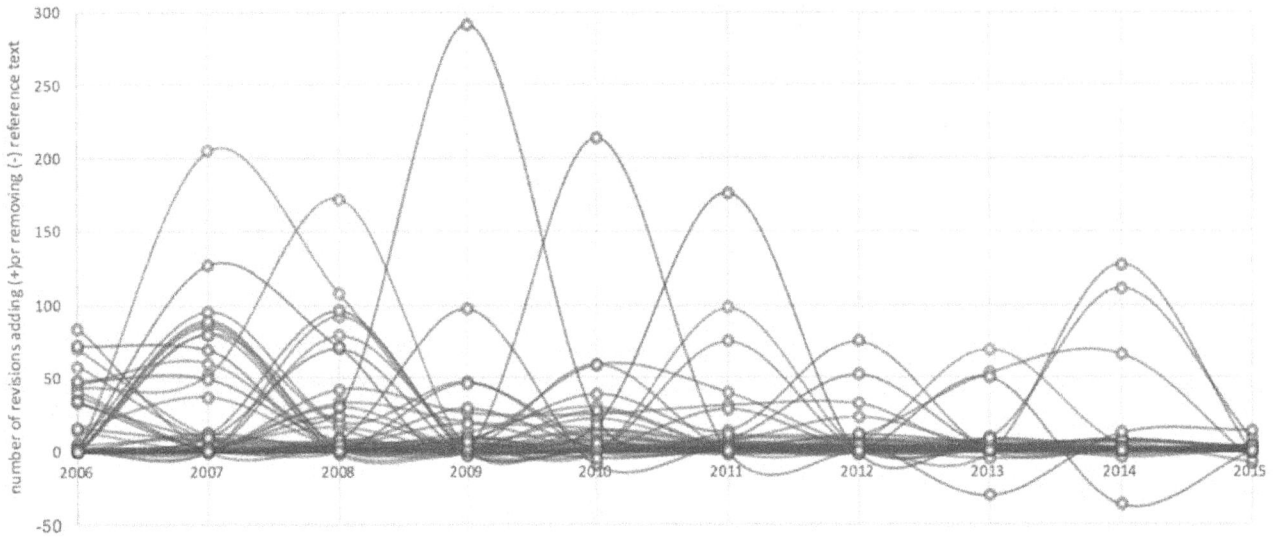

Figure 2: Revisions in which reference text was added to or removed from 50 FEATURED ARTICLES by year

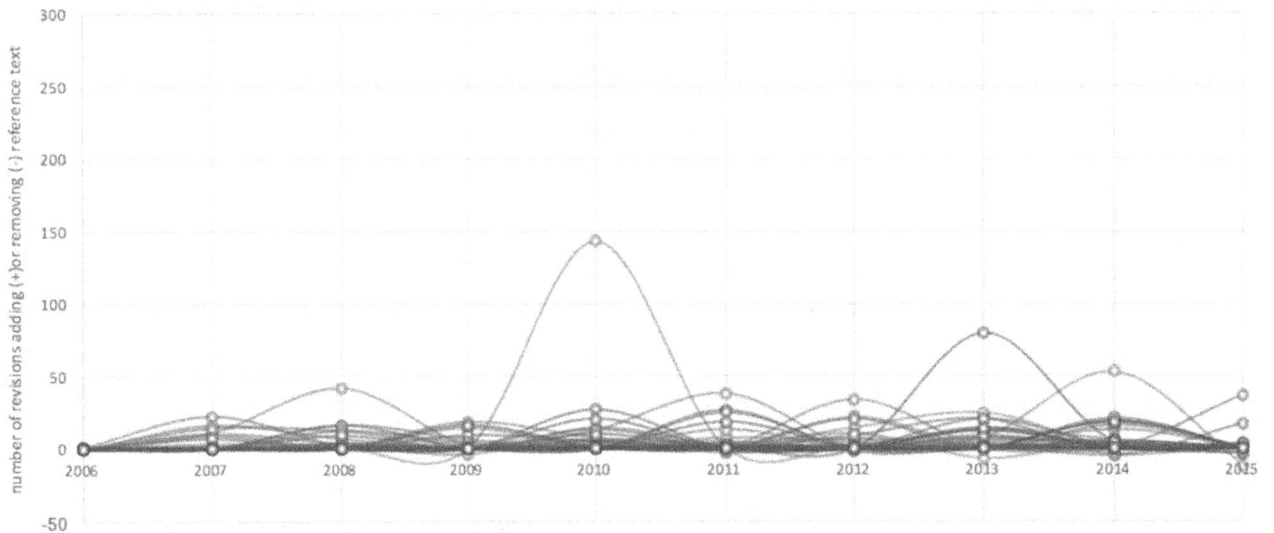

Figure 3: Revisions in which reference text was added to or removed from 50 NON-FEATURED ARTICLES by year

By examining revision data, we observed that reference-related editing activity on individual articles ebbed and flowed over years with distinct peaks and valleys (See Figures 2 and 3). As expected, non-featured articles exhibited lower peaks than featured articles. We also observed that real-world events sparked the reference activity peaks in non-featured articles, for example, the two highest peaks in non-featured article reference activity were when a volcano erupted and an actor won an award. This is consistent with observations that breaking news events precipitate fast-paced editing and dense co-author networks [15] in which well-sourced claims would be critical to the survival of text.

Manufactured controversy

Controversy doesn't always arise naturally either because of one editor challenging another or because material is deemed likely to be challenged, sometimes formal processes are initiated to ritualize the process of challenging content. These rituals are commonly referred to (both inside Wikipedia and in academic contexts) as "peer review." In Wikipedia, there are two primary forms of invoking a review of claims, one is decentralized through the insertion of a {{citation needed}} template and the other is by engaging a more centralized review process, the most rigorous of which is the nomination for Featured Article (FA) status.

Decentralized

By inserting the text {{citation needed}} into an article, editors can tag an unsupported claim and challenge the community to find a reliable source for it. In the ideal case, this attracts the attention of other editors or readers and triggers citation activity to help verify the claim. Precisely this kind of activity is described by one interviewee who recounted one occasion on which they found and added references to deter the removal of content from an article:

> someone… put a lot of 'citation needed' text on this article or removed stuff which was not referenced. And then I thought, 'okay, it's a shame that all this stuff has to be removed because it's not referenced,' and then I did some work and Googled for some references and added them (P2).

Another editor explained that if you don't know what to cite but, *"you've got a good interesting segment, you should put in a 'citation needed' flag"* (P6). Yet another interviewee's behaviors suggest that this is not always effective because, although they enjoy citation-related editing, they do not go out of their way to address claims tagged with {{citation needed}}:

> I find bad citations, or dead links, or that sort of thing all the time, but unless I feel like I can correct it pretty easily, I generally just leave that. I'd leave all the ones that say "citation needed." They pretty much just sit there for me (P5).

The same participant went on to explain that:

> There seems to be an awful lot of calls for citations—citation needed—and I don't know what happens with people… it seems like people create the article and then go away. It's like somehow when somebody else goes through it and calls for a citation or marks as a citation needed that the [original] author never comes back (P5).

Aside from randomly encountering content marked with {{citation needed}}, Wikipedia editors may use a tool called a "watchlist"[1] to keep an eye on the content they have created or have a special interest in. The excerpts above suggest that these techniques may be too haphazard or underutilized to yield desired citation activity. New tools may be needed help facilitate decentralized content review.

Centralized

Peer review is a process for subjecting content to scrutiny and inviting critique. In Wikipedia, peer review happens most centrally as an encyclopedia-wide process that culminates in Featured Article status. It also happens nested within topic-specific and thematic "wikiprojects" that maintain their own standards and review processes. On Wikipedia, much of the peer review process involves verifying whether an article is sufficiently well sourced, and standards have been refined over time:

> I could remember my first few featured articles, I had to return to a few years later and bring them up to scratch with extra citations because a lot of the stuff was un-cited, or not specifically cited. We had a different view then, this was 2007. But round

about the time, as in 2007, 2008, the idea of inline citations as a necessity became, well, it was a big issue. And it became general. And I've always followed that since. I've always been careful to cite everything. (P3).

In fact, during the featured article process, editors also commonly use {{citation needed}} tags to organize article improvement efforts. Featured Articles are considered to be the highest quality articles, but other levels of review also exist, including Good Article, A-class, B-class, and others. Initiation of a review process serves as an invitation to the community to examine an article critically and apply relevant standards. One interviewee explained how review processes helped them organize their hobby of reference cleaning and correction:

> I have a bit of a peculiar hobby of liking to look at articles, maybe that are going through a good article review, and if the references aren't perfectly formatted, I like to fix them (P1).

These kinds of helpful copyedits are distinct from sourcing activity, in that they only serve to improve the reference text itself. They account for some of the reference-related editing activity we see in graphs of Featured article reference-related revisions (see Figure 2). We did not categorize revisions to differentiate them qualitatively.

In the 100 revision histories we examined, featured article process shows up as a clear antecedent to reference-related editing activity. In figure two, the peaks and valleys associated with reference-related editing in featured articles is more pronounced than in non-featured articles. Most often, peaks directly preceded the featured article process, although in some cases peaks preceded featured article status by years. In the most extreme case, the article on Hillsboro, Oregon, peaked at 95 reference-related revisions in 2007 but was not nominated for featured status until 2009 and was not featured until seven years after the peak in 2014. In this case, other centralized quality improvement processes were responsible for the peak, namely efforts to prepare the article for "good article" status in 2007. In only one case, peak citation activity occurred after FA status: The Simpsons was featured in 2007, but in 2009 the show became the longest-running television show and the format changes and in that year citation-related revisions to the article reached a peak.

Quality and Quantity

A few themes recurred that were not related to conflict but are important because they explain important features of citation activity and can help with interpretation of revision data. All of our participants discussed the quality of sources in terms of publisher or source type (blog, news article, journal article, etc.) and mentioned the quality of the reference itself in terms of formatting, completeness, and/or consistency with other references in an article. The value of a complete and well formatted reference is important to note when interpreting data about the number of reference-

---

[1] https://en.wikipedia.org/wiki/Help:Watchlist

related edits since they may include many revisions that do not add a new source although they add new reference text.

More than once, participants mentioned the desirability of economizing references. One participant described someone with whom they stopped co-editing because: "*she used to add references to statements that were already referenced and the references she added weren't necessary at all. I said 'Hey, these references aren't very necessary' and she wasn't very happy about that at all*" (P8). Participant 3 offered a similar opinion:

> I'm dead against that, when people offer a fairly simple fact, and because that fact is in eight different books, they feel they've got to cite it to the eight different books, and I tell people not to do that. I say, 'No, one citation is enough, or two if you really want.' (P3).

A preference for few but high-quality references may also yield reference-related deletion of text.

DISCUSSION

Our findings characterize much of the citation activity in Wikipedia as an effort to protect encyclopedic content in response to real and perceived conflict. When we embarked on this project, we were familiar with citation as a knowledge construction activity. Our assumptions about the rhetorical and functional value of citation in the sciences quickly gave way as we perceived Wikipedians' tendency to describe citation as a defensive act. We use the term *information fortification* to describe citation activity designed to preserve the visible and online status of information claims in Wikipedia and which may occur online more generally in blogs, discussion threads, and elsewhere. Information fortification differs in several important dimensions from well-known theories of citation.

Information Fortification and Other Theories of Citation

Although theories of citation activity in the sciences account for some motivations similar to information fortification, the functions and meanings of citation in science typically include a layer of political and social relationships among the citers and cited that is absent in information fortification. Recall that Latour and Woolgar included two roles for citation: 1) as a tool that allows scientists to strengthen and defend knowledge claims and 2) as a currency, the accrual of which lends credibility to scientists and their work [17]. Although the first role is largely similar to information fortification, the "marketplace of credibility" that sustains practices like redundant citation (the 36% of physics citations sampled by Moravcsik and Murugesan [23]) does not appear to be present in the context of open collaboration. Or at least not among editors who cite prolifically. Participants noted that they discouraged others from citing redundantly and even removed such references. No participant mentioned the need to add citations to an article for reasons like signaling membership in a theoretical camp, to appease likely reviewers, or to prove their own expertise.

Another point where information fortification departs from commonly described citation practices in the sciences is in which statements need to be sourced. Widely known Latourian and Mertonian accounts of citation in the sciences incorporate concepts of erosion [18] or obliteration by incorporation [11]. Both of these ideas suggest that the construction of fact entails a diminishing need to provide a citation for a claim. For example, a new idea in a scientific field requires citation to substantiate the claim, but a well-accepted "fact" no longer requires citation. Information fortification obligates citation for claims regardless of how well accepted they might be, in part because the potential grounds for controversy is not bounded by a particular field of expertise. Part of what distinguishes Wikipedia as an open collaboration project is its low barrier to entry and exit—anyone who wants to contribute to the project is welcome to edit regardless of their past experience or training. This creates a review context distinct from scientific fields where "peers" are generally scientists who share at least some general disciplinary training if not deep expertise in the topic at hand. Writing an article about cell biology sourced to satisfy the information needs of all internet users is an entirely different matter than writing one to satisfy the needs of a biologist. Our interviewees described writing in a context where anyone might challenge anything at any time.

We note that an additional reason for citation that did not surface explicitly in interviews, is the need to support the information needs of readers not only as potential reviewers but also as encyclopedia users who come there to learn. In order to learn about a topic or to find information sources about a topic, people use the site to get started or as a pointer to other information sources [9, 13]. For this reason, the quality of information sources used on the site is important not only to substantiate claims in the article, but also as sources of further reading and consultation.

The Effectiveness of Stigmergic Citation

Stigmergy describes a form of indirect coordination in which one actor leaves a trace of activity in the environment that is interpreted by and prompts the activity of the next actor. We heard from interviewees that the addition of a {{citation needed}} template was used to support distributed, stigmergic verification of information claims in the encyclopedia. This tool was used both in a distributed way by editors as they wrote articles, and as a part of organized review processes.

Centralized processes like featured article review by definition produce high-quality, well-sourced articles, but the effectiveness of decentralized, stigmergic citation efforts is less clear. How appeals for citation using {{citation needed}} get resolved or not remains unexamined. When Wikipedians (or bots) assess the quality of articles, C-class and above are expected to have at least some references; however, fewer than 8% of English Wikipedia's 5.5 million articles have been rated at C-class or above [33]. That means the vast majority of articles have not undergone a centralized review process.

Recently, the tool CitationHunt[2] was deployed to encourage the addition of references to resolve instances of {{citation needed}} and reduce the number of unsupported claims. CitationHunt prompts users with an unsourced statement in Wikipedia and offers a link to edit the article where the statement appears to add a reference and remove the citation needed template. When Wikipedia editors described sourcing statements that had been originally written by others, they often described using a web search—often Google or Google Scholar—to quickly find a source that supported the claim in need of verification. This is an example of the kind of new tool we speculated may be helpful in guiding editors to pages where {{citation needed}} is used.

The question remains whether CitationHunt or the use of the {{citation needed}} template in general yields references to sources of comparable quality as those added by authors of articles who include references as they compose an article. In light of filter bubbles and the vast number of resources available to information, these practices raise the question of whether information statements written first and sourced later are more subject to confirmation bias. The question of neutrality has long been discussed in Wikipedia, where a foundational policy is NPOV (neutral point-of-view), which requires Wikipedia articles to report multiple interpretations or controversy about a concept without supporting a particular perspective. Many scholars have raised the question of whether neutrality is possible, not just in Wikipedia [22, 26], but in the production of knowledge at all [19]. The question becomes newly relevant in the context of sourcing information claims. Can citation be a neutral activity? According to Latour and Woolgar, the construction of scientific fact is a process that depends on persuasive acts of literary inscription [17]. Citation in Wikipedia may be mobilized by different interests than in the sciences, but do the biases of the cited sources remain? If Wikipedia's sources express implicit biases, can these biases be neutralized through a collaborative process of consensus building and meta-analysis that aspires to neutral representation of facts? The questions raised by this work will inform our future studies of citation activity online.

SUMMARY

Information fortification is a form of citation activity distinct from the scientific practice in which citation practices originally emerged. The fortification mindset reflects the precarious status of information statements that are asserted on Wikipedia. Social functions of citation like signaling theoretical positioning or credibility exchange were absent. Unlike scientists, Wikipedia editors do not themselves take responsibility for creating new knowledge about the world, instead they do the work of assembling information. In this context, references to sources defend information that has been integrated and curated from others who would challenge or undo that work of information assembly. The expansive grounds on which statements might be challenged in Wikipedia is a characteristic of the online open collaboration context.

ACKNOWLEDGEMENTS
This work was supported by a National Science Foundation grant (#1253302).

REFERENCES

1. Jeffrey Bardzell and Shaowen Bardzell. 2015. Humanistic Hci. *Synthesis Lectures on Human-Centered Informatics*, 8, 4, 1-185.

2. Genevieve Bell, Mark Blythe and Phoebe Sengers. 2005. Making by making strange: Defamiliarization and the design of domestic technologies. *ACM Transactions on Computer-Human Interaction (TOCHI)*, 12, 2 (2005), 149-173.

3. Mark Blythe and Paul Cairns. Year. Critical methods and user generated content: the iPhone on YouTube. In *Proceedings of the SIGCHI Conference on Human Factors in Computing Systems*.

4. Chih-Chun Chen and Camille Roth. 2012. {{Citation needed}}: the dynamics of referencing in Wikipedia. In *Proceedings of Proceedings of the Eighth Annual International Symposium on Wikis and Open Collaboration* (Linz, Austria).

5. Blaise Cronin. 1984. *The citation process. The role and significance of citations in scientific communication.*

6. Alex Csiszar. 2015. *Objectivities in Print*. Springer, City.

7. Alex Csiszar. 2010. Seriality and the search for order: Scientific print and its problems during the late nineteenth century. *History of science*, 48,399-434.

8. Heather Ford, Shilad Sen, David R Musicant and Nathaniel Miller. Year. Getting to the source: where does Wikipedia get its information from? In *Proceedings of Proceedings of the 9th international symposium on open collaboration*.

9. Andrea Forte and Amy Bruckman. 2009. Citing, writing and participatory media: wikis as learning environments in the high school classroom. *International Journal of Learning and Media*, 1, 4 (2009), 23-44.

10. Andrea Forte and Amy Bruckman. 2005. Why do people write for Wikipedia? Incentives to contribute to open–content publishing. Workshop Position Paper, ACM Conference on Groupwork (GROUP 2005).

11. Eugene Garfield. 1975. The Obliteration Phenomenon. *Current Contents*, 51-52 (1975).

12. Aaron Halfaker, R Stuart Geiger, Jonathan T Morgan and John Riedl. 2013. The rise and decline of an open collaboration system: How Wikipedia's reaction to popularity is causing its decline. *American Behavioral Scientist*, 57, 5, 664-688.

---

[2] https://tools.wmflabs.org/citationhunt/

13. Alison J. Head and Michael B. Eisenberg. 2010. How today's college students use Wikipedia for course-related research. *First Monday.*

14. Campbell Joseph. 1949. *The hero with a thousand faces.* Princeton, NJ: Princeton University.

15. Brian Keegan, Darren Gergle and Noshir Contractor. 2013. Hot off the wiki: Structures and dynamics of Wikipedia's coverage of breaking news events. *American Behavioral Scientist*, 57, 5, 595-622.

16. Aniket Kittur, Ed H. Chi and Bongwon Suh. 2009. What's in Wikipedia?: mapping topics and conflict using socially annotated category structure. In *Proceedings of Proceedings of the SIGCHI Conference on Human Factors in Computing Systems* (Boston, MA, USA, 2009). ACM.

17. B. Latour and S. Woolgar. 1986. *Laboratory Life: the Construction of Scientific Facts.* Princeton University Press.

18. Bruno Latour. 1988. *Science in Action: How to Follow Scientists and Engineers through Society.* Harvard University Press.

19. Richard Lewontin. 1996. *Biology as ideology: The doctrine of DNA.* House of Anansi.

20. Kurt Luther, Matthew Flaschen, Andrea Forte, Christopher Jordan and Amy Bruckman. Year. ProveIt: A New Tool for Supporting Citation in MediaWiki. In *Proceedings of ACM Symposium on Wikis and Open Collaboration* (WikiSym '09).

21. Max van Manen. 2014. *Phenomenology of Practice.* Left Coast Press, Walnut Creek, CA.

22. Paolo Massa and Federico Scrinzi. 2012. Manypedia: comparing language points of view of Wikipedia communities. In *Proceedings of Proceedings of the Eighth Annual International Symposium on Wikis and Open Collaboration* (Linz, Austria, 2012).

23. Michael Moravcsik and Poovanalingam Murugesan. 1979. Citation patterns in scientific revolutions. *Scientometrics*, 1, 2 (1979), 161-169.

24. Jason Priem, Dario Taraborelli, Paul Groth and Cameron Neylon. 2010. Altmetrics: A manifesto (2010).

25. W Boyd Rayward. 1997. The origins of information science and the International Institute of Bibliography/International Federation for Information and Documentation (FID). *JASIS*, 48, 4, 289-300.

26. Joseph Reagle. 2005. Is the Wikipedia Neutral?.

27. Henry G Small. 1978. Cited documents as concept symbols. *Social studies of science*, 8, 3 (1978), 327-340.

28. Besiki Stvilia, Michael B Twidale, Linda C Smith and Les Gasser. 2008. Information quality work organization in Wikipedia. *Journal of the Association for Information Science and Technology*, 59, 6, 983-1001.

29. Olof Sundin. 2011. Janitors of knowledge: constructing knowledge in the everyday life of Wikipedia editors. *Journal of Documentation*, 67, 5, 840-862.

30. Wikipedia. Citoid. https://www.mediawiki.org/wiki/Citoid. Accessed: June 30, 2017.

31. Wikipedia. Identifying Reliable Sources. https://en.wikipedia.org/wiki/Wikipedia:Identifying_reliable_sources. Accessed: 6-30-17.

32. Wikipedia. Wikipedia: Verifiability. http://en.wikipedia.org/wiki/Wikipedia:Verifiability. Accessed: 6-30-17.

33. WP 1.0 bot. Wikipedia Articles by Quality and Importance. https://en.wikipedia.org/wiki/User:WP_1.0_bot/Tables/OverallArticles. Accessed: 06/30/17.

Keynote Speaker

Jimmy Wales
Wikia, Inc. & Wikimedia Foundation

Group 2018 also welcomes Internet and technology entrepreneur Jimmy Wales, founder of the online non-profit encyclopaedia Wikipedia and co-founder of the privately owned Wikia, Inc. including its entertainment media brand, Fandom powered by Wikia. Wales serves on the board of trustees of the Wikimedia Foundation, the non-profit charitable organisation he established to operate Wikipedia. In April 2017, Jimmy launched WikiTribune — a news website involving professional journalists working alongside volunteers to curate fact checked and reliable articles. In 2006 Jimmy was named in Time magazine's '100 Most Influential People in the World' for his role in creating Wikipedia.

Jimmy Wales

GROUP 2018, January 7–10, 2018, Sanibel Island, FL, USA.
© 2018 Copyright is held by the author/owner(s).
ACM ISBN 978-1-4503-5562-9/18/01.
https://doi.org/10.1145/3148330.3148353

Twenty Thousand Leagues Above the Book: An Interactive Visual Analytics Approach to Literature

Markus Luczak-Roesch
School of Information
Management
Victoria University of
Wellington
luczakma@vuw.ac.nz

Adam Grener
School of English, Film,
Theatre and Media Studies
Victoria University of
Wellington
adam.grener@vuw.ac.nz

Emma Fenton
School of English, Film,
Theatre and Media Studies
Victoria University of
Wellington
efmfenton@gmail.com

Abstract

Here we present a novel tool for the digital humanities
that leverages temporal data mining, network science, and
visual analytics. Our initial user studies show that this
approach facilitates a new collaborative methodological
practice that is a hybrid of close and distant reading.

Author Keywords

digital humanities, text mining, network analysis

ACM Classification Keywords

H.5.m [Information interfaces and presentation (e.g.,
HCI)]: Miscellaneous.

Introduction

In recent years data-driven analysis has emerged as a
growing methodology within literary studies. These
"distant reading" practices harness available technology to
open new avenues for how we understand literary texts.
Whereas traditional literary scholarship is generally
grounded in the interpretation of the specific language of
a text or body of texts, macroanalytic approaches present
new ways of seeing texts, both individually and in the
aggregate. **Here we introduce a novel tool for
interacting with literature that transcends the
boundaries of traditional close and data-driven
distant reading.** Our approach constructs temporally

Figure 1: Deployment of our prototype on a 49" multi-touch screen. Individuals and groups can convene in front of this setup and use the tool while working with one of the analysed novels.

ordered networks of information occurrence, which we configured to match characters as the unit of information. This creates a unique view of the narrative structures within novels and opens a variety of possibilities for visual as well as information theoretic analysis. We demonstrate the application of our tool on nineteen Victorian novels.

Foundations and related work

Character networks have been a central object of analysis in computational approaches to narrative. Character networks offer visual models of texts and new perspectives on how they function [6] through a static picture of their structure and systems. In addition to aiding the analysis of plot, character networks offer a foundation for social network analysis and for understanding how novels construct relationships between characters and thus the social worlds they represent. The construction of character maps can be extremely challenging [6, 9]. Piper [9] and Elson, et al. [3] have developed programs for extracting social networks from texts by identifying character co-occurrence within paragraphs or by using dialogue interaction to establish relation. While this work reveals the inherent difficulties in reliably generating social networks with speed and ease, it has also shown the possibilities for using character networks to understand genre [8], character typology [1], and character-space [7].

Tool prototype

Our method applies the Transcendental Information Cascades (TIC) approach [4, 5] to represent a text as a temporally ordered network of information occurrence. For our prototype we used character names as the unit of information, but one can select any other information that can be extracted from text (e.g., general entities, bigrams, part-of-speech elements, and topics). As shown in Figure 2 we break the text down into "slices" of 1,000 words (with chapter breaks terminating a slice prior to 1,000 words). This slice size can be changed but our tests showed that 1,000 words slices produce networks of adequate granularity. Each slice is processed to match characters from a given dictionary. Edges signify consecutive appearances of a character in different slices of the text, which means a character does not appear in any slice between the two slices that are linked.

The central output of the data processing is a dynamic network, which represents the unfolding of the character occurrences. It can be played and paused at any point. Each edge and node in this dynamic network can be clicked to reveal details about the links between two nodes or a particular node respectively, and to jump to the full text of the novel that corresponds to a particular slice. The system also produces lists of all appearances of individual characters as well as the first and last appearance of each character, which can be used to focus the analysis on major or minor characters only for example. Figure 1 shows the deployment of our prototype, which involves a 49" multi-touch screen. Groups and individuals can convene around this setup and use the tool while working with one of the analysed novels.

Preliminary user study results

The TIC algorithm has been run on 19 novels to this point, 15 novels by Dickens, and four by other Victorian novelists for comparative purposes. An initial user study to evaluate our tool was performed involving two humanities scholars and nine university students in English literature. We held five user study sessions where first the two humanities scholars, then a group of three, and finally three groups of two students were given access to our tool. The humanities scholars were additionally provided with all the generated data visualisations as digital image files.

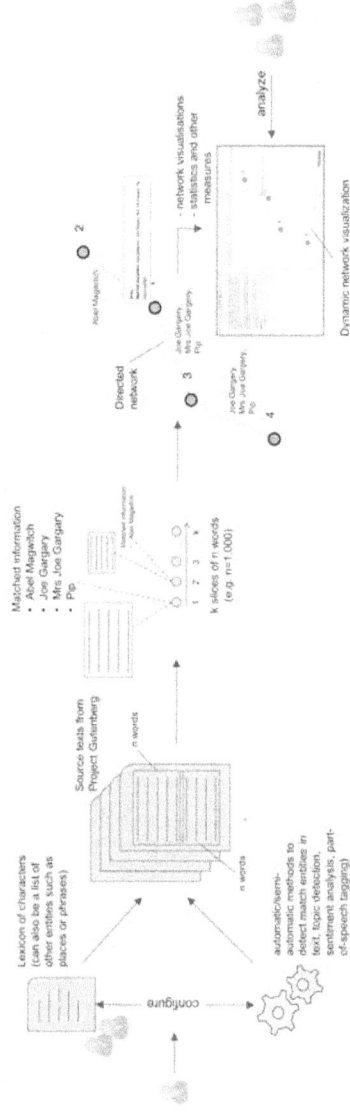

Figure 2: The analytical pipeline underlying our tool prototype applying Transcendental Information Cascades to literary works.

Although our approach draws on the methods employed by distant reading, our outputs allow for analysis in the aggregate and of individual works. From the initial results we see that our approach promises to create unique analytical value for the digital humanities by offering unique macroscopic views of corpora that also facilitate rich interaction with individual works. In addition to its linking of close reading and distant reading practices, we also want to highlight the possibility of collaborative non-linear reading [2] enabled by our tool prototype.

The two humanities scholars collaboratively produced a set of annotated graphs based on the images that were provided to them (see Figures 3 and 4 for two examples). These annotated graphs show to great detail what kind of insights humanities scholars are looking for. Annotating groups of nodes to mark up larger episodes or sequences in the novel was a common task they performed. The interactions between the derived networks and the original texts flowed both ways; the scholars began with moments of known narrative significance and moved to the network

to understand that significance, but they also identified elements of the network that presented as significant to identify areas to begin textual analysis. These observations on self-designed annotations are evidence for **an emergent methodological practice**, as the humanities scholars were given a novel tool and then developed their own analytical process around it.

The users studies also demonstrate the potential of our tool to cultivate **collaborative interpretive practices for readers**. Observations made by one user about the visualisations have prompted group consideration of the relationship between the text itself and the visualisations. For example, one user noted the relatively marginal position of Lydgate in *Middlemarch* despite their sense of his importance. The group reviewed the broader patterns of character appearance in the novel and concluded that a character's significance is not merely a product of how frequently they appear. In another instance, one user's identification of a event of narrative significance in *Great Expectations* prompted the group to use the visualisations

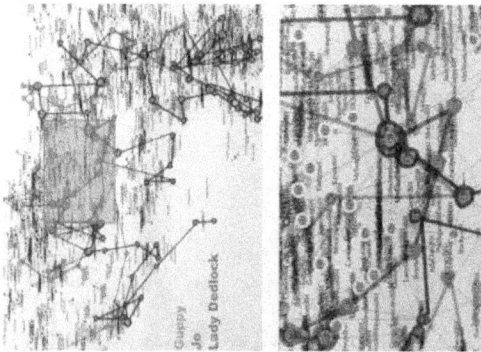

Figure 3: Manual annotation of the *Bleak House* network that identifies moments of convergence for important characters.

to connect this event to broader changes in the character dynamics of the text. These examples demonstrate the capacity of the tool to foster rich collaborative reading practices. Readers draw on their own knowledge and experience of the text, but have used the common point of analysis and discussion provided by the visualisations to facilitate a shared understanding of the text.

Conclusion and future work

Here we presented a novel method to create temporal networks representing the evolution of character occurrences in literary works. Our current research aims to analyse the various quantitative measures the method makes accessible (e.g. network properties, character entropy) so as to better understand their properties for comparative and predictive purposes (e.g. using the measures as features to determine the literary epoch of works). Further user studies will be performed to obtain more general insights into how individuals interact with abstract digital representations of literary works. The preliminary user study results presented here emphasise the desirability of annotation features to capture the notes left by users. The comprehensive paper notes produced by the two humanities scholars on printouts of the generated visualisations will guide the implementation of this and are a crucial resource in our user-centred design process. Due to the generic nature of the TIC approach, our tool provides the capacity to trace any kind of information throughout continuous texts (e.g. keywords, places, part-of-speech tokens, or even sentiments) in any language. Our software is available as open source software[1].

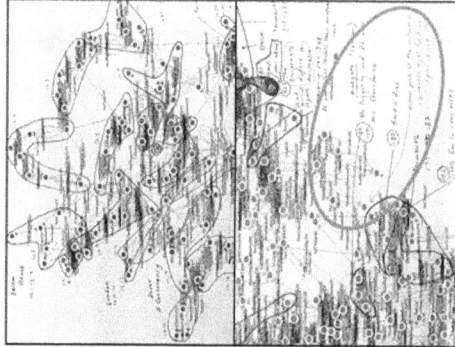

Figure 4: Manual annotations of the *David Copperfield* network that identify moments of narrative significance.

References

[1] Bamman, D., Underwood, T., and Smith, N. A. A bayesian mixed effects model of literary character. In *ACL (1)* (2014), 370–379.

[2] Burbules, N. C. Rhetorics of the web: Hyperreading and critical literacy. *Page to screen: Taking literacy into the electronic era* (1998), 102–122.

[3] Elson, D. K., Dames, N., and McKeown, K. R. Extracting social networks from literary fiction. In *Proceedings of the 48th annual meeting of the association for computational linguistics*, Association for Computational Linguistics (2010), 138–147.

[4] Luczak-Roesch, M., Tinati, R., and Shadbolt, N. When resources collide: Towards a theory of coincidence in information spaces. In *Proceedings of the 24th International Conference on World Wide Web*, ACM (2015).

[5] Luczak-Roesch, M., Tinati, R., Van Kleek, M., and Shadbolt, N. From coincidence to purposeful flow? properties of transcendental information cascades. In *Proceedings of the IEEE/ACM ASONAM conference*, ACM (2015).

[6] Moretti, F. Network theory, plot analysis. *New Left Review* (2011).

[7] Piper, A. The constraints of character. introducing a character feature-space tool. https://txtlab.org/?p=611.

[8] Piper, A. Detecting literary characters. https://txtlab.org/?p=559.

[9] Piper, A. Development of a (semi-) automatic character network tool. https://novel-tm.ca/?p=472.

---

[1]Source code repository: https://github.com/vuw-sim-stia/lit-cascades, demo instance for public use: https://stia.shinyapps.io/tlit/

A Personalized "Course Navigator" Based on Students' Goal Orientation

Prateek Basavaraj
University of Central Florida
Orlando, Florida 32826
Prateek.basavaraj@ucf.edu

Ivan Garibay
University of Central Florida
Orlando, Florida 32826
Ivan.garibay@ucf.edu

Abstract

Higher education institutions must understand students' mastery and performance goals in order to guide them in selecting suitable courses to take, so that they are successful. We propose a personalized recommendation system called "Course Navigator" for guiding undergraduate Information Technology (IT) students in selecting course curriculum based on their self-reported goal orientation and past course performance. We analyzed data from 2500 IT students at University of Central Florida (UCF) to create course recommendations. Our preliminary results show that the course recommendations for students with different goal orientations differ and may help students customize their course selections based on their goals.

Author Keywords

Science, Technology, Engineering, and Mathematics (STEM) Education; Recommendation Systems; Personalized Learning.

CCS CONCEPTS

• **Social and professional topics~Information technology education**

Introduction

Increasingly, higher education institutions are using data to improve student success through improved academic advising [1]. One way of improved academic advising is by providing personalized course recommendations to students. In this research, we developed a personalized course recommendation system called 'Course Navigator' that takes into account: (i) course performance data, (ii) program curriculum requirements and (iii) student-based surveys that take into account their (a) goal orientation and (b) program interests. The main goals of Course Navigator are: (i) to ease students' burden while making course decisions and (ii) to reduce students' cognitive load by providing suitable recommendations based on their academic background and goal orientations.

Related Work

Recommendation Systems for Personalized Learning

There are different artificial intelligence methodologies used for personalized and adaptive learning educational systems [3]. The focus of some of these educational systems has been to generate learner profiles by examining students' characteristics [3,5]. Chen [2] considered course difficulty levels and proposed a genetic-algorithm-based personalized e-learning system, which provides individualized learning paths based on the learner's incorrect testing responses. Lin et al. [4] developed a system using a decision tree approach to provide learning paths for learners. Some of the important variables analyzed by Lin in his study were creativity levels, gender and self-perception of creativity. Hill et al. [8] designed a recommendation system that uses Human-Computer Interaction, Artificial Intelligence and Big Data methods to help academic researchers, students to collaborate. Akbas et al. [1] designed a personalized course recommendation system with the application of historical data for the benefit of students and decision makers in higher educational and training institutions.

Student Goal Orientations

Goal orientation refers to the type of goal a student is working towards, which has been shown to have a significant impact on learning [6]. Based on the achievement goal orientation theory, there are two types of students: 1) *Mastery-Goal-Oriented (MGO)* and 2) *Performance-Goal-Oriented (PGO)* students [6]. MGO students work very hard, persist in the face of difficulty, try new things to challenge themselves, so

that they can master the tasks they have undertaken. In contrast, PGO students prefer to undertake tasks that they are already good at and consider making mistakes a lack of competence; therefore, they avoid taking risks where they might fail [7]. Students with performance avoidance goal orientation are negatively related to their academic standing [7]. Students who are in academic probation often adopt performance avoidance goals than those in good academic standing [7]. We considered these characteristics of students with PGO and MGO in the design of our personalized recommendation system.

A Personalized "Course Navigator"

To the best of our knowledge, the personalized recommendation system proposed in this paper is the only course recommendation system that leverages students' goal orientations, course relative importance in combination with past course performance data. The course navigator is intended to serve as a collaborative system between advisors and students. Academic advisors can use course navigator to customize students' plan of study based on their needs. Based on a recent survey of students 49% reported that the departmental curriculum provides little or no flexibility in choosing courses. The goal of course navigator is to provide more flexibility and improve student advising.

Student Survey Data

First, we inferred each student's program interests (Information Technology, Computer Science, Computer Engineering) and goal orientation (MGO, PGO) based on the student-based survey data. For this paper, we only analyzed data for the IT program.

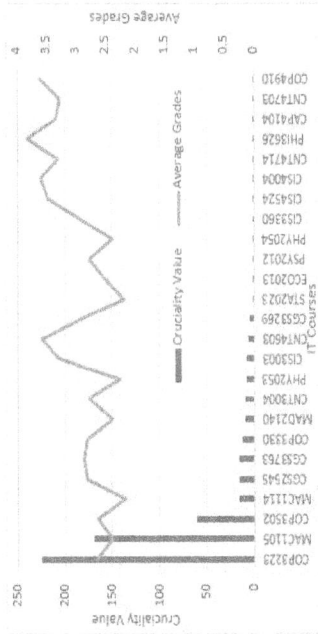

Figure 1: Representation of Cruciality values and Average Grades of IT Courses

IT Program Curricula

Next, we conceptualized the IT curriculum in the form of a directed graph by considering course prerequisite requirements. With the application of network science parameters such as betweenness centrality and path length, we calculated the cruciality value for all courses by multiplying betweenness centrality and path length of courses [5]. In general, this value helps identify the relative importance of a course in the curriculum. The cruciality values of IT courses are shown in **Figure 1**.

Student Course Performance Data

Finally, we considered student performance. We analyzed student performance data (grades) and the degree status (number of courses completed or failed). Our personalized recommendation system takes into account individual students versus their relative performance to other students in a course. Therefore, the personalized recommendations are based on both the student's GPA and average grade for each course.

Preliminary Results

Descriptive Statistics

We analyzed student survey responses of 510 IT majors. Based on the questions related to satisfaction and pleasure in learning new skills, we found that approximately 46% and 24% of students exhibit one or more characteristics of MGO and PGO, respectively. Whereas rest 30% answered neutral (0) to these questions. The IT program course catalog at UCF suggests students take courses in order as shown in Table 1.

MGO Student Recommendations

For MGO students, our system recommends courses with low or average grades (i.e. challenging) in the beginning terms. Based on the number of courses a student is willing to take in the first term, the personalized system checks the courses with no prerequisites and their cruciality values. For example, if a student wishes to enroll in four courses and his initial goal orientation is MGO then the recommendation system checks the cruciality values of courses with no prerequisites. Then the Course Navigator checks the average grades of these courses. Since student's initial goal orientation is MGO, the system recommends difficult course (MAC1114) in addition to COP3223, MAC1105 and CGS2545. The personalized recommendations for MGO's is shown in Table 2.

PGO Student Recommendations

For PGO students, our system recommends courses with high average grade (i.e. easy) in the beginning terms. The reason behind recommending easy courses was PGO students are low risk takers. For PGO, the system recommends CGS2545, CGS3763 which are easy courses in addition to MAC1105 and COP3223. The recommendations for PGO student profiles for IT program are shown in Table 3. Based on these results,

Term-1	Term-2	Term-3	Term-4
COP3223	COP3502	COP3330	CGS3269
MAC1105	ECO2013	PHY2053	STA2023
	PSY2012	CGS2545	CIS3003
	MAC1114	MAD2140	

Term-5	Term-6	Term-7	Term-8
CAP4104	CIS4524	CNT4703	COP4910
PHY2054	PHI3626	CIS4004	CNT4714
CNT3004	CGS3763	CNT4603	
CIS3360			

Table 1: UCF IT Program Catalog Recommendations

Term-1	Term-2	Term-3	Term-4
N=4	N=4	N=2	N=4
COP2223	PHY2053	MAD2140	CNT4603
MAC1114	COP3502	CIS3003	CGS3269
MAC1105	CGS3763		STA2023
CGS2545	COP3330		ECO2013

Term-5	Term-6	Term-7	Term-8
N=4	N=2	N=4	N=4
PSY2012	CNT3004	CIS4524	COP4910
PHY2054	CAP4104	CIS4004	
CIS3360		PHI3626	
CNT4714		CNT4703	

Table 2: Course Recommendations for MGO IT Students

Term-1	Term-2	Term-3	Term-4
N=4	N=4	N=2	N=4
CGS2545	MAD2140	PHY2053	PHI3626
CGS3763	CIS3003	COP3502	CAP4104
MAC1105	COP3330		CIS4524
COP2223	MAC1114		CNT4603

Term-5	Term-6	Term-7	Term-8
N=4	N=2	N=4	N=4
PHY2054	CNT4714	STA2023	COP4910
CIS3360	CNT3004	ECO2013	
CGS3269		CIS4004	
PSY2012		CNT4703	

Table 3: Course Recommendations for PGO IT Students

the recommendations differed significantly for MGO versus PGO students'. These recommendations may help both MGO and PGO students plan and successfully complete courses each term.

CONCLUSION

In this paper, we proposed a personalized course recommendation system to assist students. Our proposed approach determines students' goal orientations and analyzes the program curriculum, and course performance data. The preliminary results suggest that this proposed system helps in course selection based on their initial goal orientation. In the near future, we will study the effectiveness of our recommendation system on student success by measuring the course completion and success rates of students who followed our recommendations with those who followed program specified catalog recommendations.

Our initial work has focused on better understanding the differing self-reported goal orientation of students to identify the type of tasks that course navigator can support. The next step is to determine whether these personalized course recommendations are perceived by students and advisors as an improvement to the static course guidelines from the university catalog. Additionally, it will be important to conduct a longitudinal study on whether students who elect to adopt an MGO or PGO plan of study experience better or different learning outcomes.

Acknowledgements

We would like to also thank Dr. Pamela Wisniewski for her guidance on this work.

References

1. Mustafa Ilhan Akbaş, Prateek Basavaraj, and Michael Georgiopoulos. 2015. Curriculum GPS: An Adaptive Curriculum Generation and Planning System. In Interservice/Industry Training, Simulation, and Education Conference (I/ITSEC).

2. Chih-Ming Chen. 2008. Intelligent web-based learning system with personalized learning path guidance. Computers & Education 51, 2 (2008), 787–814.

3. Hugo Gamboa and Ana Fred. 2002. Designing intelligent tutoring systems: a bayesian approach. Enterprise Information Systems III. Edited by J. Filipe, B. Sharp, and P. Miranda. Springer Verlag: New York (2002), 146–152.

4. Chun Fu Lin, Yu-chu Yeh, Yu Hsin Hung, and Ray I Chang. 2013. Data mining for providing a personalized learning path in creativity: An application of decision trees. Computers & Education 68 (2013), 199–210.

5. Ahmad Slim, Jarred Kozlick, Gregory L Heileman, Jeff Wigdahl, and Chaouki T Abdallah. 2014. Network analysis of university courses. In Proceedings of the 23rd International Conference on World Wide Web. ACM, 713–718.

6. Marilla Svinicki. 2005. Student goal orientation, motivation, and learning. Idea Paper 41 (2005).

7. Hsieh, P., Sullivan, J. R., & Guerra, N. S. (2007). A closer look at college students: Self-efficacy and goal orientation. Journal of Advanced Academics, 18(3), 454-476.

8. Hill, S. J., Brown, K. A., Cirstea, A. I., Morgan, A. R., Mustafa, A., & Tartaro, A. (2014, November). BIG Science: A Collaborative Framework for Large Scale Research. In Proceedings of the 18th International Conference on Supporting Group Work (pp. 285-287). ACM.

Using Native Tongue Mnemonics to Enhance English Learning

Muhammad Irtaza Safi
University of Central Florida
Orlando, FL 32816, USA
irtaza.safi@gmail.com

Karla Badillo-Urquiola
University of Central Florida
Orlando, FL 32816, USA
Kcurquiola10@knights.ucf.edu

Suleman Shahid
Lahore University of Management
Sciences, Lahore, Punjab,
Pakistan.
suleman.shahid@lums.edu.pk

Zirak Zaheer
Lahore University of Management
Sciences, Lahore, Punjab,
Pakistan.
zirakz7@gmail.com

Momina Haider
Carnegie Mellon University,
Pittsburgh, PA 15213
mominah@andrew.cmu.edu

Hamza Mahmood
Lahore University of Management
Sciences, Lahore, Punjab,
Pakistan.
hamza.mahmood1993@gmail.com

ACM ISBN 978-1-4503-5562-9/18/01.
https://doi.org/10.1145/3148330.3154509

Abstract

An individual's language and culture play an important part in their learning process [9]. In this paper, we develop a mobile application called "Mnemorizer" to help international students learn English vocabulary for standardized tests. We use mnemonics and gamification to aid learning and present results that indicate that native tongue mnemonics are more effective than mnemonics in English. Initial results of this ongoing project provide motivation for our future work, which will leverage crowdsourcing techniques to build a database of mnemonic devices to support a broader subset of languages and cultures.

Author Keywords

Learning; Mnemonics; language; mobile application

ACM Classification Keywords

K.3.1 Computers and Education: Computer Uses in Education

Introduction

With globalization now mixing different cultures together, knowledge is transferred across the planet at unprecedented speeds and modern learners face a unique mixture of challenges. One such example is

Main contribution of this work

The main contribution of this work lies in designing a system to teach English vocabulary, which incorporates mnemonics and gamification, exploring whether tailoring mnemonics to a students' native tongue can enhance performance. Our application is different from existing mnemonic based solutions such as Memrise [9] because we provide 'culturally relevant' mnemonic suggestions by recording the location at which the mnemonic was submitted and then prioritizing the mnemonic 'closest' to the user's location. This allows us to provide mnemonics which are more relevant in an automated manner based on the fact that very close geographical proximity predicts culture/language proximity. Our platform is similar to Dontcheva et al [3] in that it leverages crowdsourcing and learning to improve engagement and performance.

learning English vocabulary for standardized tests. In 2014 nearly 8.2 million international students came to the United States [8], the vast majority of them being non-native English speakers. For these students, memorizing vocabulary for standardized tests is a daunting challenge.

Background

Platforms like Code Academy [10], Memrise [11] and flashcard apps, such as Magoosh [12] make successful use of gamification strategies for word vocabulary learning. Gartner [13] notes that gamification accelerates the feedback cycle by enabling users to get a quicker reward for their accomplishment. It provides clarity and focus, and gives tasks which are challenging yet achievable.

Mnemonics helps learners remember new words that may otherwise be difficult to recall [1]. Educational research has found that children learn much more effectively when taught in their native language [9] while Dontcheva et al have demonstrated how crowdsourcing can improve engagement and performance[3]. Our system combines these three approaches by building an implicitly social platform around gamification and mnemonics, allowing us to source the most "culturally effective" mnemonics for users leveraging their native language. For the purposes of this extended abstract, we only test if native language mnemonics enhance learning performance.

Methods

We employed user-centered design principles prior to designing and implementing our app. We describe this

process in the section below, as well as the design of our user study to evaluate the app.

User Centered Design Process

We disseminated an initial user discovery survey (90 responses) and conducted 13 semi-structured interviews in a bilingual university student population in Pakistan. The survey results guided the design of our app. Overall, the students were well-spoken in English as their second language with Urdu as their native tongue. 86% of our respondents claimed to be fairly good at English but still 85% of them found learning English vocabulary to be very hard. 80% of our respondents employed the use of some sort of mnemonic in helping them to learn and, interestingly, nearly 55% of them came up with a native language (Urdu) mnemonic. 45% of our users used a flashcard based learning app such as Magoosh for learning vocabulary for standardized tests.

Even though the students liked Magoosh, this platform does not provide the mechanism for native tongue mnemonics desired by our participants. The trend toward native tongue mnemonics was re-confirmed by our semi-structured interviews where users expressed deep fondness for the repetitive gamification model used in Magoosh. Words such as "sights," "sounds," "people," "celebrities," "music" came up frequently in our interviews when we asked users to elaborate on the kinds of mnemonics they used. We noticed that our participants often gave example mnemonics in Urdu instead of English. When we asked about this, participants often explained that Urdu was "familiar" to them and helped them "more easily remember" the words in English. After our user discovery had been completed, we referred back to the literature to

Figure 1: Screenshot of Mnemorizer App with English mnemonic (Group 2).

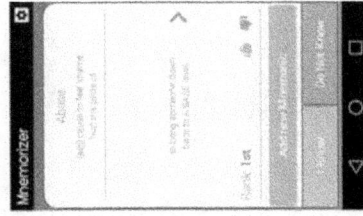

Figure 2: Screenshots of Mnemorizer App with Urdu mnemonic (Group 3).

determine if native tongue mnemonics had been studied previously in computing contexts to aid in learning. While we did not find previous work using our exact approach, Cassell et al's work [2] on virtual peers and "code-switching" between informal and formal language to aid young children learn further encouraged us to test whether we could similarly improve learning performance by using native language, and hence culturally relevant mnemonics for college students.

Mnemorizer App Design

Figures 1 and 2 show Mnemorizer's mobile app interface using the word "Abase" and displaying the English and Urdu mnemonics, respectively. While using the gamification aspect of Magoosh, the app additionally provides the word meaning and the option of scrolling through the mnemonics, rating them, and adding custom mnemonics. When the user sees a word, they 'tap to see its meaning,' if the user's assumed meaning matches with the actual meaning, they tap 'I know.' Our application cycles through a set of words until the user confirms that they 'know' the word's meaning. After one iteration has completed, the application restarts the cycle and continues this way until the deck has been exhausted. This approach introduces repeated retrieval [4] and motivational affordances [7]. Users are engaged with the app as they try to learn all the words and have their decks completed similar to how users are motivated to achieve specific goals in games[6].

User Study Design

We used the cycling mechanism to test the speed at which users learned words depending on the kinds of mnemonics presented to them. We divided a group of

15 participants into 3 groups of 5. Group 1 was provided with only the English meaning of the words; group 2 with meanings and English mnemonics; and group 3 with meanings and Urdu mnemonics. Participants went through 3 iteration cycles. When using the app, we asked users to think out loud. Mnemonics were randomly sourced from university students.

Results

Table 1 shows the results of our user study. The numbers represent the percentage of words "known" in each iteration for the respective group. As seen, the group which has been provided native language mnemonics (Group 3) recalled 80% of the words in the second iteration and 90% by the third. This suggests a faster uptake compared to Group 1 and Group 2, suggesting that the use of native language mnemonics may be more effective in reducing the time it takes to learn English vocabulary.

Table 1: Percent of Correct Words Given Each Iteration

Iteration	Group 1	Group 2	Group 3
1	25%	20%	20%
2	54%	52%	80%
3	83%	90%	90%

Additionally, users in Group 3 who thought aloud frequently remarked at how they were glad to see the mnemonic in Urdu and were quickly able to form mental associations between the words and their "own experience."

Discussion

We found that our user sample, comprised of people

Future Work: Combining Native Tongue Mnemonics with Crowdsourcing.

Far from being just a way of expressing thoughts, a language encapsulates the culture, sensibilities, trends and sensitivities of a people. In order for mnemonics to be as effective as possible, they must encapsulate all of the above and be tailored to the specific user. This is only possible if one has knowledge of the user's "cultural vicinity". By using the learner's location and obtainable metadata from the smartphone and social media, we can possibly deliver mnemonics (created by other users) which are the most culturally relevant and hence effective. In this way, our system can behave dynamically as short term shifts in the user's cultural stimulus happen. For instance, if a particular genre of music suddenly gains popularity in a region, our system will automatically adapt its mnemonic suggestions to the new "cultural vicinity".

who considered themselves strong English speakers, still learned faster when the mnemonics were in their native tongue (Urdu). We believe this is due to the Urdu language bringing in the cultural familiarity that can be so vital to learning. This leads us into the direction of using crowdsourcing from a user's local vicinity to source mnemonics. Using crowdsourcing to enhance learning is not a new concept and works such as [5] have demonstrated its efficacy. Ultimately, we hope to build a system which is sensitive to the user's language and specific culture to dynamically adapt mnemonics so they are best suited for each user.

References

1. Mohammad Amiryousefi and Saeed Ketabi. 2011. Mnemonic Instruction: A Way to Boost Vocabulary Learning and Recall. *Journal of Language Teaching and Research 2*, 1. https://doi.org/10.4304/jltr.2.1.178-182

2. Justine Cassell, Kathleen Geraghty, Berto Gonzalez, and John Borland. 2009. Modeling Culturally Authentic Style Shifting with Virtual Peers. In *Proceedings of the 2009 International Conference on Multimodal Interfaces (ICMI-MLMI '09)*, 135–142. https://doi.org/10.1145/1647314.1647338

3. Mira Dontcheva, Robert R. Morris, Joel R. Brandt, and Elizabeth M. Gerber. 2014. Combining Crowdsourcing and Learning to Improve Engagement and Performance. In *Proceedings of the SIGCHI Conference on Human Factors in Computing Systems (CHI '14)*, 3379–3388. https://doi.org/10.1145/2556288.2557217

4. J Karpicke and H Roedigeriii. 2007. Repeated retrieval during learning is the key to long-term retention☆. *Journal of Memory and Language 57*, 2: 151–162. https://doi.org/10.1016/j.jml.2006.09.004

5. Kurt Luther, Nathan Hahn, Steven P. Dow, and Aniket Kittur. 2015. Crowdlines: Supporting Synthesis of Diverse Information Sources through Crowdsourced Outlines. In *Third AAAI Conference on Human Computation and Crowdsourcing*. Retrieved November 3, 2016 from http://www.aaai.org/ocs/index.php/HCOMP/HCOMP15/paper/view/11603

6. Karen Robson, Kirk Plangger, Jan H. Kietzmann, Ian McCarthy, and Leyland Pitt. 2015. Is it all a game? Understanding the principles of gamification. *Business Horizons 58*, 4: 411–420. https://doi.org/10.1016/j.bushor.2015.03.006

7. Ping Zhang. 2008. Technical opinionMotivational affordances: reasons for ICT design and use. *Communications of the ACM 51*, 11: 145. https://doi.org/10.1145/1400214.1400244

8. 2014. SAT Test 2014: Number Of International Students Taking College Admission Exam Doubles, Student Visa Applications Up. *International Business Times*. Retrieved November 4, 2016 from http://www.ibtimes.com/sat-test-2014-number-international-students-taking-college-admission-exam-doubles-1718805

9. Mother tongue matters: local language as a key to effective learning. Retrieved November 3, 2016 from http://www-01.sil.org/literacy/mother_tongue_matters.htm

10. Learn to code. *Codecademy*. Retrieved October 31, 2016 from https://www.codecademy.com/

11. Memrise - Unlock your language learning superpowers! *Memrise*. Retrieved September 16, 2017 from https://www.memrise.com

12. Free GRE Vocabulary Flashcards - Magoosh GRE. Retrieved November 3, 2016 from https://gre.magoosh.com/flashcards/vocabulary

13. Gartner Says By 2015, More Than 50 Percent of Organizations That Manage Innovation Processes Will Gamify Those Processes. Retrieved November 3, 2016 from http://www.gartner.com/newsroom/id/1629214

Cooperative Mixed Reality: An Analysis Tool

Lisa M. Rühmann
Clausthal University of Technology
Clausthal-Zellerfeld, Germany
Lisa.Ruehmann@tu-clausthal.de

Michael Prilla
Clausthal University of Technology
Clausthal-Zellerfeld, Germany
Michael.Prilla@tu-clausthal.de

Gordon Brown
Clausthal University of Technology
Clausthal-Zellerfeld, Germany
Gordon.Brown@tu-clausthal.de

Abstract

While mixed reality scenarios are highly relevant for cooperation support, most work done in this context is on individuals. When working on cooperation support scenarios in MR, we arrived at situations in which we needed insights into the way how people used the technology to work together. To support the investigation of this question, we created a 3D analysis tool for interactive and cooperative task support in MR.

GROUP '18, January 7–10, 2018, Sanibel Island, FL, USA
© 2018 Copyright is held by the owner/author(s).
ACM ISBN 978-1-4503-5562-9/18/01.
https://doi.org/10.1145/3148330.3154510

The tool and exemplary results from applying to a visual search experiment conducted in a cooperative mixed reality setting with Microsoft HoloLens devices are presented here. We show how it can uncover interaction otherwise not or hard to discover.

Author Keywords

Augmented reality, mixed reality, cooperative tasks, visual search, HoloLens, AR analysis tool.

ACM Classification Keywords

H.5.1 Multimedia Information Systems: Artificial, augmented, and virtual realities; H.5.3 Group and Organization Interfaces: Computer-supported cooperative work.

Introduction

Augmented reality (AR) with its multiple application areas is a technology that is currently gaining more importance. Using Azuma's words, AR "allows the user to see the real world, with virtual objects superimposed upon or composited with the real world. (...) AR supplements reality, rather than completely replacing it." [1:356]. By using AR technology, users enter a mixed reality (MR) setting, in which digital and physical objects and information are tightly integrated and can be used together.

While there is potential for AR in cooperation support

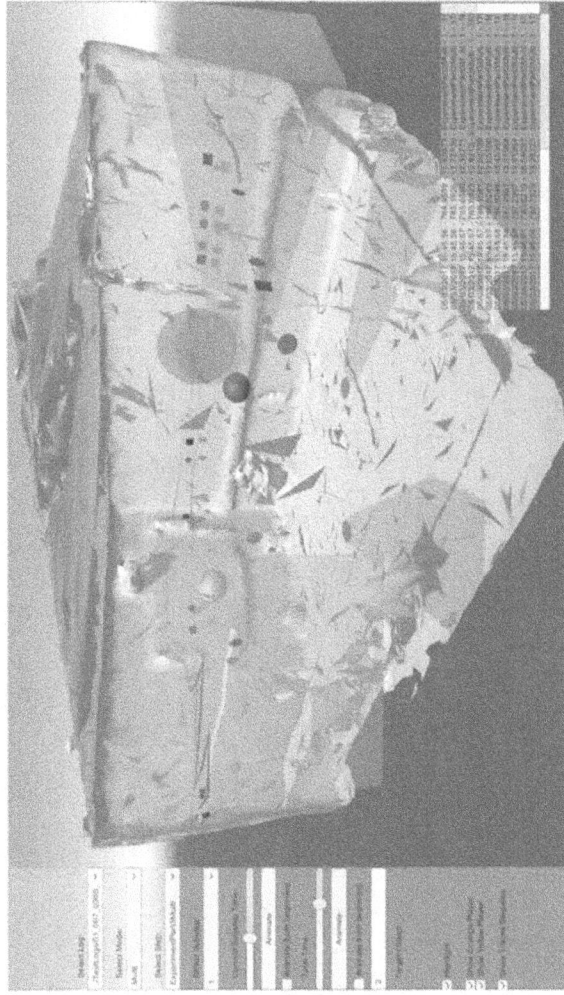

Figure 1: The AR Analysis Tool during the analysis of visual search, including the 3D model of the room, the 2D objects to be searched, the participants' field of view (shadows and cylindrical projection), the participants' positions (yellow/A, left; red/B, right), and gaze cues on the wall.

(e.g., [2,3]), observing interaction and cooperation in MR is difficult, as it needs an integrated view on the virtual and real (physical, spatial) aspects of MR. This paper presents a novel tool for this analysis. The tool uses log and sensor data of devices, connects them to the spatial environment, and visualizes individual and cooperative activities.

Augmented Reality Analysis Tool

Common means for analysis of cooperation such as videotaping the cooperators and analyzing their work cannot capture the virtual aspects of the mixed reality setting (i.e., the virtual objects), and using the first-person view as seen by actors through head-mounted AR devices makes it hard to analyze the cooperation between the actors, i.e. to see how one actor influences another (cf. Figure 2). To our knowledge, no specific tools for the analysis of cooperative AR exist that help to overcome these issues. Due to the lack of such tools, we created a new tool for cooperative AR interaction analysis that uses log data created by our applications (see Figure 1). It represents the spatial environment in which actors are working together and makes their interaction with the

MR setting available. It uses different log data created by a tool we create for Microsoft HoloLens devices:

Model of the room: In order to place virtual objects accurately, the HoloLens creates a 3D model of rooms it works in (see Figure 1).

Head movements for gaze cues: The head tracker built into the devices was used to keep track of gaze cues ([5], cf. Figure 1). This was used for detecting search behavior, and the current gaze is available in real time to cooperators.

Figure 2: As a contrast to Figure 1, these two pictures here show the same situation as to be observed from outside the MR space (leaving out the virtual contents, top) and from the point of view of one participant (losing the spatial context, bottom).

Body movements: We track movements by logging the position measured by the device. This is a very accurate way of determining the position.

Intersections with and looking at virtual objects: Movements and gaze are related to virtual objects in the room, which allows to identify where an object is in relation to a person and whether the person has looked at it, including the duration of looking at the object.

User interaction: The use of gestures for selecting and moving objects is logged for the analysis.

Application of the tool

Figure 1 shows a sample view of the tool during the analysis of a 2D search task performed by two people. Their task was to find a specific (virtual) object, which was randomly displayed amongst similar objects in a room via HoloLens devices and select it together. Figure 1 shows the heads of the two participants as balls, their gaze as cues on the wall and the virtual objects placed on the walls.

The tool offers different features for the analysis of cooperative MR (Figure 1). To support different levels of granularity for the analysis, it enables the selection of steps within an interaction such as the search task described above (i.e., repeated 2D searches). The timeframe can be manually controlled through a slider, and it features a time lapse for looking at interactions in more detail as well as selective hide and show mechanisms for virtual objects, users and gaze cues. The resulting tool provides a flexible and powerful means to analyze interaction of actors in MR. The features included in the tool currently are a subset of what may be needed, and we will discuss additions for the analysis of search patterns later on. The tool has

not been evaluated through a user study. This is a limitation we are aware of and will explore further in the future.

Exemplifying MR Analysis: Visual Search Patterns

To exemplify the usage of the tool and the benefit it creates for the analysis of interaction in MR, we describe search patterns we found by applying the tool. To identify the search patterns, we replayed the interaction during the search experiment described above and looked at gaze cues as coherent movements during search. Such cues were found to be a key to guiding co-located cooperation such as understanding other people's activities [5] and performing visual searches together [4,6]. Figure 1 shows gaze cues of two experiment participants. We also looked-for ways in which the participants of the experiment consciously worked together to carry out the search tasks. After the participants had received information on the object to look for and started to move within the search space, the identifying of the pattern began. The identification of patterns started once participants had the task presented to them and they started to move.

In 2D search we identified two patterns with different specifications, with the "Spinner" pattern being the most common strategy used among the pairs:

Spinner: The "Spinner" (cf. Figure 3) describes a circular movement throughout the complete space from the starting point to the object searched, where one of the participants turned at least around halfway.

Following: The "Following" pattern (Figure 4) refers to one participant following the other while searching. This

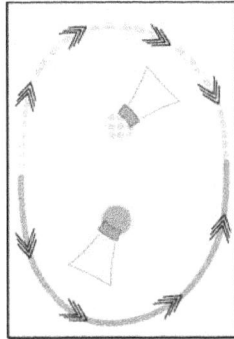

Figure 3: Depiction of Spinner Movement – the circles in the center represent the participants in their corresponding color (orange/solid (B) left, yellow/dashed (A) right) with a representation of their field of view. The lines on the outside show the gaze cues of the participants and the center shows a representation of their field of view. The arrows indicate in which direction the gaze developed over time.

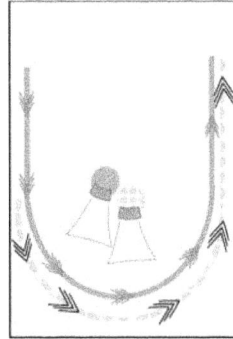

Figure 4: Depiction of a Following pattern. In this example, B is the one following and A is the leader during the search. This is shown through making the B's gaze line thinner and applying grey arrows that indicate the direction.

pattern was used to categorize the search if one participant began their motion shortly after the other participant moved and followed the other participant and the gaze cues were largely identical and did not differ from another except for the timing.

In the 3D search condition, we found three patterns:

Spinner: The "3D Spinner" pattern is similar to the Spinner described for 2D search.

Random: The "Random" search pattern refers to a search strategy in which the participants seemingly randomly and quickly looked around the search space.

Sep. Space: The "Sep. Space" (separation of space, cf. Figure 5 and Figure 6) refers to situations in which the participants only searched a specific part of the search space and neglected the other search space.
In addition to the different patterns, differences within the groups concerning the 'evolution' of the search also became apparent. The analysis of these findings is beyond the scope of this paper and will be described elsewhere.

Discussion: Analyzing MR

While the tool presented here helped us to detect patterns we may have missed otherwise, our work also points to improvements and features for the tool, which we are exploring. One area could be automatic detection of patterns. As we know the characteristics of the patterns, this can be done in real time and displayed to the researcher, who then may analyze the searches deeper. We may also add pattern learning algorithms to the tool in order to detect new patterns or expand the existing catalogue of cooperation in MR.

Another area we are looking into is the integration of audio and video into the analysis tool. Audio would be helpful to understand how participants discussed and decided on search strategies and how they coordinated their search. The integration of video would do the same for deictic communication and analyzing outer actions of the actors. We used both sources for additional analyses in this paper, and integrating them into the analysis tool would be beneficial.

Conclusion

In this paper, we presented a novel tool for the analysis of cooperative MR settings, in which people work together supported by head-mounted AR devices. With respect to the tool for analysis we presented here, we show how it enables researchers to analyze situations in which users cooperate supported by AR devices, and how it goes beyond existing means for this analysis. We also identified needs for further development of this tool. In addition, the conduction of a user study is also needed. Our future work will further investigate the aspects discussed in this paper, and we invite other researchers to help develop methods for the analysis of this setting.

Acknowledgements

We would like to thank the developers of the analysis tool and the experiment application. We would also like to thank the participants of the search experiment.

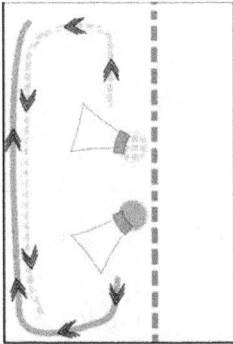

Figure 5: Depiction of the „Sep. Space (front half)". The participants only searched in the space in front of them and did not turn around wherefore the part behind their backs was not searched.

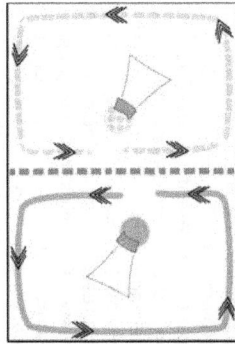

Figure 6: Depiction of "Sep. Space" with the "My Half" facet. The participants only explored the "half" of the room they were standing in.

References

1. Ronald T. Azuma. 1997. A Survey of Augmented Reality. *Presence: Teleoperators and Virtual Environments* 6, 4: 355–385.

2. Mark Billinghurst and Hirokazu Kato. 2002. Collaborative Augmented Reality. *Commun. ACM* 45, 7: 64–70.

3. Dragoş Datcu, Stephan G. Lukosch, and Heide K. Lukosch. 2016. Handheld Augmented Reality for Distributed Collaborative Crime Scene Investigation. *Proceedings of the 19th International Conference on Supporting Group Work*, ACM, 267–276.

4. Marc Pomplun, Tyler W Garaas, and Marisa Carrasco. 2013. The effects of task difficulty on visual search strategy in virtual 3D displays. *Journal of vision* 13, 3: 24–24.

5. Randy Stein and Susan E. Brennan. 2004. Another Person's Eye Gaze As a Cue in Solving Programming Problems. *Proceedings of the 6th International Conference on Multimodal Interfaces*, ACM, 9–15.

6. Yanxia Zhang, Ken Pfeuffer, Ming Ki Chong, Jason Alexander, Andreas Bulling, and Hans Gellersen. 2017. Look together: using gaze for assisting co-located collaborative search. *Personal and Ubiquitous Computing* 21, 1: 173–186.

Enhancing Collaboration in Classroom Using Smartphone in Developing Countries

Muhammad Zahid Iqbal
Information Technology University
Lahore, Pakistan
MSCS14043@itu.edu.pk

Tariq Mehmood
Virtual University of Pakistan
Tariq.ped@gmail.com

Abstract

Creating the best learning environment for students and handling a large class size is always a big challenge for the teachers in the developing countries. It creates lack of individual attention for students which resulting a higher number of dropouts in earlier school classes. Previous studies show best practices of smart technologies in the classroom. This research conducted to develop an efficient and low-cost solution to create children interaction and increasing engagement and teaching efficiency in the classroom. We developed *My Class Manager*; a Smartphone application for quiz and test marking, audio quiz for native language learning and performance management throughout the year. This application is for Android OS Smart phones. We conducted three evaluation tests of three classes of size 35, 40 and 45 students in a local school. It created a time-efficient learning environment and provided awesome feedback to develop more functionality in the application. This paper is presenting the quantitative and qualitative results of the pilot study.

Author Keywords

Design Interaction, ICT for Education, Human Centered Design, m-Learning

ACM Classification Keywords

Human Factors, Evaluation, Usability testing

Introduction

Education in the developing countries and rural areas is always a problem due to lack of resources and teachers. Due to large classes' size, teachers are unable to provide attention to students individually which leads toward poor performance.

GROUP '18, January 7–10, 2018, Sanibel Island, FL, USA
© 2018 Copyright is held by the owner/author(s).
ACM ISBN 978-1-4503-5562-9/18/01.
https://doi.org/10.1145/3148330.3154511

Smartphone is integrating rapidly in the lives. There is a big move towards the implementing these applications in the education. Distance learning has been totally changed with these applications [1]. Lots of students' engagement strategies are being adopted in the different countries which definitely bring results to a great extent [2,13,14]. Singapore & Australia have brilliant experience of ICT based solution in the early classes' school education and really get appreciated results [6,10].

Related Work

Using ICT approach lots of work done on Smartphone application to enhance the classroom learning [12]. Wankel & Charles worked with the social media, communication mediums and web 2.0 to bring an innovation in the classroom environment by developing different resources on the free hosted web [3]. Tondeur, Jo, and et al showed their finding as it is hard to implement any new technology in the classroom in the public sector because of polity restrictions [4].

Use of computer games in the classroom efficient learning [15] is tested by Ke, and Fengfeng with different goals of learning [5]. Salman Cheema, and Kurt VanLehn constructed a distributed system called FACT to facilitates the use of popular Classroom Challenges (CCs) developed by the Mathematics Assessment Project [6]. Jung, and Insung worked with ICT-Pedagogy integration in the teachers training workshop to deliver the best practices and providing ICT experience for teachers [7]. McKay, Christian designed *MakerCart* which is a mobile FabLab for the classroom to overcome the spaceand funding issues [8].

Markett, and Carina have introduced mobile phones & SMS based system to create interactivity in the classroom where students get involved with instructors using SMS [9]. Meurant, and Robert have also used SMS teaching methodology which provides quite

successful results [10]. Son Do-Lenh and Patrick Jermann suggested an ecological approach to measure the effectiveness of pervasive technologies in a classroom. They presented evaluating the *TinkerLamp*, an interactive tabletop interface to enhance the classroom ecology [11].

My Class Manager

Despite all of the above mentioned great inventions, there is no reliable work done for the classrooms of the developing countries which can create efficiency in the teaching and learning process. It creates a gap between delivery of knowledge and time efficiency. Students are losing interest in the class and increasing dropout ratio with time.

We have developed a Smartphone application named *My Class Manager* for Android OS devices which has three main features;

1. Audio Quiz/test
2. OCR based test evaluation
3. Record management
4. English Learning/Dictionary

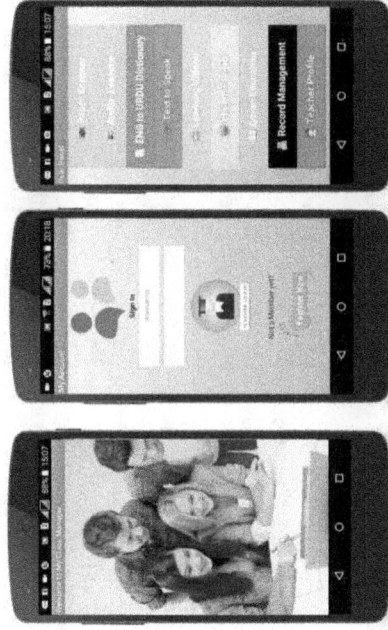

Figure 1: Right to Left, Splash Screen, Login Screen and Dashboard of Application

A server is linked with the Android application where teachers can create their quiz/tests and conduct in the classroom. When the request will be sent to the server, server will use OCR (Optical Character Recognition) to check the answer sheet with the correct answers. The concept of the audio quiz enables the teachers to manage a large class size by creating attention and delivering the quiz with native English language Ascent.

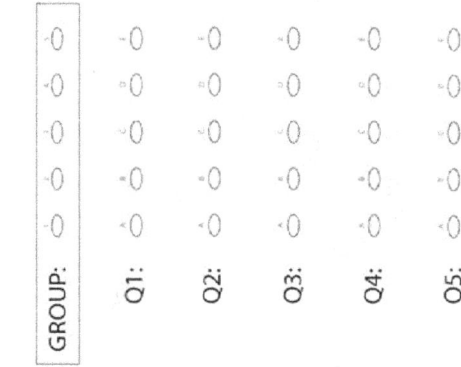

Figure 2: Sample answer sheet used for the application

Figure 3 is showing the playing of the audio quiz in the classroom. This also includes holy Quran lessons with translation for students. Teacher provides the answer sheets to the students and plays the audio quiz in the classroom as shown in Figure 3. After finishing the quiz

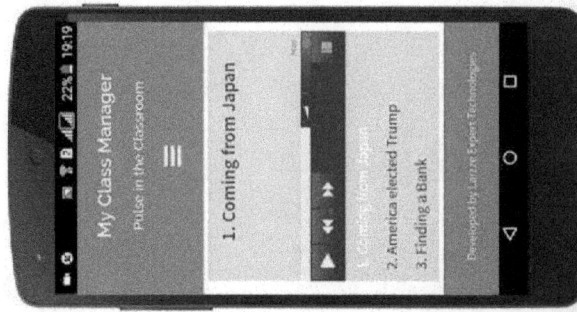

Figure 3: It shows how teacher have to play lectures/Quiz recorded by Native English Speaker in case of English Test.

time, teacher will scan the answer sheets of all the students through our application. Application sends the scanned answer sheet to server & provides the results on the base of correct answers and percentage.

Figure 4 shows how a teacher will scan the answersheet, send to the server and get response from the server with correct and wrong answers. Server provides results on the bases of the accuracy. Application saves complete record of students in the teacher's profile from where he/she can manage his classes separately. Application provides text to speak, English to Urdu dictionary for the teachers as an additional tool, shown in Figure 5.

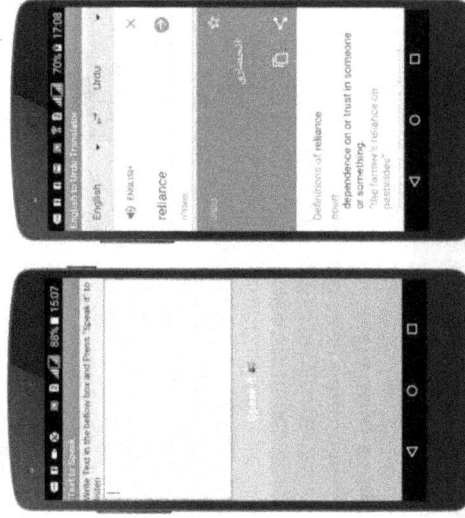

Figure 5: Showing the screenshots of built-in dictionary and text to speak for teachers

Usability Testing

To evaluate the application and measures the effectiveness of these concepts, we conducted a proper evaluation in the classrooms. Application tested in the local school with three different classes.

We conducted three tests, one in each class. These tests conducted in 6th, 7th and 8th class with class sizes of 35, 40 and 45 respectively. A Smartphone was given to every teacher with application installed inside and guided about the testing procedure of the application. Teachers were guided about the processing of the application and methodology of taking tests in classes. Contents of all the tests were taken from the syllabus of the students. Parameters used during this evaluation were time taken to completed the test and provide results and the students' behavior towards the technology interaction in the classroom. We conducted a comparison of the traditional method with the method of using our application. This data presented in Figure 6 is providing comparison of both types of tests. These tests were conducted using one page MCQ test has 30 questions in each.

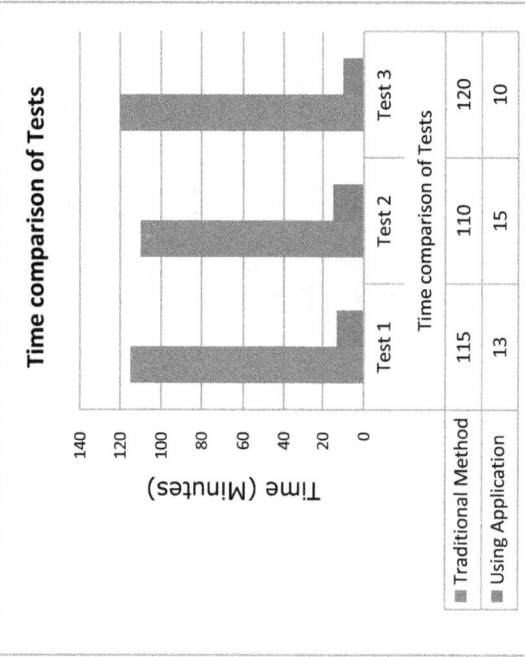

Figure 4: It shows application interface for scanning answer sheet& showing results

There were Eight (8) teachers who participated in the testing and total about 120 students who tested through application based testing. Students participated in the evaluation are 12-16 years old and belong 6th, 7th and 8th classes.

As per our evaluation data presented in Figure 6, checking class tests/quiz manually takes 100-120 Minutes while using or application it takes 10-15 minutes. This time was included spreading answer sheets and checking using application. It saved about two hours just for a simple test which helped us to evaluate the students' performance easily and provided whole class average results.

Teachers participated in evaluations had 3-7 years experience in teaching English and science subjects. As explained by a teacher who has about seven years experience in teaching English says, "*Students love technology interaction in the classroom as compared to traditional methods.*"As test evaluation is one of the most troublesome tasks for the teacher and many teachers never like to conduct quiz/tests because of this difficulty.

Conclusion

As per our consistent goal to create better classroom engagement and time efficient delivery of knowledge by latest technology integration, we have found great results. Adaptation interests from the teachers helped us to measure the solution efficiency in solving the problem. Children showed a great attraction towards this solution as a new approach in the class as a new method of teaching.

Class test & Quiz marking performance and regular assessment of the large size classes highly improved which is one of the basic needs for teachers. As for generating progress reports for parents and management of students' data for the whole years need lots of time with manual working, *My Class Manager* can do this work without any effort. We are working to develop more functionality in the application which can help the teacher more comprehensively and bring more interactivity in the classroom.

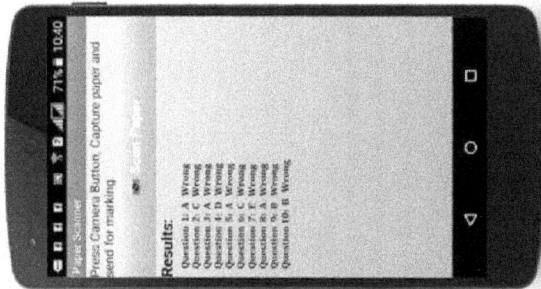

Time comparison of Tests

	Test 1	Test 2	Test 3
		Time comparison of Tests	
Traditional Method	115	110	120
Using Application	13	15	10

Figure 6: Time comparison between both methods used to evaluate the solution in three classes.

References

1. Paris, Scott G., and Alison H. Paris. *Classroom applications of research on self-regulated learning. Educational psychologist* 36.2 (2001): 89-101.

2. Christenson, Sandra L., Amy L. Reschly, and Cathy Wylie, eds. *Handbook of research on student engagement.* Springer Science & Business Media, 2012.

3. Wankel, Charles, and Patrick Blessinger. *Increasing student engagement and retention in e-learning environments: Web 2.0 and blended learning technologies.* Vol. 6. Emerald Group Publishing, 2013.

4. Tondeur, Jo, et al. *ICT integration in the classroom: Challenging the potential of a school policy. Computers & Education* 51.1 (2008): 212-223.

5. Ke, Fengfeng. *Computer games application within alternative classroom goal structures: cognitive, metacognitive, and affective evaluation. Educational Technology Research and Development* 56.5-6 (2008): 539-556.

6. Cheema, Salman, et al. *Electronic posters to support formative assessment.* Proceedings of the 2016 CHI Conference Extended Abstracts on Human Factors in Computing Systems. ACM, 2016.

7. Jung, Insung. *ICT-Pedagogy Integration in Teacher Training: Application Cases Worldwide. Educational Technology & Society* 8.2 (2005): 94-101.

8. McKay, Christian, and Kylie Peppler. *MakerCart: A mobile fab lab for the classroom. Position Paper at the Interaction Design for Children Conference (IDC).* 2013.

9. Markett, Carina, et al. *Using short message service to encourage interactivity in the classroom. Computers & Education* 46.3 (2006): 280-293.

10. Meurant, Robert C. *Cell Phones in the L2 Classroom: Thumbs up to SMS.* 2006 International Conference on Hybrid Information Technology. Vol. 1. IEEE, 2006.

11. Do-Lenh, Son, et al. *Classroom-experience evaluation: Evaluating pervasive technologies in a classroom setting. Child Computer Interaction: Workshop on UI Technologies and Their Impact on Educational Pedagogy,* the ACM International Conference on Human Factors in Computing Systems (CHI 11). No. EPFL-CONF-164658. 2011.

12. Thomas, Kevin M., Blanche W. O'Bannon, and Natalie Bolton. "Cell phones in the classroom: Teachers' perspectives of inclusion, benefits, and barriers." *Computers in the Schools* 30.4 (2013): 295-308.

13. Yamamoto, Noriyasu. "An Interactive Learning System Using Smartphone: Improving Students' Learning Motivation and Self-Learning." *Broadband and Wireless Computing, Communication and Applications (BWCCA), 2014 Ninth International Conference on.* IEEE, 2014.

14. Brotherton, Jason A., and Gregory D. Abowd. "Lessons learned from eClass: Assessing automated capture and access in the classroom." *ACM Transactions on Computer-Human Interaction (TOCHI)* 11.2 (2004): 121-155.

15. Alvarado, Diego. "Supporting non-formal learning through co-design of social games with children." *Proceedings of the 11th International Conference on Interaction Design and Children.* ACM, 2012.

Understanding Book Popularity on Goodreads

Suman Kalyan Maity
Dept. of CSE
IIT Kharagpur, India
sumankalyan.maity@
cse.iitkgp.ernet.in

Ayush Kumar
Dept. of CSE
IIT Kharagpur, India
ayush235317@gmail.com

Ankan Mullick
Bing
Microsoft India
ankan.mullick@microsoft.com

Vishnu Choudhary
Dept. of CSE
IIT Kharagpur, India
bansal.jhs@gmail.com

Animesh Mukherjee
Dept. of CSE
IIT Kharagpur, India
animeshm@cse.iitkgp.ernet.in

Copyright held by the owner/author(s).
GROUP '18, January 7–10, 2018, Sanibel Island, FL, USA
ACM 978-1-4503-5562-9/18/01.
https://doi.org/10.1145/3148330.3154512

Abstract

Goodreads has launched the Readers Choice Awards since 2009 where users are able to nominate/vote books of their choice, released in the given year. In this work, we question if the number of votes that a book would receive (aka the popularity of the book) can be predicted based on the characteristics of various entities on Goodreads. We are successful in predicting the popularity of the books with high prediction accuracy (correlation coefficient ~0.61) and low RMSE (~1.25). User engagement and author's prestige are found to be crucial factors for book popularity.

Author Keywords

book popularity; Goodreads; prediction

ACM Classification Keywords

H.4.m [Information Systems Applications]: Miscellaneous; J.4 [Computer Applications]: [Social and Behavioral Sciences]; K.4.2 [Computers And Society]: [Social Issues]

Introduction

Popularity/success of a book is important not only for the authors but also for the publishers, the professional book reviewers and the book selling platforms like Amazon, eBay etc. The initial popularity of books can have a significant impact how the eventual sales would be [5]. Understanding book popularity is a difficult task even for an expert working

Related Work

Predicting popularity of content on social media has been widely researched. Most of these studies focus on popularity prediction of various Twitter specific entities. Extensively studied among these being the hashtags. Tsur and Rappoport [7] studied popularity of hashtags based on content features of tweets only. Ma et al. in [4] proposed a framework for predicting popularity of newly emerging hashtags. Kong et al. [2] studied the burstiness (sudden rise in hashtag usage and quick fall thereafter) of hashtag on a temporal scale. Maity et al. [6] studied various factors affecting the popularity of hashtag compounds (two or more hashtags merging together). In a recent work by Maity et al. [5], the authors have studied how book reading behavior on Goodreads can determine Amazon Best Sellers.

in the publication industries. Some of the eventual award winners and best sellers have gone through one or multiple rejections before being finally accepted by a certain publisher. There are potentially many influencing factors that can impact popularity of a book. Broadly these factors can be categorized into (i) intrinsic and (ii) extrinsic factors. Intrinsic factors correspond to the content and the quality of the book like how interesting the book is, how engaging the story line is, novelty, style of writing etc. However, these quality factors of the books are very different for different genres. For example, a successful thriller requires a credible story-line, complex twists and plots, escalating stakes and tension whereas a popular romantic novel demands demonstration of strong and healthy relationship, sexual tension, happy and optimistic endings etc. A great mystery novel involves secrets, misdirection of clues, a relatable protagonist etc. [1]. Therefore, finding common grounds is difficult for quantification of the quality aspects for different genres. On the other hand, extrinsic factors include the readers' reading behaviors, social contexts, reviews by the critics etc. which are relatively easier to obtain. In this paper, we shall consider the readers' reading, reviewing characteristics for the books, engagement activities, authors' prestige etc. to understand book popularity in Goodreads. Specifically, we are interested in predicting book votes as a popularity metric.

Goodreads is a community-driven social cataloging site which has grown exponentially into one of the most popular social book reading and recommendation sites. Goodreads provides various opportunities like quizzes, trivia apart from social book reading so as to engage their users. Goodreads Readers Choice Award is such an attempt. This was first launched in 2009. From then on, Goodreads users can take part in deciding the recipients of this award by nominating as well as by voting for their nominations. There

are 20 categories like Fiction, Thrillers, Fantasy, Romance etc. of awards and in each category 15 official nominations are made. In the first round of voting, users can nominate books to be included in the awards as write-in candidates; five in each category get added to the group of official nominees, making the total 20 in each category. Using APIs and automated crawls, we gathered all the books' data prior to the start of the voting phase. In table 1, we show all the award categories.

Present work: In this study, we aim to determine the salient factors from various Goodreads entities that contribute to the popularity of books in terms of the number of votes they receive. Towards this objective, we have considered collective user engagement behavior and show that this is an important aspect to understand book popularity alongside author's prestige. The user engagements toward books characterized by the rating/review behavior, shelve characterization and organization - a very unique utility that the Goodreads platform provides to its users, are important determinant. Further, we observe that author's prestige features like – the avg. rating of an author, the number of awards received by an author of a book etc. are crucial to the book popularity.

Fiction	History & Biography
Mystery & Thriller	Science & Technology
Historical Fiction	Food & Cookbooks
Fantasy	Graphic Novels & Comics
Romance	Poetry
Science Fiction	Debut Goodreads Author
Horror	Young Adult Fiction
Humor	Young Adult Fantasy
NonFiction	Middle Grade & Children's
Memoir & Autobiography	Picture Books

Table 1: Award Categories

Discriminative features:

We use $RELIEFF$ feature selection algorithm [3] to rank the attributes. In table 2, we show the rank of the features in terms of their discriminative power for prediction. The rank order clearly indicates the dominance of the user engagement features, however author's rating seems to be the most discriminative feature. In the top 10, three of the author features find place. Among engagement features, shelve diversity, no. of books in 'read' or 'currently-reading' shelve are the important factors for popularity prediction. This suggest that Goodreads' user engagement is crucial factor for popularity prediction. Among author features, apart from rating of the author, other prestige features of the authors like no. of awards received, no. of rating received, no. of best sellers act as prominent popularity prediction features.

Factors behind Book Popularity:

In this section, we try to understand various factors driving book popularity. We consider two major types of factors: User engagement towards books - these includes various user engagement characteristics toward books like rating, reviewing, organizing in shelves etc. Author characteristics - these factors are related to the prestige of an author of a nominated book. Subsequently we shall use them as features to our prediction model.

User Engagement:

These factors are extracted from various characteristic properties of Goodreads' user engagement toward books which we have already studied earlier.

- Average rating of the book given by the users.
- Number of ratings given by the users.
- Number of 4-star ratings given to the book.
- Number of 5-star ratings given to the book.
- User rating entropy of the book.
- Number of reviews received by the users.
- Review Sentiments - We take only 30 reviews of the books and use NLTK sentiment analysis tool[1] to find sentiment of the reviews. We then take the avg. positive sentiment score, negative sentiment score, neutral sentiment score and standard deviation of these sentiment scores as features to our model. In total, we have six set of features here.
- Number of genres of the book.
- Number of different user shelves the book is present in.
- Shelve diversity of the book - Similar to rating entropy,

we calculate shelve diversity. Formally, shelve diversity (ShelveDiv) is defined as follows:

$$ShelveDiv(b) = - \sum_{j \in shelve_{s}et} s_j \times \log(s_j)$$

where s_j is the probability that the book belongs to the jth user shelve in the set of user bookshelves.

- Number of users who have added the book in 'currently reading' or 'read' shelves.
- Number of users who have added the book in 'to read' shelves.

Author Characteristics:

These factors are extracted from various characteristic properties (mostly prestige) of the authors of the nominated book.

- Number of books written by the author of the book.
- Average rating of the author of the book.
- Number of ratings received by the author of the book.
- Number of reviews received by the author of the book.
- Number of distinct awards received by the author.
- Number of 'best seller' books of the author.
- Follower count of the author.
- Number of common shelves among the authors' books.
- Number of unique shelves among the authors' shelves.

Rank	Features
1	Avg. rating of the author
2	Shelve Diversity
3	No. of users who have added the book in 'currently reading' or 'read' shelves
4	No. of awards received by the author
5	No. of different shelves the book is present in
6	No. of users who have added the book in 'to-read' shelves
7	Rating Entropy of the book
8	No. of reviews received by the book
9	No. of 5-star ratings received by the book
10	No. of ratings received by the author

Table 2: Top 10 predictive features.

---

[1] http://text-processing.com/demo/sentiment/

Prediction Framework

We shall now use the above user engagement and author characteristics as features for our prediction model.

We consider 400 books from all the 20 award categories of Goodreads Choice Award in 2015 for our prediction task. We perform a 10-fold cross-validation on the data sample. We use Support Vector Regression (SVR) for the prediction. For evaluating how good the prediction is, we use Pearson correlation coefficient (r) and root mean square error (RMSE). We achieve high correlation coefficient (~ 0.61) and low root mean square error (~ 1.25). We observe that user engagement feature type is the strongest feature type contributing to correlation coefficient of 0.59 with RMSE value of 1.29 whereas with only author features, we achieve corr. coeff. of 0.44 and RMSE value of 1.41.

Predicting the votes of the highly voted books:

Apart from overall prediction of the votes for the book nominations, we also investigate how our model performs in predicting the votes of the highly voted books. In specific, we ask if the features are able to suitably discriminate these books and if the predictions for them are better or worse than the overall prediction. We observe that our prediction model can very well predict the highly voted books' vote and the correlation coefficient is always higher than the overall case (see table 3). For predicting the votes of the top 3 most voted books, our model achieves a very high correlation coefficient of 0.83 (although the RMSE value goes a bit higher).

Award category specific prediction:

We further categorize the books into the Award categories to investigate whether such categorization helps in improving the prediction accuracy. For prediction of votes of the books in each category, we train the prediction model on all the books except for the books belonging to that category.

The set of books in this category acts as a test set for the prediction task. In table 4, we show the results of the prediction. In most of the categories, we observe significant improvement in prediction accuracy from the case with no categorization. We also observe that in some award categories, prediction accuracies fall e.g., Romance, Science & Technology, Memoir & Autobiography, Graphic Novels & Comics etc.

Conclusions and Implications

In summary, we propose a framework for predicting popularity (no. of votes) of books. Our proposed model achieves a high ccorrelation coefficient ∼0.61 with low RMSE (∼1.25). We observe that the user engagement features are the most discriminative ones compared to the others. Our prediction framework can predict votes of the highly voted books with higher accuracy than the above base case. The stratification of the books into award categories further enhances the prediction accuracies for most of the categories significantly.

Our research has important implications. It shows that initial rating, reviewing, user engagement features obtained from collective Goodreads user behavior along with authors' prestige can efficiently determine popularity of books. Our proposed system can early predict book popularity using these above features which can be easily obtainable. This early prediction can be effective in several ways - (i) act as guide for recommending appropriate books to the new users joining Goodreads and, (ii) help the book selling platforms like Amazon, eBay by forecasting early the eventual fate of a book/group of books/genre so that these platforms are able to launch proper and focused advertisements/promotional campaigns to boost up the sales.

Table 3: Prediction results for the highly voted books

	Corr. Coeff.(r)	RMSE
top 100	0.66	2.72
top 50	0.63	1.56
top 20	0.75	1.15
top 10	0.68	1.04
top 5	0.7	1.17
top 3	0.83	2.2

Table 4: Prediction results for the Award category specific prediction

Category	r	RMSE
Fiction	0.76	0.83
Mystery & Thriller	0.69	1.08
Historical Fiction	0.84	1.15
Fantasy	0.82	0.89
Romance	0.49	1.63
Science Fiction	0.67	1.19
Horror	0.73	1.11
Humor	0.7	1.25
NonFiction	0.7	1.33
Memoir & Autobiography	0.48	1.18
History & Biography	0.66	1.08
Science & Technology	0.41	1.3
Food & Cookbooks	0.61	1.77
Graphic Novels & Comics	0.39	1.39
Poetry	0.52	1.59
Debut Goodreads Author	0.87	0.82
Young Adult Fiction	0.8	0.86
Young Adult Fantasy	0.79	1.46
Middle Grade & Children's	0.61	1.2
Picture Books	0.66	1.38

REFERENCES

1. James W Hall. 2012. *Hit Lit: Cracking the Code of the Twentieth Century's Biggest Bestsellers.* Random House.

2. Shoubin Kong, Qiaozhu Mei, Ling Feng, Fei Ye, and Zhe Zhao. 2014. Predicting Bursts and Popularity of Hashtags in Real-time. In *Proc. of SIGIR.* 927–930.

3. Igor Kononenko, Edvard Simec, and Marko Robnik-Sikonja. 1997. Overcoming the myopia of inductive learning algorithms with RELIEFF. *Applied Intelligence* 7 (1997), 39–55.

4. Zongyang Ma, Aixin Sun, and Gao Cong. 2013. On predicting the popularity of newly emerging hashtags in Twitter. *JASIST* (2013), 1399–1410.

5. Suman Kalyan Maity, Abhishek Panigrahi, and Animesh Mukherjee. 2017. Book Reading Behavior on Goodreads Can Predict the Amazon Best Sellers. In *Proc. of ASONAM.*

6. Suman Kalyan Maity, Ritvik Saraf, and Animesh Mukherjee. 2016. #Bieber + #Blast = #BieberBlast: Early Prediction of Popular Hashtag Compounds. In *Proc. of CSCW.*

7. Oren Tsur and Ari Rappoport. 2012. What's in a Hashtag?: Content Based Prediction of the Spread of Ideas in Microblogging Communities. In *Proc. of WSDM.* 643–652.

MobiAssist - ICT-based Training System for People with Dementia and their Caregivers: Results from a Field Study

David Unbehaun

University of Siegen

Kohlbettstraße 15; 57072 Siegen, Germany

David.unbehaun@uni-siegen.de

Daryoush Vaziri

University of applied sciences Bonn-Rhein-Sieg

Grantham-Allee 20; 53757 St. Augustin

Daryoush.vaziri@h-brs.de

Konstantin Aal

University of Siegen

Kohlbettstraße 15; 57072 Siegen, Germany

Konstantin.aal@uni-siegen.de

Qinyu Li

University of Siegen

Kohlbettstraße 15; 57072 Siegen, Germany

Qinyu.li@uni-siegen.de

Rainer Wieching

University of Siegen

Kohlbettstraße 15; 57072 Siegen, Germany

Rainer.wieching@uni-siegen.de

Volker Wulf

University of Siegen

Kohlbettstraße 15; 57072 Siegen, Germany

Volker.wulf@uni-siegen.de

Abstract

As a result of ageing societies, the prevalence of dementia, and accordingly the need of care is increasing rapidly. Here, the use of ICT-based technologies may facilitate and promote a self-sustaining life-style for people with dementia and their caregivers. The presented poster describes early findings from the project MobiAssist and outlines the ICT-based training system. The system aims to increase the physical and cognitive capabilities of people with dementia, relief the caregivers and improve wellbeing of involved parties.

Author Keywords

Dementia; exergame; ICT; participatory design; social support; caregivers; field study

ACM Classification Keywords

J.3. LIFE AND MEDICAL SCIENCES. Health

Introduction

Demographic transition, especially in industrialized nations increases the risk of dementia disease in older adults and their need for health care services. Such health care services often involve not only professional caregivers, but relatives and informal caregivers as well. From an economic and social perspective, concepts and services to ease the burden for affected older adults, as well as for involved stakeholders are required. A promising approach here is the design of interventions to increase physical activity in older adults with dementia. Studies show that physical training improves mental health [1], cognitive performance (e.g. information processing, coordination,) [2] and physical performance [3] and thereby improve the daily competence of patients with dementia [1][4].

However, a major challenge remains long-term adherence to such interventions and their practical use in older adults with dementia [5]. A promising solution could be the integration of technology-based interventions into the daily life's of people with dementia. ICT can be a key element in terms of supporting health, social participation, safety and communication, with the overall aim to enable them a self-determined life [6][7]. Anderson-Hanley et al. assert that through use of exergames, cognitive

efficiency of older adults can be trained in a better way than with conventional exercises [8]. Exergames can effectively be utilized to improve physical and intellectual capacities for older adults [9][10].

The authors present results from an exploratory field study with an early prototype of an ICT-based training system that was tested with people with dementia and their caregivers. Early results from an 8-month field study with 31 semi-structured interviews and 70 moderated group-sessions are presented.

Methods and Data

The study was conducted in three day-care facilities and ambulatory care environments with older adults suffering from dementia. The aim of the study was to investigate the integration of an ICT-based training system into the daily routines of people with dementia and their informal and professional caregivers over a longer period of time (in total 8-months). Here, relevant aspects concentrate on sustainable effects of exergames on individual performance and social interaction. First, we conducted interviews with people with dementia, their relatives and other stakeholders such as caregivers, therapists and doctors to gain meaningful insights about the participants' daily routines, their biographical background, memory and social environment, and therapeutically successful field test methods and instruments. During the following exploratory study, we evaluated the system over a period of 34 weeks with three participants with early stage of dementia at their home setting and in three day-care centres in a group setting, where the authors trained with three to five participants with early to medium dementia in weekly sessions.

Figure 1: Using the system with other family members

System Overview

Within the project MobiAssist[1], we developed an ICT based training system to support daily life activities of people with dementia and their caregivers. The training exercises address physical, creative and cognitive areas.

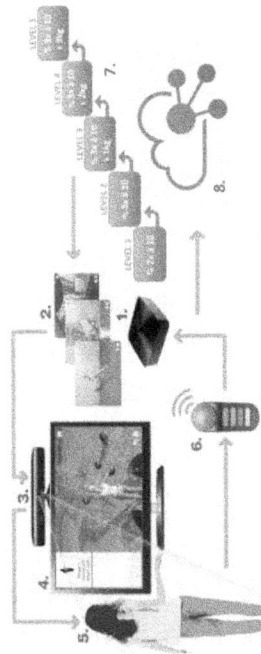

Figure 2: System overview

The system consists of several technical components that are centralised around the TV, having in mind that older adults watch more television and use less novel ICT compared to the younger generation. The motion-sensing-based exercise training program is running on a space-saving and quiet mini-computer to reduce the disturbances of using too much technology. Currently, a MS Kinect is used to detect the motions of the participant while interacting with the system, but the open implementation will allow other cameras to be used as well. To simplify the interaction with the overall system, a tablet and a PlayStation 3 Buzzer were used. The tablet shows the current exercise plan, the results of the different games and education material about the disease, while the Buzzer with its big colourful buttons is used as input device during the games.

Early Findings

The findings indicate that the participants and caregivers benefited in different dimensions. Most of the participants were able to improve their physical abilities, e.g. improvements in gait, coordination, mobility, balance and stability. These results are further complemented by the promotion of cognitive abilities that were observed with the patients, in terms of learning effects, fostered memories, increased self-consciousness and faster reaction time. In addition to the benefits for people with dementia, the relatives benefited from the use of the system, for instance by supporting the daily routines, gaining more leisure time and decreasing physical and emotional stress resulting from care. Furthermore, informal and professional caregivers recommend the ICT-system as a permanent feature at home and in day-care centers. The findings also illustrated social impacts induced by using the system. Participants developed a strong sense of advanced social collaborations. By integrating strength training, balance games and creative exergames into the daily routines and activities in their familiar environment, as well as into the day-care facilities of people with dementia, existing family and friend relationships have been strengthened, intergenerational exchange happened and therefore social responsibility was regained, and general social interaction increased. Participants showed strong motivation and enthusiasm, initiated learning processes, collaborated and understood the underlying concept of the exergames and its content.

Conclusion and Outlook

Our study has shown that participants who were involved in the exploratory study were motivated to move and exercise in front of the system either at

---

[1] http://mobiassist.info/

home or in the day-care centre setting. Feedback from the participant itself but also other stakeholders were positive with regard to the general movement and cognitive capabilities, social and cross-generative interaction, safety and therefore a relief for informal and professional caregivers. The authors can conclude that a successful integration of the system into daily routines and ongoing interaction led to positive effects such as a declining dependence in general care-activities. The results from this qualitative oriented study have illustrated that ICT-based training system for daily life support is able to increase self-confidence and social wellbeing of the relevant actors and creates opportunities to facilitate a self-determined and dignified aging. The authors presented novel empirical results and meaningful insights regarding the combination of classical intervention and daily creative and cognitive established therapy that were incorporated into an integrative ICT-based training system. The system has been evaluated over a longer period in ambulatory and day-care setting. Future research activities will analyse further usage and acceptance indicators of ICT-based training systems to support daily life of people with dementia and their caregivers and in addition, will elaborate on the challenges and requirements of IT-design processes with and for people with dementia. In this context, we therefore aim to conduct different evaluation studies across various cities in Germany.

Acknowledgements

The authors would like to thank all participants for their attendance and participation in this study. This work was partly funded by a grant of the German Ministry of Education and Research (BMBF, grant no. 16SV7330).

References

[1] P. Heyn, B. C. Abreu, and K. J. Ottenbacher, "The effects of exercise training on elderly persons with cognitive impairment and dementia: A meta-analysis," *Arch. Phys. Med. Rehabil.*, vol. 85, no. 10, pp. 1694–1704, 2004.

[2] S. Colcombe and A. F. Kramer, "Fitness effects on the cognitive function of older adults: A meta-analytic study," *Psychol. Sci.*, vol. 14, no. 2, pp. 125–130, 2003.

[3] K. Hauer, M. Schwenk, T. Zieschang, M. Essig, C. Becker, and P. Oster, "Physical training improves motor performance in people with dementia: a randomized controlled trial," *J. Am. Geriatr. Soc.*, vol. 60, no. 1, pp. 8–15, 2012.

[4] L. D. Baker *et al.*, "Aerobic exercise improves cognition for older adults with glucose intolerance, a risk factor for Alzheimer's disease," *J. Alzheimers Dis.*, vol. 22, no. 2, pp. 569–579, 2010.

[5] C. G. u.a. Blankevoort, "Review of Effects of Physical Activity on Strength, Balance, Mobility and ADL Performance in Elderly Subjects with Dementia," *Dement. Geriatr. Cogn. Disord.*, vol. 30, no. 5, pp. 392–402, 2010.

[6] P. H. Robert *et al.*, "Recommendations for the use of Serious Games in people with Alzheimer's Disease, related disorders and frailty," *Front. Aging Neurosci.*, vol. 6, p. 54, 2014.

[7] Wan, L., Müller, C., Wulf, V., Randall, D., "Addressing the Subtleties in Dementia Care: Pre-study & Evaluation of a GPS Monitoring System,"

in *CHI 2014*, New York, NY, 2014, pp. 3987–3996.

[8] C. Anderson-Hanley *et al.*, "Exergaming and older adult cognition: A cluster randomized clinical trial," *Am. J. Prev. Med.*, vol. 42, no. 2, pp. 109–119, 2012.

[9] J. A. Anguera *et al.*, "Video game training enhances cognitive control in older adults," *Nature*, vol. 501, no. 7465, pp. 97–101, 2013.

[10] J. Wiemeyer and A. Kliem, "Serious games in prevention and rehabilitation—a new panacea for elderly people?," *Eur. Rev. Aging Phys. Act.*, vol. 9, no. 1, pp. 41–50, Apr. 2012.

Why Did They #Unfollow Me? Early Detection of Follower Loss on Twitter

Suman Kalyan Maity
Dept. of CSE
IIT Kharagpur, India
sumankalyan.maity@cse.iitkgp.ernet.in

Ramanth Gajula
Dept. of CSE
IIT Kharagpur, India
ramanth139@gmail.com

Animesh Mukherjee
Dept. of CSE
IIT Kharagpur, India
animeshm@cse.iitkgp.ernet.in

GROUP '18, January 7–10, 2018, Sanibel Island, FL, USA
ACM 978-1-4503-5562-9/18/01.
https://doi.org/10.1145/3148330.3154514

Abstract

Having more followers has become a norm in recent social media and micro-blogging communities. This battle has been taking shape from the early days of Twitter. Despite this strong competition for followers, many Twitter users are continuously losing their followers. This work addresses the problem of identifying the reasons behind the drop of followers of users in Twitter. As a first step, we extract various features by analyzing the *content of the posts* made by the Twitter users who lose followers consistently. We then leverage these features to early detect follower loss. We propose various models and yield an overall accuracy of 73% with high precision and recall. Our model outperforms baseline model by 19.67% (w.r.t accuracy), 33.8% (w.r.t precision) and 14.3% (w.r.t recall).

Author Keywords

unfollow; social media; prediction

ACM Classification Keywords

H.4.m [Information Systems Applications]: Miscellaneous; J.4 [Computer Applications]: [Social and Behavioral Sciences]; K.4.2 [Computers And Society]: [Social Issues]

Introduction

Followership of users in social media is an important factor since it indicates social prestige and popularity for the

Dataset preparation We construct our dataset through web-based crawls of the profile information of 9.3 million users at two different time points – i) June 2014 and ii) September 2016. We then select those users who have at least 1000 followers in June 2014 and lost some followers by September 2016. We create two datasets based on followership gain/loss characteristics. *Dataset1* consists of users who lost at least 30% of their followers. *Dataset2* has users who lost at most 2% followers plus users who gained at most 2% followers. Our objective here is to identify features that discriminate this set (which corresponds to mostly accidental loss/gain of followers) from the set of users who incur a real loss of followers (i.e., *dataset1*). We further remove those users who did not tweet in English. We then randomly sample out 8000 users from *dataset1* and a similar number of users from *dataset2* for the subsequent study.

users. Followers have a proportional impact on how far and wide one's message spreads and the rate at which one can get social recognition in form of reposts, shares, likes etc.[1] It helps in outreach, helps in forming new social relationships. Though people have studied followership gain, there are very few studies that looked into the other side of the spectrum of this online relationship - the "unfollowing" behavior. Like gain in followership, followership loss has also important social connotation and business implications. Twitter or other social media are extensively used by media houses, various industry outlets from technology to fashion, political personalities. Therefore, followership loss of such entities could mean decrease in face value and which could directly/indirectly impact business. For instance, boxer cum politician, Manny Pacquiao lost 2 million followers over his gay comments[2], Indian prime minister Narendra Modi reportedly lost 313,312 followers after announcing demonetization of 500 and 1000 notes[3]. In our dataset containing 9.3 million Twitter users, 26% of the users are found to have suffered a net loss in a two years span. For instance, a user from our dataset who had 114K followers, tweeted only about mundane details of his day to day activities and therefore lost 85 percent of his followers. Another user who had 176K followers, lost 55% of his followers most likely because the tweets mostly portray political propaganda and the tweet frequency is as high as ∼ 200 tweets per day. Though both gain/loss in followership can be contextual to different relationships and situations, however, in this work we try to find holistically what factors - like *social behavior, textual content of posts, language usage and network structure* - lead to follower loss.

Related work: There have been few studies done by researchers to understand the dynamics of unfollowing in various OSNs. Kwak et al. [3] reported that 43% of active users unfollow at least once during 51 days. Twitter users have unfollowed those users who left many tweets within a short time, created tweets about uninteresting topics, or tweeted about the mundane details of their lives [2, 5]. Also Twitter users appreciate receiving more attention than giving when it comes to mentions, retweets etc., and this is pronounced in the act of unfollow [3]. Another popular mode of unfollowing in Twitter is burst unfollowing [6]. In this work, we propose models for early prediction of loss of followers on Twitter mainly focusing on the content and the language usage in the tweets posted by the users. In specific, we make use of the activities and the content of the tweets of the victim (i.e., the person losing the followers) only. Building such a model would enable the victim early in time to know the specific online behavior that could result in followership loss. Having such succinct clues can guide the victim as to how to contain his/her behavior to avoid loss of followers (which is usually very hard to accumulate).

Factors behind follower loss

The factors below attempt to extract the textual content and the language usage behavior of the victims.

Use of offensive/profane words in tweets: We use a list of offensive and profane words from https://www.cs.cmu.edu/~biglou/resources/bad-words.txt and manually label their offensive/badness score. We calculate badness influence per tweet as the sum of badness of the words used in the tweet normalized by the number of words in the tweet. The average badness influence of all the tweets of a user gives the *badness coefficient* of a user.

Repetitive content: word diversity: Repetitive content

---

[1] https://blog.bufferapp.com/definitive-guide-social-media-metrics-stats
[2] http://bit.ly/2yFnnHF
[3] http://bit.ly/2gxAzls

Tweet bursts: Bursts of tweets sometimes draw an unwanted attention in Twitter. An example of tweet burst includes a long story posted as a continuum of tweets. Twenty out of 22 respondents reported that they unfollowed 39 people because of burst tweets [2]. Consider the array T_u of tweets of a user u sorted according to the tweet arrival time. We define tweet burst as a maximal sub-array $T_u[i..j] \mid \forall k, i \leq k < j, t(k+1) - t(k) \leq 1000$ where $t(k)$ denotes the arrival time of the kth tweet of the user u. Time period of a burst $T_u[i..j]$ is defined as $t(j) - t(i)$. In the equation 1000 is a chosen hyper parameter. We use the following set of features extracted from tweet bursts - *mean inter-burst arrival time, avg. time period of a burst, max. time period of a burst, minimum time period of a burst, no. of bursts.*

Tweet length: We observe that users with tweets having very short length and users with tweets occupying most of the allowed space, are more likely to lose followers.

is considered generally as boring in social media, unless the content is very trendy. Let T_u be the multi-set of words from all the filtered tweets of user u and W be the set of all unique words in T_u and $p(w|T_u)$ be the probability of word w belonging to T_u. We now define content diversity as $ContentDiv(u) = -\sum_{w \in W} p(w|T_u) \times log(p(w|T_u))$

Topic diversity: Topic diversity also captures the notion of repetitive content by finding topics in the tweets of user rather than directly using the words. We use LDA [1], for the discovery of latent subtopics and calculate the topical diversity for an user u as $TopDiv(u) = -\sum_{k=1}^{K} p(topic_k|T_u) \times log(p(topic_k|T_u))$ where T_u denotes the set of tweets as a document for user u.

Tweet rate: In Twitter, users would hardly want their feeds to be overflown by the tweets from a single other user. We capture this notion using the rate at which a given user is tweeting which simply is the time difference of the first and the last tweets of the user normalized by the total number of tweets so far (in the data) of the user.

Mentions per tweet: We calculate *MentionCoeff* as the average number of mentions per tweet. Users who *mention* infrequently are able to less engage other users and might get unfollowed.

Mention entropy: The *MentionCoeff* measure might implicitly (and incorrectly) indicate that a particular user u, who mentions only a small set of people very frequently, is very less probable of losing followers. However, these users might also be prone to losing followers. For example, users who follow 1000 people communicate with only about 70 people on average [2]. We capture this notion by using *MentionEntropy*. Let M be the list of distinct users mentioned by user u and let $p(m \mid u)$ denote the probability with which user u mentions user m in his/her tweets. So,

$$MentionEntropy(u) = -\sum_{m \in M} p(m|u) \times log(p(m|u))$$

Users who have a low mention entropy are more from *dataset1* indicating that users engaging only a particular set of other users in their tweets repeatedly are prone to lose more followers in future.

Usage of urls in tweets: Urls are popular in Twitter community for redirection. However, excessive usage of urls is usually not encouraged in the community because that is often interpreted as spamming. Users of *dataset1* have more average url count per tweet indicating that people who use excessive urls are prone to loss of followers.

Profile description and verification status of user: Profile description renders authenticity to a user profile. Interestingly, in our dataset, users who had profile description were less likely to lose followers. Verification status is also an important factor. Verified users usually have a net gain of followers. 90% of the total verified users gained followers in our dataset.

Network features We have constructed the following two networks - a) mention network b) content similarity network of the users in the dataset.

a) Mention Network: We consider the mention network of users in the full dataset where the nodes are the users and a directed edge is created from a to b if a mentions b at least once in his/her tweets. Only those users who have their (in-degree + out-degree) > 0 are included in the network. ~17% of users from both datasets combined are present in this mention network. We have used various centrality and clustering based features (appropriately scaled) –*in-degree centrality, out-degree centrality, betweenness centrality, closeness centrality, eigenvector centrality, clustering coefficient* from this network.

Psycholinguistic aspects of tweets

We also perform psycholinguistic analysis of the tweets to observe if there exists any pattern leading to follower loss. The cognitive, linguistic and psychological dimensions are captured through different categories provided by the LIWC tool [7]. There are 64 different categories that LIWC extracts from the tweet texts. First, we collect the words related to each of these 64 categories. Next, we find for each category c, the number of words in the tweets of user u which belong to the category c and normalize this value by the total number of tweets of the user u. Some of the key points to note here are that users who lose more followers use more negation words, less inclusive words as well as less insightful words.

b) Content similarity network:

We consider the tweets of the users as bag-of-words. We then compute user-user similarity using the Jaccard co-efficient between the tweets. We then construct a network with nodes as users and edges indicating similarity between word usage of users. Through inspection of the distribution of similarities, we prune those edges with similarity values less than 0.3. In the resulting graph, the similarity feature for a user is extracted as follows: for a node n, all the neighboring nodes whose corresponding users are in the training set are considered and the majority class of neighbors is used as a feature. Clustering coefficient of similarity network is also used as a feature.

Prediction Framework

In this section, we present our model to early predict follower loss. Apart from the content based features, we have also used the following features - no. of followers, no. of followees, follower/follower ratio.

Baseline Model: In previous studies, many link based features from the follower-followee network like homophily, link exchange, follower overlap, tie strength [3] have been used as factors for followership loss. We create a baseline model by only using those features which are from the perspective of user who get unfollowed and we shall compare our model with this baseline model.

Our Model: Doc2vec + features Apart from the features described above, we obtain vector representation of users using the state-of-art Doc2vec model[4]. The word vectors are trained from the dataset of tweets. We feed the user vectors along with the features to feed-forward multi-layer perceptron (MLP) and train using cross-entropy loss for the classification task. We perform a 10-fold cross validation to evaluate our model. We vary the values of K^4 (number

of topics in LDA) and other hyper parameters to obtain the best results.

Table 1: Evaluation results.

Models	Accuracy	Precision	Recall	F1-score	ROC-area
Baseline Model	61%	0.65	0.70	0.67	0.62
Our Model	**73%**	**0.73**	**0.87**	**0.80**	**0.71**

Results: Table 1 summarizes the results. Our model significantly outperforms the baseline model by 19.67% (w.r.t accuracy), 33.8% (w.r.t precision) and 14.3% (w.r.t recall). To understand which features are discriminative we rank them by their χ^2 values. The top six discriminative features came out to be - *avg. tweet burst time period, max. tweet burst time period, tweet frequency, mention entropy, topic diversity, eigenvector centrality of mention graph.*

Conclusions and implications

In this paper, we identify various socio-linguistic factors behind followership loss and propose a feature-based model for followership loss prediction that achieves a good accuracy of 73% and significantly outperforms the baseline model. The most discriminative factors are related to the users' tweeting behavior - frequency of tweets, their burstiness, the engaging ability of the user and the topic diversity of the user's tweets.

Our research can be helpful for Twitter users in various ways - i) to early identify the followership loss in near future ii) enabling victims to quickly take corrective measures/actions to stop the trend of follower loss and iii) help the Twitter service as a whole to build a "tweet-properly"-like recommendation system for the subscribers to help them avoid unforeseen follower loss.

---

[4]best result for $K = 30$

REFERENCES

1. David M. Blei, Andrew Y. Ng, and Michael I. Jordan. 2003. Latent Dirichlet Allocation. *J. Mach. Learn. Res.* 3 (March 2003), 993–1022.

2. Haewoon Kwak, Hyunwoo Chun, and Sue Moon. 2011. Fragile Online Relationship: A First Look at Unfollow Dynamics in Twitter *(CHI '11)*. 1091–1100.

3. Haewoon Kwak, Sue Moon, and Wonjae Lee. 2012. More of a Receiver Than a Giver: Why Do People Unfollow in Twitter? *(ICWSM '12)*.

4. Quoc V. Le and Tomas Mikolov. 2014. Distributed Representations of Sentences and Documents. *CoRR* abs/1405.4053 (2014).

5. Sue Moon. 2011. Analysis of Twitter Unfollow: How often Do People Unfollow in Twitter and Why? *(SocInfo '11)*.

6. Seth A. Myers and Jure Leskovec. 2014. The Bursty Dynamics of the Twitter Information Network. *CoRR* abs/1403.2732 (2014).

7. Yla R. Tausczik and James W. Pennebaker. 2010. The Psychological Meaning of Words: LIWC and Computerized Text Analysis Methods. *Journal of Language and Social Psychology* 29, 1 (2010), 24–54.

Is Breaking Up Hard To Do? Managing Relationship Boundaries On Social Networking Sites

Edward Dillon
Morgan State University
Department of Computer Science
edward.dillon@morgan.edu

Xinru Page
Bentley University
Department of Computer Information Systems
xpage@bentley.edu

Pamela Wisniewski
University of Central Florida
Department of Computer Science
pamwis@ucf.edu

GROUP '18, January 7–10, 2018, Sanibel Island, FL, USA
© 2018 Copyright is held by the owner/author(s).
ACM ISBN 978-1-4503-5562-9/18/01.
https://doi.org/10.1145/3148330.3154515

Abstract

The purpose of our research is to direct more attention to two relationship privacy boundary strategies: **connection avoidance** (i.e., rejecting friend/follower requests) and **connection termination** (i.e., removing existing friends/followers). A survey study was conducted with 222 college students that examined how participants regulated these boundaries with others versus how they perceived others who regulated these boundaries with them ("self" vs. "other") on Facebook, Twitter, and Instagram. Participants reported using relationship avoidance and termination strategies more than they perceived others using these strategies against them. Overall, there were minimal impacts reported in terms of relationship changes due to others avoiding and terminating relationships. Site affordances partially explain these results, as none of the sites currently notify users when a friend request is denied or an existing friendship is severed.

Author Keywords

Social networking sites; affordances; relationship management; privacy.

ACM Classification Keywords

H.5.3 Group and Organization Interfaces (Computer-supported cooperative work)

Research Hypotheses

H1: Social media users are more likely to be aware of their own *connection avoidance* behaviors than that of others.

H2: Social media users are more likely to perceive a relational impact from *connection avoidance* behaviors of others than of themselves.

H3: Social media users are more likely to be aware of their own *connection termination* behaviors than that of others.

H4: Social media users are more likely to *avoid* new connections than they are to *terminate* existing ones.

Table 1: Research Hypotheses

Introduction

Research on the topic of social media and privacy often frames privacy as a process of interpersonal boundary regulation [4] where individuals must choose what information is appropriate to disclose to others within one's social network [3]. Less research has focused on managing our relational boundaries with others [7] through the affordances provided by social media platforms. Some research has studied the reasons why people unfriend others on Facebook; both online (e.g., inappropriate or polarizing posts) and offline factors (e.g., changes in the relationship) played a critical role in these decisions [5]. Other research has spoken to the negative emotional impact of online avoidance and ostracism [6]. When rejection occurs in interpersonal relationships [2], there is a facilitator ("rejector") and a recipient ("rejected") involved. The recipients tend to feel more upset that the relationship ended. We explore this relationship dynamic of "self" versus "other" in more depth within social networking site contexts.

Methods

Research Overview

Online relationships and boundaries management among social media users is a topic of interest within the GROUP community. Forte et al. [1] examined the strength of potentially "awkward" relationships that can occur between high school students and adults on social media sites and found that such relational ties could be beneficial to both parties. Similarly, our work examines another type of awkward social networking site interaction; specifically, we examined users' **connection avoidance** (i.e., rejecting friend/follower requests) and **connection termination** (i.e., removing existing friends/followers) strategies.

Web-based Survey Design

We distributed a web-survey that examined users' experience using three popular social networking sites: Facebook, Twitter, and Instagram. Two relationship *avoidance* ("ever turned down a friend/follower request") and *termination* ("ever removed/unfollowed someone as a friend/follower") questions were asked from the vantage point of *self* ("Have you") and *other* ("Has someone"). For the *connection avoidance* questions, we followed up on whether participants felt these actions changed their underlying relationships. Questions were repeated for each social networking platform. Measures solicited a "yes/no" response.

Research Hypotheses

To understand how participants' relationship boundary management behaviors differed from their perceptions of the relational boundary management behaviors of others, as well as the perceived impact on their relationships, four initial hypotheses were established, which are outlined in **Table 1**. We conducted the McNemar's statistical test for paired categorical data to test our hypotheses. **Table 2** shows the relative percentages of "yes" for each question and platform.

Results

Participants

The participants were college students recruited from Clemson University. The final sample (N=222) included 86 males and 136 females, ranging in age from 18 to 28 years (M=20.23, SD=1.70). **H1** was supported for all platforms. On Facebook ($X^2(df = 1, p < 0.01) = 73.11$), Twitter ($X^2(df = 1, p < 0.01) = 7.2$), and Instagram ($X^2(df = 1, p < 0.01) = 19.32$), participants reported using connection avoidance strategies (i.e., rejecting a request) significantly more often than they reported others using this strategy towards them.

	Connection Avoidance (Rejecting a Request)		Relationship Change (Avoidance)		Connection Termination (Removing Connection)	
	Self	**Other**	**Self**	**Other**	**Self**	**Other**
Facebook	97%	59%	7%	5%	94%	82%
Twitter	50%	38%	4%	3%	72%	64%
Instagram	54%	33%	4%	3%	60%	48%

Table 2: Percentage of "Yes" Responses to Survey Questions

However, the difference in perceptions between self and other for relational change due to these connection avoidance behaviors was negligible (**H2**, Unsupported), likely because reports of change were relatively low overall (ranging between 3%–7% of participants stating the avoidance behaviors caused a relational impact).

For **H3**, we found that participants significantly reported using connection termination (i.e., removing a friend/follower) more themselves than they experienced being unfriended or unfollowed by others on Facebook (X^2(df = 1, p <0.01) = 17.63), Twitter (X^2(df = 1, p = 0.01) = 6.26), and Instagram (X^2(df = 1, p<0.01) = 12.03). For **H4**, McNemar's test revealed a statistical significance for Twitter (X^2 (df = 1, p <0.01) = 24.50), but in the opposite direction than expected. Twitter users were more likely to terminate an existing relationship (i.e., unfollow someone) than to reject a request from a potential follower. This is consistent with the platform's affordances, which by default, Twitter accounts are public and allow anyone to follow another user. In order to approve followers, one has to change their privacy settings to private. **Table 3** provides an overall summary of the findings for each hypothesis.

Hypothesis Results

H1, Supported:
Connection Avoidance,
Self > Others

H2, Not Supported:
Connection Avoidance,
Relational Impact,
Self < Others

H3, Supported:
Connection Termination,
Self > Others

H4, Not Supported:
Connection Avoidance >
Connection Termination

Table 3: Summary of Findings

Discussion

Key Research Findings

The key finding from this research is that social networking site users reported using connection avoidance and termination strategies significantly more often than they perceived others using these strategies to create relationship boundaries with them. This suggests that users had a higher level of awareness of their own relationship management strategies than that of others. These results can potentially be explained by the transparency and affordances provided within the social media platforms. In all cases, Facebook, Twitter, and Instagram do not notify users when their request for a relationship connection is rejected or when an existing relationship is terminated. This lack of transparency made it difficult for social media users to know when others erect boundaries to put distance between themselves and that user. As a result, however, we believe that this helped explain why we did not see a significant difference for Hypothesis 2. Because users were not as aware of relationship boundaries created by others, they were less likely to perceive a negative relational impact.

Limitations and Future Research

We cannot definitively know whether participants' perceptions were accurate. Future research should consider finding feasible ways to reassess our findings using behavioral data. It would also be interesting to use an experimental design to test whether increased transparency of relationship boundary strategies taken by others (e.g., knowing that someone unfriended me versus me unfriending them) would significantly and negatively impact online and offline relationships. However, the ethicality of such an experiment is questionable because the intervention could potentially cause relational harm.

Conclusion

Similar to face-to-face relationships, relational ties and boundaries can also occur in social media relationships. Activities of connection avoidance and termination respectively play a role when establishing boundaries amongst social media users. Even though connection avoidance behavior is found to be prevalent, there is no indication that this particular activity influences changes to personal relationships (especially negative changes). It is also important to note that certain affordances of a social media site could play a key role in the user's decision to avoid or terminate a relationship. As future work, one aspect that remains to be examined is the correlation between connection termination and the possible relationship changes that this particular action can warrant.

References

1. Andrea Forte, Denise Agosto, Michael Dickard, and Rachel Magee. 2016. The Strength of Awkward Ties: Online Interactions Between High School Students and Adults. In *Proceedings of the 19th International Conference on Supporting Group Work (GROUP '16)*, 375–383.

2. Charles T. Hill, Zick Rubin, and Letitia Anne Peplau. 1976. Breakups Before Marriage: The End of 103 Affairs. *Journal of Social Issues* 32, 1: 147–168.

3. A. Lampinen, V. Lehtinen, A. Lehmuskallio, and S. Tamminen. 2011. We're in It Together: Interpersonal Management of Disclosure in Social Network Services.

4. Xinru Page, Alfred Kobsa, and Bart P. Knijnenburg. 2012. Don't Disturb My Circles! Boundary Preservation Is at the Center of Location-Sharing Concerns. In *Sixth International AAAI Conference on Weblogs and Social Media*.

5. C. Sibona and S. Walczak. 2011. Unfriending on Facebook: Friend Request and Online/Offline Behavior Analysis. In *2011 44th Hawaii International Conference on System Sciences*, 1–10.

6. K. D. Williams, C. K. K. Cheung, and W. Choi. 2000. Cyberostracism: effects of being ignored over the Internet. *Journal of Personality and Social Psychology* 79, 5: 748–762.

7. Pamela Wisniewski, A. K. M. Islam, Heather Richter Lipford, and David Wilson. 2016. Framing and Measuring Multi-dimensional Interpersonal Privacy Preferences of Social Networking Site Users. *Communications of the Association for Information Systems* 38, 1.

A Hot Bot: Testing Effect of Temperature on Feelings of Closeness When Interacting With a Chatbot

Victor Chue
New Jersey Institute of Technology
University Heights, GITC 5100
vc229@njit.edu

Juan Sebastian Rios
New Jersey Institute of Technology
University Heights, GITC 5100
jsr44@njit.edu

Donghee Yvette Wohn
New Jersey Institute of Technology
University Heights, GITC 5100
wohn@njit.edu

GROUP '18, January 7–10, 2018, Sanibel Island, FL, USA
© 2018 Copyright is held by the owner/author(s).
ACM ISBN 978-1-4503-5562-9/18/01.
https://doi.org/10.1145/3148330.3154516

Abstract

This study examined the effect of touching a warm or cold surface while interacting with a chatbot to see if temperature contributes to feelings of closeness with the artificial conversational agent. Our two-group experiment (N= 44) found no differences between hot and cold conditions in people's liking of the chatbot, but found a main effect of existing favorable attitudes toward chatbots.

Author Keywords

Temperature; touch; chatbot; conversational agent; haptic

ACM Classification Keywords

H.5.m. Information interfaces and presentation (HCI, User Interfaces, Input devices and strategies, Interaction styles, Haptic I/O, Voice I/O)

Introduction

In the past 20 years, there has been an ever-growing body of literature of human-robot interaction that includes audio, visual, and more recently, haptic interaction. Touch is a simple way to interact with computers. When we touch something, we feel some haptic sensations including pressure, tactile impression,

How People Treat Chatbots

- Can communicate through text or voice [6,8,10]

- Utilize electronics like Amazon Echo's Alexa, iPhone's Siri, or Window's Cortana [5]

- Used for various methods of human communication (body gestures, speech, emotions) [2,5]

- Can express and perceive emotions, communicate with high-level dialogue, and develop a distinct personality [8,13]

and temperature. The haptic research, however, has primarily focused on tactile feedback -- such as the role of vibrations for providing proper user experience to users [6]. Temperature has not played a prominent role in human-robot interactions. Studies that were done on temperature have mostly been with physical robots.

Temperature has been researched to be important in human-to-human interactions, even as far as being considered a main component of first impressions, the way we evaluate each other, and the way we behave around each other in regards to the cold-warm spectrum. This evaluation involves who we trust, help, and befriend. The colder we feel, the "colder" we act towards someone. In contrast, the warmer we feel, the "warmer" we act towards someone [12]. This "warm" feeling has been researched to improve trust [4], the chances of giving a reward versus keeping the reward [12], and even our ability to socialize and befriend those around us [14]. While temperature has been studied in HRI, there were no studies found that looked at temperature interacting with chatbots. Because of the lack of literature, our team chose to focus on how the tactile element of temperature affects people's perception of a chatbot while they interact with it.

Touch in Human-Robot Interaction

The interaction between humans and robots have become more widespread over the last two decades. Because of this, there has been an ever-growing body of literature in human-robot interaction. Haptic feedback is one major component of recent research studies [1, 14]. Some general studies include experiments revolving around a dinosaur robot [12], a robot that is used for hugging [7], and interacting with a robot's hand [6].

Touch has also been shown to be important in developing human to robot relationships [3,7]. Nakanishi found that haptic sensation was essential to social touch through the use of a robot hand [6]. Wullenkord [12] found physical contact with the robot reduced negative emotions. Both studies reveal that participants benefitted from interacting with the robot.

Temperature in Human-Robot Interaction:

As mentioned previously, few studies have been conducted in temperature research. It has been less prominent due to a lack of commercial communication technology that incorporates temperature. However, a select few studies have implemented temperature through a robot medium [1,9,11,12]. Nakanishi et al. [6] demonstrated that warmth in a robot's hand could improve connectivity with the room facilitator. Park and Lee [8] discovered that participants who interacted with the warm temperature level had a greater degree of perceived friendship when compared with the other temperature levels. Cooney, Nishio, and Ishiguro's [1] study also used a robot medium. Although temperature has played an important role in face-to-face communication, it has not been studied in depth through computer mediated communication. This is the reason why our hypothesis is focused on temperature:

Hypothesis: People will feel closer with a chatbot when exposed to warm temperature than cold temperature.

Methods

44 college students between the ages of 18-32 participated in the experiment, 31 of them were male. Participants were paid $10. After signing a consent form, participants first interacted with the "chatbot" by

answering 24 simple questions through speech with no stimulus. These questions included "What are you most passionate about?" and "Who do you admire most in your life?" During this part of the experiment, another researcher was controlling the "chatbot" with a pre-determined list of questions using the Wizard of Oz method. Following that, they answered questions about their feelings of closeness toward the chatbot on a 7-point scale. They then put both hands on a hot or cold stimulus and further interacted with the chatbot, followed by another survey about their feelings about the chatbot.

Results

We conducted a univariate analysis of variance to see the effect of the hot and cold manipulation on perceived closeness with the chatbot. Existing attitudes toward chatbots and gender were included as control variables. There was no effect of temperature ($F (1, 32) = .16, p = .69$) or gender ($F (1, 32) = 3.41, p = .07$) but a significant effect of existing attitudes ($F (1, 32) = 10.83, p = .002$). Participants in the cold condition ($M = 5.56, SD = .33$) did not feel significantly closer to the bot than participants in the hot condition ($M = 4.60, SD = .23$). These results suggest that pre-existing attitudes toward bots override effects of temperature; the temperature manipulation may not have been long or strong enough to replicate previous studies' positive effects of warm temperature.

To gain more insight into these results we analyzed participants' open-ended responses related to their thoughts on the study. Thirteen participants felt that the conversation was too "deep and personal" which made them feel uncomfortable because they knew they were talking with a bot. There was also a discrepancy in

that some participants thought the conversation was very natural and others said it felt like an interrogation or interview. Several participants mentioned that placing their hand on a cold or hot surface felt unnatural.

Discussion

It was clear that there were many elements of the experiment that were stronger than the temperature manipulation. Even though all participants had to answer the same questions audibly with the chatbot, they reacted differently to the questions. Some responded positively while others were weirded out. Future studies may want to take this into consideration and look at what factors make people feel friendlier toward chatbots. A follow-up study could be done to vary the experiment, i.e., allowing the participants to experience both the hot and cold stimulus. Previous studies of physical robots found positive effect of temperature but we did not. This could mean that the embodiment is important, but also raises questions on whether or not those studies would replicate once voice interaction is introduced to the experiment.

References

1. Martin Cooney, Shuichi Nishio, and Hiroshi Ishiguro. 2014. Affectionate Interaction with a Small Humanoid Robot Capable of Recognizing Social Touch Behavior. *ACM Transactions on Interactive Intelligent Systems 4*, 4: 1–32.

2. Stefania Druga, Randi Williams, Cynthia Breazeal, and Mitchel Resnick. 2017. "Hey Google is it OK if I eat you?" *Proceedings of the 2017 Conference on Interaction Design and Children - IDC '17*: 595–600.

3. Gijs Huisman, Merijn Bruijnes, Jan Kolkmeier, Merel Jung, Aduén Darriba Frederiks, and Yves Rybarczyk. 2013. Touching Virtual Agents: Embodiment and Mind. *IFIP Advances in Information and Communication Technology AICT-425*: 114–138.

4. Yoona Kang, Lawrence E. Williams, Margaret S. Clark, Jeremy R. Gray, and John A. Bargh. 2011. Physical temperature effects on trust behavior: The role of insula. *Social Cognitive and Affective Neuroscience.*

5. Lue Lin, Luis Fernando D'Haro, and Rafael Banchs. 2016. A Web-based Platform for Collection of Human-Chatbot Interactions. *Proceedings of the Fourth International Conference on Human Agent Interaction - HAI '16*: 363–366.

6. Hideyuki Nakanishi, Kazuaki Tanaka, Yuya Wada. 2014. Remote handshaking. *Proceedings of the 32nd annual ACM conference on Human factors in computing systems - CHI '14*, ACM Press, 2143–2152.

7. Junya Nakanishi, Kaiko Kuwamura, Takashi Minato, Shuichi Nishio, and Hiroshi Ishiguro. 2013. Evoking affection for a communication partner by a robotic communication medium. *Proceedings of the First International Conference on Human-Agent Interaction (iHAI 2013)* 34, 2: 2326.

8. Jiaqi Nie, Michelle Park, Angie Lorena Marin, and S Shyam Sundar. 2012. Can You Hold My Hand? Physical Warmth in Human-Robot Interaction. *ACM/IEEE international conference on Human-Robot Interaction*: 201–202.

9. Eunil Park and Jaeryoung Lee. 2014. I am a warm

10. Subramanian Sivaramakrishnan, Wan Fang, and Tang Zaiyong. 2007. Giving an "e-human touch" to e-tailing: The moderating roles of static information quantity and consumption motive in the effectiveness of an anthropomorphic information agent. *Journal of Interactive Marketing.*

11. L. E. Williams and J. A. Bargh. 2008. Experiencing Physical Warmth Promotes Interpersonal Warmth. *Science* 322, 5901: 606–607.

12. Ricarda Wullenkord, Marlena R. Fraune, Friederike Eyssel, and Selma Sabanovic. 2016. Getting in Touch: How imagined, actual, and physical contact affect evaluations of robots. *25th IEEE International Symposium on Robot and Human Interactive Communication, RO-MAN 2016*: 980–985.

13. Jennifer Zamora. 2017. Rise of the Chatbots : Finding a Place for Artificial Intelligence in India and US. *Proceedings of the 22nd International Conference on Intelligent User Interfaces Companion*: 109–112.

14. Ryan Schuetzer, Mark Grimes, Justin Scott Giboney, and Joseph Buckman. Facilitating Natural Conversational Agent Interactions: Lessons from a Deception Experiment. 2014. *Information Systems and Quantitative Analysis Faculty Proceedings & Presentations.* Paper 16.

Designing Social Interaction Support System with Shyness in Mind

Takeshi Nishida

Graduate School of Intercultural
Studies, Kobe University
Kobe, Japan
tnishida@people.kobe-u.ac.jp

GROUP '18, January 7–10, 2018, Sanibel Island, FL, USA
© 2018 Copyright is held by the owner/author(s).
ACM ISBN 978-1-4503-5562-9/18/01.
https://doi.org/10.1145/3148330.3154517

Abstract

Shyness have been noted as a problem of the minority,
which should be overcome on one's own. However,
surveys have shown that nearly half of the society are
introverts even in cultures believed to be extroversive.
We can see the possibility of more contribution from
the introverts if the social space is properly designed.
As an initial exploration to this design space, we report
here a field study where we held a conference banquet
with a seating arrangement system developed with
introversive participants in mind.

Author Keywords

Shyness; introverts; social interaction design;
conference support systems; seating arrangement.

ACM Classification Keywords

H.5.3. Information interfaces and presentation (e.g.,
HCI): Group and Organization Interfaces.

Introduction

Against the common belief that introverts are the small
minority, it has been reported that nearly half of the
people are introverts, not just in cultures often
described as introversive [2, 4, 8]. Reasonable
explanations to this misperception is that not a few
introverts are avoiding social opportunities or otherwise

come to act like extroverts, therefore we cannot feel their presence in daily life.

We believe that this is a sign of a large room for improvement regarding social interaction design. If social activities are designed to require less effort from the introverts, the community can expect more introverts participating and contributing, potentially leading to greater output as a whole.

Academic conferences are not the exception to this story; conferences tend to be overcrowded, making interaction difficult and tend to leave it up to individual effort. While attempts exist to technologically enhance face-to-face social interaction in conferences, they mostly focus on the efficiency finding the right person or topic [1, 3, 6], and considerations on the diverse personality of the participants seems to be insufficient.

Field Study

We report here a field study which took place at an academic conference banquet where we developed a seating arrangement system with shyness in mind. The study took place at an academic conference in Japan.

The conference had more than 20 years history of deploying experimental systems to enhance the onsite experience; for example, various chat systems have been used as a discussion backchannel during the presentation sessions [5, 7]. During the three days long conference, there are two banquets at the first two nights which was the field of this study.

As a starting point, the conference chair provided us an initial design of the system as follows:

1. Participants anonymously input to the system, who you want to talk to at the banquet.
2. The system decides the seats to satisfy as many wish as possible, and announce the result as a seating chart.
3. 3. Participants find and take a seat using the seating chart and enjoy the banquet.

Participants and their Concerns
Introversive behavior were often observed among the participants. Not a few participants, especially the younger ones and the newcomers to the community, seemed to have troubles in building new relationship.

While the initial design can help these introverts, we anticipated the following concerns. First, we took care not to make a system look like "a fun thing for the extroverts", because introverts can be afraid of events including party-like fun things. We also had to take care not to make the system look like "support for the introverts". Extroverts will not use such system because they simply don't need them, and introverts can also refuse the system because it will make them look like introverts, wasting their effort to pretend to be an extrovert. We also anticipated that anonymous collection of the wishes may not be anonymous enough for the introverts. In the initial design, collected wishes can easily be guessed by looking at the resulting seating: if someone next to you is not the one you wished to talk to, it is likely that they wanted to talk to you. This can make introverts hesitate to input their real wishes to the system.

We believe that making a system with introverts in mind is importantly different from making a system for the introverts. In this case, our design focused on providing system benefits to both introverts and extroverts, and also to provide secure anonymity where guessing the wishes from the seating chart is difficult.

Design of the Banquet Seating Arrangement System

With the above concerns in mind, we implemented a web application to collect the seating wishes from conference participants and generate seating charts. Two types of wishes were implemented.

First was the *people wish*, where the user chooses a pair of participants with the pull-down lists in the form of: I wish <participant A> and <participant B> get close seats (Figure 1). We had reasons to choose this form instead of the simpler: I want a close seat to <participant>. First, it allows participants to encourage others to interact, which can be a reason to use the system for extroverts. Second, it becomes more difficult to guess the wishes from the output seating. Login user is selected as default <participant A>, to make self-wishes easy to input.

Second was the *topic wish*, which comes in a simple form with a pull-down list: I want to talk about <topic>. Having a second type of wish is supposed to make guessing even more difficult to increase anonymity. Topic wish is also helpful for participants who have no idea who they might want to talk with. Participants could freely add new topics to this pull-down list.

Seating charts

The system decides the seating arrangement based on the wishes collected from the participants and create seating charts as shown in Figure 2. The chart shows the members of each table with a table number. Topics

is shown along with the members when it is wished by multiple members assigned to a same table.

Experience at the Conference

Data collected for analysis was the input wishes to the web application and the answers to the questionnaire collected on the last day. In addition, we had a number of random comments throughout the conference. We also had a presentation slot, just before the second night banquet, where we had an opportunity to discuss the system in public after the participants experienced the first night banquet using the system.

Input Wishes

93 out of 182 conference participants (51.1%) registered at least one wish to the system. Of the 267 wishes in total, 165 was people wishes and 102 were topic wishes. 74 participants (79.6% of who had input wishes) had at least one wish satisfied. 62/165 (37.6%) of the people wishes and 64/102 (62.7%) of the topic wishes were satisfied. People wishes were more difficult to satisfy compared to topic wishes because there were very popular participants who was wished by many participants and also there were a few participants who input very many people wishes.

27 topics were proposed in total as shown in Table 1. Most of them were typical topics for an academic conference such as technology or career related topics. We also observed a number of topics about social interaction. It seems that having a system to encourage social interaction encouraged participants to think and talk about social interaction.

Pull-down lists of all participants

Login user selected as default

Figure 1: Close look of the people wish input UI.

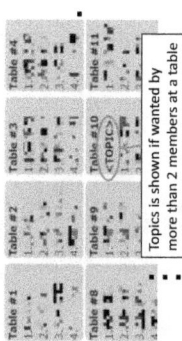

Topics is shown if wanted by more than 2 members at a table

Figure 2: Seating chart.

Technology(35)		
Strange devices(11), Programming(7)		
Career(22)		
Job hunting(10)		
Research in a company(5)		
The conference(12)		
Overview the conference history(3)		
Social Interaction(12)		
I want to talk with new people.(8)		
I want to socialize, but I'm afraid to.(4)		
Research(11)		
Alternative research output format(4)		
Other(10)		Cats(5)

Table 1: Proposed topics. Number in parentheses shows the number of people who wished the topic.

Feedback from Participants

We collected 48 answers to the questionnaire, 31 from participants who input wishes to the system and 17 from participants who didn't. Participants who used the system seemed to be more eager to provide feedbacks.

Figure 3 shows the answers to the question which asked the system impression. Majority answered that wishing is easier if guessing is designed to be more difficult, supporting our initial concerns. Participants supported our system by agreeing to questions asking that it was better to have the system than free seating, for both the first and second night banquets; however, "no opinion" was the majority answer, suggesting the difficulty to clearly feel the benefit of having the system.

One of the most thought-provoking comment appeared in public at the question time after our presentation about the seating arrangement system: *I became curious of others' wishes, so I started to ask, and then some wishes got revealed. Isn't it a problem?*

Discussion and Future Work

In contrast to prior work [1, 3, 6] which provided information to find the right person to talk with in academic conferences, we attempted to support the next step: actually talking to someone first in public. We assumed that the personality of each individual, such as shyness, to have stronger influence at this step, which guided us in carefully designing the banquet seating arrangement system.

Although we are in too early stage to derive solid design implications, we could collect feedbacks through field study to support the assumption. Initial lesson learned was: anonymous input is not comfortable

enough when the system output cannot be aggregated, which can be improved by increasing the degree of freedom of the input. However, we have to take care that secrets might make people curious.

Rooms for design improvements remained around how to make participants feel stronger that it was better to have the system. It may have been difficult to feel the benefit of the system because of the increased anonymity; while it was easy to tell that their own wish was satisfied, it was uneasy to tell that how well the system satisfied the wish of other participants.

Questions remained due to lack of data. It is still unclear that which aspect of the banquet was preferred than free seating banquet by which type of participants. It is possible that participants felt more satisfied just because they were asked their wishes. Participants might have been satisfied by randomly assigned seating. To answer the question, we need to know which participants are introverts / extroverts. For this purpose, we plan to use Gosling et al.'s Ten-Item Personality Inventory (TIPI). We also have to make clear the real concerns of introverts before such social opportunities. We plan to conduct interviews considering the different personalities and other categories (faculty / student, male / female, wish satisfied or not, etc.) in future study.

ACKNOWLEDGMENTS

We thank all the WISS participants. This work was supported by JSPS KAKENHI Grant Number 26870362.

References

1. Cox, D., Kindratenko, V., and Pointer, D. 2003. IntelliBadge: Towards Providing Location-Aware

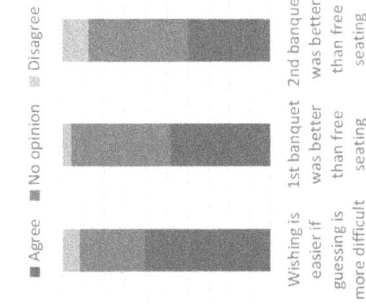

Figure 3: Answers to question asking system impression.

Value-Added Services at Academic Conferences. In Proc. UbiComp 2003, 264–280.

2. Helgoe, L. 2008. Introvert power: Why your inner life is your hidden strength. Sourcebooks, Inc.

3. McCarthy, J. F., McDonald, D. W., Soroczak, S., Nguyen, D. H. and Rashid, A. M. 2004. Augmenting the social space of an academic conference. In Proc. CSCW 2004, 39–48.

4. Morioka, M. 2013. A Phenomenological Study of "Herbivore Men". The Review of Life Studies 4, 1–20.

5. Nishida, T., and Igarashi, T. 2007. Bringing round-robin signature to computer-mediated communication. In Proc. ECSCW 2007. 219–230.

6. Numa, K., Hirata, T., Ohmukai, I., Ichise, R. and Takeda, H. 2006. Action oriented Weblog to Support Academic Conference Participants. In Proc. WBC, 26–28.

7. Rekimoto, J., Ayatsuka, Y., Uoi, H., and Arai, T. 1998. Adding another communication channel to reality: An experience with a chat-augmented conference. In CHI 98 Conference Summary, 271–272.

8. Quenk, N. L., Hammer, A. L., & Majors, M. S. 2001. MBTI Step II manual: Exploring the next level of type with the Myers-Briggs Type Indicator Form Q. Consulting Psychologists Press.

Identifying Opinion and Fact Subcategories from the Social Web

Ankan Mullick
Bing
Microsoft, India
ankan.mullick@microsoft.com

Shivam Maheswari
Dept. of CSE
IIT Kharagpur, India
shiv.maheshwari1994@
iitkgp.ac.in

Suman Kalyan Maity
Dept. of CSE
IIT Kharagpur, India
sumankalyan.maity@
cse.iitkgp.ernet.in

Pawan Goyal
Dept. of CSE
IIT Kharagpur, India
pawang@cse.iitkgp.ernet.in

Surjodoy Ghosh D
Dept. of CSE
IIT Kharagpur, India
ghosh.d.1302@iitkgp.ac.in

Srotaswini Sahoo
Dept. of CSE
NIT Rourkela, India
srotasahoo7@gmail.com

Soumya C
Dept. of CSE
IIT Kharagpur, India
soumya.cbr@iitkgp.ac.in

Abstract

In this paper, we investigate the problem of building automatic classifiers to categorize opinions and facts into appropriate subcategories. While working on two English News article datasets and two social media datasets (Twitter hashtag idioms and Youtube comments), we achieve consistent performance with accuracies in the range of 70-85% for opinion and fact sub-categorization. The proposed classifiers can be instrumental in understanding argumentative relations as well as in developing fact-checking systems. It can also be used to detect anomalous behavior such as predominant drunkers or other psychological changes.

Author Keywords

Opinion Classification, Fact Classification, Opinion-Fact Diversity, Opinion-Fact Categorization

ACM Classification Keywords

H.3.3 [Information Storage and Retrieval]: Information Search and Retrieval; H.m [Information System]: Miscellaneous

Introduction

In the online world, people post texts or pictures in social media and comment in online news articles to express their views on some events or different topics of news articles. We can broadly classify a sentence or phrase (tweet, comment etc.) into opinion (statements based on a belief or view on a fact) or fact (which can be proved true or false). Consider the following sentences: (i) *Senate voted 55-43 to confirm Robert Wilkins to the U.S. Court of Appeals for the District of Columbia* and ii) *McGreevey's lover was being paid 11000 Dollar even though he was wildly unqualified for the position.* While the first sentence is a fact, the second one is an opinion. Interestingly, all the opinion sentences may not be similar. Asher et al. [1] provide four different sub-categories of opinions - report, judgment, advise, sentiment. Similarly, Soni et al. [13] manually classify tweets into 5 fact subcategories - report, knowledge, belief, doubt, perception. However, there are no generic classifiers for categorical classification of opinions and facts as of now. Understanding fine-grained opinion and fact subcategories can be instrumental in many applications including deriving various argumentative relations such as support / attack, as well as understanding if a given sentence is fact-checkworthy.

In the modern scenario, online publishers want to increase user engagements / comments on their news articles / channels by highlighting important sentences. However, there exist no such modeling of the revenue of a newspaper based on sentence types and subtypes over different time periods. Distribution as well as flow of opinion and fact sub-categories can help in modeling the revenue generation. It will also be quite informative to examine how different categories of opinions and facts vary demographically (sex, age, region etc.), for different time frames like days of week (weekdays vs weekends), monthly (start of the month vs end of the month) or hourly (morning vs work hours vs evening vs late night). Demographic patterns of opinion and fact categories can be different for psychogenic people, predominant drunkers and others scenarios than the normal people. For example, we can identify peoples' suicidal tendencies or change in behavior in near future by tracking social media so that we can control situations accordingly. In

the field of rumors and fake news problems, it is important to study factuality or opinionatedness and how their different categorical distributions vary for rumors and fake news. At a micro level, one sentence or comment or tweet may contain multiple opinion and fact categories and separating these might be useful to derive actionable insights (Rudra et al. [10] use this for tweet summarization in disaster scenario.). In the above opinion example, "McGreevey's lover was being paid 11000 Dollar" is factual but "even though he was wildly unqualified for the position" is opinionated (judgment). Many research works focused on subjectivity or objectivity of sentence and analysis can be easier if we discover the interaction between various opinion-fact categories in the same / nearby sentences. Another important measurement is to check how sentiment analysis varies with different categories for different demographic features. Example: whether 'report' opinions are mostly neutral and 'judgment' opinions are polarized? Sentiment analysis for different subcategories of opinion categories is also interesting. To design intelligent chat-bot system, categorical classifications are important because it may help to identify mentalities of the person and each questions can be answered accordingly.

This paper takes a first step in this direction as we build two different classifiers - Bagging with Random Forest and Repeated Incremental and Pruning (Rip) for opinion and fact sub-categorizations respectively[1]. Our classifiers achieved high precision, recall, accuracy and ROC across various news and social media datasets.

Related Work

People have been working on opinion mining for the last two decades. Some works [5, 14, 15] have focused on opin-

---

[1]Due to unavailability of sufficiently labeled categories of opinions and facts, deep neural network produces poor results, and is not reported.

Dataset (#)
We have worked on four different datasets: two classical datasets (a,b) and two social media datasets (c,d) - **(a) Multi perspective Question and Answering (MPQA):** We take categorically labeled opinionated sentences from MPQA articles[6]. It contains labeled 1237 opinions and 1232 facts (786 report, 200 knowledge, 179 belief, 51 doubt, 16 perception). **(b) Yahoo news articles:** From [6], we gathered categorically labeled opinionated sentences of yahoo articles. Dataset has 470 labeled opinions and 252 facts (160,18,46,15,13). Details of (a) and (b) in [6]. **(c) Twitter Hashtag Idioms:** We collected 2942 opinionated hashtag idioms from [8] and 1480 were categorically labeled (report, judgment, advise, sentiment) with inter annotator agreement Fleiss κ=0.78. **(d) Youtube Comments:** After collecting opinions from [8], we extended the dataset up to 1540 opinions and labeled them (Inter annotator agreement Fleiss κ=0.71).

Feature Identification (#)
Our identified features can be broadly classified into three categories -

(i) POS Tag based features: We used *Stanford POS-tagger* for MPQA, Yahoo classical datasets and *CMU POS-tagger* [3] for hashtag idioms and youtube comments[a] - social media data to find no. of nouns, verb, adjectives etc, presence of adverbs etc.

(ii) Dependency parse based features (using Stanford Dependency parser): dobj (direct object), amod (adjective modifier), acomp (adjectival complement) etc.

(iii) Others - no. of characters, presence of wh-words, numbers, strong, weak adjectives, words specific to particular categories.

Different combinations of features are used for social media data (40 features) and classical data (45 features). Fact classification was done only on classical datasets[b].

[a]As CMU POS-tagger works better than Stanford POS-tagger in social media data (e.g. - tweet)[3].
[b]since the manual labeling of fact subcategories on the social media data had a very poor inter-annotator agreement.

ion mining, e.g., subjective vs. objective classification, separating facts from opinions, identifying opinion polarity, etc. Scholz and Conrad [12] extract entropy based word connections to identify word combinations, and analyze opinion tonality of news articles. Soni et al. [13] predicted factuality of tweet text, using keywords from [11].

Some graph based models have been built to identify opinions in a news article. Rajkumar et al. [9] and Mullick et al. [6] built HITS framework, modeling opinions as hub and supporting facts as authority to identify important opinions. [6] also identified top k diverse opinions, showed categorical distributions and classification of opinions into four [1] categories[2]. Mullick et al. [8] built a generic opinion-fact classifier based on classical and social media datasets and also presented how opinionatedness of various sections of news articles differs. None of the prior works have attempted building a generic classifier to identify opinion and fact subcategories that works on both news and social media. We built generic classifiers to classify opinions into four categories [1] - report, judgment, advise, sentiment, and facts into five categories [13] - report, knowledge, belief, doubt, perception.

Experiments

To handle the imbalance of datasets, we first use SMOTE [2] algorithm to make the dataset balanced (corresponding to the maximum count of the instance). After feature extraction[3], using these balanced datasets, various classifiers from Weka [4] - Naïve Bayes (NB), Logistic Regression (LR), Support Vector Machine (SVM), Repeated Incremental and Pruning (JRip, baseline model used in [6]), Logistic Boost, IBK (Instance based learning with parameter k),

[2][6] built a classifier for opinion sub-categorization only on classical news datasets, we use this as a baseline.
[3]Details of the features are in https://goo.gl/U1HrN3.

Table 1: Comparison of 10-fold cross validation testsn: Precision (P), Recall (R), Accuracy (A), Receiver Operating Characteristic (ROC) for classification of opinions into subcategories (report, judgment, advise, sentiment) for MPQA and Yahoo articles

Dataset	MPQA				Yahoo			
Classifiers	P	R	A(%)	AUC	P	R	A	AUC
NB	0.36	0.35	34.9	0.64	0.43	0.49	49.5	0.78
LR	0.43	0.43	34.9	0.68	0.58	0.47	44.5	0.69
SVM	0.61	0.61	61.7	0.74	0.56	0.57	56.6	0.71
JRip	0.74	0.71	70.1	0.73	0.63	0.70	70.1	0.65
IBK	0.79	0.79	79.2	0.86	0.68	0.69	69.1	0.80
RF	0.87	0.83	83.7	0.91	0.74	0.73	73.1	0.90
Bg+RF	**0.89**	**0.84**	**84.3**	**0.96**	**0.75**	**0.74**	**73.8**	**0.91**

Random Forest (RF), Bagging with RF (Bg+RF) were used to classify opinions and facts into their respective subcategories. The performance is measured in terms of Precision (P), Recall (R), Accuracy (A) and Receiver Operating Characteristic (ROC). Results for opinion sub-categorization are shown in Tables 1 and 2. It is clearly seen that Bagging with Random Forest (Bg+RF) produces best Precision, Recall, Accuracy and ROC for opinion sub-classification.

Table 2: Comparison of 10-fold cross validation testn: Precision (P), Recall (R), Accuracy (A), Receiver Operating Characteristic (ROC) for classification of opinions into categories (report, judgment, advise, sentiment) for idiom hashtags and Youtube comments

Dataset	Hashtags Idioms				Youtube Comments			
Classifiers	P	R	A(%)	ROC	P	R	A	AUC
NB	0.49	0.48	45.7	0.73	0.39	0.35	34.7	0.63
LR	0.46	0.51	51.3	0.83	0.47	0.47	47.3	0.72
SVM	0.60	0.60	60.5	0.77	0.58	0.59	58.6	0.72
JRip	0.78	0.76	76.4	0.89	0.57	0.51	51.8	0.48
IBK	0.77	0.78	77.5	0.85	0.63	0.62	62.1	0.63
RF	0.82	0.81	81.7	0.93	0.74	0.73	73.8	0.81
Bg+RF	**0.83**	**0.82**	**81.9**	**0.95**	**0.75**	**0.75**	**74.4**	**0.91**

Table 3: Information Gain (IG) and One Attribute Evaluation (OAE) for MPQA Opinions

Feature	IG	OAE(%)
no. nouns	0.32	44
verb	0.28	41.3
det	0.27	40.6
nsubj	0.25	39.5
no. adj	0.23	39.3

Table 4: IG and OAE for Yahoo Opinions

Dataset	Yahoo	Yahoo
Feature	IG	OAE(%)
no. nouns	0.22	44
verb	0.22	41.3
no. adj	0.21	43.4
no. mark	0.24	39.9
no. det	0.18	40.1

Table 5: IG and OAE for Hashtag Idiom opinion

Feature	IG	OAE(%)
no. nouns	0.21	38.3
verb	0.21	38.3
str adj	0.18	35.5
no. char	0.16	40.1
word	0.15	37.1

Table 6: IG and OAE for Youtube comment (YC) opinions

Feature	IG	OAE(%)
nsubj	0.19	40.0
verb	0.21	39.7
dobj	0.20	40.2
pronoun	0.17	40.2
noun	0.16	39.0

For fact classification, we used several classifiers but only top seven classifiers have been shown – apart from NB, LR, Rip we used Multi-class Classifier (MCC), Logistic Iterative Boost (LIB), Bagging with Random Forest (Bg+RF) and Sequential Minimal Optimization (SMO).

Table 7: Comparison of 10-fold cross validation testn: Precision (P), Recall (R), Accuracy (A), Receiver Operating Characteristic (ROC) for classification of facts into categories (report, knowledge, belief, doubt,perception) for MPQA and Yahoo articles

Dataset	MPQA				Yahoo			
Classifiers	P	R	A(%)	ROC	P	R	A	ROC
NB	0.54	0.59	58.7	0.64	0.55	0.50	50.4	0.59
LR	0.60	0.67	66.5	0.72	0.59	0.63	62.6	0.67
SMO	0.49	0.64	64.2	0.64	0.58	0.69	69.7	0.62
MCC	0.61	0.67	66.8	0.72	0.59	0.64	64.7	0.68
LIB	0.64	0.67	67.0	0.72	0.57	0.68	68.4	0.66
Bg+RF	0.63	0.67	66.7	0.71	0.56	0.67	66.5	0.67
Rip	**0.69**	**0.71**	**71.0**	**0.73**	**0.60**	**0.70**	**70.2**	**0.69**

For fact classification, we get the best results for Rip classifier but not for Bg+RF. Thus, we are getting two different classifiers for automatic classification of opinions and facts into categories. Tables 3, 4, 5 and 6 show Information gain and One attribute evaluation for top five features of different datasets in case of opinion classification. For fact classification, information gain and one attribute evaluation of different features for MPQA and Yahoo datasets are shown in Table 8. We see that while POS tag based features are very helpful, features from all three categories constitute the top five. For opinion classification, no. of nouns, adjectives, presence of verbs, nominal subject (nsubj) are important but for fact classification, presence of fact words, nouns, adverbs, clausal complement (ccomp) are important.

Conclusion

In this paper, we investigated the problem of opinion and fact categorical classification across several datasets. To

Table 8: Information Gain (IG) and One Attribute Evaluation (OAE) for MPQA and Yahoo fact classification

MPQA			Yahoo		
Feature	IG	OAE	Feature	IG	OAE
noun	0.24	42.1	fact words	0.25	45.5
fact words	0.23	39.2	length	0.21	40.1
ccomp	0.18	38.7	prep	0.17	37.2
adv	0.16	33.1	advcl	0.15	30.2
length	0.14	32.1	pro	0.11	30.0

the best of our knowledge, this is the first study which tries to classify facts in classical datasets and opinions in social media and classical datasets into various subcategories. Our proposed classification framework achieves good accuracy, precision, recall and ROC for various datasets. We can now use the proposed classifier to study as to how various kinds of opinions and facts are found across different datasets - (e.g. - opinionated social list hashtags [7]), and how these evolve over time. Our immediate future step is to examine various demographic distributions for different categories of opinion and fact and to be able to use this for various applications involving deep diving into argumentative relations (e.g., finding supporting / attacking / contrastive claims and opinions) or checking if a given sentence is fact checkworthy. Another future direction is to identify smaller units than a sentence by using different discourse markers (e.g., comma) and study how different opinion or fact subcategories in a sentence combine to give overall subjectivity or objectivity. Our aim is to build a generic system to identify categories over different datasets.

Acknowledgments: We would like to thank Prof. Niloy Ganguly (CSE Dept., IIT Kharagpur) for valuable feedbacks and Microsoft IDC for travel support.

REFERENCES

1. Nicholas Asher, Farah Benamara, and Yvette Yannick Mathieu. 2009. Appraisal of opinion expressions in discourse. *Lingvisticæ Investigationes* 32, 2 (2009).

2. Nitesh V. Chawla and others. 2002. SMOTE: synthetic minority over-sampling technique. *Journal of artificial intelligence research* (2002).

3. K Gimpel and others. 2011. Part-of-speech tagging for twitter: Annotation, features, and experiments. ACL.

4. Mark Hall, Eibe Frank, G Holmes, Bernhard Pfahringer, Peter R, and Ian H Witten. 2009. The WEKA data mining software: an update. *ACM SIGKDD* (2009).

5. Soo-Min Kim and Eduard Hovy. 2006. Extracting opinions, opinion holders, and topics expressed in online news media text. ACL, 1–8.

6. Ankan Mullick, Pawan Goyal, and Niloy Ganguly. 2016. A graphical framework to detect and categorize diverse opinions from online news. *PEOPLES 2016* (2016), 40.

7. Ankan Mullick, Pawan Goyal, Niloy Ganguly, and Manish Gupta. 2017a. Extracting Social Lists from Twitter. In *ASONAM*.

8. A Mullick, Shivam M, P Goyal, N Ganguly, and others. 2017b. A Generic Opinion-Fact Classifier with Application in Understanding Opinionatedness in Various News Section. In *WWW*. 827–828.

9. Pujari Rajkumar, Swara Desai, Niloy Ganguly, and Pawan Goyal. 2014. A Novel Two-stage Framework for Extracting Opinionated Sentences from News Articles. *TextGraphs-9* (2014), 25.

10. Koustav Rudra, S Ghosh, Niloy Ganguly, Pawan Goyal, and Saptarshi Ghosh. 2015. Extracting situational information from microblogs during disaster events: a classification-summarization approach. In *CIKM*. ACM.

11. Roser Saurí. 2008. *A factuality profiler for eventualities in text*. ProQuest.

12. Thomas Scholz and Stefan Conrad. 2013. Opinion Mining in Newspaper Articles by Entropy-Based Word Connections. *EMNLP* (2013).

13. Sandeep Soni, Tanushree Mitra, Eric Gilbert, and Jacob Eisenstein. 2014. Modeling factuality judgments in social media text. *ACL* (2014).

14. Janyce Wiebe and Ellen Riloff. 2005. Creating subjective and objective sentence classifiers from unannotated texts. In *CICLingLing*. Springer, 486–497.

15. Hong Yu and Vasileios H. 2003. Towards answering opinion questions: Separating facts from opinions and identifying the polarity of opinion sentences. In *EMNLP*.

Examining the Effects of Parenting Styles on Offline and Online Adolescent Peer Problems

Arup Kumar Ghosh
University of Central Florida
Department of Computer Science
arupkumar.ghosh@ucf.edu

Pamela Wisniewski
University of Central Florida
Department of Computer Science
pamwis@ucf.edu

Karla Badillo-Urquiola
University of Central Florida
Department of Computer Science
Kcurquiola10@knights.ucf.edu

Abstract

Past research has focused on investigating parenting styles in the context of various positive and negative outcomes. We examined the relationship between parenting styles and offline and online adolescent peer problems. We found that parental involvement was associated with fewer peer problems, and strictness/supervision was associated with less frequent online victimization. Higher levels of autonomy granting parenting were associated with less peer problems and online victimization. Further, teens who experienced high levels of peer problems experienced less online victimization when their parents granting them more autonomy, than parents who restricted their autonomy. The findings of this paper set a foundation for parents to consider taking more authoritative approaches to dealing with their teens' offline peer problems as to not exacerbate teens' online risk experiences.

GROUP '18, January 7–10, 2018, Sanibel Island, FL, USA
© 2018 Copyright is held by the owner/author(s).
ACM ISBN 978-1-4503-5562-9/18/01.
https://doi.org/10.1145/3148330.3154519

Author Keywords

Adolescent Online Safety; Online Victimization; Peer Problems

ACM Classification Keywords

K.4.1 [Public Policy Issues]: Ethics, Human safety, Privacy

Introduction

There has been an abundance of research concerning the influence of parenting styles on positive and negative youth outcomes [7]. Within the ACM SIGCHI community, researchers have shown that tensions exist between parents and teens when it comes to technology use and rule-setting in the home [2,8,9,10].

However, there is limited research examining how parenting style effects on both offline and online victimization. In this research, we conduct an exploratory analysis based on survey data we collected from 215 parent-teen pairs to answer the following research question: *How does parenting style effect online and offline victimization of teens?*

Background

Livingstone and Smith argue that teens are not any more vulnerable to online risks as they are to offline risks [5]. Unfortunately, there is limited research focusing on how parenting styles influence these online and offline vulnerabilities in relation to one another. For example, Eastin et al. [3] found that technological monitoring on home computers was primarily practiced by authoritarian and authoritative parents, and Ybarra et al. [11] found that such monitoring software reduced the odds of teens being exposed to sexual explicit materials online. Fewer studies have looked directly at the effects of parenting style on offline peer problems and online victimization more holistically.

Methods

Participant Recruitment

Using a Qualtrics Panel, we recruited parent and teen pairs from across the United States. Participants were sent a survey link and asked to complete the consent/assent process. Then, parents and teens completed their survey portions separately; parents first, followed by teens. In **Sidebar 1**, we describe the pre-validated constructs measured in our survey. Baumrind [1] divided parenting styles in four different categories based on parents' varying levels of responsiveness (takes care of child's needs, but promotes autonomy) and demandingness (exerts control): 1) authoritative, 2) authoritarian, 3)

permissive, and 4) neglectful. Based on these categories [1], authoritative parents are high on all three PSI scales, while authoritarian parents are only high on the strictness/supervision scale [7].

Data Analysis Approach

We used SmartPLS 3.0 [6] and Partial Least Squares Structural Equation Modelling (PLS-SEM) to understand the relationships between our constructs. A saturated model was built using all possible paths between constructs that tested both direct and indirect effects. Next, we tested for all possible moderating effects between parenting style dimensions and teen online and offline problems. Finally, we removed non-significant paths from the saturated model to get our final model, shown in **Figure 1**.

Results

Construct validity and descriptive statistics for all our model constructs are shown in **Table 1**.

Table 1: Reliability and Descriptive Statistics

Model Constructs	Cronbach's α	Mean (SD)
Parenting Styles (P)		
Involvement	0.84	4.28 (0.52)
Strictness/Supervision	0.89	4.44 (0.61)
Autonomy Granting	0.83	3.34 (0.74)
Peer Problems (T)	0.74	2.11 (0.76)
Online Victimization (T)	0.94	1.76 (1.10)

P: Parent, T: Teen; SD: Standard Deviation

Peer Problems and Online Victimization

Our structural model was statistically significant and explained 19.6% of the variance in peer problems and

Figure 1: Structural Equation Model

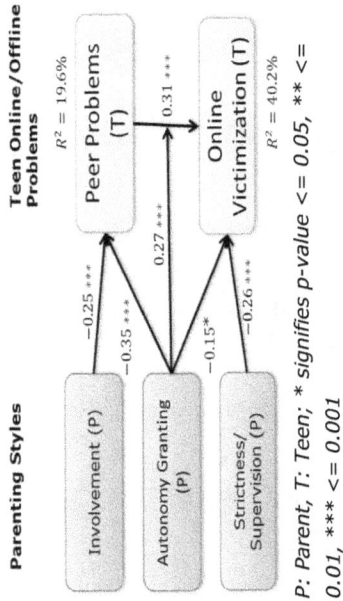

Figure 1: Structural Equation Model

P: Parent, T: Teen; * signifies p-value <= 0.05, ** <= 0.01, *** <= 0.001

Figure 2: Moderating Effect of Autonomy * Peer Problems on Online Victimization

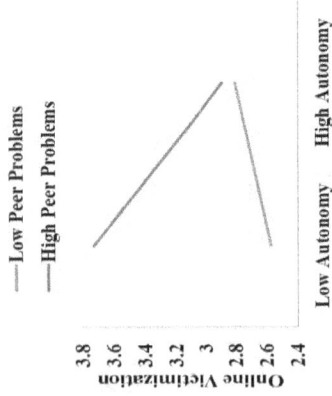

Figure 2: Moderating Effect of Autonomy * Peer Problems on Online Victimization

40.2% of the variance in teen online victimization. In **Figure 1**, peer problems and online victimization are significantly and positively correlated with one another. Parental involvement was associated with lower levels of peer problems; strictness/supervision was negatively associated with online victimization. Meanwhile, autonomy granting was associated with lower levels of both teen problem constructs.

Moderating Effects of Parenting Styles

Next, we tested for moderating effects between the different parenting style dimensions (involvement, strictness/supervision, and autonomy granting) on peer problems and online victimization. We found low autonomy granting parenting combined with an increased level of offline peer problems, was associated with the highest levels of teen online victimization, shown in **Figure 2**.

Discussion

Overall, we confirmed that *more* authoritative parenting (high involvement, high autonomy granting, and high strictness/supervision) leads to the most optimal youth outcomes - fewer peer problems and online victimization. We also found a moderating effect where low autonomy granting parenting combined with an increased level of peer problems, equated to higher levels of teen online victimization.

These findings have strong implications for supporting more optimal youth outcomes. Prior research [10] found that parents have the tendency to punish their teens and restrict their online access when they become aware of their teens online risk encounters. Yet, our results suggest that doing so may only exacerbate the problem instead of protecting teens. Instead, parents should consider taking authoritative approaches that provide the nurturing support, strictness, yet understanding and space (i.e., autonomy) that teens need, so that they can learn from their negative online risk experiences. But, unfortunately, other research shows that currently available systems (e.g., parental control apps) focus more on applying control and restriction [8].

Conclusion

The findings and implications of this paper sets a foundation for parents to consider taking more authoritative approaches to dealing with their teens' online risk experiences. Also, we confirmed that offline problems (peer) are closely related to online problems. Regarding limitations of our work, we used cross-sectional data that does not confirm causal effects. In future work, researchers should conduct longitudinal studies to explore causal effects between parenting styles and teen online/offline problems.

References

1. Diana Baumrind. 2005. Patterns of parental authority and adolescent autonomy. *New Directions for Child and Adolescent Development* 2005, 108: 61–69.

2. Lindsay Blackwell, Emma Gardiner, and Sarita Schoenebeck. 2016. Managing Expectations: Technology Tensions Among Parents and Teens. *Proceedings of the 19th ACM Conference on Computer-Supported Cooperative Work & Social Computing*, ACM, 1390–1401.

3. Matthew S. Eastin, Bradley S. Greenberg, and Linda Hofschire. 2006. Parenting the Internet. *Journal of Communication* 56, 3: 486–504.

4. Robert Goodman. 1997. The Strengths and Difficulties Questionnaire: A Research Note. *Journal of Child Psychology and Psychiatry* 38, 5: 581–586.

5. Sonia Livingstone and Peter K. Smith. 2014. Annual Research Review: Harms experienced by child users of online and mobile technologies: the nature, prevalence and management of sexual and aggressive risks in the digital age. *Journal of Child Psychology and Psychiatry* 55, 6: 635–654.

6. Christian M. Ringle, Sven Wende, and Jan-Michael Becker. 2015. *SmartPLS 3. Bönningstedt: SmartPLS.* .

7. Laurence Steinberg, Susie D. Lamborn, Sanford M. Dornbusch, and Nancy Darling. 1992. Impact of Parenting Practices on Adolescent Achievement: Authoritative Parenting, School Involvement, and Encouragement to Succeed. *Child Development* 63, 5: 1266–1281.

8. Pamela Wisniewski, Arup Kumar Ghosh, Mary Beth Rosson, Heng Xu, and John M. Carroll. 2017. Parental Control vs. Teen Self-Regulation: Is there a middle ground for mobile online safety? *Proceedings of the 20th ACM Conference on Computer Supported Cooperative Work & Social Computing*, ACM.

9. Pamela Wisniewski, Haiyan Jia, Na Wang, et al. 2015. Resilience Mitigates the Negative Effects of Adolescent Internet Addiction and Online Risk Exposure. *Proceedings of the 33rd Annual ACM Conference on Human Factors in Computing Systems*, ACM, 4029–4038.

10. Pamela Wisniewski, Heng Xu, Mary Beth Rosson, and John M. Carroll. 2017. Parents just don't understand: Why teens don't talk to parents about their online risk experiences. *Proceedings of the 2017 ACM Conference on Computer Supported Cooperative Work and Social Computing*, ACM, 523–540.

11. Michele L. Ybarra, David Finkelhor, Kimberly J. Mitchell, and Janis Wolak. 2009. Associations between blocking, monitoring, and filtering software on the home computer and youth-reported unwanted exposure to sexual material online. *Child Abuse & Neglect* 33, 12: 857–869.

Sidebar 2. Acknowledgements

This research was partially supported by the U.S. National Science Foundation under grant CNS-1018302. Any opinions, findings, and conclusions and recommendations expressed in this material are those of the author(s) and do not necessarily reflect the views of the National Science Foundation.

Carebit: A Privacy-Preserving "Step" Toward Remote Informal Caregiving

Arup Kumar Ghosh
University of Central Florida
Computer Science
arupkumar.ghosh@ucf.edu

Zaina Aljallad
University of Central Florida
Computer Science
zaina.aljallad@knights.ucf.edu

Karla Badillo-Urquiola
University of Central Florida
Computer Science
kcurquiola10@knights.ucf.edu

Pamela Wisniewski
University of Central Florida
Computer Science
pamwis@ucf.edu

Abstract

Several tele-monitoring systems have been developed
for in-home patient use. Unfortunately, many of these
systems are cost prohibitive and privacy invasive to the
patient. To overcome this problem, we designed a more
affordable and lightweight solution called *Carebit*, an
Android application that leverages the Fitbit API. We
conducted two user studies to understand ways to
improve our design. Overall, we found that the
notifications feature is the most useful feature for
users, and no concerns about privacy were mentioned.
The goal of *Carebit* is improve informal caregiving.

Author Keywords

Family Caregiving; Wearable Internet of Things; Privacy

ACM Classification Keywords

K.4.1 [Public Policy Issues]: Ethics, Human safety,
Privacy

Introduction

An informal caregiver is a family member, friend, or
neighbor, who provides unpaid services and supervision
to a loved one, someone who is ill, incapacitated, or
otherwise needs help [7]. There are approximately 43.5
million informal caregivers in the United States, out of
which 75% live within 20 minutes from their care
recipient, and 13% live in between 20 minutes and an

fees [2]. In our work, we explicitly designed our solution to reduce these barriers to user acceptance.

Carebit Implementation

The Carebit dashboard and system architecture are in shown in **Sidebar 1**. *Carebit* was implemented as a mobile app using Android Studio. The app is designed to be installed on the caregiver's mobile Android smartphone. Meanwhile, the only hardware required by patients is: 1) a Fitbit equipped with a heart rate tracker and 2) a device to sync the Fitbit via the internet (e.g., smart phone or tablet). The Fitbit is a very popular wearable fitness tracker, and costs between $150-$170 [8].

The *Carebit* app uses the Fitbit application protocol interface (API) to get pertinent health data from patients. Our solution applies Nissenbaum's contextual integrity privacy framework [4] in our design and allows the patient to control the types of information shared to a given caregiver. In order for caregivers to get access to this information, the patient must login using their Fitbit credentials and provide their consent for the caregiver to access a limited amount of the Fitbit data. For example, the last time steps were taken or current heart rate, but not sharing less relevant information, such as weight or historical data. The app is designed to keep patients' privacy in mind, but still provide the information needed for the caregiver to know if they patient may need assistance. Caregivers are free to access the application at any time to check up on their loved one and are also alerted when the patient may be in danger, which is determined using pre-defined thresholds based on the patients' vital signs (i.e., last step activity and heart rate). See **Sidebar 2.**

---

hour away [7]. Otherwise, informal caregivers often take care of loved ones as in-home patients, requiring constant attention that creates significant caregiver burden, especially when care requires constant supervision [6]. As a result, a number of tele-monitoring systems to help with in-home care have been developed [3]. Yet, a major concern with these monitoring systems is that they often require patients to give up their personal privacy for the sake of their health and safety [5].

To address this problem, we conceptualized and created *Carebit*, an Android application ("app") that leverages the Fitbit API, for informal caregiving relationships, where the patient is well enough to live independently but desires a lightweight means for another to check in on them on a daily basis. Our contribution to the broader SIGCHI community, including GROUP, is a remote caregiving solution that preserves privacy through a lightweight and low cost means. We conducted two pilot studies on an initial prototype for *Carebit*, and synthesize these results to discuss future design iterations of *Carebit* to improve informal caregiving.

Background

There have been numerous studies conducted on wearable technologies to assist in caregiving [1,5]. The common theme that emerged from all these studies is the trade-offs between privacy and the usefulness of the wearable technology. For example, in one study patients mentioned how they didn't want their loved ones knowing every single thing they were doing: "It's none of their business [5]." Another prohibitive factor was cost; many tele-monitoring solutions require investing in physical hardware and monthly monitoring

---

Sidebar 1a. Carebit Caregiver Dashboard

Sidebar 1b. Carebit System Architecture

Fitbit HR   Fitbit DB

Android Phone

CareBit
Mobile App

Methods

We conducted two pilot studies to get solicit user feedback about our initial design and prototype.

Design Probe and Interview

We showed storyboards of our initial prototype to a convenience sample of 21 participants, primarily college students and adult acquaintances. We described the main purpose of Carebit to the participants and asked the following follow-up questions:

1) Do you think an app like this might be useful to you now or in the future? Why or why not?
2) What types of notifications would you want this app to be able to give you?
3) If you were designing this app, what features would you include in the app?

The results from this probe were used to inform the design of the alert notifications implemented in the later app for a one-day user simulation.

One-Day Simulated User Study

Five college student volunteers participated in a 24-hour user simulation, acting as informal caregivers. A research assistant acted as the patient, setting off alert notifications via a Fitbit throughout the day. Volunteers were instructed to send a text message every time they received an alert, as if they were checking in on their loved one. A post-survey was administered at the end of the user simulation.

Results

Design Probe Feedback

After seeing the Carebit storyboards, about 85% of participants thought that Carebit was useful because of the following reasons: giving the patient more

independence, allowing caregivers to monitor their loved ones from afar, etc. The users also liked how the integration of technology was used to improve health. Yet, 15% did not find the app very useful as they thought the solution was very similar to existing emergency devices such as Life Alert. The most common alerts requested included irregular heartrate, low activity levels, goals achieved, and falls. Therefore, we incorporated heart rate and step activity alerts into our prototype prior to conducting a second user study.

Simulated User Study Results

The results from the second user study indicated that the participants responded a little over half of the time after receiving a notification. We found the average response time varied between 20 and 35 minutes. From the post-survey, we 60% of users stated the most useful feature was the notification alerts. Very few participants said that they checked the dashboard consistently through the day. Some participants felt the need for more alerts or alerts that persisted until they were cleared. Other felt the need to monitor more activity than just steps, such as the fall alerts that were also suggested in the prior user study.

Limitations and Future Work

Overall, our user studies showed promise that our solution may be useful and provided insights on how we can further improve Carebit. We realized that the alerts seem to be more critical for users than the dashboard itself. Yet, a major design flaw that we uncovered during the second user study was that alert notifications sometimes disappeared before participants saw them. In the future, we plan to improve this functionality and implement additional alert notifications. However, it is unlikely that Fitbit can be

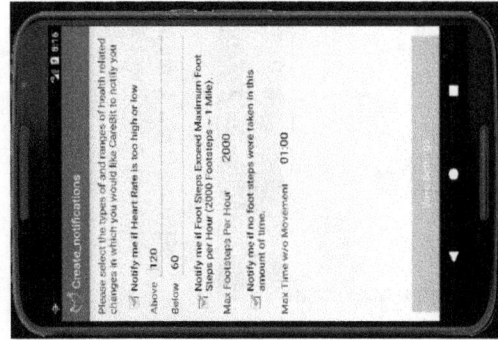

Sidebar 2. Alert Notification Settings

used to accurately detect falls. Another limitation of our pilot studies is that most of our participants were college students. For future user studies, we will recruit participants who are actually informal caregivers, as well as the loved ones they are caring for. We believe that recruiting from the intended target audience will increase engagement, as well as provide more insightful feedback on whether *Carebit* can, indeed, provide a piece of mind for individuals who desire to live independently, but need just a little bit of care.

Acknowledgements

This work is dedicated to the last author's friend Susan Riggs, who passed away due to complications from Diabetes. After being in a coma on her kitchen floor for two days before being found by a neighbor, she suffered severe lung and kidney damage, which claimed her life. Our goal is to create a production-ready version of *Carebit* for free download for friends and loved ones, who may want to watch over one another to avoid similar tragic events. We would also like to thank Kim Chen, Richard Hyman, and Joseph Prause, undergraduate students who supported development efforts. Support for this work was provided by the National Science Foundation Research Experience for Undergraduates program under Award No. 1560302. Any opinions, findings, and conclusions and recommendations expressed in this material are those of the author(s) and do not necessarily reflect the views of the National Science Foundation.

References

1. Daniel Aranki, Gregorij Kurillo, Posu Yan, David M. Liebovitz, and Ruzena Bajcsy. 2016. Real-Time Tele-Monitoring of Patients with Chronic Heart-Failure Using a Smartphone: Lessons Learned. *IEEE Transactions on Affective Computing 7*, 3: 206–219.

2. Ghassan A. Hamad and Alyn H. Morice. 2016. Telehealth in COPD: Compiling a Tele-Monitoring Package. *Chronic Obstructive Pulmonary Disease: Open Access 1*, 2.

3. Cliodhna Ní Scanaill, Sheila Carew, Pierre Barralon, Norbert Noury, Declan Lyons, and Gerard M. Lyons. 2006. A review of approaches to mobility telemonitoring of the elderly in their living environment. *Annals of Biomedical Engineering 34*, 4: 547–563.

4. Helen Nissenbaum. 2004. PRIVACY AS CONTEXTUAL INTEGRITY. *Washington Law Review* 79, 119.

5. John Vines, Stephen Lindsay, Gary W. Pritchard, et al. 2013. Making Family Care Work: Dependence, Privacy and Remote Home Monitoring Telecare Systems. *Proceedings of the 2013 ACM International Joint Conference on Pervasive and Ubiquitous Computing*, ACM, 607–616.

6. Allison Williams, Bharati Sethi, Wendy Duggleby, et al. 2016. A Canadian qualitative study exploring the diversity of the experience of family caregivers of older adults with multiple chronic conditions using a social location perspective. *International Journal for Equity in Health* 15: 40.

7. Caregiver Statistics: Demographics | Family Caregiver Alliance. Retrieved September 17, 2017 from https://www.caregiver.org/caregiver-statistics-demographics.

8. Fitbit Official Site for Activity Trackers & More. Retrieved September 21, 2017 from https://www.fitbit.com/home.

A Stakeholders' Analysis of the Systems that Support Foster Care

Karla Badillo-Urquiola
University of Central Florida
Orlando, FL 32816, USA
Kcurquiola10@knights.ucf.edu

Jaclyn Abraham
University of Central Florida
Orlando, FL 32816, USA
jaclyn.abraham@knights.ucf.edu

Arup Kumar Ghosh
University of Central Florida
Orlando, FL 32816, USA
arupkumar.ghosh@ucf.edu

Pamela Wisniewski
University of Central Florida
Orlando, FL 32816, USA
pamwis@ucf.edu

GROUP '18, January 7–10, 2018, Sanibel Island, FL, USA
© 2018 Copyright is held by the owner/author(s).
ACM ISBN 978-1-4503-5562-9/18/01.
https://doi.org/10.1145/3148330.3154521

Abstract

This paper focuses on understanding how the key stakeholders of the foster care system work together, as well as the systems that facilitate collaboration. We conducted 20 interviews with foster parents, 2 with non-profit agencies, and 1 case worker interview. Our findings suggest that each stakeholder faces their own unique challenges and sociotechnical systems put in place to assist stakeholders are not sufficient for addressing these concerns. This poster identifies the major stakeholders, their goals and needs, as well as the systems used. Our work helps identify gaps in order to design more effective systems that can better support the foster care system.

Author Keywords

Foster Care System; Stakeholders analysis; Foster Parents; Foster Teens; Caseworkers; Adolescent Online Safety

ACM Classification Keywords

K.4 COMPUTERS AND SOCIETY

Introduction

This study is part of a larger work-in-progress project on online safety for foster teens [1,2]. In conducting this larger study, we uncovered interesting complexities related to the number of different stakeholders and systems that support foster care. The goals of this

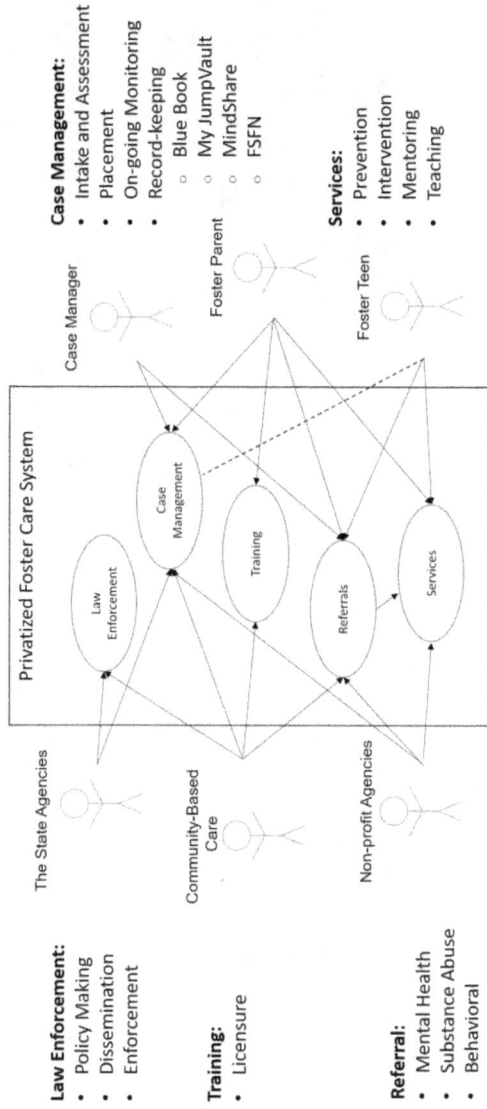

Figure 1. Use Case Diagram of U.S. Foster Care System.

research are three-fold: **RQ1)** to identify the key stakeholders and **RQ2)** understand their unique goals as they pertain to caring for foster youth, and **RQ3)** examine the systems that currently support these goals.

Background

Our recent literature review [2] on foster teens and online safety revealed a lack of empirical research on technology-based interventions that support foster youth and other foster care stakeholders. Additionally, existing programs do not adequately support the needs of foster care stakeholders, due to lack of funding and supervision [3]. In accordance with prior research within the GROUP community [5], our research will inform the design and implementation of technologies

that can support foster care stakeholders and promote organizational change.

Methods

We conducted semi-structured interviews with 20 foster parents, 3 foster care non-profit representatives, and 1 case worker. Parent interviews were conducted by phone, for about an hour, and were followed by a demographics questionnaire. Interviews were audio recorded, transcribed, and analyzed for emergent themes. Descriptive statistics are provided in **Sidebar 1**.

RQ1: Who are the primary stakeholders?

We initially identified 3 primary stakeholders—foster parents, caseworkers, and foster teens. However, throughout our interviews and research, we realized

---

Side Bar 1

Descriptive Statistics

Foster Parents:

- Most foster parents identified as White/Caucasian (15/20); only three as African American/Black, and two remained unidentified.
- Most were under the age of 50 (70%); four were between 50 and 69, and one over the age of 70.
- Mostly all foster parents were female (19/20) except for 1 male.
- Places of residence included Florida, Maine, Georgia, Kansas, New York, and North Carolina.

The non-profit representatives:

- Females
- Florida and Texas

Case worker:

- Female
- Florida

there may be additional, critical stakeholders (e.g., the state agency, community-based care agency, and non-profit agencies). To illustrate each of their roles, we developed a use case diagram (**Figure 1**) in which we present the key stakeholders (actors), as well as their main goals (ovals and lines). The state agency governs the laws, opens the case, and either passes it on to a community-based care agency (if privatized) or provides the welfare services themselves (if not privatized). Community-based care organizations are responsible for enforcing laws, licensing foster parents, and working with non-profit organizations to provide welfare services. Non-profit organizations, per insights from our representatives, assign licensed social workers to the foster teens' birth family and provide necessary support to the birth family and teen. The primary task of a licensed social worker (case manager) is to act as a "coach" for the birth family and foster teen, as well as refer them to any services that may support their needs. Foster parents are responsible for taking care of the teen, advocating for the teen's needs, and making sure the case plan (developed by the social worker) is followed. Finally, foster teens are required to follow the case plans developed by the case manager. We concluded that the system works similar to a hierarchy in which the state agency has the most power, and the foster parents and teens have the least. In the following section, we delve further into the goals and needs of each stakeholder.

RQ2: What are the goals and needs of the stakeholders?

Through our interviews, we found that the overall goal of the foster system is reunification of the teen with their birth family (though in extreme cases it may be finding a permanent home). To reach this goal, each

stakeholder focuses on their own individual goals. For instance, a caseworker's goal is for both the birth parent and foster teen to meet the goals of their case plan. The foster parent's goal is to figure out the needs of the teen to help find a permanent home. To reach these goals, stakeholders must be able to complete their tasks and perform their individual roles effectively. Unfortunately, each stakeholder has numerous unattended needs. For example, foster parents feel as though there is a "*lack of support*" from caseworkers or foster care agencies when teens are misbehaving or "*things go awry.*" (See **Side Bar 2**, FP4). However, parents also understood that the agency may have a lack of knowledge or available resources (See Side Bar 2, FP6). This perspective coincided with some of the challenges outlined by the case worker and non-profit representatives. For instance, the case worker stated that she is often overwhelmed by the numerous cases she is assigned (See **Side Bar 2**, CW 1 quote). One of the non-profit representatives also said that sometimes she feels as though the organization is trying too much, with too little resources, to help. She also mentioned that group homes can be overwhelmed at times too, reaching about 40 teens, 13 to 18 years old (when the average is typically 15 teens per group home). Though systems are put in place to help alleviate some of these challenges, there is still room for improvement.

RQ3: What systems support stakeholders' goals and needs?

During the foster parent interviews, several participants mentioned various systems of support. Since we only focused on questioning the general challenges surrounding foster care, we originally did not include questions concerning these systems in our interviews. To investigate further this emergent theme, we

---

Side Bar 2

What are the goals and needs of the stakeholders?

Lack of support: "My frustration is when the agency or the caseworker is telling you to treat them the way you would treat your child. Punish them the way you would punish your child. But yet I can't do that because they're not my child." FP4

Lack of resources: "...I think that the foster system has its hands so full... they're like, 'we hear you, and we agree that's really odd and frightening, but we have some other cases right now that are a whole lot worse than yours,' and I'm like wow! So, I think that the foster care—even if the foster care system did have a way to monitor, I don't know that they have the capacity to stay on top of all of that" FP6

Overloaded: "I handle about 30+ cases on average and yes! It's way too much." CW1, Florida

conducted a general search. The system most mentioned was the Blue Book (also known as Life book, Plan Book; See Side Bar 3, FP2). This "blue 3-inch binder" is kept throughout the course of the teens' care. It contains the child's history and placement information. It also allows the child to answer questions regarding their personal preferences and unique interests. Some states have transferred it onto online platforms like MyJumpVault (see **Side Bar 3**, FP1). Designed by foster care alumni, MyJumpVault [6] serves as a safe place to upload and manage confidential information. It also provides resources to better prepare foster care youth for the transition to adulthood. Unfortunately, when interviewing the non-profit representatives and case worker, both stated that teens either have limited access or do not get access to this system until the age of 18 (which by this age most teens have aged out of the foster care system).

Discussion and Future Research

Teens in foster care have limited access to the systems that are ultimately used to manage their lives. To increase teen engagement in the systems designed to support their needs, we recommend taking a value sensitive design (VSD) [4] approach to ensure the needs and values of *all* stakeholders are considered when developing a system of support. Prior research on VSD have implemented 3 main stages to VSD: 1) *conceptual*—identifying stakeholders and needs, 2) *empirical*—studying the context of the technical support system, and 3) *technical*—how stakeholder values are incorporated (or neglected) within the design of the system. This paper covers the first stage, conceptual and identifies the major stakeholders of the foster care system, their needs, and the technical systems of support. A limitation of our work is that most of our

participants are from Florida, and the foster care systems varies from state-to-state. To overcome some of our work's limitations and acquire a more holistic perspective, we plan to interview more case workers and non-profit organization representatives that live outside the state of Florida, as well as previous foster youth, who recently aged-out of the foster care system (at or above the age of legal IRB consent), to better understand their needs from the perspectives of VSD and sociotechnical design.

References

1. Karla A. Badillo-Urquiola, Arup Kumar Ghosh, and Pamela Wisniewski. 2017. Understanding the Unique Online Challenges Faced by Teens in the Foster Care System. *Companion of the 2017 ACM Conference on Computer Supported Cooperative Work and Social Computing*, ACM, 139–142.
2. Karla A. Badillo-Urquiola, Scott Harpin, and Pamela Wisniewski. 2017. Abandoned but Not Forgotten: Providing Access While Protecting Foster Youth from Online Risks. *The 16th International Conference on Interaction Design and Children.*
3. Jennifer Mullins Geiger and Lisa Ann Schelbe. 2014. Stopping the Cycle of Child Abuse and Neglect: A Call to Action to Focus on Pregnant and Parenting Youth in and Aging Out of the Foster Care System. *Journal of Public Child Welfare* 8, 1: 25–50.
4. Marije Nouwen, Maarten Van Mechelen, and Bieke Zaman. 2015. A Value Sensitive Design Approach to Parental Software for Young Children. *Proceedings of the 14th International Conference on Interaction Design and Children*, ACM, 363–366.
5. Michelle Partogi and Nassim JafariNaimi. 2016. Fostering Organizational Change through Co-Designing Collaborative Media. ACM, 441–444.
6. My JumpVault – Secure Document storage for Foster Youth. Retrieved September 18, 2017 from http://www.myjumpvault.org/.

Side Bar 3

What systems support stakeholders' goals and needs?

Blue Book: "Each child that comes into the home has blue book and along with the blue book normally, from early childhood or whatever, they have a book and that this is their life story or journey." FP2, Florida

My JumpVault: "they no longer use what is called a Blue Book. It is now electronic where you get a jump drive and it has all of the children's information on it, or it is sent via email to you, for you to peruse through the child's information." FP1, Florida

Designing a Video Co-Watching Web App to Support Interpersonal Relationship Maintenance

Madeline E. Smith
Leo Ascenzi
Yingsi Qin
Ryan Wetsman

Computer Science
Colgate University
Hamilton, NY 13346 USA

mesmith@colgate.edu
lascenzi@colgate.edu
tqin@colgate.edu
rwetsman@colgate.edu

GROUP '18, January 7–10, 2018, Sanibel Island, FL, USA
© 2018 Copyright is held by the owner/author(s).
ACM ISBN 978-1-4503-5562-9/18/01.
https://doi.org/10.1145/3148330.3154522

Abstract

Spending time together and enjoying everyday activities helps to support interpersonal relationships, which have many positive benefits for individuals. However, many such activities are difficult or impossible in long-distance relationships. This work aims to address that problem with one such activity: watching videos together. We describe the process we used to design our video co-watching web app. Specifically, we conducted semi-structured interviews with 10 individuals who watch videos with others to understand their current video watching activities. We analyzed those findings using affinity diagramming to identify user requirements and features. After sketching multiple wireframes and getting feedback, we developed an interactive prototype.

Author Keywords

Video co-watching; interpersonal relationship maintenance; long distance relationships; user-centered design; semi-structured interviews; prototype; web application

ACM Classification Keywords

H.5.2. Information interfaces and presentation (e.g., HCI): User Interfaces.

We took a user-centered approach to the design of an application to improve people's ability to remain connected to one another across distances while still engaging in a meaningful and fun activity, specifically co-watching videos. Intended to help people who are unable to see each other regularly (e.g., people in long-distance relationships, military families, students studying abroad, etc.) maintain their interpersonal relationships, we draw on prior work in social psychology as well as Human-Computer Interaction.

Background

Interpersonal Relationships

Interpersonal relationships have been shown to have many benefits for individuals, including increasing their psychological well-being and decreasing their likelihood of contracting physical illnesses [6]. To benefit one must maintain positive interpersonal relationships through commitment, love/liking, mutual control, benefits [5], and social exchanges [10].

Shared experiences are one way the people can increase connectedness and form positive relationships [2]. Previous research suggests that remote video co-watching is an engaging shared experience for people to feel together when physically separated [4].

Video Watching

Collocated video co-watching is popular among young people, who report enjoying company of their friends more than watching the actual videos [3]. Results of a survey of undergraduate students' TV viewing habits revealed that 25–30% of media time is spent multitasking online [1]. We therefore started our design process with the goal of emphasizing social connectedness.

Interview Study

We conducted semi-structured interviews to learn about our potential users' both solo- and group-watching behaviors.

Participant Recruitment

We sought to interview a diverse set of people with experience watching videos with others (collocated or remotely). We posted recruitment messages on our university campus and on an active neighborhood social networking site.

Potential participants filled out a screener survey, and we selected 10 participants to interview with a range of ages, genders, etc. The 10 participants we interviewed included: three participants aged 18–22, three 23–35, two 36–60, and two over the age of 60; seven were female and three were male; two live alone, three with roommates, and five with family; three of our participants were in long-distance romantic relationships; and five worked full-time.

Protocol

Our semi-structured interviews consisted of questions in three main categories: general video watching habits, solo video watching habits, and group video watching habits.

In each category, we asked about their last experience watching a video. Specifically, we asked about the types of videos they watched, the devices they used, the locations, the time of the day, if they were multitasking, the reason why they chose the above criteria, and how frequent they perform the above activities.

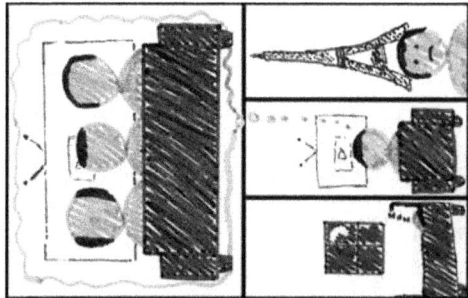

Figure 1: Long-distance friends want to watch a video together.

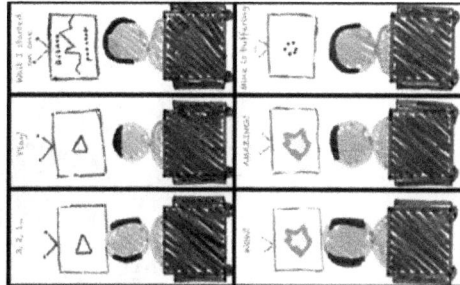

Figure 2: But they have trouble syncing their video feeds

paused to buffer. Our participants often used a single device to view the video and connecting with others.

Web Application Design

Based on the prior research and the requirements we identified in our interview study, we set out to design and develop our web application.

Prototyping

After some initial sketches and static wireframes, we used Axure to create two high-fidelity prototypes incorporating the features identified previously. We demonstrated the prototypes for a number of potential users to get feedback on the different versions before deciding which features to include in our "final" prototype.

In our design [see Figure 4], users can (1) view the streaming video, (2) see profile photos of friends watching with them, (3) chat with those friends, (4) view the webcam stream for each friend, (5) expand a friend's video, and (6) control the video and volume feeds for each friend. View a video demo of the prototype in action at hci.colgate.edu/video/demo.

Development

We are currently implementing the web application to the specifications of the prototype. Currently the front-end shell (written with HTML, CSS, and JavaScript (also Jquery) is fully functional. We are currently working on developing the back-end and connecting to existing APIs to add video and text chatting services.

There are several commercial products for co-watching videos, such as rabb.it, which are built around screen sharing and not focused on interpersonal relationships.

Figure 3: Section of the affinity diagram used to analyze interview data

For group video watching, we also asked how they communicate with each other, how often they communicate, what they communicate about, and if the communication effected video watching enjoyment.

Analysis & Findings

Interviews were fully transcribed. Notes were made and analyzed an affinity diagram was created [see Figure 1] to identify emergent themes. From those themes, we developed and ranked a set of user requirements and used those to create a set of features.

Our participants reported experiencing problems with syncing their remote video feeds (similar to [4]). Even when attempts to start the videos at the same time were successful, videos feeds sometimes lagged or

Acknowledgements

We thank the Colgate University Faculty Research Council and Office of the Dean of Faculty for funding that supported this research. In addition, we would like to thank our gracious participants and colleagues for their participation and feedback on our prototypes.

References

1. Fleura Bardhi, Andrew J Rohm, and Fareena Sultan. 2010. Tuning in and tuning out: media multitasking among young consumers. *Journal of Consumer Behaviour* 9, 4: 316–332. http://doi.org/10.1002/cb.320

2. David Cwir, Priyanka B Carr, Gregory M Walton, and Steven J Spencer. 2011. Your heart makes my heart move: Cues of social connectedness cause shared emotions and physiological states among strangers. *Journal of Experimental Social Psychology* 47, 3: 661–664. http://doi.org/10.1016/j.jesp.2011.01.009

3. Anne Jerslev. 2001. "Video nights." Young people watching videos together -- a youth cultural phenomenon. 9, 2: 2–17. http://doi.org/10.1177/110330880100900201

4. Anna Macaranas, Gina Venolia, Kori Inkpen, and John C Tang. 2013. Sharing Experiences over Video: Watching Video Programs together at a Distance. Springer Berlin Heidelberg, 73–90. http://doi.org/10.1007/978-3-642-40498-6_5

5. Brian G Ogolsky and Jill R Bowers. 2013. A meta-analytic review of relationship maintenance and its correlates. 30, 3: 343–367. http://doi.org/10.1177/0265407512463338

6. Thomas Ashby Wills. 1985. Supportive Functions of Interpersonal Relationships. In Sheldon E Cohen and S Leonard Syme (eds.). Academic Press, Inc., Orlando, FL, 61–82.

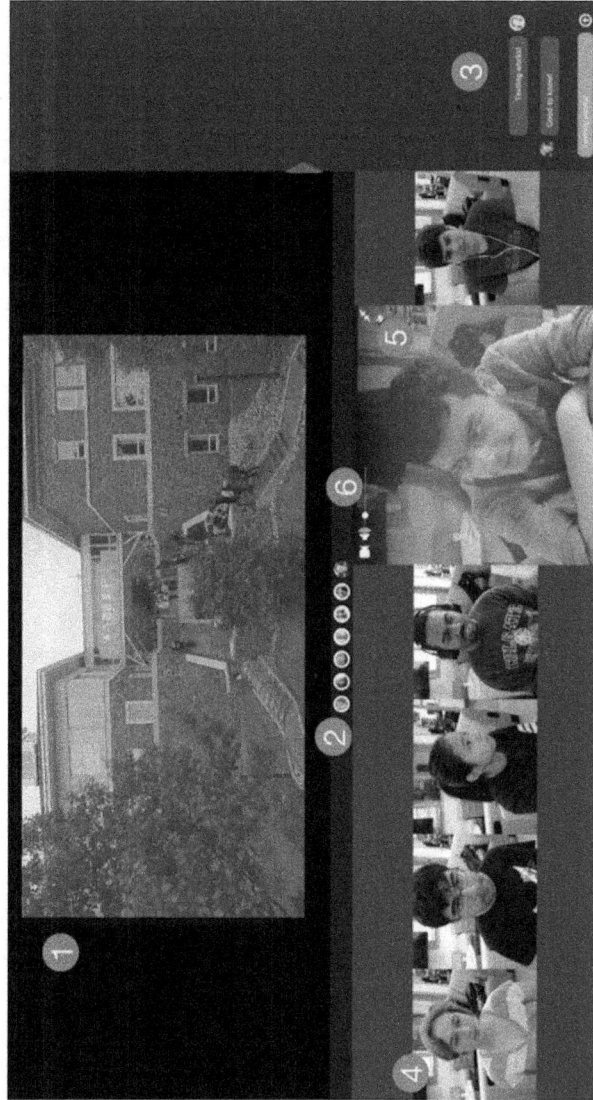

Figure 4: High-fidelity prototype of our system for remote video co-watching

Future Work

Once the current features have been developed and tested, we will conduct usability testing and refine the design as needed. We will then conduct a controlled study to evaluate the effectiveness of this app for maintaining long-distance interpersonal relationships

We would also like to add the features that were generated following our interview study but not determined to be crucial to the application. For example, we would like to create profiles and calendars so users can connect with others and schedule co-watching sessions in advance.

Regrets, I've Had A Few: When Regretful Experiences Do (and Don't) Compel Users to Leave Facebook

Shion Guha
Department of Mathematics,
Statistics and Computer Science
Marquette University
Milwaukee, WI
shion.guha@marquette.edu

Eric P.S. Baumer
Computer Science and
Engineering
Lehigh University
Bethlehem, PA
ericpsb@lehigh.edu

Geri K. Gay
Communication and
Information Science
Cornell University
Ithaca, NY
gkg1@cornell.edu

ABSTRACT

Previous work has explored regretful experiences on social media. In parallel, scholars have examined how people do not use social media. This paper aims to synthesize these two research areas and asks: Do regretful experiences on social media influence people to (consider) not using social media? How might this influence differ for different sorts of regretful experiences? We adopted a mixed methods approach, combining topic modeling, logistic regressions, and contingency analysis to analyze data from a web survey with a demographically representative sample of US internet users (n=515) focusing on their Facebook use. We found that experiences that arise because of users' own actions influence actual deactivation of their Facebook account, while experiences that arise because of others' actions lead to considerations of non-use. We discuss the implications of these findings for two theoretical areas of interest in HCI: individual agency in social media use and the networked dimensions of privacy.

Author Keywords

social media; Facebook; regret; non-use; privacy.

ACM Classification Keywords

H.5.m. Information interfaces and presentation (e.g., HCI): Miscellaneous.

INTRODUCTION

Social media serve a variety of valuable functions. People use social media for keeping in touch with friends [20], forming social groups [25], cultivating social capital [30,31,32], facilitating social grooming [63], and receiving positive social feedback [15,68].

At the same time, social media use can also have a variety

of less positive impacts. Making personal information available online (however privately) has the potential for embarrassment [43,58], regret [67], loss of face [43], bullying [13], addiction [28] and inadvertent social consequences [21, 22]. Such events, in turn, may lead to or exacerbate mental health conditions such as depression or bipolar disorder [40]. The social dimensions of these experiences have a variety of forms, depending both on whose takes action (self or other) and who is the potential recipient of the harm (self or other).

Simultaneously, a parallel strand of research has explored the non-use of social media. Notably, researchers have studied social media refusal [27], voluntary disconnection [45], reversion and relapse [13], differences between users and non-users [2, 24], motivations behind non-use [6, 48], and different experiences of non-use [14]. One common theme inferred from these studies is that social media non-use is not a strictly binary either-or proposition [7, 8] but can take a variety of forms. This line of research expands our scope of inquiry to include those who do not directly use, but may still be in some relationship with, the technologies we study and design.

This paper explores the intersection of these two research areas. Specifically, we ask: *What is the relationship between different types of regretful experiences on social media and forms of social media non-use?* This coalescence of research areas provides an important contribution in at least two ways. First, the current literature on regrets is driven by narratives around privacy [43,66]. However, other aspects of regret, both in terms of causes and in terms of effects, warrant examination. Second, people derive important value from social media. Our results speak to issues about how people balance this value with potential harms from regretful experiences.

To answer these questions, we analyzed data from an online survey (n = 515) with a demographically representative sample of US Internet users employing a mixed computational-qualitative approach. Doing so allowed us to test how different types of regretful experiences relate to different forms of non-use. Our main findings are:

1. Using computational topic modeling [11], we identified two salient themes described in open-ended survey

responses about regretful experiences. One topic deals with *actions taken by the respondent* that cause regrets, while the other deals with *actions taken by others*, regardless of whom those actions impacted.

2. Second, we examined how the occurrence of each of these two themes in respondents' data predicts different forms of use and non-use. We find that those whose regretful experiences are associated with *their own actions* are more likely to have *actually deactivated* their Facebook account, while those whose regretful experiences are associated with *others' actions* are more likely only to have *considered deactivating* their account. Thus, *different sorts of negative experiences lead to different forms of non-use* on Facebook. This finding is corroborated by analysis of closed-ended responses in our survey data.

3. Finally, we make inferences about implications to two larger theoretical areas: (a) the role of individual agency in social media (non)use [54,70], and (b) expanding beyond the individual as the unit of privacy-aware behavior to more collective, social, or networked dimensions of privacy [12,35,36,42].

The rest of this paper is organized as follows. First, we summarize the current literature from two broad areas: harms that can arise from experiences and uses of social media, focusing particularly on regret, and the literature on social media non-use. Second, we describe our study design, data collection process, and mixed computational-qualitative analytic approach. Finally, we illustrate our main findings in greater detail and define how they contribute to existing HCI scholarship.

BACKGROUND

This section is divided into three broad areas. First, we review literature from social media that concentrates on regretful aspects of social media use. Second, we review literature on social media non-use that unpacks the different forms, modalities, experiences, and effects of not using social media. Finally, we explore how frameworks of privacy have been used to explain such phenomena and bring all three threads of literature together.

Regrets on Social Media

In contrast to much prior work examining the benefit of social media use [15,20,25,30,31,32,63,68], this paper focuses on potential harm from social media. Specifically, we focus on regretful experiences. Work in social psychology [51, 52] defines regret as "a negative emotion" and states that "regret feels bad because it implies a fault in personal action." Inherently, "self-blame is a component of regret." Studying regret is important because it can lead to depression and other mental conditions [52]. Such mental health issues have also become a recently important area of study in HCI [16].

The narrative around regretful experiences in HCI is dominated by privacy [21, 43, 59, 67]. That is, experiences become regretted because they involve perceptions of

individual privacy violations, in line with the social psychology literature on regret [51].

In one seminal paper, Wang et al. [66] found that regretful experiences among Facebook users primarily occurred in four different ways: mismatches between desired and actual perceptions by others on Facebook, unanticipated social consequences, audience mismanagement (e.g. accidently sharing content to work colleagues that are more suitable for significant others), and highly emotional states while posting. Similarly, Patil et al. [43] studied (as part of a larger project) regrets in the context of location sharing by Foursquare users. They find that the three primary causes of regret are audience mismanagement, being caught lying, and dealing with an actual physical encounter after checking into its digital counterpart. Similarly, Sleeper et al. [58] found that, among Twitter users, primary causes of regret included audience mismanagement, cathartic/expressive tweets, and mismanagement of personal information. Thus, some commonalities emerge in characterization of regrets, particularly in terms of the audience's role.

Regretful experiences can subsequently impact the ways the people engage with and through social media. Wohn and Spottswood [69] studied adult Facebook users and found that regretful experiences can change the perception of ties between users depending upon the experience and its subsequent reactions. In another study, Sleeper et al. [59] found that negative experiences such as regret can lead users to reconsider how they use (or do not use) social media, but they did not study this interaction in great detail. Stern [60] studied a convenience sample of college students on Facebook and found that in that particular demographic, regretful experiences were more closely associated with self-presentation issues. While participants did not feel that these experiences represented their true self, they reported that these experiences had been valuable and had changed their online behavior in significant ways. Studying teenagers, Xie and Kang [72] similarly found that both frequency and differential patterns of social media (non) use were associated with regretful experiences. Kaur et al. [29] studied adolescents on Facebook and found that regretful experiences do influence how they use Facebook. However, they did not specifically focus on non-use.

In terms of non-use, Sleeper et al. [57] found that users would self-censor (i.e., avoid posting) certain content on Facebook if they felt that it would lead to future consequences, such as job or friendship loss. Moore and McElroy [38] studied undergraduates on Facebook and found that the Big 5 personality traits (other than openness) predict the level of regret for posting inappropriate Facebook content. Other work has linked personality with Facebook non-use [52], but connections among personality, regret, and non-use have not yet been examined.

To summarize, prior work on regret has focused primarily on the individual. This focus includes both individual attributes (personality, emotional state, demographics, etc.) and individual actions (posting content, usage frequency, self-censoring, etc.). It is not just privacy but *personal* privacy that dominates [21, 43, 58, 66]. However, significant work has highlighted the social or networked dimensions of privacy [12,35,36,42]. Similarly, regret also deals with interpersonal relationships – audience perceptions and reactions, social tie strength, etc. Thus, we may benefit from considering networked dimensions of privacy in relation to social media regret.

Social Media and (Networked) Privacy

Research on privacy in HCI taken multifaceted approaches [12,35,41, 42]. One framework [41] conceptualizes privacy as a phenomenon where information exchange between two or more parties is mediated by common norms, perceptions, and contexts. A change in any of these usually constitutes a violation of privacy. Palen and Dourish [42] call for understanding privacy beyond the individual level and in the group or network level for an increasingly intertwined and connected world.

Recently, scholars have increasingly studied the social dimensions of privacy. Some call this networked privacy [12, 35]. Networked privacy aims to treat considerations of and decisions arising from privacy concerns as a network level phenomenon. What this means is conceptually simple – we all look at our friends' activities on social media at various times and for various purposes. This practice is known as a social surveillance [34]. Networked privacy suggests that we focus on concerns arising from social surveillance, which may manifest in different ways. For instance, my friends may post embarrassing pictures of me [34,35,36] on Facebook (without my permission). My friends' privacy settings may shape my audience as much as my own privacy settings do. I may observe my social media friends engaging in regretful behavior [12]. These types of phenomena have been well studied [64], and they represent an increasingly important area of work in HCI.

Social Media Non-Use

As noted above, there has been a growing trend in the non-use of social media, especially around Facebook [6,45,48]. Calls for non-use can take many different forms. For instance, in May 2010, a campaign called Quit Facebook Day [47] encouraged Facebook users to stop using the site and to delete their accounts. Another campaign called 99 Days of Freedom [1] involved a less permanent call to action. It asked Facebook users to stop using Facebook for 99 days and to publicly signal to their networks that they were taking part in this effort. Both campaigns elicited over 45,000 responses. Moreover, there has been a slow but steady increase in more general practices of social media refusal, digital detoxification, and voluntary disconnection from social media in recent years [27, 45]. Indeed, we have also seen a few instances of public figures or "internet famous" people taking publicized breaks from social media

(or from the entire Internet) for different periods of time ranging from 25 days [62] to a full year [37, 50].

These developments have been of particular interest to researchers in HCI [7,8,53]. Many studies compare users and non-users [2,24,32,53,61,63], try to understand the motivations behind why someone would choose not to use social or communication technologies [6,45,56], or explore the different modalities and experiences that non-use can entail [2,6,14,71].

Collectively, this work has identified certain traits that set various types of non-users apart. For instance, Tufekci [63] compares college students who use SNS and those who do not. She finds that users focus more on what she conceptualizes as the "expressive internet," which is inclusive of phenomena such as social grooming, self-presentation, and other social factors. In similar work using a more generalized sample, Stieger et al. [61] found that people who quit using Facebook tend to usually have higher privacy concerns, are liable to score higher on the Internet addiction scale [74], and tend to be more conscientious in their personalities. Lampe et al.[32] find that social capital among heavy Facebook users is higher than that among both light users and non-users.

It is also important to understand social media non-users' reasoning and motivations. For instance, non-use may (or may not) be a voluntary choice [54,70]. Non-use might also be a way to make a statement about one's political identity [45] or an attempt to make better decisions about one's privacy [6,48,61]. In some cases, it might be an intentionally short term break for socio-cultural or otherwise reasons [9,56] or perhaps an option which may be desirable but not (perceived as) viable [6].

Our survey of the existing literature on social media non-use identified no prior work examining potential relationships between regretful experiences and non-use. One might expect there to be relationships between these two phenomena, since regretful experiences are often related to privacy [21, 43, 59, 66], and social media non-use is often motivated by privacy concerns [6, 45, 61].

Summary

Synthesizing across this literature review, we come to the following conclusions:

1. People have regretful experiences on social media [66]. We know how people feel about and react to these experiences, but we do not know about the longer term repercussions of such experiences on social media.

2. Many of these regretful experiences are related to privacy. Prior work on regret has examined individual aspects, but less work has considered how the networked dimensions of privacy [65] may relate to regretful experiences.

3. As a result of regretful experiences, people may stop using social media. We have some hints that this might

happen [43] but we don't really have strong evidence of the ways in which it does.

This paper fills these gaps in the literature by asking the following research questions:

RQ1: How do regretful experiences on social media relate to social media non-use?

RQ2: What role is played by the interpersonal, networked dimension of regretful experiences?

METHODS
In this section, first, we describe the overall data collection process and IRB approval. Next, we briefly summarize the online survey design, concentrating on the parts directly relevant to this paper. Finally, we describe our participant recruitment and their demographics.

Survey Design
This section briefly describes the major sections in the survey, but it focuses on the questions analyzed for this paper. The survey included three groups of questions. First, a series of questions determined the type of user for each respondent. Specific to this study, we asked each user the following two questions described below. These particular questions are theoretically important (especially in relation to Facebook) and have been described and validated in prior work [6]. The number in square brackets after each yes/no represent the total counts of such users in our sample. The text embedded in angle brackets after each question are labels for simplicity in future references.

1. Have you ever *considered deactivating* your Facebook account (yes [128]/ no [60]) <*Considered*>
2. Have you ever *deactivated* your Facebook account? (yes [70]/ no [188]). <*Deactivated*>

Note that not every question was asked of every respondent. If a respondent has never had a Facebook account, it would be meaningless to ask if she has ever deactivated it. Similarly, asking a respondent who has actually deactivated her account whether or not she has considered deactivating it would provide little to no additional information. For the respondents who did see and respond to them, these questions allow for examining the difference between *thinking* about or considering non-use (i.e., deactivating one's Facebook account) and *actually* following through.

Second, existing, well-validated scales were used to measure four constructs that may influence types of non-use First, we used the well-known Facebook Intensity Scale (FBI) (8 items) [20] to assess the overall intensity of Facebook usage. Second, the Bergen Facebook Addiction Scale (BFAS) (18 items) [3] was used to capture the six main components of addiction on Facebook, i.e., salience, mood modification, tolerance, withdrawal, conflict, and relapse. Third, for questions around Facebook Privacy Behaviors and Experiences (PBE) (10 items), we drew upon Wang et al.'s [66] prompts for examining regretful experiences on Facebook as well as their relationship to

privacy-aware behavior. Finally, we also asked questions around demographics, namely age, gender, household income, marital status, ethnicity, education, and political views. We focused on PBE questions for this study as we didn't believe that FBI or BFAS were relevant for our RQs.

Third, the survey also included several open-ended, free-text response questions. Many of these involved expanding upon responses to closed-ended questions, described below.

For the analysis of these particular research questions, we focus on a portion of the PBE section (adapted from [66]). Three questions were asked to the respondent about regretful experiences (1) that she had because of her own actions, (2) that others had because of their own actions (and which she'd seen on social media), and (3) that she had because of others' actions. We term these as "Self", "Social" and "Networked" respectively. To reiterate, "Self" refers to regretting my own actions, usually posting content. "Social" refers to someone else regretting their own actions. Finally, "Networked" refers to regrets that I had because of someone else's actions. The constructs "Social" and "Networked" are often written about in networked privacy scholarship [12, 35]. Table 1 shows the wording of each question and provides further clarification.

Since the person taking action in the Self question differs from that in the Social and Networked questions, we expect that they will have differing impacts on different types of non-use. Furthermore, since the recipient of the harm in the Social and Networked questions differs, we expect that these two types of regretful experiences will also have differing impact on non-use. Since this is exploratory work, we are reluctant to construct formal hypotheses to describe these expectations but want to acknowledge our intuition behind our data analysis strategies.

Question	Construct	Explanation
Have **you** ever posted something that **you** regretted?	Self	Content that **I** posted about **myself**.
Do you know **someone else** who posted something **they** later regretted?	Social	Content that **someone else** posted about **themselves**
Has **someone else** posted something **about you** that they later regretted?	Networked	Content that **someone else** posted about **me**.

Table 1. Description of PBE Questions

If participants responded yes to one or more of these questions, one was selected at random, and respondents were asked "Please tell us a story about this experience." These open-ended questions generated substantial textual data. On an average, each participant wrote 2 sentences containing a total of 24 words. Overall, we collected 767 sentences with a total of 19,308 words.

Participants and Data Collection

To acquire a representative sample of US internet users, we contracted with a survey and sampling agency, Qualtrics, whose recruitment and sampling procedure is outlined on their website [46]. Qualtrics' staff assembled a web panel of participants using demographic criteria derived in part from Pew's omnibus internet survey [44]. The demographic screening criteria used included gender, race/ethnicity, age, and income. At the beginning of the survey, demographic questions were used to screen respondents. For example, once we received 89 respondents age 25-34 (i.e., 17.8% of our target sample size of 500 respondents), age was used as a screening criterion for subsequent respondents, such that respondents in the age 25-34 did not pass the age criterion. Respondents who did not pass any of the screening criteria were excluded.

Recruitment continued until we had accumulated sufficient numbers of respondents for each demographic category. Ultimately, we collected a web panel of 515 participants, for which we paid $2,750. Of them, 379 participants either currently have or previously had a Facebook account.

ANALYSIS AND RESULTS

The analysis here takes a mixed methods approach. First, we start with a simple 3 x 2 contingency analysis, calculating the proportions for each type of regret (Self, Social, and Networked) versus each form of non-use (Deactivated, Considered). Second, we apply topic modeling [11] to analyze the free-text survey data. Finally, we use binary logistic regression to link these computationally identified topics about regret with forms of non-use.

The results show not only that experiences of regret increase the likelihood of non-use, but that different types of regret are more strongly associated with different forms of non-use. In short, we find that the three-way distinction among Self, Social, and Networked collapses to a two-way distinction between self-action and other-action. What matters is who takes action, *regardless* of whether the person feeling regret is the respondent or someone else.

Different Types of Regret Predict Different Forms of Non-Use

First, we consider the varying relationships between each type of regretful experience about which we asked (Self, Social, and Networked) and different forms of non-use. To do so, we first compared whether the respondent indicated that she had undergone each of the three types of privacy experiences against whether the respondent had actually deactivated her Facebook account. Figure 1 presents a visualization of this contingency table analysis. Of those respondents who indicated having Self type regret experiences, 33.7% deactivated their account. However, for those who indicated having Social type regret experiences, only 25% deactivated their account. Similarly, of those who indicated having Networked type regret experiences, only

22.7% deactivated their account. This difference is significant (Pearson's χ^2=0.404, p=<0.001).

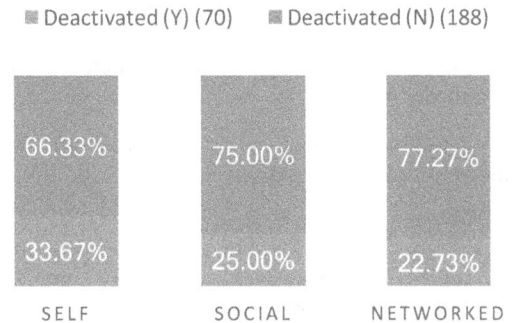

Figure 1: Deactivation is predicted by Self type of regret. The difference between Social and Networked regret is not statistically significant.

When comparing regretful experiences against whether the respondent had *considered* deactivating her Facebook account, a similar but opposite trend occurs. Self type regret experiences lead to slightly higher considered of deactivation (34.7%) than actual deactivation (33.67%). However, Social type regret experiences and Networked type regret experiences lead to much higher rates of considering deactivation (38.3% and 39.6%, respectively) than actual deactivation (25.0% and 22.7%, respectively). Figure 2 visualizes the relevant contingency table. Again, the difference among the three types of regret experiences is significant (Pearson's χ^2=0.398, p=<0.001).

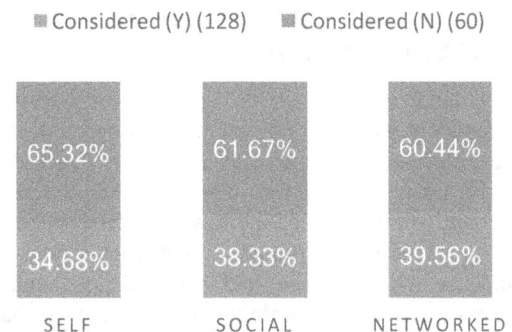

Figure 2: Consideration of deactivation predicted by Social and Networked regret. There is no significant difference between the proportions of "Social" and "Networked".

These results provide evidence that who experiences regret is not as influential as who took action to cause someone regret.

Topic Modeling and Qualitative Analysis: From Three Types of Regrets to Two Types

In recent HCI scholarship, topic modeling [11] has become a popular method [16, 17] to analyze large scale qualitative data. Briefly, topic modeling is an unsupervised approach that takes as input a collection of unlabeled documents (such as survey responses [55]) and identifies a number of underlying themes or "topics." Topic models represent each topic as a probability distribution of words that deal with that topic. Documents are represented a combination of topics in different proportions. Topic modeling algorithms attempt to infer these underlying topics from a set of unlabeled documents. Despite omitting word order, syntax, and other structural relationships, resultant topics often capture recognizable themes surprisingly well.

When applied to free-text survey responses, we can think of automatically extracted topics as "codes" that have been assigned by an algorithm rather than by human coders. Although it forgoes the linguistic and contextual knowledge of human coders, in return this approach provides a much more scalable means of analyzing large data sets.

Recent work [9, 10, 26, 39] has also advocated for combining topic modeling and related computational approaches with close qualitative reading. Thus, the work presented here uses statistical topic models, specifically Latent Dirichlet Allocation (LDA) models [11], combined with a close qualitative reading. For each topic, we inspect the top 20 words most likely to occur in documents about that topic, as well as the 50 documents (i.e., survey responses) that have the highest proportion of that topic. Doing so allows us to regain some of the human contextual knowledge often given up in topic modeling analysis.

Text Processing: Obtaining Stable Topic Models
In our analysis, each free-text response is treated as a single document. Of the three possible yes/no questions about regret (from Table 1), 100% of the participants responded yes to at least one, 62% responded yes to at least two, and 37% responded yes to all three. To reiterate, each participant wrote a free-text elaboration for only one of these questions (randomly chosen if multiple questions were answered "yes"). This leaves a total of 379 documents, one for each respondent.

We split each document into a series of tokens (words separated by punctuation and/or whitespace) and changed all the words to lowercase. In line with existing best practice on topic modeling, we removed all stopwords [33], i.e., a small set of high frequency determiners, conjunctions, and prepositions (e.g. "the", "and", "for"). Note that, because of our focus on personal and social experiences, the stopword list did not include common pronouns, such as "I", "you," "we," or "they."

We used LDA [11] to train topic models over our entire textual corpus. LDA is an approximate algorithm and can produce different results based on different initializations. Thus, we ran 10 independent instances of LDA with a consistent number of starting topics (n=5), thereby generating 10 different topic model solutions. The number of topics was chosen after experimenting with anywhere between 2 and 10 topics. We manually examined the top 100 words of each topic for each solution to determine which topics were essentially distributions of the same

words with small variations attributable to the different random initializations. We excluded all topics that exhibited more than 50% variation in word distribution across different solutions. At the end of this process, which closely resembles that used by [9], we obtained two stable topics.

For the two stable topics, we used a close qualitative inspection to understand what each topic was about. Doing so involved examining the top 50 most representative responses for each topic, i.e., the 50 documents with the highest proportion of that topic. The following two subsections provide, for each of the two stable topics, the top 20 most probable words in documents about that topic. These are followed by a selection of 5 representative responses (with each one's rank in terms of topic score) selected based on our close qualitative reading. Finally, we also assigned a high-level topic descriptor (Other-Action and Self-Action) for each topic for reference and simplicity.

Topic: Other-Action
Top 20 words: *someone, post, friend, safe, regret, else, acquaintance, upset, embarrassed, don't, want, personal, herself, himself, seen, back, posted, private, bullied, people, group.*

This topic refers to content posted by other members of the participant's social network that caused regretful experiences either for the poster (e.g., O4 below) or to the participant (e.g., O2 below). High probability words include words referring to other people (someone, friend, else, acquaintance), several third person reflexive pronouns (himself, herself), as well as verbs about specific kinds of behavior (post, embarrassed, regret, bullied). This topic suggests that participants may have used highly similar language when describing both Social and Networked experiences. In addition, representative responses for this topic occurred primarily in the questions we asked about Social and Networked types of regrets. Some exemplars:

- **O1:** "someone was bullying someone else about their weight" [rank 2]
- **O2:** "A posting about an extra marital affair was embarrassing for someone I once knew in the past" [rank 6]
- **O3:** "know someone who posted something that ended up ruining their relationship" [rank 11]
- **O4:** "Yes. Someone posted a picture of me without my permission. The picture was not an explicit picture, but I still didn't appreciate the person posting it without me knowing." [rank 18]
- **O5:** "Family member posted pictures of herself and her 'boytoy' while her husband was out of the Country on business. She announced a divorce and then wanted to stay married. Many family members were upset and embarrassed by the exposure of such personal matters." [rank 19]

Topic: Self-Action

Top 20 words: *left, never, post, stay, deleted, go, back, regretted, embarrass, quit, drama, stand, I, we, private, intrusive, comment, relationship, shared, no*

This topic refers to content and behavior posted by the participant that caused herself regrets or embarrassment (e.g., S1 below). First person pronouns appear prominently (I, we), as do numerous action verbs (left, stay, deleted, quit). The combination of first person pronouns, active voice, and the representative responses suggest individual agency as a central concept in this topic. In addition, representative responses for this topic occurred primarily in the questions we asked about Self type of regrets. Some exemplars:

- **S1:** "Okay I posted something about my relationship that I later regretted. Relationship problems or non-problems should be kept within the relationship I hate facebook for that." [rank 19]

- **S2:** "Deleted my account over some silly drama. I left because I couldnt stand it any more. I posted some stupid things and my friends started over that. After that there was not point to stay." [rank 4]

- **S3:** "posted some silly stuff about another person who used to be my friend. I was harsh in my comment so i deleted it." [rank 12]

- **S4:** "I posted about my ex and it totally blew up. I just left facebook after that and i will never go back again." [rank 2]

- **S5:** "After we informed our church family that I was pregnant with my first child we informed my mother in law that she could "tell who you want", we meant within the church, instead she posted it to Facebook. Instead of having the joy of calling out of town family and sharing the news, we were cheated of that and in return had some of those family called US asking why we didn't share the information with them. We were upset and my mother in law greatly regretted posting it. We not [*sic*] have a standard "don't post about us unless you ask" policy." [rank 9]

Topics for Different Types of Regret Predict Different Forms of Non-use

In line with the contingency analysis, topic modeling suggests that the key feature in discriminating types of regret is who takes action. We also wanted to understand if the topics obtained through the described process predicted different forms of non-use.

To recall, we asked participants two binary response questions, one about whether they had considered deactivating their Facebook accounts (*Considered*), and one about whether they had ever actually deactivated their Facebook accounts (*Deactivated*). For each participant, we

know what proportion of each topic (Other-Action or Self-Action) is prevalent in their free-text response. Therefore, we used binary logistic regressions to model the relationship between topics and non-use. We used a mean-centered log transform of the topic proportion for each topic as predictors [as in 9]. These were used in two separate logistic regression models, one with *Considered* as the dependent variable and one with *Deactivated*. Demographic variables were used as control variables in initial models. However, their absence increased the predictive power, so we selected the most parsimonious model for reporting. The procedure to calculate the mean-centered log transformed topic proportion metric is outlined in [74, equation 13]

We find that different topics affect different forms of non-use. High proportions of the topic Self-Action significantly predict Deactivated (SE=0.563, OR=1.142). In other words, a Facebook user is more likely to have *actually* deactivated her account if she experienced regretful situations caused by *her own* actions. On the other hand, high proportions of the topic Other-Action significantly predict Considered (SE=0.546, OR=1.262). This means that a Facebook user is more likely to have *considered* deactivating her account if she has experienced regretful situations caused by others' actions. The results of these models are presented in Table 2.

Model	Variables					
	Other-Action			**Self-Action**		
	Std. β	CI	Odds Ratio	Std. β	CI	Odds Ratio
Deactivated (Y)	0.41	(0.324, 0.508)	1.027	0.56	(0.409, 0.688)	**1.142****
Considered (Y)	0.55	(0.432, 0.652)	**1.262** **	0.38	(0.218, 0.593)	1.071
Fit Statistics	AIC = 481 BIC = 463			AIC = 507 BIC = 496		

Table 2. Regretful experiences arising from a respondent's actions (the Self-Action topic) increase the probability of deactivation. Regretful experiences arising from someone else's actions (the Other-Action topic) increase the probability of considering deactivation.

Summary of Results

Across the different analysis above, the results provide a coherent answer to our two research questions. First, we find that regretful experiences arising from the respondent's actions increase the likelihood of deactivation. We also find that regretful experiences arising from others' actions increase the likelihood of considering deactivation. These results are consistent across the contingency analysis of closed-ended questions and the topic modeling analysis of open-ended questions. This relationship between regret and non-use addresses **RQ1**.

Second, our survey included separate questions about other people experiencing regret (the Social questions) and others' actions causing the respondent regret (the Networked questions). Interestingly, we find that these two different experiences have the same impact on non-use – they both increase the likelihood of considering deactivation. Furthermore, our topic modeling analysis suggests limited differences, if any, in the ways that respondents described experiences related to Social types of regrets compared to Networked types of regrets, thus addressing **RQ2**.

Thus, in the relationship between regret and non-use, we find that *it matters less who experiences regret*. Instead, *it matters more who takes action* to cause regret.

DISCUSSION

The design of this study was based on the expectation (from prior work [66]) that regret oriented experiences on social media fall into three major types. First, regret experiences could originate from my own actions ("Self"). Second, I could observe others having experiences that they find regretful ("Social"). Finally, experiences may originate from content created by others about me that I find regretful ("Networked"). However, our findings suggest not only that the Social and Networked types of regret have similar impacts on non-use, but that participants' language provides little differentiation between these two types.

These results extend the foundational scholarship outlined in this paper by speaking to two main questions. First, much prior work on social media regrets emphasizes individual behavior, but our results show that many regretful actions are out of an individual's hands. How is individual agency, in terms of control and volitionality of non-use, affected by different regretful experiences? Second, prior work has established a relationship between privacy concerns and non-use [6,9,49]. How can we account for the networked dimensions of privacy as a factor influencing non-use under different regretful conditions?

Individual Agency, Control, and Volitionality of Non-use

As seen above, the Other-Action topic focuses primarily on others' actions and the Self-Action topic focuses primarily on the respondent's actions. In the former case, the respondent is often not even implicated, such as in "second-hand reports" (O3) or when "someone was bullying someone else" (O1). In the latter case, even when the response deals with other people taking action on Facebook, it often stemmed from the respondent's own actions. For example, the respondent whose mother-in-law posted on Facebook about the respondent's pregnancy did so because the respondent told her she was pregnant (S5).

These findings are particularly interesting in light of Wyatt's [70] arguments about voluntary and involuntary non-use [see also [53] on "disenfranchisement"]. Specifically, we extend the umbrella of volitionality, arguing that similar distinctions can be made among technology *users*. Consider again the examples of responses with high proportions of the Other-Action topic (O1-O5).

These statements do not place much agency in the hands of the respondent. The locus of control is elsewhere, diminishing the personal responsibility component that comprises regret [51,52]. In contrast, the representative statements for the Self-Action topic (S1-S5) describe the respondent's own actions; they may have been regretful actions, but they were the respondent's to take.

This distinction may help explain the relationship we see between each of these topics and different forms of non-use. Respondents who describe themselves in a more agentic manner (i.e., whose responses contain a higher proportion of the Self-Action topic) are more likely to have actually deactivated their Facebook account. In contrast, those who focus on the actions of others (i.e., whose responses contain a higher proportion of the Other-Action topic) are more likely to have considered deactivating their account but not actually done so. This result directly answers RQ2 and partially answers RQ1. Elsewhere, these individuals are referred to as "reluctant users" [anon under review], people who continue using a technology even though they might rather not do so. These findings suggest volitionality and sense of agency as central constructs to explaining why individuals engage in different forms of social technology use and non-use. This point applies not only to regret but also play a broader role in experiences on social media more generally.

Networked Privacy

This work also carries important implications for how we conceptualize and design for privacy in social media. In many situations, we see that regretful experiences arise not from actions of the respondent but from actions of others. Examples include the respondent who described how a "Family member posted pictures of herself and her 'boytoy'" (O5) and how this caused regret and embarrassment to the user. In another example, a respondent noted that "someone posted a picture of me without my permission" (O4) and this led to feelings of regret. Even in some situations where responses highlight their own actions (i.e., in the Self-Action topic), others' actions play a key role, such as the respondent and her church family (S5). Again, both **RQ1** and **RQ2** are intertwined here.

In recent work, some scholars have pointed to the social or "networked" aspects of privacy [35]. For instance, some teenagers "try to achieve privacy through technical means" while others socially control access by "demanding that adults keep out" [12]. However, many "have given up on controlling access to content." Instead, people try to "limit access to meaning" rather than "limit access to content," using code switching, dog whistles, and other sociolinguistic devices. Non-use, in its various forms, is one manifestation of this strategy. For example, some users leave their account deactivated at all times except when they are logged in [12]. Doing so makes it easier for these users to police content posted about them. Thus, privacy is enacted through a complex amalgam of access to meaning, use, and interpretation of actions.

Even an incredibly savvy user, a master of all possible configurations of privacy settings, does not have full control over her privacy. The interpersonal and networked nature of social media leads to situations that are not only unanticipated but, in many cases, could not have been anticipated. This is further exacerbated when people monitor each other's' activities in networks, a phenomenon termed social surveillance [22,34]. Social surveillance leads to (sometimes incorrect) impression formation [22] and unanticipated (sometimes negative) social consequences [21]. Thus, given the connectedness of modern life [12], we should position groups, communities, and networks at the center of privacy research and privacy debates, whether about regret or about other harms.

This is not to say that designers should simply throw up their hands or that we live in an era of the death of privacy. Indeed, our results show that individual action is still very important. However, they also show that the networked aspects of privacy related experiences are becoming increasingly important. Nor do we suggest that the non-users have the best strategy for ensuring their privacy. Indeed, non-users may have even *less* influence over information posted by others about them. Rather, we argue that the meaning of privacy in networks has altered. Networked privacy issues cannot be "solved" [5] through a series of configuration options and dialog boxes. In addition to novel technological interventions [65,66], which *should* be pursued, designers must *also* consider interpersonal, normative, or social interventions [4, 23] in the sociotechnical processes of boundary negotiation [42].

As a concrete example, Wang et al. have explored the idea of privacy nudges [67], which shows a randomly selected subset of the audience for a post before the post is shared. These small interventions can, and often do, encourage users to reconsider the content of their social media posts before sharing them. The framing of privacy nudges focuses on personal action, informing users that, e.g., "These people, your friends, AND FRIENDS OF YOUR FRIENDS can see your post" [68:2369]. As an alternative, one might prompt users with questions such as, "How would these people, your friends, and friends of your friends feel about seeing this post?" or "Would these people, your friends, or friends of your friends want to edit this post?" Doing so may encourage people not only to think about the individual but also the interpersonal ramifications of their actions. This provides one example of how we might design around networked privacy.

LIMITATIONS AND FUTURE WORK

This project is based on self-reported survey data on a demographically representative sample of US internet users. As in such studies, there are a number of limitations which we describe here along with proposals for future work to remedy some of these inadequacies. First, self-

report data is based upon past recollection of use. This may be inaccurate to varying degrees. A future project could remedy this by combining self-report survey data with Facebook log data. Second, we studied two forms of non-use – deactivation and consideration of deactivation – but not some of the other types such as reversion or partial use. Future work should look at a comprehensive understanding of potential harms from social media versus other kinds of non-use. Finally, this work is based on static snapshots of data in time. A dynamic, temporal analysis would uncover other nuanced patterns of how the relationship between non-use and harmful experiences plays out over time.

CONCLUSION

In this study, we investigated the link between potentially harmful experiences on social media and non-use of social media. More specifically, we investigate the link between experiencing regret and deactivating one's social media account. Using a representative sample of US internet users (n=515) and their use of Facebook, we adopted a mixed computational-qualitative method approach (contingency table analysis, topic modeling, and binary logistic regression). We find that different types of regretful experiences lead to different types of non-use. Regrets stemming from *one's own actions* increase the probability that a user will *deactivate* her account. In contrast, regrets stemming from *others' actions* increase the probability that a user will *consider* deactivating her account but not actually do so. In the latter case, it doesn't matter who experiences regret but who takes the regretful action.

These findings carry implications for at least two areas of usable privacy research. First, non-use is intimately linked with individual agency, control, and volitionally of use [23]. We show that the perceived locus of agency in regretful experiences has bearing on subsequent decisions about forms of non-use. Second, this work adds to the growing literature on networked privacy. The results here compel us to reimagine how we think about and design privacy-aware features in social media. Moving beyond the individual, the analysis here can inform designs that account for the social and networked privacy.

ACKNOWLEDGMENTS

We acknowledge funding from NSF grant no IIS-1110392. Work present here was conducted while all authors were affiliated with Cornell University. Thanks to our survey participants for their time as well as the anonymous reviewers for their valuable suggestions.

REFERENCES

1. 99 Days of Freedom. http://99daysoffreedom.com/

2. Alessandro Acquisti and Ralph Gross. 2006. "Imagined communities: Awareness, information sharing, and privacy on the Facebook." In *Privacy enhancing technologies*, pp. 36-58. Springer Berlin Heidelberg.

3. Cecilie Schou Andreassen, Torbjørn Torsheim, Geir Scott Brunborg, and Ståle Pallesen. 2012.

"Development of a Facebook addiction scale 1, 2." *Psychological reports* 110 (2): 501-517.

4. Eric Baumer, Mark Sueyoshi, and Bill Tomlinson. 2008. "Exploring the role of the reader in the activity of blogging." In *Proceedings of the SIGCHI Conference on Human Factors in Computing Systems*, pp. 1111-1120. ACM.

5. Eric P. S. Baumer, and M. Silberman. 2011. "When the implication is not to design (technology)." In *Proceedings of the SIGCHI Conference on Human Factors in Computing Systems*, pp. 2271-2274. ACM.

6. Eric P. S. Baumer, Phil Adams, Vera D. Khovanskaya, Tony C. Liao, Madeline E. Smith, Victoria Schwanda Sosik, and Kaiton Williams. 2013. "Limiting, leaving, and (re) lapsing: an exploration of Facebook non-use practices and experiences." In *Proceedings of the SIGCHI conference on human factors in computing systems*, pp. 3257-3266. ACM.

7. Eric. P. S. Baumer, Ames, M. G., Burrell, J., Brubaker, J. R., & Dourish, P. 2015. Why Study Technology Non-use? First Monday, 20(11).

8. Eric P. S. Baumer, Burrell, J., Ames, M. G., Brubaker, J. R., & Dourish, P. 2015. On the Importance and Implications of Studying Technology Non-use. Interactions, 22(2), 52–56.

9. Eric P. S. Baumer, Shion Guha, Emily Quan, David Mimno, and Geri K. Gay. 2015. "Missing Photos, Suffering Withdrawal, or Finding Freedom? How Experiences of Social Media Non-Use Influence the Likelihood of Reversion." *Social Media + Society* 1, no. 2 (2015): 2056305115614851.

10. Eric P. S. Baumer, David Mimno, Shion Guha, Emily Quan and Geri Gay. 2017. Comparing grounded theory and topic modeling: Extreme divergence or unlikely convergence? Journal of the Association for Information Science and Technology, 68: 1397–1410. doi:10.1002/asi.23786.

11. David M. Blei, Andrew Y. Ng, and Michael I. Jordan. 2003. "Latent Dirichlet allocation." *The Journal of Machine Learning Research* 3 (2003): 993-1022.

12. danah boyd. 2012. "Networked privacy." *Surveillance & Society* 10, (3/4) (2012): 348.

13. danah boyd. 2014. *It's complicated: The social lives of networked teens*. Yale University Press.

14. Jed R. Brubaker, Mike Ananny, and Kate Crawford. 2014. "Departing glances: A sociotechnical account of 'leaving' Grindr." *New Media & Society* (2014): 1461444814542311.

15. Moira Burke and Robert E. Kraut. 2014. "Growing closer on Facebook: changes in tie strength through social network site use." In *Proceedings of the SIGCHI Conference on Human Factors in Computing Systems*, pp. 4187-4196. ACM.

16. Stevie Chancellor, Zhiyuan Jerry Lin, Erica L. Goodman, Stephanie Zerwas, and Munmun De Choudhury. 2016. "Quantifying and Predicting Mental Illness Severity in Online Pro-Eating Disorder Communities."

17. Francine Chen, Patrick Chiu, and Seongtaek Lim. 2016. "Topic Modeling of Document Metadata for Visualizing Collaborations over Time." In *Proceedings of the 21st International Conference on Intelligent User Interfaces*, pp. 108-117. ACM.

18. Ben C. F. Choi Zhenhui Jiang, Bo Xiao, and Sung S. Kim. 2015. "Embarrassing Exposures in Online Social Networks: An Integrated Perspective of Privacy Invasion and Relationship Bonding." *Information Systems Research* 26, no. 4 (2015): 675-694.

19. Maeve Duggan Nicole B. Ellison, Cliff Lampe, Amanda Lenhart, and Mary Madden. 2015. "Social media update 2014." *Pew Research Center* 19 (2015).

20. Nicole B. Ellison, Charles Steinfield, and Cliff Lampe. 2007. "The benefits of Facebook "friends:" Social capital and college students' use of online social network sites." *Journal of Computer-Mediated Communication* 12.4 (2007): 1143-1168.

21. Shion Guha, and Jeremy Birnholtz. 2013. "Can you see me now?: location, visibility and the management of impressions on foursquare." In *Proceedings of the 15th international conference on Human-computer interaction with mobile devices and services*, pp. 183-192. ACM.

22. Shion Guha, and Stephen B. Wicker. 2015. "Do Birds of a Feather Watch Each Other?: Homophily and Social Surveillance in Location Based Social Networks." In *Proceedings of the 18th ACM Conference on Computer Supported Cooperative Work & Social Computing*, pp. 1010-1020. ACM.

23. Saul Greenberg, and David Marwood. 1994. "Real time groupware as a distributed system: concurrency control and its effect on the interface." In *Proceedings of the 1994 ACM conference on Computer supported cooperative work*, pp. 207-217. ACM.

24. Eszter Hargittai. 2007. "Whose space? Differences among users and non-users of social network sites." *Journal of Computer-Mediated Communication* 13, no. 1 (2007): 276-297.

25. Adam N. Joinson. 2008. "Looking at, looking up or keeping up with people?: motives and use of Facebook." In *Proceedings of the SIGCHI conference on Human Factors in Computing Systems*, pp. 1027-1036. ACM.

26. Matthew L. Jockers, and David Mimno. 2013. "Significant themes in 19th-century literature." *Poetics* 41 (6): 750-769.

27. Nathan Jurgenson. (2013). The Disconnectionists. The New Inquiry.

28. Dimitris Karaiskos, Elias Tzavellas, G. Balta, and Thomas Paparrigopoulos. 2010. "P02-232-Social network addiction: a new clinical disorder?." *European Psychiatry* 25 (2010): 855.

29. Puneet Kaur, Amandeep Dhir, Sufen Chen, and Risto Rajala. "Understanding online regret experience using the theoretical lens of flow experience." *Computers in Human Behavior* 57 (2016): 230-239.

30. Cliff Lampe, Nicole Ellison, and Charles Steinfield. 2006. "A Face (book) in the crowd: Social searching vs. social browsing." In *Proceedings of the 2006 20th anniversary conference on Computer supported cooperative work*, pp. 167-170. ACM

31. Cliff Lampe, Nicole B. Ellison, and Charles Steinfield. 2008. "Changes in use and perception of Facebook." In *Proceedings of the 2008 ACM conference on Computer supported cooperative work*, pp. 721-730. ACM.

32. Cliff Lampe, Jessica Vitak, and Nicole Ellison. 2013. "Users and nonusers: Interactions between levels of adoption and social capital." In *Proceedings of the 2013 conference on Computer supported cooperative work*, pp. 809-820. ACM.

33. Jure Leskovec, Anand Rajaraman, and Jeffrey David Ullman. *Mining of massive datasets*. Cambridge University Press, 2014.

34. Alice E. Marwick. 2012. "The public domain: Social surveillance in everyday life." *Surveillance & Society* 9(4): 378.

35. Alice E. Marwick. 2014. "Networked privacy: How teenagers negotiate context in social media." *New Media & Society* (2014): 1461444814543995.

36. Alice Marwick and danah boyd. 2014."'It's just drama': teen perspectives on conflict and aggression in a networked era." *Journal of Youth Studies* 17, no. 9 (2014): 1187-1204.

37. Paul Miller. 2013. I'm still here: back online after a year without the internet. http://www.theverge.com/2013/5/1/4279674/im-still-here-back-online-after-ayear-Without-the-internet

38. Kelly Moore, and James C. McElroy. 2012. "The influence of personality on Facebook usage, wall postings, and regret." *Computers in Human Behavior* 28, no. 1 (2012): 267-274.

39. Michael Muller, Shion Guha, Eric P. S. Baumer, David Mimno and N. Sadat Shami. 2016. Machine Learning and Grounded Theory Method: Convergence, Divergence and Combination. In Proceedings of the 19th International Conference on Supporting Group Work, 3-8. ACM, New York, NY.

40. Elizabeth L. Murnane, Dan Cosley, Pamara Chang, Shion Guha, Ellen Frank, Geri Gay, and Mark Matthews. 2016. "Self-monitoring practices, attitudes, and needs of individuals with bipolar disorder: implications for the design of technologies to manage mental health." *Journal of the American Medical Informatics Association.* doi: 10.1093/jamia/ocv165

41. Helen Nissenbaum. (2009). *Privacy in context: Technology, policy, and the integrity of social life.* Stanford University Press.

42. Leysia Palen and Paul Dourish. 2003. "Unpacking privacy for a networked world." In *Proceedings of the SIGCHI conference on Human factors in computing systems*, pp. 129-136. ACM.

43. Sameer Patil, Greg Norcie, Apu Kapadia, and Adam J. Lee. 2012. "Reasons, rewards, regrets: privacy considerations in location sharing as an interactive practice." In *Proceedings of the Eighth Symposium on Usable Privacy and Security*, p. 5. ACM.

44. Pew Internet Survey. 2015. http://www.pewinternet.org/datasets/january-2014-25th-anniversary-of-the-web-omnibus

45. Laura Portwood-Stacer. (2013). Media Refusal and Conspicuous Non-Consumption: The Performative and Political Dimensions of Facebook Abstention. *New Media & Society*, 15(7), 1041–1057.

46. Qualtrics Panels. 2016. URL: https://www.qualtrics.com/online-sample/

47. Quit Facebook Day. URL: www.quitfacebookday.com

48. Lee Rainie, Sara Kiesler, Ruogu Kang, Mary Madden, Maeve Duggan, Stephanie Brown, and Laura Dabbish. 2013. "Anonymity, privacy, and security online." *Pew Research Center* 5 (2013).

49. Lee Rainie, A Smith and Maeve Duggan. 2013. *Coming and going on Facebook. Pew Research Center.* http://www.pewinternet.org/~/media//Files/Reports/2013/PIP_Coming_and_going_on_facebook.pdf

50. D Roberts. 2014. Reboot or Die Trying. Retrieved July 31, 2015, from http://www.outsideonline.com/1926796/reboot-or-die-trying

51. Neal Roese and Summerville, A. (2005). What we regret most... and why. *Personality and Social Psychology Bulletin*, 31(9), 1273-1285.

52. Neal Roese, K. A. I. Epstude, Florian Fessel, Mike Morrison, Rachel Smallman, Amy Summerville, Adam D. Galinsky, and Suzanne Segerstrom. "Repetitive regret, depression, and anxiety: Findings from a nationally representative survey." *Journal of Social and Clinical Psychology* 28, no. 6 (2009): 671.

53. Christine Satchell and Paul Dourish. 2009. "Beyond the user: use and non-use in HCI." In *Proceedings of the 21st Annual Conference of the Australian Computer-Human Interaction Special Interest Group: Design: Open 24/7*. pp. 9-16. ACM.

54. Margaret E. Roberts, Brandon M. Stewart, Dustin Tingley, Christopher Lucas, Jetson Leder-Luis, Shana

Kushner Gadarian, Bethany Albertson, and David G. Rand. "Structural Topic Models for Open-Ended Survey Responses." *American Journal of Political Science* 58 (4) (2014): 1064-1082.

55. Tracii Ryan and Sophia Xenos. 2011. "Who uses Facebook? An investigation into the relationship between the Big Five, shyness, narcissism, loneliness, and Facebook usage." *Computers in Human Behavior* 27, no. 5 (2011): 1658-1664.

56. Sarita Yardi Schoenebeck. 2014. "Giving up Twitter for Lent: How and why we take breaks from social media." In *Proceedings of the SIGCHI Conference on Human Factors in Computing Systems*, pp. 773-782. ACM.

57. Manya Sleeper Rebecca Balebako, Sauvik Das, Amber Lynn McConahy, Jason Wiese, and Lorrie Faith Cranor. 2013. "The post that wasn't: exploring self-censorship on Facebook." In *Proceedings of the 2013 conference on Computer supported cooperative work*, pp. 793-802. ACM.

58. Manya Sleeper, Justin Cranshaw, Patrick Gage Kelley, Blase Ur, Alessandro Acquisti, Lorrie Faith Cranor, and Norman Sadeh. 2013. "I read my Twitter the next morning and was astonished: A conversational perspective on Twitter regrets." In *Proceedings of the SIGCHI conference on human factors in computing systems*, pp. 3277-3286. ACM.

59. Manya Sleeper, Alessandro Acquisti, Lorrie Faith Cranor, Patrick Gage Kelley, Sean A. Munson, and Norman Sadeh. 2015. "I Would Like To..., I Shouldn't..., I Wish I...: Exploring Behavior-Change Goals for Social Networking Sites." In *Proceedings of the 18th ACM Conference on Computer Supported Cooperative Work & Social Computing*, pp. 1058-1069. ACM.

60. Susannah Stern. 2015. "Regretted online self-presentations: US College students' recollections and reflections." *Journal of Children and Media* 9, no. 2 (2015): 248-265.

61. Stefan Stieger, Christoph Burger, Manuel Bohn, and Martin Voracek. 2013. "Who commits virtual identity suicide? Differences in privacy concerns, internet addiction, and personality between Facebook users and quitters." *Cyberpsychology, Behavior, and Social Networking* 16, no. 9 (2013): 629-634.

62. Baratunde Thurston. 2013. #Unplug: Baratunde Thurston Left the Internet for 25 Days, and You Should, Too. http://www.fastcompany.com/3012521/unplug/baratunde-thurston-leaves-the-internet

63. Zeynep Tufekci. 2008. "Grooming, gossip, Facebook and MySpace: What can we learn about these sites from those who won't assimilate?." *Information, Communication & Society* 11 (4) (2008): 544-564.

64. Jessica Vitak, Pamela Wisniewski, Xinru Page, Airi Lampinen, Eden Litt, Ralf De Wolf, Patrick Gage Kelley, and Manya Sleeper. 2015. The Future of Networked Privacy: Challenges and Opportunities. In *Proceedings of the 18th ACM Conference Companion on Computer Supported Cooperative Work & Social Computing* (CSCW'15 Companion). ACM, New York, NY, USA, 267-272.

65. Amy Voida, Stephen Voida, Saul Greenberg, and Helen Ai He. "Asymmetry in media spaces." 2008. In *Proceedings of the 2008 ACM conference on Computer supported cooperative work*, pp. 313-322. ACM.

66. Yang Wang, Gregory Norcie, Saranga Komanduri, Alessandro Acquisti, Pedro Giovanni Leon, and Lorrie Faith Cranor. 2011. "I regretted the minute I pressed share: A qualitative study of regrets on Facebook." In *Proceedings of the Seventh Symposium on Usable Privacy and Security*, p. 10. ACM.

67. Yang Wang, Pedro Giovanni Leon, Alessandro Acquisti, Lorrie Faith Cranor, Alain Forget, and Norman Sadeh. 2014. "A field trial of privacy nudges for Facebook." In *Proceedings of the 32nd annual ACM conference on Human factors in computing systems*, pp. 2367-2376. ACM.

68. Kevin Wise, Saleem Alhabash, and Hyojung Park. 2010. "Emotional responses during social information seeking on Facebook." *Cyberpsychology, Behavior, and Social Networking* 13 (5) (2010): 555-562.

69. Donghee Yvette Wohn, and Erin L. Spottswood. 2016. "Reactions to other-generated face threats on Facebook and their relational consequences." *Computers in Human Behavior* 57 (2016): 187-194.

70. Sally Wyatt. (2003). Non-Users Also Matter: The Construction of Users and Non-Users of the Internet. In N. Oudshoorn & T. Pinch (Eds.), How Users Matter: The Co-construction of Users and Technology (pp. 67–79). Cambridge, MA: MIT Press.

71. Susan P. Wyche, Sarita Yardi Schoenebeck, and Andrea Forte. 2013. "Facebook is a luxury: An exploratory study of social media use in rural Kenya." In *Proceedings of the 2013 conference on Computer supported cooperative work*, pp. 33-44. ACM.

72. Wenjing Xie and Cheeyoun Kang. 2015. "See you, see me: Teenagers' self-disclosure and regret of posting on social network site." *Computers in Human Behavior* 52 (2015): 398-407.

73. Limin Yao, David Mimno, and Andrew McCallum. 2009. "Efficient methods for topic model inference on streaming document collections." In *Proceedings of the 15th ACM SIGKDD international conference on Knowledge discovery and data mining*, pp. 937-946. ACM.

74. Young KS. 1998. Caught in the net: how to recognize the signs of Internet addiction–and a winning strategy for recovery. New York: Wiley.

FitAware: Promoting Group Fitness Awareness Through Glanceable Smartwatches

Andrey Esakia[1]   **D. Scott McCrickard[1]**   **Samantha Harden[2]**   **Michael Horning[3]**

[1]Department of Computer Science and Center for HCI
Virginia Tech
esakia|mccricks@cs.vt.edu

[2]Department of Human Nutrition, Foods, and Exercise
Virginia Tech
harden.samantha@vt.edu

[3]Department of Communication and Center for HCI
Virginia Tech
mhorning@vt.edu

ABSTRACT

Physical inactivity is a global public health concern. Community-based interventions that use strategies such as competition and cooperation, with group dynamics-based strategies at their core, are effective at improving individual physical activity behaviors, but they often rely on participants to actively seek out fitness information themselves. This work examines how technologies such as smartwatches that are designed to raise awareness of personal and group fitness can encourage positive fitness behavior within and across peer groups. This paper presents a study about smartwatch use by 27 people as part of an 8-week community physical activity intervention program with elements of competition and cooperation, seeking to understand fitness awareness and behavior of the participants. Results indicate generally high awareness levels of smartwatch information. In particular, members of most successful groups exhibited significantly higher awareness for feedback displayed on the smartwatch.

Author Keywords

Awareness; Physical activity; health informatics; group dynamics; community intervention; persuasive technology

ACM Classification Keywords

H.5.m. Information interfaces and presentation (e.g., HCI): Miscellaneous;

INTRODUCTION AND RELATED WORK

Most Americans do not meet the minimum physical activity recommendation levels [31]. These recommendations are often translated to 10,000 steps per day, and daily step counts represents an easy to-track physical activity level indicator [11,12,27]. Self-monitoring, feedback, and goal setting are the fundamental evidence-based behavior change strategies [24]. Community-based approaches are recommended for large scale interventions[24] and group

dynamics-based strategies help harness the interpersonal factors that occur in small groups [17]. Example strategies include group member cooperation, competition, and interaction toward becoming more active and improving perceptions of cohesion [6].

Group dynamics-based interventions have been shown to be effective for in-person program delivery format, but are not always optimal due to cost and reach [13,25]. Interventions delivered via web-based systems typically suffer from high dropout rates [25], with technology interaction burden cited as a key factor [18].

This paper presents a study about FitAware, a smartwatch-centered system intended to facilitate behavior change via group dynamics based feedback presented on smartwatches, featuring non-interruptive glanceable updates that inform users of personal and group step progress. Feedback includes daily personal steps, collective team steps, user rank within the team, and team rank across all teams. FitAware was deployed as a part of an 8-week community intervention, where teams of varying sizes sought to increase physical activity. Surveys and system usage logs revealed when users wear the watch, they notice display indicators, recall values from the indicators, and increase perceived awareness. These findings reveal how smartwatches can provide users with sustained awareness of group focused feedback.

Prior work has examined awareness of group-focused feedback in the web environment [23] as well as with mobile devices[2][1][21], including ones that examine cooperation, competition and social engagement in the context of socially connected pairs [7]. These examples, while effective in certain ways, all require burdensome user interaction to receive feedback—even smartphones impose barriers on the user experience [3]. This work explores how smartwatches can offer glanceable notifications with promise for increased awareness [19] [20].

THE FITAWARE SYSTEM

FitAware is a three-component system consisting of a Pebble smartwatch interface, companion Android app, and a website. The system digitizes and enhances components of FitEx, an 8-week group dynamics community-based physical activity promotion intervention [15,22]. FitEx

GROUP '18, January 7–10, 2018, Sanibel Island, FL, USA
© 2018 Association for Computing Machinery.
ACM ISBN 978-1-4503-5562-9/18/01...$15.00
https://doi.org/10.1145/3148330.3148343

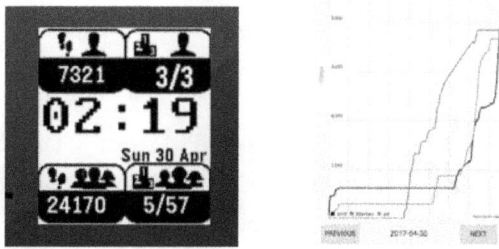

Figure 1. a) FitAware smartwatch watchface interface (Top left: personal steps. Top right: personal rank in the team. Bottom left: team steps. Bottom right: team rank). b) One of the views from the companion Android app provides detailed daily progress for the team member steps.

targets small groups in their natural environments (e.g., workplace, church, home) leveraging existing social connectedness with family, friends, coworkers, and others. The program prescribes formation of small groups (3 to 7 people) from existing social circles where one group member is encouraged to be the team captain, ideally proactive in group interaction and encouragement. Group members set individual goals, with the sum of individual goals as a group goal. They track their progress for 8 weeks, receive feedback, and compete with other teams.

The design philosophy for the smartwatch considered advantages of smartwatches for information accessibility [10,14]. Smartwatches enable faster access to information with low cognitive demand [20,28]. FitAware uses the Pebble smartwatch due to always-on display and long battery life, encouraging ease of use and glanceability important in the design. Recognizing the automaticity [4] with which users—periodically and unprompted—check smartphones [10], we provide non-interruptive passive notifications on smartwatches. Passive notifications have shown good results in the context of influencing health behaviors via smartphones [5,9]. This is preferred over interruptive updates as users react negatively to interruptions from unimportant, secondary) events [26,30]. The watchface layout (see Figure 1a) presents information in a manner that is prescribed for High Throughput Textual Displays [29]. The time and date information is surrounded by within-group (top row and bottom left) and between-group (bottom right) indicators in the four corners. *Personal steps* shows user daily step-count information computed by the smartwatch sensors. *Personal rank* shows the standing in the small team of friends or co-workers. *Team steps* show total team steps. *Team rank* shows between-team competition feedback comparing the person's team to other teams. All watchfae information resets at midnight.

Every 15 minutes, the smartwatch exchanges information via Bluetooth with a companion Android app that, in accordance with Consolvo's design considerations[8], expands the information presented on the watch face and provides more detailed information (see Figure 1b). The app exchanges data with the server to obtain group information updates and share progress and the tracked chronological logs of information displayed on the watchface and smartphone. The website also allows users to manually enter and view progress.

FITAWARE DEPLOYMENT

As outlined in the introduction, there is a need to understand how fitness smartwatches can provide sustained awareness of individual and group fitness feedback. We investigate four aspects of this issue: whether participants continually wear the smartwatch, whether smartwatches can peripherally communicate fitness information about individuals and groups, whether changes in the information are noticed, whether smartwatch wearers can demonstrate awareness of individual and team progress feedback, and whether smartwatch wearers self-report increased awareness. To investigate these questions, we conducted an eight-week field study during which some participants used FitAware.

Study

FitAware was deployed among eligible and interested FitEx participants. Prior to the start of the intervention, the participants set activity goals and completed demographics questionnaires. All study participants were assisted with website registration and FitAware setup. Study participation was voluntary with no compensation for completion.

Upon completion of the study, the participants were offered $20 to participate in a post-program survey and a debriefing interview. The survey consisted of questions aimed at capturing awareness of feedback presented on the watchface as well as the degree of group cohesion of the team measured via Physical Activity Group Environment-Questionnaire [16], used to assess the sense of competition, cooperation, interaction, and competition. The survey questions used a 7-point Likert scale, with the exception of a question asking to recall typical values for smartwatch indicators.

Participants

Nine eligible groups of participants were recruited with some assistance from community outreach organizations. These groups collectively contributed 27 FitAware users of the total 275 individuals participating in the community statewide intervention. The eligibility criteria required the groups to be composed of adults from an existing social circle, with some or all of members equipped with an Android smartphone. From the 9 groups 4 had 4 FitAware users, 2 groups had 3, another 2 had 2 FitAware users and there was one group with only one FitAware user. Of these groups two had FitAware only users while the other groups had two or more web only users(web users had to enter their progress manually).

All nine groups were composed of full-time coworkers that either shared office space, floor, or building. Occupations differed, including front desk receptionists, government clerks and university lab technicians. Participant differed in

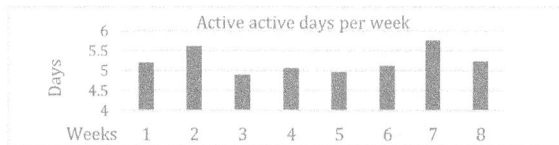

Figure 2. Average weekly active days of smartwatch use.

age (23-61 years old), gender (20 female, 7 male), and race (20 Caucasian, 5 African American, 1 Native American, 1 Asian), BMI (21 to 46) and education level (12 post college/9 college/5 some college/1 high school).

RESULTS

To explore if users could achieve awareness of information from feedback indicators of group centered information, we analyzed the system usage logs and survey responses.

FitAware use

Feedback from the smartwatch indicators requires regular smartwatch use. Of 27 participants that signed up to use the smartwatch, three dropped out early, leaving 24 participants that completed the 8-week long study. From the 24 participants that finished the study, 23 yielded usable system tracking data (one of the participants had a smartphone with faulty Bluetooth, preventing data from being received from the smartwatch), 21 responded to the survey and 20 participated in the post-survey debriefing interviews.

The system use logs show active days of wearing the watch. For these active days, we considered days during which user steps continuously increased for at least 8 hours during the day (8am-8pm) with periods of inactivity (no increase) shorter than one hour (time necessary to charge Pebble). On average, the 23 participants had 5.22 (SD=0.29) active days of smartwatch use (See Figure 2 for weekly averages) per week. Debriefing interviews revealed some of the reasons for not wearing the watches every which include leaving it charging ("*Forgot it was charging*") and forgetting to put it on ("*Simply because I would forget to put it on.*"). Correlation analysis revealed a moderate correlation between participant age and the average active days (r=-.449, p<0.05) suggesting that younger audience had more active days.

Awareness

To assess user awareness of the feedback from the four watchface indicators, a 7-point Likert survey prompted users to indicate: likelihood of visually noticing each indicator ("*Regardless of why you looked at the Pebble smartwatch display, how likely were you to notice each of the following?*"), level of awareness with the information presented from indicators ("*I was aware of the <indicator name>*"), the confidence of noticing changes in the indicators ("*I regularly noticed changes in the <indicator name>*") and the values for the indicators that they would see at the end of a typical day ("*By the end of a typical day, what were the values for the following indicators on the Pebble smartwatch display?*")

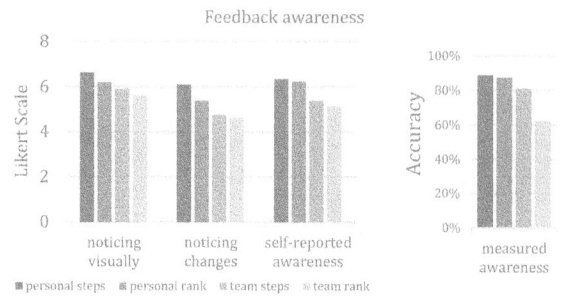

Figure 3. Results from the survey and the accuracy of measured awareness based on recall for typical indicator values at the end of day.

Peripherally noticing indicators. Visual contact with indicators should raise awareness. Participants rated the likelihood of noticing indicators for personal steps, personal rank, team steps and team rank at 6.62, 6.20, 5.90 and 5.62 (see Figure 3). Responses for personal steps and team rank were significantly different (t=4.088, P<0.01) suggesting that on average users were more likely to visually notice personal steps than team rank when looking at the watchface.

Noticing changes in indicators. Noticing changes in indicators contributes to increased awareness. Users' degree of agreement for noticing changes for personal steps, personal rank, team steps and team rank is 6.10, 5.38, 4.76 and 4.62, respectively. Responses for the personal steps indicator are significantly higher than team rank (t=4.088, P<0.01), team steps (t=3.229, P=0.03) and personal rank (t=2.096, P=0.043). User responses are reflective of indicator update frequency; personal steps update continuously while other indicators only update every 15 minutes.

Self-reported awareness. Users rated their awareness for the feedback from the four indicators comprised of personal steps, personal rank, team steps and team rank at 6.33, 6.24, 5.38 and 5.14 correspondingly. Analyzing for significant differences for the responses shows that users reported significantly higher awareness for personal steps than team steps (t=2.955, P=0.005) and team rank (t=3.344, P=0.002) but not personal rank (t=0.395, P=0.695), also the responses of personal rank are significantly higher than those for team steps (t=2.979, P=0.005) and team rank (t=3.369, P=0.002), which is suggestive of stronger within-group awareness.

Measured awareness. To measure awareness of feedback from the indicators, the survey asked participants to recall indicator values for a typical day. 21 survey participants provided responses for personal steps and personal rank, 19 for the team rank, and 17 for team steps and team rank. Shapiro-Wilk normality tests showed all 21 participants exhibited distributions close to normal for personal steps, but 4 participants did not have normally distributed end-of-day values for team steps due to some group members self-reporting progress (P<0.05), and 4 participants did not provide answers for team steps. Thus we were able to measure team step accuracy for the 13 participants.

For all participants with normally distributed 'end of the day' indicated personal and group steps we define *accuracy* as $A_s = \frac{|S_r - S_m|}{S_r} * 100\%$ where S_r is the value reported by the user and S_m is the median end of the day value for the active days (i.e. the actual 'end of the day' typical or most frequent value).For the ranking indicators we measured accuracy differently since the values are often repeated. We define *ranking accuracy* as $A_r = \frac{R_r}{R_1} * 100\%$ where R_r is the frequency of occurrence of the reported rank and R_1 is the frequency of occurrence of the most common rank that was displayed on the watchface at the 'end of the day' time indicated by the user.

Accuracy for personal steps, personal rank, team steps and team is 88.7%, 87.5%, 81%, and 62.6% respectively, see Figure 3. Independent samples t-tests reveal no significant difference between goals and reported steps (t=-1.749, P=0.088). We found significant differences between team rank accuracy and the other three indicators but no significant differences between personal steps, personal rank and team steps. This is suggestive of less overall awareness for the team rank than the other three indicators.

Variances for the accuracy measures for personal steps, personal rank, team steps and team rank are 1%, 3%, 4% and 9% respectively. Correlation analysis for team rank accuracy responses reveals significant correlations with the median of steps displayed at the end of the day (r=0.504, P<0.05) and competitiveness in the group (r=0.61, P<0.01). There is a significant correlation between the proportion of the active days during which the team rank was on the 'pedestal' (top 3 places) and accuracy of the team rank recall by the team members. The average accuracy of team rank recall for the participants whose 'end of the day' team rank indicator was in the top 3 for the most time (frequency of 50% or above) was 84.11% while other participants showed an average accuracy of 42.7%. Two tailed independent sample t-test analysis shows significant differences in the accuracy of the responses between these categories of participants (t=4.005, P<0.01). The participants in top 3 all came from the groups that had at least 3 active Android users. On average the members from these groups reported significantly higher competitiveness than participants from other groups (t=2.388, P=0.027), as well the median of steps displayed at the end of the day (t=2.289, p=0.034). There was no significant difference in the active days between the two categories of participants nor in Android app use. There were also no significant differences in terms of the self-reported awareness or noticing changes of team rank between these categories of participants.

DISCUSSION
The use of the smartwatch resulted in high awareness for personal steps and personal rank. For team steps, 4 out of 21 participants could not recall a typical value. For the remaining 13 eligible participants, strong correlation between accuracy of recalling team steps and active days suggests that, unlike personal steps and personal rank that can be 'learned' rather quickly, awareness of the typical end-of-day team steps benefits from increased exposure to the information. Survey results for self-reported awareness are reflected in recall accuracy results and suggest that users were more aware of personal steps and personal rank than of other indicators. For the team steps indicator, some users could not remember the typical values (*"Oh goodness... I will be honest I don't really remember"*) or difficult to read (*"The team steps [indicator] were hard [to read] because it is a higher number"*, *"This one [team steps] got hard to read once there were five digits"*).

For between-team information represented by team rank, the overall awareness levels were much lower than for the within-team information (personal steps, personal rank and team steps). However, the average measured awareness levels for the team rank feedback were significantly higher for the participants whose teams were in the top 3 for the most days (84.11% vs 42.7% for the other teams). The participants from these teams were also significantly more competitive and active (based on the median daily indicated step values). Another distinctive characteristic of teams with higher awareness of team rank was the presence of proactive group captains that were openly competitive (*"As the team captain I wanted to be like 'We must win!'"*), attentive to other group members (*"I liked to keep an eye [on the team steps indicator] to make sure that everyone was syncing properly"*), supportive (*"I would go and I would check with everyone to make sure their watches are syncing"*), and encouraging (*"She[captain] would say '<name>, I put you on this team because I know you walk a lot and you are not walking enough today!' [laughs]"*). This is suggestive of a positive influence from such proactive and competitive captains on feedback awareness for all group members.

CONCLUSION AND FUTURE WORK
The goal of this study was to investigate glanceable smartwatch indicators as part of group fitness program to facilitate awareness of within-group and between-group progress feedback. The results show high awareness levels for within-group feedback. Participant awareness levels for between-group feedback (team rank) revealed significant dependence on group characteristics. Participants in teams with a proactive, competitive, encouraging captain exhibited measurably stronger team rank feedback awareness as well as higher activity levels and competitiveness.

These results are encouraging as they show that passive glanceable watchface updates can facilitate awareness of the group fitness related feedback. The findings revealing the differences in the awareness levels of the feedback from the team rank indicator, motivate further exploration of how the personal and group factors influence the feedback awareness levels. Our next step is to gain a deeper understanding of how the encouragement and reminders from the team captains lead to an increased group members' awareness of the feedback, and then formulate a list of design considerations for a group-fitness oriented smartwatch centered system with a focus on communicating, augmenting and amplifying the effects of such encouragements and reminders, exemplified through a working system based on a modern smartwatch platform with better information visualization, physical activity tracking and user interface interactivity capabilities.

ACKNOWLEGEMENTS

We are grateful to Virginia Tech's Institute for Creativity, Arts, and Technology (ICAT) for supporting this work through a SEAD grant. Thanks also to everyone who worked on and participated in the FitEx program.

REFERENCES

1. Aino Ahtinen, Pertti Huuskonen, and Jonna Häkkilä. 2010. Let's all get up and walk to the North Pole: design and evaluation of a mobile wellness application. In *Proceedings of the 6th Nordic conference on human-computer interaction: Extending boundaries*, 3–12. Retrieved January 6, 2017 from http://dl.acm.org/citation.cfm?id=1868920

2. Ian Anderson, Julie Maitland, Scott Sherwood, Louise Barkhuus, Matthew Chalmers, Malcolm Hall, Barry Brown, and Henk Muller. 2007. Shakra: tracking and sharing daily activity levels with unaugmented mobile phones. *Mobile Networks and Applications* 12, 2–3: 185–199.

3. Daniel Lee Ashbrook. 2010. Enabling mobile microinteractions. Georgia Institute of Technology. Retrieved May 7, 2017 from https://smartech.gatech.edu/handle/1853/33986

4. Joseph B. Bayer, Scott W. Campbell, and Rich Ling. 2015. Connection Cues: Activating the Norms and Habits of Social Connectedness. *Communication Theory*. Retrieved January 6, 2017 from http://onlinelibrary.wiley.com/doi/10.1111/comt.12090/pdf

5. Frank Bentley and Konrad Tollmar. 2013. The power of mobile notifications to increase wellbeing logging behavior. In *Proceedings of the SIGCHI Conference on Human Factors in Computing Systems*, 1095–1098. Retrieved January 6, 2017 from http://dl.acm.org/citation.cfm?id=2466140

6. Albert V. Carron and Kevin S. Spink. 1993. Team building in an exercise setting. *Sport Psychologist* 7, 1. Retrieved January 6, 2017 from http://search.ebscohost.com/login.aspx?direct=true&profile=ehost&scope=site&authtype=crawler&jrnl=0888 4781&AN=20735419&h=R6x1x8ocUsYPW016x7C4 0%2FEiTd8skrgbuS52QihsyXm6mYwxjz8k0Gh0JFg SvBxd69%2BX5iFoi%2BKT0cdHYXGs9w%3D%3D &crl=c

7. Yu Chen and Pearl Pu. 2014. HealthyTogether: exploring social incentives for mobile fitness applications. In *Proceedings of the Second International Symposium of Chinese CHI*, 25–34. Retrieved January 6, 2017 from http://dl.acm.org/citation.cfm?id=2592240

8. Sunny Consolvo, Katherine Everitt, Ian Smith, and James A. Landay. 2006. Design requirements for technologies that encourage physical activity. In *Proceedings of the SIGCHI conference on Human Factors in computing systems*, 457–466. Retrieved January 6, 2017 from http://dl.acm.org/citation.cfm?id=1124840

9. Sunny Consolvo, David W. McDonald, Tammy Toscos, Mike Y. Chen, Jon Froehlich, Beverly Harrison, Predrag Klasnja, Anthony LaMarca, Louis LeGrand, Ryan Libby, and others. 2008. Activity sensing in the wild: a field trial of ubifit garden. In *Proceedings of the SIGCHI Conference on Human Factors in Computing Systems*, 1797–1806. Retrieved February 18, 2017 from http://dl.acm.org/citation.cfm?id=1357335

10. Bernard Desarnauts. 2015. Seconds at a time. Retrieved November 3, 2016 from https://medium.com/wristly-thoughts/seconds-at-a-time-e8762b223476#.5s634umn7

11. Mitch J. Duncan, Wendy J. Brown, W. Kerry Mummery, and Corneel Vandelanotte. 2017. 10,000 Steps Australia: a community-wide eHealth physical activity promotion programme. *Br J Sports Med*: bjsports-2017-097625. https://doi.org/10.1136/bjsports-2017-097625

12. Elizabeth G. Eakin, Kerry Mummery, Marina M. Reeves, Sheleigh P. Lawler, Grant Schofield, Alison J. Marshall, and Wendy J. Brown. 2007. Correlates of pedometer use: Results from a community-based physical activity intervention trial (10,000 Steps Rockhampton). *International Journal of Behavioral Nutrition and Physical Activity* 4, 1: 31.

13. Diane K. Ehlers, Jennifer L. Huberty, and Gert-Jan de Vreede. 2015. Can an evidence-based book club intervention delivered via a tablet computer improve physical activity in middle-aged women? *Telemedicine and e-Health* 21, 2: 125–131.

14. Andrey Esakia, Shuo Niu, and D. Scott McCrickard. 2015. Augmenting Undergraduate Computer Science Education With Programmable Smartwatches. In *Proceedings of the 46th ACM Technical Symposium on Computer Science Education*, 66–71. Retrieved January 6, 2017 from http://dl.acm.org/citation.cfm?id=2677285

15. Paul A. Estabrooks, Michael Bradshaw, David A. Dzewaltowski, and Renae L. Smith-Ray. 2008. Determining the impact of Walk Kansas: applying a

team-building approach to community physical activity promotion. *Annals of Behavioral medicine* 36, 1: 1–12.

16. Paul A. Estabrooks and Albert V. Carron. 2000. The Physical Activity Group Environment Questionnaire: An instrument for the assessment of cohesion in exercise classes. *Group Dynamics: Theory, Research, and Practice* 4, 3: 230.

17. Paul A. Estabrooks, Samantha M. Harden, and Shauna M. Burke. 2012. Group dynamics in physical activity promotion: what works? *Social and Personality Psychology Compass* 6, 1: 18–40.

18. Gunther Eysenbach. 2005. The law of attrition. *Journal of medical Internet research* 7, 1: e11.

19. Wayne CW Giang, Liberty Hoekstra-Atwood, and Birsen Donmez. 2014. Driver engagement in notifications a comparison of visual-manual interaction between smartwatches and smartphones. In *Proceedings of the Human Factors and Ergonomics Society Annual Meeting*, 2161–2165. Retrieved January 6, 2017 from http://pro.sagepub.com/content/58/1/2161.short

20. Rúben Gouveia, Fábio Pereira, Evangelos Karapanos, Sean A. Munson, and Marc Hassenzahl. 2016. Exploring the design space of glanceable feedback for physical activity trackers. In *Proceedings of the 2016 ACM International Joint Conference on Pervasive and Ubiquitous Computing*, 144–155. Retrieved January 6, 2017 from http://dl.acm.org/citation.cfm?id=2971754

21. Xinning Gui, Yu Chen, Clara Caldeira, Dan Xiao, and Yunan Chen. 2017. When Fitness Meets Social Networks: Investigating Fitness Tracking and Social Practices on WeRun. In *Proceedings of the 2017 CHI Conference on Human Factors in Computing Systems*, 1647–1659. Retrieved from http://dl.acm.org/citation.cfm?id=3025654

22. Samantha M. Harden, Sallie Beth Johnson, Fabio A. Almeida, and Paul A. Estabrooks. Improving physical activity program adoption using integrated research-practice partnerships: an effectiveness-implementation trial. *Translational Behavioral Medicine*: 1–11.

23. Rodney P. Joseph, Nefertiti H. Durant, Tanya J. Benitez, and Dorothy W. Pekmezi. 2014. Internet-based physical activity interventions. *American journal of lifestyle medicine* 8, 1: 42–67.

24. Emily B. Kahn, Leigh T. Ramsey, Ross C. Brownson, Gregory W. Heath, Elizabeth H. Howze, Kenneth E. Powell, Elaine J. Stone, Mummy W. Rajab, and Phaedra Corso. 2002. The effectiveness of interventions to increase physical activity: A systematic review. *American journal of preventive medicine* 22, 4: 73–107.

25. Emily L. Mailey, Jennifer Huberty, and Brandon C. Irwin. 2016. Feasibility and Effectiveness of a Web-Based Physical Activity Intervention for Working Mothers. *Journal of physical activity & health*. Retrieved January 10, 2017 from http://europepmc.org/abstract/med/26999823

26. D. Scott McCrickard, Christa M. Chewar, Jacob P. Somervell, and Ali Ndiwalana. 2003. A model for notification systems evaluation—assessing user goals for multitasking activity. *ACM Transactions on Computer-Human Interaction (TOCHI)* 10, 4: 312–338.

27. W. Kerry Mummery, Grant Schofield, Anetta Hinchliffe, Kelly Joyner, and Wendy Brown. 2006. Dissemination of a community-based physical activity project: the case of 10,000 steps. *Journal of Science and Medicine in Sport* 9, 5: 424–430.

28. Stefania Pizza, Barry Brown, Donald McMillan, and Airi Lampinen. 2016. Smartwatch in Vivo. In *Proceedings of the 2016 CHI Conference on Human Factors in Computing Systems* (CHI '16), 5456–5469. https://doi.org/10.1145/2858036.2858522

29. Zachary Pousman and John Stasko. 2006. A taxonomy of ambient information systems: four patterns of design. In *Proceedings of the working conference on Advanced visual interfaces*, 67–74. Retrieved from http://dl.acm.org/citation.cfm?id=1133277

30. Alireza Sahami Shirazi, Niels Henze, Tilman Dingler, Martin Pielot, Dominik Weber, and Albrecht Schmidt. 2014. Large-scale assessment of mobile notifications. In *Proceedings of the SIGCHI Conference on Human Factors in Computing Systems*, 3055–3064. Retrieved January 6, 2017 from http://dl.acm.org/citation.cfm?id=2557189

31. Products - NHIS Early Release - 2015. Retrieved April 19, 2017 from https://www.cdc.gov/nchs/nhis/releases/released20160 5.htm

Psychological Wellbeing as an Explanation of User Engagement in the Lifecycle of Online Community Participation

Donghee Yvette Wohn
New Jersey Institute of Technology
University Heights, GITC 5100
Newark, NJ 07102
wohn@njit.edu

Cliff Lampe
University of Michigan
4322 North Quad, 105 S. State St.
Ann Arbor, MI 48109
cacl@umich.edu

ABSTRACT

This study documents users' changes in psychological wellbeing across the lifecycle of their participation in an online community. Through in-depth interviews with 30 long-term users of Everything2.com, and content analysis of their posts, we found that psychological wellbeing plays a large role in the evolution of how users participate in the community over time. Everything2 is a long-running user-generated content site framed as an open encyclopedia. Results suggested that negative psychological wellbeing, such as loneliness and low self-esteem, fueled initial participation; validation and criticism from other users on one's content motivation continued content contribution; but ultimately feelings of relatedness with the community, unrelated to content contribution, was what retained users. Absence of social connections in the online community, as well as improved wellbeing offline, led to exit.

Author Keywords

Online community; psychological wellbeing; motivation; emotional support; feedback

ACM Classification Keywords

H.5.m. Information interfaces and presentation (e.g., HCI): Miscellaneous.

INTRODUCTION

In this paper, we examine the role an individual's psychological wellbeing plays in their participation of an online community. How does it influence their entry into the community, the experiences they have as an active member, and their exit from that community?

Psychological wellbeing is a term used to refer to general

mental health and wellness [35]. There are many dimensions of psychological wellbeing, some of which include an individual's positive evaluation of himself or herself (self-acceptance), satisfaction with life, having a purpose in life, self-determination [4], and positive relationships with other people [30-32].

Online communities can enhance positive psychological states by nurturing emotional support. While online communication is now dominated by tools like Facebook and Twitter that support existing relationships [16] there are still many examples of online spaces where networks form, and where emotional support from strangers, often in the form of pseudonymous interaction, is an important component. For example, there are many "mommy blogs" like YouBeMom and UrbanBaby that provide frank and forthright emotional support for women with the shared experience of parenting [33]. Large communities like Reddit have multiple boards where people engage in relational self-disclosure [37] and offer emotional support to one another. Online health communities have strong elements of emotional support, a key feature of this growing genre of online interaction [14, 22]. Even in "extreme communities" like those that promote commonly stigmatized illnesses like anorexia, emotional support has been seen to be an important aspect of participation [46].

While people are using these systems for emotional support, the systems themselves are rarely designed with the explicit intention of facilitating emotional support. In fact, all of the systems described above have the commonality of being an online space where people contribute information—the emotional support that results from online interactions is a result of people utilizing the affordances of the technology in unintended ways. How do people reinterpret and reuse features of an online community to facilitate emotional support?

In order to address questions of psychological wellbeing and online community features, we studied a mature, ongoing user-generated content community, Everything2. This site has persisted for more than 17 years, though its most active time period was in the early 2000s. People who contributed to the site often did so over long periods of time. Through interviews with long-term users, as well as an assessment of their site activity, we looked at how they used the site to meet emotional support needs. We show that for some online community members, social support from other users can provide a very important motivation for committing to the community, and that the features of the system play an essential role in signaling that social support.

The Effects of Lifecycles of Participation

Online communities persist over long periods of time, and users are likely to change their participation in different ways over both their individual tenure within the community, as well as over the lifecycle of the community itself. Iriberri and Leroy [11] focus on how you measure successful outcome of a community over time, but did not consider outcomes for users in that lifecycle. Preece and Shneiderman [26] articulate the "Reader to Leader" framework in which they show how people move between different roles within a community, though they do not discuss in depth how motivations and outcomes are affected by those changes in roles, focusing on the functional elements of the roles. Velazquez et al. [41] extend the Reader to Leader model to talk about motivations associated with change over time, but do not address outcomes for participants in terms of their perceived benefits – like psychological wellbeing.

We are thus interested in the ecology of online community participation and how psychological wellbeing plays a role throughout the entire lifecycle of a user:

RQ1: How does a person describe their changes in psychological wellbeing over the course of their time in an online community?

EMOTIONAL SUPPORT IN ONLINE COMMUNITIES

User-generated content communities are often seen through the lens of their functionality, or through operational processes like member recruitment, rather than for their ability to provide social support for participants.

However, a previous generation of research and reflection did explore the affective benefits of online communities, and theories of affordances over the past decades also show why these processes are as salient in a social media environment as they were in earlier forms of online interaction.

Early online communities, which were largely text-based and pseudonymous, had multiple narratives that showed how emotional support was an important outcome for participants. Rheingold [29] described many incidents in the online community THE WELL where participants offered emotional support to each other. Horn [10] showed how participants in Echo, an early online community in New York City, received emotional support, and in many cases had emotion-based conflicts on the site. Pfaffenberger [25] describes in USENET how pseudonymous interaction

led to both misbehavior as well as relational disclosure and emotional support in online communities.

Another aspect of early online community research was how pseudonymous interactions allowed for identity play and exploration. Turkle [40] pointed out in her classic work that pseudonymous interactions allowed for people to try on identities that they weren't able to explore in other areas of their life. For example, people could explore relatively benign identities like a science fiction fan, or express identities that were much riskier in their main interactions. For example, Shaw [37] talks about how early online communities like IRC were important for gay men to meet others like them, especially when there were not many other gay men in their area. Reid [27] described IRC communities where gender swapping was a common activity with a variety of social goals. These platforms described above, though covering a range of different technologies, shared in common a dependency on pseudonymous interaction (enabling identify control) and to some extent independence from geographic proximity, enabling participants to meet like-minded others independent of distance.

Emotional Support in Online Health Communities

Online health communities are another example of online communities that leverage independence from geography and freedom to manage identity. Online communities allow people to share emotional support with those who are geographically distant [12], but share the same health issue. Maloney-Krichmar and Preece [21] did an in-depth description of one online health community and found that strong feelings of social support and mutual reciprocity were expressed by members of the community, which supported people who might not have been able to share their common struggles without fear of being judged. Massimi et al. [22] studied a range of health communities covering different types of illnesses and found that emotional support was often an important feature of use, in that once an acute illness faded, or a person became more used to their situation, their participation would change.

Health communities also show how the threat of stigma makes control over identity signals very important. Newman et al. [24] describe how people are unwilling to share health problems on "real identity" sites like Facebook because of the potential stigma of those illnesses, which could indicate why mostly pseudonymous online health support communities are still such a prevalent and important part of the online social space. Li et al. [20] found a similar result in that people were more likely to participate in a weight loss discussion in a pseudonymous online community as it was less ego-threatening than to do so on Facebook. In a study of "pro-ana" online communities – groups that share tips, support, and advocacy for eating disorders – participants felt like the community was the only place they could go as their motivations were too stigmatized in other relationship contexts [46]. In a study comparing hypotheses that online communities helped to relieve or avoid stigma, Lawlor and Kirakowski [18] found that participants in these communities were more likely to seek formal help.

Both the early generations of text-only online communities and health-based online communities show that emotional support can result from people who share a common identity (including one established by an illness) where online participation facilitates those interactions.

Re-Use of Communities and Features

There has been growing interest in the HCI community about how to design for wellbeing [39], and an active interest in designing communities for psychological wellbeing and emotional support [19]. Studying how people re-use technical and social features of online communities may help inform how to engage in that design.

In many of the cases described above, people are going to a community for the purpose of sharing information, but often engage in activities that promote psychological wellbeing as a side effect of that activity. In order to show social support in these communities, it may be important to repurpose tools to provide signals of emotional support. Ellison et al. [5] show how "signals of relational investment" on Facebook, like sending birthday greetings or liking comments, is positively associated with perceptions of social support on the site. Burke et al. [3] also found that people who engaged in interactive behaviors on the site (as opposed to consumption only) had better psychological outcomes. This has often been related to the concept of "social grooming" in that use of tools in systems can be a way of signaling attention or support in a cue sparse environment. Lampe [15] argues that features of systems are often reinterpreted by users of those systems to meet their own goals.

RQ2: How are participants using features of the site to send and receive signals of emotional support?

Study Context: Everything2

We conducted in-depth interviews with 30 long-term users of Everything2, an online user generated content community that has existed for more than 17 years. Everything2 was a reasonable site in which to situate this research because its long history enabled us to talk to long-term users. This was important because most prior research focused on initial participation [2,13,17] which made it difficult to have insight into users who have already been engaged in the community for a long period of time. In addition, one of the authors was a long-term participant user of the community, which provided insight into community norms, shared repertoire, and processes. Moreover, some of the users were current users while others were no longer users of the site, which was useful in understanding why people exited the site.

Everything2 is a user-generated content community that allows users to post any kind of content they want, but the community norm tends to focus more on creative writing (e.g., essays, fiction, anecdotes) than factual articles. The site is a collection of independent articles rather than a collaborative effort to create and edit. Users can post content, called "write-ups" and these posts are arranged into topics, which are called "nodes." Each article is written by a single individual, who retains ownership and attribution for their content. The site is almost entirely based on text.

Although Everything2 never reached the size of large-scale user-generated content communities such as Reddit or Wikipedia, users have been consistently active on the site since its inception. Through in-site messaging, offsite communication like email and instant relay chat (IRC), and occasional in-person meetings, users, who refer to themselves as Noders, have a long history of social interaction with each other on the site [41].

METHOD

Participant Recruitment

Semi-structured in-depth interviews were conducted with long-term members of Everything2. Participants were recruited through snowball sampling; we started with one established member of the Everything2 community that knew a great number of connections in the site and asked for a referral to other long-term users. We continued this referral method until we began to see saturation in response. In addition, to avoid the homophily bias of snowball sampling [9] we recruited some users based on server logs of their usage. Some users were selected because they used private messages frequently but contributed few articles, while others were recruited because they were avid writers, but did not engage in messaging. We included both current users as well as those who had not logged in for months to get diverse users (users who were no longer active on the site could still be reached via email). We also contacted users whose content was deleted by administrators. We used this sampling method in order to maximize diversity and to characterize in rich detail a variety of user experiences—this does not imply that these users are representative of a larger population, but rather that they reflect diverse types of users.

Potential participants were sent a message through the site messaging system, or by email to accounts listed on their profile and were directed to an online screening questionnaire. They were then contacted and interviewed by telephone. Before the interview, researchers described the goal of the research and the types of data being collected to the respondent, and received their informed consent. The study was approved by the IRB of the institution where data was collected. Usage log data were provided by the administrator of the site, and all participants were aware of that access as part of the informed consent process.

Respondents also were informed that researchers had looked over their early public posts.

Interviews and Analyses

One-hour semi-structured interviews were conducted using a key-point interview guide [9]. We asked participants about their motivations to participate in their site, and why and how their participation evolved over time. In particular, we asked about different periods in the lifespan of their use and the relationships they had with other users of the site both online and offline. To help users remember their activities, we extracted information of their entire usage history from the site's servers. This information included what kind of write-ups they posted, when they were posted, their voting activity, and their messaging activity. For the sake of individual privacy, we did not look at the content of their messaging activity. We also looked at the public posts that were accessible through the user's public profile. For example, a user would be asked a series of questions like, "The first time you posted was on April, 2001, and it was about XXX. Do you remember this? Can you tell me what was going on with your life when you posted this? What kind of reaction did you get from the community?"

Three coders read through all of the transcripts and iteratively analyzed them by assigning subject codes, or tags, using the software package Atlas.ti [23]. The first few rounds of coding were mainly based on how participants used the site's different features, such as their motivation to post something, interaction with other users, and interaction with administration. This resulted in five overarching themes with a total of 24 categories and more than 60 tags.

Once we saw an emergent pattern of participants discussing psychological wellbeing factors such as loneliness, happiness, and self-confidence in relation to different activities on the site, we went back and coded by users' psychological state. After identifying their psychological state when they joined, any changes during their lifecycle, and when they left the community, we looked at what kind of motivations, writing content, social responses (e.g., voting, social support or lack thereof, social activities on and off the site), and external factors (factors unrelated to the website) were tied to that state. This data was organized as a matrix in a spreadsheet.

RESULTS

Psychological Wellbeing and Early Stages of Membership

There were many different reasons people joined Everything2, some of which include social influence ("my friends made me join") and boredom ("I had 3 hours every afternoon where I didn't have classes so I wound up just killing time in the afternoon"). However, when describing the circumstances of their life when they joined the site, many participants reported being in a state of low psychological wellbeing, desiring companionship and recognition. These users had experienced a major life change (e.g., going to college, moving to a new place) or some life event (e.g., death of a close person, unemployment, poor health) that was associated with negative psychological states and were thus using the site as a shoulder to cry on.

When Henry[1] joined Everything2, he was in poor health and was seeking an alternative social venue. "I found that when I was very ill, my social circle was very uncomfortable with that and they did not want to come around and see me when I was sick because I looked so terrible, but over the Internet that didn't matter," he said. One of Henry's earliest posts was a long entry about Crohn's disease. The first seven paragraphs are factual statements about the disease, very much resembling a post that one would find on Wikipedia. In the final two paragraphs, however, he related his own experience, divulging extremely sensitive personal information:

```
CROHN'S DISEASE HAS TAKEN A LOT FROM
ME OVER THE YEARS. I'VE BEEN POINTED
AT, TEASED, TAUNTED, EXCLUDED FROM
SOCIAL GATHERINGS, AND EVEN BEEN
ACCUSED OF USING MY ILLNESS FOR
PERSONAL GAIN. HOWEVER, CROHN'S HAS
GIVEN ME A LOT AS WELL. SINCE I WAS
DIAGNOSED AT THE AGE OF THIRTEEN, I
LEARNED QUICKLY THAT I WAS NOT
INVINCIBLE, SOMETHING THAT MANY TEENS
TAKE YEARS AND A NUMBER OF STUPID
MISTAKES TO LEARN.
```

In the case of Mike, his father had just passed away and he was home without a job: "[Everything2] was a grieving method for me in a lot of ways," he said. His early entries echoed Mike's melancholy state and contained subject matter such as tragic novels, alcohol, smoking, solitude, and tragic stories. One entry, titled "Pictures of my father," reflects his mindset at the time. Unlike his other factual entries, this one is comprised of short sentences, almost like poetry:

```
PHOTOGRAPHS OF MY FATHER REST IN PILES
ON   THE PIANO AND   THE DINING   ROOM
TABLE. WE MAKE A COLLAGE ON POSTER
BOARDS OF OUR FAVORITES, OUR DEAREST.
PICTURES TO REMEMBER THE LEGACY OF HIS
LIFE; SCHOOL PICTURES, FROM VIETNAM,
SKINNY,     WITH    A BEARD,    AT
OUR GRADUATIONS, MY SISTER'S WEDDING.
MOMENTS CAPTURED AGO, WHICH NOW, (IN
VAIN) TRY TO EXPRESS HIM. THEY JUST
DON'T GIVE ENOUGH. THE POSTER BOARDS
WERE PUT ON EASELS AT THE FUNERAL
HOME. AN OPEN ESCAPE FROM THE OMINOUS
COFFIN   NEARBY.   A   CHANCE   TO
FORGET DEATH FOR    A    MOMENT
AND REMEMBER.
```

---

[1] All usernames were randomly converted to different pseudonyms that were consistent with gender.

Participants explained that interacting with others online was an effort to share the burden. Frank, who wrote about his grandfather's death, said that the act of sharing the negative experience helped alleviate his mood. "If you share your pain with someone else, then the pain is halved, but if you share your joy with someone else, it basically gets doubled," he said.

Others, however, did not have a specific traumatic event—they were just lonely and desiring some form of socialization. "I joined because I wanted feedback. It is critical to me and is the glue that holds a lot of this together," Denise said.

Denise's early posts were mostly fiction, dealing with subjects such as vengeance, rape, and death. These posts elicited much feedback from other users, mostly in the form of private messages, according to one of her posts about her appreciation for Everything2.

Lonely users had different ways of coping. Some sought out the site to find people to talk to. Gwen described how her most active time on the site was when she started college. She said that when she first got to college, she had what she thought was an awesome roommate. The two of them built a social circle, but the roommate was later put on heavy anti-psychotics that turned all of their mutual friends away. She said she was in a deep state of melancholy when she joined Everything2:

> I was just honestly looking for a place to belong, looking for people to pay attention to me and give me some comfort and make me feel less alone. I felt that Everything2 was the only place I could go and feel safe and people there wanted to "hang out" with me. I spent a lot of nights up talking to people and I really think it helped me get through that.

Other users, however, were not going to the site to seek friends, but rather to pour out their emotions, much like one would write in a journal. Recalling his first year on Everything2, Nate said, "I was living in this tiny little attic apartment and I had nothing going on—literally nothing going on, so I was just sitting in my room at night for like, five or six hours, and I know Everything2 was a big part of that time I spent online." In the first year he joined Everything2, Nate wrote 244 posts, a quarter of which were posted after midnight.

For Sam, most of her early posts were either short, factual entries, or deeply personal anecdotes about her deceased mother and estranged father. Across several entries, she talks about her hatred and fear of men, her psychological state well expressed in the following excerpt:

```
SOMETIMES IT'S ALL I CAN DO TO FIGHT
THE HATE AND RAGE THAT WELLS UP IN ME
AND I WANT TO ATTACK SOMETHING,
SPITTING FIRE AND FISTS FLYING. MAYBE
THIS IS WHY I HAVE BARELY EVER DATED,
WHY MY FIRST KISS CAME SO LATE, AND
```

```
WAS A "KISS AND RUN." COULD HE FEEL
THE PAST ON MY LIPS? DID HE TASTE THE
POISON OF WHAT MY EYES HAVE ABSORBED?
```

Some users, like Frank, titled entries with dates rather than a subject matter, indicating their usage of Everything2 as a personal log. However, unlike a private diary, these users were seeking an audience. Sam said she shared emotional anecdotes because she desired feedback. "If I didn't care about others' responses, I would just keep a private journal," she explained.

Increasing Psychological Wellbeing through Feedback and Attention

A salient theme among the participants we interviewed was the relationship between positive feedback and subsequent feelings of pride, self-confidence, and status. "As trivial and childish as it is, the voting and the cooling system is extraordinarily psychologically rewarding, especially for someone who is just starting out," Rob said, "Getting that sort of positive feedback even on top of the negative feedback, which was pretty acerbic sometimes, was a huge gut punch of super gold pep."

Gerald recalled how his initial write-ups were very well-received by the Everything2 community. "I respected the writing of other things I saw get cools and upvoted so when something I wrote got that, it was validating," he said.

Henry said that the community felt very encouraging and positive, especially in comparison to other sites: "There were always insightful comments. So much of the Internet, if you read comments that people post on other websites, it's 'you're stupid,' or 'you suck' but on Everything2 you get actual feedback on how to make something better."

Increasing self-esteem by participating in the site was a recurring theme in the interviews, especially among participants who were unsocial (offline) at the time they joined the site. Several participants used the term "popularity" to describe how they felt about their status on the site. This was especially salient among participants who described themselves as having never been in the center of attention in offline situations.

"I've never been popular in my life and it was so cool to have people want to meet me after reading something that I wrote. It gave me a confidence that I had never had before and it made me feel like I was part of something for the first time ever in my life," Bob said.

Similarly, Alice talked about how she garnered reputation on the site and a lot of interest from male users, which encouraged her to write more:

> A very long time ago I had one of the most popular nodes out there. It was named, 'How I nearly killed myself masturbating. A lot of boys wanted to get to know me because I wrote that node. I loved being popular.

Feedback had aspects of both quantity and quality; in other words, more feedback mattered, but the type of feedback mattered too. Many participants talked about how receiving a lot of upvotes or cools made them feel good. However, a few participants also pointed out that they were affected by individual users who communicated positive feedback through private messages. "I remember there was one particular user who was very encouraging," Kent recalled, "I was very self-deprecating but she said that what I was doing was great and that I should continue doing it."

Many users talked about how they gained confidence from positive feedback for factual write-ups and began writing more personal things or fiction. These more-or-less "subjective" write-ups generated more appeal for those who had social connections on the site because they were writing for a more specific audience. Rachel talked about how the ties with the community influenced her desire to contribute content:

> Folks who were actively participating in the community side of things weren't writing for the sake of writing. You were writing for this particular audience of people that you cared about and if you had a falling out with them it made you want to take your content away.

Rachel's posts in her first month of joining Everything2 were mostly factual posts related with biology. Some examples of the titles of her post include 'psychobiology' and 'cortical stimulation mapping.' After a month, however, she began to write more personal things. Her first post that had personal content was simply titled with the date, "October 4," and starts out with: "I saw someone who had been hit by a bus." She goes into detail about how she felt as a witness and her feeling of helplessness in the situation:

```
PEOPLE WERE STANDING AROUND, LOOKING AT
THEIR WATCHES, ON THEIR CELL PHONES.
THEY DIDN'T LOOK DISTURBED. I WAS
DISTURBED. I KEPT THINKING ABOUT HOW
COLD THE SURFACE OF THE ROAD WOULD BE
ON A MORNING LIKE THIS. I WONDERED WHAT
IT WOULD BE LIKE TO BE IN HIS PLACE. I
JUST HOPE HE WASN'T SCARED. I HOPE HE
DIDN'T FEEL ALONE.
```

In her first three months, Rachel wrote 39 posts—after that, she did not write as much—less than 10 a year—but she actually became more involved in the community. In 2000, she sent 0 private messages, but this number increased to 103 in 2001 and 1011 in 2002. This indicates that while Rachel was not contributing more content, she was engaging in conversation with other members.

The effect of positive ratings, however, seemed only to apply to the early stages of users' membership. Lola described how she was initially driven by reputation, to "show that I was there for a reason." However, once she started to become socially involved with other users, she started posting less and communicating more with other

users both online and offline. "What wound up happening is that I made some of the best friends I've ever had. I don't consider them noders anymore. Yeah, I met them because of Everything2, but now I consider them family," she said.

Sense of Community Enhancing Psychological Wellbeing

Use of Diverse Features to Connect

There were several characteristics that made the community in Everything2 seem unique to our interview participants: the common interest in writing, instantaneous nature of feedback, openness of the members, and diversity of users. Many participants described the site as tightly knit community. "It's a dynamic, edgy community and the combination of having a database of writings along with a message board and a chat box was novel and appealing," Leo described.

Lightweight feedback played an important role in introducing and integrating users to the community aspect of the site. "Obviously votes and cools can start a new friendship. If a group of people voted five times on your posts, at one point you will jump into chat with them," Kent explained. In particular, users bonded over discussions that were based on socially sensitive topics, such as having a miscarriage or watching a close friend or family member commit suicide, as they were able to commiserate with others who shared similar experiences.

Roy said, "It was the first time where I was part of an organization and could reach out and communicate with someone in virtually every aspect of professional and personal lifestyles where everybody had this common interest that allowed them to communicate. That was something that I hadn't experienced before and really the heart of social networking."

Flora admitted that she was "actually pretty shy back then" so she would watch people chat but rarely reach out to others. However, she eventually found herself conversing with people who wanted to talk to her about the things that she had posted:

> People would message me about things that I had written, asking questions, or saying, 'Hey that was a great write up, you forgot to include a comma, you may want to fix that.' As I started having people reach out to me, I started messaging more.

This sense of community was present even in people who did not write or talk with other users on the site. Tim, who called himself a "lurker," described how he was engaged in site for several years before he started writing, by just reading what people posted and chatted about. He said that watching people interact on the site showed him that there were certain norms and "unspoken rules" governing a site, which helped get his "foot in the door."

The feeling of belonging to a group was stronger for long-term users. "Ultimately, it was a sense of community; you could talk to someone you didn't know and find if you had something in common," Erin said. In fact, information was what lured people to site, but it was not the factor that made them stay. As Jack put it:

> The nodes were much more interesting to me as a catalyst for the community, an anchor to the community that is a monument that we can build... it was absolutely about interacting with each other rather than people contributing to this static compendium.

One unique aspect of Everything2 was that the sense of community also spilled over into organization of in-person events. Many participants talked about attending meetings (called noder-meets); ranging from large gatherings that took place over several days to city-wide scavenger hunts and smaller, more spontaneous dinners. Almost every participant conveyed an anecdote related to their noder-meet experience. Flora recalled:

> I was amazed by people's willingness to trust a large group of complete strangers in their home because oftentimes the larger gatherings were 30, 40, 50 people and you're basically sending out an open invitation to people who may be serial killers or rapists.

Pseudonymity Facilitating Community

Everything2 allows users to create pseudonyms, which enabled people to be anonymous, yet create a distinct persona. The anonymous aspect enabled people to write freely about any topic without fear of judgment. Isis said that the anonymity in Everything2 made her more comfortable about writing about private things. Isis' posts tended to be peppered with profanity, rants, rhetorical questions, and sharp critiques of society, especially regarding women's body image. "There are certain times in my life when things happen to me and I don't feel like I have anywhere to express how I actually feel about them so I end up coming back to Everything2," she said.

Participants noted that the content was able to become the springboard for social interactions thanks to the design of the system. Erik pointed out that he had more emotional investment in Everything2 than Wikipedia because the content is linked to a specific person or profile:

> Wikipedia's model does great for peer-reviewed factual writing if you don't mind being completely anonymous or near anonymous, but on Everything2, it's that human factor behind each writeup. I can look at a writeup written by Ta**x or Pa**se and it's not just a piece of fiction—it's a piece of fiction written by someone that I care very deeply about.

With pseudonymity, the collection of writings under a person's profile enabled others to learn more about them in a meaningful manner. These profiles were more than a static page of self-presentation. By reading someone's work over a long period of time, participants said that they were able to gain an understanding of that person.

Quinn said that knowing people through Everything2 was different from other online communities because she had a good sense of who they were as a person. She said that this made her feel comfortable about meeting some Everything2 people offline:

> I friended a lot of random strangers on Facebook so I can send them little free gifts from my flash games and they'll send stuff back. I have no sense of who they are, I don't know anything about them, there's no community, there's no interaction, there's no getting to know them. For me Twitter is the same way, you can't get a sense of a person in 140 characters. I've not met anybody through Twitter or Facebook that I'd actually want to get to know or meet in person.

Posting content through a pseudonym was also a way for participants to convey information about themselves in an indirect, yet rich way. Linda explained:

> I got emotionally involved with people on the site because they liked my mind and the way it worked, and they just understood my thought process and where I came from and my experiences by reading my nodes.

Exit Reasons

People discontinued or made major changes to their patterns of participation on the site for largely two reasons. For people who had low psychological well-being, "feeling better" made them use the site less—sometimes the alleviation could be attributed to the site, but other times it was a change in off-site situations, such as getting married or getting a job.

On the other hand, people were also leaving because being on the site lowered their psychological wellbeing—either because the people they loved were no longer present, or they felt like an outsider, which lowered their feelings of self-worth and emotional connection.

Losing Friends and Feelings of Relatedness

For people who had high psychological well-being and were socially active—social problems with site members or departure of online friends lowered their psychological well-being and made them use the site less. Henry commented: "As much as I enjoyed the writing, the longer I was there, the more it was about the community to me—the more it was about the people. And when the people that I knew, left, I didn't really see any need to continue," Henry said. "The site is kind of an empty room; nothing happening much, kind of like an echo," Bob said.

Loss of the feeling of togetherness caused people to lose a feeling of purpose to be on the site, even when it came to contributing content, because the perceived audience was no longer there. Several of participants who used to be active members but were no longer so, explained that loss of people they considered their "friends" in the community discouraged them to write. "A lot of my content was silly and the people that would read it are not really there anymore. So why would I go write up something silly that 10 or 20 people may read, of which none of them are people I know?" Erin explained. She said that she still occasionally logged in to check her inbox, but that she no longer felt a need to contribute content to the site.

Similar to Erin, Bob said that he still goes to the site to read but does not have the same investment in the site as before because the people on the site have changed. "There was so much going on at one point... it was a big crowded room and you knew everybody. Now, the way I look at the site, it's a kind empty room...few people are here and there but it does not feel like an interesting community as there are not lot of intelligent conversation going on," he said.

For these users, even though they eventually left the site, they still harbored strong feeling of fondness towards the site. Because they left the site because the people they considered their close contacts were no longer on it, it was different from situations such as leaving one site for another. Moreover, many participants continued friendships forged through Everything2.

Pete attributed his time on Everything2 as a very important chapter of his life that he considered a positive experience:

> I look on it fondly, it's a part of my life, it made me who I am today, I wouldn't be the same person if it weren't for these people, and it wasn't really the site so much as was the people on there, and like some of these people are seriously dear and I don't know what I'd do without them.

Feeling Like an Outsider
The favorable feeling toward the site was not present, however, with users who left because they felt peripheral to the social groups. The strong mini communities within the site came with negative aspects such as gossiping, strained relationships, and feeling isolated if one was not part of certain groups. "It's so funny, it was almost like a high school social clique in cyberspace," Mary recalled. She said that people were sometimes gathered in the chat room making fun of other users and talking about the people rather than the content that they wrote on the site. "It ended up being a reversion back to high school, which made it interesting; most of the things people talked about were personal, social stuff," she said.

While participants like Jack loved Everything2 for all of the inside jokes, people who did not understand these jokes felt left out. Carol also described Everything2 as being a "series of cliques" that she felt like she was not a part of. Living in Alaska, she felt isolated from the community because she was not able to participate in the offline meetings:

> They would meet up and hook up and have great parties. It informed so much of what was going on with the site but here in the last outpost of the Pacific Northwest, all you had was to read the subtext in the comments. It was kind of like everyone was playing a game I didn't get to participate in.

The feeling of being an outsider was not only about social interactions, but also in relation to content contribution. Gwen, who was a content editor, talked about how she was upset because her suggestions regarding administrative aspects of the site were being ignored: "It felt like the direction and the way I use the site was being thrown by the wayside and wasn't important." Frank said he was upset that people he disliked were being supported by others: "There were people whose writing I didn't like and I felt they were being too accepted because I didn't think they were good writers but others were worshipping them. There was one that I really didn't like and he became an editor and I left," Frank said.

DISCUSSION
While interaction on social media sites, which are dominated by "real name" identity tools, has become a default mode of online interaction over the last decade, sites where pseudonymous interaction is the default mode still represent a major part of the online community ecosystem. We use quotations in the term "real identities" as several scholars have pointed out that 1) people can have multiple identities, and 2) pseudonyms are an authentic expression of identity, even if not used in other contexts [1]. Our results indicate that people may use these pseudonymous interactions in order to seek out emotional support in online communities, and become active members because they feel safer in an environment where they are not judged by others, while still being able to maintain a constant identity within the site.

We found that relatedness—the sense of belonging—was extremely important in keeping users engaged on the site. Our interviews suggested that only those people who feel a social connection to the site persisted. This also had negative effects, however, such that some people who felt they were not a part of a subgroup were reminded of cliques in high school and felt like they were an outsider. This was particularly salient for individuals who were more interested in factual content than emotional content.

Reduced Cues Afford Intimacy

One major difference between interactions in online communities, versus the broader category of social media, is the use of so-called "Real Identity". Sparse cues afforded by text-only environments could lead to the identity play identified by Turkle, but could also lead to misbehavior like flaming and trolling that was often associated with the process of "deindviduation" [38]. In other words, the theories of the time were based in a "cues filtered out" mode, where text-only environments led to mostly negative emotional outcomes between people interacting in online communities.

However, newer theories of how the features of online communities can support interpersonal interaction show that, over time, emotional support can be improved by technology mediation. Walther [42, 43] proposed the "hyperpersonal model" to explain how reduced cues could support online interpersonal intimacy. In his framework, text-based online communities allow people to control their "cues given off", unlike in other environments. For example, people in online environments can create a pseudonym that is able to express negative emotions or non-normative beliefs that might lead to sanctions in other contexts.

Finally, reduced cues available to people in online communities may be simpler for appropriation by those participants. We found that people in Everything2 would repurpose features of the site intended for content production to signal emotional support, including ascribing meaning to simple one-click positive feedback. This was very consistent with other research on how people find meaning in the recipient of simple feedback mechanisms through paralinguistic digital affordances such as Likes on Facebook [45] and provided a qualitative explanation for why feedback in early stages of community participation would explain long-term engagement in online communities [34]. Sites that allow for re-use of features might enable users to engage in more creativity in offering social support to each other.

Increased Cues Afford Intimacy

In what seems like a paradox, we found that increased cues also afford intimacy, but only for those who had already established some baseline level of respect and/or closeness. The strong communities formed in Everything2 were not necessarily confined to cyberspace. We found that people were also extending their online bonds to offline meetings, which in turn strengthened their online relationships. This could extend our understanding of the hyperpersonal model in that in initial phases of the relationship, reduced cues could support intimacy, but once the relationship is formed, then the "richer" cues may serve to solidify the bond.

Recommendations for Practice

In many online communities, design practice is centered around the efficient delivery and production of tasks. While this task-based focus likely does meet the needs of some participants, tools that allow users to go "off-topic" and offer emotional support to one another may be another important consideration for designers of user generated content communities. In particular, the analysis above shows that features that promote social grooming can help foster feelings of social support and thus a person's commitment to the community.

Having a range of affordances that have different "weights" in terms of how much effort it takes to engage in that behavior, can provide users with more versatility. For example, simple behaviors that require a mere click—in Everything2 this was voting, but it could be Liking on Facebook or Favoriting on Twitter—provide a relatively low barrier to signaling interest and support, as supported in other work on social media [8].

Pseudonymity may be optimal to guarantee the initial anonymity but allow the potential for more intimate connection through the constant identity. However, Resnick [28] describes the use of pseudonyms as a benefit in online environments, but warns that when pseudonyms are too easy to abandon or create, they may lead to more negative behavior [7]. He describes how tools like reputation systems can lead to commitment to a pseudonym, without removing the benefits of identity-control enabled by these features. This may be useful in the context of communities that want to facilitate emotional support among its users at a more systematic level.

Limitations

It is important to interpret these results in the context of this particular user-generated content community, as things may be very different in other contexts. In the case of need fulfillment of relatedness, Everything2 was ideal in that there were many features built into the site that facilitated interaction among users. The communication features in Everything2 are also diverse in terms of instantaneousness (instant messaging vs. in-system emailing) and effort (voting vs. sending a message). The interactivity of the community could have been what contributed most to users' feeling of relatedness. However, it could also be that the content of the site, which despite it being described as an open encyclopedia, focused more on personal and subjective content rather than factual content, also contributed to the feeling of relatedness. Factual content can be dry whereas personal content is expressive and conveys more about the writer; not just by the content itself but the writing style and use of vocabulary.

It is unclear whether or not these are features that could be incorporated into communities with other types of content. Many participants talked about how they appreciated the quality of content on Everything2; however, since most of the content is creative, it was uncertain how much emotional attachment to the community would contribute to the quality of content were it more factually oriented.

Another limitation of our study is that when participants talked about how their wellbeing improved through usage of the site, there are confounding factors that make it difficult to attribute the positive outcomes to a specific factor. While we presume that social interactions played a large part in enhancing psychological wellbeing, this is primarily based on the participants' self-reports. The act of expressive writing has been shown in prior research to have therapeutic effects; it could be that the writing, or a combination of writing and socializing, contributed to better wellbeing. To determine true causality, one would have to take a more structured, experimental approach. In addition, these interviews were conducted with established members of the community, whose use had persisted over time. This leads to two potential limitations. First, recall of early motivations and experiences are likely shaped by current impressions of the site. Second, experiences of this group likely were different from people who left the site after negative initial interactions.

CONCLUSION

Interviews with long-term users suggested that initially, positive feedback played a large part in why they continued to stay on the site because it made them feel good about themselves. This was consistent with prior research [6,44]. However, in discussing why they continued to stay on the site, interviewees talked about how the site became a social experience, and how they were gratified not by the metric-driven aggregate feedback of the site's rating system, but one-to-one social experience shared with other users.

In summary, we found that people who used the site as a way to escape from, or release negative emotions, were able to increase their psychological wellbeing through positive feedback, which mostly happened during the early stage of participation, but later positive feelings were built through social connections.

Systems like those described above are often designed for information sharing; rarely do they have explicit designs that promote emotional support. However, people may be using unintended affordances of online technologies – like reduced cues in text environments in the form of upvotes and downvotes – to get emotional support.

Our work contributes to design as we know more deeply about how psychological factors influence people's involvement in the community, as well as what psychological factors were important for maintaining users over a long period of time. For newer users, giving them more autonomy may increase their engagement with content. However, at the end of the day, feeling emotionally connected with other people was the only motivation that was positively associated with long-term usage.

In the context of this particular community, the "novelty" of sharing or getting new content did not seem to be what motivated long-term users. This suggested that to retain long-term users, user-generated content community

administrators should consider incorporating features that facilitate interpersonal connections rather than mere repositories of information, because the people who "stick around" were not really there to share knowledge. In fact, information was the wing-man that lured people to site, but it was not the factor that made them stay. As Patrick said, "I came there and got involved because of writing, but in the end of it, I stayed because of the people."

ACKNOWLEDGMENTS
This work was partially supported by NSF grant IIS-HCC-0812429.

REFERENCES
1. boyd, d. 2012. The politics of real names. *Communications of the ACM* 55, 8: 29-31.

2. Moira Burke, Cameron Marlow and Thomas Lento. 2009. Feed me: Motivating newcomer contribution in social network sites. In *Proceedings of ACM Conference on Human Factors in Technical Systems (CHI'09)*, 945-954.

3. Moira Burke, Cameron Marlow and Thomas Lento.. 2010. Social network activity and social wellbeing. In *Proceedings of the 28th international conference on Human factors in computing systems (CHI'10)*, 1909-1912.

4. Edward L. Deci and Richard M. Ryan. 2000. The "what" and "why" of goal pursuits: Human needs and the self-determination of behavior. *Psychological inquiry*, 11, 4: 227-268.

5. Nicole B. Ellison, Jessica Vitak, Rebecca Gray and Cliff Lampe. 2014. Cultivating social resources on social network sites: Facebook relationship maintenance behaviors and their role in social capital processes. *Journal of Computer-Mediated Communication* 19, 4: 855-870.

6. Andrea Forte, Niki Kittur, Vanessa Larco, Haiyi Zhu, Amy Bruckman and Robert E. Kraut. 2012. Coordination and beyond: social functions of groups in open content production. In *Proceedings of the ACM 2012 conference on Computer Supported Cooperative Work (CSCW'12)*, 417-426.

7. Eric J. Friedman and Paul Resnick. 1997. The Social Cost of Cheap Pseudonyms. *Journal of Economics and Management Strategy* 10, 2: 173-179.

8. Rebecca A. Hayes, Caleb T. Carr and D. Yvette Wohn. in press. One click, many meanings: Interpreting paralinguistic digital affordances in social media. *Journal of Broadcasting and Electronic Media*

9. Douglas D Heckathorn. 1997. Respondent-driven sampling: a new approach to the study of hidden populations. *Social problems* 44, 2: 174-199.

10. Stacy Horn. 1998. *Cyberville: Clicks, Culture, and the Creation of an Online Town*. Warner Books, New York, NY.

11. Alicia Iriberri and Gondy Leroy. 2009. A life-cycle perspective on online community success. *ACM Computing Surveys (CSUR)*, 41, 2: 11-29.

12. Grace J. Johnson and Paul J. Ambrose. 2006. Neo-tribes: the power and potential of online communities in health care. *Communications of the ACM*, 49, 1: 107-113.

13. Elisabeth Joyce and Robert E. Kraut. 2006. Predicting Continued Participation in Newsgroups. *Journal of Computer-Mediated Communication*, 11, 3: 723-747.

14. Amy Jo Kim. 2000. *Community Building on the Web: Secret Strategies for Successful Online Communities*. Peachpit Press, Berkeley, CA.

15. Cliff Lampe. 2015. Gamification and Social Media. in Waltz, S.P. and Sebastian Deterding (eds.) *The Gameful World: Approaches, Issues, Applications*, MIT Press, Cambridge, MA, 463.

16. Cliff Lampe, Nicole Ellison and Charles Steinfield. 2006. A Face(book) in the Crowd: Social Searching vs. Social Browsing. In *Proceedings of ACM Special Interest Group on Computer-Supported Cooperative Work (CSCW'06)* , 167-170.

17. Cliff Lampe and Erik Johnston. 2005. Follow the (Slash) dot: Effects of Feedback on New Members in an Online Community. In *Proceedings of International Conference on Supporting Group Work (GROUP '05)*, 11-20.

18. Aideen Lawlor and Jurek Kirakowski. 2014. Online support groups for mental health: A space for challenging self-stigma or a means of social avoidance? *Computers in Human Behavior* 32: 152-161.

19. Reeva Lederman, Greg Wadley, John Gleeson, Sarah Bendall and Mario Álvarez-Jiménez. 2014. Moderated online social therapy: Designing and evaluating technology for mental health. *ACM Transactions on Computer-Human Interaction (TOCHI)* 21, 1

20. Victor Li, David W. McDonald, Elizabeth V. Eikey, Jessica Sweeney, Janessa Escajeda, Guarav Dubey, Kaitlin Riley, Erika S. Poole and Eric B. Hekler. 2014. Losing it online: characterizing participation in an online weight loss community. In *Proceedings of the 18th International Conference on Supporting Group Work (GROUP'14)*, 35-45.

21. Diane Maloney-Krichmar and Jennifer Preece. 2005. A multilevel analysis of sociability, usability, and community dynamics in an online health community. *ACM Transactions on Computer-Human Interaction (TOCHI)*, 12 2: 201-232.

22. Michael Massimi, Jackie L. Bender, Holly O. Witteman and Osman H. Ahmed. 2014. Life transitions and online health communities: reflecting on adoption, use, and disengagement. In *Proceedings of the 17th ACM conference on Computer supported cooperative work & social computing (CSCW 2014)*, 1491-1501.

23. Thomas Muhr and Susanne Friese. 2004. User's Manual for ATLAS. ti 5.0. *Berlin: ATLAS. ti Scientific Software Development GmbH.*

24. Mark W. Newman, Debra Lauterbach, Sean A. Munson, Paul Resnick and Margaret E. Morris. 2011. It's not that i don't have problems, i'm just not putting them on facebook: challenges and opportunities in using online social networks for health. In *Proceedings of the ACM 2011 conference on Computer supported cooperative work (CSCW 2011)*, 341-350.

25. Brian Pfaffenberger. 2002. A Standing Wave in the Web of Our Communications: Usenet and the Socio-Technical Construction of Cyberspace Values. in Lueg, C. and Fisher, D. (eds.) *From Usenet to CoWebs: Interacting with Social Information Spaces*, Springer Verlag, New York, NY.

26. Jennifer Preece and Ben Shneiderman. 2009. The reader-to-leader framework: Motivating technology-mediated social participation. *AIS Transactions on Human-Computer Interaction* 1, 1: 13-32.

27. Elizabeth M. Reid. 1991. Electropolis: Communication and Community on Internet Relay Chat *Department of History*, University of Melbourne, Melbourne.

28. Paul Resnick. 2001. Beyond Bowling Together: SocioTechnical Capital. In Carroll, J. (ed.) *HCI in the New Millenium*, Addison-Wesley.

29. Howard Rheingold. 2000. *The Virtual Community: Homesteading on the Electronic Frontier*. MIT Press, Cambridge, MA.

30. Richard M. Ryan and Edward L. Deci. 2001. On happiness and human potentials: A review of research on hedonic and eudaimonic wellbeing. *Annual review of psychology*, 52, 1: 141-166.

31. Carol D. Ryff. 1995. Psychological wellbeing in adult life. *Current directions in psychological science*, 99-104.

32. Carol D. Ryff and Burton Singer. 1998. The contours of positive human health. *Psychological inquiry* 9, 1: 1-28.

33. Sarita Yardi Schoenebeck. 2013. The secret life of online moms: anonymity and disinhibition on YouBeMom. com. In *Proceedings of ICWSM*, (

34. Chandan Sarkar, Donghee Yvette Wohn, Cliff Lampe. 2012. Predicting length of membership in online community "Everything2" using feedback. In *Proceedings of CSCW*, 207-210.

35. Martin E.P. Seligman and Mihaly Csikszentmihalyi. 2000. *Positive psychology: An introduction*. American Psychological Association.

36. David F. Shaw. 1997. Gay men and computer communication: A discourse of sex and identity in cyberspace. *Virtual culture: Identity and communication in cybersociety*. 133-145.

37. Martin Shelton, Katherine Lo and Bonnie Nardi. 2015. Online media forums as separate social lives: A

qualitative study of disclosure within and beyond Reddit. In *iConference 2015 Proceedings*. Retrieved from http://hdl.handle.net/2142/73676

38. Lee Sproull and Stephanie Kiesler. 1991. *Connections: New ways of working in the networked organization*. MIT Press, Cambridge, MA.

39. Anja Thieme, Madeline Balaam, Jayne Wallace, David Coyle, Sian Lindley. 2012. Designing wellbeing *Proceedings of the Designing Interactive Systems Conference*, 789-790.

40. Sherry Turkle. 1994. Constructions and reconstructions of self in virtual reality: Playing in the MUDs. *Mind, Culture, and Activity* 1, 3: 158-167.

41. Alcides Velasquez, Rick Wash, Cliff Lampe and Tor Bjornrud. 2014. Latent users in an online user-generated content community. *Computer Supported Cooperative Work* 23, 1: 21-50.

42. Joseph B. Walther. 2007. Selective self-presentation in computer-mediated communication: Hyperpersonal

dimensions of technology, language, and cognition. *Computers in Human Behavior* 23, 5: 2538-2557.

43. Joseph B. Walther. 1996. Computer-mediated communication: Impersonal, interpersonal, and hyperpersonal interactions. *Communication Research*, 23: 1-43.

44. Donghee Yvette Wohn. 2015. The effects of feedback and habit on content posting in an online community. In *Proceedings of iConference 2015*, 1-8.

45. Donghee Yvette Wohn, Caleb T. Carr, and Rebecca A. Hayes. 2016. How affective is a "Like"?: The effect of paralinguistic digital affordances on perceived social support. *Cyberpsychology, Behavior, and Social Networking 19*, 562-566.

46. Daphna Yeshua-Katz and Nicole Martins. 2013. Communicating stigma: The pro-ana paradox. *Health communication* 28, 5: 499-508.

Re-thinking Traceability: A Prototype to Record and Revisit the Evolution of Design Artefacts

**Marisela Gutierrez Lopez, Gustavo Rovelo Ruiz, Kris Luyten,
Mieke Haesen, Karin Coninx**

Hasselt University – tUL – imec
Expertise centre for Digital Media
Hasselt, Belgium
firstname.lastname@uhasselt.be

ABSTRACT

Keeping track of design processes is a cumbersome task due to the apparently unconstrained and unstructured nature of creative work. Traceability is fundamental to revisit and reflect on the *design narratives* that describe artefact evolution. In this paper, we aim to identify what characteristics are necessary to facilitate traceability of creative design processes. For this end, we use a functional prototype to connect artefacts, design rationale, and decisions in a shared workspace. We evaluated this prototype for 15 weeks with six pairs of students engaged in a user-centered design project. Our findings show that having a lean repository of artefacts annotated with design rationale can facilitate tracking progress in different phases of the process. We found that creating a record of the participants' design work is useful to reflect *on* and *for* team agreement, ensure consistency of evolving artefacts, and help in planning future steps in the design project.

Author Keywords

Traceability; user-centered design; design artefacts.

ACM Classification Keywords

H.5.m. Information interfaces and presentation (e.g., HCI): Miscellaneous.

INTRODUCTION

Artefacts are "almost anything that provides a visual and spatial forum for design ideas" [35]. They are used by design teams to ground communication, boost creativity, and justify design decisions [26,35]. Nevertheless, artefacts provide only a partial representation of design work. The turning points taken by design teams to evolve artefacts in an iterative way is what contains the most valuable information about the design process [5]. Keeping track of artefact

evolution helps to create a *project memory* [17], which contains the experiences and knowledge gained during the process.

Many design practitioners are reluctant to adopt tools that track the evolution of artefacts, since they tend to formalize design activities in a specific way. Constraining the design activities can potentially have a negative impact on design thinking [12], which is essential for finding creative, innovative solutions. Nevertheless, keeping track of the evolution of artefacts is useful in many ways. First, it can create a shared representation and understanding of the experiences acquired during a project [17]. Furthermore, it can improve the design process in three ways [20,25]: (1) by ensuring consistency of artefacts since results from one phase of the process are connected to the next phase, (2) by promoting reusability of previously generated knowledge, and (3) by providing a means for design teams to reflect on their approach and progress.

Existing tools that capture the evolution of design artefacts emerge largely from the engineering domain. These tools focus on supporting *traceability* of the design process, a term that is rarely used for creative design practices. Traceability enables design teams to pinpoint where a certain element was introduced into the process, and explore the reasons for its ultimate adoption or rejection [17], which in turn can help to reflect on the co-evolution of design problems and solutions [5]. In this paper, we adopt the concept of traceability for creative design activities. We frame this concept in user-centered design processes, and adapt it according to the needs and working style related to design activities. We explore our solution in a longitudinal study with students that work on a design project with external stakeholders.

User-centered design (UCD) approaches involve an iterative process to design and develop interactive systems. Teams working in UCD adopt multidisciplinary perspectives, where communication is based on a variety of artefacts [13]. However, the strengths of this process also introduce associated drawbacks. These limitations include keeping track of the evolution of design artefacts and their rationale, and for multidisciplinary teams, getting the same understanding about these artefacts [9,28]. When it comes to traceability of UCD processes, there is a tension to retain a degree of formalism and at the same time offer enough flexibility for creativity [9]. In our research, we investigate how design teams document and retrieve information about artefact evolution during a user-centered design process. We explore how the concept of traceability can be used into a creative design process. Our goal is twofold: *(1) understand how teams document and retrieve their ongoing work, and (2) identify what characteristics are necessary in an application in order to facilitate traceability in creative design.*

Achieving these goals requires understanding how teams generate, communicate, and retrieve their ideas over the duration of a project. Thus, we framed a study around a design task that follows the lifecycle of user-centered design, from initial idea generation to high-fidelity prototype. Our study consisted of a 15-week longitudinal study involving six pairs of students whose assignment was to redesign an interactive application for tax calculations. This project had the involvement of the external stakeholders in several stages. To investigate how teams document and retrieve their ongoing work, we asked them to record their collaborative design process using a functional prototype named *Helaba*. This tool supports recording design rationale and decisions in a shared workspace.

We designed and developed Helaba following the guidelines described in our previous research [10] to address the need of designers to keep track of their design rationale in a simple and flexible way. Using this tool, we gathered the artefacts, communications, and decisions produced by the participants during the design process. Additionally, we periodically collected the feedback of participants to gather information about their experiences. This procedure allowed us to create an extensive picture of the design process followed by each team, thus allowing us to explore traceability.

Findings of our study revealed that documenting UCD processes in Helaba was useful to support progress of the different stages in a flexible way. More specifically, it helped participants to keep track of their process by providing a (1) lean structured repository and (2) a shared workspace to keep annotated artefacts and design decisions in a common workspace. We extend previous research by using traceability as a mean to bridge creative and engineering design perspectives. Furthermore, we contribute with a longitudinal evaluation on how design rationale and traceability can be used in UCD processes.

FRAMING TRACEABILITY IN UCD PROCESSES

Conceptualizing User-centered Design
Design is better considered as a process rather than a set of isolated activities or outcomes. Swan et al. [31] describe design as *processional* given its "unfolding and contingent" nature. The design problems co-evolve together with solutions [5]. During this co-evolution, *wicked* design problems – to which there is no clear solution – are explored and refined [1]. Artefacts are valuable since they embody this *processional* nature, being refined in an incremental manner

and shaped by what was done before [31]. However, the most useful information is found not in the artefacts themselves, but on the discussion that led to their creation [35] and the knowledge that they reflect [29]. In this way, artefacts portray a partial picture, that serve the purpose of making ideas visible, and providing a space to communicate and refine those ideas [35]. Artefacts and the narrative of their evolution serve to understand the design process. Thus, it is valuable to capture and reflect upon the way artefacts are created and refined [3].

There is an ongoing discussion to the degree in which artefacts and creative design processes can be articulated and made explicit to others [8,9,35]. Fallman [8] proposes three opposing accounts for positioning design: romantic (artistic process), conservative (much as in scientific or engineering domains), and pragmatic (ill-defined process creative by nature). Each of these accounts provide valuable interpretations of how to conceptualize the design process, and how it can be articulated and made explicit to others. In HCI, part of this discussion is oriented towards the differences in positioning user-centered design as mostly an engineering or a creative design endeavor [23,35]. The former implies that design can be formal and systematized; while in the latter, it is considered a loosely defined process that does not constrain design thinking.

While there is a tendency to position UCD as part of the conservative account [2,9,35], there is limited evidence that structured design processes capture or support the work practices of designers successfully [9,35]. Accordingly, it has been suggested that the focus in UCD practice should be shifted from engineering towards a more creative one [2,9,23]. However, UCD projects often require producing an interactive application that can be deployed and tested with end-users [13]. This implies that tools to support UCD processes should provide a balance between supporting "good practices" in engineering and accommodating the unconstrained nature of creativity.

Bridging Design Accounts to Support Traceability
The Oxford Dictionary defines traceable as something that is "able to be found or discovered" or "able to be followed on its course or to its origin" [36]. Being able to "trace every step along the way of how a problem is transformed into a solution, including intermediate results and findings" is important for both science and engineering [7]. In engineering design, traceability relates to the history of a design, as it enables identification of where certain information was introduced into the process [25]. According to Neven et al. [20], traceability is useful as guidance to look forward and frame the process, and backtracking to follow the origin of design elements.

According to Tang et al. [32], being able to trace back design rationale is relevant for the design process as it involves artefacts in constant evolution. Design rationale captures the ideas behind why an artefact is the way it is [12]. Thus, traceability and design rational are concepts often associated to facilitate capturing and revisiting design knowledge. However, a single final design rationale is not enough for traceability, as there should exist a link between the rationale and progression of artefacts over time [25]. This is especially relevant for the early stages of design, where a large amount of ideas and artefacts are explored and defined [29].

Engineering Design and Traceability

The concept of traceability has been widely explored in engineering design. Solutions emerging from this perspective focus on formalizing models and steps for recording the design process [17]. Some of the explored solutions include:

- *Requirement modelling* to track the evolution of requirements and their integration into development and maintenance tasks [22].
- *Design rationale* to structure design argumentations using formal models to surface the connections between discourses and artefacts [15,25,32,33].
- *Group decision support* to identify knowledge that needs to be integrated and traced, and handle the links to support decisions [19].

Some reported benefits from these solutions are [20,27]: (1) early detection of potential conflicts or discrepancies in the design process, (2) communicate and justify design decisions to team members from different disciplines, and (3) facilitate reuse and analysis of design knowledge. Limitations are related to the fact that these solutions assume that design discourse can be made uniform and standardized [25,32]. However, there is little empirical evidence to support how this approach works in practice [9,12].

Creative Design and Traceability

Traceability has not been explicitly explored within creative design. However, previous research reports the potential value/benefits of tools to keep track of design evolution over time [3]. Therefore, there are a number of solutions proposed to support reusing, documenting, and inspiring the design process. Some relevant solutions include:

- *Open spaces* to document ongoing design processes, which act as a source of collective creativity and inspiration, promoting free exchange of ideas and feedback between designers [18,31].
- *Shared workspaces between teams* to ground communication and to document design knowledge for facilitating its reuse [3,14,21].
- *Typical design artefacts* such as sketches [16,24] and storyboards [34] to collect, share, and access previous ideas, supporting reuse and inspiration.

The value of these solutions is that they integrate the creative, progressive nature of design, and avoid constraining the thinking process of designers. As with these solutions, we aim to explore design work in consideration of the existing practices of designers, and avoid imposing a structure to it. We extend these solutions by exploring how the concept of traceability could be fitted into creative practices, and used to bridge these to engineering design practices.

Off-the-Shelf Tools to Support Traceability

A number of (commercial) off-the-shelf solutions have some kind of useful support for traceability. These tools are adapted to the needs of design teams working in commercial, fast-paced projects, where design outcomes are communicated to a large number of actors. We reviewed 16 of these tools in order to understand what is available for designers in terms of traceability. It is not our intention to create an exhaustive list of available tools, but to explore what commercial applications for designers support traceability. Thus, we reviewed applications that support traceability based on the reports of tools used by professional designers and evaluated them according to the design guidelines proposed by [10]: support artefact-based communication, gather feedback in a shared workspace, and enable awareness of artefact evolution. See Appendix A for a summary of the assessment we did from the 16 commercial tools and their URL.

All these applications highlight the need of supporting remote, multidisciplinary design work. Ten out of sixteen tools include a shared workspace that can be used to trace back the history of artefacts. However, none of these applications explicitly target traceability or reuse of designs because they do not make the link between pieces of knowledge evident. Conversely, the focus is on supporting ongoing conversations, feedback, and reduce "approval times" of design proposals. The tools that include a shared repository also support teams to organize their files in different ways, such grouping files into projects. Nine tools include team or task management features, such as the possibility to create Kanban boards, or to assign tasks to different team members. Eight tools offer the possibility to be linked with third-party tools to support project management and team communication. While these off-the-shelf solutions offer interesting and seemingly beneficial features, it is not clear how they support ongoing design processes. Furthermore, there is no evidence in literature of their proven efficiency for supporting design work, or how (and if) they could be optimized for traceability.

EXPLORING TRACEABILITY WITH HELABA

In order to investigate traceability, we use a solution named *Helaba*. The target users of our system are designers from different levels of experience, as well as other stakeholders of the UCD process (e.g. managers, clients, etc.). This tool is a functional prototype that allows design teams to connect artefacts, design rationale, decisions, and feedback in a shared workspace. Online shared workspaces facilitate being aware of the activities of others and contextualizing individual activities [6,14]. In the early stages of design, artefacts are essential to generate and refine conceptual ideas [28]. Therefore, shared workspaces in design help to capture and revisit ideas generated, and to improve team collaboration [14]. We contextualize the functionalities of Helaba with the guidelines that were used to inform its design and development [10]. A rough relation between the guidelines and core elements of Helaba is shown in Table 1.

	Design guidelines	Core elements
G1	Support artefact-based communication	Notes
G2	Gather feedback in a shared workspace	Lean repository, Notes
G3	Enable awareness of artefact evolution	Decision cards and Lean repository

Table 1: Design guidelines and core elements of Helaba.

Notes

Helaba supports artefact-based communications with *Notes*. The Notes are annotations that can be attached to an artefact, in analogy with traditional post-it notes. The goal of this feature is to support designers to externalize ideas and comments that can be related to a specific part of an artefact. This link between artefacts and annotations can promote engagement with artefacts [16], and serve to document design rationale [25]. Individual Notes can also be used to start a *conversation thread*, where team members can discuss about the artefact at hand. Figure 1 presents an artefact and its attached Notes (top), and a zoom-in of a conversation thread (below).

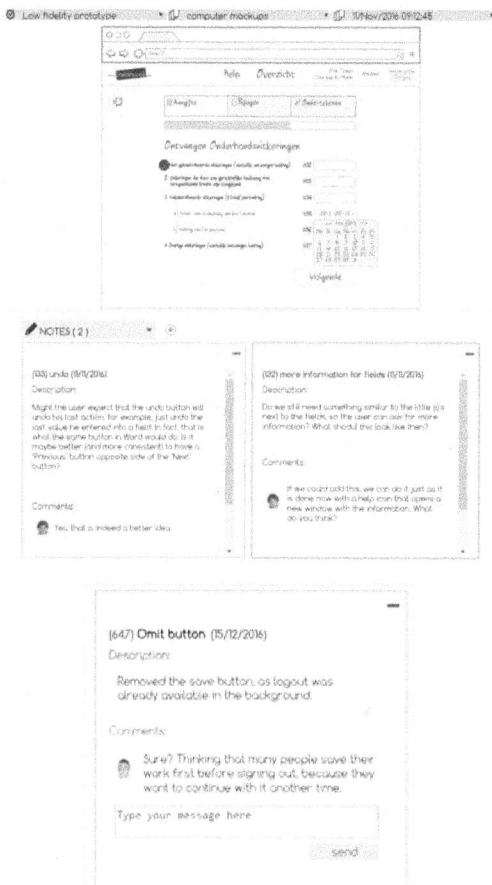

Figure 1: Artefact annotated with *Notes* (top) and *conversation thread* (below).

Decision Cards

Decision cards, depicted in Figure 2, are meant to externalize individual or collective ideas and otherwise tacit knowledge about decisions. This includes information on *why* a decision was taken and *who* was involved in taking the decision. Each given visual artefact can have any number of Decision cards. The granularity of the decisions is determined by the designer, and can range from conceptual or preliminary ideas to concrete technical requirements. Decision cards do not constrain how or what to externalize as a design decision to ensure maximum freedom. For early stages in the process, this is essential as many ideas and concepts are still not well developed, and to minimize the threshold for designers to use the system.

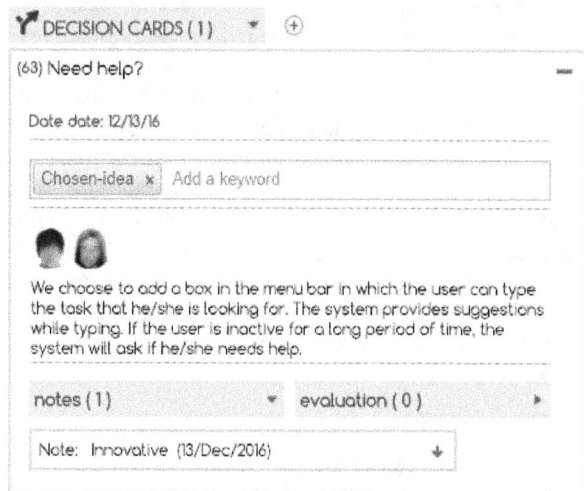

Figure 2: Decision cards include information about *why* a decision was taken and *who* was involved in taking the decision.

Lean Artefact Repository

Another feature to help design teams to be aware of artefact evolution is the Lean artefact repository, illustrated in Figure 3. A repository for documenting the design work provides access to insights into ongoing processes [31].

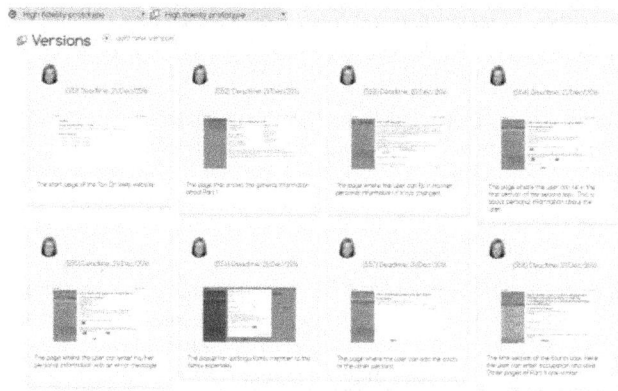

Figure 3: Overview of the Lean artefact repository.

Helaba provides a space for storing and organizing artefacts in a hierarchical structure. With this structure, we aim to offer design teams tools to organize files in a more intuitive way. The principle we use in the Lean repository is that design work can be divided in four levels: *projects*, *tasks*, *artefacts*, and *versions*. Each project contains one or more tasks, each task contains one or more artefacts, and each artefact contains one or more versions or elements of the same artefact. For instance, the overview in Figure 3 illustrates a high-fidelity prototype task of a project, together with different screens as versions.

METHOD

Participants and Assignment

A total of 12 participants between 21 and 25 years old joined our study (10 male, 2 female). Participants were computer science students (Master level), enrolled in an academic course where the goal was to create an application while following a UCD approach. For this academic course, six teams of two students were formed. The assignment was to re-design an interactive application for tax calculations. A group of six members of the Federal Ministry of Finance was involved as external stakeholders (i.e. *clients*) for this project. This group of clients included experts from both computer science and finances. The students had to go through five phases that characterize some of the typical steps taken in a UCD project (see Table 2). Notice that Helaba is designed for supporting UCD processes, but implies no restrictions on the way the UCD process is executed in practice (e.g. phases to follow, artefacts to add…).

Phase	Activities
User analysis	Interview end-users and clients; Analyze and define initial requirements; Create *personas* and *scenarios*
Task analysis	Explore existing application; Create *task* and *dialog models*
Low-fidelity prototype	Create *early prototypes* to explore alternative solutions; Usability evaluation of prototypes (involving UX experts); Present a preliminary solution to clients
High-fidelity prototype	Workshop to generate new ideas; Create an *interactive prototype* of the chosen solution; Usability evaluation of the prototype (involving end-users)
Final system	Prepare a deliverable of prototype to client; Create *final reports* (both team and individual)

Table 2: Phases of the assignment, mapped with activities followed and artefacts created by students.

We selected this project as a basis for our study as it involves: (1) a real-life design case, (2) external stakeholders (i.e. end-users, clients, and UX experts), (3) collaborative design work, and (4) follows the life-cycle of the UCD process, from initial exploration to final solution.

Experimental Design

At the start of the academic course, we invited the participants to join voluntarily our study, which required them use Helaba to document their design activities. We explained the system functionalities, and asked them to use

it for their collaborative activities "in the best way possible". To promote neutrality and encourage participants to record as much content as possible, it was agreed that the content uploaded to the system would not be evaluated in any form unless explicitly stated. As an incentive, we offered an extra point in the project's grade for participating in the study.

The study had a duration of 15 weeks, which is the length of an academic semester and aforementioned course. In addition, two weeks of holidays between semesters were included, but no tasks were assigned during this period. During this time, we gathered information of the process followed by each team by monitoring the content they uploaded to the system. In addition, we collected participants' feedback at regular intervals to learn about their experiences during the study. After each phase of the UCD process, students either participated in an interview or filled-in an online survey. Figure 4 presents the monitoring techniques used throughout our study: interviews, online surveys, and focus groups. We alternated between monitoring techniques to collect information on different levels. However, we asked similar questions in each phase of the study in order to draw comparisons, such as frequency and purpose of use of Helaba, and other tools used.

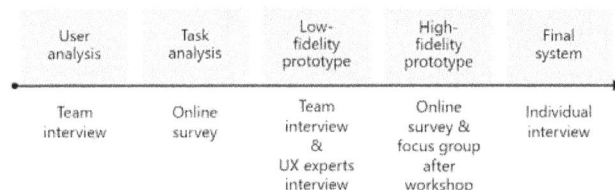

User analysis	Task analysis	Low-fidelity prototype	High-fidelity prototype	Final system
Team interview	Online survey	Team interview & UX experts interview	Online survey & focus group after workshop	Individual interview

Figure 4. Monitoring techniques used in each UCD phase.

The interviews were used in key phases of the project to explore in-depth the practices of the participants. For instance, interviews held during the user analysis and low-fidelity prototype were in pairs, as we wanted to contextualize their collaborative design work. The final interview was individual to explore the perception of each participant about how Helaba facilitated teamwork and self-reflection. Furthermore, we interviewed the three UX experts who performed usability evaluations during the low-fidelity prototype phase. The UX experts were experienced HCI researchers, with an average of seven years of experience. The interviews with the UX experts talked about their experiences using Helaba during the usability evaluation process. Additionally, we conducted first a workshop and then a focus group during the high-fidelity prototype phase. In the workshop, participants used Helaba to revisit previously explored, but discarded ideas to generate new features for their prototypes. The focus group involved all students, and was used to gather their opinions and experiences during the workshop.

Online surveys were used to collect the same information as in the interviews, but in a more concise way during the task analysis and high-fidelity prototype phases (see Figure 4). The online surveys were taken undertaken individually or as a team. We asked teams to fill-in one survey per team, but some teams found easier to fill them individually. In 4 instances (11% of responses), we detected a discrepancy between the answers of teams who filled-in the survey individually. For instance, one team member reported to "upload all artefacts" while the other reported to "upload some artefacts". For these instances, we took a conservative approach and reported the least positive answer.

Our experimental design allowed us to monitor key aspects of the design processes followed by participants (e.g. goals of the project, deliverables produced, and timing). Since all teams received the same instructions and worked under the same conditions, this approach enables us to compare results across teams regardless of the amount, type, and quality of content they recorded. This experimental design would be very difficult – if not impossible – to achieve in an "in-the-wild" design project (e.g. with professional designers in a design consultancy) due to the highly unpredictable nature of design projects [30]. Furthermore, the selected project and population allow us to explore a full cycle of UCD project with novice designers, which we believe can benefit from traceability of their processes.

Data Gathering and Analysis

We gathered data by recording audio and video of the interviews conducted through the study. The workshop and focus group were also audio and video recorded, and two observers took notes. We completed our dataset with the responses given by participants to the surveys. We compiled the data gathered to create a matrix of responses according to the UCD phase in which they were captured. We did a thematic analysis looking for similarities and differences in the responses of participants across different teams for each phase of the process. This analysis allowed us to find patterns in the work style of each team, and to understand how they used Helaba throughout the study. We describe the findings of this analysis in the sections below.

DOCUMENTING A UCD PROCESS WITH HELABA

The assignment guided participants through the typical phases of a user-centered design process. While all teams had similar tasks, each team used a particular tactic and set of tools to facilitate teamwork. For instance, when remotely located, one team used either Skype or Facebook chat to communicate, while another team only used Slack for their conversations. All teams reported to use a similar tactic and set of tools in similar ways through the process. For instance, the team who used Slack as a remote communication tool used it as such through the entire project. This means that a particular tactic for communication was followed regardless of the differences in the activities of each phase. The participants selected the tools they use according to their needs, instead of adopting new tools according to the phase of the project. This finding is consistent with how professional designers select and adopt tools in commercial design settings [11].

Unlike other tools mentioned by the participants, the reported uses of Helaba changed during the study. During the

first half of the project, participants reported to use it mostly as a repository of artefacts, adding a limited number of annotations to them (i.e. Notes and Decision cards). The total number of artefacts and annotations added in Helaba supported these comments from the participants. As illustrated in Figure 5, more content was added in the second half of the project, when the core design tasks and bulk of discussion took place. This evolved for all teams in a similar manner.

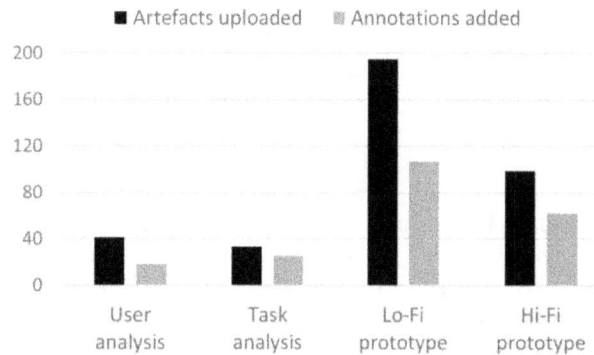

Figure 5. Artefacts uploaded and annotations added to Helaba in the different stages of the UCD process.

Regardless of the work style that each team used, the two core strengths of Helaba for all teams were: (1) keep a record of previous and future work and (2) create a space to access the work of others. The specific work style of each team was accommodated in Helaba. The tool supported teamwork in different ways during different stages, according to the tasks and priorities of each stage. To answer the question of *what characteristics are required in a system to facilitate traceability,* we discuss our findings based on the design guidelines that were used to create Helaba (see Table 1).

G1: SUPPORT ARTEFACT-BASED COMMUNICATION

The first guideline indicates the need to have a *visual connection between artefacts and communication related to the artefact.* We explored this guideline with the Notes feature of Helaba. Notes are digital post-its pinpointed to a specific part of an artefact. We found that the Notes were used to build a narrative of their design process, especially in relation to how artefacts linked to each other.

The value of the Notes for participants was to record the *content* generated during their design work. The content included information about design alternatives and choices. Information regarding the *process* associated to their design work was recorded to a lesser extent, for instance with tasks to be undertaken by each team member. Recording the content and process helped participants to build a narrative of their project. This narrative was easy to record, since the Notes did not impose a structure nor constrained their way of thinking. The participants used Notes to record:

- Agreements reached
- Rationale of design choices
- Next steps to iterate an artefact
- Discarded design alternatives

When it comes to traceability, the narrative built using Notes facilitated to document the rationale of their design work (e.g. what was done and why). The content recorded by the teams in the Notes reveals mostly convergence moments. Similarly, participants did not use Helaba to discuss their designs directly, but to record the topics and outcomes of their discussion. We illustrate this finding with a quote by T1: *"We selected [to record] the discussions that we thought that were important for the further design and the progress of the project". [T1; Task analysis].*

Divergent ideas were discussed either face-to-face or using synchronous communication tools, such as Facebook chat or Skype. Moreover, even though Notes are enabled as conversation hotspots (e.g. for asynchronous communication), we found a limited amount of conversations – only 24% of Notes had a conversation attached. Participants preferred using familiar communication tools (e.g. Slack, Facebook chat), and recording the outcome of their conversations into Helaba. This tactic relates to the well-documented fact that recording design rationale can be overwhelming [12], as reported by T4: *"We recorded some [discussions] on Helaba. However, since we discussed a great amount of it through Skype and face-to-face, it would be double work to add all what was said to Helaba..." [T4; Task analysis].*

To evaluate the utility of Helaba to capture design discussions, we asked participants about the type of information they registered in the system, how they registered it, and how often they recorded their team discussions. Participants reported that most of these discussions were recorded as Notes, and included a mixture between design alternatives, decisions, and upcoming tasks. The answers of participants, illustrated in Figure 6, reflect on the proportion of discussions that students perceived to record (as Notes) across the different phases of the study.

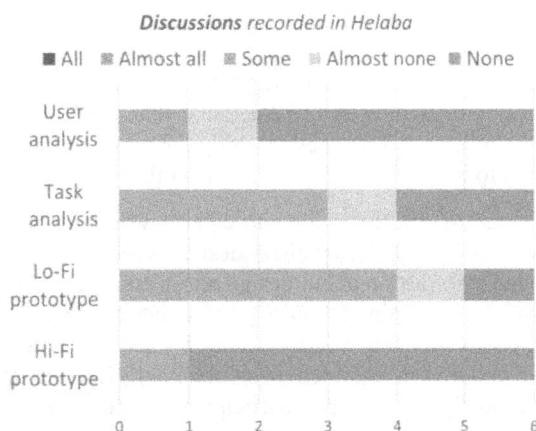

Figure 6. Responses to the question: "How much of your *team discussions* during [phase] were recorded in Helaba?" mapped to the different phases of the UCD process.

During the user analysis phase, four teams did not record any Note. The reason given by these teams for not creating Notes was that their conversations took place in a different setting (e.g. face-to-face or other tool), and it seemed redundant to add their discussions to Helaba. However, there was a shift in the usage during the task analysis and low-fidelity prototype phases, as most teams added Notes actively. This finding shows that Notes were especially useful during convergence moments. In other words, where more dialog was required to create an artefact, more Notes were included, and more convergence moments were recorded.

G2: GATHER FEEDBACK IN A SHARED WORKSPACE

The second guideline points out the need for *sharing and receiving feedback from team members and stakeholders of the project in a shared workspace*. We explored how Helaba facilitates traceability with a shared workspace organized around artefacts. Through the shared workspace, we found that teams used the system to gather feedback at two levels: *internal feedback* and *external feedback*.

Participants reported using Helaba to record feedback when working in remote, asynchronous setting. This type of content was added to clarify or give feedback about the work done by the other team member. Thus, we refer to it as *internal feedback*. Notes were mostly used to record internal feedback, as they allowed pinpointing a comment to specific elements of the artefacts. For example, Student A uploaded a new version of an artefact, and added Notes to let Student B know what changes were made and where. In response, Student B added comments to these Notes to either accept the changes or give feedback about them (see *conversation threads* in Figure 1).

Teams used the shared workspace actively to receive or record *external feedback* from clients, UX experts, and end-users. All teams reported discussing the feedback from external sources, and recording the outcomes that were used to guide the next iterations. Having a centralized space for capturing feedback from externals was especially relevant in the late stages of the project, when feedback gathered was used to retrospectively describe design choices (e.g. write final report, defend choices with clients). Making decisions in line with previous knowledge generated during the project was facilitated by having information about previous stages and a log of "what others say". For instance, this log was used to reflect on how the contribution of the stakeholders influenced the design process, as illustrated by T2: *"The discussions we had [with the client] were added to the artefact" [T2; Lo-Fi Prototype]*

We used the shared workspace for gathering feedback by asking the UX experts to use the tool for conducting their usability evaluations. A total of 465 Notes were created in the scope of these evaluations. Around 10% of these Notes included a direct conversation between the teams and the UX experts to either clarify feedback or ask follow-up questions. This is more Notes and conversations than in any of the phases of the design process (see Figure 5). They focused on documenting enough information to make the evaluation as complete and useful as possible. The UX experts thought Helaba is a useful tool to understand the rationale of design choices when contextualized by other explored alternatives. This information helped the UX experts to grasp the struggles of the participants and come up with meaningful feedback. After the usability evaluations took place, all teams reported to access frequently the comments of the UX experts to guide their work. This reflects on traceability for externals of the design process, who can be informed in an easy way of previous design choices using the system.

G3: ENABLE AWARENESS OVER ARTEFACT EVOLUTION

The third guideline specifies that teams need to *maintain awareness over artefact evolution and previous design decisions*. We explored this guideline with the Lean repository and Decision cards features as they enabled participants to capture, retrieve, and revisit information from key points of the design process. For instance, as illustrated in a quote by T3, participants used the information recorded to inform the next steps of their design work: *"[We used Helaba to] check on decisions/notes on low fidelity prototypes and use it to make decisions on how to create/design the high fidelity prototypes." [T3; Hi-Fi prototype]*.

Lean Repository for Coherence and Consistency

All teams consistently mentioned that Helaba was useful as a repository to overview their project evolution. One of the strong points of our tool for participants was being able to organize different artefacts and versions together with annotations and decisions. This facilitated traceability as it enabled participants to retrieve artefacts and their rationale, make connections between different artefacts, and iterate them in a coherent way.

The structure used to organize artefacts within Helaba was similar for all teams. For instance, the *tasks* created by participants were consistent with the stages of the UCD process: all teams had a specific task for each of the phases, with the exception of two groups who did not uploaded their high-fidelity prototype. The pre-defined structure (i.e. *projects*, *tasks*, *artefacts*...) allowed participants to organize files in a more intuitive and useful way than with other file storage services, such as Google Drive. The reason for this increased usefulness was that uploading artefacts together with annotations facilitated to be aware of the changes done by others, as mentioned by T4: *"If it was useful to put [an artefact] on Helaba for the team partner. Especially if not all changes were discussed or approved by the other". [T4, Hi-Fi prototype]*

To find out how participants selected what artefacts to upload (or exclude) from Helaba and why, we asked them to report the proportion of artefacts that they uploaded in each phase. As illustrated in Figure 7, the participants uploaded to a considerable proportion of artefacts created during the different phases of the design process. This reflects on the fact that students became more proficient in using our tool, but also on that more artefacts were created during these phases.

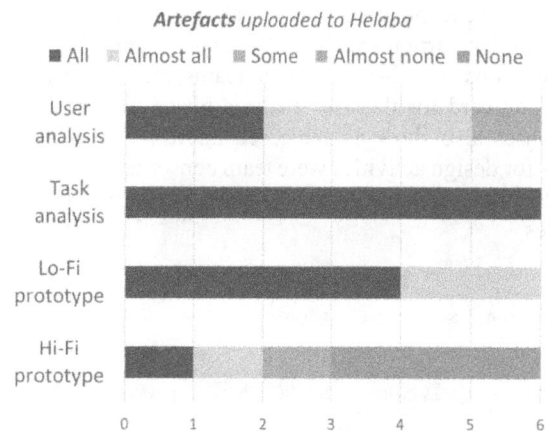

Figure 7. Responses to the question: "How many of the artefacts you created for [phase] were recorded in Helaba?" mapped to the different phases of the UCD process.

The participants defined a *version* as: (1) a new screen in the system, (2) a milestone where they reworked a screen thoroughly, (3) an artefact whose direction changed in a significant way, or (4) a finalized deliverable. Keeping record of a variety of versions facilitated to keep track of changes and their rationale over time.

Decision Cards for Consensus and Milestones

The Decision cards were useful to externalize team consensus in an explicit way. One core strength of Decision cards is that they supported teams to capture the agreements that emerged from their discussions, without influencing the reasoning process. In comparison to the Notes, participants felt compelled to reflect upon their design choices before creating a Decision card. In this way, while participants did not felt "forced" to record or address each of the decisions, they were cautious of what content they externalized as a decision.

A reason for this is that consensus is not simple nor easy to articulate. Thus, participants created Decision cards only to capture what they perceived as a milestone in the process, as mentioned by T6: *"We only made a Decision card of the hardest problem" [T6, Task analysis]*. When prompted to explain what information was recorded as a decision, participants mentioned that they captured in Decision cards those decisions that:

- Were perceived as major and difficult
- Involved several steps to be executed
- Involved reworking large parts of the artefacts, such as entire screens
- Documented intensive discussions
- Included ideas to be explored in the next versions of the artefact
- Resolved external feedback (i.e. comments from UX experts or clients)
- Had a larger impact in the overall design

We asked participants to report the proportion of decisions recorded in Decision cards during each phase of the UCD process. The responses to this question, depicted in Figure 8, confirm that participants recorded a conservative proportion of decisions. For instance, four teams did not create any Decision card for the user analysis phase. However, these responses also show an increased interest in the Decision cards for design activities were team consensus is required to create a determinative artefact, such as in early prototyping phases.

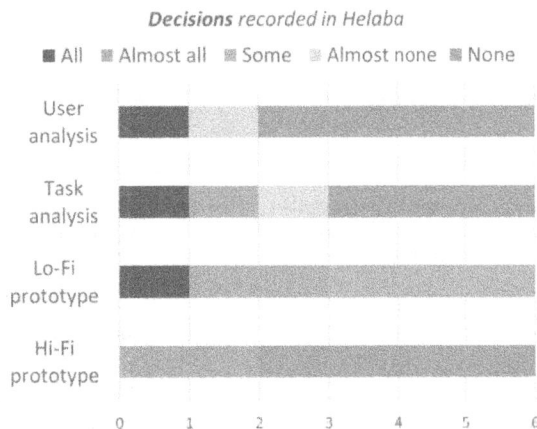

Figure 8. Responses to the question: "How much of your decisions [per phase] were recorded in Helaba?" mapped to the different phases of the UCD process.

What teams perceived as minor decisions remained implicit or were kept as Notes. Thus, the decisions included in the Decision cards are conscious reflections about the challenges and milestones of the ongoing design process. Having a combination of features to record annotations (Notes and Decision cards) led the participants to consider Helaba as a "repository of decisions". What is more, the participants felt motivated to keep "good track" of decisions for traceability, as illustrated by T6: *"We wanted Helaba to be an extensive database of all our decisions [for this phase], so we recorded all of them". [Hi-Fi prototype, T6]*

CORE ASPECTS TO SUPPORT TRACEABILITY IN CREATIVE DESIGN

The way participants engaged with Helaba helped us to identify three core aspects to facilitate traceability in creative design: *make and revisit a design narrative, display curated design artefacts,* and *integrate team contributions.*

Make and Revisit a Design Narrative

Consistent guideline G1, we introduced a flexible, artefact-based approach to document design rationale. Participants include narratives for the artefacts, "telling their story" throughout the different steps of the UCD process. The narratives situated the artefact with respect to the *content* that is captured by the artefact, as well as the *process* of design activities that lead to the artefact [30]. Consequently, all narratives included information about the design knowledge (e.g. design rationale, decisions) and teamwork coordination (e.g. to do lists).

The flexibility of Helaba helped participants to implement their own workflow within the UCD process, such as we

intended to when designing the system. All teams applied an incremental and iterative working style, as is suggested by the UCD process. Helaba was used to structure and capture the subsequent iterations of their work, and helped them to refine gradually subsequent evolutions of the artefacts. The collection of previously documented knowledge became increasingly more valuable for the participants towards the end of the project. Especially when they had to motivate their decisions to both the stakeholders and the educational team.

Two features were used for creating the narrative: Notes and Decision cards. The Notes served as diary for the project to document design knowledge associated with artefacts and convergence moments. As described by Lindley et al. [16], annotated artefacts were used as a *team memory*. The participants considered the Notes as the core feature to make and contextualize the narrative of their design process. The reason for this was the strong association between Notes and artefacts, and the level of freedom that they provided to record information. The Decision cards were considered more suitable to record milestones in the project, but were less essential than Notes to build the narrative. Decision cards were also useful to reflect and articulate team consensus: teams often used them to capture important steps that have a significant influence on the evolution of the artefacts.

The narratives created by the participants acted as *emergent boundary objects*, as proposed by Dalsgaard et al. [4]. In contrast to the original conception of boundary objects, the *emergent* characteristic of boundary objects indicates that they are "dynamically being transformed in collaborative practices" [4]. In this sense, the narratives were transformed across the different phases of the UCD process. Furthermore, the narratives aided to record temporary ideas, which helped concrete concepts to emerge in collaboration with others (i.e. team members, clients, UX experts). Recording and being able to trace these emergent boundary objects was used to reflect on the process (*why* a decision was taken, *when* a concept emerged…) and justify decisions during and at the end of the project.

Display Curated Design Artefacts

Design activities typically produce a large quantity of artefacts, which has only increased because it has become so easy to create digital ones [29]. We found that instead of just uploading every source of inspiration and artefact created to Helaba, participants selected those that they considered meaningful to represent their process. In this way, all teams used the shared workspace to display a "curated" selection of the artefacts, which represented milestones shaped by team interactions.

The lean repository of Helaba served as a canvas to organize the artefacts that were representative for the design process. Accordingly, participants used this feature to populate a coherent, albeit simplified, visual narrative of their process. As previous research [29], we found that participants were more interested in reviewing the work of others to become aware of their actions, than in revisiting their own work. Having a curated selection of artefacts was useful to ensure consistency and coherence in the process. Participants knew that the content in Helaba was relevant for both their team member and the process. In combination with the narrative, these artefacts helped to build a cohesive story of the project milestones over time. In this sense, as stated by design guideline G3, it was vital for the success of the projects to enable awareness of the artefacts evolution among the team members.

We believe that having a designated space to record the relevant "turns and twists" of the design process is useful to visualize the co-evolution of problems and solutions [5]. Being able to select those moments to record (e.g. not enforcing the kind of artefacts or content to record), helped participants to record the "bursts of development" [5] and milestones of the project (e.g. Decision cards), which is vital knowledge to produce and record when it comes to traceability [17] .

Integrate Team Contributions

Design guideline G2 highlights the importance of gathering feedback in a shared workspace. Including the point of view of different team members in a single workspace was a key aspect to support traceability during the study. We did not design Helaba to replace existing established communication tools, and as such, day-to-day communication happened in channels other than Helaba. Discussions happened most of the time in a face-to-face setting, with team members being present in the same location, or discussing issues using tools such as Slack or Skype when collaborating remotely. The shared artefact-centered workspace offered each team the tools to stay up-to-date with the work of each other. Participants collaborated in the system more actively in those phases where more dialog was required to reach a solution, where the problem spaces were larger, and where more unknowns required to be explored. By reviewing the work of others, participants engaged in an *ongoing* reflection, which helped them to think on solutions based on the content recorded in Helaba. Furthermore, the design knowledge they recorded helped participants to frame their activities to reflect *on* previous agreements and ideas (e.g. retrospective thinking), and *for* finding new courses of action (e.g. prospective thinking).

The limited amount of discussions and conversations recorded puts forward the question of whether Helaba should include different sorts of communication channels (e.g. chat, video). We argue that in a tool like ours, *recording the design process* must remain pivotal. The strength of the system was not that all conversations took place in there, but that it brought together different actors in one "designated" space to discuss crucial aspects about the design. This finding reflects on the commercial, off-the-shelf tools to support remote, multidisciplinary design work described earlier in the paper (summarized in Appendix A). We believe these tools would benefit of features that help to record and scaffold the design process, instead of being comprehensive

communication suits. Furthermore, forcing users to use one single communication tool instead of those already familiar and highly specialized, could result in reduced acceptance of the system. Traceability is better supported with communication based on artefacts, in a shared workspace where relevant design knowledge is easily accessible. We suggest that it would be interesting to let the user import information from different tools in a seamless way to avoid "double work". For example, importing a decision that happen in an external chat application into Helaba, rather than copying or typing (again) an entire conversation. This will allow designers to create a curated information flow.

LESSONS LEARNT ABOUT HELABA AND FUTURE WORK

Recording design rationale is a particularly controversial task given the extra effort that it requires [12]. The minimal structure imposed by Helaba facilitated to create this record. However, the flexibility in systems such as ours also requires a strong support to warrant that user can add, organize, and retrieve content in an efficient way. In our study, participants decided freely when to record information in the system and the type of information to record in a curated manner.

The flexibility and openness enabled by Helaba was fundamental for the participants of our study. Participants captured their design work with the granularity they felt appropriate, and felt free to change directions as required. This reflects of the fact that participants were able to adapt the tool to their own processes, rather than being limited to strict rules imposed by the system. Assessing the quality or creativeness in the outcomes of the participants' projects was out of the scope of our study. However, we believe that the freedom offered by Helaba allowed participants of the study to focus on the creative aspects of the process, rather than on managing the process itself.

Considering this context when discussing our results, it is worth to highlight the logic next step: validate the findings we present here with different design teams working in projects of diverse duration and level of complexity. We believe this study is a necessary first step towards understanding how to integrate traceability into the design process in professional settings, where teams have variable sizes and composition. We are certain that Helaba allowed each team to create a narrative of their process that was relevant and valuable for them, both visually and conceptually. Finally, we demonstrated that it is not required to have a systematic or formal approach to support traceability. Thus, we believe this is a first step towards offering tools that balance formal and creative approaches in user-centered design.

ACKNOWLEDGEMENTS

This research was supported by the COnCEPT project, funded by the European Commission 7th Framework ICT Research project (no. 610725). We would like to thank Gilbert Cockton for the insightful discussions and feedback on early drafts of this paper.

APPENDIX A

	Shared workspace				Artefact-based communication		Awareness of artefact evolution		
	Shared workspace	Connected with external tools	Track recent activities of the team	Team and task management	Annotations in artefact	Synchronous / asynchronous communication	File structure	Version control/ management	Record decisions explicitly
ConceptShare	Yes	No	Yes	Yes	Yes	Yes	Yes	Yes	No
Notable	No	No	Yes	No	Yes	Yes	Not clear	No	No
Firefly	No	No	No	Yes	Yes	Yes	Yes	Yes	No
Skwibl	Yes	Yes	Yes	Yes	Yes	Yes	Yes	Yes	No
Designdrop	No	No	Not clear	No	Yes	Yes	No	Yes	No
Govisually	Yes	Yes	Yes	Yes	Yes	Yes	Yes	Yes	Yes
Concept inbox	Yes	Yes	Yes	Yes	Yes	Yes	Yes	Yes	No
Redpen	Yes	Yes	Yes	No	Yes	Yes	Yes	Yes	No
Realtime board	Yes	Yes	Yes	Yes	Yes	Yes	Yes	Yes	No
InVision	Yes	Yes	Yes	Yes	Yes	Yes	Yes	Yes	No
Wake	Yes	Yes	Yes	Yes	Yes	Yes	Yes	Yes	No
Conceptboard	Yes	Yes	Yes	Yes	Yes	Yes	Yes	Yes	No
Prevue	Yes	No	Not clear	Not clear	Yes	Yes	Yes	Not clear	No
Apollo	No	No	No	No	Yes	Yes	No	Yes	No
Redmark	No	No	No	No	Yes	Yes	No	Yes	No
Bounce	No	No	No	No	Yes	Yes	No	No	No

https://www.conceptshare.com   https://www.designdrop.io   https://realtimeboard.com   https://prevue.it
http://notableapp.com   http://www.govisually.com   https://www.invisionapp.com   http://www.useapollo.com
https://www.fireflyapp.com   http://conceptinbox.com   https://wake.com   http://redmark.com
http://skwibl.com   https://redpen.io   https://conceptboard.com   http://www.bounceapp.com

Appendix A: Summary of (commercial) off-the-shelf design tools that have some kind of useful support for traceability.

REFERENCES

1. Richard Buchanan. 1992. Wicked Problems in Design Thinking. *Design Issues* 8, 2: 5–21.

2. Gilbert Cockton. 2014. A Critical, Creative UX Community: CLUF. *Journal of Usability Studies* 10, 1: 1–16.

3. Peter Dalsgaard and Kim Halskov. 2012. Reflective Design Documentation. In *Proceedings of the Designing Interactive Systems Conference* (DIS '12), 428–437. http://doi.org/10.1145/2317956.2318020

4. Peter Dalsgaard, Kim Halskov, and Ditte Amund Basballe. 2014. Emergent boundary objects and boundary zones in collaborative design research projects. In *Proceedings of the Designing Interactive Systems Conference* (DIS '14), 745–754. http://doi.org/10.1145/2598510.2600878

5. Kees Dorst and Nigel Cross. 2001. Creativity in the design process: co-evolution of problem-solution. *Design Studies* 22, 5: 425–437. http://doi.org/10.1016/s0142-694x(01)00009-6

6. Paul Dourish and Victoria Bellotti. 1992. Awareness and Coordination in Shared Workspaces. In *Proceedings of the ACM conference on Computer-Suported Cooperative Work* (CSCW '92), 107–114. http://doi.org/10.1145/143457.143468

7. Alexander Egyed. A scenario-driven approach to traceability. In *Proceedings of the International Conference on Software Engineering* (ICSE '01), 123–132. http://doi.org/10.1109/ICSE.2001.919087

8. Daniel Fallman. 2003. Design-oriented human-computer interaction. In *Proceedings of the SIGCHI Conference on Human Factors in Computing Systems* (CHI '03), 225–232. http://doi.org/10.1145/642651.642652

9. Bengt Göransson, Jan Gulliksen, and Inger Boivie. 2003. The usability design process - integrating user-centered systems design in the software development process. *Software Process Improvement and Practice* 8, 2: 111–131. http://doi.org/10.1002/spip.174

10. Marisela Gutierrez Lopez, Mieke Haesen, Kris Luyten, and Karin Coninx. 2015. Helaba: A system to highlight design rationale in collaborative design processes. In *Proceedings of the International Conference on Cooperative Design, Visualization, and Engineering* (CDVE '15) 175–184. http://doi.org/10.1007/978-3-319-24132-6_21

11. Marisela Gutierrez Lopez, Mieke Haesen, Kris Luyten, and Karin Coninx. 2015. Study and analysis of collaborative design practices. In *Proceedings of the 4th Participatory Innovation Conference* (PIN-C '15), 176–183.

12. John Horner and Michael E Atwood. 2006. Design Rationale : The Rationale and the Barriers. In *Proceedings of the Nordic conference on Human-*

computer interaction (NordiCHI '06), 341–350.
DOI=http://dx.doi.org/10.1145/1182475.1182511

13. Wendy Ju, Arna Ionescu, Lawrence Neeley, and Terry Winograd. 2004. Where the wild things work: capturing shared phsyical design workspaces. In *Proceedings of the ACM Conference on Computer-Supported Cooperative Work* (CSCW '04), 533–541. http://doi.org/10.1145/1031607.1031696

14. Xavier Lacaze and Philippe Palanque. 2007. DREAM & TEAM: A tool and a notation supporting exploration of options and traceability of choices for safety critical interactive systems. In *Proceedings of the 11th IFIP TC 13 International Conference On Human-Computer Interaction* (INTERACT '07), 525–540. http://doi.org/10.1007/978-3-540-74800-7_48

15. Siân Lindley, Xiang Cao, John Helmes, Richard Morris, and Sam Meek. 2013. Towards a tool for design ideation: insights from use of SketchStorm. *Proceedings of theInternational BCS Human Computer Interaction Conference* (BCS-HCI '13), Article 14.

16. Nada Matta, Myriam Ribière, Olivier Corby, Myriam Lewkowicz, and Manuel Zacklad. 2001. Project memory in design. In *Industrial Knowledge Management*, Rajkumar Roy (ed.). Springer, London, 147–162.

17. Mark Meagher, Kate Bielaczyc, and Jeffrey Huang. 2005. OpenD: supporting parallel development of digital designs. In *Proceedings of the Conference on Designing for User eXperience* (DUX '05), Article 25.

18. Kannan Mohan and Balasubramaniam Ramesh. 2007. Traceability-based knowledge integration in group decision and negotiation activities. *Decision Support Systems* 43, 3: 968–989. http://doi.org/10.1016/j.dss.2005.05.026

19. Pavković Neven, Štorga Mario, Bojčetić Nenad, and Dorian Marjanović. 2013. Facilitating design communication through engineering information traceability. *Artificial Intelligence for Engineering, Design, Analysis and Manufacturing* 27, 2: 91–105.

20. Lora Oehlberg, Kyu Simm, Jasmine Jones, Alice Agogino, and Björn Hartmann. 2012. Showing is sharing: building shared understanding in human-centered design teams with Dazzle. In *Proceedings of the Designing Interactive Systems Conference* (DIS '12), 669–678. http://doi.org/10.1145/2317956.2318057

21. International Standards Organization. 2010. *ISO 13407. Human Centred Design Process for Interactive Systems*. Geneva, Swiss.

22. Ipek Ozkaya and Omer Akin. 2007. Tool support for computer-aided requirement traceability in architectural design: The case of DesignTrack. *Automation in Construction* 16, 5: 674–684. http://doi.org/10.1016/j.autcon.2006.11.006

23. James Pierce, Phoebe Sengers, Tad Hirsch, Tom Jenkins, William Gaver, and Carl DiSalvo. 2015. Expanding and refining design and criticality in HCI. In *Proceedings of the SIGCHI Conference on Human Factors in Computing Systems* (CHI '15), 2083–2092. http://doi.org/10.1145/2702123.2702438

24. Cecil Piya, Vinayak, Senthil Chandrasegaran, Niklas Elmqvist, and Karthik Ramani. 2017. Co-3Deator: A team-first collaborative 3D design ideation tool. In *Proceedings of the SIGCHI Conference on Human Factors in Computing Systems* (CHI '17), 6581–6592. http://doi.org/10.1145/3025453.3025825

25. Colin Potts and Glenn Bruns. 1988. Recording the Reasons for Design Decisions. In *Proceedings of the International Conference On Software Engineering (ICSE '88)*, 418–427.

26. Donald A. Schön. 1983. *The Reflective Practitioner*. Temple Smith, London.

27. Jami J Shah, Dae K Jeon, Susan D Urban, Plamen Bliznakov, and Mary Rogers. 1996. Database infrastructure for supporting engineering design histories. *Computer-Aided Design* 28, 5: 347–360. http://doi.org/10.1016/0010-4485(95)00054-2

28. Moushumi Sharmin and Brian P. Bailey. 2011. Making sense of communication associated with artifacts during early design activity. In *Proceedings of the 13th IFIP 13 TC International Conference on Human-computer Interaction* (INTERACT '11). 181–198. http://doi.org/10.1007/978-3-642-23774-4_17

29. Moushumi Sharmin, Brian P Bailey, Cole Coats, and Kevin Hamilton. 2009. Understanding knowledge management practices for early design activity and its implications for reuse. In *Proceedings of the SIGCHI Conference on Human Factors in Computing Systems* (CHI '09), 2367–2376. http://doi.org/10.1145/1518701.1519064

30. Joachim Stempfle and Petra Badke-Schaub. 2002. Thinking in design teams - an analysis of team communication. *Design Studies* 23, 5: 473–496. http://doi.org/10.1016/S0142-694X(02)00004-2

31. Laurel Swan, Diana Tanase, and Alex S Taylor. 2010. Design's processional character. In *Proceedings of the Designing Interactive Systems Conference* (DIS '10), 65–74. http://dx.doi.org/10.1145/1858171.1858186

32. Antony Tang, Yan Jin, and Jun Han. 2007. A rationale-based architecture model for design traceability and reasoning. *Journal of Systems and Software* 80, 6: 918–934.

33. Antony Tang, Peng Liang, Viktor Clerc, and Hans Van Vliet. 2011. Traceability in the co-evolution of architectural requirements and design. http://doi.org/10.1007/978-3-642-21001-3_4

34. Shahtab Wahid, Stacy M Branham, Lauren Cairco, D Scott McCrickard, and Steve Harrison. 2009. Picking

up artifacts : storyboarding as a gateway to reuse. In *Proceedings of the 12th IFIP TC 13 International Conference on Human-Computer Interaction* (INTERACT '09), 528–541. http://dx.doi.org/10.1007/978-3-642-03658-3_57

35. Tracee Vetting Wolf, Jennifer A Rode, Jeremy Sussman, and Wendy A Kellogg. 2006. Dispelling design as the "black art" of CHI. In *Proceedings of the SIGCHI Conference on Human Factors in Computing Systems* (CHI '06), 521–530. http://dx.doi.org/10.1145/1124772.1124853

36. Oxford English Dictionary. 2017. *Traceable*. Retrieved July 1, 2017 from https://en.oxforddictionaries.com/definition/traceable

Danmaku vs. Forum Comments: Understanding User Participation and Knowledge Sharing in Online Videos

Qunfang Wu
School of Information Studies,
Syracuse University
Syracuse, USA
qwu114@syr.edu

Yisi Sang
School of Education,
Syracuse University
Syracuse, USA
yisang@syr.edu

Shan Zhang
School of Information Studies,
Syracuse University
Syracuse, USA
szhang44@syr.edu

Yun Huang
School of Information Studies,
Syracuse University
Syracuse, USA
yhuang@syr.edu

ABSTRACT

Danmaku is a new video comment feature that is gaining popularity. Unlike typical forum comments that are displayed with user names below videos, danmaku comments are overlaid on the screen of videos without showing users' information. Prior work studied forum comments and danmaku separately, and little work compared how these two features were used. We collected 38,399 danmaku comments and 16,414 forum comments posted in 2017 on 30 popular videos on Bilibili.com. We examined the usage of these two features in terms of user participation, language used, and ways of sharing knowledge. We found that more users posted danmaku comments, and they also posted these more frequently than forum comments. Even though, in total, more negative language was used in danmaku comments than in forum comments, active users appeared to post more positive comments in danmaku. There was no such correlation in forum comments. It is interesting to find that danmaku and forum comments enabled knowledge sharing in a complementary manner, where danmaku comments involved more explicit knowledge sharing and forum comments exhibited more tacit knowledge sharing. We discuss design implications to promote social interactions for online video systems.

Author Keywords

Danmaku comments; forum comments; anonymous; synchronous; knowledge sharing; explicit knowledge; tacit knowledge.

ACM Classification Keywords

H.5.2. Information Interfaces and Presentation (e.g. HCI): User Interfaces.

INTRODUCTION

Danmaku, a new video commentary feature, originated in Japan and now is very popular on Chinese video websites (e.g., Bilibili.com, AcFun.cn) [5], especially among young people. Unlike traditional video forums where comments are displayed below the video, danmaku comments fly from right to left on the video screen. Users can send danmaku comments anonymously and see other users' danmaku comments while they are watching the videos. Figure 1 illustrates the typical design of displaying the two types of comments using an example on Bilibili.com [5] (the most popular danmaku video website in China).

Compared to the forum design, which has been widely applied to the majority of video websites across different nations (e.g., YouTube), danmaku was adopted by video websites mainly in Asia. There has been increasing interest in the CSCW and CHI communities over the new social phenomena created by danmaku [45, 53, 28]. However, these two features (forum vs. danmaku) have been studied separately. For example, scholars found that users posted forum comments for varying purposes, e.g., sharing ideas, networking, and answering questions [32], as well as debating [46]. Regarding danmaku, Ma and Cao discovered that users applied different strategies to communicate effectively using danmaku, e.g., using different colors to distinguish user groups [28]. Yao et al. also conducted a survey study to understand the perceived benefits and drawbacks of danmaku [53]; e.g., users perceived that danmaku made the video more fun but also contained a large number of critiques and insulting language [53]. Little research compared the usage of the two comment features.

To address this gap, we collected 38,399 danmaku comments and 16,414 forum comments posted in 2017 on 30 recent and popular videos on Bilibili.com. We compared these two types of comments in terms of user participation, language patterns

Figure 1. User interface of displaying danmaku and forum comments on Bilibili.com. For example, Bilibili.com offers the following three danmaku modes: 1) Rolling danmaku, the default mode, where users' danmaku comments fly from right to left on the screen; 2) Top danmaku centers the comments on the top of the screen; 3) Bottom danmaku centers danmaku comments at the bottom of the video window. Users can select different display modes, colors and fonts for their danmaku comments.

and ways of knowledge sharing. Our work makes the following major contributions by providing empirical evidence of new knowledge: (1) the new danmaku feature promoted user participation compared to traditional comment features using forums; (2) even though there was more negative language in danmaku than in forum comments overall, active users posted more positive danmaku instead of forum comments; and (3) the ways of sharing knowledge in danmaku and forum comments are complementary, where more explicit knowledge is shared in danmaku. Our findings shed light on future design possibilities for online video websites.

RELATED WORK

Compared to forum comments, danmaku has two major perceived features: (1) building a "Pseudo-Synchronized" communication experience [41], where danmaku may make users feel like they are co-watching the video at the same time even though they can post danmaku comments at different times [28] and (2) posting anonymously. In this section, we review relevant literature on how synchronous and anonymous interactions impact user participation in online communities.

In addition, both studies on traditional forum [32, 46] and danmaku [28, 8] found that users posted comments for different purposes, including to answer questions [28, 32], to share opinions [53, 46], etc. Thus, we also review relevant literature on knowledge sharing in online communities, and develop our hypotheses.

Synchronization and Anonymity in Online Communication

Providing synchronous communication media is predicted to improve user participation [40]. For example, in an online business writing classroom, students generated a significantly larger amount of discussions when interacting with each other via the synchronous conference option [31]. It was also found that users wrote significantly more sentences in synchronous online discussions than in asynchronous discussions [18]. Yu et al. conducted a qualitative study to compare two alternative comment media, danmaku's Synchronous Overlay and Adjacent Scrollable, and found that the former promoted a stronger sense of togetherness [54].

Anonymity is also found to have a positive impact on user participation [23, 17, 14]. For example, Kilner et al. analyzed an online forum of practice for U.S. soldiers and found that removing anonymity options led to significantly fewer comments [23]. In a web forum for a basic undergraduate technology course, students who were anonymous were approximately five times more likely to provide critical suggestions than those who were not anonymous [17]. Through a scenario-based experimental study, researchers found that anonymous groups participated significantly more in chatting than identified groups [14].

Given that anonymous danmaku creates pseudo-synchronous experiences, and the above literature on user participation, we developed the following hypothesis.

H1: Users send more danmaku comments than forum comments.

Anonymity not only provides a safe way to interact but also results in lack of accountability [34]. This loss of accountability results in an increased level of toxic disinhibition, consequently promoting impulsive, aggressive, and abusive behaviors [10]. According to Tucey's study, anonymous discussion can be of a lower quality than its counterpart; it can lead to flaming, rudeness, and less thoughtful contributions to the debate because participants feel that they have less responsibility for their words [49]. On the contrary, a more revealed identity yields less swearing, less anger, more affect words, more positive emotion words and less negative emotion words in comments [36]. Kilner and Hoadley observed that the prohibition of anonymous posts on a military professional education site almost completely eliminated negative comments [23]. Based on the literature, we developed our second hypothesis as below.

H2: Danmaku comments are more negative than forum comments.

Knowledge Sharing in Online Communities and Social Networks

Prior studies found that users posted danmaku comments for crowdsourcing captions [30], explaining terminologies [26] and debating [26]. Forums, e.g., on YouTube, can be a public space for answering questions [32], engaging in debates and exchanging opinions about various topics [46]. These two types of commenting provide different ways of knowledge sharing on video websites, however, little research investigates if/how users shared knowledge differently through these two types of comments on video websites.

Scholars have been using Brown's definitions of explicit knowledge and tacit knowledge to differentiate ways of knowledge sharing [6], e.g., in healthcare systems [42, 1], e-government [37], and social media [39].

Explicit knowledge is referred to as "know-what" knowledge and expressed in words, numbers or symbols, and stored in databases, memos, notes, or documents, etc. This type of knowledge is formalized and codified, thus it is easier to identify, store, retrieve and communicate [52]. Tacit knowledge is referred to as "know-how" knowledge. It can be defined as experiences, beliefs, values, intuitive feeling, mental model, skills and observation in people's minds [11, 39]. The key to acquiring tacit knowledge is through sharing experience or people's thought processes [24].

For example, studies found that the social web paradigm was helpful for tacit knowledge sharing through interactive and collaborative technologies, such as social networking and online discussion forums [1]. Happer et al. found that on social Q&A sites, users asked informational questions and conversational questions which aimed to simulate discussions for sharing expression and opinions [15], promoting tacit knowledge sharing. Panahi et al. claimed that characteristics of social media, e.g., user-generated content, peer-to-peer communication and multimedia oriented, can support tacit knowledge sharing [39].

In this paper, we collected archived danmaku and forum comments to test the following hypothesis.

H3: Both danmaku and forum comments exhibit the same pattern of knowledge sharing where more tacit knowledge is shared than explicit knowledge.

METHOD

We collected archival data from Bilibili.com, and annotated the collected comments in terms of the type of knowledge sharing, then we performed both quantitative and qualitative methods to test our hypotheses.

Data Collection and Processing

We used the Bilibili official API to crawl both danmaku and forum comments. In Bilibili.com, there are six popular genres of videos: anime, dramas, games, lectures, sports, and TV shows. For each of the six genres, we selected five popular videos that were uploaded recently. To make a fair comparison between the two types of comments, for each video, we analyzed the two data sets in the same time frame. The data collection was conducted between March and May in 2017. Finally, we collected 38,399 danmaku comments and 16,414 forum comments from 30 videos. Table 1 shows basic information regarding the videos and comments according to the genres. Each collected forum comment is provided with the real user identifier that is used to log in to the website, but each danmaku comment contains a pseudonymous identifier of the comment creator.

Genre	Video in Total	Average Video Length (mins)	Average Viewers	Danmaku Comments in Total	Forum Comments in Total
Anime	5	20	32,620	9,163	2,518
Drama	5	28	18,997	6,591	4,806
Game	5	15	233,974	7,143	1,684
Lecture	5	24	194,650	3,541	4,581
Sports	5	21	201,507	4,294	1,658
TV show	5	22	36,757	7,667	1,167

Table 1. Basic information regarding the videos and collected comments according to the six genres.

Data Analysis

To test the proposed hypotheses, we performed statistical tests to examine the characteristics of danmaku comments and forum comments. For example, when comparing the level of user participation in sending danmaku and forum comments, we conducted the t-test if the test statistic followed a normal distribution, otherwise we employed the Wilcoxon-Mann-Whitney test. We applied the Pearson's product-moment correlation method to test the relationship between comment sentiment score and user post frequency, and ran the Chi-square test to examine the interaction between the type of knowledge sharing (i.e., explicit and tacit) and the type of comments (i.e., danmaku and forum).

We also conducted content analysis to gain a better understanding of users' commentary behavior including: what danmaku comments active users made; what language patterns emerged in danmaku comments; and how knowledge was shared in danmaku and forum comments.

Annotation of Knowledge Sharing

To understand the type of knowledge shared in danmaku comments and forum comments, we adopted the definitions of explicit and tacit knowledge [6] to annotate the comments.

For example, the fact-based comment "The BGM (background music) is Victory" and the terminology definition comment "Islam's stone punishment is burying a person's lower body into the soil and then killing the person by throwing stones" were annotated as explicit knowledge sharing. Comments that described users' own experiences, e.g., "The cell phone signal of China Telecom works well in the dorms of my university", and "The commentor [of the ice hockey game] is too subjective! He is not professional," were annotated as tacit knowledge sharing.

Initially, we randomly selected 500 danmaku comments and 500 forum comments, and asked two coders to independently annotate them into three categories: explicit knowledge, tacit knowledge or non-knowledge. For each comment, if both of the two coders annotated them into either explicit or tacit knowledge, we affirmed it was knowledge; otherwise it was non-knowledge. Then, we calculated two coders' agreement on explicit knowledge and tacit knowledge. The kappa value is 0.86 for danmaku knowledge and 0.87 for forum knowledge, both of which show substantial agreement (0.61 ∼ 0.80) [51]. Finally, a third coder resolved the disagreement with the first two coders together using the "majority rule" approach.

FINDINGS

In this section, we present our findings in order of answering the proposed hypotheses.

User Participation

There were 20,887 unique users involved in 38,399 danmaku comments and 10,148 unique users involved in 16,414 forum comments.

To test the first hypothesis, we applied statistical methods to compare the count of comments, the number of unique users, and users' post frequency in danmaku and forum comments for the 30 videos. We also applied qualitative analysis to present how active users used the two comment features.

Total Comments

First, we applied the Shapiro-Wilk's method to test the distribution of danmaku comment counts and forum comment counts for the 30 videos. Neither of the samples followed a normal distribution (the counts of danmaku comments: $N = 30$, $W = 0.68$, $p < 0.001$; the counts of forum comments: $N = 30$, $W = 0.59$, $p < 0.001$). Thus, we applied the Wilcoxon-Mann-Whitney test to compare the counts of danmaku and forum comments. The counts of danmaku comments ($N = 30$, $Mean = 1,280$, $SD = 1,200$) were significantly larger than the counts of forum comments ($N = 30$, $Mean = 547$, $SD = 797$, $V = 400$, $p < 0.01$). (**H1 supported**)

User Counts and Post Frequency

Similarly, we applied the Shapiro-Wilk's method to test the distribution of the numbers of unique users in danmaku comments ($N = 30$, $W = 0.82$, $p < 0.001$) and the numbers of unique users in forum comments ($N = 30$, $W = 0.77$, $p < 0.001$) for the 30 videos. Neither followed a normal distribution. Therefore, we applied the Wilcoxon-Mann-Whitney test to conduct the comparison. The result showed that the numbers of unique users involved in danmaku ($N = 30$, $Mean = 707$, $SD = 527$) were significantly larger than that in forum ($N = 30$, $Mean = 343$, $SD = 366$, $V = 392$, $p < 0.01$).

We also compared user's post frequency in danmaku and forum comments. Due to unequal sample sizes and unequal variances for the two kinds of comments, we conducted Games-Howell tests [25] for post-hoc pair-wise comparisons. The number of danmaku comments posted per user ($N = 20,887$, $Mean = 1.91$, $SD = 0.84$) was significantly larger than the number of forum comments posted per user ($N = 10,148$, $Mean = 1.45$, $SD = 0.42$, $t = 2.72$, $df = 44$, $p < 0.01$).

Unique Active Users in Danmaku

There were not only more comments but also more users active in danmaku than forum. To address why there were more active users in danmaku, we reviewed the top 20 active users in both danmaku and forum respectively to examine how they made comments. Interestingly, these active users in danmaku comments conducted one or two functions constantly in their comments.

We identified four major groups of active users that emerged as a result of the unique interaction design of danmaku, i.e., overlaying comments on video displays. They include video caption providers, plotters, community norm regulators and parasocial commentors.

First, caption providers, who unofficially translate foreign languages to Chinese using danmaku comments, formed the major active user group. In danmaku, they are called "Caption-Kun" (Kun is a respectful call in Japanese). Interestingly, we found that, sometimes, multiple users collaboratively created Chinese captions by posting the danmaku comments. For example, an active Caption-Kun wrote 51 comments in a Norwegian TV play, among which 48 comments were captions, but the user did not finish translating the whole video. After many other users called for "Caption-Kun" by sending danmaku comments, such as "Caption-Kun, please come", "Ah, I can't understand [the language]", etc. a second Caption-Kun showed up and finished creating the rest of the video captions. Both caption providers positioned their danmaku comments at the bottom of the screen, where official video captions were displayed typically. This has been a norm for video caption providers to follow.

Second, plotters are the users who watch the same video more than once and send hints of the forthcoming plots. For instance, a game video user posted 43 comments in two different days. In the second day's comments, he forecasted plots using danmaku comments, such as "High-energy reaction ahead!!!" (i.e., the following plot is very exciting), "High-energy reaction ahead, please wear a helmet!!!" (i.e., the following plot is very exciting and intense, please be prepared mentally), "Tut tut, see the end from here" (i.e., the end can be guessed through this plot). These plotters are different from spoilers. They don't disclose detailed plots in comments but provide hints, which make videos more interesting and attractive. It's also time-saving for the users who are seeking specific information in videos, e.g., scientific lectures.

Third, community norm regulators are those users who try to maintain the danmaku posting norms. For example, one active user, who posted 39 comments, was devoted to promoting polite language in danmaku communities. He posted: "↓ please report this user who posted danmaku in yellow" (the yellow danmaku user made a statement that discredited women). The down arrow was used to indicate who the user was. Another active user with 34 danmaku comments sent: "Everyone reported the meaningless danmaku at the bottom [of the video screen]" (danmaku comments at the bottom of the screen usually cover captions).

In addition to the above typical user groups, there was also another group of active users, who exhibited parasocial interactions. Parasocial interaction (PSI) is defined as "an imaginary social relationship, an imaginary friendship, an illusion of face-to-face relationship and an interpersonal interaction between the media user and the consumed media" [22]. For example, a user sent 40 danmaku comments in an online game competition video. These comments revealed that the user assumed the roles in the game himself/herself and made an imaginary conversation. For example, the user commented, "Childe: Beating you is a piece of cake", "Dio Ye: God knows what happened to me", and "Kris: Folks, please get your eyes checked with an ophthalmologist" (Childe, Dio Ye, and Kris are all roles in the game). However, such parasocial users rarely appeared.

Language Style
Sentiment Analysis
To conduct sentiment analysis, we used a tool called SnowNLP, which has been applied for sentiment analysis of microblog comments in Chinese [38]. Microblog comments, danmaku comments and forum comments are all oral and short text. Each comment is an input and will be rated a positive sentimental score from 0 to 1. The comment is more positive if its score is closer to 1, and more negative if closer to 0. As a result, danmaku comments ($Mean = 0.580$, $SD = 0.072$, $25^{th} percentile = 0.402$, $75^{th} percentile = 0.825$) were more negative than forum comments ($Mean = 0.615$, $SD = 0.115$, $25^{th} percentile = 0.329$, $75^{th} percentile = 0.956$). Due to unequal sample sizes and unequal variances of sentiment scores for the two kinds of comments, we conducted Games-Howell tests for post-hoc pair-wise comparisons. The results also showed that danmaku comments were significantly more negative than forum comments ($t = 11.90$, $df = 26$, $p < 0.001$). (**H2 supported**)

Active Users Posting Positive Comments in Danmaku
We further tested the correlation between sentiment score and user participation by applying the Pearson's product-moment correlation method. For each comment, the value of user participation was calculated by the number of comments each user sent. In danmaku, the sentiment variable had a positive correlation with the user participation variable ($t = 9.95$, $df = 38,397$, $p < 0.001$), which suggests that active users tend to send positive anonymous comments. However, in forum comments, there was no significant correlation between the sentiment score and the user participation ($t = 1.52$, $df = 16,412$, $p = 0.130$).

Terms and Language Patterns
The use of danmaku terms forms a unique danmaku culture [29]. Danmaku terms originate from various sources, e.g., several popular videos, slang terms online, and other languages or cultures (Japanese, Korean) [13]. These terms are used gradually by more and more users in danmaku comments. To investigate how danmaku terms were used in danmaku comments and forum comments, we searched danmaku slang terms on two popular encyclopedia websites, i.e., Baidu Baike [4] and Moegirlpedia [33]. Baidu Baike is a mainstream online encyclopedia which provides an encyclopedia term list, "Danmaku Terms", containing up to 123 danmaku terms. Moegirlpedia is another crowdsourced encyclopedia which creates up-to-date popular "Danmaku" terms.

We combined the danmaku terms from the two sources into a comprehensive collection of 1,134 slang terms in total. To pre-process the comment data, we applied a popular Chinese tokenizer, Jieba, which allows to upload a self-developed library. When analyzing the data, we took the slang term collection as the self-developed library that successfully avoided Jieba tokenizer from separating slang terms into separate tokens. Then we counted the frequency of terms used in danmaku comments and forum comments respectively.

There were 364 slang terms used in the 38,399 danmaku comments, and each term was used 26.88 times on average ($SD = 128.74$). Similarly, there were 337 slang terms used in the 16,414 forum comments, and each term occurred 18.02 times on average ($SD = 41.22$). Slang terms were used more frequently in danmaku comments than in forum comments.

Most danmaku terms were used to express emotions or opinions related to the video content. For example, users used many special characters which were easier to type, e.g., "233333" (laugh out loud), "hhhhhh" (onomatopoeic words to imitate laugh sounds), and "666666" (compliment to the roles), to express stronger emotions towards the video content compared with traditional comment language. It is found that danmaku users entertain each other to meet their psychological need and they aren't concerned with whether these emotions or opinions can create actual utility (e.g., persuading others) [19].

We also found that several terms were used to interact with other users. These danmaku terms tend to be brief and flexible. For example, to ask other users questions related to the videos, users typed "BGM" (background music) or "OP" (Opening Song); to invoke a call for action, they commented "If magic has colors" (a term to call for a large number of danmaku comments with different colors to cover the video screen) or "Subtitle group" (call for subtitle translation); to provide information, they commented "[There is] high-energy reaction ahead" (spoilers) or "Progress bar" (to indicate the remaining time); to show one's own opinions to other users or debate with others, they entered "1" (agree with previous comments). These danmaku terms were used by the users to construct a norm in the danmaku community.

We further compared the text length of danmaku comments and forum comments. Due to unequal sample sizes and unequal variances of comment length for the two kinds of comments, we then conducted Games-Howell tests for post-hoc pair-wise comparisons. The result showed that danmaku comments ($Mean = 9.33$, $SD = 39.1$) were significantly shorter than forum comments ($Mean = 45.23$, $SD = 4,920$, $t = 65.6$, $df = 17$, $p < 0.001$).

Knowledge Sharing

Explicit Knowledge and Tacit Knowledge
After annotating the comments, we identified 667 cases of knowledge sharing in danmaku comments, out of which 463 (69.42%) cases were explicit knowledge and 204 (30.58%) cases were tacit knowledge. In forum comments, we identified 734 cases of knowledge, where 212 (28.88%) cases were explicit knowledge and 522 (71.12%) cases were tacit knowledge. Table 2 presents the distribution of explicit and tacit knowledge for different video genres in danmaku comments and forum comments.

A Chi-square test of independence was calculated to compare ways of knowledge sharing in danmaku and forum comments. Danmaku and forum were significantly different in the way of sharing knowledge, i.e., explicit knowledge was shared more in danmaku comments and tacit knowledge was shared more

Genre	Danmaku Knowledge				Forum Knowledge			
	Explicit		Tacit		Explicit		Tacit	
Anime	18	55%	15	45%	57	80%	14	20%
Drama	190	84%	36	16%	91	27%	246	73%
Game	34	40%	50	60%	5	56%	4	44%
Lecture	62	63%	37	37%	30	14%	180	86%
Sports	97	73%	35	27%	20	51%	19	49%
TV show	62	67%	31	33%	9	13%	59	87%
Total	463	69%	204	31%	212	29%	522	71%

Table 2. The distribution of explicit and tacit knowledge in different video genres.

in forum comments ($X^2 = 228.33$, $df = 1$, $p < 0.001$). (**H3 not supported**)

Knowledge Sharing in Danmaku

There were various types of explicit knowledge and tacit knowledge shared in danmaku comments.

More specifically, we observed explicit knowledge sharing on a variety of topics, including: (1) Natural Science, e.g., "[This is a] high-dimension space", "Sleeping soft tissue fluid comes from the kidneys", "Electromagnetic waves could be transmitted in vacuum"; (2) Social Science, e.g., "The race does not determine the culture, but the culture determines the attributes of human beings", "England is a united kingdom, it indeed consists of four countries, not four districts", and "The nature of comedies is satire"; (3) Technology, e.g., "[The pictures] whose visual are round were taken by wide-angle lens", "This is not a dynamic wallpaper, it's called Live Photos", and "The signals of the three telecom operators might be different even at the same place, so the same place can't be the control condition of the test"; and (4) Other Information, e.g., "The lady in blue cheongsam is an actress in the movie Mr. Donkey", "The back ground music is River Flows in You", and "[The boxer] with blue gloves is from China" (one user asked which boxer was from China).

For tacit knowledge, we observed (1) Opinion, e.g., "It's been proved as a norm that commentary is a personal live broadcast but not a television program relay, so it will come along with subjective emotions", "In order to fully show the proper respect and manner to one's country, everyone from any country should take off their hats during national flag raising", and "Respect women but not support the materialistic feminism, women should be protected"; (2) Experience, e.g., "The dubbed laughter here serve as a purpose to enhance the voice effect on this program, this is certainly a talk show 누_누 (an emoji to express speechless)", "Personally, I prefer the home button on the Samsung phone", and "[This was] made by Keynote. Those pages were easy to make by Magic Move"; and (3) Community-based, which means specific knowledge (rules, norm) in danmaku context, e.g., "Please keep in mind that it is extremely disrespectful to mention other uploaders" (Uploader is who uploaded videos), and "Folks, please actively report the insulting comments".

Case Studies of Knowledge Sharing in Danmaku and Forum

To understand if danmaku and forum comments shared knowledge differently, we selected comments that shared knowledge regarding the same topics in both danmaku comments and forum comments of a video.

For example, in the video, entitled *"As a women, I feel really sorry for it"*, the topic of feminism was commented in both danmaku and forum. The video was made by clipping several famous feminist movies or dramas and triggered heated discussion among users.

In danmaku comments, the major topic was to define "feminism". Many users held the same view that "feminism meant equal rights between men and women, not femdom". Besides the discussion of "feminism", users also commented about this short video. Users shared the names of the movies or dramas, e.g., "[the movie shown] just now is Blind Mountain (a Chinese movie)", or the names of actresses, e.g., "This is Yuanyuan (a Chinese actress)". They also introduced the stone punishment which was used to punish women in Iran, e.g., "[This is] Iranian Stoning Penalty". Several users also recommended other related movies or dramas in comments, "Please add Malena (a famous Italian movie which is also about feminism)". Interestingly, users also shared where the video title *"I feel really sorry for it"* came from and came up three different answers. For example, one user thought that it came from a movie *"Memories of Matsuko"*. Though they did not have an agreement, other users received more perspectives by reading the danmaku. We also noticed that users addressed each other directly in several danmaku comments, i.e., "Greetings to the previous user [who made the last danmaku comment], the women in cheongsam is [the role] in the movie Mr. Donkey", to answer questions that was brought by a previous user.

However, in forum comments, we observed that the topics were extended from defining feminism to a variety of other topics. For example, users commented in the forum regarding marriage, DINK (Double Income No Kids), female in politics, female discrimination in workplace, and equality of men and women in China, etc. Users shared more arguments (e.g., their own experiences, or laws) to demonstrate their opinions, and the arguments were longer than those in danmaku.

As another example, an educational video, entitled *"China Eye Plans to Shock the World, Hawking Has Repeatedly Warned to Stop, Jealousy?"*, was about Chinese FAST (the biggest spherical radio telescope) program. In danmaku comments, users mainly discussed what FAST was used for, and its scientific, ethic and political issues in the exploration of outer space. In addition, users also shared their opinions about extra-terrestrial intelligence. It's worth mentioning that the users also shared a popular science fiction, "The Three Body Problem", and the "Dark Forest Law" in it – "Once be found [by each other], only one side can remain alive". In forum comments, we found that the users tended to explain further more about why China developed FAST program and Hawking's theory.

DISCUSSION

We developed and tested three hypotheses to compare danmaku and forum comments in terms of user participation (**H1**), sentiment of language used (**H2**), and knowledge sharing (**H3**). In this section, we reflect on our findings, and discuss design implications and limitations.

Unique User Groups and Interaction using Danmaku

Anonymity encourages users' early and continued participation [3] and the sense of security provided by anonymity can encourage students to share their thoughts more freely[50]. Therefore, it is not surprising that there were more anonymous danmaku comments than user-identified forum comments (**H1**).

However, we expanded the understanding of user participation by providing new empirical evidence and claims that more unique users engaged in danmaku and they were more actively posting danmaku comments. We further identified four groups of users, who made new types of interactions with online videos and their danmaku peers, as a result of the unique user interaction design of danmaku.

For example, the pseudo-synchronous interaction of danmaku allows caption providers to create video captions by posting danmaku comments. In fact, there has been a large online community, called Fansub (fan subtitling) [12, 27, 47] who volunteer to translate foreign TV shows and programs. These online users could contribute directly to co-create video content by using the danmaku features. Plotters' comments not only raise other video users' awareness of the upcoming video content, but also catalyze users' interest to continue watching and find out the answers. Users who have parasocial interactions by posting imaginary story comments also enrich the content of the video [35]. Comments of community norm regulators can alert users who violated the "rules". For example, we found that users tried to build the norms regarding where to position danmaku by posting danmaku comments, e.g., "Could you not post the danmaku at the bottom? it bothers me from reading the captions :)", or "The danmakus at the bottom are really annoying".

Active Users Posting Positive Comments in Danmaku

Even though danmaku comments were significantly more negative than forum comments overall (**H2**), our results also showed that active users sent more positive and anonymous danmaku comments than less active users. However, there was no such association discovered in forum comments. A survey study reported that in virtual communities, reputation and reciprocity have a positive impact on posters' participation [16], however, our findings can not be well explained by existing literature which typically claimed anonymity resulted in more negative comments [49, 36, 23].

We also observed that active users in danmaku tended to express their emotion. For example, to express emotion, active users sent numeric characters such as "2333" and alphabetical characters such as "hhhhhh" to express their happiness. They also seemed post the same comments repeatedly or type longer comments to express stronger emotion, e.g., "Ah ha ha ha ha ha ha ha ha ha", "Oh my god ha ha ha ha ha ha ha ha ha", and "Holy crap, laughing my fat ass off". We also found that the top one active user wrote 120 similar danmaku comments to express his love to certain movie characters or happiness when watching a drama video, e.g., "___yoyo____",

"_cp____", "_____". Interestingly, the top two and top three active users also used many comments with underlines in the same videos, e.g., "__William _____ ⊙", "ò__ ⊙" to mimic a smiling face. In fact, once a commenting style was created, other users tended to quickly learn the "languages". Given that the numeric character comments received neutral sentiment scores and the happy comments received positive sentiment scores, their frequent emotion sharing comments for fun [53] may help explain the language patterns we observed.

The above language patterns were very similar to that in online chat [2], where abbreviations, taboo words, short and simple sentences are frequently used. The unique features of danmaku comments are that users can also leverage colors and posting modes to support their expressions of different comments. For example, when they want to alert others, they post danmaku comments in bright colors. Video caption providers typically post their danmaku comments at the bottom of the screen.

Complementary Knowledge Sharing

We applied Brown's definitions of explicit knowledge and tacit knowledge to differentiate ways of knowledge sharing [6] in online video websites. The findings rejected our hypothesis regarding knowledge sharing on danmaku (**H3**).

Our finding–the traditional forum comments involved more tacit knowledge sharing–was aligned with the prior literature [15, 39]. However, interestingly, danmaku–as a new social commenting feature–promoted explicit knowledge sharing, instead of tacit knowledge sharing. These two comment features provide venues for knowledge sharing in a complementary manner on video websites.

Previous studies regarding the impact of asynchronous and synchronous online communication on knowledge sharing may be helpful to understand the finding. For example, Im and Lee demonstrated that synchronous communication could not develop into more serious learning stages beyond socialization, whereas asynchronous discussions were more topic-related and yielded more discussion about the posted topics [21, 18]. If we examine the data more closely, according to Table 2, more explicit knowledge sharing seemed occur in video genres such as drama and sports, and much less explicit knowledge were shared in games and anime videos. In future work, we plan to test if users shared knowledge differently when commenting on different video genres.

Design Implications

A recent online survey study of 213 Chinese online users suggested that danmaku could be leveraged to better facilitate user engagement and interaction in an online learning environment [53]. Our findings in terms of the improved user participation, positive sentiment of comments, and complementary knowledge sharing further showed danmaku's potential in online video learning.

First, caption providers can help address video accessibility issues [20] by posting captions using the danmaku feature. Student plotters may help other students better understand the structure of the video lectures by making forecasting comments.

Even though there may be negative comments in danmaku unavoidably, active users' positive comments will help improve users' watching experiences by making the videos more fun to watch, which is one of the major perceived benefits of danmaku [53, 28]. Danmaku terms can be provided and gradually created in a danmaku dictionary, which will facilitate their communication with other users more effectively.

The complementary knowledge sharing promoted by danmaku and forum suggests that we should keep the discussion forum feature of the current online video learning system when introducing the danmaku feature. On one hand, danmaku design can make online users feel socially and emotionally connected with others and users may be able to construct and confirm meaning quickly through sending short danmaku comments. On the other hand, online students can engage in deeper conversations and debates on discussion forums.

Limitations and Future Work
We collected danmaku and forum comments from the most popular danmaku video website, Bilibili.com. The findings need to be further evaluated using other danmaku websites. We only examined how danmaku and forum comments addressed explicit or tacit knowledge sharing. In the future, we will apply more comprehensive measurements to evaluate the informativeness of comments in danmaku and forum, e.g., measuring informativeness priority, classifying information intention, and clustering themes [9]. Due to the anonymous danmaku design and layout, users cannot reply to individual users, thus we were not able to construct conversations among the danmaku users. We plan to conduct qualitative studies to gain a better understanding of how users interact with each other through danmaku comments.

In this paper, we compared danmaku and forum comments, which were both asynchronously created, in a Chinese video website. Recently, social network websites (e.g., Facebook Live Video streaming) released danmaku-like features for video sharing. It is worth investigating if/how the genres of the videos on social media and the cultural background of the users impact the use of danmaku features. For example, in the U.S., social TV [7, 48] and YouTube live broadcast [43, 44] are popular. A recent preliminary study showed that compared to adjacent strollable (design of YouTube live broadcast), danmaku's synchronous overlay would make users recall more comments of interest [54]. Comparing knowledge sharing in danmaku and synchronous live comments may yield interesting findings as well.

CONCLUSION
Using both quantitative and qualitative methods, we compared 38,399 danmaku comments and 16,414 forum comments posted in 2017 on 30 popular videos on Bilibili.com. More users were involved in danmaku communication and they posted danmaku comments more frequently than forum comments. Certain active users made unique interactions with online videos or their peer users by posting danmaku

comments, e.g. caption providers created video captions voluntarily. Overall, danmaku contained more negative comments than forums; however, active users made more positive comments in danmaku instead of in forum comments. Slang terms and shorter comments were more found in danmaku comments. One of the most important findings is that danmaku and forum comments enabled knowledge sharing in a complementary manner. More specifically, more explicit knowledge was shared in danmaku comments and more tacit knowledge sharing was involved in forum comments. We discussed the great potential of danmaku in the context of online learning using videos.

ACKNOWLEDGEMENTS
The contents of this publication were developed under a grant from the National Institute on Disability, Independent Living, and Rehabilitation Research (NIDILRR grant number 90DP0061-01-00). NIDILRR is a Center within the Administration for Community Living (ACL), Department of Health and Human Services (HHS). We thank Zhiyuan Xu and Qiuyan Liu for collecting the sample data from Bilibili.com and facilitating data analysis. We also thank Xiaojuan Ma and anonymous GROUP reviewers for their thoughtful feedback on this paper.

REFERENCES
1. Syed Sibte Raza Abidi, Salah Hussini, Wimorat Sriraj, Somboon Thienthong, and Allen G Finley. 2009. Knowledge sharing for pediatric pain management via a Web 2.0 framework.. In *MIE*. 287–291.

2. Rami A Al-Sa'Di and Jihad M Hamdan. 2005. "Synchronous online chat" English: Computer-mediated communication. *World Englishes* 24, 4 (2005), 409–424.

3. Dorine C Andrews. 2002. Audience-specific online community design. *Commun. ACM* 45, 4 (2002), 64–68.

4. Baidu Baike. 2017. Danmaku Terms. http://baike.baidu.com/item/%E5%BC%B9%E5%B9%95%E6%9C%AF%E8%AF%AD/18061202?fr=aladdin. (2017). Accessed by 07/02/2017.

5. Bilibili. 2009. Bilibili Danmaku Video Website. (2009). http://www.bilibili.com/ Accessed by 07/02/2017.

6. John Seely Brown and Paul Duguid. 1998. Organizing knowledge. *California management review* 40, 3 (1998), 90–111.

7. Pablo Cesar and David Geerts. 2011. Past, present, and future of social TV: A categorization. In *Consumer Communications and Networking Conference (CCNC), 2011 IEEE*. IEEE, 347–351.

8. Yue Chen, Qin Gao, and Pei-Luen Patrick Rau. 2015. Understanding Gratifications of Watching Danmaku Videos–Videos with Overlaid Comments. In *International Conference on Cross-Cultural Design*. Springer, 153–163.

9. Seungwoo Choi and Aviv Segev. 2016. Finding informative comments for video viewing. In *Big Data (Big Data), 2016 IEEE International Conference on.* IEEE, 2457–2465.

10. Kimberly M Christopherson. 2007. The positive and negative implications of anonymity in Internet social interactions: "On the Internet, Nobody Knows You're a Dog". *Computers in Human Behavior* 23, 6 (2007), 3038–3056.

11. Ritesh Chugh. 2015. Do Australian Universities Encourage Tacit Knowledge Transfer?.. In *KMIS*. 128–135.

12. Tessa Dwyer. 2012. Fansub Dreaming on ViKi: "Don't Just Watch But Help When You Are Free". *The Translator* 18, 2 (2012), 217–243.

13. Yangchun Fu. 2014. The Studies of Bullet Curtain Language in Bilibili. (November 2014).

14. Russell Haines, Jill Hough, Lan Cao, and Douglas Haines. 2014. Anonymity in computer-mediated communication: More contrarian ideas with less influence. *Group Decision and Negotiation* (2014), 1–22.

15. Maxwell F Harper, Daniel Moy, and Joseph A Konstan. 2009. Facts or friends?: distinguishing informational and conversational questions in social Q&A sites. In *Proceedings of the SIGCHI Conference on Human Factors in Computing Systems.* ACM, 759–768.

16. Shwu-Min Horng. 2016. A study of active and passive user participation in virtual communities. *Journal of Electronic Commerce Research* 17, 4 (2016).

17. Craig D Howard, Andrew F Barrett, and Theodore W Frick. 2010. Anonymity to promote peer feedback: Pre-service teachers' comments in asynchronous computer-mediated communication. *Journal of Educational Computing Research* 43, 1 (2010), 89–112.

18. Stefan Hrastinski. 2008. The potential of synchronous communication to enhance participation in online discussions: A case study of two e-learning courses. *Information & Management* 45, 7 (2008), 499–506.

19. Huixian Huang and Jie Zhu. 2015. Danmaku Community's Meaning Construction and Psychological Needs to Danmaku Language. *Young Journalists* 9 (2015), 73–74.

20. Yun Huang, Yifeng Huang, Na Xue, and Jeffrey P Bigham. 2017. Leveraging Complementary Contributions of Different Workers for Efficient Crowdsourcing of Video Captions. In *Proceedings of the 2017 CHI Conference on Human Factors in Computing Systems (CHI '17).* ACM, New York, NY, USA, 4617–4626. DOI: http://dx.doi.org/10.1145/3025453.3026032

21. Yeonwook Im and Okhwa Lee. 2003. Pedagogical implications of online discussion for preservice teacher training. *Journal of research on technology in education* 36, 2 (2003), 155–170.

22. Seung-A Annie Jin and Namkee Park. 2009. Parasocial interaction with my avatar: Effects of interdependent self-construal and the mediating role of self-presence in an avatar-based console game, Wii. *CyberPsychology & Behavior* 12, 6 (2009), 723–727.

23. Peter G Kilner and Christopher M Hoadley. 2005. Anonymity options and professional participation in an online community of practice. In *Proceedings of the 2005 conference on Computer support for collaborative learning: learning 2005: the next 10 years!* International Society of the Learning Sciences, 272–280.

24. Alice Lam. 2000. Tacit knowledge, organizational learning and societal institutions: An integrated framework. *Organization studies* 21, 3 (2000), 487–513.

25. Alexander Leichtle. 2012. The Games-Howell Test in R. (2012). http://www.gcf.dkf.unibe.ch/BCB/files/BCB_10Jan12_Alexander.pdf Accessed by 10/01/2012.

26. Chen Li. 2015. Can danmaku interation be introduced into live telecast? *News World* 95-96 (2015), 80–80.

27. X Liu and G de Seta. 2014. Chinese fansub groups as communites of practice: an ethnography of online language learning. *Asien: the German journal on contemporary Asia* (2014).

28. Xiaojuan Ma and Nan Cao. 2017a. Video-based Evanescent, Anonymous, Asynchronous Social Interaction: Motivation and Adaption to Medium. In *Proceedings of the 2017 ACM Conference on Computer Supported Cooperative Work and Social Computing.* ACM, 770–782.

29. Xiaojuan Ma and Nan Cao. 2017b. Video-based Evanescent, Anonymous, Asynchronous Social Interaction: Motivation and Adaption to Medium. In *Proceedings of the 2017 ACM Conference on Computer Supported Cooperative Work and Social Computing (CSCW '17).* ACM, New York, NY, USA, 770–782. DOI: http://dx.doi.org/10.1145/2998181.2998256

30. Zhihao Ma and Jinping Ge. 2014. The Review of The Japanese Animation Barrage: A Perspective of Parasocial Interaction. *Journal of International Communication* 8 (2014), 116–130.

31. Mark Mabrito. 2006. A study of synchronous versus asynchronous collaboration in an online business writing class. *The American Journal of Distance Education* 20, 2 (2006), 93–107.

32. Amy Madden, Ian Ruthven, and David McMenemy. 2013. A classification scheme for content analyses of YouTube video comments. *Journal of documentation* 69, 5 (2013), 693–714.

33. Moegirlpedia. 2017. Danmaku Terminologies. (2017). https://zh.moegirl.org/%E5%BC%B9%E5%B9%95 Accessed by 07/02/2017.

34. Helen Nissenbaum. 1999. The meaning of anonymity in an information age. *The Information Society* 15, 2 (1999), 141–144.

35. Rachel O'Donovan. 2016. 'To boldly go where no psychologist has gone before" : effects of participation in fandom activities on parasocial relationships. *Journal of Applied Psychology and Social Science* 2, 1 (2016), 41–61.

36. Eli Omernick and Sara Owsley Sood. 2013. The impact of anonymity in online communities. In *Social Computing (SocialCom), 2013 International Conference on*. IEEE, 526–535.

37. David Osimo. 2008. Web 2.0 in government: Why and how. *Institute for Prospectice Technological Studies (IPTS), JRC, European Commission, EUR* 23358 (2008).

38. Xiaofu Ouyang. 2016. *Study on Xiamen Tourist Environment Image Based on Visitors' Microblog Data Analysis*. Ph.D. Dissertation. Xiamen University.

39. Sirous Panahi, Jason Watson, and Helen Partridge. 2012. Social media and tacit knowledge sharing: Developing a conceptual model. *World academy of science, engineering and technology* 64 (2012), 1095–1102.

40. Lionel P Robert and Alan R Dennis. 2005. Paradox of richness: A cognitive model of media choice. *IEEE transactions on professional communication* 48, 1 (2005), 10–21.

41. Hamano Satoshi. 2008. How information systems have been designed so far. In *Architecture of the Ecosystem*. BIGART. ISBN: 978-4-7571-0245-3.

42. Katharina Steininger, David Ruckel, Ewald Dannerer, and Friedrich Roithmayr. 2010. Healthcare knowledge transfer through a web 2.0 portal: an Austrian approach. *International Journal of Healthcare Technology and Management* 11, 1-2 (2010), 13–30.

43. Emily Sun, Rodrigo de Oliveira, and Joshua Lewandowski. 2017. Challenges on the Journey to Co-Watching YouTube. In *Proceedings of the 2017 ACM Conference on Computer Supported Cooperative Work and Social Computing*. ACM, 783–793.

44. John C Tang, Gina Venolia, and Kori M Inkpen. 2016. Meerkat and periscope: I stream, you stream, apps stream for live streams. In *Proceedings of the 2016 CHI Conference on Human Factors in Computing Systems*. ACM, 4770–4780.

45. Yan Tang, Yibing Gong, Li Xu, Qingheng Zhang, Huaxin Liu, Sheng Wang, Qian Wang, and Xiaofeng Gao. 2017. Is Danmaku an Effective Way for Promoting Event based Social Network?. In *Companion of the 2017 ACM Conference on Computer Supported Cooperative Work and Social Computing*. ACM, 319–322.

46. Mike Thelwall, Pardeep Sud, and Farida Vis. 2012. Commenting on YouTube videos: From Guatemalan rock to el big bang. *Journal of the American Society for Information Science and Technology* 63, 3 (2012), 616–629.

47. Yuan Tian. 2011. *Fansub cyber culture in China*. Georgetown University.

48. Peiyun Tu, Meiling Chen, Chilan Yang, and Haochuan Wang. 2016. Co-Viewing Room: Mobile TV Content Sharing in Social Chat. In *Proceedings of the 2016 CHI Conference Extended Abstracts on Human Factors in Computing Systems*. ACM, 1615–1621.

49. Cindy Boyles Tucey. 2010. Online vs. face-to-face deliberation on the global warming and stem cell issues. (2010).

50. Dorothy Van Soest, Robert Canon, and Darlene Grant. 2000. Using an interactive website to educate about cultural diversity and societal oppression. *Journal of Social Work Education* 36, 3 (2000), 463–479.

51. Anthony J Viera, Joanne M Garrett, and others. 2005. Understanding interobserver agreement: the kappa statistic. *Fam Med* 37, 5 (2005), 360–363.

52. Jerry Wellman. 2009. *Organizational learning: How companies and institutions manage and apply knowledge*. Springer.

53. Yaxing Yao, Jennifer Bort, and Yun Huang. 2017. Understanding Danmaku's Potential in Online Video Learning. In *Proceedings of the 2017 CHI Conference Extended Abstracts on Human Factors in Computing Systems*. ACM, 3034–3040.

54. Bingjie Yu and Leon Watts. 2017. Designing Commenting Mechanisms for Dynamic Media: Synchronous Overlay and Adjacent Scrollable. In *Proceedings of the 2016 ACM Conference Companion Publication on Designing Interactive Systems*. ACM, 18–22.

Open Data Standards for Open Source Software Risk Management Routines: An Examination of SPDX

Robin Gandhi ⓘ
University of Nebraska at Omaha
Omaha, NE, USA
rgandhi@unomaha.edu

Matt Germonprez ⓘ
University of Nebraska at Omaha
Omaha, NE, USA
mgermonprez@unomaha.edu

Georg J.P. Link ⓘ
University of Nebraska at Omaha
Omaha, NE, USA
glink@unomaha.edu

ABSTRACT

As the organizational use of open source software (OSS) increases, it requires the adjustment of organizational routines to manage new OSS risk. These routines may be influenced by community-developed open data standards to explicate, analyze, and report OSS risks. Open data standards are co-created in open communities for unifying the exchange of information. The SPDX® specification is such an open data standard to explicate and share OSS risk information. The development and subsequent adoption of SPDX raises the questions of how organizations make sense of SPDX when improving their own risk management routines, and of how a community benefits from the experiential knowledge that is contributed back by organizational adopters. To explore these questions, we conducted a single case, multi-component field study, connecting with members of organizations that employed SPDX. The results of this study contribute to understanding the development and adoption of open data standards within open source environments.

Author Keywords

Risk Management; Open Source Software; Standardization; Practice Theory; Routines; Case Study; Interviews

ACM Classification Keywords

D.2.3 [Software Engineering]: Coding Tools and Techniques—Standards

INTRODUCTION

Organizations are using open source software (OSS) at increasing rates. This includes use in internal development processes, upstream contributions to open source communities, and redistribution in delivered products and services. While the benefits for engaging with open source communities have been well documented [5,8,11,12], engagement with OSS exposes an organization to a number of legal, intellectual property, and security risks. To manage

these complex risk factors, organizations have developed routines that include tracking open source assets throughout an organization, creating cross-functional teams to vet OSS licenses, and partnering with open source foundations to support risk management routines. To assist with the complexities of OSS risk management during software exchange in a supply chain, the Software Package Data Exchange (SPDX®) specification was established by the Linux Foundation's SPDX workgroup. SPDX is a community of organizational members who have co-created and applied the SPDX specification from which OSS risk related routines can be enacted. We refer to these practicing and contributing organizational members in the SPDX workgroup as the "SPDX community."

The SPDX specification is quite simply a specification in the way that HTML or IEEE 802.11g are specifications. SPDX intends to support the supply chains that rely on OSS for seamless exchange of software. It is defined by the community, yet the specification does not detail the distributions and engagements of users that work with it locally. As such, engagement with any specification, including SPDX, takes different forms, depending on local organizational situations. An organization using SPDX prepares "SPDX documents" by examining OSS packages. An SPDX document captures metadata information about a software package and is structured according to the SPDX specification. SPDX documents include fields for the name of the software package, version number, license of the software package, URLs to locate vulnerability announcements, and the relationships of the package to other packages (i.e., is a copy_of or prerequisite_for). Figure 1 illustrates the relationship between the SPDX specification, an OSS package, and the resulting SPDX document. The routines of interest in this paper enact this relationship.

GROUP '18, January 7–10, 2018, Sanibel Island, FL, USA
© 2018 Copyright is held by the owner/author(s).
ACM ISBN 978-1-4503-5562-9/18/01.
https://doi.org/10.1145/3148330.3148333

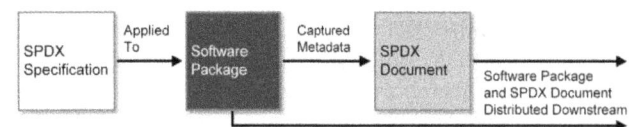

Figure 1. The SPDX specification is applied to a software package to capture its metadata in a standard form in the SPDX document (an instance of the data standard). The SPDX document and the software package are distributed together to downstream users.

In this paper, we explore interactions in the SPDX community through routines. Specifically:

Locally Structured Routines: In response to the growth of the SPDX community, this research explores how the SPDX specification - one particular artifact produced by the SPDX community - is used to guide improvements to OSS risk management routines in participating organizations. We consider how the SPDX specification serves as both a source of inertia and inflexibility and at the same time offers opportunities for flexibility and change to organizational members considering their own, local OSS risk management routines [7].

Communally Structured Routines: Organizations contribute to the SPDX specification by discussing their own routines and negotiating how these routines will be supported in the SPDX specification. For example, the first version of the SPDX specification was untested and based on assumptions about what OSS risk management routines might look like and how those routines should be captured in a shared specification. After each release, the implementation experience and feedback from organizational members helped improve and evolve the SPDX specification to suit real world OSS risk scenarios.

Routines, such as OSS risk management routines, are dualities [7]. They are, in part, their fixed, organized, and structured aspects. This could include the list of steps to accomplish a particular task, the driving directions between two points, or the instructions for baking a cake. Routines are also, in part, their patterns of behavior when interpreting and enacting the structured instructions. These negotiated aspects are reflected in the task workarounds, the driving shortcuts, and the deflated cake. Both parts inform each other. In this research, we present a single case, multi-component study to understand how OSS risk management routines are advanced through the combination of local interpretation and communal routines, leading to our research questions:

RQ1: How do organizations participating in the SPDX community describe their local interpretations of communally structured OSS risk management routines?

RQ2: How do these local interpretations influence the extent of their SPDX adoption?

RQ3: How do these member organizations seek to guide the advancement of the shared SPDX specification?

THE SPDX COMMUNITY
Since 2010, SPDX has become a community of diverse organizational members – software, systems and tool vendors, foundations, and systems integrators – who collaborate in developing the SPDX specification. The history of the SPDX community dates back to 2007, when the original founders raised the issue of software pedigree and authenticity associated with the exchange of OSS. The SPDX community is currently supported by the Linux Foundation, as one of its core workgroups aimed at advancing the use and distribution of OSS. Similar to other projects at the Linux Foundation, SPDX development work is shared among the organizations volunteering their expertise and who have the interest and capacity in using the specification in their own risk related OSS routines.

To manage different activities in the SPDX community, teams are organized to share responsibilities. The Technical Team develops the SPDX specification, documentation, templates, samples, and tools. The Legal Team manages the SPDX License List, a subset of the full SPDX specification that provides a standardized short identifier for OSS licenses. The Outreach Team coordinates public appearances and promotion of SPDX, including participation in events and maintaining the website. The activities of all teams are coordinated at the monthly SPDX General Meeting via a conference call. Within this structure, organizations participate in the SPDX community and contribute their individual experience and expertise where they best can.

EXCHANGING ORGANIZATIONAL ROUTINES
Routines are sets of actions executed repeatedly with reliable outcomes and routines have both fixed and negotiated aspects [7,22]. Fixed aspects are embodied in artifacts, workflows described in references, standardized forms, or other tools used for executing the routines. The fixed aspects of routines can be explicitly stored, shape expectations for behavior, and allow multiple people to carry out actions in coordinated, repetitive, and recognizable patterns [22]. However, routines are constantly adapted and negotiated to circumstances – slightly differently each time [22].

Organizations can exchange routines that were developed elsewhere and thus not have to invent their own routines [23]. In such exchanges, routines are often transferred in a codified form such as handbooks, software, and proprietary standards. The encoding is influenced by the originating organization and its specific context, culture, and understanding. Organizations must overcome the knowledge boundary resulting from differences in organizational contexts and backgrounds before integrating external routines [19,23]. Challenges also exist for implementing off-the-shelf routines (e.g., embedded in commodity software) from vendors where the organization needs to unpack the codified knowledge and integrate it with existing organizational knowledge [21]. Knowledge embedded in artifacts will likely be misunderstood [22,23] and employees will have difficulty applying the exchanged routine [19].

Creating Shared Routines through Shared Standards
An alternative to adopting external routines is to create shared routines that accommodate the organizational needs of all involved [21]. In the case of creating shared routines, accommodating the broad needs of all members is necessary and builds communal support and shared understanding of those routines [19]. Yet, even as routines are created in a shared setting, fixed and negotiated aspects remain present.

Industries create shared routines to achieve compatibility of practices or save costs in the exchange of products or data. For example, the act of sharing data between organizations requires a standardized format and shared understanding to ensure that a receiver can accurately interpret encoded data. Before an industry agrees on a standard way of expressing routines, a negotiation for standardization occurs in which participants engage in complex negotiations [1] over which aspects of technologies and practices are included in the jointly created standard. This negotiation extends beyond the participants involved in the standardization and includes downstream users who engage the published standard in their own meaningful ways, which can inform future versions of the standard [6].

Standards represent fixed aspects of routines that are considered uniform across adopting organizations but the differing local contexts and backgrounds may lead to unexpected implementations due to deviating interpretations [2]. Adoption of standards often depends on the cultural fit [2] and whether organizations can develop compliant local routines associated with the standard [18]. The adoption of standards is an internal process to organizations and unless audited and certified, business partners can often not judge whether local implementations are uniform [17].

Organizations can benefit from investing and engaging in standardization processes [15]. Benefits arise from coupling internal product development with shared standard development to ensure future conformance by adjusting product development or by influencing standards based on a product strategy. Further, participants of the standardization process can express organizational expectations for a standard and through the contact with other experts learn to apply the standard in more effective and productive ways [15]. Specifically, organizations engaged in the standardization process benefit from the expertise gained by employees in the negotiation with other organizations which helps to overcome knowledge boundaries [19,21].

Standards can be developed within open source communities [25] which provide platforms for new forms of shared innovation, particularly for technologies that can benefit all involved participants [11]. Standard development in open source communities enhances the process through early implementation, testing, and experience-based evaluation and refinement [25]. Issues associated with formal standards are mitigated in communally developed standards, including lack of clarity of the specification, licensing and patent issues, and deviating implementations [9].

When developing standards communally, organizational engagement varies [5]. One approach uses communal standards internally but does not interact with the community in their development. This approach is encouraged, since some users might later decide to contribute back, spread the word, or contribute in invisible ways, e.g. educate others on their use [3]. Another approach provides direct engagement with the community through bug submission, new feature requests, and descriptions of how the standard has been implemented locally. This often entails dedicating employees who participate in the community, to engage in operational and strategic discussions, and to even provide resources to the community such as hardware or funding [5].

To adopt standards, organizations might have to change their own practices, find a way to work around the limitations of a standard to support local routines, or seek guidance from the standards community directly. We focus our research to understand how members of an open data standard community play a role in the interpretations of communally defined routines, how these interpretations influence the adoption of routines, and finally, how organizations guide the advancement of the routines within a community – specifically in the context of SPDX.

RESEARCH DESIGN AND METHODS

This case study is part of a four-year, qualitative field study regarding organizational engagement with open source communities. Research team members actively engaged with the SPDX community and were contributing members to the development of the SPDX specification for over two years. Additionally, members from the research team presented and discussed their SPDX community development work at ten Linux Foundation conferences, and ran focus groups at three Fortune 500 companies on organizational engagement with open source communities. Finally, the research team hosts open source tooling related to the deployment and use of the SPDX specification. As such, we leveraged our longstanding direct engagement with the SPDX community members to construct an assurance case design approach [10] that we used to define our interview questions.

Assurance Case Design Approach

Stemming from our direct engagement, we identified recurring claims regarding engagement with the SPDX specification and community. The researcher-identified claims did not determine the answers to our research questions. Instead, the claims provided a logical starting point from which to construct our structured argumentation method based on Goal-structuring Notation (GSN) and derive our interview questions [16].

The explicit and logical argumentation structure of GSN combined with defeasible logic [14] produces an assurance case. In our application of an assurance case, a top-level claim regarding engagement with SPDX was created and further refined into sub-claims through a series of rebuttals that can introduce doubts in the top-level claim. The rebuttals were informed by our longstanding direct engagement with the SPDX community.

Through sub-claims, the rebuttals (i.e., doubts) are addressed and eventually substantiated or countered via evidence collected through empirical observations – interviews and a focus group in our case. As sub-claim doubts are eliminated, the assurance in the top-level claim increases [14]. Such induction promotes high assurance by surfacing and addressing critical issues rather than supporting the top-level claim merely by observing similar repetitions through enumerative induction.

The assurance case design approach is novel. Unlike hypothesis testing, our approach does not develop *a priori* hypotheses and does not evaluate their truth statement. Rather, the assurance case ensured rigor and internal validity in the development of the interview protocol with a top-level question that reflects the intended purpose of the SPDX community. The creation and existence of SPDX is predicated on the fact that it will improve OSS risk management in organizations. This is not a hypothesis that the researchers (us) came up with. The interview protocol was developed to further investigate if this is actually happening based on the SPDX community activities and organizational engagement in those activities.

Structuring the Assurance Case

From the assurance case approach, the how and why research questions were analyzed to derive a top-level claim per the assurance case notation. Our top-level claim captured OSS risk management routines in an organization:

> **Top Claim C0:** Use of the SPDX specification improves OSS risk management routines in an organization.

Sub-claims in the assurance case stem from the top-level claim and direct attention towards the specific characteristics of the research questions. As part of this process, we introduce rebuttals that challenge the top-level and sub-claims. Each rebuttal expresses a reason for doubting that claim. This argumentation continues until a sub-claim can be directly supported by concrete evidence. One branch of this logical argumentation produced these rebuttals and claims:

> **Top Claim C0:** Use of the SPDX specification improves OSS risk management routines in an organization.
>
> **Rebuttal R1:** Unless the SPDX specification is deemed complex for operational needs of local OSS risk management routines.
>
> **Sub-claim C1:** Stakeholders have necessary guidance to correctly interpret the SPDX specification for adopting it in their local OSS risk management routines.
>
> **Rebuttal R1.1:** Unless SPDX adoption into local routines is ad-hoc.
>
> **Sub-claim C1.1:** Stakeholders have access to vetted strategies for SPDX adoption into their local routines.
>
> **Evidence E1.1:** List of strategies to adopt SPDX in local routines.

To develop the interview protocol, each claim and sub-claim is explicitly linked to a question in the interview protocol. For the claims above, the associated interview questions are:

> **Claim C0 → Question Q0:** In the context of software exchange, could you describe your organization's OSS risk management routines?
>
> **Claim C1 → Question Q1:** How did your organization become familiar with or adopt SPDX?
>
> **Claim C1.1 → Question Q1.1:** Can you speak about SPDX adoption strategies in your organization and how those strategies have been informed (i.e., through the SPDX website, discussions in the SPDX community, upstream and downstream vendors, or elsewhere)?

Responses to the interview questions created evidence. All questions were general enough to invite answers that provided insights beyond the evidence we hoped to collect. Through the GSN argumentation structure, the evidence was explicitly linked to the claims that they support or reject. Interviewees, when asked an open-ended question whether they could think of a question we did not ask but should have asked, were satisfied with the breadth and depth of the interview – providing face validity on the interview protocol.

To offset concerns that the assurance case may not be representative of organizational OSS risk management, we performed a preliminary validation with representatives of the Linux Foundation and incorporated their feedback. The full argumentation structure is available online.[1]

Data Collection and Validation

We relied on semi-structured interviews to collect evidence for the assurance case. The interview protocol is available online.[2] All 15 interviewed organizations agreed to be named including, ARM Ltd., Black Duck Software Inc., Dimension Data North America Inc., GitHub Inc., Intel Corporation, Micro Focus International plc, NexB Inc., Palamida Inc., Qualcomm Technologies Inc., Red Hat Inc., Siemens AG, SUSE plc, Texas Instruments Incorporated, and Wind River Systems Inc. We recorded and transcribed a total of 14 interviews, resulting in approximately 10 hours of recording, and had two interviewees decline recording where we relied on copious notes. Immediately after the interviews, interviewers wrote personal debriefs to capture personal perceptions, observations, and thoughts from the interview.

Following the interviews, we created a practitioner-oriented slide deck[3] to present the collected data to SPDX community members. Two members from our research team attended the 2017 Linux Foundation Open Source Leadership Summit and presented the interview data as part of a one-hour focus group as a way to share and collect comments on the data broadly. We presented recurring sentiments gathered from the interview data, without expressing how we, as a research team, understood how the SPDX specification influences or is influenced by organizational risk management routines. A total of 15 SPDX members attended the focus group, some of whom were interviewed in the project earlier. The focus group did not dispute the recurring sentiment outlined in the

---

[1] https://github.com/SPDX-CaseStudy/files/raw/master/AssuranceCase.png

[2] https://github.com/SPDX-CaseStudy/files/raw/master/InterviewProtocol.docx

[3] https://github.com/SPDX-CaseStudy/files/raw/master/FocusGroup.pptx

presentation, generating discussion, not questions, about the data – providing face validity on the data itself.

Data Analysis

Data analysis was performed by all three members of the research team. The transcribed interviews were imported into NVivo software and recurring themes were coded in-vivo. These themes were the basis of the presentation given to the SPDX members to verify the validity of our data [20]. The presentation included the themes and supporting quotes from the interviews.

As the general analytic strategy for the study we chose to rely on theoretical propositions [26] as manifest in our assurance case. The assurance case builds a bridge between the dualities of routines for OSS risk management centered around SPDX. Through the assurance case, specific patterns of behavior in an organization in interpreting and using the fixed aspects prescribed by the SPDX specification are investigated. Each sub-claim and related interview question in the assurance case were designed to investigate the synergy and breakdowns in the patterns of behavior when enacting an OSS risk management routine.

For answering our research questions, we composed an effects matrix of direct quotes [20] to display answers to each interview question across our dataset and followed the pattern matching analytic technique [26]. Every company is represented by one row for each evidence in the assurance case with three columns: supporting evidence, additional information, and counter example. The matrix display allowed us to visually validate the prevalence of themes and sentiment towards our claims [20]. The content of the effects matrix directly provides evidence for the assurance case. The case study is presented in the linear-analytic structure [26].

FINDINGS

Stemming from our top-level claim – use of the SPDX specification impacts OSS risk management routines in an organization – we found that the communally developed SPDX specification has impacted the local OSS risk management routines. The organizations we interviewed are engaged in the development of the SPDX specification and are preparing their organizations to be SPDX compliant. Some started providing SPDX documents with their software to customers for learning and educating customers on SPDX. In an effort to further support this top-level claim, we next discuss the five top-level rebuttals that challenge the claim.

Top Claim C0: Use of the SPDX specification improves OSS risk management routines in an organization.

Rebuttal R1: Unless the SPDX specification is deemed complex for operational needs of local OSS risk management routines.

This rebuttal reflects the communal pressure on internal OSS risk management routines. The pressure comes from a large, complex and formal specification to be interpreted and

adopted. If the specification is too complex, the goal of achieving compatibility of practice and cost savings might be impeded because local interpretations are made difficult.

When asked about the SPDX specification, organizations referred to the complexity of the specification as a barrier to initial feasibility and adoption. The complexity is perceived in the large number and partially optional fields that the specification supports and the formatting of the SPDX doument which requires tooling to generate and use.

Excessive complexity is getting in the way of adoption.[4]

Despite the discussed complexity of the SPDX specification, organizations that worked with it found the specification straight forward in how it should be used and get support from the SPDX community to overcome knowledge barriers for implementing the external routine locally.

[The SPDX specification] is quite a document. It took me awhile to read. Actually, what you need to output is understandable when you get down to it.

Further, interviewees identified cases where the SPDX specification integrates with their OSS risk management routines. This includes, being able to produce and import SPDX documents.

Our business driver was to reduce the cost of distributing license information which we achieved by switching to SPDX documents only.

In many interviews, we found that a key strategy towards SPDX adoption was the use of the SPDX License List even prior to the ability to produce and import SPDX documents. As a subset of the full SPDX specification, the SPDX License List reduces OSS risk information complexity through short identifiers for open source licenses (e.g., BSD-3-Clause). The short identifiers allow developers to replace long license text in each source file with the SPDX short identifier to indicate the applicable license. Such use of the short identifiers improves the quality of automatically scanned license reports because ambiguity is eliminated. The License List is perceived as highly valuable in simplifying OSS risk management routines, for example in inter-personal communication where the shared understanding of the short identifiers improves clarity, eliminates unnecessary verbosity, and avoids uncertainty.

First of all, was adopting the standardized license names and identifiers. We had all [open source license names] in a non-standard way and we said, let's do a mapping of all the different ways to name a license. To standardize, let's switch the names to be the standard license names and surface those short hand identifiers because those are so much easier to communicate.

To summarize evidence for rebuttal R1 – unless the SPDX specification is deemed complex for operational needs of local OSS risk management routines – we found that the

---

[4] In most cases, only one representative quote is chosen in our analysis.

complexity of the specification was a significant barrier to adoption upfront. This finding should caution the SPDX community to discuss ways to address specification complexity and bloating. The SPDX specification is well-defined and community support helps with implementation, but does not provide well-defined gradations for organizations that perceive varying levels of OSS risk or are at different levels of maturity with respect to their OSS risk management routines. A full scope SPDX document is going to be onerous for organizations that do not have a large portfolio of OSS exchanges in supply chains or OSS use in mission critical applications. Specification complexity was easy to overcome for organizations that were engaged in the SPDX community or had started to use SPDX short identifiers in their organizational routines. Many of these early adopter organizations also had a clear business driver or opportunity associated with OSS risk management.

> **Top Claim C0:** Use of the SPDX specification improves OSS risk management routines in an organization.

> > **Rebuttal R2:** Unless the information recorded in an SPDX document does not support local OSS risk management routines.

This rebuttal reflects the pressure that local routines put on the SPDX specification. If the SPDX document supports local OSS risk management routines, then the shared creation of the standard succeeded. Conversely, an SPDX document that is useless to organizations can indicate that either the shared routines created through SPDX do not meet local needs or that the SPDX specification is an insufficient compromise between divergent local interpretations.

SPDX released version 2.1 early 2017. Many organizations we interviewed were still working with version 1.2 of the SPDX specification. In version 2.1, expression of relationships between package elements was a major addition. Version 2.1 also added the ability to record any known vulnerabilities in the described package. The organizations we interviewed were involved to various degrees in the development of the new versions of SPDX specification. As such, they had insight into the intentions of the new SPDX specification and how it could be applied in the organizational OSS risk management routines.

> *I would say right now we're kind of just using all of the basic required fields up to the 1.2 spec level. We're not yet using things like relationships or anything like that just because we haven't really grown into it. We see that kind of stuff being useful, especially for our customers in the future.*

Some organizations perceived the specification as being too rigorous or sophisticated while others saw value in most information recorded in SPDX documents. The match between the features of the specification and the needs for the local OSS risk management routines are important in the consideration for adopting the SPDX specification. The two representative quotes exemplify the divergent views:

> *I think it strikes me as being more rigorous than is necessary.*

> *I think most of the information which is required, or what the standard has defined, [is] really necessary.*

As such, the data captured in an SPDX document was not universally aligned with local OSS risk management routines. The relationships between SPDX documents and the level of tracking software artifacts varied. The following quotes show again the variety of uses that the SPDX specification supports and that the value some perceive from tracking licenses at the level of code snippets is not seen favorably by others who cannot justify the extra effort.

> *It would be rare for me to think of situations where I would go beyond the file level (one aspect of the specification). - I actually found from experience that if we try to describe package licensing at too detailed a level, we get information that is too complex to be useful.*

> *We found that file level is not enough, that there are often snippets that could have an effect on our file and on the entire package.*

Further, organizations pointed out that SPDX documents were not designed to be used for internal OSS risk management routines but that it is an exchange format that is only relevant when providing the information downstream. For internal OSS risk management routines, organizations are using their own data format or databases that aligns best with other operations or data management routines. The SPDX specification combines the many local practices through a process of combining innovations.

> *[In the SPDX group] we talked about the merits of different fields, how to characterize them, and how to serialize formats.*

However, organizations reported that the development and advancement of their internal data structures and routines are influenced by the SPDX specification. The naming of internal data fields was aligned with SPDX fields where appropriate. Ultimately, to produce SPDX documents, the data from internal data structures has to be mapped to SPDX fields. This is done through transformations where needed.

> *When I hear my guys having modeling discussions, I often say, "look at SPDX, if it's a coin flip what to call this field, let's go with the standard.'*

In response to rebuttal R2 – unless the information recorded in an SPDX document does not support local OSS risk management routines – we found that organizations use different subsets of the entire SPDX specification depending on what makes sense in their local routines. Although the use of SPDX documents may not fully be part of internal routines, the information required to create such a document is being recorded in internal artifacts. For organizations that advance their OSS risk management routines, the SPDX specification seems to provide standard information that an organization can record to be compatible.

> **Top Claim C0:** Use of the SPDX specification improves OSS risk management routines in an organization.

> > **Rebuttal R3:** Unless the organization does not require SPDX documents upon supply or intake.

This rebuttal reflects the level of adoption across the open source supply-chain ecosystem. Shared routines through standards are evident in the use of standard-compliant artifacts such as SPDX documents, that are transferred and understood between organizations. A lack of exchanging of SPDX documents could indicate that local interpretations of the standard are not aligned across organizations and that local routines are unaffected by the creation of the shared standard.

Organizations did not require SPDX from upstream suppliers. The consensus is that producing SPDX documents requires a tool, is too much work, and, consequently, cannot be expected from open source suppliers which may be mostly communities of volunteers.

[We don't require SPDX] from our suppliers, in that outside of open source we don't use a lot of third party content within our products. It's not really relevant from that perspective.

For many organizations, there was no advantage to being an early adopter. Organizations had reservations for asking SPDX documents from commercial suppliers as the SPDX specification is not yet well understood and the adoption of SPDX is limited.

We're not asking them to do it because I don't think we've fully figured it out ourselves and I'm not going to ask a vendor to [provide SPDX documents] until we've got it nailed down and really understand what it means.

For some organizations, a business driver for SPDX adoption is that they have to provide licensing information about their products to every customer and prior to SPDX there was no standard way to do so. SPDX documents allowed to reduce the work in supplying this information in a unique format for each customer. Customers were educated in the use of SPDX documents and the benefits of switching to the standard format.

The cost of distributing license information was our business driver for adopting SPDX.

Others have started experimenting with SPDX and shipping SPDX documents with a limited set of products. The purpose is to learn how SPDX can be integrated in their OSS risk management routines. These efforts uncover challenges with SPDX, including the ability to produce and consume SPDX documents.

Very recently, we've started providing an SPDX summary of those licenses alongside copies of the licenses with one product. I'm not sure we entirely know how we want this stuff formatted ourselves. There's experimentation going on to learn what we want before we start [with] other products. Because once you do that it's really hard to change later.

In response to rebuttal R3 – unless the organization does not require SPDX documents upon supply or intake – we found organizations experimenting with supplying SPDX documents but that challenges remain. SPDX adoption is not wide spread in software supply chains and when used, the patterns of behavior have yet to crystalize. The process of

organizational compliance with SPDX requires organizations to reconsider their OSS risk management routines and make changes within their OSS supply-chain.

Top Claim C0: Use of the SPDX specification improves OSS risk management routines in an organization.

Rebuttal R4: Unless SPDX does not integrate well in to organizational training programs.

This rebuttal reflects organizational commitment to the SPDX specification. The local interpretation is influenced using individuals and their understanding of how the standard impacts their routines. Through training, an organization ensures that the local interpretation is consistent across employees, reflects best practices, and is aligned with intended use cases. A lack of training can lead to divergent understandings, inconsistent and non-standard use or avoidance of the SPDX specification, which defeats the purpose of the standard.

We found that the SPDX specification is rarely integrated in developer training. One of the reasons is the limited use of the SPDX specification in software exchanges.

Until the day comes when we would attempt to adopt the SPDX specification, I don't see how it would enter into our developer training.

In many organizations, developers are not required to interact with SPDX documents, because specialized departments are responsible for reviewing license compliance and creating SPDX documents for software package exchanges.

[Developers] know about the fields that they have to fill in their request, about license and stuff like that. I'm not sure they are aware of SPDX.

When SPDX is integrated in developer training, the focus is on the aforementioned license short identifiers and the remaining SPDX specification is only mentioned. Participants often point out that the short identifiers simplify communication and developers are required to use them in their daily work.

I definitely mention SPDX as the standard. We don't go through its breakdown, of the fields and the structure.

In a few organizations, mainly tool vendors that implement SPDX as part of their service, we did find that the SPDX specification is an integral part of developers' training and daily routines. The training is informal and knowledge about SPDX is shared through everyday work routines.

Our training is relatively informal so it's mainly when we have weekly [meetings] and our audit of our internal and external work. It's part of just an ongoing discussion. We're members [of the SPDX community], we follow the standards, so it's not a particularly formal training. We use Slack for our business and there's an SPDX chat, and so we're constantly talking about things that are going on in SPDX.

In response to rebuttal R4 – unless SPDX does not integrate well in to organizational training programs – we found that the SPDX License List does find its use in training but broadly, developers are not trained on the SPDX specification. Many participants indicated that SPDX was only mentioned in developer trainings.

> **Top Claim C0:** Use of the SPDX specification improves OSS risk management routines in an organization.

> > **Rebuttal R5:** Unless engagement with SPDX community is difficult.

This rebuttal reflects the importance of engagement in a community of practice. Participation in the standards development process is perceived as beneficial for (1) influencing the standard to meet local needs, and (2) learning how to use the standard and reflecting on local interpretations with the community. The former reflects the process of shared innovation and the creation of shared routines through standards. The latter informs how organizations interpret and implement the standard.

Some interviewees were co-founders or long-standing members of the SPDX community and made significant contributions. For these members, the community is a place to meet like-mined people, to exchange best practices, and codify them in a specification.

I look at SPDX as, to a certain extent, our primary trade association. So, all of us in the business, little guys like us and the big ones like Black Duck were all there, we all know each other from there.

Other interviewees had a more "arm's length" perspective. They described themselves as community observers. They are interested in staying up to date with how the industry is shaping up and evaluate for themselves whether or not to use SPDX. Some reported that they have introduced features into the SPDX specification to better support their own OSS risk management routines.

I guess, my impact is that I feed stuff into the License List on occasion and give a bit of a review comment on the technical side, on the specification and things that I find ambiguous or

don't really know how to implement. It's nice to see some of those fitting into future specifications.

Additionally, some reported that the development of the SPDX specification is going in the wrong direction or that it was becoming too complex. Some stay silent about their concerns because others appear to derive value from certain feature, while others voice their concerns explicitly.

The other thing is that SPDX, and I made this point also in the general SPDX meeting, at least in my opinion - it's evolving in the wrong direction.

Finally, engagement with the community has changed perspectives in some cases on OSS risk management and helped improve local risk management routines.

I've actually adjusted my thinking about what we need to provide. So, we weren't collecting copyright statements before. Seeing that in the SPDX specification has sort of encouraged me to start collecting those. It's helping to push us to a better situation.

In response to rebuttal R5 – unless engagement with SPDX community is difficult – we found that the organizations who are participating derive value from the conversations and are able to help shape the SPDX specification to support their local OSS risk management routines. The organizations that do not participate in the creation of shared routines but engage as observers stay up to date on the development, arrive at their own interpretation of the specification, and consequently determine how to implement SPDX to support their local routines. Some organizations are comfortable with only proxy representation through consultants engaged in the SPDX community. Their local OSS risk routines are not burdened by limitations or the complexity of SPDX as the translations to local routines is skillfully taken care of by consultants. This strategy may also alleviate some of the concerns mentioned in previous rebuttals. See Table 1 for summary of all rebuttals and what we found.

Rebuttal	Elimination Summary
Rebuttal R1: Unless the SPDX specification is deemed complex for operational needs of local OSS risk management routines.	**Rebuttal R1** is not eliminated for organizations just starting with SPDX. Organizations engaged in the SPDX community for a long time easily address the rebuttal.
Rebuttal R2: Unless the information recorded in an SPDX document does not support local OSS risk management routines.	**Rebuttal R2** is eliminated in most organizations by mapping parts of SPDX to local OSS risk management routines.
Rebuttal R3: Unless the organization does not require SPDX documents upon supply or intake.	**Rebuttal R3** is not eliminated in most organizations as SPDX adoption in OSS supply chains is not widespread. Few organization are starting to use and ship SPDX to customers.
Rebuttal R4: Unless SPDX does not integrate well in to organizational training programs.	**Rebuttal R4** is partially eliminated by the inclusion of License List in developer training and best practices. However, there is only mention of SPDX in formal training.
Rebuttal R5: Unless engagement with SPDX community is difficult.	**Rebuttal R5** is eliminated in organizations that directly participate, observe, or engage through proxy representation in the SPDX community. SPDX community is perceived as open and inviting.

Table 1. Rebuttals and summary of findings.

DISCUSSION

In this research project, we explored questions of (1) how organizations participating in the SPDX community described their local interpretations of communally structured OSS risk management routines, (2) how these

local interpretations influenced the extent of their SPDX adoption, and (3) how these member organizations sought to guide the advancement of the shared SPDX specification. Sensibly, organizations described their local interpretation of the SPDX specification differently. The local interpretation sparked a number of responses, including the full standard used for exchanging licensing information, the standard becoming a guiding influence in the advancement of local OSS risk management routines, and the standard being questioned as too complex for local needs. The most common engagement came from the SPDX License List short identifiers which simplify internal routines and the exchange of information. Even when the SPDX specification was not fully used, it influenced many organizations' thinking, data collection, and governance.

The duality of routines – as both influencing and being influenced by community engagement – was apparent in the ways that SPDX members shared and deployed the specification. The business driver appeared to be a deciding factor for the extent to which an organization engaged with the SPDX specification and aligned its routines. While extant literature treated external routines that are taken into the local context as codified knowledge that is easily misunderstood and difficult to deploy [19,21,22], we found contrary information in open communities. Organizations involved with the SPDX community shared their experiences and interpretations with other community members and negotiated changes to the shared routines by suggesting changes to the SPDX specification itself. Misunderstandings were resolved in the negotiation process. The divergent implementations resulting from different contexts and backgrounds in each organization became a source of innovation that was shared with the community and reflected in updated releases of the specification [6,7]. The challenge that the SPDX specification may now face is to balance which innovations to include [12], while containing the complexity that could impede use by new and existing adopters.

In the case of SPDX, leveraging open source communities for standards development: (1) advances the specification to better align with local routines and (2) improves local routines based on the codified specification. Within this duality, communal negotiation over features exemplified that the specification was a source of flexibility by accommodating the different forms of risk related work by members, while at the same time serving as a source of inflexibility by requiring those engaged with the specification to be attentive to communally agreed upon features.

Co-creating Risk Related Best Practices

Observations related to OSS risk and SPDX share parallels with other risk related data exchange standards. We found that organizations attempted to address OSS risks close to delivery. This is also observed with security risk. While it is better to consider security early in the software development lifecycle, it is often done much later and closer to software delivery [13]. Similarly, with OSS risk management, rather than integrating and spreading the responsibility throughout the product lifecycle, it tends to be addressed primarily towards the end – using automated license scanning mechanisms. These automated mechanisms often fall short. An organization that we interviewed had much success by federating the OSS risk responsibility to every developer and every process in product development. Thus, eliminating the need for heavy weight processes closer to software release.

In response, it may be advisable to build a more granular data standard adoption scheme with built-in gradation for different levels of OSS risk management maturity. Most successful security risk frameworks, starting with orange book,[5] have gradation built into them to accommodate different perceived design basis threats. With SPDX, a majority of the fields are optional to allow for gradation in maturity. However, this is not explicitly reflected in the specification. There has been community discussion around a SPDX lite version that reflects this sort of need.[6]

Design in a Responsive and Brokered Engagement

In complex software ecosystems that include both proprietary and OSS, the design of software is responsive to a highly dynamic landscape [12]. Software design is not a solitary experience, accomplished within a single organization. Instead, software design is a shared experience where participants are responsive to the environmental conditions that define choices. Similar to the way a flooded road defines a travel route, risk-related elements (e.g., licenses and vulnerabilities) define software design decisions, along with other elements including intellectual property management, corporate strategy, and community health. The creation of the SPDX specification is an improvement of the road markers that better declare potential risks inherent in OSS.

Interestingly, SPDX not only helps stabilize the complexities inherent in software design by allowing open source participants to respond more appropriately to software risks. SPDX itself entails responsive design as members engage in the duality of routines, informing and being informed by others in the community. The design of the SPDX specification entails a suite of communal responses to the wants and needs of members in mitigating risk-related concerns in OSS design.

To manage the complexity of the many voices and the commercial needs in the design of open source artifacts, neutral brokers such as the Linux Foundation now play important roles [24]. OSS design now readily exists in professional contexts [8], resulting in needs for community governance, codes of conduct, and marketing support. In these brokered engagements, design becomes considerably more structured and considerably less egalitarian [4].

SPDX is one community as part of an intentional collection of such communities. Within the Linux Foundation, other brokered communities include those that manage core

---

[5] http://csrc.nist.gov/publications/history/dod85.pdf

[6] https://wiki.spdx.org/view/Legal_Team/Minutes/2012-07-25

infrastructure (e.g., Network Time Protocol), provide open source training (e.g., OpenStack Fundamentals), and maintain commercially critical operating systems (e.g., the Linux kernel). Together, one community not only serves its own needs but can support aspects of partner communities (e.g., SPDX providing license declarations for the Linux kernel). As such, design in brokered engagements can include the intrinsic needs of any single community and extrinsic needs of a brokering foundation.

CONCLUSION

This paper makes four contributions. First, this paper contributes to research on routines by uncovering the complexity involved in the development of communal risk related open data standards. We demonstrated how a communal standard codifies aspects of OSS risk management routines deemed as best practices and how organizations engage with the standard to improve their local routines. Organizations engage in the standard development to test their local routines and compare them with other implementations to learn about better ways to accomplish the same goals. Engagement in the SPDX community was essential to ensure that the standard would satisfy organizational needs, inform local interpretations, and codify those interpretations for others to share. The embodiment of the shared routine in the SPDX specification served as a starting point for organizations to adopt the shared routine and engage in negotiation with others about how to interpret and implement the standard.

Second, this paper contributes to open source research by reporting how the SPDX project is changing the open source ecosystem by developing shared routines and encoding their fixed elements in the SPDX specification. The open source ecosystem is often viewed as a collection of communities that build on each other's code but are otherwise independent. Routines often spread through the use of shared tools, such as git, that become shared fixed elements in local routines, or through boundary spanning community members. We found that the SPDX members, through their engagement with the SPDX community, co-create routines that span organizations and open source communities but are not bound to the use of specific tools and rather define the fixed elements collectively.

Third, this paper contributes to standard setting literature by demonstrating how shared practices shape standards. Often, standards precede implementation and serve as fixed aspects of lived routines. We reported a case where the standard responded to the local interpretations, thus introducing a new perspective on the role of standards in routines. The definitions in the SPDX specification provide fixed aspects of local routines but through the community engagement the interpretation was negotiated and adjusted to meet changing local needs. The standard is fully developed in an open source community, not by the rules of a formal standard setting organization.

Fourth, this paper makes a methodological contribution by demonstrating the use of the assurance case driven case study design as proposed by Gandhi and Lee [10]. The assurance case guided the development of the interview questions and provided confidence that we addressed all challenges to the claims. Further, the assurance case facilitated the discussion of the research team, uncovered differing understandings, and ensured that detailed aspects were explored together. The assurance case served as an artifact in our own research routines – as a source of structure and knowledge.

Several questions and avenues for future research remain. Future research can investigate the details by which communally created routines and their embodiment in standards are locally interpreted and implemented. Future research can also investigate how the community driven standard development process compares to the process of standard setting organizations and consequently how these differences affect the local interpretation and adoption. Finally, this study was bound by a focus on SPDX community members, however, we know that SPDX is being adopted and used by organizations that do not participate with the SPDX community. We believe that including such organizations can reveal new lines of inquiry as the specification is deployed across the vast landscape of OSS engagement.

ETHICS

The study was reviewed and approved by our Institutional Review Board.

ACKNOWLEDGEMENT

Authors contributed equally and are listed in alphabetical order.

This project received funding through the National Science Foundation's Virtual Organizations as Sociotechnical Systems and the Innovation and Organizational Sciences Programs [VOSS-IOS: 1122642].

ORCID

Robin Gandhi ⓘ orcid.org/0000-0002-2632-1692
Matt Germonprez ⓘ orcid.org/0000-0003-2326-5901
Georg J.P. Link ⓘ orcid.org/0000-0001-6769-7867

REFERENCES

1. James Backhouse, Carol W. Hsu, and Leiser Silva. 2006. Circuits of power in creating de jure standards: Shaping an international information systems security standard. *MIS Quarterly* 30: 413–438.

2. Anna Canato, Davide Ravasi, and Nelson Phillips. 2013. Coerced practice implementation in cases of low cultural fit: Cultural change and practice adaptation during the implementation of Six Sigma at 3M. *Academy of Management Journal* 56, 6: 1724–1753. https://doi.org/10.5465/amj.2011.0093

3. Jocelyn Cranefield, Pak Yoong, and Sid Huff. 2015. Rethinking lurking: Invisible leading and following in

a knowledge transfer ecosystem. *Journal of the Association for Information Systems* 16, 4: 213–247.

4. Kevin Crowston, Qing Li, Kangning Wei, U. Yeliz Eseryel, and James Howison. 2007. Self-organization of teams for free/libre open source software development. *Information and Software Technology* 49, 6: 564–575. https://doi.org/10.1016/j.infsof.2007.02.004

5. Linus Dahlander and Mats G. Magnusson. 2005. Relationships between open source software companies and communities: Observations from Nordic firms. *Research Policy* 34, 4: 481–493. https://doi.org/10.1016/j.respol.2005.02.003

6. Ben Eaton, Silvia Elaluf-Calderwood, Carsten Sørensen, and Youngjin Yoo. 2015. Distributed tuning of boundary resources: The case of Apple's iOS service system. *MIS Quarterly* 39, 1: 217–A12.

7. Martha S. Feldman and Brian T. Pentland. 2003. Reconceptualizing organizational routines as a source of flexibility and change. *Administrative Science Quarterly* 48, 1: 94–118. https://doi.org/10.2307/3556620

8. Joseph Feller, Patrick Finnegan, Brian Fitzgerald, and Jeremy Hayes. 2008. From peer production to productization: A study of socially enabled business exchanges in open source service networks. *Information Systems Research* 19, 4: 475–493. https://doi.org/10.1287/isre.1080.0207

9. J. Gamalielsson and B. Lundell. 2013. Experiences from implementing PDF in open source: Challenges and opportunities for standardisation processes. In *2013 8th International Conference on Standardization and Innovation in Information Technology (SIIT)*, 1–11. https://doi.org/10.1109/SIIT.2013.6774572

10. Robin A. Gandhi and Seok-Won Lee. 2009. Assurance case driven case study design for requirements engineering research. In *Requirements Engineering: Foundation for Software Quality*. Springer Science + Business Media, 190–196. https://doi.org/10.1007/978-3-642-02050-6_16

11. Matt Germonprez, J. P. Allen, Brian Warner, Jamie Hill, and Glenn McClements. 2013. Open source communities of competitors. *ACM Interactions* 20, 6: 54–59. https://doi.org/10.1145/2527191

12. Matt Germonprez, Julie E. Kendall, Kenneth E. Kendall, Lars Mathiassen, Brett Young, and Brian Warner. 2016. A theory of responsive design: A field study of corporate engagement with open source communities. *Information Systems Research* 28, 1: 64–83. https://doi.org/10.1287/isre.2016.0662

13. Karen Mercedes Goertzel. 2013. A twenty-five year perspective. *CrossTalk - The Journal of Defense Software Engineering* 26, 4: 8–15.

14. John B. Goodenough, Charles B. Weinstock, and Ari Z. Klein. 2013. Eliminative induction: A basis for arguing system confidence. In *Proceedings of the 2013 35th International Conference on Software Engineering (ICSE)*, 1161–1164.

15. John Hurd and Jim Isaak. 2005. It standardization: The billion dollar strategy. *International Journal of IT Standards & Standardization Research* 3, 1: 68–74.

16. Tim Kelly and Rob Weaver. 2004. The goal structuring notation – A safety argument notation. In *Proceedings of the Dependable Systems and Networks 2004 Workshop on Assurance Cases*.

17. Andrew A. King, Michael J. Lenox, and Ann Terlaak. 2005. The strategic use of decentralized institutions: Exploring certification with the ISO 14001 management standard. *Academy of Management Journal* 48, 6: 1091–1106. https://doi.org/10.5465/AMJ.2005.19573111

18. Tatiana Kostova and Kendall Roth. 2002. Adoption of an organizational practice by subsidiaries of multinational corporations: Institutional and relational effects. *Academy of Management Journal* 45, 1: 215–233. https://doi.org/10.2307/3069293

19. Julia Kotlarsky, Harry Scarbrough, and Ilan Oshri. 2014. Coordinating expertise across knowledge boundaries in offshore-outsourcing projects: The role of codification. *MIS Quarterly* 38, 2: 607–A5.

20. Matthew B. Miles and A. M. Huberman. 1994. *Qualitative data analysis: An expanded sourcebook.* Sage Publications, Thousand Oaks.

21. Jeppe Agger Nielsen, Lars Mathiassen, and Sue Newell. 2014. Theorization and translation in information technology institutionalization: Evidence from Danish home care. *MIS Quarterly* 38, 1: 165–A7.

22. Brian T. Pentland and Martha S. Feldman. 2008. Designing routines: On the folly of designing artifacts, while hoping for patterns of action. *Information and Organization* 18, 4: 235–250. https://doi.org/10.1016/j.infoandorg.2008.08.001

23. Etienne Wenger. 1998. Communities of practice: Learning, meaning, and identity. Cambridge University Press.

24. Joel West and Siobhán O'mahony. 2008. The role of participation architecture in growing sponsored open source communities. *Industry and Innovation* 15, 2: 145–168. https://doi.org/10.1080/13662710801970142

25. S. A. Wright and D. Druta. 2014. Open source and standards: The role of open source in the dialogue between research and standardization. In *2014 IEEE Globecom Workshops (GC Wkshps)*, 650–655. https://doi.org/10.1109/GLOCOMW.2014.7063506

26. Robert K. Yin. 2008. *Case study research: Design and methods.* SAGE Publications, Inc, Los Angeles, Calif.

Crisis Informatics for Everyday Analysts: A Design Fiction Approach to Social Media Best Practices

Dharma Dailey
University of Washington
Seattle, USA
ddailey@uw.edu

Robert Soden
University of Colorado Boulder
Boulder, USA
robert.soden@colorado.edu

Nicolas LaLone
Bellevue University
Bellevue, USA
nlalone@bellevue.edu

Abstract

The importance of social media usage during crisis has been well established in academic and practitioner communities. Yet, the promise of rendering insights from social media for responders in a consistent and reliable manner remains a challenge and accepted standards of practice have yet to emerge. Inspired by a May 2017 workshop consisting of 15 Crisis Informatics practitioners from 3 continents, we imagine a training curriculum aimed at developing the necessary skills to harness social media data during a crisis. We call the recipients of that training Crisis Informatics Research Technicians (CIRT). We offer this design fiction to stimulate a conversation among Crisis Informatics scholars, Human-Computer Interaction scholars, crisis response professionals, and the public on best practices, tools, limitations, and ethics of using social media to improve crisis response.

Author Keywords

Crisis Informatics; Social Computing; Design Fiction; Social Media.

ACM Classification Keywords

K.4.1 Public Policy Issues; K.4.3. Organizational Impacts.

INTRODUCTION

Because such a large swath of the public uses social media, there are now many kinds of workers responsible for monitoring, analyzing, and rendering insights from SM data pertaining to crises. Initial use of social media (SM) during crisis was informal and emergent [8, 17, 32, 37]. Over time, information work enabled by SM has become its own form of crisis response. For example, digital humanitarians collaborate via SM to amplify important information and curb misinformation [6, 29]. Crisis mappers use collaborative ICT tools and SM to curate damage assessments after major disruptions [15, 26, 33, 45]. Similarly, all types of government entities increasingly task staff to monitor SM for risks to public safety.

Despite growing acceptance of its importance, rendering insights from SM that can consistently and predictably guide crisis response activity remains challenging. SM use by the public continues to evolve. The platforms themselves constantly change. Techniques and tools of collecting, curating, and understanding SM data are also evolving. Even as the research community and the public are becoming more attuned to the challenges of deriving insights from SM numerous commercial, academic, and community-driven tools aimed at supporting SM analysis in crises have been introduced [33, 45, 52]. Concerns over demographic biases, platform biases, and biases in the analytic tools rise as when SM data is mined for a crisis insights [2].

There are currently no standards for what good data analysis looks like from SM [27]. There are also few attempts to integrate SM data with other kinds of knowledge during a crisis response in real time [24]. To summarize, understanding SM trends is now an essential

part of crisis response, but best practices for doing this work are very much a work in progress.

One group steeped in the opportunities and challenges of using SM to understand crises are Crisis Informatics researchers. Coined in 2006, Crisis Informatics (CI) refers to a branch of human-computer interaction research that is strongly informed by crisis and disaster sociology. Like those fields, much of CI research is driven by fieldwork with researchers frequently working directly with volunteer, non-profit or government response organizations. Though CI is by no means strictly about SM, early on CI researchers recognized that SM was both an important new realm of crisis information work as well as a new type of data to inform crisis response itself [13, 36, 49]. Therefore, many CI researchers have developed significant expertise in collecting and analyzing SM crisis data.

In May of 2017, 15 Crisis Informatics researchers and analysts from 3 continents and 9 institutions gathered at the University of Colorado to discuss Grand Challenges in Crisis Informatics. The workshop provided space for collective reflection on what the CI field has accomplished in its first decade, where it stands, and where it is headed. The themes that emerged from the workshop were a direct inspiration for the design fiction we present here. This design fiction is meant to open and extend elements of the conversation we started at the workshop. Specifically, we invite others to imagine:

1) What productive, ethical, and scientifically grounded analysis of SM crisis data looks like.
2) How to highlight and promote essential knowledge, best tools, and best practices to everyday analysts.

In this design fiction, we offer a certification-training curriculum that results in a new Crisis Informatics Response Technician (CIRT). We draw on emergency response trainings offered to the public in the United States and abroad to imagine a five-day introductory training that presents skills and knowledge we deem necessary to perform the role of CIRT. By constraining the time given to the training, we hope to elicit perspectives on essential skills and knowledge required to render insights from SM data pertaining to crises. In the next section, we present much of the text of a brochure advertising the training to potential CIRT trainees.

Becoming a CIRT: A Certification Overview

What is a CIRT?

A Crisis Informatics Response Technician (CIRT) leverages social media to support crisis response in real time. Since its creation in 2019, CIRT training has provided thousands of citizens with new skills and procedures to meet the promise of internet communication technologies, social computing, and social media in crisis response.

Because social media analysis can be done from anywhere with an internet connection, a CIRT can provide off-site or on-site support to:

- Distributed teams of digital humanitarians;
- Volunteer organizations that support formal response such as Virtual Operation Support Teams (VOSTs);
- Within emergency management agencies;
- In companies or non-profits that either need or can supply analysis of social media crisis data.

CIRTs are trained in many different types of internet-based communication tools. Training introduces best practices from scientific and practitioner communities for leveraging social computing for emergency applications. This includes tools, techniques, limitations, and ethical considerations.

To be effective, a CIRT should also be aware of general human behavior in crises; the many uses (and non-uses) of social media during crises; and incident management systems as they pertain to different types of crises that CIRTs may be called upon to support.

CIRTs work in many different capacities. Some examples of their tasks include:

- Analyzing social media during crises;
- Developing tools, or techniques for leveraging social media during crises;
- Shaping institutional policies and practices on leveraging social media post-response.

Who Certifies CIRTs?

The CIRT training program is a nationally recognized course within the Federal Emergency Management Agency (FEMA). The CIRT training program is also an essential course of the United Nations Development Programme (UNDP) focus on Crisis Response.

How Do I Become Certified?

All training materials are freely available online. However, qualifying CIRT Training is offered through many partner agencies and fees may apply. This training is a 5-day process that covers 1 Unit, organized by thematic area, each day. Intense, 1-day CIRT boot camps can also be attended for rapid certification when an active crisis response requires additional support.

Each Unit except the first is evaluated through a simulated crisis response exercise where CIRTs in training are required to apply the key lessons of the Unit in real life scenarios.

What Will I Study?

Reflecting the many kinds of knowledge required to leverage social media data in large-scale crises, CIRT training integrates the knowledge of five core areas, organized as individual Units. Certification is awarded after successfully completing training in each Unit.

Curriculum

Unit 1: Human Behavior and Types of Crises

To gain insights from social media during crises, it is helpful to first survey the social scientific research on crisis and disaster. This unit introduces the human response to crises in three ways 1) how people behave in crises, 2) typology of different kinds of crises, and 3) the crisis management cycle.

Well-attested findings into human behavior during crises are introduced from individual, organizational, and cultural perspectives. It is international in focus, reflecting the global nature of the CIRT training program. As a CIRT, you may not always be asked to engage data from your country of origin.

A typology of crises is also introduced. This background is essential for interpreting the information needs and information flows during a crisis. Different types of crises produce different kinds of information and necessitate different forms of response and recovery. For example, a bombing and the pursuit of a bombing suspect will require a different set of skills than identifying potential geographic areas that need assistance after a flooding event.

Successful crisis response extends beyond the immediate emergency period. Preparation and mitigation prior to a crisis will influence long-term recovery and resilience. This unit concludes with different theories of the crisis management cycle with an emphasis on the interconnection between each phase.

Learning Goals:

- Participants will become familiar with the history of disaster management and will demonstrate understanding of contemporary practices and controversies in this area.
- Participants will learn to apply lessons of disaster sociology to accounts presented in social media and mainstream news outlets.
- Participants will be able to demonstrate understanding of key concepts such as resilience, hazard, risk, and vulnerability.
- Participants will be able to describe how context shapes the information needs of the public and formal emergency responders related to disaster.

This unit typically takes between 10 and 12 hours to complete and is the most reading intensive of the units.

Unit 2: Formal Response Mechanisms and Internal Data Hierarchies

This training incorporates a basic introduction to U.S. emergency management processes and crisis response procedures known as the "Incident Command System." It incorporates FEMA training IS-100.b: Introduction to Incident Command System, which provides participants with foundational understanding of formal emergency response practices. The Unit then builds on that basic knowledge to cover the way information is managed within the Command as well as how information is intended to flow between the Command and the public. Because volunteers—whether spontaneous or organized—often fill gaps in formal response, this unit will benefit a CIRT regardless of whether they intend to work directly within formal response or not.

Learning Goals:

- Participants will become familiar the structure of formal response activities between types of crises.
- Participants will become familiar with the terminology used by different types of government agencies around the world.
- Participants will be able to critically evaluate information management practices of responders working in different types of crises.
- Participants will be familiar with key challenges in developing effective crisis communication between the public and government response agencies.

This unit typically takes between 5 to 10 hours to complete.

Unit 3: Social Computing Platforms, Everyday Use and Extraordinary Use

Building on the general knowledge of human behavior in crises gained in Unit 1, this unit looks closely at how people employ SM in crisis. This unit explores social computing platforms in three ways 1) Common SM platforms used in crises, 2) patterns of mass participation and collaboration in crises, and 3) Mass participation crisis communities.

This lesson first provides an overview of major social computing platforms. These platforms include Facebook, Instagram, OpenStreetMap, Pinterest, Snapchat, Twitter, Reddit, Wikipedia, WhatsApp, and Weibo. For each platform, the technological affordances, demographics, cultures, and practices of users are considered. Commonalities and differences in information flows are emphasized.

People's use of technology and their trust of information sources are strongly conditioned by their everyday experience. This everyday experience informs behavior of individuals during a crisis response effort. The second part of this unit explores day-to-day SM practices as well as extraordinary use during a crisis response.

This unit concludes by examining community participation in crisis response efforts in two ways. First, in the last decade, several patterns and behavioral repertoires among SM users have emerged that follow from one crisis to the next. For example, hashtags such as #Prayfor<name of place> or the creation of memorial Facebook pages occur within minutes of a disaster. Some of these are "prosocial" such as repertoires for fundraising and some are "anti-social" such as repertoires for spreading disinformation. Second, highly organized, digital teams like the digital humanitarians, Virtual Operation Support Teams (VOSTs) and crisis mappers have solidified behaviors, practices, and tools. Each will be explored.

Learning Goals:

- Participants will become familiar with current trends in social computing.
- Participants will become familiar with the self-organizing behaviors present on social computing platforms.
- Participants will be able to critically evaluate the resources needed to harness different platforms given the availability of resources in a particular kind of crisis.
- Participants will be able to identify falsehoods and rumors and separate them from useful, awareness enhancing data made by people on the ground.

This Unit typically takes 8 hours to complete and requires a smart phone, tablet, or laptop.

Unit 4: Leveraging Social Media Data

This Unit covers the two basic approaches to leveraging SM data for crisis 1) the curation model and 2) large scale data analysis.

Much crisis-specific SM analysis is achieved through tools and practices that will be familiar to most SM users. These include cultivating and curating follower-following relationships with trusted information sources and monitoring keywords such as crisis-specific hashtags. We call this the Curation Model of SM analysis and we introduce several exemplars of this model as it is employed by different sets of volunteers, NGOs, and emergency management organizations.

Large-scale analysis of SM data is a field of active innovation among academics, practitioners, and developers. We introduce a number of approaches to large-scale data analysis as employed by practitioners and researchers emphasizing the opportunities and challenges of each.

An important feature of this Unit is consideration of common sources of error in interpreting social media data. This includes biases shaped by demographic limitations, SM participation, how SM platforms are arranged (algorithmic biases), how SM data is collected and analyzed, and assumptions of the analyst.

Learning Goals:

- Participants will become familiar with key information streams produced by social computing.
- Participants will be introduced to common tools used to analyze data produced by social computing.
- Participants will be able to critically evaluate social computing data and apply that knowledge to a live dataset.

- Participants will be able to identify key points of information that enhance coverage of activity on the ground.

This Unit typically takes 8 hours to complete and will be the most technologically immersive aspect of the training. A pre-unit knowledge quiz and study guide is provided in the online study materials.

Unit 5: Crisis Data Ethics

An important aspect of the still-evolving usage of SM in crises pertains to the vulnerabilities it can expose for users. In over a decade of SM use in crises, there are numerous examples of life-saving aid and assistance mediated through SM. There is increasing awareness that SM information needs to be handled with care to protect the safety and privacy of individuals.

Past examples of social media usage in crisis have highlighted important concerns related to SM usage. For example, during the VA Tech shooting in 2007, college students presumed that their Facebook posts were within their own social network and were not aware that posts would be of interest to media and other external audiences. In the Mumbai attack of 2008, terrorists used SM posts to locate victims. The trade-offs of making information available publicly are complex and context specific. Though public understanding and perceptions continue to evolve, it is important for CIRTS to be aware of the risks their analysis may pose.

Learning Goals:

- Participants will become familiar with how crisis response influences safety and privacy and the ethics of data use.
- Participants will be able to identify key aspects of data security.

- Participants will be able to critically evaluate data warehousing efforts and relevant ethical concerns.
- Participants will be able to identify ethical issues and tactics for addressing them during crisis response efforts.
- Participants will be familiar with important strategies for self-care used by CIRT practitioners who may be called upon to work long hours in emotionally difficult or stressful situations.

This unit typically takes 4 to 6 hours to complete. Post unit readings consisting of case studies and past CIRT work within ethics are available in the study materials.

The Crisis Informatics Workshop

This training was developed by the Crisis Informatics Workshop (CIW), a community of academics and practitioners who work together to innovate how social computing can support crisis response. The yearly workshop is a gathering through which members share best practices of analysts working across widely varying contexts.

CIW is an independent non-profit that curates and maintains training materials and other resources developed by practitioners and researchers. Maintenance and curation are paid for by training fees and donations. CIW encourages bottom up innovation and rapid transfer of knowledge in a fast-evolving field.

CIRT trainings focused on U.S response efforts are developed in coordination with the Federal Emergency Management Agency (FEMA). A multinational training unit has been developed in coordination with the United Nations Development Programme (UNDP) and the International Federation of Red Cross & Red Crescent Societies (IFRC).

Author's Statement

The imagined curriculum for a Crisis Informatics Response Technician (CIRT) is inspired by an assessment of current themes in Crisis Informatics (CI). These themes were identified by a workshop of CI scholars at University of Colorado Boulder in the spring of 2017[1]. In this section, we link our design fiction to some of the major themes that emerged during discussion. We express them here as four commitments related to Crisis Informatics research and practice that we identified attendees as expressing at the workshop

Commitment to Multiple Knowledges

Our imagined curriculum draws from several knowledge areas that CI researchers use in their research. The necessity for drawing upon multiple epistemological traditions were expressed during the discussion in two ways. First, in discussions of the various methodological commitments researchers in the field make in their own research. Second in frustration over how CI work can be misinterpreted by audiences outside of the field who lack one or more of the knowledge areas that CI draws on.

SM often makes visible slices of both formal and informal crisis response that would otherwise be challenging for researchers to study (e.g. [48]). An early insight of CI was that SM both made visible the emergent work that publics do in crises while simultaneously changing how that work occurs [18, 35-37, 44, 46, 47, 49]. So far, new behaviors and practices visible through SM extend but do not circumvent core insights from sociology of crises and disaster. Therefore, our imagined curriculum first introduces a primer on social science research on crisis.

---

[1] Grand Challenges for HCI Crisis Informatics Researchers Workshop, May 6, 2017.

CI researchers can attest to the fact that misconceptions about how people behave in crisis prevail among those not primed in the sociology of crises. For example, the stereotype that humans are little more than panicked animals during a crisis is as common among our peer reviewers as it is among the public. However, the reality is that decades of social science research in disasters have shown that during times of disaster, people tend to be calm, rational, and cooperative [9, 14]. Once their immediate safety has been secured, they seek to help others as well as obtain information on the condition of their family, friends, and neighbors [7]. They converge, both physically, and digitally on "the scene" in an effort to find out what happened and assist affected people. In short, to interpret SM data in crises, it helps to understand how emergent self-organization and cooperative behavior generally work in crises [9, 10, 30, 40]. SM analysts are disadvantaged if they are unaware of common human behaviors in crises.

Depending on your point of view, formal crisis response mechanisms either fill the gap of emergent informal response or vice versa. Either way, SM analysts focusing on crisis should understand how formal response works [3, 20, 31]. Though formal response training gives some background on the sociology of crises, formal response training necessarily emphasizes the mechanics of emergency response. This can leave those in formal response organizations with a gap in understanding emergent online behavior in crises.

Another important feature of the curriculum is introducing a typology of different kinds of crises. This typology should emphasize that different kinds of crises result in (and require) different patterns of information sharing. This is essential for effective response to specific crises. Through this fact, it should be noted that CI

professionals are often pressured to generalize across crises in a manner that is not empirically supported.

Disaster sociology is only one of the traditions that CI relies upon. A good deal of discussion at the CI workshop concerned the nuances of interpreting SM data. This is a strong focus in not only CI, but also many kinds of data science. CI Researchers were early adopters of exploiting SM data for research. As such, many CI researchers have become specialists in working with SM able to make methodological contributions to SM research in other thematic areas.

SM are far from neutral technologies. It takes considerable work to understand each platform. Each socio-technical system is vastly different. Here, another cornerstone of CI is important, awareness of Human Computer Interaction theory. HCI theory helps to explain and amplify the numerous innovations that have taken place among crisis practitioners.

In addition, as a research community with over a decade of experience in trying to do science with large-scale SM data, we are well aware of the opportunities and challenges such data presents. Even the mechanics of collection are fraught with potential pitfalls (and therefore an object of ongoing study and innovation) [1, 34]. The landscape of what can be collected, what the public is willing to share, and the mechanics of doing so continues to evolve, therefore our methods continue to shift.

As data science becomes more popular, increasingly complex tools to aggregate and analyze information are marketed to those without a background in computer or data science. It is important for domain specific researchers who work with large-scale data to take leadership in fostering methodological transparency. By pushing a curriculum that includes methodology and tools for interpreting SM specific to a domain, the possibility for wide-scale interrogation of methods is opened to a broader public than the methods sections of peer-reviewed papers.

Commitment to Ethical Research and Practice

Workshop participants also expressed strong interest in navigating the ethical implications of Crisis Informatics research and practice. A concern in this context is the value-vs.-vulnerability trade-off created by publicly available information about crisis-affected communities. This is highly context dependent. Data about crisis affected (and therefore potentially vulnerable) populations are made available by the public themselves. These data are then available for professional crisis responders as well as the public. Yet, the potential for trouble increases as wide-scale of SM data becomes more widespread.

Workshop participants felt that the situatedness of different crises and the vulnerabilities of different populations made uniform rules about aggregation and disclosure unhelpful. However, an intermediate step could be to work collectively toward developing decision-making heuristics and sensitizing questions. Analysts could use this work as a values lever [23, 43] or moment that creates a consideration for the ethical consideration of a design or decision. The safety and privacy implications of large-scale data about crisis are still unfolding, but the central importance of this theme is expressed in our curriculum through the inclusion of a Unit dedicated to ethical considerations of crisis data.

Commitment to the Long View

A major frustration for workshop participants is the sense that CI research is boxed in by "the event." The outsized attention that crisis events receive in the media and our politics as compared to the long periods of preparing for or recovering from them, carries over to how CI research is funded and to how and when those outside the field take an interest in its findings. A landslide becomes an international story when it kills 43 people, but this "event" would not have occurred at all if the county planning board had interpreted risk assessments differently years earlier [11, 12]. The CI researchers at the workshop were cognizant that mitigating future crises demands a long view of crisis mitigation, preparedness, response, and recovery.

Crises are the result of complex interactions between naturally or socially produced hazards and societally constructed vulnerabilities to those hazards. The factors that shape these vulnerabilities influence how and when disasters strike, who is affected, and long-term patterns of recovery [28]. These factors also shape what technologies are available to communicate once an event disrupts that region. Even if CI remains boxed by telling stories of "the event" those stories will be most impactful on mitigating future crises if the interrelations between information needed before, during and after considered [42]. Therefore, our imagined curriculum introduces several versions of the crisis management "cycle."

Commitment to the Global Community

The Crisis-Informatics Workshop included scholars from 3 continents and while we would like to say this is normal, in many ways it is not. With some important exceptions, much Crisis Informatics work has focused on the United States. Bombings [39, 48], Hurricanes [5, 16, 22, 50, 51], Mass Shootings [25, 37, 49], and different kinds of crisis like veteran re-integration [41] or public transit disruption in rural areas [38] all focus on the

United States and its brand of response. This extends to web communities and web platforms as well [21]. As we constructed this curriculum, each of the authors (by extension of the CIW's geographic dispersion) felt the limitations of that epistemological limitation. As such, we focused on international focuses like the creation of international VOSTs [4, 6, 19].

The causes and effects of crisis are global in nature. Efforts to understand and mitigate crisis must therefore also be informed by international perspectives. By focusing on CIRT as an internationally leaning certification, our design fiction highlights the need to increase the intersectionality of this type of work.

CONCLUSION

Our imagined curriculum allows us a new way to assess, carry forward, and communicate a discussion of important challenges and trends within Crisis Informatics research. Through consideration of what the role of CIRT could play within crisis response and what types of expertise would be needed to facilitate such a role, we were able to articulate some of the issues at stake, think through the trade-offs of prioritizing various training content, and speculate about what new partnerships between formal and informal crisis response might coalesce around.

By suggesting a certification that combines multiple threads of expertise into a single crisis-focused curriculum, we invite conversation with the academic research community, practitioners, and the wider public. Specifically, we offered a vision of 1) What productive, ethical, and scientifically grounded analysis of SM crisis data might look like and 2) How to highlight and promote essential knowledge, best tools, and best practices to both professional and lay analysts.

ACKNOWLEDGMENTS

The authors would like to thank the Grand Challenges in HCI Crisis Informatics Researchers Workshop participants: Jennings Anderson, Ken Anderson, Melissa Bica, Olga Bolchak, Julie Demuth, Nicolas Lalone, Brian Keegan, Marina Kogan, Thomas Ludwig, Wendy Norris, Leysia Palen, Konstantinos Papangelis, John Robinson, Bryan Semaan, and Ashley Walker.

REFERENCES

1. Kenneth M Anderson and Aaron Schram. 2011. Design and implementation of a data analytics infrastructure in support of crisis informatics research: NIER track. in *Software Engineering (ICSE), 2011 33rd International Conference on*, IEEE, 844-847.

2. Danah Boyd and Kate Crawford. 2012. Critical questions for big data: Provocations for a cultural, technological, and scholarly phenomenon. *Information, communication & society*, 15 (5). 662-679.

3. Dick A Buck, Joseph E Trainor and Benigno E Aguirre. 2006. A critical evaluation of the incident command system and NIMS. *Journal of Homeland Security and Emergency Management*, 3 (3).

4. Monika Büscher and Michael Liegl. 2014. Connected communities in crises. *Social Media Analysis for Crisis Management* (1).

5. Cornelia Caragea, Anna Squicciarini, Sam Stehle, Kishore Neppalli and Andrea Tapia. 2014. Mapping Moods: Geo-Mapped Sentiment Analysis During Hurricane Sandy. in *11th International Conference on Information Systems for Crisis Response and Management (ISCRAM 2014)*, University Park, PA, USA.

6. Camille Cobb, Ted McCarthy, Annuska Perkins, Ankitha Bharadwaj, Jared Comis, Brian Do and Kate Starbird. 2014. Designing for the deluge: understanding & supporting the distributed, collaborative work of crisis volunteers. in *Proceedings of the 17th ACM conference on Computer supported cooperative work & social computing*, ACM, 888-899.

7. Dharma Dailey, John Robinson and Kate Starbird. 2016. Sharing food, gathering information: the context and visibility of community information work in a crisis event. *IConference 2016 Proceedings*.

8. Sharon Dawes, Anthony Cresswell and Bruce Cahan. 2004. Learning From Crisis: Lessons in Human and Information Infrastructure From the World Trade Center Response. *Social Science Computer Review*, 22 (1). 52-66.

9. Thomas E Drabek and David A McEntire. 2003. Emergent phenomena and the sociology of disaster: lessons, trends and opportunities from the research literature. *Disaster Prevention and Management: An International Journal*, 12 (2). 97-112.

10. Russell R Dynes. 1990. Community emergency planning: false assumption and inappropriate analogies.

11. Kai Erikson. 1995. *A new species of trouble: The human experience of modern disasters*. WW Norton & Co.

12. Kai T Erikson. 1976. *Everything in its path*. Simon and Schuster.

13. Laz Etamike and Ben Agah. 2011. Information Communication Technology (ICT) and Crisis Management: An Imperative for Developing Countries. *Raziskave in Razprave, 4* (2). 95.

14. Henry W Fischer. 1998. *Response to disaster: Fact versus fiction & its perpetuation: The sociology of disaster*. University press of America.

15. Sean Goggins, Christopher Mascaro and Stephanie Mascaro. 2012. Relief work after the 2010 Haiti earthquake: leadership in an online resource coordination network. in *Proceedings of the ACM 2012 conference on Computer Supported Cooperative Work*, ACM, 57-66.

16. Aditi Gupta, Hemank Lamba, Ponnurangam Kumaraguru and Anupam Joshi. 2013. Faking sandy: characterizing and identifying fake images on twitter during hurricane sandy. *Proceedings of the 22nd international conference on World Wide Web companion*. 729-736.

17. Teresa M. Harrison, Theresa A Pardo, J Ramón Gil-García, Fiona Thompson and Juraga Dubravka. 2007. Geographic Information Technologies, Structuration Theory, and the World Trade Center Crisis. *Journal of the American Society for Information Science and Technology*, 58 (14). 2240-2254. 10.1002/asi

18. Amanda Lee Hughes and Leysia Palen. 2009. Twitter adoption and use in mass convergence and emergency events. *International Journal of Emergency Management*, 6 (3). 248-260.

19. Amanda Lee Hughes and Andrea H Tapia. 2015. Social media in crisis: when professional responders meet digital volunteers. *Journal of Homeland Security and Emergency Management*, 12 (3). 679-706.

20. Jessica Jensen and William L. Waugh. 2014. The United States' Experience with the Incident Command System: What We Think We Know and What We Need to Know More About. *Journal of Contingencies and*

Crisis Management, 22 (1). 5-17. 10.1111/1468-5973.12034

21. Brian Keegan, Darren Gergle and Noshir Contractor. 2013. Hot off the wiki: Structures and dynamics of Wikipedia's coverage of breaking news events. *American Behavioral Scientist*, 57 (5). 595-622.

22. Marina Kogan, Leysia Palen and Kenneth M Anderson. 2015. Think local, retweet global: Retweeting by the geographically-vulnerable during Hurricane Sandy. in *Proceedings of the 18th ACM conference on computer supported cooperative work & social computing*, ACM, 981-993.

23. Nicolas LaLone. 2014. Values levers and the unintended consequences of design. in *Proceedings of the companion publication of the 17th ACM conference on Computer supported cooperative work & social computing*, ACM, 189-192.

24. Nicolas LaLone, Andrea Tapia, Christopher Zobel, Cornelia Caraega, Venkata Kishore Neppalli and Shane Halse. 2017. Embracing human noise as resilience indicator: twitter as power grid correlate. *Sustainable and Resilient Infrastructure*. 1-10.

25. Alexander C Leavitt. 2016. Upvoting the News: Breaking News Aggregation, Crowd Collaboration, and Algorithm-Driven Attention on reddit.com *Annenberg School for Communication and Journalism*, University of Southern California.

26. S Liu and Jen Ziemke. 2013. From cultures of participation to the rise of crisis mapping in a networked world. *The participatory cultures handbook*. 185-196.

27. Alan M MacEachren, Anthony C Robinson, Anuj Jaiswal, Scott Pezanowski, Alexander Savelyev, Justine Blanford and Prasenjit Mitra. 2011. Geo-twitter analytics:

Applications in crisis management. in *25th International Cartographic Conference*, 3-8.

28. Gloria J Mark, Ban Al-Ani and Bryan Semaan. 2009. Resilience through technology adoption: merging the old and the new in Iraq. in *Proceedings of the SIGCHI conference on human factors in computing systems*, ACM, 689-698.

29. Patrick Meier. 2015. *Digital humanitarians: how big data is changing the face of humanitarian response*. Crc Press.

30. Laura G. Militello, Emily S. Patterson, Lynn Bowman and Robert Wears. 2006. Information flow during crisis management: challenges to coordination in the emergency operations center. *Cognition, Technology & Work*, 9 (1). 25-31. 10.1007/s10111-006-0059-3

31. Donald P Moynihan. 2009. The network governance of crisis response: Case studies of incident command systems. *Journal of Public Administration Research and Theory*. mun033.

32. Dhiraj Murthy. 2013. New media and natural disasters: Blogs and the 2004 Indian Ocean tsunami. *Information, Communication & Society*, 16 (7). 1176-1192.

33. Ida Norheim-Hagtun and Patrick Meier. 2010. Crowdsourcing for crisis mapping in Haiti. *innovations*, 5 (4). 81-89.

34. Leysia Palen, Kenneth M Anderson, Gloria Mark, James Martin, Douglas Sicker, Martha Palmer and Dirk Grunwald. 2010. A vision for technology-mediated support for public participation & assistance in mass emergencies & disasters. in *Proceedings of the 2010 ACM-BCS visions of computer science conference*, British Computer Society, 8.

35. Leysia Palen and Sarah Vieweg. 2008. The emergence of online widescale interaction in unexpected events: assistance, alliance & retreat. in *Proceedings of the 2008 ACM conference on Computer supported cooperative work*, ACM, 117-126.

36. Leysia Palen, Sarah Vieweg, Jeannette Sutton, Sophia B Liu and Amanda L Hughes. 2007. Crisis Informatics: Studying Crisis in a Networked World. in *Third International Conference on e-Social Science*, Ann Arbor, MI.

37. Leysia Palen, Sarah Vieweg, Sophia B Liu and Amanda Lee Hughes. 2009. Crisis in a networked world: Features of computer-mediated communication in the April 16, 2007, Virginia Tech event. *Social Science Computer Review*, 27 (4). 467-480.

38. Konstantinos Papangelis, Nagendra R Velaga, Fiona Ashmore, Somayajulu Sripada, John D Nelson and Mark Beecroft. 2016. Exploring the rural passenger experience, information needs and decision making during public transport disruption. *Research in Transportation Business & Management*, 18. 57-69.

39. Liza Potts and Angela Harrison. 2013. Interfaces as rhetorical constructions: reddit and 4chan during the boston marathon bombings. in *Proceedings of the 31st ACM international conference on Design of communication*, ACM, 143-150.

40. Yan Qu, Philip Fei Wu and Xiaoqing Wang. 2009. Online community response to major disaster: A study of Tianya forum in the 2008 Sichuan earthquake. in *System Sciences, 2009. HICSS'09. 42nd Hawaii International Conference on*, IEEE, 1-11.

41. Bryan C Semaan, Lauren M Britton and Bryan Dosono. 2016. Transition Resilience with ICTs:'Identity Awareness' in Veteran Re-Integration. in *Proceedings of the 2016 CHI Conference on Human Factors in Computing Systems*, ACM, 2882-2894.

42. Bryan Semaan and Gloria Mark. 2011. Technology-mediated social arrangements to resolve breakdowns in infrastructure during ongoing disruption. *ACM Transactions on Computer-Human Interaction (TOCHI)*, 18 (4). 21.

43. K. Shilton. 2012. Values Levers: Building Ethics into Design. *Science, Technology & Human Values*, 38 (3). 374-397. 10.1177/0162243912436985

44. Irina Shklovski, Leysia Palen and Jeannette Sutton. 2008. Finding community through information and communication technology in disaster response. in *Proceedings of the 2008 ACM conference on Computer supported cooperative work*, ACM, 127-136.

45. Robert Soden and Leysia Palen. 2014. From crowdsourced mapping to community mapping: The post-earthquake work of OpenStreetMap Haiti. in *COOP 2014-Proceedings of the 11th International Conference on the Design of Cooperative Systems, 27-30 May 2014, Nice (France)*, Springer, 311-326.

46. Jeannette N Sutton, Leysia Palen and Irina Shklovski. 2008. *Backchannels on the front lines: Emergency uses of social media in the 2007 Southern California Wildfires*. University of Colorado.

47. Jeannette Sutton, Leysia Palen and Irina Shklovski. 2008. Backchannels on the front lines: Emergent uses of social media in the 2007 southern California wildfires. in *Proceedings of the 5th International ISCRAM Conference*, Washington, DC, 624-632.

48. Andrea H Tapia, Nicolas LaLone and Hyun-Woo Kim. 2014. Run amok: group crowd participation in identifying the bomb and bomber from the boston marathon bombing. *Proceedings of the 11th ISCRAM*.

49. Sarah Vieweg, Leysia Palen, Sophia B Liu, Amanda L Hughes and Jeannette Sutton. 2008. Collective intelligence in disaster: An examination of the phenomenon in the aftermath of the 2007 Virginia Tech shootings. in *Proceedings of the Information Systems for Crisis Response and Management Conference (ISCRAM)*.

50. Joanne I White, Leysia Palen and Kenneth M Anderson. 2014. Digital mobilization in disaster response: the work & self-organization of on-line pet advocates in response to hurricane sandy. in *Proceedings of the 17th ACM conference on Computer supported cooperative work & social computing*, ACM, 866-876.

51. Michael J Widener, Mark W Horner and Sara S Metcalf. 2013. Simulating the effects of social networks on a population's hurricane evacuation participation. *Journal of geographical systems*, 15 (2). 193-209.

52. Jen Ziemke. 2012. Crisis mapping: The construction of a new interdisciplinary field? *Journal of Map & Geography Libraries*, 8 (2). 101-117.

What Would *You* Do? Design Fiction and Ethics

Eric P. S. Baumer
Timothy Berrill
Sarah C. Botwinick
Jonathan L. Gonzales
Kevin Ho
Allison Kundrik
Luke Kwon
Tim LaRowe
Chanh P. "Sam" Nguyen
Fredy Ramirez
Peter Schaedler
William Ulrich
Amber Wallace
Yuchen Wan
Benjamin Weinfeld
Computer Science & Engineering
Lehigh University
Bethlehem, PA 18015, USA
ericpsb@lehigh.edu

GROUP '18, January 7–10, 2018, Sanibel Island, FL, USA
© 2018 Copyright is held by the owner/author(s). Publication rights licensed to ACM.
ACM 978-1-4503-5562-9/18/01…$15.00
https://doi.org/10.1145/3148330.3149405

Abstract

Design fiction can be highly effective at envisioning possible futures. That envisioning enables, among other things, considering ethical implications of possible technologies. This paper highlights that capacity through a curated collection of five short design fiction pieces, each accompanied by its own author statement. Spanning multiple genres, each piece highlights ethical issues in its own way. After considering the unique strategies that each piece uses to highlight ethical issues, the paper concludes with considerations of how design fiction can advance broader discussions of ethics in computing.

Author Keywords

Design fiction; ethics.

ACM Classification Keywords

H.5.m. Information interfaces and presentation (e.g., HCI): Miscellaneous.

Introduction

Recent years have seen a flourishing of interest in design fiction within HCI and related areas [6,10–12,16,26,29]. This development is perhaps unsurprising, given the multitude of purposes that design fiction can serve. Perhaps most notably, design fiction enables, or at times even forces, thinking through the specific details and ramifications of a technology without actually figuring out implementation, conducting a study, analyzing the results, etc. [10]. Interestingly, Dunne and Raby's [18] formulation of critical design describes it as a sort of value fiction. While some work has extended this sensibility to design and to implement speculative artifacts [51], writing and analyzing design fiction can serve many valuable purposes.

Much of design fiction's unique capacities come from its implicit nature. For example, a review for a fictional book can conjure various sorts of impressions about a

submissions for such a curated collection [http://www.fictionalconference.com/].

After establishing some background on different fundamental approaches to ethics, this paper presents the five short design fiction pieces. Each piece is accompanied by an author statement, written by the authors of that piece, as well as a curator's note, written by the author who curated these pieces. Both the curator's note and the author statement serve to highlight the different ways that ethics are highlighted in each fiction. The paper concludes by considering both the strengths and weaknesses of design fiction as a means of facilitating debate about ethical issues in computing.

Background: Ethics

Different traditions define and constitute the purview and function of ethics in varying manners. This section reviews three dominant approaches to normative ethics, i.e., determining what people should do.

First, according to virtue ethics, one determines what one should do by following certain precepts, or virtues. These virtues are less rules per se but more particular aspects of one's character. These aspects are revealed in response to certain situations, especially challenging moments. For instance, Aristotle [2] describes courage as a virtue that one might demonstrate in response to fear-inducing situations. One who lacks the virtue of courage would, in the face of fear, instead demonstrate the vice of cowardice. Alternately, one who exhibits excessive or unwarranted confidence exhibits the vice of rashness or recklessness.

Second, according to duty ethics, one determines what one should do by fulfilling one's duties. In some approaches [e.g., 42,43], specific duties constrain and guide our actions. Examples include duty to others (e.g., treating people as equals) or duty to self (e.g., caring for one's body by avoiding gluttony or excessive

book (that does not exist) without needing to actually create the book itself [48]. Indeed, the reader creates for herself or himself imagined details of the book, and different readers may come away imagining different details. In many ways, this implicit aspect resembles what Blythe and Encinas [12] refer to as ambiguity. Rather than being explicitly didactic, these types of fictions leave much interpretation (and interpolation) to be done by the reader. The reader is given the opportunity to consider, given a hypothetical scenario, what s/he would.

Ethical issues provide a prime opportunity to take advantage of these unique aspects of design fiction. In some ways, all (design) fiction might be considered ethical, in so far as both ethics and fiction deal with what people, real or imagined, either should or would do in specific scenarios. For any issue, there are multiple different kinds of arguments that one could make about how to proceed ethically. Design fiction essentially allows us to take a designerly approach [cf. 15] to issues of ethics and technology. In so far as design revolves around simultaneous consideration and exploration of different possible paths forward [14,17], design fiction provides an opportunity to consider different means of ethical judgments and decision making.

To levy this multiplicity more fully, this paper presents a curated collection of five short design fiction pieces. In this way, the approach resembles other recent design fiction efforts. For instance, Blythe and Encinas [12] present four different design fiction pieces, all within the same future world but each highlighting a different aspect of the design fiction genre. Similarly, both Baumer et al. [6] and Penzenstadler et al. [39] present collections of fictional abstracts for papers to appear in future conference proceedings. In one case, an entire fictional conference was created to garner

drinking). Other approaches formulate all ethical decisions in terms of a single duty. For instance, Kant's categorical imperative [25] suggests that human life should not be treated as a means to an end. Stealing would be ethically wrong, as it uses someone else's work as a means to benefit one's self. Similarly, suicide would be ethically wrong, as it would essentially treat one's own life as a means to alleviate one's own suffering. In yet another take, duties emerge because of one person's obligation to fulfill the rights of others. For example, Locke [30] argued that all humans have the rights of life, health, liberty, and possessions. Thus, people have a correlative duty to uphold and not harm anyone else's life, health, etc. The influence of this line of thinking can be seen in the American "life, liberty, and the pursuit of happiness" or in the French "liberté, égalité, fraternité."

Third, according to consequentialist ethics, one determines what one should do by weighing the consequences of one's actions. To take an example from above, gluttony could be seen as resulting in negative consequences both to one's self (e.g., becoming overweight and developing various medical conditions) and to others (e.g., the family and friends who end up needing to care for the gluttonous eater). This consequentialist approach can be applied in different ways. In some approaches, one considers the consequences of individual actions [7], tallying both the positive and negative outcomes of any given choice. For example, watching television might be less desirable than volunteering for charity because of the sum positive benefits of the latter. Other approaches [32] focus not on individual actions but on the consequences of broader moral rules. For instance, a rule prohibiting stealing could be seen as ethical because it produces the most favorable outcomes for the greatest number of people, as opposed to allowing stealing which would provide benefit to the powerful few who could steal without fear

of retribution. In many ways, this line of thinking resembles utilitarianism, which seeks to provide the most good for the greatest number of people and the least detriment to the fewest number of people.

This review is far from exhaustive. Other perspectives bring different intellectual traditions to bear. Speculative fabulation [23] applies concepts from feminist thought [24] to explore, among other things, the ethics embedded in the stories, the fables, that people tell each other. A postmodernist approach avoids codification of ethical codes in favor of relying on a fundamental human moral impulse that, it is argued, serves as the foundation for all sociality. Afrofuturism [33,54] as a literary and artistic movement suggest that ethics of technology should consider, among other things, sociocultural dimensions. Thoroughly covering every existing approach to ethics far exceeds the scope of this paper. Instead, this section seeks to establish what we mean by ethics and, moreover, what counts as an ethical issue. This groundwork helps demonstrate how the short fiction pieces below highlight ethical issues.

Context and Writing Process

The short fiction pieces below were all written by students in a course on the social and ethical dimensions of computing. The class dealt with a number of topics and issues, from persuasive technology [8,20,44], to social media use and non-use [5,22,41], to privacy and surveillance [34,36,47], to algorithmic bias and discrimination [1,4,50]. A full syllabus for the course is available at http://ericbaumer.com/wp-content/uploads/2012/10/CSE252Spring2017Syllabus.pdf.

During the final week of class, students were assigned a reading on design fiction [9] as well as a related piece of fiction [49]. During class, students were then asked to form small groups and write a piece in the genre of design fiction. The ostensible goal for the assignment was to suggest something about the nature of the relationship between technology and society. Although the course focused on ethical issues, students were not explicitly asked to write about ethics. However, every one of the pieces that students wrote raised ethical issues.

Students were asked to write approximately 100 to 200 words, but many students wrote more. Students were also informed that this assignment was inspired by the GROUP Design Fiction track and given a link to the call for submissions. During the final several minutes of class, some of the pieces were read aloud by the students who wrote them and discussed by other students.

Curated Collection

After reviewing all twelve short fictions, the first author invited eight for inclusion here. These were chosen on the basis of which most effectively used the format to highlight ethical tensions. Of these eight, five had at least one contributor who was willing to write an author statement. All students who contributed to the short fictions included here are listed as authors on this paper.

User Reviews of "Know Yourself"
See sidebar for product description.

User Review 1 ★★★☆☆: I guess this app is okay. I used it when I was trying to switch majors in college. It gave me some advice, but most of what it told me I already knew. It's nice to have the option of using this app tho.

User Review 2 ★☆☆☆☆: Would give 0 if I could. This app doesn't tell me shit! It makes assumptions about my personality and interests without knowing who I truly am. Like it says I could be a doctor, but doesn't take into account I can't afford med school! Sad! It's

From the Product Description: Know yourself is an app that uses all data available on a user (Google, Facebook, Amazon, iMessages, etc) along with groundbreaking machine learning algorithms to compile an incredibly comprehensive personality report. These reports can be used to find friends with similar personalities, discover your dream job, pick out the perfect vacation spot, and so much more!

presumptuous and discriminatory. Would not recommend.

User Review 3 ★★★★★: I was a senior in high school with no idea what I was going to do in college but my school made us all use this app and it told me to be an engineer and I've never looked back. It even matched me with people that I would get along with so I didn't have to worry about making friends in college, we just found each other on Facebook, created a GroupMe before we got to campus, and didn't talk to anyone else. Know Yourself has my whole life figured out!

User Review 4 ★★☆☆☆: A company I was applying to made me share my 'know yourself' results. My personality apparently didn't line up with what they were looking for so they canceled my interview :(

AUTHOR STATEMENT

Reviews from the app 'Know Yourself' highlight some of the dangers and benefits of a future in which massive amounts of personal data from various sources can be aggregated and analyzed to paint a detailed picture of a person. While some people may seek out this information to learn more about themselves and are happy with the results, others feel the data doesn't portray them fairly. This misportrayal raises larger ethical issues when seeing the powerful influence the data has over certain situations, such as companies making hiring decisions.

We decided to present this information in reviews of an app because it is a concise, relatable way to display differing views of the technology. Reviews range from a user hating the app to a user loving the app, including viewpoints where users were on the fence. This format makes it unnecessary to write blocks of text when a short statement, like from User review 4, is enough to showcase the user's poor experience. App reviews allows the reader to put themselves in the place of a po-

Radio Advertisement for Medi-Check

Don't go another day without getting your individualized Medi-Check. A new, revolutionary medical technology designed to monitor your health at all times. Medi-Check is painlessly injected into your neck by professionally trained staff members at your local office. Immediately after the procedure you will reap a wealth of benefits from this advanced technology.

Medi-Check will automatically monitor your blood sugar, cholesterol, blood pressure, heart rate, iron and vitamin levels and report to you via free downloadable application. If measurements become problematic, your primary care physician will be contacted and informed of the issue. The days of waiting forever in the doctor's office are over.

But that's not all! Hypersensitive isolated nerve trackers can detect localized physical injuries such as broken bones, lacerations, burns and sprains. Medi-Check will immediately contact emergency medical professionals based on the severity of the injury.

Parents, never worry if your children are safe again. With the parental control app, constantly monitor your child's health and activities. Automated drug and blood alcohol content measurements will ensure your kids stay safe and out of trouble. Physical fitness monitoring that outstrips any other product makes sure your child stays active and healthy.

Most importantly, in dire medical circumstances your Medi-Check can administer emergency automatic defibrillation that could save your life.

Don't wait until it's too late, get your Medi-Check today!

tential downloader of "Know Yourself". Which reviewer would you side with? Would you download the app after reading? These questions provoke readers to think about data sharing and privacy, without explicitly saying so.

CURATOR'S NOTE

This piece clearly draws inspiration from work on inferring individual traits from social media data [55]. Through the different reviews, it asks in what ways someone might actually make use of such technologies. These differing uses lead to a whole variety of issues: privacy [34,36], accuracy, accountability/transparency [4], socioeconomic status [1,50], filter bubbles [38], etc.

This piece emphasizes a consequentialist approach. Each review gestures toward different set of potential consequences from the Know Yourself system. Each of these consequences highlights different potential benefits or detriments to different individuals or groups. In line with consequentialist reasoning, the reader is implicitly asked to weigh each of these benefits and detriments in assessing Know Yourself.

Part of the piece's strength comes from leveraging the common trend of every product receiving both lauding and damning reviews, it provides a unique format to deploy ideas of multiplicity and plurality in interpretations of technology [3,40,46]. Furthermore, the reader brings yet another perspective. Review 3 writes glowing praise for Know Yourself while seemingly unaware of the constraints the system may place on social interaction. Juxtaposition against the other reviews allows the reader to identify Reviewer 3 as the classic unreliable narrator [13]. It is also likely quite intentional that Review 3 is an engineer.

AUTHOR STATEMENT

The idea of the Medi-Check came when thinking about the invasion of privacy of a person's current state of health. We wanted to question what is too much when considering keeping current on a person's health. It is like an extreme version of a Fitbit which also monitors different aspects of a user's health.

CURATOR'S NOTE

The Medi-Check advertisement employs what might be called a slippery-slope style argument. Essentially, it progressively adds layer upon layer of ethically dubious functionality. Monitoring glucose levels, cholesterol, blood pressure, and heart rate all seem fairly innocuous. However, automated drug and alcohol testing becomes reminiscent of the Quantified Toilets critical making intervention during the CHI 2014 conference [http://quantifiedtoilets.com/]. Similarly, the physical interventions Medi-Check purports to be able to make would make it similar to Fit4Life [44]. The advertisement asserts that these invasive functionalities are actually in the user's best interest and may even save her or his life.

These arguments belie a combination of consequentialist and duty ethics. Clearly, Medi-Check should be interpreted in terms of its consequences. Functionally, it purports to improve health through self-monitoring. Societally, it normalizes surveillance [21]. However, Medi-Check also makes appeals to the various responsibilities or duties that one has: to care for one's own body, to report on one's health to one's doctor, to monitor the health of one's children. The advertisement implicitly asks readers to consider the extent to which a device such as Medi-Check would actually help fulfill these duties, and, moreover, whether they would use such a technology.

Part of what becomes compelling, then, is where and how the line is drawn. At what point does Medi-Check start to become ethically questionable, either in terms of fulfilling duties or in terms of its consequences? At what point does it become ethically objectionable? Both where and how the reader draws these lines helps reveal the reader's own ethical decision making processes around (health) technology.

SkyNet API

SkyNet is an online service available to all users of the Internet, providing a simple, programmable interface for many aspects of daily life. Because of the open nature of SkyNet, there is no need for authentication tokens or other security mechanisms. Anyone can make an HTTP request to any of the following endpoints. These requests make use of SkyNet's vast amounts of resources and technologies to organize, request, and provide information about various aspects of the current state of life, along with the past and future. See sidebar for a few examples.

AUTHOR STATEMENT

We came across this idea when thinking about the current state of technology. With products like the Amazon Echo and Google Home, we can check the weather, schedule appointments, and buy groceries, all without lifting a finger. Our vision of the future was a world where machines like the Echo and Home did all of the mundane tasks in our lives, but also had the power to go even further and alter time and space. Rather than just receiving information, our SkyNet API allows users to update information on anything, whether that is the current state of traffic or the current level of water in your glass. The idea can then be extended further to changing people's personalities or family history to give a level of customizability that only SkyNet could provide. We presented the idea in the form of an API document to emphasize the ease and flexibility with which people can achieve such tasks in the future.

```
//#! Last Updated 2017-05-02
15:33:27 UTC-5

/get/weather?location=place
Retrieves weather forecast at place.

/post/weather?location=place&u
pdate_key=key&update_value=val
ue

Provides user-submitted update of
weather forecast at place.

/get/traffic?location=place
Retrieves state of transportation at
or near current place.

/post/traffic?location=place&u
pdate_key=key&update_value=val
ue

Provides user-submitted update of
traffic at place.

/get/info?person=name
Retrieve current status of an entity
person.

/post/info?person=name&update_
key=key&update_value=value
Update current status of an entity
person with attribute update_key
and new value.

/get/history?person=name
Retrieve historical records of an en-
tity person.

/post/history?person=name&upda
te_key=key&update_value=value
Update historical records of an enti-
ty person for a given time/date and
the event that occurred.

Sample Request:
curl
https://skynet.google.com/post
/info?person=epsb&update_key=w
ater_bottle_level&update_value
=100%

Response:
{
    status: 200
}
```

In addition, there is the added benefit of needing no security in the API because anyone can adjust anything about it. Any potential security issues can be fixed by a friendly developer or user of the API. However, this is flawed thinking, and a satirical comment on how some real-world developers may treat computer security without proper knowledge of the subject. Ultimately, we want readers to consider the potential reach of technology (particularly "Internet of Things" devices) and how security is an important consideration when developing these devices. An API like ours demonstrates the importance of privacy and security in technology and how necessary they are in our interconnected society.

CURATOR'S NOTE

Much in the SkyNet API is reminiscent of Wikipedia. For example, the anyone-can-edit model similarly carries the concomitant notion that errors or vandalism could be easily corrected/reverted by others, e.g., through the /post/history endpoint. The fact that people are indexed by name suggests that this piece may be written in a distant future, or perhaps an alternate reality, where a person's name is unique enough to serve as a database key.

These points suggests a virtue-oriented take on ethics. In the potentially threatening situation of cyber attacks, SkyNet responds with the virtue of openness; "there is no need for authentication tokens or other security mechanisms." This framing implicitly suggests security as the complementary vice to openness. In doing so, it echoes a recurring theme in both popular media and scholarly research intimating a future without privacy [19,27,45,52].

EULA for Kohai Meets Senpai (Companionship Site)
Please read this End-User License Agreement carefully before clicking the "I agree" button and using this companionship site.

By clicking "I Agree" button, you are agreeing to be bound by the terms and conditions of this Agreement. The agreement is between you, the user, and Kohai Meets Senpai, Inc. (referred to as KMS from this point forward).

If you do not agree to the terms of this Agreement, do not click on the "I Agree" button and miss out on a chance to find happiness in this world.

Other than that, feel free to find your senpai!

Warning!! If you join this companionship site, you will find that you may not be able to handle the multitude of attention that will be coming your way. We are not liable for the amounts of dates you will be asked out on or for the many new people you will meet.

Licensing: The companionship site grants you a revocable, limited license to join and use solely for your personal, non-commercial purposes strictly in accordance with the terms of this Agreement. Redistribution of profiles is forbidden and will result with the immediate termination of said profile along with a $500.00 fine to both distributor and the person receiving, as well as the deed to your house. This, in turn, includes everything you own.

Warranties: This internet companionship site is set to update every day. New pictures, profiles, and statuses are made constantly. So, in order to allow this, you must have the latest version of Javascript. 4rend LLC is not responsible for any damages to your accessing device. This includes but is not limited to water damage to device, full on 40-episode battles, kamehameha waves, and/or complete destruction.

Liability: KMS is not responsible for any feelings of fever, severe cold, sudden hotness, sudden nausea, sudden

I am writing this letter to notify the entire organization of Iota Eta Pi that they are currently under investigation. As of the beginning of the year, Wossamotta University has been granted privileges to monitor and collect all GroupMe messages sent and received while using WoU Wifi. All messages have been sorted and analyzed greatly. After much deliberation, it was evident that I Eta Pi has been involved in many activities that go against our code of conduct. The University will take all necessary and reasonable steps to stop the alleged conduct and provide support to the complainant, the respondents, and as necessary, to other members of the University community. The data we have uncovered is extremely disappointing, and we will be taking all consequences very seriously. Investigations will be conducted and all members involved in the disorderly messages will be punished accordingly. Furthermore, any signs of illegal activity found within the messages will also be sent to the authorities for further investigation.

den coldness, and inability to logout of the virtual environment.

Laws: The biggest law that users must be aware of is having any "companionship" with a minor and vice versa. In different states, these laws vary greatly, users are responsible for doing research in their own local area on this aspect. 4rend LLC is not responsible for any arrest in regards to using the service.

AUTHOR STATEMENT
EULA for Kohai Meets Senpai highlights ethical issues in user agreements. Because people rarely read EULAs, they can end up agreeing to many unreasonable statements. Although you usually still own content you post to sites such as Facebook, you also grant them a license to use that content in almost any way they want. In turn, because they did not read the EULA, users do not really know what they agreed to.

CURATOR'S NOTE
This piece relies heavily on virtue ethics. The company 4rend LLC exhibits several Aristotelian [2] vices in this EULA. A combination of malice and greed is shown by the company's willingness not noly to fine its users but also to seize "the deed to your house, [which], in turn, includes everything you own." This EULA could also be said to exhibit cowardice in its disownment of responsibility for a multitude of different effects that may result from use of Kohai Meets Senpai. Despite this emphasis on virtue, the piece also asks the reader to consider a duty ethics perspective. What duty or responsibility *should* such a company have to its users?

Clearly, this piece relies heavily on parody and exaggeration. However, these exaggerations and parodies are effective primarily because they are grounded in and inspired by actual corporations and business practices. The relationship between Kohai Meets Senpai and 4rend LLC feels reminiscent of the relationship between

Google and its parent corporation Alphabet, Inc. The suggestion that using a companionship site could result in physical symptoms from fever to nausea seems surprising, until it is suggested that the site uses, or perhaps takes place in, a virtual environment.

Most notably, the notion that a user who redistributes profiles from the site agrees to give up "the deed to your house [and] everything you own" seems absurd. However, prior work has found that people willingly agree to sign up for social media websites even when the user agreement includes, for instance, giving up one's first born child as payment to use the site [35]. The point is not that people actually agree to these terms, the point is that they do not read them. This is perhaps unsurprising, given that the volume of text in the privacy policies to which most people agree in a year far exceeds the amount of time most people have available to spend reading such policies [31]. This piece implicitly asks which of the above clauses are most ridiculous (e.g., those dealing with "kamehameha waves") and which might actually find their way into real EULAs.

Letter of Disorderly Conduct
Iota Eta Pi, 123 Greek Rd., Anytown, XY 99999

To the members of Iota Eta Pi: (see sidebar for text)

Sincerely,

Office of the Code of Conduct, Wossamotta University, 1 Admin Way, Anytown, XY 99999

AUTHOR STATEMENT
Our intent with this piece was to address the ownership of information privacy. Students across the world use wireless devices to interact with one another and the world around them, and most students believe that communication through their own devices is private. As

social media sites have done with their services, it is possible for a university to offer wifi under a policy that entitles them to access users' information. Because so much information flows through wireless devices on a college campus, the conduct letter is intentionally vague to leave the student wondering about their possible violations. It is a scary thought that your university could be monitoring all of your online activity on campus, but it is entirely possible. In April, 2015, the Alpha Delta Pi Sorority at George Washington University was placed on disciplinary probation after a chapter member posted inappropriate material about their philanthropy on social media [37]. This showed that a university can and sometimes will punish students for their conduct online. Conduct letters like this one are a common occurrence on many college campuses with greek life. A story like this could instill great fear in university students' minds since it is both feasible and relatable.

CURATOR'S NOTE

This piece's greatest strength comes from its vagueness. As the author statement notes, quality derives from actual letters that Greek organizations have received. In actual conduct sanction letters, the motivation for such vagueness is unclear. In the piece here, that vagueness becomes a source of ambiguity [12], leaving the reading to surmise exactly what sort of activities the administration observed that ran contrary to the institution's code of conduct.

That vagueness also extends to the ethics of the situation depicted here. The letter most directly raises questions about the ethics of surveillance. On the one hand, if members of Iota Eta Pi were in fact engaging in objectionable behavior, it seems important and perhaps even valuable that Wossamotta U identified and sanctioned these behaviors. Indeed, many universities have policies about what constitutes acceptable use of their

networking and internet resources. On the other hand, these policies often deal with bandwidth usage or illegal activities, with file sharing services being a prime example of both. Less often do these policies deal with the content of such communication. One could consider the question being raised in terms of a consequentialist means-end analysis [25]. That is, the piece implicitly asks the reader whether the goal of detecting and sanctioning conduct violations justifies the surveillance of individual students' communications with one another? Again, the intentional vagueness and ambiguity here – of the nature of Wossamotta U's policy, of Iota Eta Pi's conduct, of the mechanisms by which surveillance is conducted – make it even more difficult for the reader to determine what s/he would do in such a situation.

Concluding Remarks

Each of the above short fictions uses different strategies to highlight ethical issues. The curator's note intentionally avoids assessing the strengths or weaknesses of each piece, instead emphasizing the different kinds of ethical issues raised by each. Although they might not address the question individually, these pieces collectively point out some of the unique challenges particular to the ethics of computing.

First, one of the main difficulties comes from the displacement or translation of agency [28]. Many of the approaches to ethics described above assume that individuals are taking actions, based either on their duties or obligations [25,30,42,43], on the expected consequences [7,32], or on the individual's underlying virtues and vices [2]. When an action is performed by, say, Medi-Check, it is less clear that duty, consequences, or virtues are as relevant. The situation becomes even murkier with technologies such as Know Yourself or the SkyNet API. When technologies are created by one person or persons, then used by others (possibly in an unintended manner), whom do we interrogate?

Second, fairly blurry boundaries divide questions of ethics from those of politics and power [53]. In Letter of Disorderly Conduct, the issues have less to do with the specific implementation details of any one technology and more to do with the use of technology as an exercise of authority [21]. Similar questions are raised by the satirical EULA, both with respect to reasonable or expected consequences that might arise from making use of some technology and with respect to the designers' or implementers' ability to abdicate responsibility for those consequences.

Third, this paper offers design fiction as a means of engaging students in technically-oriented courses. The pieces presented here demonstrate students' ability to use this genre in novel and compelling ways. While this paper emphasizes ethical issues, the approach may be viable for highlighting other types of sociotechnical issues.

To be sure, there is a certain power to the presence of an actual artifact and to stories of what actual people actually did with it [51]. Design fiction provides just one of many potential formats for raising and debating ethical issues in computing. Each of these different formats has their own strengths and weaknesses in terms of working through the consequences of different kinds of underlying commitments and values [3,18]. While physical artifacts can leverage rich implementation details to afford multiple interpretations [46], they also require advanced design skill. Design fiction, then, may prove more accessible means for students, who may not yet have completed their technical training or have significant implementation experience, to consider how we think about and work through the ethics of computing.

Acknowledgments

Thanks to all the students enrolled in Lehigh's CSE 252 Computers, the Internet, and Society course during spring semester of 2017; and to the anonymous reviewers for constructive comments.

References

1. Julia Angwin, Jeff Larson, Surya Mattu, and Lauren Kirchner. 2016. Machine Bias. *Pro Publica*. Retrieved from https://www.propublica.org/article/machine-bias-risk-assessments-in-criminal-sentencing

2. Aristotle. 350AD. Nicomachean Ethics. In *The Internet Classics Archives*, D. C. Stevenson (ed.). Retrieved July 1, 2017 from http://classics.mit.edu/Aristotle/nicomachaen.html

3. Shaowen Bardzell. 2010. Feminist HCI: Taking Stock and Outlining an Agenda for Design. In *Proceedings of the ACM Conference on Human Factors in Computing Systems (CHI)*, 1301–1310.

4. Solon Barocas and Andrew D. Selbst. 2016. Big Data's Disparate Impact. *California Law Review 104*, 3: 671–732.

5. Eric P. S. Baumer, Phil Adams, Vera D. Khovanskaya, Tony C. Liao, Madeline E. Smith, Victoria Schwanda Sosik, and Kaiton Williams. 2013. Limiting, Leaving, and (Re)Lapsing: An Exploration of Facebook Non-use Practices and Experiences. In *Proceedings of the ACM Conference on Human Factors in Computing Systems (CHI)*, 3257–3266. https://doi.org/10.1145/2470654.2466446

6. Eric P. S. Baumer, June Ahn, Mei Bie, Elizabeth M. Bonsignore, Ahmet Börütecene, Oğuz Turan Buruk, Tamara Clegg, Allison Druin, Florian Echtler, Dan Gruen, Mona Leigh Guha, Chelsea Hordatt, Antonio Krüger, Shachar Maidenbaum, Meethu Malu, Brenna McNally, Michael Muller, Leyla Norooz, Juliet Norton, Oguzhan Ozcan, Donald J. Patterson, Andreas Riener, Steven I. Ross, Karen Rust, Johannes Schöning, M. Six Silberman, Bill Tomlinson, and Jason Yip. 2014. CHI

2039: Speculative Research Visions. In *Extended Abstracts of the ACM Conference on Human Factors in Computing Systems (CHI EA)*, 761–770. https://doi.org/10.1145/2559206.2578864

7. Jeremy Bentham. 1789. Introduction to the Principles of Morals and Legislation. In *The Works of Jeremy Bentham*, John Bowring (ed.). London.

8. Daniel Berdichevsky and Erik Neuenschwander. 1999. Toward an ethics of persuasive technology. *Communications of the ACM* 42, 5: 51–58.

9. Julian Bleecker. 2009. *Design Fiction: A Short Essay on Design, Science, Fact and Fiction*. Near Future Laboratory, Venice Beach, CA.

10. Mark Blythe. 2014. Research Through Design Fiction: Narrative in Real and Imaginary Abstracts. In *Proceedings of the ACM Conference on Human Factors in Computing Systems (CHI)*, 703–712. https://doi.org/10.1145/2556288.2557098

11. Mark Blythe. 2017. Research Fiction: Storytelling, Plot and Design. In *Proceedings of the ACM Conference on Human Factors in Computing Systems (CHI)*, 5400–5411. https://doi.org/10.1145/3025453.3026023

12. Mark Blythe and Enrique Encinas. 2016. The Co-ordinates of Design Fiction: Extrapolation, Irony, Ambiguity and Magic. In *Proceedings of the ACM Conference on Supporting Group Work (GROUP)*, 345–354. https://doi.org/10.1145/2957276.2957299

13. Wayne C. Booth. 1961. *The Rhetoric of Fiction*. University of Chicago Press, Chicago.

14. Bill Buxton. 2007. *Sketching User Experiences: Getting the Design Right and Getting the Right Design*. Morgan Kaufmann, San Francisco, CA.

15. Nigel Cross. 2006. *Designerly Ways of Knowing*. Springer-Verlag, London.

16. Paul Dourish and Genevieve Bell. 2014. "Resistance is futile": reading science fiction alongside ubiquitous computing. *Personal and Ubiquitous Computing* 18, 4: 769–778. https://doi.org/10.1007/s00779-013-0678-7

17. Steven P. Dow, Alana Glassco, Jonathan Kass, Melissa Schwarz, Daniel L. Schwartz, and Scott R. Klemmer. 2010. Parallel Prototyping Leads to Better Design Results, More Divergence, and Increased Self-efficacy. *ACM Transactions on Computer-Human Interaction* 17, 4: 18:1–18:24. https://doi.org/10.1145/1879831.1879836

18. Tony Dunne and Fiona Raby. 2001. *Design Noir: The Secret Life of Electronic Objects*. Birkhäuser, Berlin.

19. Martin Enserink and Gilbert Chin. 2015. The end of privacy. *Science* 347, 6221: 490–491. https://doi.org/10.1126/science.347.6221.490

20. BJ Fogg. 1998. Persuasive Computers: Perspectives and Research Directions. In *Proceedings of the ACM Conference on Human Factors in Computing Systems (CHI)*, 225–232. https://doi.org/10.1145/274644.274677

21. Michel Foucault. 1977. *Discipline and Punish: The Birth of the Prison*. Vintage Books.

22. Ellie Harmon and Melissa Mazmanian. 2013. Stories of the Smartphone in Everyday Discourse: Conflict, Tension & Instability. In *Proceedings of the ACM Conference on Human Factors in Computing Systems (CHI)*, 1051–1060. https://doi.org/10.1145/2470654.2466134

23. Donna J. Harraway. 2013. SF: Science Fiction, Speculative Fabulation, String Figures, So Far. *Ada: A Journal of Gender, New Media, and Technology*, 3. Retrieved October 26, 2017 from http://adanewmedia.org/2013/11/issue3-haraway/

24. Alison M. Jaggar. 1983. *Feminist Politics and Human Nature*. Allenheld, Totowa, NJ.

25. Immanuel Kant. 1985. *Grounding for the Metaphysics of Morals*. Hackett Publishing Company, Indianapolis.

26. Ben Kirman, Conor Linehan, Shaun Lawson, and Dan O'Hara. 2013. CHI and the future robot enslavement of humankind: a retrospective. In *Extended Ab-*

stracts of the ACM Conference on Human Factors in Computing Systems (CHI EA) (alti.chi), 2199–2208.

27. Michal Kosinski, David Stillwell, and Thore Graepel. 2013. Private traits and attributes are predictable from digital records of human behavior. *Proceedings of the National Academy of Sciences* 110, 15: 5802–5805. https://doi.org/10.1073/pnas.1218772110

28. Bruno Latour. 1992. Where Are the Missing Masses? The Sociology of a Few Mundane Artifacts. In *Shaping Technology / Building Society: Studies in Sociotechnical Change*, Wiebe E. Bijker and John Law (eds.). MIT Press, Cambridge, MA, 225–258.

29. Conor Linehan, Ben J. Kirman, Stuart Reeves, Mark A. Blythe, Joshua G. Tanenbaum, Audrey Desjardins, and Ron Wakkary. 2014. Alternate Endings: Using Fiction to Explore Design Futures. In *Extended Abstracts of the ACM Conference on Human Factors in Computing Systems (CHI EA)*, 45–48. https://doi.org/10.1145/2559206.2560472

30. John Locke. *Two Treatises.* Cambridge University Press, Cambridge.

31. Aleecia M. McDonald and Lorrie Faith Cranor. 2008. The Cost of Reading Privacy Policies 2008 Privacy Year in Review. *I/S: A Journal of Law and Policy for the Information Society* 4: 543–568.

32. John Stuart Mill. 1991. Utilitarianism. In *Collected Works of John Stuart Mill*, J. M. Robson (ed.). Routledge, London.

33. Alondra Nelson. 2002. *Afrofuturism.* Duke University Press, Durham, NC.

34. Helen Nissenbaum. 2011. A Contextual Approach to Privacy Online. *Daedalus* 140, 4: 32–48. https://doi.org/10.1162/DAED_a_00113

35. Jonathan A. Obar and Anne Oeldorf-Hirsch. 2016. The Biggest Lie on the Internet: Ignoring the Privacy Policies and Terms of Service Policies of Social Networking Services. In *The Research Conference on*

Communications, Information, and Internet Policy (TPRC). https://doi.org/10.2139/ssrn.2757465

36. Leysia Palen and Paul Dourish. 2003. Unpacking "privacy" for a networked world. In *Proceedings of the ACM Conference on Human Factors in Computing Systems (CHI)*, 129–136. https://doi.org/10.1145/642633.642635

37. Eva Palmer. 2015. Eight Greek life chapters sanctioned for conduct violations. *The GW Hatchet.* Retrieved July 1, 2017 from https://www.gwhatchet.com/2015/09/04/eight-greek-life-chapters-sanctioned-for-conduct-violations/

38. Eli Pariser. 2011. *The Filter Bubble: What the Internet Is Hiding from You.* Penguin Press, New York.

39. Birgit Penzenstadler, Bill Tomlinson, Eric Baumer, Marcel Pufal, Ankita Raturi, Debra Richardson, Baki Cakici, Ruzanna Chitchyan, Georges Da Costa, Lynn Dombrowski, Malin Picha Edwardsson, Elina Eriksson, Xavier Franch, Gillian R. Hayes, Christina Herzog, Wolfgang Lohmann, Martin Mahaux, Alistair Mavin, Melissa Mazmanian, Sahand Nayebaziz, Juliet Norton, Daniel Pargman, Donald J. Patterson, Jean-Marc Pierson, Kristin Roher, M. Six Silberman, Kevin Simonson, Andrew W. Torrance, and André van der Hoek. 2014. ICT4S 2029: What Will Be The Systems Supporting Sustainability in 15 Years. *Proceedings of the 2014 conference ICT for Sustainability* 2, 10.2991/ict4s-14.2014.4: 30–39.

40. Trevor J. Pinch and Wiebe E. Bijker. 1987. The Social Construction of Facts and Artifacts. In *The Social Construction of Technological Systems*, Wiebe E. Bijker, Thomas P. Hughes and Trevor J. Pinch (eds.). MIT Press, Cambridge, MA, 17–50.

41. Laura Portwood-Stacer. 2013. Media refusal and conspicuous non-consumption: The performative and political dimensions of Facebook abstention. *New Media & Society* 15, 7: 1041–1057. https://doi.org/10.1177/1461444812465139

42. Samuel Pufendorf. 1672. *De Jure Naturae et Gentium (Of the Law of Nature and Nations)*. London.

43. Samuel Pufendorf. 1673. *De Officio Hominis et Civis Juxta Legem Naturalem (The Whole Duty of Man According to the Law of Nature)*. London.

44. Stephen Purpura, Victoria Schwanda, Kaiton Williams, William Stubler, and Phoebe Sengers. 2011. Fit4Life: The Design of a Persuasive Technology Promoting Healthy Behavior and Ideal Weight. In *Proceedings of the ACM Conference on Human Factors in Computing Systems (CHI)*, 423–432. https://doi.org/10.1145/1978942.1979003

45. Jed Rubenfeld. 2008. The End of Privacy. *Stanford Law Review* 61, 1: 101–161.

46. Phoebe Sengers and Bill Gaver. 2006. Staying Open to Interpretation: Engaging Multiple Meanings in Design and Evaluation. In *Proceedings of the ACM Conference on Designing Interactive Systems (DIS)*, 99–108.

47. Irina Shklovski, Janet Vertesi, Emily Troshynski, and Paul Dourish. 2009. The Commodification of Location: Dynamics of Power in Location-Based Systems. In *Proceedings of the International Conference on Ubiquitous Computing (Ubicomp)*, 11–20. https://doi.org/10.1145/1620545.1620548

48. M. Six Silberman. 2016. Reading Elinor Ostrom In Silicon Valley: Exploring Institutional Diversity on the Internet. In *Proceedings of the ACM Conference on Supporting Group Work (GROUP)*, 363–368. https://doi.org/10.1145/2957276.2957311

49. Bruce Sterling. 2011. Maneki Neko. *Lightspeed*, 11.

50. Latanya Sweeney. 2013. Discrimination in online ad delivery. *Communications of the ACM* 56, 5: 44–54. https://doi.org/10.1145/2460276.2460278

51. Ron Wakkary, William Odom, Sabrina Hauser, Garnet Hertz, and Henry Lin. 2015. Material Speculation: Actual Artifacts for Critical Inquiry. In *Decennial Aarhus Conference on Critical Alternatives*. https://doi.org/10.7146/aahcc.v1i1.21299

52. Reg Whitaker. 1999. *The End of Privacy: How Total Surveillance Is Becoming a Reality*. The New Press, New York.

53. Langdon Winner. 1980. Do Artifacts Have Politics? *Daedalus* 109, 1: 121–136.

54. Ytasha L. Womack. 2012. Afrofuturism: An Aesthetic and Exploration of Identity. *Institute for Ethics and Emerging Technologies: Ethical Technology*. Retrieved October 26, 2017 from https://ieet.org/index.php/IEET2/more/womack201201 04

55. Wu Youyou, Michal Kosinski, and David Stillwell. 2015. Computer-based personality judgments are more accurate than those made by humans. *Proceedings of the National Academy of Sciences* 112, 4: 1036–1040. https://doi.org/10.1073/pnas.1418680112

LiveDissent: A Media Platform for Remote Participation in Activist Demonstrations

William A. Hamilton
Interface Ecology Lab
Texas A&M University
College Station, TX, USA
bill@ecologylab.net

Andruid Kerne
Interface Ecology Lab
Texas A&M University
College Station, TX, USA
andruid@ecologylab.net

Nic Lupfer
Interface Ecology Lab
Texas A&M University
College Station, TX, USA
nic@ecologylab.net

Abstract

Social media platforms such as Twitter and Facebook have become a critical tools for the coordination of activist movements and demonstrations. Additionally, live streaming platforms like Periscope have started to emerge as modalities for reporting on and remotely experiencing activist activities. In this design fiction, we present LiveDissent, a fictional media platform that leverages both established and emerging technologies to support remote participation in activist demonstrations. These technologies include mobile live streaming, telepresence robots, unmanned aerial vehicles, and digitally augmented picket signs. LiveDissent brings these technologies together into an aggregated platform for remotely watching and participating in demonstrations. We discuss a planned in the wild study at an upcoming demonstration, through which we will explore the design and implications of social media and telepresence for participation in activism. Finally, our authors' statement connects to related prior work and explores potential research and ethics questions.

Author Keywords

activism; telepresence; mobile live streaming; social media

ACM Classification Keywords

H.5.m [Information interfaces and presentation (e.g., HCI)]: Miscellaneous

GROUP '18,, January 7–10, 2018, Sanibel Island, FL, USA
ACM 978-1-4503-5562-9/18/01.
https://doi.org/10.1145/3148330.3149406

Figure 1: Drone footage of police using water cannons on protesters during freezing weather conditions. The video was captured by activists using private drones during the North Dakota Access Pipeline demonstrations. Credit: Myron Dewey MA, Digital Smoke Signals, Professor/Drone Pilot/Filmmaker

Introduction

The means of activism and political participation are changing. Over the past decade, we have seen social media platforms such as Twitter and Facebook emerge as critical tools for the organization, reporting, and experiencing of activist movements and demonstrations [16, 4, 19, 20, 9]. Similarly, during the past two years, mobile live streaming has been widely adopted as a means for activists to broadcast demonstrations in real time to remote participants [3, 14]. Beyond just sharing these experiences, live streaming has proven to be a effective tool for spreading awareness of issues, promoting the accountability of authorities, and providing a means for remote participants to engage in activist experiences they wouldn't otherwise be able to. In this work, we explore research questions regarding supporting activism with the next generation of media technologies.

For example, one emerging technology that is already significantly impacting activism in practice is unmanned aerial vehicles (UAVs) or drones. UAVs have been a tool commonly used by law enforcement agencies and the military for foreign and domestic surveillance [17]. However, in recent protests, there have been reports of increasing numbers of private drones equipped with streaming video capabilities. The drones have seemingly been owned and operated by local activists to capture aerial footage of authorities and help document police and activist activities (Figure 1) [5]. In some cases, authorities have employed counter measures such as shotguns [15] and surface to air missile defense systems [1] against activist drone activity.

In addition to aerial drones, we imagine the potential impact of other emerging technologies at demonstrations. For example, telepresence robots, such as the Beam Pro [7], could be used to proxy for remote activists potentially hundreds of miles away. Other technologies like pico projector

[18] powered picket signs could be dynamically configured to show images or video created by online participants (Figure 2). These kinds of technologies stand to give remote participants new opportunities to participate in activism and affect social and political change.

The emergence of these technologies and phenomena have stimulated us to address new research questions including: 1) How do emerging media and telepresence technologies enhance participation in demonstrations for both in-person and online actors? 2) How do we support coordinating participation around and through these technologies? 3) What are the effects, consequences, and safety concerns of telepresence technologies such as UAVs and robots at activist demonstrations? 4) What are the rights and responsibilities of local and remote participants, device owners, and the authorities during telepresence augmented activist demonstrations?

To explore these questions, we are designing LiveDissent, a media platform for supporting enhanced local and remote participation in activist demonstrations. In the following sections, we present the design of a LiveDissent prototype. Subsequently, we propose an explorative fictional field study to investigate the above research questions through deployment of a LiveDissent prototype at a demonstration.

LiveDissent Prototype

We have designed LiveDissent as a fictional media platform to support participation in political and social demonstrations by remote and on-the-ground activists. The LiveDissent prototype would be implemented as an online, desktop and mobile platform for organizing, coordinating, and participating in activist demonstrations through live streaming media and telepresence technologies. The LiveDissent research prototype incorporates a fleet of digital picket signs, video streaming capable UAVs, and telepresence robots which are made available to participants during active demonstrations. To support remote participation, the prototype provides democratic mechanisms for remote activists to access and use these devices at demonstrations. In the following sections, we present and motivate the design of each LiveDissent modality.

Mobile Live Streaming

Similar to Periscope and Facebook Live, the LiveDissent mobile app allows users to upload live video streams to a web platform. Each live stream will be tagged as belonging to a specific event, enabling remote participants to browse streams by event. Each stream will also incorporates real time text chat, which remote participants can use to communicate with each other and local participants.

Additionally, live streamers can choose to provide their GPS location and camera orientation. This will enable present-

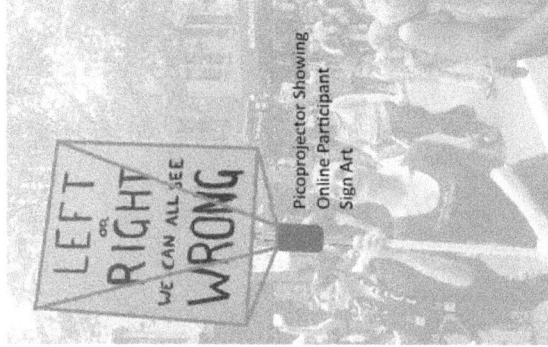

Figure 2: Digital picket signs use pico projectors to display remote participant submitted art on protest signs. Original Credit: 99% Australia

ing ongoing live streams on top of a map of the event, in order to provide awareness of available camera perspectives and overall coverage. Remote viewers are then able to use the real-time map to help coordinate positioning of on-the-ground streamers, to ensure that important angles are covered.

Digital Picket Signs

The LiveDissent prototype also supports the use of digital picket signs. A digital picket sign will incorporate a lightweight pico projector, attached to the handle of a blank picket sign. The projector is then used to display custom images and video on the sign (Figure 2). This pico projector is driven by a Raspberry Pi with a cellular data connection, which polls the LiveDissent web service for a set of images and videos to display. The sign will then cycle through the submitted content as the on-the-ground activist carrying the sign participates in the demonstration.

We want the digital picket signs to serve as a highly visible means for remote participants to have impact at demonstrations. To that end, remote and on-the-ground users can submit their sign designs as images or short animated gifs using the LiveDissent web and mobile apps. This content is then downloaded and displayed by the on-the-ground picket signs.

Participant submitted sign content for each event will be posted to an online sign board (Figure 3). This sign board is similar in function to the social media site Reddit, with activists being able to up and down vote sign content that they think supports the cause. Signs with a higher vote count will subsequently be shown with more frequency on digital picket signs at the demonstration. We hypothesize that by being able to vote on sign media sources, participants will be able to collaboratively moderate their content. Creative and appropriate signs will be voted to the top, while

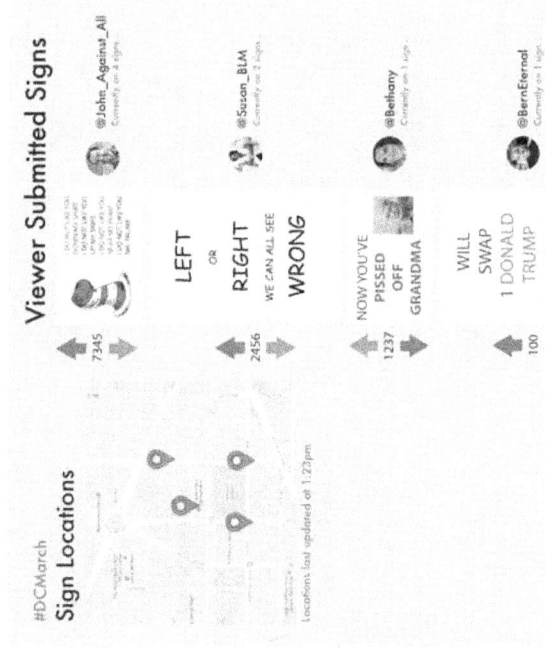

Figure 3: The sign board enables participants to vote on participant submitted sign content and see current digital picket sign locations. The map shows the current locations of the active digital picket signs for the #DCMarch in progress. On the right is a list of the current top sign images along with the user who submitted them.

counter-productive signs will down voted and not shown on picket signs. The digital picket sign also have a veto button on the handle, giving the on-the-ground sign carriers an option to not show sign messages they find inappropriate to the demonstration or which they personally do not wish to represent.

Unmanned Aerial Vehicles

A fleet of UAVs will be made available to activists to provide aerial video streams of demonstrations. While operating, UAV camera video is streamed to the LiveDissent platform, where it will be presented in coordination with other on-the-ground live streams. Aerial video will help provide more coverage of a demonstration and promote the accountability of authorities.

The LiveDissent prototype supports two methods for controlling UAVs during demonstrations. First, UAVs can be checked out by a specific participant, who can then directly control their location and camera angle. Alternatively, UAVs can be shared among a collection of participants, who then democratically control the UAV through a voting system. Users are able to vote on specific locations using a map interface of the demonstration area. The system then directs the UAV to fly to the specified location and pan the camera over the surrounding area.

To promote the safe operation of UAVs and compliance with Federal Aviation Administration (FAA) regulations, we design the LiveDissent UAV control system to provide a few initial safety measures. First, drones utilized by LiveDissent will be equipped with real time collision avoidance capabilities, so that they are not accidentally or maliciously driven into participants, bystanders, officers, vehicles, buildings, or other obstacles on the ground. The UAV control system will also enforces a minimum and maximum flight height to ensure the safety of participants on the ground, as well

as other aircraft in the area. The system independently manages drone take off and landing procedures at designated landing zones. UAVs low on power are no longer controlled by LiveDissent participants; they will be automatically guided to landing zones to prevent crashes or drone failures in unsafe areas.

Figure 4: A remote activist confronts police via a LiveDissent telepresence robot. Original Credit: AP Photo/Max Becherer

Telepresence Robots

In addition to UAVs, LiveDissent provides a fleet of telepresence robots which are available on location for planned demonstrations. These robots are available for use by remote participants through the LiveDissent web app. During the demonstration, remote participants can control the robot's position and orientation. They can then use their webcam to engage with local activists and participate in the demonstration (Figure 4). This not only enables remote participants to interact with activists as if they were actually at the demonstration. It further allows local activists to see and feel the support of people from all over the world, who support the same cause. If there are no available devices, remote participants will be placed into a waiting queue until the next device becomes available.

Telepresence robots will have their activity automatically streamed to the LiveDissent web app. This includes the live audio and video of the operator, the live audio and video captured from the robot, and its location and orientation. Other remote viewers are able to watch along as the operator interacts with activists on the ground. To prevent any one user from dominating a telepresence robot, a maximum time is enforced for robot operators. Additionally, to support democratic moderation, online viewers are able to vote to extend the time of or kick the current operator.

Similar to the UAVs, LiveDissent telepresence robots implement some safety and quality measures. The robots have a maximum speed to prevent them from being used as ramming devices or in other potentially harmful ways. When low on power, they automatically return to a designated charging location. In the event that a robot is incapacitated, a LiveDissent volunteer is alerted of its location so they can either fix the issue or return the robot to the designated retrieval location.

Online Coordination Platform

The LiveDissent online platform will serve as an aggregation point for viewing and participating remotely in activist demonstrations. Each of the modalities—including mobile live streams, digital protest signs, UAV footage, and telepresence robots—will be aggregated, coordinated, and presented together through the LiveDissent web interface. A coordinating map interface will show the location, orientation, and status of each the devices active around a particular demonstration. From here, participants can focus on particular streams, or select multiple streams to watch together, to experience the demonstration from multiple concurrent views (Figure 5).

Additionally, LiveDissent will provide both demonstration-wide and stream-specific chat channels for participants to communicate through. These channels are accessible to both local and remote participants, using the web and mobile apps respectively. Participants can post text, images, links, and videos to these channels to communicate with participants in the demonstration at large or with the specific audiences of each video stream.

By viewing the map for a demonstration, remote participants will be able to maintain a different kind of awareness not available to those on the ground. Remote participants will have easier access to other information sources around the demonstration, such as news outlets and social media. Remote participants will then be able to use this awareness to help alert those at the event of significant events and issues that spontaneously emerge. We hypothesize that this kind of crowdsourced coordination will serve as a rewarding participatory experience for remote activists, leading to more informed, effective, and safer demonstration efforts.

We note here that remotely participating in demonstration via the LiveDissent prototype will be open to the public. All participants will be able to vote in the democratic mechanisms available for participating via digital picket signs, UAVs, and telepresence robots. However, privileges such as user timeouts and banning will be provided for demonstration organizers so that they are able to moderate behavior undermining the cause.

Proposed Field Study

To observe emergent use of the LiveDissent prototype in a situated demonstration context, we will be conducting an in the wild deployment at the upcoming March for Universal

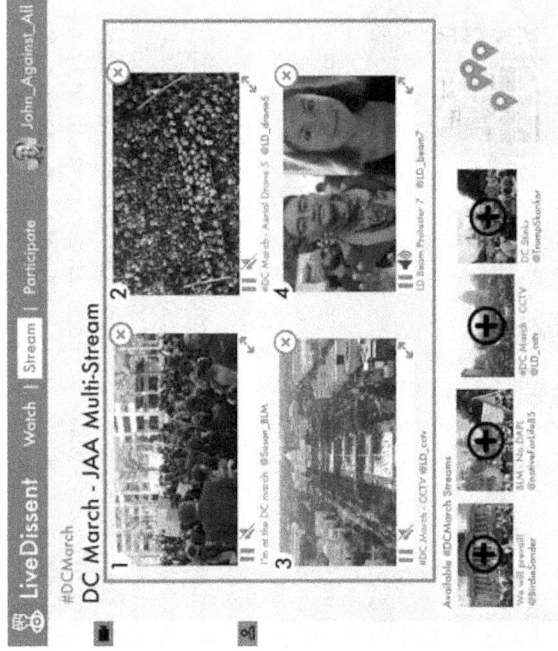

Figure 5: The LiveDissent multi-stream view enables participants to watch multiple mobile live mobile streams, aerial drone video streams, and telepresence robot streams simultaneously. Participants are also presented with a map showing the real time locations of stream sources.

Health Care in Washington, DC. Researchers will be on the ground at the demonstration observing as well as distributing and maintaining devices. During the march, we will be deploying 20 digital picket signs, 3 UAVs and 5 telepresence robots for use by local and remote participants.

The LiveDissent research team has been communicating with the demonstration organizers to coordinate the locations of UAV launching zones and robot recharging stations. We are also enlisting the help of demonstration organizers to help distribute, observe the use of, and secure prototype devices throughout the event. We have received the planned route for the march. Using this data, we have pre-programmed flight path boundaries for the UAVs as to avoid restricted no-fly-zones and to keep them within a set radius of the planned route. Similar demonstration specific boundaries have also been developed for telepresence robots.

To recruit participants, demonstration organizers have been advertising the availability of the LiveDissent prototype as part of their campaigning. To attract remote participants, we will be posting march specific links to the LiveDissent web app on social media just prior to the start of the march and will continue to do so until the march is over.

During the deployment all video streams will be recorded. The interactions of remote participants through the mobile and web LiveDissent app will also be anonymously logged for later analysis.

After the demonstration is over, we will be contacting those who participated with LiveDissent for follow-up interviews about their experiences. These participants will include local demonstrators who held digital picket signs, produced mobile live streams, and interacted with telepresence robots. Additionally, we will contact remote demonstrators who manned the telepresence robots, submitted content for the picket signs, communicated in global or stream-specific chats, and participated controlling LiveDissent UAVs. Through these semi-structured interviews we aim to elicit qualitative data regarding users' experiences as they relate to our research questions.

Authors' Statement

We present the fictional LiveDissent research prototype to evoke a discussion of new forms of participation in political activism. In recent months and years, we have seen increasing occurrences of activist demonstrations, in the

United States and elsewhere, involving political and social movements, such as Black Lives Matter, Arab Spring, Occupy Wall Street, the Dakota Access Pipeline, and the Anti-Trump Resistance. It is clear that social media forms play an increasingly important role in the organization, reporting, and experiencing of activist movements and demonstrations [16, 4, 19, 20, 9].

Beyond Twitter and Facebook, mobile live streaming via apps like Facebook Live and Periscope have recently emerged as means for sharing and reporting on activist activities [3, 14]. While Dougherty explored the production of mobile live streaming as a form of civic engagement [2], more research is required to investigate emerging mobile live streaming practice at activist events. Further, recent research has found that the aggregation of multiple live media streams together around events can lead to increased opportunities for participation and engagement [6]. However, there are additional potential implications for the design of live social media channel aggregation, in situated activist contexts, such as protests.

There are many open questions involving the design of social media and live-streaming to support activism. For example, we imagine that emerging technologies—such as telepresence robots and UAVs—have the potential to further impact political activism in practice. One obvious change is that telepresence technologies afford new capabilities for remote participants' embodied presence.

Significant prior research has investigated the use of telepresence technology at work [10, 12], in health care applications [11, 10], and at academic conferences [13]. Recent work is also starting to explore the use of drones for collaboration and sharing experiences [8]. However, there is less work investigating use of telepresence devices in the wild, at emotionally charged events such as political protests.

What are the potential implications of participating in activist experiences through these types of technologies? Does participation become more meaningful, rewarding, and impactful for remote and on-the-ground participants? We hypothesize that, yes, it would, but the specific implications for individuals and activist movements as a whole are unclear.

When these new forms of remote participation become more available, we imagine a plethora of emergent research questions, concerning how we should design computational tools and media to support activists.

- How will it be decided who gets to participate and how?

  - First come first serve?
  - Pay to participate?
  - Crowd voting?
  - Should people be allowed to remotely participate in demonstrations in other countries? Is it even possible to prevent this?

- What are the benefits and dangers of centralized aggregations of activist media and communication? Publicizing the identities and locations of activists may directly pose a threat to their privacy and safety. Additionally, centralizing activist communication channels and media may make it easier to disrupt their activities and ultimately undermine their efforts.

- Are there gate keepers to activist media and telepresence tools? And if there are, who are they?

  - Protest organizers?
  - Government agencies?
  - Private media platform owners?

- How do we support the organization and acquisition of these kinds of resources? While technologies like UAVs and pico projectors are becoming more affordable, they still cost hundreds of dollars. Meanwhile, telepresence robots cost thousands of dollars. All of these technologies also require some technical expertise to setup and safely use.

- Is it dangerous to enable humans to control UAVs or telepresence robots at political demonstrations?

  - Will remote activists operate devices responsibly, given their physical removal from the situation?
  - What are the risks of malicious actors hijacking devices and attempting to instigate violence?
  - What safe guards should be in place to protect local activists and authorities?

- New forms of participation in political activism will not be able to address all peoples or needs equally. As researchers, how should we prioritize our objectives?

In this work, we presented the potential design and evaluation of the LiveDissent media platform to explore new ways of supporting remote and local participation in activism. The fictional prototype describes how new technologies can be integrated to create new experiences around activism and raises questions about this research area, many being ethical in nature. Ultimately, it is still unclear if these technologies and the experiences they afford will impact and empower activist movements in a positive and safe way.

REFERENCES

1. David Axe. 2017. National Guard Deploys Missile Launchers to Dakota Access Pipeline to 'Observe'

Protestors. (17 January 2017).
http://www.thedailybeast.com/national-guard-deploys-missile-launchers-to-dakota-access-pipeline-to-observe-protestors [Accessed: 1 July 2017].

2. Audubon Dougherty. 2011. Live-streaming Mobile Video: Production As Civic Engagement. In *Proceedings of the 13th International Conference on Human Computer Interaction with Mobile Devices and Services (MobileHCI '11)*. ACM, New York, NY, USA, 425–434. DOI: http://dx.doi.org/10.1145/2037373.2037437

3. Emily Dreyfuss. 2016. As Standing Rock Protesters Face Down Armored Trucks, The World Watches on Facebook. (27 October 2016). https://www.wired.com/2016/10/standing-rock-protesters-face-police-world-watches-facebook/ [Accessed: 1 July 2017].

4. Jennifer Earl, Heather McKee Hurwitz, Analicia Mejia Mesinas, Margaret Tolan, and Ashley Arlotti. 2013. This protest will be tweeted: Twitter and protest policing during the Pittsburgh G20. *Information, Communication & Society* 16, 4 (2013), 459–478.

5. April Glaser. 2016. The FAA banned drones from flying at the Standing Rock oil pipeline protest. (28 November 2016). https://www.recode.net/2016/11/28/13767216/faa-bans-drones-standing-rock-dakota-access-pipeline-video [Accessed: 1 July 2017].

6. William A. Hamilton, John Tang, Gina Venolia, Kori Inkpen, Jakob Zillner, and Derek Huang. 2016. Rivulet: Exploring Participation in Live Events Through Multi-Stream Experiences. In *Proceedings of the ACM International Conference on Interactive Experiences for TV and Online Video (TVX '16)*. ACM, New York, NY, USA, 31–42. DOI: http://dx.doi.org/10.1145/2932206.2932211

7. Suitable Technologies Inc. 2017. Beam Pro Telepresence Robot. (2017). https://www.suitabletech.com/products/beam-pro [Accessed: 3 July 2017].

8. Brennan Jones, Kody Dillman, Richard Tang, Anthony Tang, Ehud Sharlin, Lora Oehlberg, Carman Neustaedter, and Scott Bateman. 2016. Elevating Communication, Collaboration, and Shared Experiences in Mobile Video Through Drones. In *Proceedings of the 2016 ACM Conference on Designing Interactive Systems (DIS '16)*. ACM, New York, NY, USA, 1123–1135. DOI: http://dx.doi.org/10.1145/2901790.2901847

9. Andrea Kavanaugh, Steven D. Sheetz, Hamida Skandrani, John C. Tedesco, Yue Sun, and Edward A. Fox. 2016. The Use and Impact of Social Media During the 2011 Tunisian Revolution. In *Proceedings of the 17th International Digital Government Research Conference on Digital Government Research (dg.o '16)*. ACM, New York, NY, USA, 20–30. DOI: http://dx.doi.org/10.1145/2912160.2912175

10. Annica Kristoffersson, Silvia Coradeschi, and Amy Loutfi. 2013. A Review of Mobile Robotic Telepresence. *Adv. in Hum.-Comp. Int.* 2013, Article 3 (Jan. 2013), 1 pages. DOI: http://dx.doi.org/10.1155/2013/902316

11. Annica Kristoffersson, Silvia Coradeschi, Amy Loutfi, and Kerstin Severinson-Eklundh. 2011. An Exploratory Study of Health Professionals' attitudes about robotic telepresence technology. *Journal of Technology in Human Services* 29, 4 (2011), 263–283.

12. Min Kyung Lee and Leila Takayama. 2011. "Now, I Have a Body": Uses and Social Norms for Mobile Remote Presence in the Workplace. In *Proceedings of the SIGCHI Conference on Human Factors in Computing Systems (CHI '11)*. ACM, New York, NY, USA, 33–42. DOI: http://dx.doi.org/10.1145/1978942.1978950

13. Carman Neustaedter, Gina Venolia, Jason Procyk, and Daniel Hawkins. 2016. To Beam or Not to Beam: A Study of Remote Telepresence Attendance at an Academic Conference. In *Proceedings of the 19th ACM Conference on Computer-Supported Cooperative Work & Social Computing (CSCW '16)*. ACM, New York, NY, USA, 418–431. DOI: http://dx.doi.org/10.1145/2818048.2819922

14. Tess Owen. 2016. DeRay McKesson live-streamed his arrest during a Black Lives Matter protest in Baton Rouge. (10 July 2016). https://news.vice.com/article/deray-mckesson-live-streamed-his-arrest-during-a-blacklivesmatter-protest-in-baton-rouge [Accessed: 1 July 2017].

15. Lauren Sigfusson. 2016. Drone Pilot and FAA Comment on Drone Shooting at North Dakota Pipeline Protest. (5 December 2016). http://drone360mag.com/news-notes/2016/10/drone-pilot-and-faa-comment-on-drone-shooting-at-north-dakota-pipeline-protest [Accessed: 1 July 2017].

16. Kate Starbird and Leysia Palen. 2012. (How) Will the Revolution Be Retweeted?: Information Diffusion and the 2011 Egyptian Uprising. In *Proceedings of the ACM 2012 Conference on Computer Supported Cooperative Work (CSCW '12)*. ACM, New York, NY, USA, 7–16. DOI: http://dx.doi.org/10.1145/2145204.2145212

17. Tyler Wall and Torin Monahan. 2011. Surveillance and violence from afar: The politics of drones and liminal security-scapes. *Theoretical Criminology* 15, 3 (2011), 239–254.

18. Max L. Wilson, Dan Craggs, Simon Robinson, Matt Jones, and Kristian Brimble. 2012. Pico-ing into the Future of Mobile Projection and Contexts. *Personal Ubiquitous Comput.* 16, 1 (Jan. 2012), 39–52. DOI: http://dx.doi.org/10.1007/s00779-011-0376-2

19. Volker Wulf, Konstantin Aal, Ibrahim Abu Kteish, Meryem Atam, Kai Schubert, Markus Rohde, George P. Yerousis, and David Randall. 2013a. Fighting Against the Wall: Social Media Use by Political Activists in a Palestinian Village. In *Proceedings of the SIGCHI Conference on Human Factors in Computing Systems (CHI '13)*. ACM, New York, NY, USA, 1979–1988. DOI: http://dx.doi.org/10.1145/2470654.2466262

20. Volker Wulf, Kaoru Misaki, Meryem Atam, David Randall, and Markus Rohde. 2013b. 'On the Ground' in Sidi Bouzid: Investigating Social Media Use During the Tunisian Revolution. In *Proceedings of the 2013 Conference on Computer Supported Cooperative Work (CSCW '13)*. ACM, New York, NY, USA, 1409–1418. DOI: http://dx.doi.org/10.1145/2441776.2441935

Ad Empathy: A Design Fiction

Michael Skirpan
University of Colorado Boulder
Boulder, CO
michael.skirpan@colorado.edu

Casey Fiesler
University of Colorado Boulder
Boulder, CO
casey.fiesler@colorado.edu

Abstract

Industry demand for novel forms of personalization and audience targeting, paired with research trends in affective computing and emotion detection, puts us on a clear path toward emotion-sensitive technologies. Written as API documentation for an AI marketing solution that provides "emotion-sensitive marketing decisions," this design fiction presents one possible future application of today's research. Offering a demonstrable grey area in technology ethics, Ad Empathy should help to ground debates around fair use of data, and the boundaries of ethical design.

Author Keywords

advertising; API; design fiction; emotion; ethics; social computing; speculative fiction; neural networks; machine learning; target marketing

ACM Classification Keywords

H.5.m. Information interfaces and presentation (e.g., HCI): Miscellaneous

Product Introduction

Today's competitive attention economy requires brands to reach customers in personal and affective ways. Years of research and experience establish that personalization is effective for ad targeting and affecting user and consumer attitudes [20]. However, personalization is also a saturated approach. The relative ease of obtaining consumer preference data makes it common for online advertisers to know *what* a customer wants. Companies wanting the competitive edge now need to know *when* a product is best advertised and *how* it should be framed. Knowing this demand, we are happy to launch Ad Empathy, an AI marketing solution supporting brands to make emotion-sensitive marketing decisions.

Our API Resources are designed to help our clients generate content for ad impressions, catering to the dynamic needs of the diverse individuals in their audience. We work with most major social media platforms and search engines to create connected profiles of customers that can be accessed from any ad client via the Ad Empathy API. For each advertising platform you would like to integrate with Ad Empathy, simply add your company's registered OAuth tokens using the Ad Empathy Dashboard and within 48 hours we will have trained models for each of your customers and customer types. From that point onward, you can use the Ad Empathy API to design your ad and impressions on any connected platform. To use Ad Empathy as a full-cycle marketing platform, you may also register your product inventory with our platform to track emotional responses to product-specific brand interactions and improve our models.

Getting Started

Before making any requests using our models, you should contact a member of our Sales Team to discuss pricing options or obtain a free trial. All API Resource requests must contain a valid token pair <client-token> and <client-secret>, a <cookie-id> for the user, and optionally a <platform-id> to specify the ad client platform. Developers building platform-agnostic services can use our Accounts API to obtain valid <cookie-id>'s for building cross-platform ad campaigns and event triggers.

API Resources

Once you have obtained valid token pairs, integrated your external ad platform's tokens, and see the green check mark at the top corner of your Ad Sense Dashboard, you can begin using any API Resource.

MOOD

get - *GET* /mood/now/<cookie-id>

Returns current emotional state (mood) of user as a list of top ten moods by confidence

list - GET /mood/list/*<cookie-id>*

Returns a list of frequencies for all moods categories that Ad Empathy has related to the specified user.

MOOD.PRODUCT

list - *GET* /mood/product/<product-id>/<cookie-id>

Returns a list of product IDs and the mood that is most positively associated with a customer interaction.

MOOD.TOPIC

list - *GET* /mood/topic/<cookie-id>

Returns a list of content topics and our highest confidence mood association for that topic.

TREND

get - GET /trend/now/<cookie-id>

Returns the predicted emotional states, ordered by confidence, for upcoming 30-minute time interval.

list - GET /trend/daily/*<cookie-id>*

Returns a list of 30-minute time intervals over 24-hours with the most common emotional state associated to each interval.

RESPONSE

get - GET /response/<product-id>/<cookie-id>

Returns the user's last cached online emotional response to an interaction with <product-id>. (API Resource available only to customers using Ad Empathy Trackers for their product inventory)

EXPRESSION.TEXT

get - GET /expression/single/<emotion>/*<cookie-id>*

Returns the syntax tokens most commonly associated with the user's online expression of the emotion.

list - GET /expression/all/<cookie-id>

Returns a paginated list of emotional states, sorted by their frequency, and the most common syntax tokens associated to that state.

How Does It Work?

Ad Empathy is a state-of-the-art multi-model AI ecosystem that leverages the volume and velocity of online behavioral data by training user-specific machine learning models. The core of the system is a Long Short Term Memory (LSTM) neural network trained specifically to predict the evolution of moods using temporally-structured data coming from online activities (e.g., text from posts, click content, reactions to others' posts). Our company began training this model nearly five years ago when researchers first found Gated Recurrent Units as a solution to cutting through the noise of online data [15]. After years of fine-tuning and learning how to transfer models between different users and incorporate multi-modal data, we found we had sown the seeds of something much bigger than a mood prediction model. In short, this core model became the heart of a system of interacting models. Developing our expertise in model transfer allowed our team to take layers of our novel LSTM model and combine them with convolutional layers or other Recurrent, language-processing layers, and train them as Generative Adversarial Networks to blossom the wide functionality of novel content creation you see today.

When your company opens an account with Ad Empathy, our system begins by data mining all social media

content and brand interactions available for your customer base. After mining all historical data about your customers, we place their user accounts into our reactive event loop that keeps tabs on new activities across any connected platform. Prior to training, we run all the data through a noise reduction network trained specifically to identify relevant emotional content. Using the filtered data set, we fork fresh versions of our base model and begin training a unique mood model for each of your customers. This training continues until the confidence of our predictions meets a certain threshold. Testing is done using a data set we capture and separate during the data-mining phase. Our central model (the one underneath the Mood API) takes in time-structured online activity for a user and outputs a likely current mood given the most recent observation. This model is then transferred into our second network, which chunks your users' history into 24-hour segments and trains a model that predicts the upcoming 24-hour emotional cycle (and provides the backbone of our Trends API!).

Once we have accurate models for our Moods and Trends API, we do fine-grain analysis on specific data such as text and photos. This process starts by performing a topic-modeling analysis on all user text and browsing history to break up each user's history into topic-specific data sets. Further, each user photo is analyzed for facial expression, object detection, and captioning to develop visual insights into the personal aesthetics of your customer's emotions. A core value that Ad Empathy offers is recognizing that each product a customer purchases is embedded in a different context and thus requires a different cognitive model to understand underlying emotional relationships. We develop those models along many dimensions that account for complex relationships between emotions and brand sentiments.

Important to understanding how Ad Empathy works is that each API your team uses is operating with different custom models and parsing techniques that branch out from of our central mood-recognition network. Our *Expression* API, for instance, uses sentiment analysis in tandem with a generative adversarial network to parse user text and then learn how to generate novel text that expresses the same sentiments while staying within the known vernacular of your customer. The adversarial network is trained against the core mood model, which allows rapid exploration of the syntax space observed and parsed from your customers' online platforms.

If your company would like to learn even more about the inner-workings of Ad Empathy, feel free to make an appointment with our Machine Intelligence Team to discuss specifics or let us know how you think we could improve our process.

Example Use

Working with customers, we have found solutions that mix and match our APIs to help you generate the relevant content and design marketing campaigns most appropriate to your products. We explain some of our most successful applications below:

Time Cycling
Our research has shown that many customers have predictable emotional response patterns based on time of day. It is often reliable that a customer will elicit more positive emotions to food around 11AM; however, this response will diminish leading up to around 2PM as it becomes more likely they already ate lunch. For this reason we recommend *time cycling* campaigns for products with emotions that are highly correlated to temporal patterns.

For this, we recommend analysis of your products with our *Trends* Resource to discover your most temporally stable products and to make inferences about how they are associated across time. Then using our *Expressions* Resource, you can design context-sensitive Content Ads that can portray your product regularly at the times associated to the emotion best suited for your product.

A/B Emotional Testing
Not sure whether your product is better fit to when your customer feels happy or angry? Try A/B Testing emotions instead of features. Combining our Impressions and Response APIs, your team can try your ad impressions against different emotional conditions to see what elicits the most positive response. This can improve how you understand how your product is being perceived and better inform our models.

For well-modeled user profiles, your team may try running simulations using our Impressions and Expressions APIs. You can pilot your A/B tests, discovering correlations between ad impression and emotional responses and designing ad impressions with the right emotional language.

Appropriate Use of Ad Empathy
The purpose of Ad Empathy is to support businesses in employing emotional insights as they create online advertisements. We love seeing our customers rapid prototyping new ad campaigns and trying out new combinations of our models to maximize the utility emotions and timing play in your ad impressions. Ad Empathy, however, is *not* meant to be used as a research platform, nor should it be used to target specific customers and invade their privacy. We do not approve of customer-specific analysis that exposes potentially

sensitive vulnerabilities related to private dimensions of a customer's mental state.

Ad Empathy should also never be used in relation to medical data or to support mental health inference relative to emotional trends. Similarly, our insights should remain in the realm of marketing and should not be used in decision-making algorithms related to employment, education, housing, or health. Though we are proud of the accuracy of our system, it is not appropriate to use such predictions to make firm decisions that could negatively impact your customers. If your company is focused on biomedical or employment-related inference, please contact our Customer Relations Team to discuss fair uses of data and how to access our models for purposes outside of our available products. Projects that are funded by a government agency should speak to an Ad Empathy representative before using our products. If your use of Ad Empathy goes beyond marketing, we offer consulting services to help your company develop an ethical and accurate system that incorporates emotional insights.

Thank you again for using Ad Empathy!

Author's Statement

The goal of this design fiction is to structure discussion around a technology that is at the cusp of creation, regardless of whether it emerges in this exact form. Industry demand for novel forms of personalization and audience targeting paired with research trends in affective computing and emotion detection puts us on a clear path toward emotion-sensitive technologies. With both the capability and economic incentives in place, we must, as a community, carefully define lines between what we consider fair marketing applications of

technology versus unwelcome and unfair intervention or even exploitation.

Design fiction is one way to consider these possible futures. As a conflation of design, science fact, and science fiction, the medium is a method for exploring ideas, implementation strategies, and consequences [6]. Importantly, as Baumer points out in an introduction to a set of fictional conference abstracts, these visions of tomorrow can help shape the research directions of today [3]. Lindley further proposes design fiction as a methodology for considering the ethics of radical digital interventions [12]. Proposing our design fiction as an ethical provocation and a starting point for conceptualizing complex problems ahead in our socio-technical future, we ask: how could a vision of tomorrow inform the ethical considerations of the research we are conducting today? Where is the line between research and privacy, utilizing data insights and manipulation?

Written as an API, the piece situates itself both in technical and social literatures of computing. Questions have already been raised about the ethics of corporate experimentation and the fine line between product testing and harmful intervention [13]. Research has shown that users may not really understand what they are consenting to when agreeing to a terms of service [2,10]. They may also find certain uses of their data to be "creepy" or invasive when it comes to behavioral advertising [19]. When asked about the process of data merging and aggregation, users tend to feel they are not the ones receiving a true benefit [5].

Though these user attitudes may raise red flags, research and industry continue expanding our capabilities in this area. In computer vision, deep neural nets have been a boon for new models that aid in extracting emotion from facial images posted online [4,11]. Text is no different as research continues to improve our ability extract emotional insights from syntax tokens [1,14]. Separately, researchers have proven capabilities to make mental health inferences using social media data [7,8]. Typically, future directions for this kind of work involve technology design for helping people. However, there are other potential uses for this technology, including online marketing tactics.

If we consider the bleeding edge of marketing and artificial intelligence, we see very similar forms of emotional targeting being brandished as the next wave [16]. Yet, when users actually find out how they are being classified on psychological and emotional terms, it foments anger and is seen as "overstepping boundaries" [17]. In academic circles, researchers such as Zeynep Tufekci and Kate Crawford have stoked debate around new kinds of privacy harms caused by advancements in AI and algorithmic methods [9,18]. Their concern is based on the fact that predictive inference is now able to go beyond what users openly disclose about themselves.

Ad Empathy and its API Resource offer a demonstrable grey area in technology ethics. The product very clearly meets the path we are trending toward, yet it should provoke some sense of caution or discomfort in its ability to find users at their most vulnerable moments. Without a doubt, this kind of system will become possible and machines will continue pushing the limits of our cognitive capacity to recognize manipulation, presenting ethical issues that are worthy of close consideration and skepticism. As a discussion piece, the Ad Empathy design fiction should work to ground debates around fair use of data, and the boundaries of ethical design. We hope Ad

Empathy offers a point of negotiation around how to move forward relative to this plausible future.

References

1. Ameeta Agrawal and Aijun An. 2012. Unsupervised emotion detection from text using semantic and syntactic relations. In *Proceedings of the IEEE/WIC/ACM International Joint Conferences on Web Intelligence and Intelligent Agent Technology*.

2. Yannis Bakos, Florencia Marotta-wurgler, and David R Trossen. 2009. Does Anyone Read the Fine Print? Testing a Law and Economics Approach to Standard Form Contracts. *New York University Law and Economics Working Papers* Paper 195. Retrieved from http://lsr.nellco.org/nyu_lewp/195

3. Eric P S Baumer, et al. 2014. CHI 2039 : Speculative Research Visions. ACM CHI 2014.

4. C. Fabian Benitez-Quiroz, Ramprakash Srinivasan, and Aleix M. Martinez. 2016. EmotioNet: An accurate, real-time algorithm for the automatic annotation of a million facial expressions in the wild. In *Proceedings of the IEEE Conference on Computer vision and Pattern Recognition (CVPR)*.

5. Igor Bilogrevic and Martin Ortlieb. 2016. "If You Put All The Pieces Together..." Attitudes Towards Data Combination and Sharing Across Services and Companies. ACM CHI 2016.

6. Julian Bleecker. 2009. Design Fiction: A Short Essay on Design, Science, Fact and Fiction. *Near Future Laboratory*: 4–97.

7. Stevie Chancellor, Zhiyuan Lin, Eric L. Goodman, Stephanie Zerwas, and Munmun De Choudhury. 2016. Quantifying and predicting mental illness

severity in online pro-eating disorder communities. ACM CSCW 2016.

8. Munmun De Choudhury, Scott Counts, and Eric Horvitz. 2013. Predicting postpartum changes in emotion and behavior via social media. ACM CHI 2013.

9. Kate Crawford and Jason Schultz. 2013. Big Data and Due Process: Toward a Framework to Redress Predictive Privacy Harms. *Boston College Law Review* 55, 1.

10. Casey Fiesler, Cliff Lampe, and Amy S. Bruckman. 2016. Reality and Perception of Copyright Terms of Service for Online Content Creation. ACM CSCW 2016.

11. Youngsung Kim, ByungIn Yoo, Youngjun Kwak, Changkyu Choi, and Junmo Kim. 2017. Deep generative-contrastive networks for facial recognition. *arXiv (working paper)*. Retrieved from https://arxiv.org/abs/1703.07140

12. Joseph Lindley. 2015. Operationalising Design Fiction for Ethical Computing. *ACM SIGCAS Computers and Society* 45, 3: 79–83.

13. Michelle N. Meyer. 2015. Two Cheers for Corporate Experimentation: The A/B Illusion and the Virtues of Data-Driven Innovation. *Colorado Technology Law Journal* 13: 273–332.

14. Myriam Munezero, Calkin Suero Montero, Maxim Mozgovoy, and Erkki Sutinen. 2013. Exploiting sentiment analysis to track emotions in students'

learning diaries. In *Proceedings of the Koli Calling International Conference on Computing Education.*

15. Rajib Rana. 2016. Gated Recurrent Unit (GRU) for Emotion Classification from Noisy Speech. *arXiv (working paper)*. Retrieved from https://arxiv.org/abs/1612.07778

16. Gargi Sharma. 2017. How emotion detection technology can make marketing more effective. *ParallelDots*. Retrieved from http://blog.paralleldots.com/technology/changing-marketing-with-emotion-detection-technology/

17. Olivia Solon. 2017. "This oversteps a boundary": Teenagers perturbed by Facebook surveillance. *The Guardian*. Retrieved from https://www.theguardian.com/technology/2017/may/02/facebook-surveillance-tech-ethics

18. Zeynep Tufekci. 2015. Algorithmic Harms Beyond Facebook and Google: Emergent Challenges of Computational Agency. *Colorado Technology Law Journal* 13: 203–218.

19. Blase Ur, Pedro Giovanni Leon, Lorrie Faith Cranor, Richard Shay, and Yang Wang. 2012. Smart, useful, scary, creepy: Perceptions of online behavioral advertising. In *Symposium on Usable Privacy and Security (SOUPS)*.

20. David Jingjun Xu. 2006. The influence of personalization in affecting consumer attitutdes towards mobile advertising in China. *Journal of Computer Information Systems* 47, 2: 9–19.

Creating, Reinterpreting, Combining, Cuing – Paper Practices on the Shopfloor

Peter Heinrich
ZHAW, School of
Management and Law
Winterthur, Switzerland
heip@zhaw.ch

Alexander Richter
IT University of
Copenhagen
Copenhagen, Denmark
aric@itu.dk

Lars Rune Christensen
IT University of
Copenhagen
Copenhagen, Denmark
lrc@itu.dk

Gerhard Schwabe
University of Zurich
Zurich, Switzerland
schwabe@ifi.uzh.ch

ABSTRACT

Despite the advent of a flurry of digital technologies, paper prevails on manufacturing shopfloors. To understand the roles and value of paper on the shopfloor, we have studied the manufacturing practices at two state-of-the-art automotive supplier facilities, applying ethnographic fieldwork, in-depth interviews, as well as photo and document analysis. We find that paper has unique affordances that today's digital technologies cannot easily supplant on current shopfloors. More specifically, we find four paper practices: (1) creating and adapting individual information spaces, (2) reinterpreting information, (3) combining information handover with social interaction, and (4) visual cuing. We discuss these practices and the unique affordances of paper that currently support shopfloor workers and also consider the limitations of paper, which are becoming increasingly apparent, since more tasks increasingly depend on real-time information.

Authors Keywords

Paper Practices; Shopfloor; Manufacturing; Affordances; Digital Artifacts

ACM Classification Keywords

H1.1; H.4.1; K.4.3; K.6.1

INTRODUCTION

Already in the 1980s, scholars and practitioners have discussed replacing paper on the shopfloor with digital technologies [5]. Proponents have argued that paper has significant limitations as a collaboration medium, because it is slow and has limited capacity (e.g. [10]). Recent literature also corroborates this view of paper, stressing the same shortcomings of using paper such as slow information transfer, high workload of managing paper documents, outdated information, and loss of synchronization (e.g. [19]). Nonetheless, many highly successful and profitable manufacturing companies still substantially use paper on

their shopfloors. Why?

Research into the substitution of paper by digital technologies brings to mind similar expectations of paper's future in office environments. At least as early as the mid-1970s, the *paperless office* was becoming a popular catchphrase, and many predicted that it was only a matter of time before our office environments would become paperless. But paperless office is still rather vision than reality [12].

The missing of the paperless shopfloor and the paperless office could be explained by reference to so-called *demographic factors*. In this view, paper continues to be used, because the generations of people brought up with paper documents find it difficult to move towards screen-based documents and new technological tools. As this generation gradually retires, it has been argued, digital documents will replace paper. Also, the argument goes, investment in technology and more user-friendly technology will ensure the eventual paperlessness of offices and shopfloors [29]. However, paper is still used heavily in today's office environments and studies indicate that there is very little evidence of a link between age cohort and preference for paper [29]. Also, (massive) investments in new digital technologies for working with documents have not eliminated the use of paper in collaborative work. This is true in both office environments and shopfloors.

The research suggests that the reason why paper continues to be key in collaborative work relates to its *interactional properties*, or the physical aspects of paper that shape the ways in which it can be used in a wide range of task types [6]. These may be thought of as the affordances of paper.

Based on insights from the literature on the affordances of paper in cooperative work, we investigate the affordances of paper in a particular setting type – the shopfloor of future *smart factories*. The manufacturing industry is moving towards smart factories: changing demands in global markets are increasingly leading manufacturing companies to transform previously mass-produced items into individualized products [20], making flexibility a key success factor of the 21th century [22].

For the shopfloor context, this requires less routine work, and dynamic and efficient collaboration by highly skilled shopfloor workers. That is, while much traditional manual shopfloor work is becoming automated, shopfloor workers in smart factories are gaining more autonomy as flexible problem-solvers and decision-makers [1]. We focus on the affordances of paper on the shopfloor of current or future smart factories.

The article's empirical material originates from two studies of shopfloor work at automotive suppliers seeking to move into the smart manufacturing paradigm: (1) ETOC, a company in Slovenia that manufactures large tools for sheet-metal transformation, and (2) a division of Mass Production Company (MPC) in Germany that manufactures mechanical parts for automotive engines. While both are in the automotive sector, ETOC manufactures one-off individual machine parts, while MPC mass-produces engine parts. Studying these two companies offers us a broad view across different manufacturing settings and at least some differences in cultural background. Without claiming completeness, both settings provide a broad spectrum of paper affordances across different manufacturing contexts. [1]

Our study highlights paper's affordances on these two factories' shopfloors, arguing that aiming to make these shopfloor types paperless is largely uncalled for. We also analyze paper's limitations on smart factory shopfloors, which for instance surface in the context of decision-making, when the process requires rapid distribution of large amounts of data. The upshot is that paper has a place on the shopfloor of modern smart factories provided that the usage of paper artifacts is appropriately integrated with digital tools.

Given paper's widespread uses in companies and private life, there are various possible perspectives on its uses and purposes. We look at paper practices as ways to create and maintain local information spaces, through which workers store, retrieve, and share information. *Information space* relates to "a set of concepts and relations among them" [23]. We consider which concepts of information space workers relate to and how they store, retrieve, and share them in their environment.

Our study is structured as follows. First, we account for related research on affordances in general and the paper's affordances in particular. Second, we account for methods and settings. Third, we introduce the two cases, followed by the analysis, where we unpack the affordances of paper on the shopfloor. We then discuss our findings in light of the literature and the notion of future smart shopfloors.

PAPER AFFORDANCES AND PRACTICES

The concept of affordances originates from ecological psychology, and was proposed by James Gibson [9] to

denote action possibilities provided to an actor by an environment. In the late 1980s, Norman [24] suggested that affordances be taken advantage of in design. The suggestion strongly resonated with designers' concern about making possible uses of their products immediately obvious; the concept soon came to play a key role in interaction design and human-computer interaction (HCI).

Affordances are seen as a way to bring materiality back into the analysis by highlighting technology's physical characteristics without succumbing to technological determinism. Hutchby [16,17] underlines that technologies should be understood as artifacts that are both "shaped by and shaping of" [17:444] human practices. In line with this, he defines technology affordances as the "… functional and relational aspects which frame, while not determining, the possibilities for argentic action to an object" [17:444]. Further, affordances may differ between persons and between contexts, and are in this sense relational. For instance, a computer with a working integrated development environment (IDE) has the affordance of writing code, compiling it, and executing it, but only if the user is a skilled programmer that knows the appropriate programming language, and so on. Relatedly, the use of complex paper artifacts on the shopfloor also requires skills on the parts of the user, and certain affordances are only visible to the trained eye rather than a novice. This implies that individuals must first 'learn' affordances before they can gain awareness on them [16].

Research into paper practices [30] has for instance shown that paper affords ease of marking. This is important when people are reviewing a document's contents, allowing them to write and comment on the text as they read. Paper also affords flexible cross-referencing between multiple documents, allowing users to spread out pages in physical space and to read and write across documents. This is crucial when one seeks to compare and contrast between documents or seeking to extract and integrate information across documents. Paper also affords complex, two-handed navigation within and between documents. This enables readers to effectively 'get to grips' with a document's structure by allowing them to flick through quickly and get a feel for the content [25]. Paper also affords us opportunities to interact and communicate with one another by physically passing and delivering documents rather than e-mailing them [11]. Further, paper can be used to organize work in time and space, including being placed conspicuously in order to impress others [6]. It may make a significant difference whether or not an artifact is paper-based or digital [7,21]. For instance, in her seminal ethnography of paper flight strips in air traffic control, MacKay showed that replacing paper with digital tools in this safety-critical environment is a non-trivial challenge [21]. The affordance of paper contrasts with the affordance of for instance software applications to an extent where a one-to-one substitution may be impractical and in some cases undesirable [3,7,21]. Studies from other domains,

---

[1] The continued development of smart manufacturing is especially important in Europe and in the remainder of the Western world, where the wage premium – compared to the emerging economies – is a disadvantage and every aspect of the manufacturing process must be improved so as to remain competitive. This study is based on EU funding for strengthening smart factory work.

including for instance microfinance, have also pointed to paper's enduring value. For instance, the study of microfinance, Ghosh et al. [7] have shown that paper is able to deliver valuable context-specific information that derive from paper's affordances. This research may help explain why people generally use paper as well as in complex cooperative work settings, and why replacing paper with newer digital technology may be a challenge – if desirable at all.

In contrast to this research, scholars and practitioners have proposed to replace paper on the shopfloor with digital technologies [5,15,26] owing to paper's limitations. It has been argued that paper has significant limitations as a collaboration medium, because (1) the data streams are too broad to be transmitted by paper, (2) the feedback loops are too slow, (3) human input is too error-prone, and (4) the interpretability of information would rise to unacceptable levels [10]. Some recent literature corroborate this view of paper, stressing the same shortcomings of using paper such as slow information transfer, high workload of managing the paper documents, outdated information, and loss of synchronization [19].

With this short summary of the literature, we see that paper has unique affordances, but we also see that these affordances simultaneously shape paper usage's limitations. We will now explore paper's affordances in two cases of factory shop work, with the aim to provide a balanced view of paper's affordances and account for the opportunities of and challenges to its uses in future manufacturing settings.

METHODS

This study is a part of the international research project Facts4Workers [4], which seeks to create attractive and intelligent workplaces in a factory of the future. We initially studied how shopfloor practices can be supported via human-centered IT solutions. A deep understanding of workers' individual practices has been our basis to deliver suggestions (in the form of requirements) for sociotechnical solutions that support smarter work.

Our study is based on ethnographic fieldwork oriented to informing design of information technology. The development of technologies for cooperative work, in our case smart factories, is ultimately what our approach is about. Applying ethnographic methods may afford us insights into practices that we would otherwise be unaware of. This is a key justification in that we cannot know in advance what a practice's relevant features are, let alone how they are relevant for technology development and prospective users. Analytical findings based on ethnography may ground a technology development process by providing a framework in which it can be conducted, explored, critiqued, and evaluated. Sociotechnical theory is an apparatus of the mind, a technique of perception and reflection that helps its processors see, discuss, and ultimately act on phenomena [2]. In this vein, this study's ethnographic findings are (partly) intended to ground

possible future technology development processes in a context that may make designers sensitive to certain phenomena such as the affordances of paper and may provide a vocabulary or conceptual apparatus for thinking about design opportunities and design challenges.

Our study is based on ethnographic fieldwork collected over 14 months, conducted as several multiday, on-site data collection sessions from February 2015 to April 2016. (Further data collections are ongoing but don't form part of this study). Our data collection followed the principle of triangulation [31:291]. We obtained data from observations, field notes, focus groups, and interviews.

The fieldwork at ETOC included observations of shopfloor work, eight employee interviews (with an average length of about 40 minutes), two focus groups, and the collection of documents such as bills of materials, technical drawings, and component lists. The study of MPC's shopfloor included 12 days of observations of shopfloor work, eight interviews with workers, and four interviews with management (with an average length of about 38 minutes), three focus groups with management, and the collection of documents spanning the machines' information spaces. During the interviews, we adopted the role of neutral observers [32]; although we know this does not make us unbiased, we sought to obtain answers from different perspectives that were as frank as possible. Whenever the interviews were conducted in other languages, we translated these into English.

Our data analysis and interpretation followed the principle of the hermeneutic circle, which suggests that "we come to understand a complex whole from preconceptions about the meanings of its parts and their interrelationships" [18:71].

CASE STUDY 1: ETOC

Case Context

ETOC is a Slovenian manufacturer of tools for sheet-metal transformation. Its customers insert these tools into large presses on their properties and use them to stamp sheet metal to create automotive metal parts (i.e. parts of cars' bodywork). The tools can have dimensions of up to 6 metres by 4 metres. Consisting of two assemblies, the matrix and the stamp, a finished tool houses up to several hundred individual components and sensors.

Figure 1: ETOC's Shopfloor

Except for some large cast-iron frames and some standard parts, the components are all manufactured in-house using both computer numeric control (CNC) machinery and manual operations (see Figure 1). Given these products' highly application-specific natures, the company has an engineer-to-order process. Normally only a single unit is designed and manufactured for any given order. A condensed overview of the production of a sheet-metal transformation tool on the shopfloor of ETOC may look something like this: After the design phase, the build process starts with the arrival of the large cast-metal frames from an external supplier that will later house all the components. These frames are first machined to close dimensions, as they later provide the support structure for all other parts. In parallel, the workshop begins to machine the custom metal parts, which will later be mounted on the cast-iron frame.

This process is time-consuming and involves several complex machining steps such as laser-cutting, milling, drilling, turning, hardening, and grinding. As soon as parts are finished on the machines, assembly workers begin to assemble the parts. There is no separate warehouse involved – either the assembly workers pull the components directly from the machine operators, or they are stacked beneath the assembly workplace. The same holds true for all standard parts, which are ordered from external suppliers.

Paper Affordances and Practices on ETOC's Shopfloor

At several junctures in this process, paper and its affordances are key to this shopfloor work. That is, key shopfloor operations are managed with paper. Documents are mainly printed by employees in project management or production management. The printouts are based on data available from the computer-aided design (CAD) or enterprise resource planning (ERP) system. Documents include for instance large-scale assembly drawings and bills of materials (BOMs) for assembly workers and production orders for machine operators. The printouts are then handed to the shopfloor workers and later, where appropriate (e.g. completed production orders), recollected, filed, and imported back into the ERP system so as to update the data. Thus, updates in the ERP system can easily be delayed for up to 24 hours.

A use of paper we observed was the creation of individual, ad hoc information spaces. We found that paper has unique properties that facilitate this process: It is very malleable and can be attached to objects or bent around them, is available in large sizes, can be cut into pieces and is always readable if there is sufficient light. These are some of paper's properties. Workers place paper where it seems appropriate to them and stack paper documents upon each other to make their interconnections easily visible. Further, given paper's easy mobility, they put it directly on the tool they are building or on top of other components. We may say that the workers blend the paper-based information into their work environment. With paper documents, workers

can place the information directly where they need to consume it: directly where the work is done or where sufficient space is available for large-scale printouts. The amount of dirt on paper (see Figure 2 and Figure 3) may give an impression of usage frequency and usage intensity in this harsh environment.

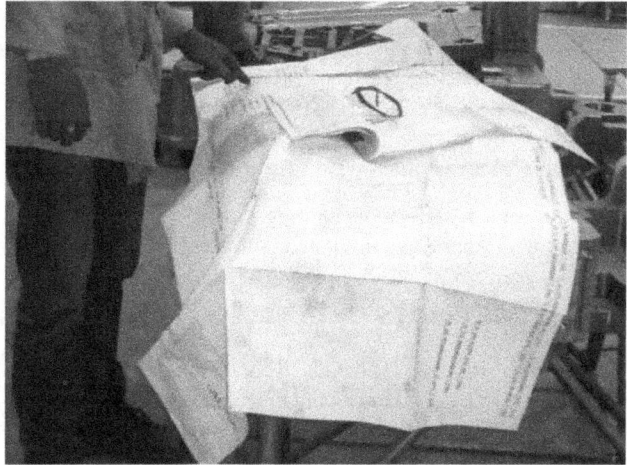

Figure 2: Paper's Malleability

Workers also alter the content of the presented information by adding their own extensions in the form of markings and notations. As one can see in Figure 3, a worker transformed a bill of material into an assembly checklist and into a progress indicator, simultaneously. This is a recurring practice. The paper-based BOM is especially interesting for its different uses: Besides its traditional use as a components list, ETOC extended information with a rough trajectory through the various machining steps. Thus, the BOM also provides a map on which workers see where these parts could reside if not found in the intended place. However, as this information is not real-time, ETOC only labeled the rough production steps, not the machine performing the operation. Since there are often several machines with equal capabilities, the parts are dynamically scheduled to them. Nonetheless, this augmented BOM provides some hints when workers need to search for parts. Workers also extend the information on paper using their own notations. Sometimes the BOMs are used as a 'script', and workers tick off the parts they have already assembled.

On this shopfloor, paper documents also trigger personal interaction during handoffs. For instance, the machine operators don't retrieve the production orders by themselves.

A machine operator told us: *"Yes, the boss [the production manager] comes in with a list of what will be produced on the machine." (I4).*

This allows the production manager and the machine operators to talk, engage in micro-adjustments of their work, clear up potential misunderstandings, ask questions, and so on. Thus, the information on paper is also accompanied by a brief face-to-face interaction. The machine operators are approached by assembly workers, who want to retrieve updated information when their parts are completed. As shown, the information on the BOM is either too unspecific on paper or is already outdated.

At first sight, this just delays production. But it also sparks social interactions between an assembly worker and machine operators, allowing for further micro-adjustments. While larger deviations from an original production plan (such as reprioritization of the production sequence) would require the production manager to engage in the decision-making process, minor adaptions (such as a quick reworking of a part that doesn't fit) might not be a problem.

In addition to the opportunities for blending with the environment, marking, and personal interactions, paper may also be said to have limitations – there are challenges associated with the medium. Generally speaking, a paper-based organization of the work process runs the risk of not being able to fully provide timely and synchronized information access. A project manager notes: *"Sometimes, I don't have an overview of the whole project. Sometimes, I don't get the full information, or I get it at the wrong time, mostly too late." (I5).*

To address this challenge of working with paper and printouts, at the start of each shift, the project manager manually compares the BOM to the de facto progress on the shopfloor. The information he gets from different paper sources is incomplete and references different points in time: *"[...] we have a [computer program] on which they can solve it. But it is not for all parts, it is not real data. Some workers don't fill it in." (I5).*

The idea is that the workers must enter their paper-based information from the various worksheets and other documents back into the ERP system. However, this is not done consistently by everyone, which causes problems, to a degree where the information in the ERP system cannot be relied on.

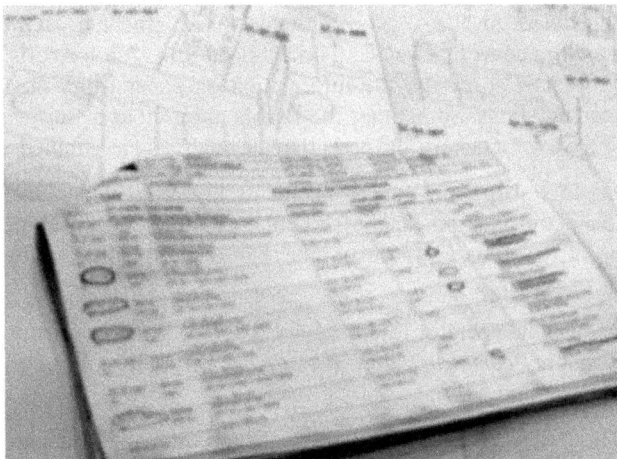

Figure 3: Augmenting a BOM with Custom Information

Further, the shopfloor operations scheduling is done manually, using primarily paper-based documents. Thus, most of the planning-related information remain with certain persons, for instance, the project manager, and are not readily accessible to others, such as other managers or assembly workers. This means that either the person interested in this information must directly approach the corresponding co-worker and must ask him face-to-face, or must search for this information in the physical environment, which is often time-consuming. A typical morning start for the project manager for instance involves getting a picture of the progress made during the last shift. This takes about an hour. To do this, he checks the general workshop status, which pieces are missing, and the status of the finishing process. Once awareness of the overall situation is lost (or perceived to be lost), a complete reassessment of the situation must be done. This reassessment, as done by the project manager, currently involves tracking numerous pieces of information distributed across the shopfloor.

This type of challenge of building awareness with paper is one faced not only faced by the project managers; the machine operators and assembly workers also repeatedly try to regain sufficient awareness so as to be able to continue working. For instance, the assembly workers collect the necessary parts for an assembly step before an operation begins. If parts are not yet available, they talk to the machine operators, who are the only ones who can provide predictable short-term information on which parts will be finished next. If rescheduling is required (e.g. to meet deadlines), the production manager is involved, to acknowledge the rescheduling. Although the BOM provides hints about a particular piece's machining sequence, the current stage is not provided on paper, since this would require constant updates. The workers don't have the current machining operation on their list and must search for it themselves.

In sum, this case shows that paper readily affords the creation of personal information spaces via easy bending, placing, marking, and annotating of paper-based resources such as printouts; it also affords a personal touch when it is handed off. However, the case also shows that paper has trouble transferring information in a timely and predictable manner; especially the distribution of key documents (with markings and annotations) across the shopfloor challenges the establishment of a real-time overview or awareness for managers and workers.

CASE STUDY 2: MPC

Case Context
MPC is an automotive supply company. While it operates globally, we conducted fieldwork at a German plant, where (amongst others) different models of high-quality chain-tensioners are manufactured to tight specifications. Since these components are critical to engine reliability, the company's main objective is to deliver components that are 100% fault-free.

Although many production and assembly steps run fully automated and are controlled by sophisticated PLC systems, the human workforce is still needed throughout the shopfloor. Staff members' main task is to operate the machines, handle the pieces produced, and keep the machines clean and in good condition. They also perform regular maintenance, quality control operations, and complex retooling operations whenever they need to produce a batch of different types on the machines.

An outline of the manufacturing process of chain-tensioners on the shopfloor of MPC may look like this: The production is divided into several groups, each of which produces items for the final product and is part of the value stream. One of the main challenges is the just-in-time production, establishing compliance with the quantities and timelines without creating large stocks. The production runs 24 hours in a three-shift operation. The operator, tool-setter, and team leader roles basically describe the task within a shift. Operators work directly on the machines and maintain the production process. Tool-setters monitor the quantities and quality of the multiple machines, set up and retool the machines if necessary, and support the operator when required. Team leaders coordinate the operators and the tool-setters in every production area, and report to the product managers.

A typical day starts with shift handover, which involves operators, setters, and team leaders. During the handover, they – orally and in writing – exchange key information to the next shift. Owing to the large number of documents, information management is a major challenge, especially across multiple shifts or over longer time periods. For instance, several physical and digital shift logs document any occurrences during the shifts. After handover, the setters carry out the necessary maintenance procedures and document them. Also, the machines are calibrated and retooled to meet the current order requirements. The team leader records the product quantities several times a day in a paper template and compares these with the nominal number of production orders. Counting pieces is very time-consuming, and prone to errors owing to media breaks. If the required product quantities are reached, the machines must be retooled for the following order. At the shift's end, handover to the next shift takes place. The exchange of information between employees mostly occurs orally and is not well structured, which means the sharing and traceability of key information over longer periods cannot be guaranteed. Further, it is not possible to access relevant information centrally and efficiently.

Paper Affordances and Practices on MPC's Shopfloor

While MPC is arguably a high-tech and high-profit production company, we found that it deliberately relies on paper in many places on the shopfloor and paper has fixed positions throughout. The documents are fairly short (1 to 2 pages) and are visible under a protective film in close proximity to the workspace. Thus, the information spaces around the machines are designed to match the specific tasks. The documents fulfill different purposes – some are purely informative (e.g. efficiency statistics), while others coordinate recurring actions and have a checklist character (see Figure 5). The document in the middle is a checklist where employees place their signature when they have performed the required maintenance and cleaning operations. Documents that relate to each other are mounted in close proximity so as to ease information interlinking. Also note the different areas, where information is provided in a very structured way, mixed with empty spaces for unstructured information such as simple handwritten logs.

The large document boards (see Figure 4) support management discussions. This configuration allows several persons to have continuous access to all information in parallel, and the presence of paper serves as a reminder to talk about certain issues.

Paper documents facilitate social interactions during handovers. For instance, during handover, shift documentation is passed along and discussed. Further, paper fosters personal responsibility. Employees sign that they have performed certain steps and thereby deeply identify with the task. This activity is also tightly bound to the place of action and is therefore connected to the physical reality. If it were to digitalize these processes, managers would face a dilemma.

Figure 4: A Management Meeting Board on the Shopfloor with All Relevant Aggregated Shopfloor Data Displayed

They recognize the benefits of vertical information integration, yet fear that digitization would reduce this coupling to the physical reality. Employees could take actions more light-handedly on digital artifacts than signing off at the work location immediately after a task has been performed: *"Who ensures that the workers don't tick the checkboxes later on their mobile phones in the cafeteria?" (I9)*

While workers enter certain information directly into the ERP system so as to speed up processes, they still need to enter the same values on their paper forms by hand. Using barcodes, workers tag the documents so that they can be referenced from within the ERP system once archived (digitally scanned). Some of these paper-based documentation processes and archiving activities are also required by their customers.

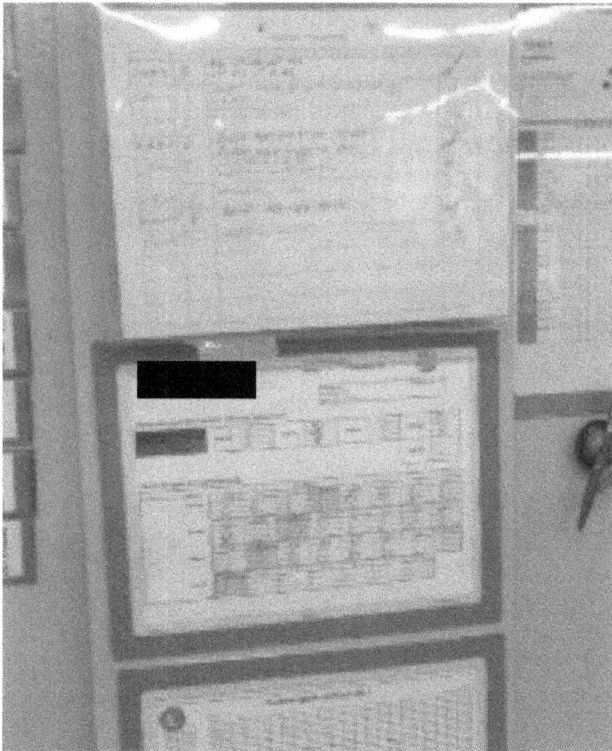

Figure 5: On an Assembly Line, Documents for Shift Entries, Quality Control, and Performance Data

Some workers don't trust the systems: *"[...] some dispatchers [...]don't feel comfortable if they haven't manually sorted all this again according to their own rules. That is my concern here, to also have this effect when giving rigid instructions from the system" (I11).*

Especially the quality assurance (QA) setting has proven insightful, since we observed very different stakeholders with different information-sharing needs. Already, QA workers act as problem-solvers and autonomous decision-makers, supporting the machine operators and tool-setters whenever quality-related problems arise.

However, it is hard to plan these operations, since (1) errors arise unpredictably and (2) it is hard to exactly time regular QA activities. These regular activities include for instance assistance from QA personnel when a machine is retooled to produce a different part. While the retooling is a planned process, given the complexity of such a process, it is hard to exactly time events, which simply emerges as a result.

From the perspective of a QA employee, this relates to the problem of insufficient information availability to make accurate predictions. As a result, the loads on these employees vary significantly. What the QA employees would need is a coherent picture of the current state of the shopfloor and a projection of future QA-relevant events. But the environment is spatially too distributed to be easily recognizable to them, and the available feedback information transport based on paper and direct face-to-fact communication is either too slow or too unpredictable.

In addition, providing spontaneous assistance to tool-setters and machine operators is difficult in terms of providing awareness. The quality assurer may visit the machine with close to zero awareness of what the progress status is. *"[...], he simply needs a better perception of the process, to be better integrated and to be able to better accompany, control, and influence it" (I3).*

The information this quality assurer received beforehand per telephone is often insufficient. Thus, as a first and time-consuming step, he needs to build a picture of the situation by talking to the staff at the machine to find out how the problem surfaced and what they have already tried. At the time of the interviews (2015), the quality assurer planned to start using a paper document to transport this information in the form of a ticket on which it would be mandatory to fill a description of the problem and the steps performed to resolve it – in other words, using the paper to convey situation awareness information. Here, the quality assurers actively try to manage the problem of perceived unpredictable feedback information quality by standardizing the format in which this information must be submitted.

In sum, our study of the MPC shopfloor shows that, also in a mass production environment, paper has a place and that its properties allow for effective designs of large information spaces, facilitates the integration of different documents, and explicates liability, thereby creating high information quality.

However, looking into the practices of QA employees, the task is so demanding from an information-sharing perspective that a paper-based approach doesn't seem feasible. Thus, employees use other media (such as telephone or direct face-to-face communication) to perform their tasks. Hence, digital technology must not only match the performance of paper but must significantly outperform it in order to yield the expected benefits.

DISCUSSION

We have studied the use of paper as a key information source and transport medium in two automotive supplier shopfloors.

These two companies differ in their manufacturing strategy (engineer-to-order vs. make-to-stock/build-to-order), are located in different countries (Slovenia and Germany), and have fundamentally different personnel costs and different shopfloor organization schemes (dynamic self-organization and hierarchical control). Still, paper's roles on both shopfloors are similar. Thus, we argue that paper's use in factory environments is neither a question of how advanced and innovative a company is, which basic organizational model it applies, or if it is in a high-wedge or low-wedge country. Rather, as shown, the value of paper derives from its interactional affordances for the cooperative actors on these shopfloors.

Notably, this argument runs parallel to the findings of MacKay [21] and of Ghosh et al. [7], who similarly underscore the key value and importance of paper's affordances in shaping practice, albeit in difference circumstances and settings. The specific practices of for instance air traffic control, microfinance, and – in our case – smart factories are inextricable connected to paper's affordances. We may assume that ending the use of paper in shopfloor settings would fundamentally change the practices applied there, too. This is because paper fundamentally shapes each of these practices. Further, we may observe that paper's affordances seem to be valuable in both the technology-rich settings of smart factories and for instance in the comparably technology-poor setting of microfinance in a developing region [7]. Arguably, the value of paper persists across diverse settings because its value derives from general interactional affordances, which may lend themselves to practices as diverse as smart factories in Europe and microfinance in Africa. This says something about paper's flexibility and how it may be fundamental to many types of contemporary practices. Having said this, we may also note differences across settings. That is, where paper's uses in smart factories and air traffic control [cf. 21] is mainly a question of efficiency and practicality, paper's uses in microfinance [cf. 7] is also encouraged by low cost, which is especially important in a development context.

We summarize our findings concerning the smart factory context as follows: we found four paper practice categories in both shopfloor settings: (1) creating and adapting individual information spaces, (2) reinterpreting information, (3) combining information handover with social interaction, and (4) visual cuing. In all these aspects, current digital alternatives are no match. We will now elaborate on this.

Creating and Adapting Individual Information Spaces

In both industrial cases, we have observed that individuals or teams deliberately design their information spaces to match their requirements by distributing the different documents in their physical environment. Many of these documents have a low page count and their entire content displays at once. This is notable, since it reflects the flat nature of the information hierarchy used to provide the information. In contrast to that, digital alternatives either feature visualizations such as *wizards* or *zoom and filter* [cf. 28] metaphors that deliberately hide information so that the entire content is never visible at once. The difference between the observed cases is the responsibility of the creation and arrangement of elements in the information spaces. While at MPC, the arrangement is largely predetermined by management and supervisors, at ETOC, the creation of information spaces happens dynamic. Another common observation is the *always-on* arrangement in the field of vision that also provides visual cues and reminders of unfinished documents and open tasks. Especially paper's flexible nature and robustness allows one to embed documents directly into the manufacturing process. This flexibility is hard to recreate in current digital systems, since this would require massive screen space. Augmented reality human-machine interfaces (HMIs) could be helpful here, but it should be noted that these entirely lack paper's haptics [30]. Further, a common cognitive task is to relate to and integrate different documents into the work environment dominated by machinery and physical objects. This is currently enabled by paper's malleability, which is wholly unmatched in today's digital alternatives.

Reinterpreting Information

As illustrated above shopfloor workers face the challenge of how to integrate many different information sources. We also observed how the workers update these many documents. Some of the documents are simple forms, and workers just fill them out as required. But first, several documents can be managed in parallel. Second, and more importantly, paper documents can be re-purposed by annotations. This differs from the known practices in the office world where annotation aids text comprehension [cf. 25] and shifts the meaning of a document (e.g. a bill of material) from something map-like to something script-like [cf. 27] and use as a checklist by simply marking what has already been processed. There were some differences in the observed cases. While MPC supplied its workers with much more predetermined checklist-style documents, ETOC provided more map-like documents. The interesting observation here is that paper provides easy transitioning from maps to checklists via annotation and from checklists to maps via complete representation that is always visible. Thus, questions like *What is the current state and progress of the construction process?* or *Which activities and tasks do we need to perform during machine retooling?* are easy to answer with paper documents, even if their initial character did not target this interaction. Since digital alternatives are much less malleable, the initially intended use is 'enforced' much stronger, and even the simplest interaction such as extending documents with arbitrary content becomes impossible if not initially accounted for in software.

Combining Information Handover with Social Interaction

Besides these personal practices, paper also facilitates social processes. In both case studies, we found support for Sellen and Harper's [29] assertion that document handover can initiate and support face-to-face discussion between a sender and a receiver. In the context of manufacturing, this exchange of additional information fills the gaps in the incomplete information on paper and also bonds people to the according processes. Knowing and meeting the person who is waiting for a part (see ETOC) differs from merely reading information on a digital device. Thus, care should be taken to retain these established social protocols when digitalizing such processes. Both at ETOC, when the production orders are distributed by the production manager, and at MPC, when teams hand over shifts, documents support social interaction.

Visual Cuing

So far, we have already carved out that taking paper away from people must be a well-considered decision. However, depending on the specific shopfloor, there are already problems when the information distribution speeds hits its limit via paper-based processes. Besides negatively affecting overall shopfloor performance, it primarily affects decision-making by impairing a decision-maker's capability to effectively gain sufficient situation awareness.

The unpredictable feedback issue also affects awareness in terms of perceptions of the environment [13,14]. When the information provided to a practitioner is incomplete or doesn't reflect the environment's state at a point in time, it cannot be utilized to generate a consistent overview of the current state of a shopfloor. The challenge is that, although shopfloor environments can be designed to supply a large stream of information simultaneously from several sources (e.g. by combining information sources with large information spaces), it hits limits with paper-based processes in terms of latency.

Once lost, situational awareness must be rebuilt. Given the size of typical shopfloors and the diversity and focus of an employee's work situational awareness, breakdowns happen at every major shift in activity (e.g. the service technician approaching a faulty machine or the assembly worker switching between two projects they are working on). If situational awareness is not efficiently conveyed, it must be obtained from interaction with the environment. But even if the information is available at the right time, synchronized, and well accessible, we may see breakdowns in terms of the prediction of future events. As the information updating speed of a paper-based process is low, it makes no sense to include data into the documents that immediately become invalid or inconsistent. Especially with paper, having this strict document co-notation, only information is provided in the first place that is correct and remains correct – facts from the past or information that is time-invariant altogether. In combination with the low latency, paper fails to deliver the real-time information required for predicting upcoming events on a shopfloor.

Nonetheless, there is still more room for purposeful uses of digital technology in manufacturing workplaces. Especially at some ETOC cases, workers fell back to paper use although their software offers the required capabilities. This may well be owing to a lack of organizational support and training on new procedures, resulting in outdated and missing pieces of information in systems. But, again, paper can be advantageous here, since one can work even with partial information only, while a software solution would need to explicitly account for it to function.

In sum, digitalization is a two-sided coin. On the one hand, focusing just on efficiency aspects [10,19] neglects all the positive aspects of working with paper that are deeply embedded in our society and workplaces. On the other hand, one cannot overlook the emerging problems of the slow paper-based processes. For the proclaimed new role of the human worker as a problem-solver and decision-maker, real-time information is vital.

CONCLUSION

By studying paper practices at two automotive supplier shopfloors, we were able to illustrate paper's roles as an information source and communication medium. Using the theoretical lens of affordances, we have discussed these roles from a material and a social perspective and have also elaborated on workers' need for situation awareness, which may increase in the years to come and may make the reliance on paper a growing problem.

This research has focused on the general problem of using paper in decentralized control environments. While we have been able to empirically ground our findings in only two case studies here, we know from other cases in the FACTS4WORKERS project the problem is more widespread and poses a risk to digitalization efforts in every manufacturing company. We do not claim that our results are representative. We are aware that our arguments' significance is limited owing to qualitative research's – well-known – restrictions. To assess the rigor of our research, we sought to meet quality demands such as multiple data collection methods, controlled deductions, and analytical generalizability [8].

We have identified several valuable paper practices that are at risk if the transformation process in a company is not human-centered, although we are only at the start of transitioning to smart factories. Further research is needed into how to retain the benefits of traditional paper-based systems while providing the real-time support, which only a digital system can offer.

Based on the results from these case studies, we currently work on developing exemplar shopfloor solutions, trying to retain a maximum of the established practices while supporting the workers with real-time information. Further, we plan to expand our study scope so as to get deeper insights into the phenomenon of companies staying with paper from other perspectives, such as from different firms or industries.

7 ACKNOWLEDGEMENTS

This study is part of the FACTS4WORKERS project which has received funding from the European Union's Horizon 2020 research and innovation programme under Grant Agreement n° 636778. We further thank Benedikt Bleyer, Christian Buchberger, Maria Herdt, Matjaž Milfelner, Luis Schüller and Jennifer Studer for their efforts in the data-collection.

REFERENCES

1. Gianni Campatelli, Alexander Richter, and Alexander Stocker. 2016. Participative Knowledge Management to Empower Manufacturing Workers: *International Journal of Knowledge Management* 12, 4: 37–50.

2. Lars Rune Christensen. 2014. Techno-anthropology for Design. In *What is Techno-anthropology?*, Tom Børsen and Lars Botin (eds.). Aalborg University Press.

3. Lars Rune Christensen. 2016. On Intertext in Chemotherapy: an Ethnography of Text in Medical Practice. *Computer Supported Cooperative Work (CSCW)* 25, 1: 1–38.

4. Jonathan Denner, Peter Heinrich, Constantin Heldman, and Alexander Richter. 2015. *First version of requirements of workers and organisations. Project Report - FACTS4WORKERS: Worker-Centric Workplaces in Smart Factories.*

5. Manocher Djassemi and James A. Sena. 2006. The Paperless Factory: A Review of Issues and Technologies. *International Journal of Computer Science and Network Security* 6, 12: 185.

6. Mateusz Dolata and Gerhard Schwabe. Paper Practices in Institutional Talk: How Financial Advisors Impress their Clients. *Computer Supported Cooperative Work (CSCW):* 1–37.

7. Ishita Ghosh, Jay Chen, Joy Ming, and Azza Abouzied. 2015. The Persistence of Paper: A Case Study in Microfinance from Ghana. In *Proceedings of the Seventh International Conference on Information and Communication Technologies and Development* (ICTD '15), 13:1–13:10.

8. Michael Gibbert, Winfried Ruigrok, and Barbara Wicki. 2008. What passes as a rigorous case study? *Strategic management journal* 29, 13: 1465–1474.

9. James J. Gibson. 1979. The ecological approach to visual perception Houghton Mifflin.[rGRL, SR].

10. Joel D. Goldhar and Mariann Jelinek. 1985. Computer Integrated Flexible Manufacturing: Organizational, Economic, and Strategic Implications. *Interfaces* 15, 3: 94–105.

11. Richard Harper. 1998. *Inside the IMF: an ethnography of documents, technology and organisational action.* Routledge.

12. Richard Harper and Brian Shatwell. 2002. Paper mail in the home of the 21st century: An analysis of the future of paper mail and implications for the design of electronic alternatives. *Interactive Marketing* 3, 4: 311–323.

13. Christian Heath and Paul Luff. 1992. Collaboration and control: Crisis management and multimedia technology in London Underground Line Control Rooms. *Computer Supported Cooperative Work (CSCW)* 1, 1: 69–94.

14. Christian Heath, Marcus Sanchez Svensson, Jon Hindmarsh, Paul Luff, and Dirk Vom Lehn. 2002. Configuring awareness. *Computer Supported Cooperative Work (CSCW)* 11, 3: 317–347.

15. George Q. Huang, Y. F. Zhang, and P. Y. Jiang. 2008. RFID-based wireless manufacturing for real-time management of job shop WIP inventories. *The International Journal of Advanced Manufacturing Technology* 36, 7–8: 752–764.

16. Ian Hutchby. 2001. *Conversation and technology: From the telephone to the Internet.* Polity Press.

17. Ian Hutchby. 2001. Technologies, texts and affordances. *Sociology* 35, 2: 441–456.

18. Heinz K. Klein and Michael D. Myers. 1999. A set of principles for conducting and evaluating interpretive field studies in information systems. *MIS quarterly:* 67–93.

19. Jürgen Kletti. 2015. *MES - Manufacturing Execution System: Moderne Informationstechnologie unterstützt die Wertschöpfung.* Springer-Verlag.

20. Yoram Koren. 2010. *The Global Manufacturing Revolution: Product-Process-Business Integration and Reconfigurable Systems.* John Wiley & Sons.

21. Wendy E. MacKay. 1999. Is Paper Safer? The Role of Paper Flight Strips in Air Traffic Control. *ACM Trans. Comput.-Hum. Interact.* 6, 4: 311–340.

22. Steven Nahmias and Tava Lennon Olsen. 2015. *Production and Operations Analysis: Seventh Edition.* Waveland Press.

23. Gregory B. Newby. 1996. Metric multidimensional information space. In (TREC).

24. Donald A. Norman. 1988. *The psychology of everyday things.* Basic books.

25. Kenton O'hara and Abigail Sellen. 1997. A comparison of reading paper and on-line documents. In *Proceedings of the ACM SIGCHI Conference on Human factors in computing systems,* 335–342.

26. Mark G. Remson. 1991. Paperless manufacturing-a challenge now and in the future. In *Semiconductor Manufacturing Science Symposium, 1991. ISMSS 1991., IEEE/SEMI International,* 89–94.

27. Kjeld Schmidt. 1997. Of Maps and Scripts—the Status of Formal Constructs in Cooperative Work. In *Proceedings of the International ACM SIGGROUP Conference on Supporting Group Work: The Integration Challenge* (GROUP '97), 138–147.

28. Ben Schneiderman. 1996. The eyes have it: A task by data type taxonomy for information visualizations. In *Visual Languages, 1996. Proceedings., IEEE Symposium on.*

29. Abigail Sellen and Richard Harper. 1997. Paper as an analytic resource for the design of new technologies. In *Proceedings of the ACM SIGCHI Conference on Human factors in computing systems,* 319–326.

30. Abigail Sellen and Richard HR Harper. 2003. *The myth of the paperless office.* MIT press.

31. David Silverman. 2006. *Interpreting qualitative data: Methods for analyzing talk, text and interaction.* Sage.

32. Geoff Walsham. 2006. Doing interpretive research. *European journal of information systems* 15, 3: 320–330.

Reflections on Operators' and Maintenance Engineers' Experiences of Smart Factories

Daniela Wurhofer[1,2]**, Thomas Meneweger**[1]**, Verena Fuchsberger**[1,2]**, Manfred Tscheligi**[1,2]

[1]Center for Human-Computer Interaction, University of Salzburg, Salzburg, Austria

[2] AIT Austrian Institute of Technology GmbH, Center for Technology Experience, Vienna, Austria

[1]firstname.lastname@sbg.ac.at   [2]firstname.lastname@ait.ac.at

ABSTRACT

In production environments, the number of distributed, networked, and automated systems has grown rapidly and is expected to continue to grow in the future. This affects humans' work fundamentally, in terms of their tasks and routines. Increasing automation and digitalization leads to a substantial change of human-machine interactions on the shop floor, raising the question about humans' role in highly automated environments. In this paper, we shed light on how work in increasingly automated and digitalized factories is experienced, drawing on interviews with operators and maintenance engineers from three different industrial contexts. By reflecting on actual and anticipated developments in smart production environments, we point out how workers will experience those contexts. We finally discuss resulting challenges and leverage points for smart factories, i.e., areas where HCI and CSCW can contribute to positively influence workers' experiences in times of increasing automation and digitalization.

ACM Classification Keywords

H.5.m. Information Interfaces and Presentation (e.g. HCI): Miscellaneous;

Author Keywords

Smart Factory; Factory of the Future; Industry 4.0; Work; Experience.

INTRODUCTION

Modern production environments are characterized by increasing automation and digitalization. Systems in the factory are interconnected with other systems and working procedures are more and more automated. This change does not only concern production modes and routines, it also affects humans' everyday working routines in fundamental ways. The trend towards digitalized, networked, and automated systems is referred to as *smart factories, factories of the future, fourth industrial revolution,* or *industry 4.0.* Thereby, an academic as well as a public discourse started to take place, discussing economic, social, societal, and political consequences.

GROUP '18, January 7–10, 2018, Sanibel Island, FL, USA

© 2018 ACM. ISBN 978-1-4503-5562-9/18/01...$15.00

DOI: https://doi.org/10.1145/3148330.3148349

What is less discussed is how humans' interactions with systems and technologies are affected by these changes. Systems are increasingly interconnected and may be difficult to separate. Systems' operations become more complex and are harder to understand; processes are automated and cannot be intervened easily. Accordingly, workers' tasks and routines may need to be adapted, completely changed, or may even become obsolete. However, what does such a change of work mean for humans' role in production environments? How is the relation of humans and systems configured? How do humans experience working in increasingly automated and digitalized production environments?

This work contributes a reflection on workers' experiences in highly automated and digitalized factories. In particular, we explored how increasing automation and digitalization is experienced and anticipated by workers on the shop floor, relying on interview data from 10 operators and 22 maintenance engineers from three different industrial contexts in Central Europe. Based on our results, we point out areas where research and design can play a considerable role in promoting positive experiences in smart factories. These areas address control, workload, qualification and knowledge, as well as involvement and responsibility. Looking beyond single interactions in the factory, we envision the factory context from an experiential, holistic perspective [52], pointing out challenges and potentials of the fourth industrial revolution from an experiential point of view.

Our paper is structured as follows. First, we present related work regarding smart factories to demarcate and motivate our work. Next, we describe our research context, as well as the applied method and analysis. Then, we describe characteristics of work building on interviews with operators and maintenance engineers. Finally, we reflect on the results, point out challenges and leverage points to enhance workers' experiences, and discuss our insights.

BACKGROUND

In this section, we provide a brief overview of the historical development of manufacturing, point out promises and visions coming along with increasing digitalization and automation (including potential consequences for humans), and indicate how Human Computer Interaction (HCI) and Computer Supported Cooperative Work (CSCW) are involved in these developments.

A Historical Perspective on Fabrication

When considering the evolution and development of fabrication from a historical perspective, four industrial revolutions can be distinguished [43]. Beginning in the late 18th century, the first industrial revolution used water and steam power to mechanize production. Textile industry was the first to be affected by it. Tasks previously done laboriously by hand in hundreds of weavers' cottages were brought together in a single cotton mill and the factory was born. The second industrial revolution used electric power to create mass products. With moving assembly lines and the division of labor, mass products could be fabricated. With the third industrial revolution, electronics and information technology were used to automate production: digital technology found its way into factories.

Now a fourth industrial revolution is becoming apparent. This current revolution is characterized by a fusion of technologies, blurring the lines between the physical, digital, and biological spheres [43]. So-called cyber-physical systems (CPS) are introduced in traditional industries, meaning that many purely mechanical devices have evolved into computer-controlled and networked electromechanical systems [9]. The Internet allows communication between humans and machines in cyber-physical systems throughout large networks [8]. Whereas the first, second, and third industrial revolution are describing historical evolutions, the fourth industrial revolutions is rather a future vision or direction for factory environments, based on current technological developments and opportunities.

Smart Factories: Promises & Visions

Referring to the above mentioned fourth industrial revolution, the German government introduced the term *Industry 4.0* in 2011. This term summarizes "all technologies, trends and developments which serve to advance production plants" [47, p.1] and emphasizes the development of factories towards automation and digitalization. Similarly, the terms *smart factory* or *factory of the future* represent keywords to denote highly technological developments of factories [8]. In the following sections, we explain what increasing automation and digitalization mean from a technology-focused as well as from a human-focused perspective.

Technology-Focused Perspective

According to Broy and Schmidt [9], highly technological developments involve cyber-physical systems (i.e., control of mechanical activity through embedded computing) and advanced visualization techniques of data via virtual reality. Further, systems are aware of the environment and other objects through sensors and can interact with the environment through actuators. Thus, systems are dynamic and context-sensitive. Networking and connectivity are other important characteristics regarding smart factories. Systems are no longer located at a specific, unique place but distributed over several places, communicating with each other via networks. Smart factories come along with visions and promises of virtualization, decentralization, and network building [8].

Technological challenges associated with the new developments include individualized production (e.g., personalized mass products, modularization), collaborative networks (e.g., networks of legally independent organizations that share competencies in order to exploit a business opportunity), or end-to-end digital integration (e.g., advanced methods of communication and virtualization) [8]. Unquestionably, these technological developments already affect and will affect modern production environments and their socio-economic contexts. Thus, a range of disciplines is concerned with factories and their future, shaped by different foci and research interests: economics and sociology (e.g., [10, 19, 25]), computing, engineering and technology (e.g., [8, 9, 47]), or human factors and ergonomics (e.g., [12, 21, 22, 41]).

Human-Focused Perspective

With regard to human actors, different structural levels like shop floor, engineering, or management can be distinguished. Each of these structural levels is characterized by specific socio-technical constellations and system requirements. In the light of increasing automation and digitalization, it is uncertain if humans are still needed in smart factories. A common opinion is that humans will still be necessary; however, work and tasks will change [8]. This change could result in an *upgrading of qualifications* through the automation of simple and low-level tasks [55]. This can be considered as *skill-biased technical change*, meaning that the winners of increased automation are those who have already higher qualifications and resources [10]. In particular, there is an increasing need for coordination [8], requiring operators on the shop floor to be skilled in decision making (e.g., to solve problems in case of unforeseen events). The role as decision maker or coordinator comes along with an increase of work content for the single worker, making experience-based trouble shooting a main task of workers in future factories [25].

The increasing gap between complex tasks requiring high-qualified workers and simple tasks requiring low-qualified workers, with decreasing importance of qualifications on a mid-level, is considered as *polarization of qualifications* [25]. Jobs requiring such mid-level qualifications will be unnecessary or substituted by automation. In contrast to the upgrading hypothesis, simple activities will not disappear but new simple activities will evolve with increasing automation [10]. Overall, a polarized work environment will evolve, which could be considered as an environment which provides either *lousy or lovely jobs* [19].

Regarding humans in relation to machines, different philosophies exist. According to the *prosthesis design* philosophy, the machine expert is in complete control of the processes [38]. This means that the human is no longer needed to operate processes or carry out tasks. Considering the *human in the loop* philosophy, the human can actively intervene in processes. That means that the typical *safety valve* to manage problems is to keep a person "in the loop", requiring the person to apply his or her expertise in making the final decision on what actions to take [45]. Another philosophy considers *humans and machines complementing each other* [12, 25]. The effectiveness of such joint systems depends on the ability of both human and machine agents to coordinate and capitalize upon the unique abilities and information to which each agent has access [12].

The present paper takes a human-focused perspective, investigating and reflecting on workers' experiences in smart factories. Thereby, the above mentioned philosophies represent perceptions of human-machine relations which may be indicative for workers' experiences of smart factories. Relations between humans' experiences in smart factories and the above stated philosophies should be explicitly considered and discussed for that reason.

Human-Machine Interaction in Factories

Especially the CSCW community emphasizes the importance of investigating new technologies in the field (for an overview see [3]). For example, Brahe and Schmidt [6] ask for investigating how workflow technologies "are developed, deployed, appropriated, amended, used, redeveloped in the wild". Or, as Harrison and Dourish [23] point out "The placeness [...] is an evolved set of behaviours rooted in our ability to creatively appropriate aspects of the world, to organise it, and to bend it to our needs", emphasizing the shared understandings of appropriate use, and the social interpretation of cues in the physical environment. Regarding recent developments like for example digital fabrication, Ludwig et al. [31] also point out the importance of investigating practices of appropriation in the field to make technologies more sociable. Considered from a historical perspective, the so-called Francophone Ergonomics tradition put workers in the centre of work, paying particular attention to field studies, especially focusing on the effects of increased mechanization and automatic control systems. Attention was paid to working conditions of highly automated control systems as well as cognitive and organizational requirements related to decision making in technically complex work settings (e.g., supervisory process control in time- and safety critical work) [3].

Research on CSCW often focuses on work practices and work organization in a variety of contexts. The integration of IT systems or workflow management systems in relation to existing work practices and work organization was for example investigated in medical or financial contexts (e.g., [6, 20, 39]), as well as in the context of trouble shooting at call centers [11]. Other studies in the medical context investigated work organisation related to roles and practices (e.g., [5, 42, 46]. Collaborative practices and the integration of technology was also studied in the context of aircraft [50]. Further topical areas of CSCW research are mobile knowledge work [15] or crowd working [24, 35]. Summing up these studies, they point out the importance of aspects like control, communication, situation awareness or involvement of workers as well as the possibility of active intervention. Further, they emphasize the need for organizational implementation of new ways of working, the configuration of work as a means to provide influence and responsibility for work, or the awareness and visibility regarding changing work practices when introducing a new technology at work.

Previous work in human-centered automation and man-machine studies (e.g., [1, 38, 44, 45]) discusses potential consequences for workers regarding future factories. One such consequence is for example that simple presentations of low-level data become insufficient as they produce high cognitive load due to rising complexity and autonomy, considered as "data availability does not equal informativeness" [12, p.5]. It is essential that the human maintains an understanding of the problem from the system's perspective (e.g., solution

tactics) to let humans intervene appropriately in critical situations [12, 38]. According to Hirsch-Kreinsen [25], increasing complexity of systems is related to a limited controllability of systems, coming along with functional and economical challenges and unanticipated requirements due to lacking experiences of workers. This leads to a so-called *functional and informational distance* between workers and systems [25], which makes it difficult for workers to accumulate new knowledge, control systems, and take over responsibility of system processes. Digitalization and automation may lead to a loss of practical (tacit) knowledge, experience, and problem solving skills (which is especially relevant in case of unexpected errors). For example, monitoring tasks without direct contact to physical and material processes on the shop floor lead to an elimination of "the informal feedback associated with vibrations, sounds, and smells that many operaters relied upon" [28, p.419]. Further, detailed instructions regarding tasks and working procedures make detailed knowledge unnecessary and convey a loss of know-how [25]. Hancock [22] considers operators' overreliance on automation as *automation bias*, pointing out that employees and management have too much trust in the ability of digital systems to automate and support work procedures. Especially in case of unexpected (and mostly inevitable) incidents, highly automated processes lead to problematic situations which are difficult to solve and hard to cope with due to their routinous nature. Already in 1983, Bainbridge [1] considered this as *ironies of automation*.

Smith [45] describes this as *brittleness*, i.e., the occurrence of situations and incidents which cannot be handled by the system, requiring a person to be in the loop (i.e., to apply his or her expertise in making the final decision on what actions to take). Thus, the human's role is to amplify the machine's adaptability of dealing with unexpected conditions [38]. This was also shown by Meneweger et al. [33], pointing out the necessity of humans to adapt to the automated systems and compensate failures in processes or task procedures. Regarding difficult and complex problems or failure situations, the human is mostly left with his own resources without any tools. This can be related to the informational distance described above: attempts to take the user out of the problem-solving loop can inadvertently increase the user's burden by requiring to handle the difficult cases without the benefit of experience and the practice of solving the simpler ones [16, 51].

Building on existing research from the CSCW community as well as man-machine studies, we take a closer look on an experiential perspective of work in the following. Especially in highly automated and digitalized factory contexts, such a perspective is often missing, in particular regarding operators' and maintenance engineers' experiences when working with smart manufacturing systems.

User Experience in Smart Factories

Humans are expected to be needed in smart factories, though in changing roles and for changing tasks [4]. This is based on the assumption that traditional processes and structures may (partly) remain in companies due to technological limitations. Further, short-term orientation and organizational structures of companies impede long-term oriented innovation [25]. It is, therefore, questionable if there will ever be a completely new production environment with no "ancient" structures. Rather, hybrid structures are more likely to characterize smart factories.

That means that different stages of development may exist next to each other: Fully automated/digitalized systems, partly automated/digitalized systems, as well as systems which are not automated/digitalized at all.

Since the human is expected to be an essential part of future factories (as mentioned earlier), it is important to discuss how the developments towards the fourth industrial revolution will change humans' working routines and practices in smart production environments. This change of working routines, in turn, strongly impacts how humans' experience related technology usage in everyday factory work. Within HCI, this experiential view is subsumed under the umbrella term *User Experience* (UX) [18] and is also relevant for human-machine interaction in the factory. Regarding daily factory work, the relevance of workers' UX (e.g., [34]), as well as contextual influences on it (e.g., [53]) - comprehensively considered as Contextual User Experience [53] - have already been shown. For industrial settings in particular, the need to understand industrial user experience [36] has been pointed out. Further, creating value for companies through UX research [48] and the importance of defining UX goals [26] have been emphasized.

Changing work routines and practices impose challenges for UX in smart factory work regarding meaningfulness [30], joy [22], and positive experiences when interacting with technology [26]. For example, increasing automation could create high cognitive load and lead to a feeling of excessive demand due to increased complexity of processes. Tasks requiring passive monitoring of processes could represent a lack of challenge and lead to a feeling of boredom. Collaborating with advanced systems like robots could change interaction and communication at the workplace [40] and consequently affects workers' experience.

Although there is some research on UX in the factory, research focusing on the understanding of operators' and maintenance engineers' experiences in smart factories is missing. Potential effects of automation and digitalization on the workers' experience, i.e., the experience of workers on smart shop floors, is considered as an increasingly important topic to be investigated by the HCI and CSCW community. In particular, we address the exploration of challenges and opportunities that research and design will be confronted with in smart factories.

EXPLORING FACTORIES IN THE WILD

For our reflections on smart factories, we are drawing on qualitative interview data gathered in three different industrial contexts: automotive, electronics, and logistics sectors. Our studies took place in three facilities, one developing systems and solutions for inbound logistics (e.g., warehouses), one automotive supplier, and one operating in the area of semiconductor fabrication, i.e., producing micro chips. The studies were conducted within two nationally funded projects where we investigated human-machine interactions at industrial facilities, which consider themselves as Industry 4.0 contexts

(i.e., deploying digital, interconnected, and automated technologies). Within these projects, we focused on humans on the shop floor, e.g., on operators and maintenance engineers in factories, or stakeholders in close contact with them (e.g., shift leads, trainers).

Qualitative Interviews

The reason for focusing on employees involved in operating and maintaining activities is that their work (directly involved in the production activities) will be mostly affected by changes coming along with increasing digitalization and automation on shop floors [29]. We conducted two waves of interviews, i.e., two interview studies with the first interview study taking place in April 2014 and the second taking place in May 2016. In both studies, interviewees were affected by the introduction of a new system. This was used as a trigger for interviewees' narrations regarding their experiences and anticipations in the light of increasing digitalization and automation. The first interview study was conducted at the semiconductor production site, focusing on daily work of human operators in the chip production, aiming to explore how operators experience working together with a newly deployed automated (robotic) system on the shop floor. The second interview study focused on maintenance engineers from all three industrial facilities, investigating how they experience working together with an intelligent assistive system. The insights presented in this paper are based on a sample of 32 participants from all three industrial partners. All interviews lasted about one hour.

Within the first study, we conducted 10 narrative interviews. Narrative interviews are open-structured qualitative interviews that aim to evoke reports of personal experiences by the participants [17]. The people interviewed were affected by the deployment of an automated (robotic) system. The system deployed was a robotic arm, which is able to load and unload machines for chip production. For the production of micro chips, a waver must undergo several production steps where it is treated by different machines. The robotic arm puts the wavers into the machines and puts it out from the machines after the procedure has finished. Before the introduction of the robotic arm, these loading and unloading tasks were done manually by human operators. We interviewed seven operators, two shift leads, and one dispatcher, all working together with the automated (robotic) system. In the interviews, we focused on workers' experiences regarding the newly deployed system. We were interested in expectations regarding the new system, actual changes of working routines, as well as anticipations for future factory work considering increasing automation and digitalization. Participants' mean age was 40 years ($SD = 12$), ranging from 22 to 57 years. Eight workers were male and two female. Their average working experience in the factory was 16 years ($SD = 11$), ranging from 0.5 to 30 years.

Within the second study, we conducted 22 semi-structured interviews [17]. Eight people were interviewed at project partner A working in the logistics context; eight people at project partner B working in the automotive domain, and six people at project partner C working in the semiconductor factory. In all three industrial contexts, a prototype of an intelligent assistive system for supporting experienced and inexperienced maintenance engineers was deployed. The interactive prototype was implemented on a mobile device (tablet) which provided different functionalities for assisting maintenance engineers in their daily work such as step-by-step guidance for specific maintenance tasks or error diagnostics support. To evaluate the system, the participants had to perform standardized maintenance tasks in the respective context by using the prototype for assistance (e.g., step-by-step guidance was provided). Afterwards, we interviewed the 10 maintenance engineers being familiar with service activities (in the specific context), and the 12 employees not being familiar with the specific maintenance task (e.g., working at the IT department, persons responsible for training or documentation)i.e., stakeholders indirectly involved in maintenance. On the one hand, the interviews focused on the assistive system prototype and its potentials for work. On the other hand, we explored maintenance engineers' daily working routines as well as actual and expected changes of their work due to technological innovations and increasing automation at production sites. The mean age of the participants was 41 years ($SD = 11$), ranging from 18 to 62 years; 20 employees were male and two female. Their average working experience in the company was 14 years ($SD = 9$), ranging from 1.5 to 32 years.

Analysis

The qualitative interviews were audio recorded, transcribed verbatim, and analyzed following a thematic analysis approach [7]. This analysis approach is used to organize qualitative data sets by identifying different themes within the collected data. For our purpose, we aimed to structure and describe the participants' statements about their experiences with and anticipations regarding new systems by revealing the prevalent thematic issues facing an increasingly digitalized and automated industry context.

In a first step, we selected relevant data with regard to the question how employees anticipate and experience changes. Then, the collected data was structured by assigning initial categories. In a next step, the categories were summarized into more general themes that aimed to describe people's experiences and assessments regarding the deployment of automated systems or smart technologies. Overall, from an operator's point of view, four main themes, and from a maintenance engineer's point of view, five main themes were identified. Based on the identified themes in the qualitative interviews, the findings were then interpreted in relation to their relevance for research and design. The outcomes of these reflections are presented after the next section, which shows the main insights from the interviews.

FINDINGS

In this section, we provide insights on how work in smart factories is described from both operators' and maintenance engineers' perspectives. Quotations have been translated from german to english.

Operators' Experiences

Below, we present experiences of operators that came along with increasing automation and digitalization in the studied factories. Selected quotations of operators are denoted accordingly from O1 to O10.

Monotony and Complexity

Working with automated systems was often associated with monotony. Such monotony can either be seen negatively or positively. When considered negatively, working with automated systems was experienced as more repetitive and monotonous, which was associated with a decrease of mental effort. One participant (O10) put it like this: *"It has made work boring... because it simply withdraws our tasks"*. In contrast, some of the workers saw monotony in a positive way, as monotony was linked to a decrease of mental effort and workload. One participant stated it in the following way: *"It has reduced working speed. Many handles [i.e., movements] can be omitted [...]. That is positive from my point of view"*. Next to monotony, an increase of complexity was linked to the introduction of automated systems. Ever since the deployment of automated systems, some procedures were experienced as more complex than before. Workers had to adjust their behavior to the system's behavior, including the anticipation of or reaction to the system's behavior. This made some working routines (e.g., the deposit of specific tools) more complicated for workers.

Adaption and Control

Regarding the collaboration with automated systems, the question who adapts to whom or controls whom was arising. Often, operators pointed out the necessity to adapt to the automated systems. That means that in practice, the operators had to adjust their working routines to the systems' work. In order to anticipate the system's behavior and execute their work properly, the operators had to constantly focus on what the system was doing. Thus, the human could act as a back-up for the automated system in case of defects/errors, i.e., the human replaced the automated system in case of problems to ensure that the production continued. Such an adaption represented a constraint in the operator's behavior and workflow. In our case study, the deployment of automated systems led to physical constraints for the operators, i.e., a limitation of space. Workers had to take care where to position things as the new systems required physical space, which was not demanded before. For example, one participant (O6) remarked: *"And the space is also [limited]... at some point you don't know where to place things"*. Another issue linked to the need to adapt to the system is the feeling of control. When talking to operators, they often stated that they experience no possibility to contribute to or influence the system's behavior. This leads to a feeling of non-involvement and lack of control. One participant (O2) stated it in the following way: *"Regarding the robot [...] you don't have any influence"*. Similarly, another participant (O10) pointed out that *"you should not intervene in the robot's actions [...]. You stand alongside and look at it [the system] until it is finished"*.

Knowledge Acquisition and Trouble Shooting

Knowledge is a central topic when introducing new systems and technologies in a factory. Operators' knowledge on how to handle these systems is crucial in daily work. Acquiring knowledge and skills in handling new systems is especially important for problem solving, as in case of problems direct interaction with the system is needed. When knowledge is not provided sufficiently in trainings, trial and error strategies are often applied on-site to learn more about the automated system. This was described as follows by one participant (O10): *I mean, I have to say, we found out a lot by ourselves, because at night no one is here and we are doing overnight shifts. This means we have to be able to find solutions by ourselves and, thus, we were able to fix some errors with the manual, the electronic one, thankfully. Also without the technicians".*

As learning happens while doing, mainly targeting the most important functionalities of the system, informal knowledge is especially important. This means that knowledge about the automated system was gained by asking or observing others (mainly other operators as well as technicians). This was pointed out by the following statement (O1): *"There have been trainings, but most information had been shared from worker to worker".* In this study, direct interaction with the automated system was closely linked to trouble shooting. This means that in case of errors and problems, the automated system had to be actively operated (i.e., the system's routines have to be interrupted). Thus, knowledge acquisition was especially important for problem solving and trouble shooting.

Emotions and Feelings
Regarding operators' emotions and feelings, there were different fears linked to working with automated systems. Often, fear of being replaced was mentioned. This means that operators were afraid that humans are replaced by machines and not needed any more in the factory. For example, one participant (O1) stated: *"Clearly, this is linked to fear, as it* [the robot] *should replace the human somehow".* Automated systems were often considered as taking away tasks from the operators: The automated system carried out tasks that were previously conducted by operators. Another issue was fear due to uncertainty of future developments. It was often unclear for operators what the deployment of new systems meant for their work. One participant (O1) pointed out that the number of automated systems will steadily increase by stating the following: *"How is that going on? If it begins like this it can only get worse'.* However, the operators also reported ambiguous feelings towards to the robots, since they were aware that innovation was needed and emphasized the necessity to keep track with technological progress.

Maintenance Engineers' Experiences
In this section we describe experiences of maintenance engineers, and stakeholders involved in maintenance. Selected quotations of maintenance engineers and involved stakeholders are denoted accordingly from M1 to M22.

Connectedness and Complexity
Employees and workers associate smart factories with increasing connectedness of systems and higher complexity. One participant (M13) considered this increasing connectedness as one of the biggest challenges regarding smart factories: *"The overall connection of all systems coming from different subsystems [...] drawing conclusions somehow and provide them to others [...]. I think this is the great challenge now, which*

we hopefully can cope with passably". Increasing automation was linked to increasing complexity, or, as one participant (M7) mentioned, *"a high level of automation is coming along with many new requirements".* There were also concerns regarding the comprehension of increasingly interconnected and complex systems. For example, one participant (M2) indicated that the *"comprehension of the system could get lost [...] however, this is essential for trouble shooting".* Another issue contributing to complexity is the integration of existing - and often old - systems. For example, one participant (M13) stated that *"we need also solutions for old facilities. I think this is the challenge."* Related to the connectedness of systems is the possibility to access information constantly (e.g., in the cloud). The extensive amount of available information in turn increased complexity, making it more difficult to select and provide the right information.

System Control and Monitoring
The supervision of systems - in the sense of monitoring and controlling them - play an increasingly important role in smart factories. On one hand, this should prevent problems beforehand, considered as *"the attempt to recognize problems preventively"* (M10). On the other hand, supervision of systems means the remote access and control of systems. In particular, this could mean that one remotely logs into a system for *"accessing equipment via the laptop"* (M22). Condition monitoring is another term mentioned in this context. Therefore, the current state of a system was checked constantly, and, if there is a specific abrasion, this information was passed on or displayed. One participant (M17) mentioned that in the past years, the control over systems (i.e., remotely accessing and controlling them) had increased, which, in turn, allowed to better trace and document systems' operations and performance. This participant further reported about a feeling of being monitored by the system, e.g., through the increasing need to document tasks and activities. This was perceived as *"surveillance"* (M17).

Increased Mobility and Permanent Availability
Changes for employees were often induced by an increase of mobile technologies like smartphones, laptops, or tablets. In relation to this, higher convenience of work due to reduced ways was mentioned. Mobile technologies often reduced ways, as necessary information was available on the mobile device. For example, one participant (M9) pointed out that *"the deployment of tablets for maintenance has made maintenance engineers' work much more comfortable, respectively, they have to walk much less than before".* Closely related to this was the possibility to work remotely. Often, workers could access systems remotely, thus also saving time and pathways. As one participant (M10) stated, the possibility to work mobile and remote also has drawbacks as physical activity and movement is reduced: *"Much of the things for which someone had to go somewhere is in the meanwhile possible without moving".* Further, this provided the opportunity to work from everywhere - even from home or from the airplane. Such a permanent availability may provide advantages and drawbacks at the same time; one participant (M13) considered it as *"a blessing as well as a curse".* Some of the participants complained about the permanent availability at work due to mobile

phones, as this would interrupt them during work. One participant (M22) stated for example: *"Regarding mobile phones, it's the permanent availability. That is necessary especially during the night shifts, I know, but if you are getting thirty calls on the phone you are frustrated, eventually"*.

Availability of Expertise and Documentation

In the interviews, knowledge, information, and documentation of knowledge were central topics regarding smart factories. One participant (M11) stated it like this: *"Having access to experts is getting increasingly important as technology is developing very quickly and new customers are constantly joining"*. Expertise in maintenance and trouble shooting related to technological developments and innovations was found to be an important aspect. Similarly, availability of information was another important aspect mentioned by the workers. Workers and employees were increasingly interconnected via networks (e.g., internet), which, in turn, makes it possible to access information easily. Such an availability of information provided advantages as well as disadvantages and, thus, had to be organized in a way that is not too complex but easy to locate.

Related to that was a growing need for (appropriate) documentation. With increasing automation and digitalization, there were a lot of new products which have to be documented. When documenting, products, technologies, processes and context had to be understood in order to properly explain and report. The organization of processes was related to documentation. As one participant (M11) stated, *"if the product changes, the documentation has to change, too"*, meaning that increasing digitalization did not only affect production and products, but also the way processes were reported. One participant (M12) pointed out a trend towards mobile documentation which could be realized via information units. Information units could be considered as chunks of information that can be put together modularly. In order to be successfully applied, such a new approach (i.e., information units) would require new structures and strategies which are modular and flexible.

Emotions and Feelings

Emotions and feelings were also mentioned regarding maintenance work in smart factories. The fear of increasing unemployment was often pointed out. Further, employees and workers reported about the loss of personal contact. Feeling monitored by systems was also an impression. One participant (M17), for example, stated *"this did not take place in the past, this kind of surveillance"*. Reliefs were also coming along with increasing automation. For example, one participant (M3) described that *"everything is going on faster, and everybody wants faster responses. The advantage is that you can send photos or contact the technician on-site. That is a relief"*. However, at the same time, stress had increased, e.g., due to constant availability. Stress associated with constant availability was often linked to smart phones which were used as a work tool. As one participant (M21) stated, *"the [smart]phone is a stress factor which we did not have in former times"*. Overall, permanent availability seemed to induce stress in workers and employees, whereas remote access to systems may represent a relief (i.e., reducing the need to be on-site).

Summary

Based on the interviews, we identified the following characteristics regarding *operators' experiences and anticipations considering smart factories*: (1) monotony and complexity; (2) adaption and control; (3) knowledge acquisition and trouble shooting; (4) emotions and feelings. From *maintenance engineers'* point of view, the following themes denoted their *experiences and anticipations related to smart factories*: (1) connectedness and complexity; (2) system control and monitoring; (3) increased mobility and permanent availability; (4) availability of expertise and documentation; (5) emotions and feelings. In the next section, we reflect on the above listed themes and point out challenges and leverage points for research and design in smart factories.

DISCUSSION & REFLECTION

The introduction of new technologies in work environments in the sense of increased automation, digitalization and connectedness of systems is related to a spectrum of experiences workers have with these technologies. In the previous chapter, we showed how operators and maintenance engineers of three production facilities experienced an increase in automation. In this chapter, we reflect on our results in regards to workers' experiences in smart factories and resulting challenges and leverage points related to technological developments as well as humans' experiences, values and meaningfulness of work. The topics described in this section represent central categories which we will summarize and discuss in the following with regard to challenges and leverage points for CSCW and HCI.

Control

In the interviews with the operators as well as in the interviews with the maintenance engineers, control was discussed throughout. From a maintenance engineers' point of view, control seemed to be mostly related to the control of systems, in the sense that the system state is monitored or that systems are increasingly controlled remotely. In contrast, for operators it was questionable who is in control of whom, as operators often had to adapt to the automated system or were not allowed or able to control the system. In the production facilities we researched, the maintenance engineers actively controlled the systems, whereas operators rather seemed to be passive with regard to autonomous systems in the factory. They hardly had any influence or control but rather had to adapt their routines to the system's actions. Thus, control can range from the extreme of having total control over the system to the extreme of being totally obedient to the system.

In line with related work, it has been reported that humans strive for a feeling of control. According to Rosso et al. [37], the feeling of personal control represents one source for making work meaningful. Work with little space for action and decision-making negatively effects a person's well-being and intellectual capacity [49]. In a broader sense, this can be considered as self-efficacy, i.e., individuals' beliefs that they have the power and ability to produce an intended effect [2]. Striving for control in relation to the introduction of new technologies was for example shown by Brahe and Schmidt [6], who studied the introduction of a workflow management system in a large financial institution. Regarding human-machine interaction in the factory, Kaasinen et al. [26] mentioned a sense of control over the system as relevant to transform negative feelings like anxiety or uncertainty into positive experiences. This may be an especially important aspect when considering operators who had to adapt their working routines and practices to the automated system. As this passivity may convey feelings that one's work is not important or can be replaced by automated systems, fears and uncertainties were often mentioned in relation to increasing automation and digitalization. Increasing complexity (e.g., through networked, distributed systems) makes it more and more difficult to understand processes and limits the controllability of systems [25].

From a technological perspective, which is shaped by the possibilities and requirements of machines, the need to control systems will decrease with increasing automation and digitalization. This in turn may limit humans' feeling of being in control over the system. From an experience-centered perspective, a feeling of control is crucial for the workers' self-esteem and meaningfulness of work.

Challenges and Leverage Points
A pressing question is *how to give workers (a feeling of) control whilst not counteracting technological developments regarding increasing automation and digitalization.* The following examples provide suggestions of how to convey a feeling of control in workers.

- *Possibility for human interventions:* Enabling workers to overrule the system in specific cases and situations gives them a feeling of control towards the system. For example, in case of errors, also operators (not only maintenance engineers and technicians) should have the possibility (e.g., knowledge and permissions) to take actions.

- *Transparency of system activity:* Knowing what a system is doing (instead of experiencing it as a black box) is essential to control systems [38]. Information about the system's state and activities provides a feeling of control in workers. For example, displays that allow to track system activities support transparency and control.

Workload
Our interviews showed that aspects like monotony, complexity, or permanent availability might come along with increasing automation and digitalization. In particular, maintenance engineers reported about increasing complexity, coming along with a range of new requirements and challenges. They experienced processes and systems as increasingly complex. Related to the introduction of new technologies, some maintenance engineers felt stressed and overstrained due to permanent availability (e.g., permanent calls on the phone). With regard to operators, increasing automation of processes led to boredom as tasks got monotonous and repetitive, or workers had long waiting times between tasks. For both, operators and maintenance engineers, knowledge about systems and processes declines as a result of increasing automation. This is in line with existing literature, claiming that due to the omission of the first order feedback loop (e.g., drawing, milling, grinding, drilling, handling, etc.), the worker is able to attend to a wider segment

of the total transformation process and the required domain knowledge becomes more extensive and more complex [41]. Machines will increasingly take over tasks which were conducted by humans beforehand, changing workers' processes and routines. Related to increasing automation, workload can vary from low to high, meaning that workers' experiences may range from boredom to excessive demand. According to Goos [19], increasing automation and digitalization creates a divide between jobs which are not challenging at all and jobs which are very challenging, pointing out the spectrum of how workload may be experienced.

From an experience-centered perspective, adequate workload and challenge are important for positively experiencing work. Ideally, humans are stimulated by work, i.e., work allows them to optimally apply their abilities in a way that neither overstrains nor underchallenges them.

Challenges and Leverage Points
A challenge is *how to contribute towards an individualized, optimal level of workload for workers.* Below, we provide exemplary suggestions how boredom as well as excessive demand can be reduced towards optimal, well-balanced workload, creating a flow experience [13].

- *Assistive systems to reduce overstrain:* Providing technological support in form of assistive systems can help to reduce cognitive load of human workers. For example, assistive systems can offer step-by-step instructions for specific tasks, support humans in trouble shooting, or store information which can be dynamically requested.

- *Challenge and dispersion against boredom:* Bringing new input for workers can counteract boredom induced by monotonous or repetitive tasks. Such a new input could be gamification [14] of work, i.e., playful or challenging approaches for workers in relation to their (and other workers') work activities.

- *Mental and physical training to compensate inactive times:* We suggest to use non-active times for facilitating mental and physical activities, having a positive effect on work (as workers are better informed and/or healthier). For example, online courses and trainings may contribute to further education of workers, or physical trainings might compensate long standing or sitting.

Qualification and Knowledge
In our interviews, knowledge and expertise were considered as important by both operators and maintenance engineers, especially with regard to errors and unexpected incidents. Both, operators and maintenance engineers pointed out that the need of handling errors will rise with increasing automation and digitalization. Further, it will get more difficult to handle errors due to increasing connectedness of systems and increasing complexity. For operators, knowledge on how to handle new systems was crucial especially when errors occur; however, they reported that trainings were often insufficient so that they had to acquire knowledge informally or by trial and error. For maintenance engineers, access to knowledge was also an important topic; they mainly accessed expertise remotely

or via documentation. The statements of both operators and maintenance engineers showed the importance of knowledge, pointing out the important and differentiating role of education and constant access to knowledge in smart factories.

In line with related work, failures of machines are a crucial element of industrial work [45]. Mostly, failures represent unexpected situations which have to be handled by the human, requiring the so-called human in the loop [25]. Being prepared to handle unexpected situations is closely related to vigilance, i.e,. the need for sustained attention over a longer period of time, e.g., required for air traffic control [32]. When referring to humans in smart factories, most of the time experienced, educated and highly qualified workers are meant [47]. This is related to increasing complexity and the fact that problem solvers and trouble shooters may become increasingly important. In other words, "The more we depend on technology and push it to its limits, the more we need highly-skilled, well-trained, well-practised people to make systems resilient, acting as the last line of defence against the failures that will inevitably occur." [4, p. 65]. In accordance with the polarization hypothesis [10], simple jobs will also remain, as new simple activities will evolve with increasing automation. Thus, the gap between highly qualified and low qualified activities will increase.

From an experience-centered perspective, knowledge on how to solve errors is crucial [11]. As shown in our interviews, workers strive for diversification and self-determination. At best, work should be more than troubleshooting or passively reacting to pitfalls and errors. When not having the necessary knowledge to counteract errors and troubles, workers are likely to feel helpless or frustrated. Ideally, humans have access to knowledge (e.g., on systems, processes, products) whenever necessary. Knowledge acquisition can be either facilitated on-site by sufficient training or by access to necessary information.

Challenges and Leverage Points
A challenging topic is *how to provide workers with necessary knowledge and information tailored to the individuals' expertise.* We indicate exemplary suggestions for design in order to offer workers the possibility to gather the knowledge or training they need or would like to have.

- *Flexible learning approaches:* Offering the possibility of further education for workers in a flexible manner promotes knowledge acquisition [27]. Such trainings should be available in different modes so that a worker can choose according to what type of training is most adequate. For example, eLearning could be used as a means to train workers, with the mode of on-site (directly on the system) as well as online training.

- *Dynamic access to knowledge:* Providing the possibility to access knowledge whenever needed supports workers in handling situations which require specific expertise and knowledge, expanding existing qualifications. For example, assistive systems could dynamically provide knowledge dependent on the specific situation as well as on the qualification of the worker.

Involvement and Responsibility
Involvement and responsibility seem to be an important issue of work in increasingly automated and digitalized contexts for both operators and maintenance engineers. For operators, feeling involved in decision processes and developments was crucial regarding the deployment of new systems; not involving them led to uncertainties and fears regarding future developments. For maintenance engineers, responsibility was often associated with stress, which was even increased due to permanent availability related to new technologies such as mobile phones.

Consequently, responsibility and involvement might be crucial for workers' experience, being in the tension of high responsibility and non-involvement. Involvement and responsibility in the sense of decision making and space for action is crucial for one's well-being and intellectual capacity [49]. Being involved and having influence does not only convey a positive experience, it further promotes an understanding of the complexity of the involved systems and increases acceptance of new systems [6, 54]. According to Grote et al. [21], responsibility should come along with the possibility to change something, otherwise it will be frustrating. With increasing complexity, responsibilities are often no longer directly assignable. Christoffersen and Woods [12] consider this as directability, asking who owns the problem.

From an experience-centered perspective, providing the feeling of responsibility can reduce fears and uncertainties. Too much responsibility, however, can be linked to overstrain and stress. Thus, involvement of humans should be given but has to be balanced.

Challenges and Leverage Points
An important question is *how to achieve that workers feel responsible while not being overstrained.* Below, we point out exemplary suggestions for design in relation to workers' experiences.

- *Participation:* Actively involving workers in decision processes and deployment of new technologies counteracts uncertainties, fears and rumors. Workers should not be passively confronted with technological innovations but actively involved in decision processes [33]. For example, design decisions can be discussed and iterated in workshops with workers who will be affected by the new system.

- *Transparency of processes:* Whenever changes in everyday work occur (e.g., change of existing structures, processes, or work flows; introduction of new systems; hiring of new workers), workers should be able to prepare themselves beforehand instead of being immediately confronted with the new situation. This preparation does not only include information about the time frame, potential changes or reasons for the change; it also includes necessary knowledge acquisition (i.e., training) to be optimally prepared for new challenges coming along with innovation.

Limitations & Contribution
We are aware that our insights are bound to the three industrial contexts under consideration. The proposed challenges are

therefore a first collection of topics related to human-machine interactions in smart factories. With this, we open up a special application context to a broader audience and discuss opportunities for experience-centered design in increasingly automated and digitalized contexts. Beyond this, the presented challenges and potentials may be also relevant for humans' experiences with automated systems in other contexts. For example, with regard to the application area of (semi-)autonomous driving, designers are also confronted with the challenge to design for optimal, well-balanced workload of drivers.

Envisioning the future of production needs to consider that technological innovation is intertwined with existing, even outdated, technology. Even in highly automatized and digitalized shop floors, humans are expected to be needed, though in changing roles and for changing tasks [4]. Next to high-qualified workers who plan, introduce, supervise, and maintain the systems, practically experienced operators are needed to compensate automation deficiencies which are very likely to occur in the future. Autonomy and self-organization of systems will probably be partly applicable in the factory [10], so that proven and traditional forms of work will likely also remain [25]. Even with increasing automation and digitalization, industrial work in the factory will probably never be fully automated and digitalized; rather, we will find mixed forms of automation and digitalization that design needs to face, raising the question of how to optimally unite human and system competences. Therefore, smart factories have to be considered in constant transition between the first and the fourth industrial revolution, i.e., between mechanical and cyber-physical production.

Our findings are mostly in line with related work (e.g., [1, 4]), showing for example that monitoring and error-handling tasks increase with increasing automation. We extend existing research by looking at smart factories from a human-centric perspective, taking into account how humans interact with technologies in smart factories. Therefore, we explicitly consider experiences of workers with (new) systems in the factory (e.g., boredom, excessive demand, or loss of control) and discuss them in relation to challenges and leverage points for enhancing work experience. This connection between future tasks on the shop floor, experiences of workers, and resulting challenges has not been explicitly discussed in related work on factories (of the future) so far. Such a linkage provides insights and promotes further research regarding humans' role, experiences and the relation of humans and systems in smart factories and other highly automated and digitalized contexts.

CONCLUSION

In this paper, we critically discussed the role and associated experiences of workers and presented design challenges for increasingly automated shop floors. Our reflections are based on interviews with 10 operators and 22 maintenance engineers from three different industrial contexts. In relation to the introduction of new technological systems, we had the opportunity to interview them about their work experience and anticipations of the future. We discussed challenges arising in smart factories, i.e., areas where design can contribute to posi-

tively influence workers' experiences in times of increasing automation and digitalization.

Overall, we understand increasing automation and digitalization in factories as having both advantages and drawbacks. Changing work routines and practices impose challenges for the design of systems, interactions, and work environments. We see the role of design to cope with the changing work routines and practices in a way that workers' experience is taken into account and shaped towards positive experiences [26]. An exemplary potential for experience-centered design in relation to the above mentioned challenges is to design for perceived control. This could be for example achieved by enabling human interventions or providing transparency of activities and processes. Designing for balanced workload is another experiential goal that could be addressed, e.g., by facilitating technological support, offering challenging activities, or supporting mental and physical training. Further, designing for information provision could positively influence workers' experiences, e.g., by offering further education or flexible learning, or by providing dynamic access to knowledge. Assigning responsibility to workers may be another way how design could positively shape experiences, e.g., by allowing active involvement of users or providing contextual information.

Assuming that we can positively shape workers' experiences, we stress the importance of a holistic perspective on smart factories. We have to be aware that the fourth industrial revolution comes along with economical, political, educational, and social changes. These changes provide challenges and opportunities that have to be considered when discussing smart factories in general and the role of design in particular. For example, jobs and working hours may become more flexible and dynamic. Thus, work performance may be defined in other ways, as the measurement of working hours may not be adequate any more. With more flexible jobs, individuality of workers can be better considered so that humans can work in a way that best fits their strengths. Jobs in the factory may probably change, making existing differentiations between roles of operators, maintenance engineers, or technicians outdated and requiring new job descriptions. Further, education may also be defined differently, with work as an inclusive space for education and training.

The above mentioned issues point out the challenges and potentials of the fourth industrial revolution from a human-centered view. We hope that researchers and practitioners step into the complex context of smart factories and engage in the design of workplaces of the future, affecting not only work but human life in all its facets.

ACKNOWLEDGMENTS

The financial support by the Austrian Federal Ministry of Science, Research and Economy and the National Foundation for Research, Technology and Development is gratefully acknowledged (Christian Doppler Laboratory "Contextual Interfaces"). The financial support by the Austrian Ministry for Transport, Innovation and Technology is gratefully acknowledged. The program "Produktion der Zukunft" is operated by the Austrian Research Promotion Agency FFG.

REFERENCES

1. Lisanne Bainbridge. 1983. Ironies of automation. *Automatica* 19, 6 (1983), 775–779.

2. Albert Bandura. 1977. *Social learning theory*. Englewood Cliffs, NJ: Prentice Hall.

3. Liam Bannon, Kjeld Schmidt, and Ina Wagner. 2011. Lest we forget. In *ECSCW 2011: Proceedings of the 12th European Conference on Computer Supported Cooperative Work, 24-28 September 2011, Aarhus Denmark*. Springer, 213–232.

4. Gordon Baxter, John Rooksby, Yuanzhi Wang, and Ali Khajeh-Hosseini. 2012. The Ironies of Automation: Still Going Strong at 30?. In *Proceedings of the 30th European Conference on Cognitive Ergonomics (ECCE '12)*. ACM, New York, NY, USA, 65–71. DOI: http://dx.doi.org/10.1145/2448136.2448149

5. Claus Bossen and Martin Foss. 2016. The Collaborative work of Hospital Porters: Visibility, Accountability and IT Hospital Logistics. In *Proceedings of the 2016 Conference on Computer Supported Cooperative Work*. Association for Computing Machinery.

6. Steen Brahe and Kjeld Schmidt. 2007. The story of a working workflow management system. In *Proceedings of the 2007 international ACM conference on Supporting group work*. ACM, 249–258.

7. Virginia Braun and Victoria Clarke. 2006. Using thematic analysis in psychology. *Qualitative research in psychology* 3, 2 (2006), 77–101.

8. Malte Brettel, Niklas Friederichsen, Michael Keller, and Marius Rosenberg. 2014. How Virtualization, Decentralization and Network Building Change the Manufacturing Landscape: An Industry 4.0 Perspective. *International Journal of Mechanical, Aerospace, Industrial, Mechatronic and Manufacturing Engineering* 8, 1 (2014), 37 – 44.

9. Manfred Broy and Albrecht Schmidt. 2014. Challenges in Engineering Cyber-Physical Systems. *Computer* 47, 2 (2014), 70–72. DOI: http://dx.doi.org/10.1109/MC.2014.30

10. Erik Brynjolfsson and Andrew McAfee. 2014. *The Second Machine Age: Work, Progress, and Prosperity in a Time of Brilliant Technologies*. Norton & Company.

11. Stefania Castellani, Antonietta Grasso, Jacki O'Neill, and Frederic Roulland. 2009. Designing Technology As an Embedded Resource for Troubleshooting. *Comput. Supported Coop. Work* 18, 2-3 (June 2009), 199–227. DOI:http://dx.doi.org/10.1007/s10606-008-9088-1

12. Klaus Christoffersen and David D. Woods. 2002. How to make automated systems team players. *Advances in human performance and cognitive engineering research* 2 (2002), 1–12.

13. Mihaly Csikszentmihalyi. 1990. *Flow: the psychology of optimal experience*. Harper & Row, New York.

14. Sebastian Deterding. 2012. Gamification: Designing for Motivation. *interactions* 19, 4 (July 2012), 14–17. DOI: http://dx.doi.org/10.1145/2212877.2212883

15. Ingrid Erickson and Mohammad Hossein Jarrahi. 2016. Infrastructuring and the challenge of dynamic seams in mobile knowledge work. In *Proceedings of the 19th ACM Conference on Computer-Supported Cooperative Work & Social Computing*. ACM, 1323–1336.

16. A Finegold. 1984. The engineer's apprentice. *The AI Business: The Commercial Uses of Artificial Intelligence, MIT Press, Cambridge, MA* (1984).

17. Uwe Flick. 2009. *An introduction to qualitative research* (fourth ed.). Sage.

18. Jodi Forlizzi and Shannon Ford. 2000. The building blocks of experience: an early framework for interaction designers. In *DIS '00: Proceedings of the 3rd conference on Designing interactive systems*. ACM, New York, NY, USA, 419–423. DOI: http://dx.doi.org/10.1145/347642.347800

19. Maarten Goos and Alan Manning. 2007. Lousy and Lovely Jobs: The Rising Polarization of Work in Britain, The Review of Economics and Statistics. (2007).

20. Maren Sander Granlien and Morten Hertzum. 2009. Implementing new ways of working: Interventions and their effect on the use of an electronic medication record. In *Proceedings of the ACM 2009 international conference on Supporting group work*. ACM, 321–330.

21. Gudela Grote, Johannes Weyer, and Neville A. Stanton. 2014. Beyond human-centred automation – concepts for human–machine interaction in multi-layered networks. *Ergonomics* 57, 3 (2014), 289–294. DOI: http://dx.doi.org/10.1080/00140139.2014.890748 PMID: 24670142.

22. Peter A Hancock, Richard J Jagacinski, Raja Parasuraman, Christopher D Wickens, Glenn F Wilson, and David B Kaber. 2013. Human-automation interaction research past, present, and future. *Ergonomics in Design: The Quarterly of Human Factors Applications* 21, 2 (2013), 9–14.

23. Steve Harrison and Paul Dourish. 1996. Re-place-ing space: the roles of place and space in collaborative systems. In *Proceedings of the 1996 ACM conference on Computer supported cooperative work*. ACM, 67–76.

24. Kenji Hata, Ranjay Krishna, Li Fei-Fei, and Michael S Bernstein. 2016. A Glimpse Far into the Future: Understanding Long-term Crowd Worker Quality. *arXiv preprint arXiv:1609.04855* (2016).

25. Hartmut Hirsch-Kreinsen. 2016. Digitization of industrial work: development paths and prospects. *Journal for Labour Market Research* 49, 1 (2016), 1–14. DOI: http://dx.doi.org/10.1007/s12651-016-0200-6

26. Eija Kaasinen, Virpi Roto, Jaakko Hakulinen, Tomi Heimonen, Jussi PP Jokinen, Hannu Karvonen, Tuuli Keskinen, Hanna Koskinen, Yichen Lu, Pertti Saariluoma, and others. 2015. Defining user experience goals to guide the design of industrial systems. *Behaviour & Information Technology* (2015), 1–16.

27. Alice Y. Kolb and David A. Kolb. 2009. The SAGE Handbook of Management Learning, Education and Development. (2009). DOI: http://dx.doi.org/10.4135/9780857021038

28. John D. Lee and Bobbie D. Seppelt. 2009. *Springer Handbook of Automation*. Springer Berlin Heidelberg, Berlin, Heidelberg, Chapter Human Factors in Automation Design, 417–436. DOI: http://dx.doi.org/10.1007/978-3-540-78831-7_25

29. Till Alexander Leopold, Vesselina Ratcheva, and Saadia Zahidi. 2016. *The Future of Jobs : Employment, Skills and Workforce Strategy for the Fourth Industrial Revolution*. Report. World Economic Forum, Cologny. http://www3.weforum.org/docs/Media/WEF_Future_of_Jobs_embargoed.pdf

30. Yichen Lu and Virpi Roto. 2015. Evoking meaningful experiences at work – a positive design framework for work tools. *Journal of Engineering Design* 26, 4-6 (2015), 99–120. DOI: http://dx.doi.org/10.1080/09544828.2015.1041461

31. Thomas Ludwig, Oliver Stickel, Alexander Boden, and Volkmar Pipek. 2014. Towards Sociable Technologies: An Empirical Study on Designing Appropriation Infrastructures for 3D Printing. In *Proceedings of the 2014 Conference on Designing Interactive Systems (DIS '14)*. ACM, New York, NY, USA, 835–844. DOI: http://dx.doi.org/10.1145/2598510.2598528

32. Lindsey K. McIntire, John P. McIntire, R. Andy McKinley, and Chuck Goodyear. 2014. Detection of Vigilance Performance with Pupillometry. In *Proceedings of the Symposium on Eye Tracking Research and Applications (ETRA '14)*. ACM, New York, NY, USA, 167–174. DOI: http://dx.doi.org/10.1145/2578153.2578177

33. Thomas Meneweger, Daniela Wurhofer, Verena Fuchsberger, and Manfred Tscheligi. 2015. Working Together with Industrial Robots: Experiencing Robots in a Production Environment. In *Proceedings of the 24th IEEE International Symposium on Robot and Human Interactive Communication (RO-MAN)*.

34. Marianna Obrist, Wolfgang Reitberger, Daniela Wurhofer, Florian Förster, and Manfred Tscheligi. 2011. User experience research in the semiconductor factory: a contradiction?. In *Proc. of INTERACT'11*. Springer-Verlag, Berlin, Heidelberg, 144–151.

35. Giovanni Quattrone, Martin Dittus, and Licia Capra. 2017. Work Always in Progress: Analysing Maintenance Practices in Spatial Crowd-sourced Datasets. Association for Computing Machinery (ACM).

36. Mikko J. Rissanen, Kari Rönkkö, and Sanjay Tripathi. 2011. Understanding Industrial User Experience: An Excerpt from 1st International Workshop on Industrial User Experience (WIndUX 2011). In *Proc. of IndiaHCI '11*. ACM, 75–78. DOI: http://dx.doi.org/10.1145/2407796.2407807

37. Brent D Rosso, Kathryn H Dekas, and Amy Wrzesniewski. 2010. On the meaning of work: A theoretical integration and review. *Research in organizational behavior* 30 (2010), 91–127.

38. Emile M. Roth, Kevin B. Bennett, and David D. Woods. 1987. Human Interaction with an "Intelligent" Machine. *Int. J. Man-Mach. Stud.* 27, 5-6 (Nov. 1987), 479–525. DOI:http://dx.doi.org/10.1016/S0020-7373(87)80012-3

39. Aleksandra Sarcevic and Randall S Burd. 2009. Information handover in time-critical work. In *Proceedings of the ACM 2009 international conference on Supporting group work*. ACM, 301–310.

40. Allison Sauppé and Bilge Mutlu. 2015. The Social Impact of a Robot Co-Worker in Industrial Settings. In *Proceedings of the 33rd Annual ACM Conference on Human Factors in Computing Systems (CHI '15)*. ACM, New York, NY, USA, 3613–3622. DOI: http://dx.doi.org/10.1145/2702123.2702181

41. Kjeld Schmidt. 1991. Computer support for cooperative work in advanced manufacturing. *International Journal of Human Factors in Manufacturing* 1, 4 (1991), 303–320.

42. Kjeld Schmidt, Ina Wagner, and Marianne Tolar. 2007. Permutations of cooperative work practices: a study of two oncology clinics. In *Proceedings of the 2007 international ACM conference on Supporting group work*. ACM, 1–10.

43. Klaus Schwab. 2016. The fourth industrial revolution: What it means, how to respond. *URL http://www. weforum. org/agenda/2016/01/the-fourth-industrial-revolution-what-it-means-and-how-to-respond* (2016).

44. Thomas B. Sheridan. 1992. *Telerobotics, Automation, and Human Supervisory Control*. MIT Press.

45. Philip J Smith, C Elaine McCoy, and Charles Layton. 1997. Brittleness in the design of cooperative problem-solving systems: The effects on user performance. *Systems, Man and Cybernetics, Part A: Systems and Humans, IEEE Transactions on* 27, 3 (1997), 360–371.

46. Allan Stisen, Nervo Verdezoto, Henrik Blunck, Mikkel Baun Kjærgaard, and Kaj Grønbæk. 2016. Accounting for the invisible work of hospital orderlies: Designing for local and global coordination. In *Proceedings of the 19th ACM Conference on Computer-Supported Cooperative Work & Social Computing*. ACM, 980–992.

47. Alexander Stocker, Peter Brandl, Rafael Michalczuk, and Manfred Rosenberger. 2014. Human-centred ICT tools for smart factories. *e & i Elektrotechnik und Informationstechnik* 131, 7 (2014), 207–211. DOI: http://dx.doi.org/10.1007/s00502-014-0215-z

48. Heli Väätäjä, Marko Seppänen, and Aija Paananen. 2014. Creating value through user experience: a case study in the metals and engineering industry. *International Journal of Technology Marketing* 9, 2 (2014), 163–186. DOI:http://dx.doi.org/10.1504/IJTMKT.2014.060093

49. Walter Volpert and Walter Georg. 1981. *Psychologische Aspekte industrieller Arbeit*. Fernuniv., Gesamthochsch.

50. Stephanie Wong and Carman Neustaedter. 2017. Collaboration and awareness amongst flight attendants. In *Proceedings of the 2017 ACM Conference on Computer Supported Cooperative Work and Social Computing*. ACM, 948–961.

51. David D Woods, Leila Johannesen, and Scott S Potter. 1991. Human interaction with intelligent systems: an overview and bibliography. *ACM SIGART Bulletin* 2, 5 (1991), 39–50.

52. Peter Wright and John McCarthy. 2010. Experience-centered design: designers, users, and communities in dialogue. *Synthesis Lectures on Human-Centered Informatics* 3, 1 (2010), 1–123.

53. Daniela Wurhofer, Roland Buchner, and Manfred Tscheligi. 2014. Research in the Semiconductor Factory: Insights into Experiences and Contextual Influences. In *Proceedings of 7th International Conference on Human System Interaction (HSI)*. 129–134.

54. Daniela Wurhofer, Thomas Meneweger, Verena Fuchsberger, and Manfred Tscheligi. 2015. Deploying Robots in a Production Environment: A Study on Temporal Transitions of Workers' Experiences. In *Proceedings of Interact 2015*.

55. Shoshana Zuboff. 1988. *In the Age of the Smart Machine: The Future of Work and Power*. Basic Books, Inc., New York, NY, USA.

Infrastructural Grind: Introducing Blockchain Technology in the Shipping Domain

Karim Jabbar
University of Copenhagen
Copenhagen, Denmark
karim@di.ku.dk

Pernille Bjørn
University of Copenhagen
Copenhagen, Denmark
pernille.bjorn@di.ku.dk

ABSTRACT

In this paper, we present ethnographic data unpacking three different accounts of how Blockchain technology gets introduced into the shipping domain. The results demonstrate that the shipping industry is based upon an information infrastructure with a socio-technical kernel comprising transaction practices between shippers, freight forwarders, ports, shipping lines, and other actors in the shipping industry. These practices are based upon standards, which have evolved over time and are embedded within the installed base of the infrastructure. We find that because of the inertia of the shipping infrastructure, Blockchain technology cannot be seamlessly introduced directly into the shipping domain. Instead, we introduce Infrastructural Grind as the activity by which domains (e.g. shipping) intersect with new technological infrastructures (e.g. Blockchain). Infrastructural grind occurs as a result of various infrastructuring activities taking place at different intersections between the two infrastructures, and is constituted of the sum of these manifestations. We propose that infrastructural grind is enacted through activities expressing elements of consolidation, permeability, and velocity.

Author Keywords

Information Infrastructures; Entrepreneurship; Embeddedness; Socio-technical; Blockchain; Shipping; Supply chain

ACM Classification Keywords

H.5.3. Group and Organization Interfaces [Computer-supported cooperative work].

INTRODUCTION

Blockchain is a technical protocol that fosters trust among users through the transparent recording of transactions in an immutable and tamper-proof shared duplicated ledger. When looking at Blockchain, and its growing number of protocol extensions, in the shape of user-facing applications, it can be seen as an information infrastructure

[16] growing through the entrepreneurial actions of multifaceted actors involved in the infrastructure. While Blockchain is primarily known in the area of cryptocurrencies [41] [20] [12], such as Bitcoin [26], the technology is also being considered to be used in various other domains not directly linked to currency or finance [3]. Shipping is one of these domains [17].

The shipping domain is comprised of a multitude of actors distributed along a complex supply chain, who are directly and indirectly collaborating with each other in order to process shipments across the globe. Shipping can therefore be seen as an information infrastructure [9] [35], where the actions of individual shippers, freight forwarding companies, trucking companies, customs and dock workers, shipping lines, underwriting financial institutions, and insurance companies are contributing to *infrastructuring* [27] the domain. This global and distributed collaboration among trading entities is supported by a technological installed base comprising legacy systems and standardized procedures, which have consolidated over time. The consolidation results in embeddedness [37], by which implicit shared understanding of mundane trading practices is learnt as part of shipping apprenticeship [35]. Thus, the introduction of Blockchain in shipping will have to deal with possible socio-technical constraints occurring at the intersection of the emerging Blockchain information infrastructure, and the shipping domain. With a focus on the points of intersection between these two infrastructures, we ask the following research question:

What characterizes the process whereby Blockchain technology gets introduced into the shipping domain?

In this paper, we present data gathered over the past 20 months, focusing on the activities of heterogeneous actors operating in the shipping domain, as well as within the emerging Blockchain information infrastructure. Examining our empirical data, we find that because of the inertia of the installed base of the shipping infrastructure, Blockchain technology cannot be seamlessly introduced directly into the shipping domain. As these two infrastructures (blockchain technology, and shipping domain) converge towards each other, an Infrastructural Grind takes place, and an area of reflexive permeation is created. The infrastructures rub off on each other so to speak. The process of infrastructural grind comprises the amalgamation of various infrastructuring activities taking place at different intersections between the two infrastructures. We propose that infrastructural grind is enacted through activities expressing elements of consolidation, permeability, and velocity. These infrastructuring activities taking place at the points of intersection between infrastructures can thus simultaneously reinforce the existing infrastructural consolidation, permeate into the domain that the technology seeks to enter, and do so at varying speeds depending on the level of infrastructural push-back. The contribution of this paper is a theoretical concept that can be used to better understand the activities occurring at the intersection of converging large-scale information infrastructures, and that can supplement existing user-centric accounts in HCI/CSCW of how technology gets appropriated in various settings.

The paper is structured as follows: Firstly, we provide a background on the literature on Blockchain in HCI, and cover the related literature in the field of information infrastructures with a focus on the intersections between infrastructures. Secondly, we present our method, and account for our data collection, analysis, and limitations. Thirdly, we unpack three empirical accounts of Blockchain in shipping, each displaying different manifestations of infrastructural grind. Finally, we discuss our findings in connection to the existing literature, highlight our contribution, and conclude.

BACKGROUND

Blockchain in HCI

In the literature on human-centered computing, accounts of Bitcoin and Blockchain are beginning to emerge. Here the focus of the work has primarily been on cryptocurrencies, for instance emphasizing how users in the United States understand Bitcoin principles [12], what motivates Bitcoin users in Malaysia [34], and design implications based on interviews with Bitcoin users and non-users [12] [34]. In a recent CHI paper, Bitcoin has also been used in the design of a technology probe, Bitbarista, aiming at foregrounding the data complexities that are often black-boxed in the design of connected devices [28]. Here the focus was not on Bitcoin per se, but an investigation into the perceptions of users about the data transactions occurring in IoT devices. While these investigations and their theoretical contributions enhance our understanding of user interaction with Bitcoin, they tell us little about the complex process by which the underlying technology of Bitcoin – namely Blockchain can be propagated into diverse domains such as energy and shipping [3] [17]. Blockchain technology has potential beyond cryptocurrency, and our interest is to understand the very work which goes into bringing Blockchain technology into new types of domains, exemplified by the shipping context.

Blockchain as an Information Infrastructure

The process by which new technology is colliding with new domains of use is not easily captured and understood, thus we need analytical concepts, which can help us to illuminate the challenges. Analytically, we explore the process of propagating Blockchain to the domain of shipping as investigating the intersection between two converging information infrastructures.

Information infrastructures is a socio-technical relational construct [9], which emphasizes the connections across technologies, artefacts, and standards, which serve as the foundation for interaction, yet blend with the background and become unnoticed [35]. Infrastructure is the underlying technological bedrock, which serve to support multiple applications. However, it is more than the technical foundation, it also includes the foundational ever-evolving and dynamic set of socio-technical relationships that are replicated and sustained through *infrastructuring* [27]. Infrastructuring activities growing the *Bitcoin* information infrastructure have in recent literature been articulated as the mixture of self-directed entrepreneurial actions performed by heterogeneous actors pursuing each their individual goals and respective business agendas [16]. What makes the Bitcoin information infrastructure different from our study of the intersections between Blockchain and the shipping domain is, that Bitcoin is one instance of a Blockchain information infrastructure. Bitcoin is one example (the most famous) of how the Blockchain technology can be used in a particular domain (in this case cryptocurrency). However, the use-case of Blockchain goes beyond Bitcoin, and can fundamentally evolve into different types of domains. However, when we refer to the Blockchain information infrastructure, we include the Bitcoin information infrastructure as well as the hundreds of others specific instances of Blockchain technology (e.g. Ethereum, Hyperledger, Tendermint, Corda, Cosmos, Polkadot, as well as private Blockchains and Distributed Ledger Technologies developed by start-ups). Thus, when we explore the intersections between the Blockchain information infrastructure and the information infrastructure of the shipping domain, we are considering the multiple instances of Blockchain technologies (public or private; permissioned or permissionless, interoperable or closed-off, etc.), which serve as the landscape of technologies [16], which are potentially intersecting with new domains of use.

Information infrastructures are embedded into multiple socio-technical arrangements, such as technological, organizational, or interpersonal arrangement [4] [37]. Such embeddedness includes the standards, legal frameworks, policies, and procedures involved in the particular domain (in the case of shipping the legal framework, paper trails, and international law structuring shipping across international ports). Standardization of information infrastructures can thus be seen as "*a process that increases irreversibility and decreases interpretative flexibility of the technologies while supporting flexibility of use and openness to further changes*" [15]. The existence of standards and procedures infrastructuring the work, also serve as enablers or constraints for further infrastructural development [30]. Standards and structures allow for certain changes but not for others. Infrastructuring work is thus consolidated as the information infrastructure evolves, and its installed base gains inertia [30]. Although embeddedness is a dynamic concept, whose relational features get reinforced, and evolve over time, the concept primarily focuses on a single information infrastructure in a current state of affairs, and how it historically has been embedded into socio-technical assemblages [38] [1] [2]. Our focus is different.

We are interested in understanding the *dynamic change*, or lack of change, which is involved in the initial infrastructural activities. We want to understand what the work of infrastructuring looks like, *prior* to the achievement of embeddedness into standards and policies, and entanglement with other information infrastructures [25]. We are exploring the infrastructuring [27] work of Blockchain into shipping *in the making* – before it reaches saturation. Interestingly, this also means that while the shipping domain has a clear information infrastructure developed over many years based upon numerous of standards, policies etc. – the Blockchain information infrastructure is new and malleable and involved in an ongoing development of its kernel [30] – as its installed base gains inertia. This mean that, when we explore the intersections, where the Blockchain and shipping information infrastructures collide, we must consider how actors are synergizing [4] and aligning objectives, artefacts, and practices with relevant stakeholders, and leveraging previously developed technological, relational, and organizational networks. Further, we must also consider the potential negative impacts - the reverse synergizing process [21] - that can potentially damage the long-term stability of an information infrastructure, when the adding of incompatible new actors cracks the inertia of the infrastructure.

METHOD

Introduction of Blockchain to the shipping domain is taking place at multiple sites globally. Thus, we cannot simply go to one place in order to study Blockchain in shipping, but instead we must attend to the various sites of design [6], which manifest the different ongoing initiatives. Inspired by multi-sited ethnography, we trace the intersections of Blockchain and shipping within different settings as a cultural phenomenon in diverse socio-technical situations [23]. To gain access to the core of where Blockchain in shipping in being created, we volunteered and became part of the community which drives this interest, and we thus engaged in participant-observations [13]. It was only through the dedicated engagement with the field, which makes it possible to be where the decisions are made, that we are able to study the infrastructuring work involved in introducing Blockchain to the shipping domain.

Data collection

Our data collection includes 15 interviews, as well as 150 hours conducting participatory observations in various types of companies involved in the shipping industry. This includes interviews and observations in both established technology companies and in start-ups that specifically design blockchain-based solutions for the shipping industry. The individuals and companies that we engaged with are geographically distributed all over the world, in countries such as Denmark, Sweden, the Netherlands, the United Kingdom, the Unites States, Israel, Hong Kong, and Australia. In terms of area of business, the companies were freight forwarders, ports, shipping lines, trucking companies, technology vendors, and start-ups. We conducted fifteen interviews, of no less than one hour, with these informants over Skype, and followed up with field visits and observations on-site in Denmark, the Netherlands and the United Kingdom. In certain cases, we came back to the same site several times to elaborate on our previous findings. The data collection design emerged as the data collection process unfolded. While some of the initial interviews were kept very structured and were not followed up on by other activities, others created opportunities for referrals to other stakeholders, or invitations to come visit. This happened intuitively as relationships developed with the informants and could not have been anticipated. We spent in excess of 150 hours observing the work of the companies, hereunder joining in and participating in various business meetings, internal strategy meetings, technology demonstrations, and speaking events at various conferences. By being active participants in the everyday routines of several of these informants, we were able to get a nuanced understanding of the type of work involved with the introduction of Blockchain in shipping. As a supplement to our interviews and our participant observations, we also looked at the online communication of issues related to Blockchain in shipping, as well as the related discussions on the topic in various media such as Reddit, coindesk.com, and porttechnology.org. By doing so, we could follow the digital traces left by relevant stakeholders in specific fora. Data was captured in field notes, documents, downloads of discussion fora, news articles, and audio-recorded interviews, which were later transcribed.

Data analysis

Because of the intuitive and unpredictable development of relationships with informants, we performed our data analysis simultaneously with ongoing data collection, rather than sequentially [7]. On an ongoing basis, we would work with the data available up to that point, through interview transcripts, observations notes, recording of business meetings, and so on. We worked at finding categories and concepts that would help explain the infrastructuring work going on at the intersection between the two converging infrastructures (Blockchain and shipping). Thereafter we organized possible categories by recurring themes and developed interpretative write-ups of the data that could serve as the basis for further engagement with the informants, old as well as new. Through this process, we could iteratively validate our findings regarding the observed infrastructuring practices taking place as Blockchain is introduced in the shipping domain. Throughout our analyses, we had to reorient the overall framing and underlying categorizations a number of time until we reached the final results, as presented in this paper.

RESULTS

In the following we will present our empirical findings in the shape of three different accounts of how Blockchain technology is being introduced to the shipping domain. The accounts will show that the process whereby this emerging technology is appropriated by the established shipping information infrastructure can be characterized as an *infrastructural grind* between the established installed base of the shipping infrastructure and the emerging Blockchain information infrastructure. We will show how this grind is expressed differently in each one of these accounts, and how it is constituted by various degrees of infrastructure consolidation, and permeability to Blockchain technology, as well as variable adoption velocity.

Port-to-port shipping: Blockchain as a way to digitize shipping documentation

Today, international shipping is structured around a streamlined process ensuring that a specific shipping containment can be moved efficiently from a point of origin to a specific delivery address at any other global location. This process whereby goods are shipped around the world relies heavily on the maritime sector, which funnels these goods onboard containers from port to port via fleets of increasingly large specialized ocean vessels. This practice of transporting goods across seas and oceans has become the subject of industry consolidation, standardizations and efficiency gains, particularly with the advent of container shipping, intermodal transport, and IT supported smart-ports. While the physical means of transportation across the oceans, and means of handling cargo at the ports have become more efficient and automated, the underlying methods of handling documentation requirements pertaining to specific shipping consignments have remained roughly the same. The type of paperwork required for the legal international shipment of consignments (stamps, lists, papers etc.) is built upon decades, if not centuries, of international policies and negotiations and we are constantly witnessing how additional requirements for shipping documentation is continuously increasing. Today processing an export consignment requires up to four separate contracts covering (i) export sales, (ii) carriage, (iii) finance, and (iv) cargo insurance. Within these four contracts up to 37 different official documents will need to be added (an average consignment will have more than 20 different related documents). These documents cover all aspects related to the commercial transaction, transportation, finance, and not least government documents such as certificates of origin, import and export

licenses, sanitary certificates, documents claiming preferential tariff or VAT rebate, etc.

Processing the documentation for export consignments was a largely manual process until the advent of digital shipping portals in the late 1990's, which connect the shippers and freight forwarders to the global ocean shipping digital infrastructure. Today three large privately-owned portals, INTTRA, Cargosmart, and GT Nexus, handle the bulk of data transfer between supply chain actors in the shipping industry. The underlying technology of these portals is not based on data sharing, but rather data relaying though EDI messages (Electronic Data Interchange). More specifically two global standards for EDI messages set the framework for exchange in the shipping industry: ASC X12 in the United States, and UN/EDIFACT in most other parts of the world. Both standards provide a set of syntax rules to structure, an interactive exchange protocol, and provide a set of standard messages, which allow multi-country and multi-industry exchange of electronic business documents. Currently there are over 200 specific EDIFACT messages covering all aspects of the shipping industry. On the Graphic User Interface level of the shipping portals, the users can fill in data or import it from an XML format. The systems will then create and send the appropriate EDIFACT messages, and allow for the automatic generation of important documents.

It is against this backdrop, that the world's largest shipping company Maersk Line, in collaboration with IBM, recently announced that they had finalized a Proof of Concept project, in which they had shown the potential value of Blockchain technology in digitizing the extensive and fractured paper trail in the shipping industry. For the "paper trail project", IBM and Maersk have worked with a number of trading partners, government authorities and logistics companies, in order to collectively test the use of a Blockchain-based shared ledger aiming at simplifying the process by which the numerous required documents are currently being attached to a specific shipping consignment. More specifically the project involved shipping various goods on specifically selected port-to-port stretches, and collaborating with the producing companies, as well as customs in the port of origin and at the destination port. These participating actors would have access to view and/or amend the transactions on the shared Blockchain ledger as the shipment moved from one location to the next. An example of this, is that when a shipment of electronics goods on a Maersk Line container vessel is transported from the Port of Rotterdam to the Port of Newark, involving the Customs Administration of the Netherlands, the U.S. Department of Homeland Security Science and Technology Directorate, and U.S. Customs and Border Protection – all the transactions and documents are saved on the shared Blockchain ledger, making it possible for all actors to track all data in secure ways, without the need of a portal with transaction costs.

The main focus of the 'paper-trail' Blockchain project is the core of shipping, namely the port-to-port of the shipping supply chain. The port-to-port part of shipping is incidentally also the most standardized and structured part of the whole shipping industry in terms of existing legacy systems connected by standardized EDIFACT message relaying. This was highlighted by the Maersk head of IT strategy, describing the project in an interview a few months before the project became public:

> *"From a Maersk Line perspective, we started out this project in quite a restricted way. We have looked at full container loads, and primarily port-to-port"* (Head of IT Strategy, Maersk Line, Interview, January 4th 2017)

By adopting this project framing, IBM's Blockchain solution faces the constraints of the existing installed base of the shipping information infrastructure. Namely, a web of legacy systems, established procedures and business practices, communication protocols (e.g. UN-EDIFACT and ASC X12), which have been entrenched though decades of ongoing standardization in the shipping industry.

This legacy of practices, systems, and competitive considerations, has in the past been a constraint for digitization efforts in the shipping industry. Maersk has, in fact, previously experienced the difficulties and dilemmas associated with being first movers in rolling out new digital solutions for the industry at scale. According to the Maersk's Head of IT strategy, the company has also in the past been a first mover on new digital solutions in the industry, thus they known about the potential challenges in getting industry buy-in.

> *"[Maersk] spent decades trying to roll out such solutions (...) INTTRA being one of the very large ones. A shipping portal. We were one of the founding members and we have performed equity dilution along the way, and let in other companies."*. (Head of IT Strategy, Maersk Line, Interview, January 4th 2017)

Then, as now, the highly competitive situation between shipping companies results in a default distrust reaction to industrywide collaboration initiatives initiated by a single large player. This gives us a good indication that the Maersk/IBM Blockchain project was initially created as a technology push, and not so much as a "business-first" project. Rather than taking broader implementation challenges into consideration, such as the willingness of all involved parties i.e. freight forwarders, customs, ports, shipping lines, and so on, to migrate their current systems onto the proposed Blockchain, the Maersk/IBM project seems to have primarily been designed by IBM to prove the technical feasibility of a Blockchain solution. In so doing IBM and Maersk are showcasing the possibility of Blockchain to simplify the paper trail process in the shipping industry, and are given the opportunity to market their Blockchain solution, which is now available on IBM Bluemix cloud servers. This was corroborated by the Maersk Head of IT:

> *"IBM is really eager to introduce Blockchain technology to the project... We are playing along. We have IBM as a technology partner. We do not have any objections against it. But we also do not want to take a technological risk on it. If IBM can make a compelling case, then fine. We will then go forward.".* (Head of IT Strategy, Maersk, Interview, January 4th 2017)

Blockchain technology is potentially a solution to the problem of distrust among industry players, as it does not rely on a commercial third party, but on a network of equal peers. However, while IBM's proposed solution, which is based on the Linux Foundation's Hyperledger Fabric Blockchain, is today available for corporate clients on IBM's Bluemix cloud service, the uptake among actors in the shipping industry does not seem to be happening. This can be interpreted as a strong "push-back" from the installed base of the information infrastructure. Over the past decades, the current infrastructure underlying the shipping industry has been consolidated both in terms of its overall IT architecture based on EDIFACT messaging, and in terms of the practices, perceptions, and competitive considerations that perpetuate the current system. The push back by the installed base of the shipping infrastructure is thus manifested in a basic distrust in the solution provided by Maersk/IBM resulting from previous similar efforts, as well as generalized perception that the current EDIFACT-based system, despite its shortcomings in terms of administrative documentation burden and lack of transparency, works well enough.

Bill of Lading, anonymous trading, and compliance: Could Blockchain be a solution?

The *Bill of Lading* is arguably the single most important document in the shipping industry, since it acts as a cargo receipt, contract of carriage, as well as a document of title across the stages of the supply chain. Currently, the Bill of Lading can be traded as the shipment is under way. This is, for instance, very common for bulk shipping of commodities. The owner of the cargo might be a financial speculator, and the title of ownership to various cargos will thus be bought and sold all while the shipment is still under way. Basically, goods are traded during transportation in the same way as stocks and bonds are traded in the financial sector. It is part of the characteristics of shippers and traders that they usually want to remain anonymous. The wish for anonymity is not necessarily a reflection of the fact that they have something to hide, but rather an indication of the fact that they are entitled to keep their trading positions a secret from their competitors. Because of this trading practice, it is currently not possible for the public, hereunder the actors in the shipping supply chain, to know the actual real-time ownership of a given cargo at any specific time during its journey across the seas. The manual transaction of physical bills of lading is perfectly legal, and implies that the holder of an original copy of a given Bill of Lading, which has been acquired through speculative trading, will have access to the cargo upon arrival to the destination port by mere presentation of the physical document. The identity of the final cargo owner will therefore only then be revealed to the broader public. In order to ensure that it is possible for whoever has acquired a Bill of Lading for a particular cargo, through speculation or otherwise, to be in possession of it at the time of arrival of the shipment to the destination port, it is common practice to air courier all the Bills of Lading connected to a specific ship via DHL or other similar services to the final port. Needless to say that this is a costly practice.

While the current system surrounding the Bill of Lading, and the possibility of trading it anonymously, is a good protection for those engaging in speculative trade of a cargo, it also represents a compliance challenge for the banks, who are underwriting a specific shipping consignment through current trade finance mechanisms. In its simplest form, trade finance works by reconciling the divergent needs of an exporter and importer. While an exporter would prefer to be paid upfront by the importer for an export shipment, the risk to the importer is that the exporter may simply pocket the payment and refuse shipment. Conversely, if the exporter extends credit to the importer, the latter may refuse to make payment or delay it inordinately. A common solution to this problem in the area of trade finance is through the issuing of a letter of credit, which is opened in the exporter's name by the importer through a bank in his home country. The letter of credit essentially guarantees payment to the exporter by the bank issuing the letter of credit upon receipt of documentary proof that the goods have been shipped. In the context of a bulk commodity cargo being traded multiple times while the shipment is under way, the banks find themselves in a situation where it is difficult for them to fully live up to their legal requirements pertaining to KYC/AML (Know your customer / Anti-money laundering). These international rules, to which banks are subjected, are designed to curb criminal financial practices, and require banks and other financial institutions to do a thorough due diligence when onboarding new customers, and to have compliance procedures in place, which allow them to track the provenance of the financial flows that they facilitate. In the current situation, the banks find themselves in a grey zone, which could potentially be remedied by a Blockchain technology solution for shipping focusing on trade finance.

In December 2016, a consortium of actors from across the shipping supply chain joined a project under the Dutch Institute for Advanced Logistics (TKI Dinalog), aiming at creating a Blockchain technology solution in specific trade finance use cases for shipment. The consortium is made up of 16 partners the main ones being ABN AMRO (bank), Port of Rotterdam (port), SmartPort (private-public

organization), Royal Flora Holland (florist conglomerate), and the Technical University of Delft. The project is an initiative by the Dutch Ministry of Economic Affairs, which is part of a broader effort to create a Netherlands Blockchain Centre of Excellence. The mandate of the project is to investigate use cases within trade finance, and to develop Proof of Concept pilots based on identified problems, and a tailored technical solution based on Blockchain. In this connection, TU Delft will be looking into building an open-source Blockchain that can be tested developing a Prof-of-Concept.

One of the members of the Blockchain team at the Port of Rotterdam tells us that the consortium so far has mainly been driven by the Dutch bank ABN AMRO, and that it is them that have been pushing to get trade finance on the agenda. Furthermore, he tells us that one of the bank's current concerns is particularly linked to issues of not knowing the identities of the parties that they are underwriting as a bank. He explains:

> "From the perspective of ABN, they want to know who is the owner (of the consignment). Who are they dealing with? If the owner ends up being on a list of companies that we cannot trade with, well then ABN has a problem... and we will know it only (the identity of the owner) when the shipment arrives here at the port". (Member of the Blockchain Team at the Port of Rotterdam, Field Visit, March 14th 2017)

Clearly the concern for full transparency of the identity of shippers is driving ABN AMRO to push for a solution that will allow the bank to live up to its compliance requirements. Simultaneously the bank seeks to de-risk its letter of credit engagements with customers in the shipping industry through a smart contract feature in the proposed Blockchain solution, which would trigger automated payments upon delivery, thus making the current letter of credit process less cumbersome, and less risky.

Our informant at the Port of Rotterdam exemplifies this:

> "That's the main focus of our project currently. We want to attach automatic payments through smart contracts. So, for example, if Maersk offloads a container in the (port) terminal, then at that specific moment they can get paid. Or at every stage of the shipment events could trigger other specific payments." (Member of the Blockchain Team at the Port of Rotterdam, Field Visit, March 14th 2017)

The ongoing discussion within the consortium is currently figuring out which technical capabilities the ideal Blockchain solution for the consortium should have in order to address the challenges described above. This means that fundamental issues, such as whether the Blockchain should be private or public is not decided yet. Private means creating a consortium Blockchain, which only partners have access to (e.g. Hyperledger), while public mean that the solution will be based upon an existing Blockchain to which everyone can post any transactions (e.g Ethereum). A public Blockchain would ensure that no specific actor would own the solution, instead it would be shared broadly as a sort of public good on which various players in the industry could potentially build the needed applications. However, there are a number of constraints both technological and legal, that would make it impossible to build a solution for shipping based on one of the established public Blockchains. One major technological constraint inherent to current public Blockchains pertains to the issue of scalability, which for Bitcoin and Ethereum for instance, means that the current technological features of these Blockchains would not be able to handle transactions in the thousands per second [15], which would be necessary if all the current trade finance transactions should be put on one of these specific Blockchains. Furthermore, legal requirements in terms of data storage would dictate that personal and sensitive data about a company's customers must be stored on servers (physical or cloud) that are fully controlled by the company itself, and not a shared ledger that is public and "ownerless". Likewise, the territoriality of transactions would ultimately also become an issue if current public Blockchains were used at scale in shipping, in the sense that these Blockchains currently do not have the capability to record the specific location of transactions. This could have legal implications in terms of which jurisdiction possible disputes would fall under. As our source at the Port of Rotterdam puts it:

> *"Yes, there are quite a number of constraints. I see a semi private or private Blockchain as a faster way to go forward, both from a scalability side and also from a security or Know Your Customer side"* (Member of the Blockchain Team at the Port of Rotterdam, Interview, March 14th 2017)

A private Blockchain would indeed not be as constrained technologically. It would be able to scale faster because it could be designed with a much higher blocksize cap (allowing for more transactions per block), and it would most importantly be able to provide transparency about the identity of the participants, which today is a legal requirement in finance, as we have seen. Paradoxically, this added transparency of the identity of participants might actually be a prohibitive factor in the mass adoption of such a Blockchain solution. Traders speculating in bulk shipments might indeed value their anonymity of transaction more than the simplified trade finance element than a potential Blockchain solution designed along those lines would afford. Based on past cases in the industry, one can indeed see that previous attempts at digitizing the Bill of Lading (Bolero, Essdocs) have not really succeeded at a larger scale. In these systems, generating and trading a Bill of Lading requires a registration with a validated identity, which might in itself deter bulk traders from using these systems. This point has been corroborated with several of our industry informants, hereunder the Head of IT Strategy at Maersk Line.

Container-weight rules: an opportunity for Blockchain implementation at the fringes?

In 2016, the International Maritime Organization (IMO) implemented a new regulation aimed at improving the safety onboard container ships, by putting in place reporting requirements that would ensure a proper weight balancing of containers as they are being loaded onto vessels. The intension behind this initiative by the maritime industry was to prevent accidents due to improper loading, and to avoid the loss of lives at sea. Practically speaking, this new regulation, called SOLAS VGM (Safety of Lives at Sea - Verified Gross Mass), requires an EDI data transmission of the weight of each container to the shipping line prior to the container's arrival to the loading port. This will ensure that the port can plan the loading sequence of containers in advance and be certain that the overall load balance of the vessel is within a tolerable safety range. While this regulation seems to make a lot of sense from a safety and process management perspective, it turned out that the required reporting of container weight was not enabled by the existing IT infrastructure of the shipping industry. So, as the date of entry into force of this regulation got closer, actions needed to be taken in order to update the existing infrastructure. The shipping portals and shipping lines were slow to amend their systems, thus opening up an opportunity for start-ups to build applications that could solve this imminent problem.

Marine Transport International (MTI), a UK freight forwarder and technology solutions provider, saw this imminent regulation requirement as an opportunity to introduce a Blockchain-enabled application to the market, which simultaneously aims at solving the problem of weight reporting, and as an added bonus, at fundamentally re-designing the reporting flow in the industry. The MTI solution, named SOLAS VGM to reflect the specific need it addresses, aims at leveraging the new legal requirements in order to extend the reach of the shipping infrastructure into the landside of operations, and to connect previously disconnected actors in the shipping infrastructure. As MTIs founder and CEO puts it:

> *"What really came as an opportunity to us, was the SOLAS VGM requirements. We now had a hook into the market that would allow us to introduce our Blockchain-based solution to the landside of the shipping supply chain".* (Founder and CEO of MTI, Field Study, London, April 12th 2017)

The landside of the shipping supply chain, that the MTI founder refers to, is comprised of the multitudes of operators and intermediaries that channel the flow of physical goods from the source, be it a factory, warehouse, farm, mine, or private household downstream until the point where the goods are loaded onto an ocean vessel. During this journey, the goods will typically be subjected to so-called intermodal exchange whereby the contents of the cargo is transferred from one mode of transportation to the next. Cargo for instance, arriving on a freight train, can get transferred to a truck via a transloader. The truck then drives the cargo to a freight forward processing terminal. Here it gets added to other cargo items and put into in a standard shipping container, which is then transported to a weighbridge and then driven to the port for customs clearance, and loading onto a high tonnage container ship destined to another country or continent. This flow of goods from multiple sources and via various modes of transport is not as streamlined as the one taking place on ocean vessels travelling between major ports. The Founder of MTI explains that

> "The port-to-port part of the supply chain is well established. It might be old-school and rely on EDIFACT messaging between data silos, but it works. Getting people to change their ways will be hard". (Founder and CEO of MTI, Field Study, London, May 30th 2017)

The coordination between actors involved in the port-to-port portion of shipping is indeed very much standardized by interoperable IT systems and notification procedures between relevant entities at the relevant time. The need for tugboat and piloting services, for instance, is mostly known by the ports in advance prior to the arrival of a ship, and likewise the contents of the shipments is often sent in advance for customs clearance at the destination port even prior to the departure of the vessel from the port of origin. This is particularly true for the customs procedures related to importing goods into the United States. In fact, under the rules of the US Customs and Border Protection Agency, a so-called import security filing (ISF) is required no later than 24 hours prior to loading the cargo onto the US-bound sea vessel. These examples illustrate how the highly-integrated kernel of the shipping infrastructure, albeit based on a "simple" EDI data relay structure, stands in contrast to the fragmented and unsynchronized landside supply chain that is characterized by numerous stakeholders with sporadic coordination. This lack of coordination is what MTI's Blockchain-based solution aims at addressing.

More specifically, SOLAS VGM allows for the integration with already existing weighbridges via API, and using these weighbridges as data collection points from where weight data is recorded onto a Blockchain and transmitted to the specific shipping lines in any format required. In doing so, the weighed containers will be automatically cleared to enter the loading port, the truckers using the system will avoid bottlenecks at the port gates, and they will simultaneously improve safety on the roads as overloaded trucks will be detected at an early stage. The ports will in advance know the provenance of the containers driving towards the port, and will thus be better able to plan their resources accordingly. In order to onboard users, i.e.

shippers and freight forwarders on the landside, MTI offers a solution that at the application level looks exactly like what they would be familiar with, and that solves a very specific imminent problem, namely transmitting weight data. In other words, MTI primarily focuses on highlighting the simplicity and narrow practical application of their SOLAS VGM solution. However, what in reality happens at the weighbridges, is that weight data is not the only thing being recorded on the Blockchain. The mandatory weighing is in fact used as an opportunity to record more than 40 different data points that are relevant for the ongoing journey of the container downstream. These data points include, but are not limited to, container size, type and number, shipping line, haulier, commodity and its description, plus all associated paperwork, including any regulatory and customs clearance documentation. This means that an added benefit to using the SOLAS VGM system is that it not only transmits the required VGM information, but also allows to connect a whole range of upstream actors that have traditionally been unconnected due to the multitude of individualized systems used to manage various small-scale operations. In the words of MTI's founder:

> "For us, it doesn't matter if customers work with legacy EDIFACT systems or have API connectivity. We can connect people together, whether they're carriers, agents, hauliers, ports, shippers, consignees or forwarders, sharing one version of the truth through the blockchain." (Founder and CEO of MTI, Interview, Skype, December 6th 2016)

Practically speaking, this means that while MTI underplays the importance of the underlying technology that their solution is built on, in order to attract users for a specific imminent use-case (reporting of container weight), it is in reality working at transforming the documentation flow in the shipping industry. It is creating a "one-stop shop" for capturing all relevant data pertaining to a shipment consignment, and avoiding push back by the established system, by offering seamless interoperability with all actors through APIs. Furthermore, it is connecting actors on the landside and providing transparency into the supply chain further upstream than what was previously possible.

MTI's end goal is in many ways similar to other players in the domain, namely to transform the old EDI-based system, and allow for better data sharing and new revenue stream opportunities. The road leading to this goal is however different. Instead of focusing their attention right at the kernel of the shipping infrastructure, which we have shown has a tendency to push back, MTI is employing a roll-out strategy aimed at the fringes of the shipping information infrastructure. Furthermore, instead of focusing on the technical features of the underlying Blockchain technology, MTI is starting at the application-level first by addressing a specific problem with a user-friendly application.

DISCUSSION

Interestingly, and perhaps not surprising, our data clearly demonstrates that to fully comprehend the potential of bringing in new technology into shipping industry, we have to address the complex socio-technical infrastructure, which makes up the very foundation of shipping. In fact, our data shows that the shipping information infrastructure has a socio-technical kernel [30] comprised of transaction practices between a diverse set of trading actors, which allow them to organize the transportation of goods across the globe. This organization of trade flows also allows for the ongoing trading of assets being shipped while en-route, as well as facilitating financial settlements related to specific shipping consignments. Furthermore, the current infrastructure is not something which is simply altered. Instead, we found that the installed base of the technologies supporting interaction in the shipping domain is based upon standards which have evolved and have been embedded [37] over time. As the actors in the shipping industry go about their mundane daily routines of processing consignments along predefined transportation pathways, by using EDIFACT-based message relaying systems, they are making the resources of the infrastructure available [30] to the millions of private shippers and business entities relying on their services. So, one could say that by compiling the required paperwork connected to a particular shipping cargo, hereunder the very important Bill of Lading, the shippers and freight forwarders are enacting a standardized procedure that will allow an exporter of a shipment of goods to have it delivered to a specific geographical location in the world.

These standardized procedures make access available to the shipping information infrastructure in terms of efficiency, intermodal integration, and legal compliance. Simultaneously, these same procedures also reinforce the existing installed base of the information infrastructure, which allow it to be sustained over time, while also unlocking enablers as well as constraints for further infrastructural embedding [4] [37]. For instance, we can argue that it is the pre-existing installed base of standardization work, embodied in a commonly agreed upon protocol and syntax (UN-EDIFACT), which has allowed for the emergence of shipping portals such as INTTRA, through which the shippers and freight forwarders can push EDI messages to the next link in the supply chain. While the creation of INTTRA reinforces the shipping information infrastructure and sustains its installed base, it also creates constraints, as we saw in the case of Blockchain. It is the installed base of the shipping information infrastructure, which makes it difficult for Blockchain to be implemented in the shipping domain, because the inertia does not allow for penetration, such as we saw in the account of the IBM/Maersk "paper trail" project.

In order to better explore the characteristics of the ongoing interplay taking place when entrepreneurial actions [16]

'push' the Blockchain information infrastructure and the shipping information infrastructures against each other, we have introduced the notion of *Infrastructural Grind*. Infrastructural grind refers to the processes by which two information infrastructures grind against each other, and potentially how new technological infrastructures succeeds in penetrating the new domain. By introducing infrastructural grind, we propose a new way to look at the process through, which emerging technology is appropriated in established business domains.

Previous work on infrastructuring often focuses on the process by which a specific infrastructure is created and maintained through socio-technical actions [27]. However, our interest is a little different. While our overall interest is to understand the specificities of the Blockchain infrastructure, it is important that, when we study how the Blockchain infrastructure is created and maintained, we also direct our attention to the *intersection between infrastructures* (technology and domain), since the very work of constructing and evolving Blockchain is a process by which the technology wrestle with domain specific infrastructures. Infrastructural grind helps us to focus on the concrete ways this process unfolds.

Our three empirical accounts each depicted a unique case of how Blockchain technology is placed into infrastructural grind with the shipping industry with different results. Each case is thus a manifestation of an ongoing grind between infrastructures, whereby the properties of each respective infrastructure come into contact and "rub off" on each other. Infrastructural grind is different from synergizing activities [4] and reverse synergizing activities [21], in the sense that synergizing focuses on how a particular infrastructure is shaped while shaping a field, while grind activities focus on the dynamic reciprocal interplay occurring when two infrastructures intersect and exchange. In other words, the grind occurs as a result of various infrastructuring [27] activities taking place at different intersections between infrastructures, and is constituted of the sum of these manifestations. Infrastructural grind can therefore be seen as the aggregate of the simultaneously occurring processes whereby the features of Blockchain become part of the installed base of the shipping information infrastructure. To be sustainable, the infrastructural grind between infrastructures (domain and technology) must support a process of longitudes [31] [19], where every smaller attempt or experiment adds so the potential long-terms results making the Blockchain infrastructure sustainable.

Importantly, this grind not only results in Blockchain features being appropriated by the shipping domain, but also impacts the process whereby Blockchain technology itself creates new features to its kernel. As we have shown in our three accounts, Blockchain technology is not a monolithic entity, but rather a patchwork of independent and interconnected implementations catered to specific use cases. More specifically, we have shown that different technical solutions are used as underlying Blockchain, be it Hyperledger Fabric, a custom-made university-designed blockchain, or a solution developed by a small start-up. This illustrates that as infrastructural grind occurs, the actors involved in introducing Blockchain to the shipping domain will continuously develop new features to their Blockchain, and refine their specific codebase to address the specific requirements emerging from the ongoing infrastructural grind.

Our empirical accounts have shown us that the ongoing process of infrastructural grind takes place differently at different infrastructural intersections, and might take shorter or longer time to result in infrastructural embeddedness [37]. The grind can, for instance, result in a push back by the installed base of the shipping infrastructure, as we have seen in the IBM/Maersk case, where the solution has not so far moved beyond proof-of-concept. Differently, the grind can also provide an immediate opportunity to address issues of actors currently underserved by the current shipping infrastructure, as we have seen in the MTI case, where new legal issues concerning 'weight' turned out to be a way to enter the shipping infrastructure. Clearly, our three cases provide us with nuances inherent to infrastructural grind activities, so let us explore these in more details. Based on our data, we found that infrastructural grind was enacted through three different expressions, namely *consolidation, permeability,* and *velocity*. At each particular intersection in which the grind takes place, these enacted expressions will combine in different ways resulting in different manifestation of Blockchain in shipping. In the IBM/Maersk account, for instance, the intersection between technology and domain was centered at the core of the kernel of the shipping infrastructure. Here the level of consolidation in the existing installed base is high and its permeability on the part of a new technology such as Blockchain low. As a result of this the outcome has so far been restricted to a Proof-of Concept, and large-scale implementation of the proposed technological solution has not materialized. As we have seen the MTI account tells a different story, in which the entrepreneurial actions undertaken by the start-up have led it to address the fringe of the shipping infrastructure, where consolidation is weaker, and permeability higher, resulting in an onboarding of smaller previously underserved players on the landside of the shipping infrastructure. In these cases, the velocity at which the embedding of Blockchain technology into the installed base of the shipping information infrastructure occurs varies greatly.

As such, infrastructural grind does not have prescriptive properties, meaning that the concept and its constituting elements are not meant to imply favoring one type of enactment over another. It simply frames the infrastructuring activities taking place at the intersection of converging infrastructures (technology and domain) as an amalgamation of enactments displaying properties of consolidation, permeability, and velocity. All these enactments happen simultaneously as they are undertaken by a range of heterogeneous actors pursuing entrepreneurial goals. As this happens, permeation of Blockchain into the shipping domain will occur differently at different points of intersection, and at different speeds. This in turn results in the Blockchain information infrastructure itself appropriating elements gained from the infrastructural grind, which are then added to the collective imaginary of what Blockchain technology is, and leveraged [4] in future grinds with other domains.

Infrastructural Grind and its dimensions of consolidation, permeability, and velocity can thus be seen as theoretical concepts that can help us better understand the complex activities taking place as information infrastructures converge. Going forward, we see opportunities for further research in HCI and CSCW that aims at contextualizing occurrences of infrastructural grind in empirical cases that go beyond the shipping domain and Blockchain technology. Such mappings of infrastructural patterns of consolidation, permeability and velocity could, for instance, supplement more user-centric approaches for explaining the appropriation of a given technology into a pre-existing setting [18], and highlight the simultaneousness of ongoing entrepreneurial activities and associated enablers and constraints, which contribute to infrastructural embeddedness.

CONCLUSION

In this paper, we had a very specific interest in examining the process through which Blockchain technology is introduced to the shipping domain. Our focus has therefore specifically been aimed at the points of infrastructural intersection between technology and domain. Firstly, we found that shipping is an information infrastructure with a socio-technical kernel that is consolidated over time though the infrastructuring activities of freight forwarders, trucking companies, ports, shipping lines, financial institutions underwriting cargo transactions, insurance companies, and other stakeholders in the shipping industry. This consolidated infrastructural kernel tends to push back at emerging new technologies attempting to enter and become part of its installed base. Secondly, we proposed *infrastructural grind* as a concept to understand the activities taking place at the intersection between converging information infrastructures, in this case the Blockchain and the shipping information infrastructure. Infrastructural grind is the process whereby two converging infrastructures rub-off on each other though heterogeneous infrastructuring activities, which are enacted at various points of intersection between the two infrastructures. Thirdly, we've shown that the infrastructuring activities taking place at these points of intersection are displaying elements of *consolidation, permeability*, and *velocity*. This means that infrastructural grind is enacted at different points of intersection between infrastructures through a specific combination of these elements. Depending on the specific intersection, the grind will result in consolidation of existing installed bases, such as when the port-to-port portion of the shipping supply chain is the target of Blockchain deployment, or permeation, such as when Blockchain technology is aimed at the fringes of the industry and the previously unserved by the current infrastructure. These two simultaneously occurring activities result in a multi-velocity path toward embeddedness of Blockchain in shipping. Slow at the core of the infrastructure, and faster at the fringes. Collectively, these deployment activities all result in the further development of Blockchain technology per se, and the expansion of the collective understanding of what Blockchain is, and what it can do, which in turn will inform future infrastructural grinds with other domains.

REFERENCES

1. Madeleine Akrich, Michel Callon, and Bruno Latour. 2002. The key to sucess in innovation Part 1: The art of interessement. *International journal of innovation management* 6(2): 187-206.

2. Madeleine Akrich, Michel Callon, and Bruno Latour. 2002. The key to success in innovation Part 2: The art of choosing good spokespersons. *International journal of innovation management* 6(2): 207-225.

3. James Basden, and Michael Cottrell. 2017. How Utilities Are Using Blockchain to Modernize the Grid, *Harvard Business Review*, March 2017.

4. Matthew Bietz, Eric P. S. Baumer, and Charlotte P. Lee. 2010. Synergizing in cyberinfrastructure development. *Computer Supported Cooperative Work* (JCSCW).

5. Pernille Bjørn, and Carsten Østerlund. 2014. Sociomaterial-Design: Bounding technologies in practice. Springer.

6. Pernille Bjørn, and Nina Boulus-Rødje. 2015. The multiple intersecting sites of design in CSCW research. *Computer Supported Cooperative Work (CSCW): An International Journal* 24(3): 319-351.

7. Pernille Bjørn, and Nina Boulus. 2011. Dissenting in reflective conversations: Critical components of doing action research. *Action Research Journal* 9(3): 282-302.

8. Jeanette Blomberg, and Helena Karasti. 2013. Reflections on 25 Years of Ethnography in CSCW. *Computer Supported Cooperative Work* (CSCW) August 2013, Volume 22, Issue 4, pp 373-423.

9. Geoffrey C. Bowker, and Susan Leigh Star. 1999. Sorting things out – Classifications and its consequences. MIT Press.

10. Geoffrey C. Bowker. 1994. Science on the run: Information management and industrial geophysics at Schlumberger, 1920–1940. Cambridge: The MIT

11. Paul N. Edwards, Geoffrey C. Bowker, Steven J. Jackson, and Robin Williams. 2009. Introduction: an agenda for infrastructure studies. Special Issue on e-Infrastructure of the *Journal of the Association for Information Systems*, 10(5), 364–374.

12. Xianyi Gao, Gradeigh D. Clark, and Janne Lindqvist. 2016. Of Two Minds, Multiple Addresses, and One Ledger: Characterizing Opinions, Knowledge, and Perceptions of Bitcoin Across Users and Non-Users, *Proceedings of the 2016 CHI Conference on Human Factors in Computing Systems* Pages 1656-1668.

13. R. Stuart Geiger, and David Ribes. 2011. Trace Ethnography: Following Coordination through Documentary Practices. *Proceedings of the 44th Hawaii International Conference on System Sciences.*

14. Ole Hanseth, and Margunn Aanestad. 2003. Design as bootstrapping. On the evolution of ICT networks in health care. *Methods of information in medicine* 42 (4), 384-391.

15. Ole Hanseth, Eric Monteiro, and Morten Hatling. 1996. Developing information infrastructure: the tension between standardisation and flexibility. *Science, Technology and Human Values*, 11(4), 407–426.

16. Karim Jabbar, and Pernille Bjørn. 2017. Growing the Blockchain Information Infrastructure, *Proceedings of the 2017 CHI Conference on Human Factors in Computing Systems.*

17. Karim Jabbar, Deanna MacDonald, Simon Ousager. 2017. Token Gesture? *FutureNautics*, Issue 15, Q2 2017, Quaterly.

18. Margaret Jack, Jay Chen, and Steven J. Jackson. 2017.. Infrastructure as Creative Action: Online Buying, Selling, and Delivery in Phnom Penh, *Proceedings of the 2017 CHI Conference on Human Factors in Computing Systems.*

19. Helena Karasti, Karen S. Baker, and Florence Millerand. 2010. Infrastructure time: long-term matters in collaborative development. *Computer Supported Cooperative Work* (JCSCW).

20. Erol Kazan, Chee-Wee Tan, and Eric T. K. Lim. 2015. Value Creation in Cryptocurrency Networks: Towards a Taxonomy of Digital Business Models for Bitcoin Companies. *PACIS 2015 Proceedings. Pacific Asia Conference on Information Systems.*

21. Tue Odd Langhoff, Mikkel Hvid Amstrup, Peter Mørck, and Pernille Bjørn. 2016. Infrastructures for healthcare: From synergy to reverse synergy. *Health Informatics Journal.*

22. Charlotte P. Lee, Paul Dourish, and Gloria Mark. 2009. The human infrastructure of cyberinfrastructure. *Proceedings of the 2006 20th anniversary conference on Computer supported cooperative work* (pp. 483 – 492). New York: ACM Press.

23. George E. Marcus. 1995. Ethnography in/of the World System: The Emergence of Multi-Sited Ethnography. *Annual Review of Athropology, Vol. 24, 95-117.*

24. Bill Mauer, Taylor C. Nelms, and Lana Swartz. 2013. "When perhaps the real problem is money itself"!: the practical materiality of Bitcoin. *Social Semiotics*, 2013

25. Eric Monteiro, Neil Pollock, Ole Hanseth, and Robin Williams. 2013. From Artefacts to Infrastructures. *Computer Supported Cooperative Work: The Journal of Collaborative Computing (JCSCW),* 22(4), 575–607.

26. Satoshi Nakamoto. 2008. Bitcoin: A Peer-to-Peer Electronic Cash System. Retrieved form bitcoin.org (5 February 2016).

27. Volkmar Pipek, and Volker Wulf. 2009. Infrastructuring: towards and integrated prespective on the design and use of information technology. *Journal of the association of information systems.*Volume 10, issue 5, May 2009, 306 – 332.

28. Larissa Pschetz, Ella Tallyn, Rory Gianni, and Chris Speed. 2017. Bitbarista: Exploring Perceptions of Data Transactions in the Internet of Things, *Proceedings of the 2017 CHI Conference on Human Factors in Computing Systems.*

29. David P. Randall E. Ilana Diamant, Charlotte P. Lee. 2015, Creating Sustainable Cyberinfrastructures, *Proceedings of the 33rd Annual ACM Conference on Human Factors in Computing Systems* Pages 1759-1768.

30. David Ribes. 2014. The Kernel of a Research Institution. *Proceedings of the 17th ACM conference on Computer supported cooperative work & social computing.* Pages 574-587.

31. David Ribes, and Thomas A. Finholt. 2009. The long now of infrastructure: Articulating tensions in development. In P. Edwards, G. C. Bowker, S. Jackson, & R. Williams (Eds.), Special Issue on eInfrastructure in the *Journal of the Association for Information Systems*, 10 (5), 375–398.

32. David Ribes, and Thomas A. Finholt. 2007. Tensions across the scales: Planning infrastructure for the long-term. *Proceedings of the 2007 international ACM*

conference on Supporting group work, Sanibel Island, Florida, USA (pp. 229 – 238). New York: ACM Press.

33. David Ribes, and Charlotte P. Lee. 2010. Sociotechnical Studies of Cyberinfrastructure and e-Research: Current Themes and Future Trajectories. *Computer Supported Cooperative Work* (2010) 19:231–244.

34. Corina Sas, Irni Eliana Kahairuddin. 2017. Design for Trust: An Exploration of the Challenges and Opportunities of Bitcoin Users, *Proceedings of the 2017 CHI Conference on Human Factors in Computing Systems.*

35. Susan Leigh Star, and Karen Ruhleder. 1996. Steps toward an ecology of infrastructure: design and access for large information systems. *Information Systems Research*, 7 (1), 111–134.

36. Susan Leigh Star. 1999. The ethnography of infra-structure. *American Behavioral Scientist*, 43, 377–3.

37. Susan Leigh Star, and Geoffrey C. Bowker. 2002. How to infrastructure. In L. A. Lievrouw & S. Livingstone (Eds.), The Handbook of New Media (pp. 151–162). London: SAGE Publications.

38. Susan Leigh Star, and James R. Griesemer (1989). Institutional ecology, translations and boundary objects: Amateurs and professionals in Berkeleys museum of Vertebrate Zoology, 1907-39. *Social Studies of Science* 19: 387-420.

39. David Tilson, Kalle Lyytinen, Carsten Sørensen. 2010. Digital Infrastructures: The Missing IS Research Agenda. Research Commentary. *Information Systems Research*, Vol. 21, No. 4, December 2010, pp. 748-759.

40. Ann Zimmerman, and Thomas Finholt. 2007. Growing an Infrastructure: The Role of Gateway Organizations in Cultivating New Communities of Users. *Proceedings of the 2007 international ACM conference on Supporting group work.* Pages 239-248.

41. Aviv Zohar. 2015. Bitcoin under the Hood. *Communications of the ACM*, September 2015, Vol 58, No 9, 104-113.

Disaggregating the Impacts of Virtuality on Team Identification

Lionel P. Robert Jr.
School of Information
University of Michigan
Ann Arbor, MI 48109 USA
lprobert@umich.edu

Sangseok You
School of Information Studies
Syracuse University
Syracuse, NY 13088 USA
syou03@syr.edu

ABSTRACT

Team identification is an important predictor of team success. As teams become more virtual, team identification is expected to become more important. Yet, the dimensions of virtuality such as geographic dispersion, reliance on electronic communications and diversity in team membership can undermine team identification. To better understand the impact of virtuality, the authors conducted a study with 248 employees in 55 teams to examine the complex and codependent effects of virtuality. Results indicate that although geographic dispersion and perceived differences can undermine team identification, reliance on electronic communications increases team identification and weakens the negative relationship between perceived differences and team identification.

Author Keywords

Team identification; virtual team; virtuality

ACM Classification Keywords

H.4.3; H.5.3; K.6.0

INTRODUCTION

Virtual teams allow organizations to assemble diverse sources of knowledge across organizational and geographic boundaries [22,57,62,78]. Many of these teams have diverse members who are geographically dispersed and rely primarily on some forms of electronic communication [47,48,55,65]. The use of these teams has increased with the availability of electronic communication technologies [2,50,62]. This has led to the emergence of what are often labeled virtual teams [23,36]. Despite the advantages, these teams also face tremendous difficulties and challenges [35,44,66]. One such challenge is their ability to maintain a strong team identity [7,17,74].

Team identification can be described as the oneness that individuals feel toward their team [42]. It represents an emotional attachment to the team [53,54]. Team

GROUP '18, January 7–10, 2018, Sanibel Island, FL, USA
© 2018 Copyright is held by the owner/author(s). Publication rights licensed to ACM.
ACM 978-1-4503-5562-9/18/01...$15.00
https://doi.org/10.1145/3148330.3148337

identification is associated with higher levels of teamwork, lower levels of conflict and better team performance. In turn, when team members have low levels of team identification they are *less* willing to put forth effort on behalf of the team and often focus on their own personal interests. Therefore, it is not surprising that team identification is seen as an essential element to promoting successful teams [7,55].

Although team identification is an important predictor of team success, it has also been found to be more difficult to develop in virtual environments [17,55]. Prior literature indicates that the frequency of day-to-day contact and feelings of similarity between members promote identification in teams. Yet, teams today are often composed of members with different backgrounds and skills and who rarely, if ever, meet face-to-face [14,21,57]. Therefore, it is not surprising that geographic dispersion, reliance on electronic communication, and the effects of diversity are often used to explain why team identification is harder to develop and yet more important in virtual teams [7,21,30,55,59,74].

However, prior literature has used one measure to represent geographic dispersion, reliance on electronic communication, and the effects of diversity, or some combination of these factors [21,29,30]. In doing so, these studies assumed that all these factors have a similar negative impact on team identification. This is problematic for several reasons. First, electronic communications can actually promote identification and facilitate team coordination [77]. Second, the effects of team diversity are not always salient and in many cases team diversity has no effect on teamwork [25]. Many scholars suggest that perceptions of differences are needed to know when diversity has triggered the in-group out-group processes associated with the negative effects of diversity [26]. In all, electronic communications and team diversity may not make it harder to identify. This suggests that one construct to represent all three factors may be at best inaccurate or at worst misleading. Given both the theoretical and empirical importance of this topic, it becomes imperative to better understand the challenges associated with team identification in virtual teams.

To address these issues, in this paper we took a different approach from previous studies. First, we separately examined the impacts of geographic dispersion, reliance on electronic communication (i.e. email, chat, voice, and video), and diversity on team identification. We chose these three factors because they have typically and consistently been used to explain why virtual teams have trouble achieving high levels of team identification [17,21,27,29,30]. Second, unlike prior researchers who have examined actual diversity (e.g., nationality; [19,21]), we examined perceived differences among team members. Research has found that perceptions of differences are what drive the negative impacts of actual diversity [25,26]. Third, we proposed and examined the interplay between each of the impacts of virtuality on team identification. It could be quite possible that the impact of each factor related to virtuality varies depending on the others. If this were true, then the impact of the use of electronic communications would be dependent on team dispersion and vice versa.

In this paper, we present and empirically test a research model that explains how each dimension of virtuality influences team identification, separately and then jointly. We conducted a study involving 248 individuals in 55 teams with varying degrees of virtuality. Results generally support the research model. Overall, this paper contributes to the GROUP literature by highlighting the complex role of virtuality on team identification.

This paper contributes to the literature in the following ways. First, this study contributes by highlighting the complex ways in which virtuality can influence team identification. In doing so, this study goes beyond existing literature on virtuality and team identification. Second, this research contributes to our understanding of the relationship between electronic communications and team identification by demonstrating electronic communications' positive impacts on team identification. Third, this research enhances our understanding of the effects of diversity on team identification. Research has consistently shown that perceived differences are one way that team diversity can negatively impact team performance [26,47,48]. This study demonstrates how geographic dispersion and the use of electronic communications can weaken the negative effects of perceived differences on team identification. Finally, the results of this study have several implications for designers.

RELATED WORK

Team Identification

Team identification can be described as a sense of belonging or oneness that individual team members feel toward their team [4,59]. Social identity and self-categorization theories are often used to explain team identification [32,68]. An individual's social identity defines who he or she is in comparison to others. Self-categorization is a process by which individuals place themselves and others into in-groups and out-groups. Individuals place those who seem to be like themselves into in-groups and those who do not seem to be like themselves

into out-groups. When a team member places himself/herself and other team members into the same in-group, identification with the team is said to have occurred [16,73].

Team identification has important benefits for all teams. In general, the more individuals identify with a team the more they adopt norms and behaviors of that team [31,69,71,73]. Team identification may be more important in virtual teams. Dimensions of virtuality such as geographic dispersion, electronic dependence and team diversity may hamper team identification [17]. Yet, these very same dimensions of virtuality may make identification more important in virtual teams [76]. Team identification can work as the glue that bridges members in different locations by creating affective ties among team members [43]. Moreover, the disadvantages from dispersion, such as a low visibility and trust, can be overcome by inducing cohesion and a sense of shared faith [29,65]. Team identification promotes these things and ultimately leads to better team performance [7,74].

Impacts of Virtuality

There are many ways to conceptualize virtuality (see [21] for a review). However, traditionally researchers have conceptualized virtuality as either present or not (i.e. virtual or face-to-face). This binary view of virtuality is still valid but it has at least one disadvantage. Binary approaches lump together things like geographic dispersion, reliance on electronic communications, and issues related to diversity (e.g., perceived differences) into one bucket. This assumes that all three elements of virtuality have similar effects, when in fact they may not. Martins and colleagues wrote one of the first papers to suggest that all teams can be defined as more or less virtual [44]. They argued that virtuality should be viewed as a continuum rather than the traditional binary view (i.e. simply present or not).

There is another view of virtuality that conceptualizes it as separate and distinct dimensions. This view separates the effects of dispersion from those associated with electronic communications [29]. For example, Gibson and Gibbs conceptualized and operationalized virtuality as separate and distinct dimensions that included geographic dispersion, reliance on electronic communications, and team diversity [21]. They identified these dimensions by reviewing the "Web of Science" and extracting dimensions based on the highest frequency of appearance in virtual team studies. Results of their study confirmed that each dimension had independent effects on team innovation. O'Leary and Cummings and Cummings et al. also put forth the idea that the effects of virtuality could be taken apart and examined independently [12,49]. In doing so, many scholars argue that dispersion can be associated with reductions in face-to-face communications but does not completely eliminate them and that reliance on electronic communications is one dimension of virtuality [36,44].

Researchers who have conceptualized virtuality as separate dimensions each along a continuum have found that the impacts of virtuality vary greatly [3,40,61]. For example, it is widely known that geographic dispersion can deteriorate team performance by increasing coordination effort and decreasing communications [3]. But other studies have found that dispersion also facilitates more open discussions [39,40]. There are ongoing debates with regard to whether electronic communications are beneficial or problematic for teams [5,17,76]. Likewise, the impacts of diversity have normally been assumed to be harmful to virtual teams [17,35,66]. Yet, Ye and Robert [79] discovered that diversity actually increased creativity in virtual teams high in collectivism. Taken together, it is required to examine interplay among the different aspects of virtuality to better predict their influence on virtual team performance.

This paper builds on previous literature that has conceptualized virtuality as separate dimensions each along a continuum. In this paper, we refer to these dimensions or elements as "the impacts of virtuality." The impacts of virtuality are related but distinct ways in which the effects of virtuality materialize. Virtuality has many impacts but in this paper we are only interested in examining a subset of them in the literature. This subset comprises the three most commonly studied impacts of virtuality: geographic dispersion, reliance on electronic communications, and team diversity.

The effects of geographic dispersion, reliance on electronic communications and team diversity were selected in this study to represent virtuality. Most scholars agree that geographic dispersion and reliance on electronic communications are two important factors of virtuality [3,21,33,56,59,65]. In addition, the literature provides strong evidence with regard the effects of diversity on virtual teams [9,21,47,48,60]. Therefore, we included the impacts of diversity in the form of perceived differences. Perceived differences are beliefs about how different team members believe they are from one another [63,79]. Such perceptions can be invoked by surface-level diversity aspects (e.g., gender and nationality) or deep-level aspects (e.g., personality and values) [26,47,48].

Taken together, geographic dispersion, reliance on electronic communications, and perceived differences capture many aspects associated with virtuality (Figure 1).

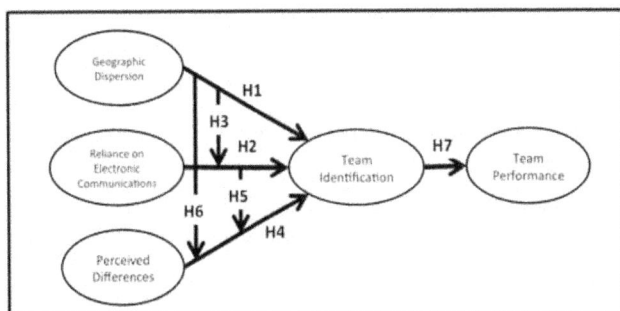

Figure 1 Research Model

RESEARCH MODEL

Geographic Dispersion and Team Identification
Although there are many views on the effects of virtuality on team identification, most scholars agree that geographic dispersion itself can be detrimental to team identification [11,17,21,28]. We believe geographic dispersion is negatively related to team identification for several reasons.

First, the identification process normally occurs through a series of interactions among team members [17,32,70]. In general, the more interactions among team members the more likely team members are to identify with the team [70]. Research has consistently shown that distance matters [50]. Geographic dispersion reduces the amount of communication and interactions between individuals [50]. In general, people communicate less with distant others than they do with individuals who are geographically closer [47]. This lack of communication and interactions can undermine the social psychological processes underlying identification [28,50,70].

Second, geographic dispersion is often associated with coordination problems. Cummings et al. [12] showed that geographic dispersion can cause delays in teamwork processes and make coordination more difficult. They argued that geographic dispersion makes it harder for teams to divide and sequence tasks [12]. This is in part because geographic dispersion makes it difficult for team members to know when members are available [11]. Coordination problems often lead to conflict, which has been shown to be negatively related to team identification [17,28,30].

Taken together, the lack of communication, coordination problems, and attribution theory all seem to indicate that geographic dispersion reduces team identification.

H1) Geographic dispersion is negatively related to team identification.

Reliance on Electronic Communications and Team Identification
Many scholars disagree about the impact of electronic communications on teamwork. As we mentioned, communication and interactions are strong predictors of identification. Some scholars believe that electronic communications are not as effective in transmitting meaning or supporting relationships across distances [13,64]. However, these studies tended to focus on what is often referred to as lean versus rich media [58]. When such classifications fell out of favor, scholars began to rethink the impact of electronic communications on identification and other social–emotional constructs [17,75,77].

Despite this, many studies have found a negative relationship between electronic communications and process and outcome variables similar to team identification (see [5]). However, we believe this is due to the fact that many studies often lump together both geographic dispersion and the reliance on electronic communications.

In fact, many scholars believe electronic communications can have positive impacts on team relationships [17,75,77].

Electronic communications offer affordances that support team identification. To start, electronic communications can support more equal participation among team members during team communications [59]. This allows more than one individual to effectively speak at the same time. This allows everyone the opportunity to participate in team discussions. Prior research has confirmed that the use of electronic communications has been associated with more equality during team discussions [52,59]. Higher levels of equality in team discussions should be positively related to team identification.

Electronic communications have additional benefits that should increase team identification. The use of electronic communication technologies can facilitate more communication among team members. Regardless of the geographic location of team members, individuals often find it difficult to schedule meetings when everyone is available. Electronic communications can increase the effectiveness of team communications. Because most electronic communications technologies afford recording and restoring features, members in virtual teams can review communication history and revise messages for future interaction, which raises comprehensibility of communications and readability of messages, respectively [10]. Both the ability to communicate more often and increases in communication effectiveness can be particularly critical to building team identification [45].

H2) Reliance on electronic communications is positively related to team identification.

Geographic Dispersion and Reliance on Electronic Communications and Team Identification
The positive relationship between reliance on electronic communications and team identification should become stronger as teams become more geographically dispersed. We posit that the more dispersed a team is, the more likely electronic communications are to become members' primary means of communication. The less dispersed the team members, the less likely they are to rely on electronic communications.

Initially, electronic communication can be problematic, but experience regarding the electronic communication technology, team, and task can create a situation where electronic communications can better support the social–emotional processes needed to facilitate team identification when teams have no other means of communication [75] (see [76] for a review). This is most likely to occur in teams that have to rely on electronic communications rather than face-to-face communications as their primary means of communication. Many studies have supported the enriching aspects of electronic communication in dispersed teams that rely on it as their primary means of communications [15,23,58,59].

Therefore, we propose that the impact of electronic communications on team identification is relative to the team's dispersion. The more dispersed teams are, the stronger the use of electronic communications will have on team identification. In teams that are highly dispersed, electronic communications are more likely to be their primary means of communication. Communications should be positively related to team identification. For example, electronic communications have been found to be a strong predictor of organizational identification when employees are dispersed [77].

H3) The relationship between reliance on electronic communications and team identification is stronger as geographic dispersion increases.

Perceived Differences and Team Identification
Perceived differences represent the perceptions of interpersonal differences among team members in values, attitudes and beliefs [26]. Differences among team members have been found to have negative implications for both face-to-face and virtual teams. For example, Kankanhalli et al. found that cultural diversity and functional background diversity increased conflict in global virtual project teams [35]. Similarly, Staples and Zhao found that cultural diversity resulted in lower satisfaction and cohesion in virtual teams [66]. Gibson and Gibbs discovered that national diversity reduced team innovation [21].

The negative effects associated with perceived differences are directly related to the identification process. As we mentioned earlier, individuals place others and themselves into in-groups and out-groups. Team identification occurs in part because individuals place themselves and their teammates into the same in-group. This means that individuals believe that they are similar to their teammates rather than different [72]. However, when team members believe they are different from their teammates the identification process is undermined.

The problems associated with perceived differences explain why many scholars thought identification would be difficult for virtual teams [43]. In general, virtual teams are composed of people from different locations with different knowledge, skills and beliefs that are also more likely to be demographically diverse [19,29,30]. Many scholars have argued that these negative implications of team diversity are often in part transmitted through perceptions of differences [26]. Therefore, perceived differences should be negatively related to team identification [20,21,24,51,55].

H4) Perceived differences are negatively related to team identification.

Perceived Differences, Geographic Dispersion, and Reliance on Electronic Communications and Team Identification
Although distance among team members is often seen as a negative, it could be a good thing. Individuals prefer to

interact less often with those they believe are different and more often with those they believe are similar [26,47,48]. This idea is derived from the similarity-attraction paradigm [8]. This paradigm posits that perceptions of similarity between teammates in values, beliefs, and attitudes engender greater interpersonal trust and collaboration while perceptions of dissimilarity between teammates in values, beliefs, and attitudes reduce trust and collaboration (e.g., [26,41]). In general, individuals do not prefer to interact with those they believe are different from them. This explains why perceptions of differences are negatively reduced to team identification.

The negative relationship between perceived differences and team identification should be weakened by the reliance on electronic communications and geographic dispersion. Electronic communications can be less personal than face-to-face interactions [59]. Electronic communications can also allow team members to communicate or not communicate with their teammates if and when they choose. The use of electronic communications allows individuals to minimize their personal interactions with their teammates. Therefore, as teams rely on electronic communications, team members do not have to personally meet with dissimilar others. The reduction of face-to-face contact should weaken the negative relationship between perceived differences and team identification.

Geographic dispersion also reduces contact among team members [50]. This should benefit teams with members who perceive that they are different from their teammates. When teammates are physically dispersed they are less likely to meet face-to-face with their teammates. Geographic dispersion provides distance among teammates. Although this reduces the frequency of contact among team members, which reduces team identification, it can have a calming effect when team members believe they are different.

H5) The negative relationship between perceived differences and team identification decreases as reliance on electronic communications increases.

H6) The negative relationship between perceived differences and team identification decreases as geographic dispersion increases.

Team Identification and Virtual Team Performance
Team identification should lead team members to engage in positive behaviors to achieve collective objectives. According to social identity theory, as mentioned, individuals tend to enhance their identity as a member of a team by reinforcing the value of being on the team. In general, when team members identify with the team, they tend to comply with team goals and are more motivated to work on behalf of the team. When team members identify with the team, potential conflicts can be reduced and satisfaction can be increased [55]. Team identification positively influences coordination effectiveness and

productivity [37]. Additionally, team members can be more motivated to participate in the team tasks that increase team performance [80].

Several studies have found that team identification increases the performance of teams regardless of their level of virtuality. For example, Robert et al. found that identification was important to the performance of both collocated teams who performed tasks in a face-to-face setting and dispersed teams who performed tasks using a type of electronic communication [59]. Robert also found in a multi-level study that team identification increased team performance in virtual teams [55]. As such, theories and empirical findings imply that team identification should be positively related to performance in virtual teams.

H7) Team identification is positively related to team performance.

METHOD

Participants
The participants were employees of an information technology (IT) solution vendor that focuses on providing human resources software and IT support for clients. Team tasks consisted mainly of problem-solving related to one of two sets of responsibilities: installation and implementation, or maintenance. Installation and implementation involved either bringing a new system online, installing a new module of an existing system or upgrading the existing system. Maintenance involved handling client issues related to the problems associated with the existing software. For example, if the clients were having trouble with their system the team would address the technical issues.

Although some team members worked at a client's site temporarily, most worked remotely from home to address client issues online. Members of these teams were dispersed and relied on electronic communications.

No formal leaders were assigned to the teams, but each team was assigned a client group advocate. These advocates were not a member of the team and were primarily responsible for maintaining the relationship with the client and evaluating the team's work. The organization participated in a study to determine the effectiveness of remote work. As part of their participation agreement, one of the researchers agreed to provide a white paper to members of the executive team.

A total of 470 employees in 70 teams were targeted for participation. We employed two team surveys and received responses from more than 50% of the members of 60 teams across both surveys. However, five teams were dropped because we could not obtain performance ratings for them. As a result, we were left with 248 individuals in 55 teams with an average response rate of 70% per team. Participant ages ranged from 26 to 52 with a mean age of 37 years. The size of the teams ranged from 6 to 8 with a mean of 6.7.

Data Collection

We collected data via two online surveys. The first survey, sent via email, was up for 1 month and had questions regarding control variables — perceived differences, dispersion, and use of electronic communications. The second survey was sent 3 months later and had questions regarding team identification. We obtained performance ratings using a third survey that went only to client group advocates. In all three cases, we sent follow-up email reminders to encourage participation. In addition, client group advocates were instructed by upper management to encourage all employees to participate.

The surveys were web-based and all individual responses were confidential and only seen by the research team. The surveys used well-established multi-item scales, which we summarize in the measurements section. We used a seven-point Likert scale to measure team identification and perceived differences. The second survey was typically administered about 1 week before the project was due.

Measurements

Control Variables

We used several control variables to reduce the possibility of alternative explanations. Because research has found that team tenure, organizational tenure, size, and age can impact team outcomes, we included these as control variables [21,36]. Team tenure was the number of years the team was together and team individual average tenure was the number of years the average team member had been employed.

Independent Variables

Reliance on electronic communications was determined by asking individuals how much they collaborated via face-to-face meetings, email, chat, phone, and video (see Table 1 for a breakdown of scores across all communication types). All team members had access to each of the technologies via software provided by the company. However, employees were not limited to that particular software and the questions were not intended to assess their use of that software system.

Team Electronic Communications	Percentage
Face-to-face meeting	10
Email	41
Chat	18
Phone/voice only communications	19
Video communications	12

Table 1 Breakdown of scores of all communication types

To calculate the score for reliance on electronic communications, we averaged the scores across all three items seen below. (1) How frequently did your team engage in collaborative interactions through electronic communications (i.e. email, chat, voice only, and video)? (2) How openly did your team engage in collaborative interactions through electronic communications (i.e. email, chat, voice only, and video)? (3) How extensively did your team engage in collaborative interactions through electronic communications (i.e. email, chat, voice only, and video)? The aggregation of electronic communications was consistent with previous literature on virtuality [21,29,36,46].

To create a multi-item measure of geographic dispersion we used an item from [67] and [12]. The first item asked team members "To what extent did your teamwork take place at different locations?" Answers ranged from (1) never, (2) almost never, (3) very rarely, (4) occasionally, (5) often (6) almost always (7) always. The second item from [12] asked team members to indicate the extent to which they were physically separated from other members of their team. The scale consisted of the following ranges: (1) same room, (2) different room on the same hallway, (3) different hallways, (4) different floor, (5) different building, (6) different city and (7) different country. At the team level, we computed the average dispersion among members to determine the extent to which the team was dispersed.

To measure the perceived differences, we adapted items from Harrison et al. [26]. Team members rated on a seven-point scale (1-strongly disagree to 7-strongly agree) how different they thought their team members' work styles were. The items included: (1) Members of my team have different work ethics, (2) Members of my team have different work habits, (3) Members of my team have different communication styles, (4) Members of my team have different interaction styles, and (5) Members of my team have different personalities.

Dependent Variables

There were two dependent variables, team identification and team performance. Identification with the team was based on a four-item scale taken from [34]. Items included: (1) I talk up this team to my friends as a great team to work in, (2) I am very committed to my team, (3) I am proud to tell others that I am part of this team, and (4) I feel a sense of ownership for this team.

We obtained team performance data from client group advocates. They were asked to rate three statements with regard to a particular team: (1) This team was efficient in providing services and support to its clients, (2) This team was effective in providing services and support to its clients, and (3) This team met or exceeded my expectations in fulfilling its overall objectives.

RESULTS

We obtained all latent construct measures at the individual level of analysis. To justify aggregating the data to the team level, we used an intra-class correlation coefficient (ICC) to measure the between-team variance. The ICC indicates how much variance in the individual response is from team membership. Higher values indicate that team membership accounts for more individual variance. ICC values at or above .08 provide justification for aggregating the data [6,38]. Team identification had an ICC of .45, perceived differences had a .40, use of electronic communications had

Variable	Mean	Std. Dev.	Reliability	1	2	3	4	5	6	7	8	9	10
1 Geographic Dispersion	5.00	0.75	0.83										
2 National Diversity	0.60	0.20	N/A	-0.11									
3 Perceived Diversity	2.50	0.72	0.88	0.07	-0.30 *								
4 Reliance on Electronic Communications	4.20	0.90	0.85	-0.54 ***	-0.10	-0.20							
5 Team Average Age	37.00	4.90	N/A	-0.07	-0.16	0.02	0.02						
6 Team Identification	4.80	0.91	0.92	0.06	-0.06	-0.27 *	0.29 *	0.14					
7 Team Individual Average Tenure	6.30	3.00	0.92	-0.10	0.06	-0.29 *	0.19	0.35 **	0.40 **				
8 Team Performance	5.70	0.56	N/A	-0.02	-0.32 *	0.03	0.07	0.34 *	0.38 **	0.07			
9 Team Size	6.50	1.40	N/A	0.24	0.22	0.07	-0.28 *	-0.06	-0.15	-0.05	-0.25		
10 Team Tenure	6.30	3.00	N/A	-0.11	-0.10	0.05	0.06	0.36 **	0.13	0.03	0.21	0.04	

Notes:
1. M = Mean; SD = Standard Deviation
2. Significance of correlations: *p<.05; **p<.01;*** p<.001
3. N = 55

Table 2 Means, Standard Deviations, Reliabilities, and Correlations of Continuous Variables

a .40 and geographic dispersion had an ICC score of .42. All ICC values were above the .08 threshold, providing justification for aggregating the data [6,38].

We assessed convergent and discriminant validity through factor loading (Table 2). All items loaded at the .70 or above level on each of their constructs while no cross-loadings were above .35. These are all indications of convergent and discriminant validity [18]. All reliabilities were above .70. Means, standard deviations and reliabilities are all listed in Table 3.

Item	1	2	3	4	5
Geo. Dispersion 1	**.85**	.29	.21	.26	.21
Geo. Dispersion 2	**.89**	.28	.09	.19	.09
Electronic Comm. 1	.24	**.85**	.17	.13	.17
Electronic Comm. 2	.20	**.88**	.01	.10	.11
Electronic Comm. 3	.30	**.83**	.01	.11	.08
Team identification 1	.20	.11	**.91**	.22	.21
Team Identification 2	.25	.12	**.78**	.14	.09
Team Identification 3	.21	.15	**.95**	.13	.18
Team identification 4	.24	.20	**.85**	.01	.01
Team Performance 1	.15	.11	.20	**.96**	.17
Team Performance 2	.23	.12	.19	**.97**	.09
Team Performance 3	.14	.22	.20	**.93**	.15
Perceived Differences 1	.23	.19	.25	**.88**	**.88**
Perceived Differences 2	.20	.11	.17	.05	**.91**
Perceived Differences 3	.23	.12	.09	.04	**.89**
Perceived Differences 4	.21	.20	.07	.16	**.94**
Perceived Differences 5	.30	.29	.18	.21	**.80**

Note: Principal Component Analysis was used for extraction method.

Table 2 Factor Loading

Hypotheses were tested using partial least squares structural equation modeling (PLS). PLS is robust structural equation modeling (SEM) technique with small sample sizes [59]. Significance tests were conducted using 1,000 bootstrap resampling. To reduce the possibility of multicollinearity, as recommended by Aiken and West [1], we standardized all continuous variables in the model (Table 4).

Independent Variables	Team Identification			R^2
	1	2	3	
Step 1: Control Variables				
National Diversity	-.07	-.03	-.10	
Team Average Age	.15	.13	.10	
Team Ind. Aver Tenure	.33*	.23	.18	
Team Size	-.17	-.23	-.20	
Team Tenure	.18*	.13	.10	
				.18**
Step 2: Main Effects				
Geographic Dispersion		-.20*	-.03	
Reliance on Electronic Comm.		.32*	.10	
Perceived Differences		-.21*	-.67**	.36***
Change in R^2				.18***
Step 3: Interaction Effects				
GD × EC			.44**	
PD × EC			.48***	
PD × GD			.62**	.66***
Change in R^2				.48***

N=55 Standardized regression coefficients are reported (Beta weights). Continuous variables were standardized.
GD = Geographic Dispersion; EC = Reliance on Electronic Communications; PD = Perceived Differences
*p<.05; **p<.01; ***p<.001

Table 4 Results of Team Identification

Model 1 shows the effects of control variables on the dependent variable. Model 2 shows the main effects of the independent variables. Model 3 shows the impact of the two-way interaction effects on team identification. The final model predicted a significant amount of the variance for team identification. We also found that there was a significant increase in the amount of variance explained by the inclusion of the interaction effects.

The results for the models examining team performance are shown in Table 5. Model 1 shows the effects of control variables while Model 2 shows the main effects of the independent variables. Results show that Model 2 explained a significant amount of the variance of team performance.

	Team Performance		
Variables	**1**	**2**	**R^2**
Step 1: Control Variables			
National Diversity	.27**	.24*	
Team Average Age	.15	.23**	
Team Ind. Aver Tenure	.33**	.16*	
Team Size	-.17	-.16*	
Team Tenure	.18*	.11	.13
Step 2: Main Effects			
Team Identification		.32**	.38**
Change in R^2			.25
N=55 Standardized regression coefficients are reported (Beta weights). Continuous variables were standardized.			
*p<.05; **p<.01; ***p<.001			

Table 5 Results of team performance

Among the control variables shown in Table 4, only average team individual tenure and team tenure were significant predictors of team identification. However, in Table 5, all the control variables were significant predictors of team performance in Models 1, 2 or 3.

Hypothesis 1, which posited that geographic dispersion would be negatively related to team identification, was supported. Model 2 included the main effects of independent variables (Table 4). From the regression analysis, geographic dispersion was negatively related to team identification (β = -0.20, p < 0.05). This result indicates that team identification was reduced as geographic dispersion increased. Hypothesis 1 was supported.

Hypothesis 2 posited that reliance on electronic communications would be positively related to team identification. Model 2 shows that reliance on electronic communications was positively related to team identification. The main effects of reliance on electronic communications were significant in both Model 2s (β = 0.30, p < 0.05). Therefore, hypothesis 2 was supported.

Hypothesis 3 posited that the effects of geographic dispersion and reliance on electronic communications would interact. Model 3 shows that there was a significant two-way interaction effect on team identification (β = 0.44, p < 0.01).

Details of the interaction effect are shown in Figure 2. One standard deviation above and below the mean was used to represent high and low conditions for both the moderator and independent variable. Reliance on electronic communications increased team identification as dispersion increased. This supports hypothesis 3.

Hypothesis 4 stated that perceived differences are negatively related to team identification. Results shown in Table 4 indicate that there was a significant main effect of

perceived differences on team identification in Model 2 (β = -0.21, p < 0.05). Therefore, hypothesis 4 is supported based on our data.

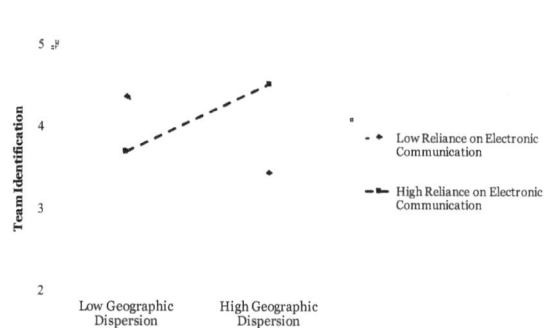

Figure 2 The two-way interaction effect between geographic dispersion and reliance on electronic communications on team identification

Hypotheses 5 and 6 stated the relationship between perceived differences and team identification would be moderated by the reliance on electronic communications (H5) and geographic dispersion (H6). The results demonstrate that there was a significant two-way interaction between perceived differences and reliance on electronic communications (β = 0.48, p < 0.01). Details of the interaction effect are shown in Figure 3. Similar to Figure 2, one standard deviation above and below the mean was used to represent high and low conditions. Thus, hypothesis 5 is supported. The interaction effect with geographic dispersion was also statistically significant (β = 0.62, p < 0.01). Thus, hypothesis 6 was also supported. Details of the interaction effect are shown in Figure 4.

Last, hypothesis 7 posited that team identification would be positively related to team performance. Table 5 indicates the results of linear regression analyses of the control variables and the independent variables with team performance as the dependent variable, respectively, in Model 1 and Model 2. We also included the control variables to demonstrate that team identification had an effect over and above those variables. As shown in Table 5, there was a significant main effect of team identification on

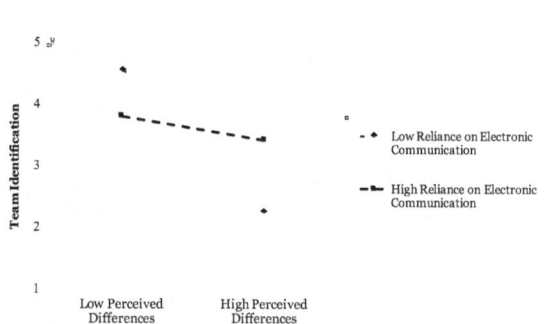

Figure 3 The two-way interaction between perceived differences and reliance on electronic communications on team identification

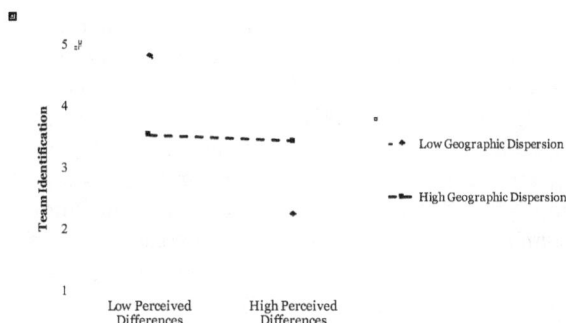

Figure 4 The two-way interaction between perceived differences and geographic dispersion on team identification

team performance in Model 2 ($\beta = .32$, $p < 0.01$). The results show that team identification increases team performance. Hypothesis 7 was supported.

Overall, the research model was supported by the data. All hypotheses were supported. Table 6 summarizes the results of hypothesis testing.

H1) Geographic dispersion is negatively related to team identification.	**Yes**
H2) Reliance on electronic communications is positively related to team identification.	**Yes**
H3) The relationship between reliance on electronic communications and team identification is stronger as geographic dispersion increases.	**Yes**
H4) Perceived differences are negatively related to team identification.	**Yes**
H5) The negative relationship between perceived differences and team identification decrease as reliance on electronic communications increases.	**Yes**
H6) The negative relationship between perceived differences and team identification decreases as geographic dispersion increases.	**Yes**
H7) Team identification is positively related to team performance.	**Yes**

Table 6 Results of the hypothesis testing

LIMITATIONS

Before discussing the implications of our findings, it is important to acknowledge the limitations of this study. First, all data were collected within one organization. Additional research is needed to determine whether our findings could be generalized to teams in other organizations. Another limitation of this study concerns internal validity. Many measures were gathered through self-reports. Although we employed two surveys to reduce common method variance, this should be considered a potential limitation. In addition, we aggregated all types of electronic communications into one construct. Although this was consisted with previous literature (see [21,29,36,46]), future studies could consider how specific types of electronic communication might alter the impacts.

For example, video communications may not have the same suppressive impacts as electronic mail.

DISCUSSION

This paper presents a research model that examines three distinct but related impacts of virtuality: geographic dispersion, reliance on electronic communications, and perceptions of differences. Results of this study demonstrate that geographic dispersion and perceptions of differences are associated with reductions in team identification but reliance on electronic communications is associated with increases in team identification. However, the effects are more complicated: the positive relationship between reliance on electronic communications and team identification is much stronger when teams are collocated. When teams are dispersed, the positive relationship between reliance on electronic communications and team identification is greatly reduced. In addition, reliance on electronic communications can reduce the negative relationship between perceived differences and team identification. In fact, the negative relationship between perceived differences and team identification occurs when teams rely more on face-to-face interactions than on electronic communications.

Implications for Research

This research contributes to the literature in several ways. First, it contributes to our understanding of the relationship between the reliance on electronic communications and team identification. Reliance on electronic communications has several positive impacts on team identification. It is directly associated with increases in team identification and more so when teams are collocated. Reliance on electronic communications also reduces the negative relationship between perceived differences and team identification. Prior conceptualizations of virtuality that lumped reliance on electronic communications along with geographic dispersion have found a negative relationship between virtuality and team identification. The negative impacts have been associated with both geographic dispersion and reliance on electronic communications [5,15]. However, by separating the two, this study goes beyond prior literature by demonstrating the positive relationship between reliance on electronic communications and team identification rather than the negative relationship implied by prior literature.

Second, this research enhances our understanding of the effects of team diversity. Perceived differences can be invoked by many different types of team diversity. This study demonstrates how the use of electronic communications can weaken the negative effects of perceived differences. This tells us that the effects of perceived differences depend largely on the amount of electronic communication and geographic dispersion among team members.

Finally, this study contributes to the literature on virtuality by highlighting the complex ways in which virtuality can influence team identification. This study goes beyond existing studies of virtuality that separate dimensions of virtuality by highlighting that the impacts of virtuality are often co-dependent. Therefore, it is not enough to just separate the effects of virtuality. This study tells us that one has to consider them in the relation to the other dimensions of virtuality.

Implications for Designers

The results of this study have several implications for designers. First, although the use of electronic communications was associated with higher levels of team identification, geographic dispersion was not. This may mean that the use of electronic communication technologies such as email, chat, phone, or video does not fully address the problems associated with geographic dispersion. The problems associated with geographic dispersion are due, in part, to a lack of contextual information [11]. Therefore, electronic communication systems have to be designed to better promote the sharing of contextual information. We believe that contextual information is exchanged best through informal rather than formal interactions. New systems should be designed to encourage informal interactions rather than simply formal task-related interactions. This could be done in part by having new systems prompt team members to share more information.

Second, new systems should take into account the location of team members at any given time. Although there are teams whose members are dispersed who never meet face-to-face and teams whose members are collocated and who primarily rely on face-to-face interactions, most teams probably exist between these two extremes at any given moment. For example, collocated teams may have members who are, at any given time, temporarily dispersed. New systems should recognize the location of team members and adapt their capabilities to prompt the sharing of more contextual information when team members are dispersed and perhaps scale down such prompting when members are collocated.

Finally, electronic communication technologies should be designed to promote team identification. Although the effects of perceived differences were weakened by electronic communications, designers should envision a much more active role for such technologies. For example, Newell et al. designed a collaboration system that prompted users to complete an online profile about their individual characteristics and preferences [47,48]. The system selected the individual characteristics and preferences among team members that were similar within each team and suppressed or hid the information about individual characteristics and preferences that were dissimilar. They found that when team members received similar information about their teammates they had higher levels of social integration and performed better [47,48].

Implications for Managers

Our study also has managerial implications. Team identification has clear performance benefits for teams regardless of the geographic location of team members. However, geographic location seems to be a barrier to team identification and the use of electronic communications seems to benefit collocated teams more than dispersed teams. One approach to overcoming the problems associated with geographic dispersion is to encourage the sharing of contextual information through informal interactions. To facilitate the sharing of such information managers should encourage informal interactions among dispersed team members. This may mean setting up online gaming pools such as NCAA brackets or encouraging other informal activities. Once team members are convinced of the importance of the contextual information, they should be more likely to share this information.

CONCLUSION

Team identification is an important predictor of team success and is seen as more important as teams become more virtual. However, the dimensions of virtuality can undermine team identification. The results of this study found that the impacts of virtuality are more complex than originally thought. More work is needed to fully understand the impacts of virtuality on team identification specifically and team relationships in general.

ACKNOWLEDGMENTS

We gratefully acknowledge the financial support from the National Science Foundation grant CHS-1617820.

REFERENCE

1. Leona S. Aiken, Stephen G. West, and Raymond R. Reno. 1991. *Multiple regression: Testing and interpreting interactions*. Sage.

2. Omar A. Alnuaimi, Lionel P. Robert, and Likoebe M. Maruping. 2010. Team size, dispersion, and social loafing in technology-supported teams: A perspective on the theory of moral disengagement. *Journal of Management Information Systems* 27, 1: 203–230.

3. N. D. Anh, D. S. Cruzes, and R. Conradi. 2012. Dispersion, coordination and performance in global software teams: A systematic review. In *Proceedings of the 2012 ACM-IEEE International Symposium on Empirical Software Engineering and Measurement*, 129–138.

4. Blake E. Ashforth and Fred Mael. 1989. Social identity theory and the organization. *Academy of management review* 14, 1: 20–39.

5. Boris B Baltes, Marcus W Dickson, Michael P Sherman, Cara C Bauer, and Jacqueline S LaGanke. 2002. Computer-Mediated Communication and Group Decision Making: A Meta-Analysis. *Organizational Behavior and Human Decision Processes* 87, 1: 156–179.

6. Paul D. Bliese. 2000. Within-group agreement, non-independence, and reliability: Implications for data aggregation and analysis.

7. Nathan D. Bos, Ayse Buyuktur, Judith S. Olson, Gary M. Olson, and Amy Voida. 2010. Shared identity helps partially distributed teams, but distance still matters. In *Proceedings of the 16th ACM international conference on Supporting group work*, 89–96.

8. D. E. Byrne. 1971. The Attraction Paradigm. Vol. 11. *Academic Pr.*

9. Laku Chidambaram. 2005. Diversity: Is there more than meets the eye? A longitudinal study of the impact of technology support on teams with differing diversity. In *System Sciences, 2005. HICSS'05. Proceedings of the 38th Annual Hawaii International Conference on*, 48a–48a.

10. Herbert H. Clark and Susan E. Brennan. 1991. Grounding in communication. *Perspectives on socially shared cognition* 13, 1991: 127–149.

11. Catherine Durnell Cramton. 2001. The mutual knowledge problem and its consequences for dispersed collaboration. *Organization science* 12, 3: 346–371.

12. Jonathon N. Cummings, J. Alberto Espinosa, and Cynthia K. Pickering. 2009. Crossing spatial and temporal boundaries in globally distributed projects: A relational model of coordination delay. *Information Systems Research* 20, 3: 420–439.

13. Richard L. Daft, Robert H. Lengel, and Linda Klebe Trevino. 1987. Message equivocality, media selection, and manager performance: Implications for information systems. *MIS quarterly*: 355–366.

14. Alan R. Dennis, Lionel P. Robert, Aaron M. Curtis, Stacy T. Kowalczyk, and Bryan K. Hasty. 2012. Research Note-Trust Is in the Eye of the Beholder: A Vignette Study of Postevent Behavioral Controls' Effects on Individual Trust in Virtual Teams. *Information systems research* 23, 2: 546–558.

15. Alan R. Dennis and Barbara H. Wixom. 2002. Investigating the moderators of the group support systems use with meta-analysis. *Journal of Management Information Systems* 18, 3: 235–258.

16. Jane E. Dutton, Janet M. Dukerich, and Celia V. Harquail. 1994. Organizational images and member identification. *Administrative science quarterly*: 239–263.

17. C. Marlene Fiol and Edward J. O'Connor. 2005. Identification in face-to-face, hybrid, and pure virtual teams: Untangling the contradictions. *Organization science* 16, 1: 19–32.

18. Claes Fornell and David F. Larcker. 1981. Evaluating structural equation models with unobservable variables and measurement error. *Journal of marketing research*: 39–50.

19. Robert C. Giambatista and Anita D. Bhappu. 2010. Diversity's harvest: Interactions of diversity sources and communication technology on creative group performance. *Organizational Behavior and Human Decision Processes* 111, 2: 116–126.

20. Jennifer Lee Gibbs. 2002. *Loose coupling in global teams: Tracing the contours of cultural complexity*. University of Southern California.

21. Cristina B. Gibson and Jennifer L. Gibbs. 2006. Unpacking the concept of virtuality: The effects of geographic dispersion, electronic dependence, dynamic structure, and national diversity on team innovation. *Administrative Science Quarterly* 51, 3: 451–495.

22. Sandeep Goyal, Likoebe Maruping, and Lionel P. Robert. 2008. Diversity and Conflict in Teams: A Faultline Model Perspective. In *Academy of Management Proceedings*, 1–6.

23. Terri L. Griffith, John E. Sawyer, and Margaret A. Neale. 2003. Virtualness and knowledge in teams: Managing the love triangle of organizations, individuals, and information technology. *MIS quarterly*: 265–287.

24. Donald C. Hambrick, Sue Canney Davison, Scott A. Snell, and Charles C. Snow. 1998. When groups consist of multiple nationalities: Towards a new understanding of the implications. *Organization studies* 19, 2: 181–205.

25. David A. Harrison, Kenneth H. Price, and Myrtle P. Bell. 1998. Beyond relational demography: Time and the effects of surface-and deep-level diversity on work group cohesion. *Academy of management journal* 41, 1: 96–107.

26. David A. Harrison, Kenneth H. Price, Joanne H. Gavin, and Anna T. Florey. 2002. Time, teams, and task performance: Changing effects of surface-and deep-level diversity on group functioning. *Academy of management journal* 45, 5: 1029–1045.

27. Guido Hertel, Susanne Geister, and Udo Konradt. 2005. Managing virtual teams: A review of current empirical research. *Human Resource Management Review* 15, 1: 69–95.

28. Pamela J. Hinds and Diane E. Bailey. 2000. Virtual team performance: Modeling the impact of geographic and temporal virtuality. In *Academy of Management Meeting*, 47.

29. Pamela J. Hinds and Diane E. Bailey. 2003. Out of sight, out of sync: Understanding conflict in distributed teams. *Organization science* 14, 6: 615–632.

30. Pamela J. Hinds and Mark Mortensen. 2005. Understanding conflict in geographically distributed teams: The moderating effects of shared identity, shared context, and spontaneous communication. *Organization science* 16, 3: 290–307.

31. Michael A. Hogg and Dominic Abrams. 1988. Social identifications.

32. Michael A. Hogg and Deborah I. Terry. 2000. Social identity and self-categorization processes in organizational contexts. *Academy of management review* 25, 1: 121–140.

33. Sirkka L. Jarvenpaa, Kathleen Knoll, and Dorothy E. Leidner. 1998. Is anybody out there? Antecedents of trust in global virtual teams. *Journal of management information systems*: 29–64.

34. Karen A. Jehn, Gregory B. Northcraft, and Margaret A. Neale. 1999. Why differences make a difference: A field study of diversity, conflict and performance in workgroups. *Administrative science quarterly* 44, 4: 741–763.

35. Atreyi Kankanhalli, Bernard CY Tan, and Kwok-Kee Wei. 2007. Conflict and performance in global virtual teams. *Journal of Management Information Systems* 23, 3: 237–274.

36. Bradley L. Kirkman and John E. Mathieu. 2005. The dimensions and antecedents of team virtuality. *Journal of management* 31, 5: 700–718.

37. Aniket Kittur, Bryan Pendleton, and Robert E. Kraut. 2009. Herding the cats: the influence of groups in coordinating peer production. In *Proceedings of the 5th international Symposium on Wikis and Open Collaboration*, 7.

38. Steve WJ Kozlowski and Katherine J. Klein. 2000. A multilevel approach to theory and research in organizations: Contextual, temporal, and emergent processes.

39. Chinmay Kulkarni. 2014. Making Distance Matter: Leveraging Scale and Diversity in Massive Online Classes. In *Proceedings of the Adjunct Publication of the 27th Annual ACM Symposium on User Interface Software and Technology* (UIST'14 Adjunct), 25–28.

40. Chinmay Kulkarni, Julia Cambre, Yasmine Kotturi, Michael S. Bernstein, and Scott R. Klemmer. 2015. Talkabout: Making Distance Matter with Small Groups in Massive Classes. In *Proceedings of the 18th ACM Conference on Computer Supported Cooperative Work & Social Computing* (CSCW '15), 1116–1128.

41. Kenneth D. Locke and Leonard M. Horowitz. 1990. Satisfaction in interpersonal interactions as a function of similarity in level of dysphoria. *Journal of personality and social psychology* 58, 5: 823.

42. Fred Mael and Blake E. Ashforth. 1992. Alumni and their alma mater: A partial test of the reformulated model of organizational identification. *Journal of organizational Behavior* 13, 2: 103–123.

43. Elizabethc A. Mannix, Terri Griffith, and Magaret A. Neale. 2002. The phenomenology of conflict in distributed work teams. *Distributed work*: 213–233.

44. Luis L. Martins, Lucy L. Gilson, and M. Travis Maynard. 2004. Virtual teams: What do we know and where do we go from here? *Journal of management* 30, 6: 805–835.

45. Jessica R. Mesmer-Magnus, Leslie A. DeChurch, Miliani Jimenez-Rodriguez, Jessica Wildman, and Marissa Shuffler. 2011. A meta-analytic investigation of virtuality and information sharing in teams. *Organizational Behavior and Human Decision Processes* 115, 2: 214–225.

46. Mark Mortensen and Pamela J. Hinds. 2001. Conflict and shared identity in geographically distributed teams. *International Journal of Conflict Management* 12, 3: 212–238.

47. Jaime Newell, Lionel P. Robert, Cynthia Riemenschneider, and Likoebe Maruping. 2009. Influencing Individual Perceptions of Deep Level Diversity in Virtual Learning Teams (VLT). In *System Sciences, 2009. HICSS'09. 42nd Hawaii International Conference on*, 1–10.

48. Jamie Newell, Likoebe Maruping, Cynthia Riemenschneider, and Lionel P. Robert. 2008. Leveraging E-Identities: The Impact of Percieved Diversity on Team Social Integration and Performance. *ICIS 2008 Proceedings*: 46.

49. Michael Boyer O'Leary and Jonathon N. Cummings. 2007. The spatial, temporal, and configurational characteristics of geographic dispersion in teams. *MIS quarterly*: 433–452.

50. Gary M. Olson and Judith S. Olson. 2000. Distance matters. *Human-computer interaction* 15, 2: 139–178.

51. Judith S. Olson and Stephanie Teasley. 1996. Groupware in the wild: lessons learned from a year of virtual collocation. In *Proceedings of the 1996 ACM conference on Computer supported cooperative work*, 419–427.

52. Stephen A. Rains. 2005. Leveling the Organizational Playing Field—Virtually A Meta-Analysis of Experimental Research Assessing the Impact of Group Support System Use on Member Influence Behaviors. *Communication Research* 32, 2: 193–234.

53. Michael Riketta. 2005. Organizational identification: A meta-analysis. *Journal of vocational behavior* 66, 2: 358–384.

54. Michael Riketta and Susanne Nienaber. 2007. Multiple identities and work motivation: The role of perceived compatibility between nested organizational units*. *British Journal of Management* 18, s1: S61–S77.

55. Lionel P. Robert. 2013. A multi-level analysis of the impact of shared leadership in diverse virtual teams. In *Proceedings of the 2013 conference on Computer supported cooperative work*, 363–374.

56. Lionel P. Robert. 2016. Monitoring and Trust in Virtual Teams. In *Proceedings of the 19th ACM Conference on Computer-Supported Cooperative Work & Social Computing* (CSCW '16), 245–259.

57. Lionel P. Robert, Alan R. Denis, and Yu-Ting Caisy Hung. 2009. Individual swift trust and knowledge-based trust in face-to-face and virtual team members. *Journal of Management Information Systems* 26, 2: 241–279.

58. Lionel P. Robert and Alan R. Dennis. 2005. Paradox of richness: A cognitive model of media choice. *Professional Communication, IEEE Transactions on* 48, 1: 10–21.

59. Lionel P. Robert, Alan R. Dennis, and Manju K. Ahuja. 2008. Social Capital and Knowledge Integration in Digitally Enabled Teams. *Information Systems Research* 19, 3: 314–334.

60. Lionel P. Robert and Daniel M. Romero. 2015. Crowd Size, Diversity and Performance. In *Proceedings of the 33rd Annual ACM Conference on Human Factors in Computing Systems*, 1379–1382.

61. Lionel P. Robert and Daniel M. Romero. 2017. The influence of diversity and experience on the effects of crowd size. *Journal of the Association for Information Science and Technology* 68, 2: 321–332.

62. Lionel P. Robert and Sangseok You. 2013. Are you satisfied yet? Shared leadership, trust and individual satisfaction in virtual teams.

63. Meir Shemla, Bertolt Meyer, Lindred Greer, and Karen A. Jehn. 2016. A review of perceived diversity in teams: Does how members perceive their team's composition affect team processes and outcomes?: PERCEIVED DIVERSITY IN TEAMS. *Journal of Organizational Behavior* 37: S89–S106.

64. John Short, Ederyn Williams, and Bruce Christie. 1976. The social psychology of telecommunications.

65. S.-S. Srinivasan, Likoebe M. Maruping, and Lionel P. Robert. 2012. Idea Generation in Technology-Supported Teams: A Multilevel Motivational Perspective. In *System Science (HICSS), 2012 45th Hawaii International Conference on*, 247–256.

66. D. Sandy Staples and Lina Zhao. 2006. The effects of cultural diversity in virtual teams versus face-to-face teams. *Group Decision and Negotiation* 15, 4: 389–406.

67. Ayoung Suh, Kyung-shik Shin, Manju Ahuja, and Min Soo Kim. 2011. The Influence of Virtuality on Social Networks Within and Across Work Groups: A Multilevel Approach. *Journal of Management Information Systems* 28, 1: 351–386.

68. Henri Tajfel and Serge Moscovici. 1972. Introduction à la psychologie sociale. *Paris, Larotzsse*: 260–278.

69. Henri Tajfel and John C. Turner. 2004. The Social Identity Theory of Intergroup Behavior.

70. Sherry MB Thatcher and Xiumei Zhu. 2006. Changing identities in a changing workplace: Identification, identity enactment, self-verification, and telecommuting. *Academy of Management Review* 31, 4: 1076–1088.

71. John C. Turner, Michael A. Hogg, Penelope J. Oakes, Stephen D. Reicher, and Margaret S. Wetherell. 1987. *Rediscovering the social group: A self-categorization theory.* Basil Blackwell.

72. John C. Turner, Penelope J. Oakes, S. Alexander Haslam, and Craig McGarty. 1994. Self and collective: Cognition and social context. *Personality and social psychology bulletin* 20: 454–454.

73. Rolf Van Dick, Oliver Christ, Jost Stellmacher, Ulrich Wagner, Oliver Ahlswede, Cornelia Grubba, Martin Hauptmeier, Corinna Hoehfeld, Kai Moltzen, and Patrick A. Tissington. 2004. Should I stay or should I go? Explaining turnover intentions with organizational identification and job satisfaction*. *British Journal of Management* 15, 4: 351–360.

74. Amy Voida, Nathan Bos, Judith Olson, Gary Olson, and Lauren Dunning. 2012. Cross-cutting faultlines of location and shared identity in the intergroup cooperation of partially distributed groups. In *Proceedings of the 2012 ACM annual conference on Human Factors in Computing Systems*, 3101–3110.

75. Joseph B. Walther. 1996. Computer-mediated communication impersonal, interpersonal, and hyperpersonal interaction. *Communication research* 23, 1: 3–43.

76. Joseph B. Walther. 1997. Group and interpersonal effects in international computer-mediated collaboration. *Human Communication Research* 23, 3: 342–369.

77. Batia M. Wiesenfeld, Sumita Raghuram, and Raghu Garud. 1998. Communication patterns as determinants of organizational identification in a virtual organization. *Journal of Computer-Mediated Communication* 3, 4: 0–0.

78. Jaime B. Windeler, Likoebe M. Maruping, Lionel P. Robert, and Cynthia K. Riemenschneider. 2015. E-profiles, conflict, and shared understanding in distributed teams. *Journal of the Association for Information Systems* 16, 7: 608.

79. Teng Ye and Lionel P. Robert Jr. 2017. Does Collectivism Inhibit Individual Creativity?: The Effects of Collectivism and Perceived Diversity on Individual Creativity and Satisfaction in Virtual Ideation Teams. In *Proceedings of the 2017 ACM Conference on Computer Supported Cooperative Work and Social Computing* (CSCW '17), 2344–2358.

80. Haiyi Zhu, Robert Kraut, and Aniket Kittur. 2012. Effectiveness of shared leadership in online communities. In *Proceedings of the ACM 2012 conference on Computer Supported Cooperative Work*, 407–416.

Towards Professionalization in an Online Community of Emerging Occupation: Discourses among UX Practitioners

Yubo Kou and Colin M. Gray

Purdue University

West Lafayette, IN 47906

{kou2, gray42}@purdue.edu

ABSTRACT

The occupational landscape of the digital economy is rapidly changing, resulting in the emergence of multidisciplinary occupations. Emerging occupations such as user experience (UX) design are in high demand, but these occupations lack clear boundaries and have yet to develop into a profession with a specified, coherent body of knowledge. While traditional occupations such as medicine and law successfully claimed their professional jurisdiction and high social power and status long before the Internet, how do these emerging occupations work towards professionalization, particularly as they are increasingly supported by and through online communities? In this paper, we investigate an online UX community to understand how UX practitioners specify their occupational knowledge and professional boundaries. Using this case as an example and provocation, we discuss how online communities support the emergence of new occupations and may play an indispensable role in modern day patterns of professionalization.

Author Keywords

Professionalization; online communities; community of practice; user experience design; UX; discourse analysis.

ACM Classification Keywords

H.5.3. Group and Organization Interfaces: Web-based interaction; H.5.m. Information interfaces and presentation (e.g., HCI): Miscellaneous.

INTRODUCTION

The computer-supported cooperative work (CSCW) community has been largely concerned with collaborative work of professionals such as designers, engineers, and scientists within organizational settings, with a few scholars mentioning professionalization but not as the primary

GROUP '18, January 7–10, 2018, Sanibel Island, FL, USA

© 2018 Association for Computing Machinery.

ACM ISBN 978-1-4503-5562-9/18/01...$15.00

https://doi.org/10.1145/3148330.3148352

research focus [27,28]. Today rapid technological changes are transforming the character of existing work and informing the creation of new occupations that are yet to be defined and specified. These nascent occupations are defined by the United States Bureau of Labor Statistics as *emerging occupations*, which become "numerically important or emerging due to technological change" [10].

CSCW researchers have previously recognized the important role of online communities in supporting amateurs and professionals in the collaborative creation and development of knowledge in areas such as software development [45], graphic design [44], and fanfiction [19]. However, most research has focused on the professional development of individuals within existing occupational or hobbyist domains, with a few exceptions such as Pace et al.'s [48] study of handcrafters on Etsy.com who desired to professionalize their art and craft practices. As shifts in technological capability continue to shape the types of occupations and professions that exist, there is a need for more research that examines the role of online communities in supporting, shaping, and defining professionalization processes in relation to emergent occupations.

In this paper, we focus on one emerging occupation, user experience (UX) design, and one related online community, the '/r/userexperience' subreddit, to document and analyze the discursive practices of UX professionals as they articulate and specify relevant knowledge and the occupational boundaries this knowledge may represent. While aspects of UX practice have existed for decades, we consider this occupation to still be in the process of professionalization because it lacks a coherent body of disciplinary knowledge [38] and only very recently have a few universities recognized the necessity to create UX academic programs at the undergraduate level [3]. Through thematic analysis [9,13], we identify how UX professionals in this online community discussed the status and development of this occupation.

The contributions of this study are three-fold. First, we discuss discursive activities within this online community, revealing potential connections among online interactions and community cohesion. Second, we characterize the interaction and knowledge-sharing practices of practitioners that indicate a tendency towards professionalization, describing the kinds of knowledge work that are necessary to construct appropriate and beneficial occupational boundaries. Third, we demonstrate the bridging of a methodological gap between existing sociological work on professionalization and CSCW knowledge about online communities, resulting in a fuller understanding of the potential role of online communities in professionalization.

RELATED WORK

Occupations and Professions
While *occupations* "represent the organization of productive labor into the social roles by which tasks are performed" [23], *professions* are organized occupational groups whose members have shared identity, commitment, as well as control over defining and regulating their work [23,39,56]. Professionalization can be understood as "the process whereby an occupation works toward becoming a profession" [56]. It is important for the CSCW community to investigate emerging occupations from the perspective of professionalization to understand how technologies can best support individual professional development as well as the production, consolidation, and circulation of occupational knowledge, both within and without formal organizations.

In the sections that follow, we describe how UX design, as one example of an emerging occupation, relates to these constructs of occupation and profession, and the ways in which these constructs become salient in the construction and performance of online communities.

UX as an Emerging Occupation
User experience has emerged as a distinct discipline [18,32], and at the same time, remains closely tied to the disciplines of human-computer interaction (HCI) and interaction design. The emergence of UX can be attributed to multiple reasons such as the ubiquity of technologies in everyday life, and increasing attention to users' interactive experience, which exceed the focus areas of related disciplines such as marketing, graphic design, interaction design, or product design [30]. More recently, the incorporation of UX into digital and physical products has been considered a strategic advantage in knowledge-based companies [20].

Despite rapid job growth, UX faces substantial learning and educational challenges due to a lack of consensus over required disciplinary knowledge [52]. Few higher education institutions have developed UX-specific undergraduate academic programs, and graduate UX academic programs have roots in and thus are heavily influenced by distinct disciplinary traditions such as computer science, library science, and information science. Although licensure and certification programs have become more common and accessible in recent years, their legitimacy and usefulness is still contested among practitioners. Consequently, newcomers and enthusiasts find few concrete paths to become a UX professional; and existing practitioners must continuously maintain and develop their UX competency.

UX is interdisciplinary, drawing from many disciplinary perspectives, identifying common problems, and generating new knowledge [35,40]. The UX discipline has absorbed a wide range of knowledge, theories, methodologies from disciplines such as computer science, engineering, sociology, and psychology [22], resulting in a fusion of interests related to interaction and service (e.g., [7]). Hassenzahl and Tractinsky [30] argued that "UX is about technology that fulfils more than just instrumental needs in a way that acknowledges its use as a subjective, situated, complex and dynamic encounter. UX is a consequence of a user's internal state, the characteristics of the desired system and the context within which the interaction occurs." Law et al.'s survey study among 275 UX researchers and practitioners [42] concurs with this view of UX as a discipline that engages with dynamic, context-dependent, and subjective problems and outcomes. In this regard, UX is distinguishable from user interface (UI) design, which is primarily concerned with the development and testing of visual interfaces. This range and diversity of disciplinary interests present in UX practice reflects the occupation's emerging state and its potential future growth of influence.

Professionalization of Occupational Practices
Professionalization indicates that a specific occupational group is able to establish a "market monopoly," or exercise control over certain services that excludes other occupations. Much research on the professionalization of traditional work such as architecture design [8], teaching [31], medicine [1], and management [49] has adopted a historical lens, valuing the long-term development through which professionalization had been accomplished over years or decades.

The professionalization of medicine provides insight into this development process, as described by Conrad and Schneider. In the early 19th century, medicine began to develop into a full-time profession [12]. At first, anyone could claim to be a doctor and practice medicine, but as practitioners with different skillsets and training arose, around 1,800 physicians persuaded state legislators to pass laws that limited access to practice to practitioners based on specified levels of training. In 1847 regular physicians founded the American Medical Association (AMA) to promote medicine within the society, marginalizing unskilled medical practice and establishing and enforcing standards and ethics of medical practice. Scientific breakthroughs in the last three decades of the 19th century allowed medical professionals to demonstrate their superior effectiveness in treatment and healthcare, which aided the formation of new licensing laws that created regular medicine as a "legally enforced monopoly of practice" [16]; This medical monopoly was further enhanced in 1910 when medical Abraham Flexner visited nearly all the medical schools in the U.S., found medical education insufficient, and suggested the closings of most schools. Flexner's recommendations helped create a "near total AMA monopoly of medical education in America" [12]; to secure a monopoly, the AMA also pushed for professional dominance in the sense that Medicine could define its own territory and evaluate itself based on its own standards.

While medicine represents only one trajectory towards professionalization, sociological studies across many domains of practice have revealed multiple factors that impact the process of professionalization. For instance, professionalization drivers include the desire of the occupational groups that were previously marginalized to seek more power and control and obtain higher social status [8,17,26,57]. In addition, international pressures from other economic competitors with more developed education and training of certain professions or internal political ideologies have stimulated professionalization [49].

Previous studies have stressed the important role of traditional institutions in either facilitating or constraining the professionalization of traditional work, including tensions between a taught vocationalism that is too specific and technical, and the need to create a space for profession-specific knowledge production that is acknowledged by broader societal and governmental structures [23,39]. For example, in managerial studies, Reed and Anthony highlighted that universities should incorporate reflection, thoughtfulness, and responsibility in the curriculum, rather than retreat into "a narrow vocationalism" that emphasizes functional and technical skills [49]. Türegün found that the professionalization of Canadian settlement work with immigrants relied upon the continuity of governmental funding and broader social support for the profession [55].

It is important to note that professionalization does not occur in every occupation, but is conditioned by the occupation's organizational and historical development [57]. For example, it would be implausible for the occupational group of low-rank clerks to claim a specific body of knowledge and skill, although these groups might organize in other ways (e.g., labor unions). In addition, professionalization is not always an ideal trajectory. For example, Silin warned that the professionalization of early childhood education might "entail a loss of control for teachers as the design and implementation of curriculum become two discrete functions" [33]. In the context of vision care, Stevens et al. reported that the division of labor brought about by professionalization actually weakened inter-professional coordination and lowered occupational satisfaction among vision caregivers [51].

Professionalization and the Development of Online Communities of Practice (CoPs)

Digital technologies facilitate communication, coordination, and opinion expression among workers, which can have an empowering effect and promote the development of online communities [43]. These online communities have the potential to become sites of interaction and socialization for groups of individuals with shared occupational interests, but also frequently create opportunities and infrastructure for professional learning [14,34].

In extant CSCW and HCI research, the concept of Community of Practice (CoP) has been highly influential in allowing researchers to interpret and analyze knowledge production and social structure in these online communities. Lave and Wenger introduced the concept of CoP [41] as an extension of traditional learning practices and validation of informal learning, marking a departure from only understanding formal educational settings as appropriate places to study learning and professional development. According to Amin and Roberts, CoPs comprise "*relatively stable communities of face-to-face interaction between members working in close proximity to one another, in which identity formation through participation and the negotiation of meaning are central to learning and knowledge generation*" [4]. These communities can be found in multiple contexts, and individuals can belong to multiple such communities at any given time [59].

In previous research, HCI and CSCW scholars and practitioners have researched and implemented systems to support the development of online CoPs in a variety of domains [21,46,47,54,58], building on expectations of knowledge exchange, leadership, and community cohesion around a key area of community identity. The most relevant quality of CoP for this study is its emphasis on the communication between practitioners, through which people share tips, best practices, learn from each other, ask questions, and seek support from each other. The CoP lens supplies us a general framework for understanding the online community of UX practitioners in our specific context of occupational interaction, informal learning practices, and the development of consensus towards occupational professionalization.

METHOD

We draw on case study methodology [59] to deeply describe and analyze the interactions within one emergent occupational online community. A single case study approach was chosen to deeply investigate one bounded system, a subreddit focused on UX design, and within that bounded system, provide a rich and nuanced account of phenomena of interest—in this case, the emergence of occupational focus and professionalization.

The Online UX Community Under Study

Reddit was the 4th most popular website in the United States and 7th in the world by the time of writing this paper [2]. Initially designed as a source for socially curated news, Reddit has accumulated more than one million subreddits supporting a diverse range of communities [48]. The '/r/userexperience' subreddit supports a vibrant, growing UX community. In a 13-month period of community interactions captured in our data collection across over a dozen related subreddits, this subreddit had accumulated more threads than all the other UX-related subreddits combined. In addition, UX practitioners in this community exhibited substantial engagement in terms of the number of authors and comments: this subreddit had the largest number of unique authors and the largest average number of comments per post among all of the related subreddits. This subreddit supports an egalitarian community where students, junior designers, and senior designers with varied educational backgrounds and work experiences socialize and discuss a range of UX-related topics.

Data Collection

We used PHP and the official Reddit API to retrieve posts, comments, as well as the metadata from the subreddit, which were stored in a local MySQL database for further analysis. The final dataset included 1,790 posts and their 11,373 associated comments from January 19, 2016 to February 16, 2017. The metadata of each post included the title, author, timestamp, content, shared URL (if applicable), number of comments, and score. Comment metadata contained the content, author, timestamp, upvote number, and score. Connections between posts and comments, and among comments were maintained through a relational key. The dataset also included 2,933 distinct users who had either made a post or a comment, with 1,010 having made at least one post and 2,576 having commented at least once.

Data Analysis

Because interactions in online communities are highly conversational, taking place among two or more UX practitioners, we decided to focus on those posts that had at least one comment for data analysis. Within the initial set of 1,790 posts, there were 670 posts having 11,373 comments.

We employed thematic analysis [9] to analyze the final dataset. We began by questioning how UX practitioners in this community defined and discussed UX knowledge, given its volatile nature. Two researchers engaged in reading and analyzing those posts and comments, and met weekly to discuss relevant themes. We took note of interactions that related to UX as an emerging occupation, such as the professional identity of UX professionals, the selection of entry points or career paths of becoming a UX professional, and the discussion of the general public's understanding of UX. We gradually recognized that while most conversations regarded individual UX professionals goal of acquiring UX knowledge and skills and obtaining a well-paid job in industry, the overarching theme within this particular community was the movement towards professionalization of UX through defining, redefining, and specifying boundaries around UX knowledge.

Keeping the central question of professionalization in mind, we began using an open coding approach to understand how the statements of UX practitioners were related to the production, development, and circulation of UX knowledge. Through memoing and constant comparison with existing codes [13], we iteratively and inductively developed a list of codes. We then used axial coding to connect and consolidate discovered codes, which were eventually developed into three major interactional themes: highlighting the emerging nature of UX, specifying UX knowledge, and enhancing societal recognition. Each theme

includes sub-themes that contain connected ideas. When we report quotes from forum threads, we use pseudo-username (e.g., U1, U2…) to represent UX practitioners.

FINDINGS

UX practitioners in this online community discussed how UX was becoming an important area of industry focus in recent years, but was still in a developmental stage in terms of professionalization. Many of the members' discourses—covering various UX topics such as trends, design tools, and general design heuristics—expressed the desire and anticipation of practitioners' that the body of UX knowledge and its relevance for industry become concrete and bounded. They also discussed actionable strategies for practitioners to increase the recognition of UX as a unique approach to industry partners and the general public.

Highlighting the Emerging Nature of UX

On this subreddit, UX was widely considered to be of important value for the success of companies. As one practitioner wrote, "It's 2016. If your company doesn't get UX you can either look for a new job now or when they go out of business." Practitioners considered UX to be a still emerging, young field in which much remains undefined. In the following conversation, two users discussed the boundaries of UX as a design field, particularly in relation to the contexts in which UX would be appropriate.

U1: I am trying to find out if the term "user experience design" can be used for anything that involves a user, customer, or and type of end-user using a service or product. To increase an end-user's satisfaction. I just find it odd how "UX design" only applies to computers or refers to computers only. Isn't there a term that encompasses how to improve [UX] design for any type of product, service, etc. regardless what of what industry?

U2: I honestly think that it's just a result of the field being young and people are still figuring out what to call stuff. Older design disciplines don't really break every part of the design process into its own special snowflake of a discipline (as far as I know). I think/hope that we will eventually just say "I'm a software designer" [...] or "I'm a software designer and I specialize in layout."

In this excerpt, U1 found inconsistency within the UX terminology and its potential scope, seeking others' opinions on this issue. U2 attributed such inconsistency to "the field being young." U2 envisioned that future usage of the term "UX design" will be simultaneously expanded and made more precise to overcome the present issues recognized by U1. Even the term "UX design," as discussed by practitioners, does not have a consensual meaning: "keep in mind that 'UX design' in the job market today is very ambiguous in meaning, and can mean any combination of marketing, graphic design, development, and IA/IxD."

Practitioners also recognized the increasing popularity of UX in technology-related industries, both as shorthand for being current and trendy, and as a pointer towards a specific philosophic commitment within the organization to be customer-centered in a holistic way:

U3: A couple of weeks ago i saw a vacancy for a "Helpdesk UX lead", which basically boiled down to being the team leader of a helpdesk [...]. I think the people who come up with these titles are people who do not really understand what UX really is, but have heard enough about it to think of it as some kind of buzz word they can just put into job titles to makes them more in keeping with current trends.

U4: Yeah it's a buzz word and companies are exploiting it so they can say they are following newest trends and competing in showing bigger diversity numbers.

In this excerpt, both practitioners observed that due to the emerging nature and popularity of UX, companies want to hire relevant professionals but lack basic understanding of this emerging occupation. While the sentiment of "UX" in the context of an IT helpdesk aligned with philosophic commitments towards the end user in similar ways as traditional UX roles, this conversation demonstrates the permeability of UX and its disjointed or inconsistent use.

Practitioners expressed their dissatisfaction with the status of UX in companies, and the need to constantly justify the role of UX designers and the value of UX to the enterprise:

Since I've been in UX, [...]we have been trying to prove value of UX. They have come around to see UX as important. But we still have to work on showing the value of user research. I guess it will always be something.

Another practitioner detailed many difficult situations that a UX practitioner might encounter in organizational settings where the practitioner has to negotiate with other roles regarding the same product:

Fighting corporate apathy and inertia. Getting devs to build what you want, not what they know. Getting the graphic artists to draw EXACTLY what you sketched, without adding their own interpretations that piss the boss off [...]. The constant begging for a budget to do some meaningful testing. Joining a project one month before UAT when there was no previous UI or UX consideration, and being told "just clean it up a bit, but don't make any big changes because we don't have time." Getting stakeholders to treat you like an expert [...].

Practitioners were generally experienced in industry, and were thus aware of the immaturity of UX as an occupation; this immaturity was manifest both in conceptual thinking and in practice. Dissatisfaction and complaints were common sentiments within practitioners' conversations, laying ground for professionalization efforts.

Specifying UX Knowledge

We identified three major activities where practitioners sought to specify UX knowledge. They listed essential UX knowledge and skills that made this occupation *unique—*

not merely a cobbling together of existing occupational perspectives and knowledge. Practitioners regularly shared practical UX knowledge as a means of discussing criteria or standards for conducting UX work, and these conversations frequently included instances of boundary work, where practitioners attempted to define what knowledge or skills belong to UX, often as contrasted with other occupations.

Stressing the Uniqueness and Importance of UX

We observed many occasions where practitioners raised and reinforced a common argument regarding UX—namely that effective practice requires a combination of diverse skills, rendering this occupation challenging for many.

I think being a good UXer requires a combination of skills which are often kind of polar opposites. You have to be logical but also empathic. You need have technical skills as well as being personable and easy to talk to. A lot of people fall into logical & technical OR empathic and personable but not both.

In this account, the practitioner underlined the "specialness" and rarity of the combination of these skills using the description "polar opposites." These descriptions not only identify a specific set of characteristics unique to UX as an occupation, but also underscore practitioners' views of themselves as a unique type of professional or individual as well. One practitioner described their UX approach:

Along with the skills of knowing how to design and conduct quality research, I also have to know how to work with vendors and a ton of other logistical/practical aspects... When my research helps to save a hundreds of hours of time [...] by either doing something right the first time or not building a bad product to begin with my position pays for itself many times over. User feedback has been critical in educating users and preventing problems that result not only in a better overall experience, but drastically reduce the burden on our CX team. Identifying unmet needs in the current product has increased engagement, growth, and retention.

In this account, the practitioner described how their UX research approach and skills facilitated other teams' work, creating substantial value for the organization. This form of legitimization of UX not only relied upon knowledge of specific skills and methods (e.g., user research), but also the power of this knowledge in producing outcomes that are desirable in industry (e.g., cost savings). While these arguments regarding value are powerful, practitioners generally agreed that this occupation is not easy to enter:

Unless your walking in the door with a Masters in HCI or some other related field [...], I highly doubt the first gig you get will be in UX. UX is not a field of study where you simply kick down the door and get started.

To this practitioner, a Master's degree in a related field was a necessity for entering the UX field. As practitioners' conversations around their occupations underscored the uniqueness of UX as an approach or philosophy of action, they also noticed the trend towards specialization, where aspects of UX work are pointing towards more niche roles:

U5: Sure, not all projects require research, just as not all require a high fidelity prototype, but you're still not a UXer if you don't know how to do Qual and Quant, you're a visual designer. I was a visual designer for 6yrs, and only in the last 2yrs been UX. The only difference between the roles has been the research.

U6: What you describe is not the case for the companies I have worked for/with or am very familiar with the folks in their UX team [...]. UX needs research, but it should be done by a researcher and not a designer. [...] At places like Google these are all separate and distinct roles: UX designer, visual designer, motion designer, UX researcher. Of course they all work together as a team, but only the last one does research...

In this conversation, U5 and U6 engaged in hot debate regarding the already present specialization of UX roles into UX designer and UX researcher. This specialization has implications for the boundaries of UX more broadly, and the requisite skills needed for areas of specialization.

Sharing Practical Knowledge

In the previous subsection, we showed how practitioners exchanged their industry-informed perspectives around high-level questions regarding UX. In this subsection, we identify online conversations where participants shared practical advice on concrete topics, such as the standard UX tools that a practitioner shall master. Here is an example:

U7: A UX designer should be using photoshop and illustrator. Nobody, not even a dev, should be using dreamweaver.

U8: We use Sketch for all of our UX stuff now. I use Illustrator and Photoshop to work on assets, but design is all done with Sketch. We'll try out Comet once it is available too. Dreamweaver isn't installed on a single machine in our office. I don't even know what possible argument anyone would make to justify using Dreamweaver over all the other better options out there.

In this example, two practitioners detailed their rationale behind choosing certain tools while rejecting others. The strong phrases such as "not even a dev" and "isn't installed on a single machine" included normative judgments towards tool choice in UX, serving as a means of establishing standards in this emerging occupation. It is interesting to note that tool choice was not a sufficient boundary in itself, but also underscored the kinds of thinking and visualization that were possible in these tools.

Experienced practitioners also shared highly practical knowledge derived from their many years of industry experience. In this conversation, diversity and years of experience was used as a way of establishing expertise,

while also demonstrating the often unusual pathways towards UX practice.

U9: I've run teams [...] and I could care less about the school they came from. It's really unimportant. Why? because you know theory, methodology and that's about it... Source: 18+ year UX Architect / Sr. UI Designer.

U10: If you have advice on how to get an internship without school or where to get solid certification, please let me know.

U11: You might be lucky and find a job where you have a senior UX practitioner who can really help hone your own practice, but this is going to be rare. Grad school isn't just about education, it is also exploring the breadth of the field and discovering what you like and don't like, an opportunity to do your own research, and maybe most importantly, learning how to advance research in UX. The discipline to write papers and explore what it means to contribute to the field of knowledge [...]is a huge skill you won't get in industry work but it resonates well with industry and will make you a better practitioner yourself... Source: 25+ years in the software industry in leadership roles as a developer, ux designer, ux researcher, and university HCI educator.

In this conversation regarding the necessity of graduate education for UX and the potential of certifications or other forms of experience outside of formal academic settings, both U9 and U11 attempted to be more convincing by showing their experience in the UX field. The conversation drew heavily from U9 and U11's individual practices to generate practical knowledge that could help to inform U10 of proper or reasonable career paths in UX. Interestingly, U11 uses academically-focused examples from graduate school as a lever to discuss what skills or ways of thinking would make a practitioner more successful in industry

Conducting Boundary Work

Practitioners attempted to draw clear lines between UX and other related concepts or fields, often delving into definitional work surrounding the "user" or "experience" and its relation to existing occupations.

U12: UX is about designing for a person's experience specifically. It's certainly a very broad field. But you can design many things without ever considering the experience somebody has. Design is just doing something with intent. Your intent need not be concerning the experience of a user. It might be designing an efficient system, or designing a store layout to maximise the money you make. It might be designing the architecture of some software. This isn't UX design, but it is design.

U13: I disagree. The purvey of "user experience" has to stop somewhere, or it becomes a useless term. It's highly useful in the realm of digital design [...], and 90+% of its usage is within that realm, so let's keep it specific and

useful. Design is always for a purpose, and it's always for humans, already.

In this example, U12 and U13 articulated their own understandings of UX and design in order to draw a distinction. However, it is also clear that different disciplinary language is being used to show the uniqueness of UX as an *approach* that is relevant in all areas, and not as a context- or outcome-bound occupation. Similarly, another practitioner sought to define the boundary, but in a more succinct manner:

UX != design/UI. UX is a broad term. Everything should consider UX: interface design, car design, [...] API design, furniture design... You get it.

Practitioners' intentions to identify clear boundaries among different occupations was also manifest in their reflection on the current status of the UX field:

Most UX jobs in the software industry are UX/UI frankly. UX =/= UI because UX is much broader, but when a big chunk of your user experience involves software the vast majority of UX designers are going to be making wireframes to various levels of fidelity. [...] The objection to the UX/UI phrase is not that those roles don't exist, it's the confusion it represents that UX is just UI design.

This practitioner was aware of the popular job descriptions that placed UX and UI together, but expressed a clear rejection of this conflation because it might introduce confusion about these two occupations' different functions. However, not all conversations were oriented towards defining boundaries between UX and others. In contrast, some practitioners found the boundaries to be diffuse, and that blurring the lines could be beneficial:

U14: This is why "user experience" is a really goofy term to begin with. If a user is someone who uses something and an experience is some combination of interaction, perception, and emotion, then really all disciplines of design add up to create a user experience.

U15: [...] I think it vaguely works well for digital because of the terms: "user" is a standard software industry term for the, well, user of the product; and experience usefully differentiates an interactive digital experience from a static or non-digital one. [...] More specific might be "digital interactive design" or something (hey that's not so bad).

Here U14 and U15 critically assessed the term of UX, noting its vagueness, particularly in relation to other disciplinary perspectives that can be more easily defined or bounded. While conversations like this contributed to a better articulation of what UX is or could be among practitioners, these comments also rejected traditional notions of disciplinary boundary in that UX represents a superset of disciplines or trans-discipline that could be applied as an approach in numerous areas of design.

Enhancing Societal Recognition

Practitioners discussed ways to gain greater social recognition of UX and its value within their organizations as well as in a broader societal context. These interactions contain actionable strategies that enable UX practitioners to gain power and control over their own work, describe their approach to other stakeholders, and ultimately distinguish UX as a legitimate and valuable way of approaching design.

Negotiating with Other Teams in Organizational Settings

Practitioners who worked in an environment with little recognition of UX's role or importance often faced challenges in demonstrating the value of their work. Many junior practitioners sought suggestions from others regarding coping strategies to effectively claim and communicate the value of UX as an approach, including the importance of identifying and implementing aspects of UX practices into organizations that were hostile or indifferent towards its inclusion.

U16: How do I introduce more UX into my role? My main issue is that the place is very much development driven. They build first, and ask questions later. How do I go about changing this? [...] Design decisions should come to our design team first for advice, but they don't.

U17: [...] your company is fairly immature when it comes to UX and before you can really bring about a change you need to "wake them up". The best way to accomplish this is to force them to see how users can't use what they develop. Often this is done through usability testing [...]. Once they see that their product don't work, they might say things like "those users are stupid, we don't want them to use our product". you then need to explain that excluding "stupid" users, have a significant impact on the revenue. after you have waked them up, you'll most likely have a chance to run one project the "right way". [...] Once you have done this you will have more ability in your role.

In this example, U16 described a situation where their working environment placed an undue focus on meeting development targets, with insufficient emphasis on or understanding of UX. U17 provided a strategy through which U1 could improve the recognition of UX within the work environment, both as an approach that brought value to the organization (e.g., expanding the pool of potential users) and as specific professional role and set of strategies that could uncover these kinds of opportunities in the future.

This finding about how UX practitioners discussed ways to improve social recognition within organizations echoes the findings from Gray et al.'s interview study [26], where designers had to both build their own competence in relation to UX as a design leader and contribute to organizational change that allowed the recognition of UX.

Promoting UX in the Public

Practitioners recognized that UX was not yet widely accepted as a legitimate, standalone occupation. This lack of broad awareness also meant that UX was not well understood by many businesses. It is against this backdrop that practitioners discussed the importance of publicly promoting UX as a means of self-preservation, thereby gaining the power that results from defined occupational roles and outcomes. As a practitioner wrote:

UX has the power to improve everyone's life, through designing solutions based on actual needs [...]. But we can't aim that high if we can't even convince small business owners that UX can help them have more loyal and satisfied customers.

The practitioner noticed great potential in the benefits and scope of UX as a practice, but also pointed out the necessary path that UX as an occupation must take in order to achieve that potential. This indicates a need not only to convince large businesses of the value of UX as a professional perspective, but also the need for grassroots understanding of UX by small business owners. An interesting practice among practitioners on the subreddit was to share strategies of how they might describe UX to a layperson. These strategies were frequently framed as a means of informing the public about UX.

U18: How do you describe what you do (to those who don't know UX)?

U19: I take complicated information and simplify it so that even your 70yr old grandma knows exactly what she should be clicking, tapping, or buying.

U20: I say I design phone interfaces. If that fails, I leave it at 'I work in computers.'

U21: I design user interfaces.

U22: I take out my smart phone and hold it up: "I design the apps you use." [...] I sometimes go into greater detail; but, giving people a vague understanding is sufficient.

U23: I say "I make it so people can use products without trouble."

Ultimately, these strategies of informing the public demonstrated the contested nature of UX as an occupation, and the difficulty in communicating the transdisciplinary nature of UX as an approach. Even though practitioners were bothered by the conflation of UX and UI in other discussions, explanations that centered on UI and usability seemed to be common and accepted in this community. UX practitioners in this subreddit choose to use umbrella terms to explain their work, and did not focus on specifying disciplinary differences between UX and UI. This is likely due to the clear distinctions shared among these community members between these terms, and the self-selected audience of participation in a UX-focused subreddit.

DISCUSSION

We have described how UX practitioners' professional discourses on the '/r/userexperience' subreddit reveal the emergent nature of UX and barriers in its drive towards professionalization. Practitioners perceived that both organizations and broader society did not give UX sufficient recognition that would be necessary to communicate value and ultimately establish a space for professionalization. Discourses exhibited a tendency towards consolidating UX knowledge by specifying normative guidelines (e.g., essential skills, paths to becoming a professional), but practitioners also outlined actions that could enable both individual practitioners as well as the UX occupation to gain more social recognition and control over the production process in industry contexts.

Despite the decades of existence of practices related to UX, it can still be considered as an emerging occupation that has just begun to reach rapid growth. Only in the past few years has job demand begun to outstrip supply, and in reaction, UX-specific academic programs at both undergraduate and graduate levels have appeared at a rapid pace. While academic programs for related occupations or disciplines (e.g., HCI, interaction design, UI design) have existed for some time, none of them have led to a clear path towards professionalization. In the present industry climate, UX practitioners appear dissatisfied with their current status, seeking to initiate changes that could supply more autonomy and power. As one element of this desire for power and legitimacy, UX practitioners have made efforts towards debating and clarifying the boundaries of their disciplinary knowledge, tools, and methods, including how these elements should be expressed as a unique professional approach. UX practitioners' professionalization efforts mirror many bottom-up actions from other occupations, such as the professionalization of medicine [12]. Both UX practitioners and doctors continuously identified existing issues in their occupation and attempted to resolve them, making efforts to specify and develop more sophisticated forms of domain knowledge. While interactions on this subreddit do not represent the entire UX occupation, these conversations indicate the desire of some practitioners to professionalize their work, including concrete strategies and steps they have taken to do so.

We refrain from suggesting that UX will or should be as professionalized as law or medicine. The larger social, cultural, and organizational contexts have changed dramatically. Today the emergence of UX, concurrently with other technological occupations, are a timely response to trends in evolving technologies and user needs, which are highly conditioned by neoliberal and consumerist philosophies [11,29]. Our findings concur with previous literature [57] that UX practitioners, employed by corporate organizations, are subject to the influence of stakeholders and practitioners in potentially overlapping occupational domains (e.g., developers, marketers, visual designers). Traditional occupations may want to seize power and authority to define UX and how it relates to existing forms of production and design activity. The transdisciplinary nature of UX foregrounds an approach that champions knowledge discovery and action independent of context as opposed to a specific means or outcomes, making the drive towards professionalization difficult, and the resulting boundaries and liminal spaces problematic to draw, communicate, and defend. These obstacles to professionalization are unprecedented when compared to law and medicine.

In this paper, we do not presume a final, optimal state that UX will eventually evolve into. Rather, we use "towards professionalization" in the title to stress the ongoing movements in which UX practitioners endeavor to develop their work and grow power within organizations and society. While these processes might grow stronger or fade in the future, at the present time, the directions of these processes are unanimous, and in alignment with the major changes in the UX discipline and industry, such as more universities are establishing UX academic programs at both undergraduate and graduate levels. Although the notion of professionalization may no longer hold the same meanings and connotations, it offers a useful perspective to examine professional work, highlighting the inner tensions, desires, and values within one occupational group, and paying attention to its development trajectory.

"Bubbling Up" Through Practice-led Research

HCI researchers have long recognized the existing research-practice gap between the academic community and the industry [50], and some have made calls for more research to understanding the actual practices of practitioners [53]. We align this study with Stolterman's [52] call to further understand design complexity from the perspective of practitioners. While the initial drivers of the *turn to practice* literature [37] were focused on physically collocated design practices, our approach towards UX practitioners' online conversations focuses on the digitally-mediated competency-building practices that point towards the professionalization of UX. This indicates both an expansion of the turn to practice research agenda and a deeper investigation regarding UX practitioners' *rationality resonance* [52] that impacts the professionalization of the UX community. The practitioners in this community engaged in a designerly practice of negotiating new knowledge and deciding how—or *if*—that knowledge was resonant with their understanding of UX practice. This example of designerly discourse indicates that the turn to practice literature could productively engage with the distributed interaction activities of practitioners. Previous research [36,37] demonstrates that this social yet professional space for knowledge sharing *informs* practice while also *enabling* that practice in direct, pragmatic ways.

It is against this backdrop that Gray et al. [25] proposed the need for knowledge to be bubbled-up from practice to academia—where "efforts are taken to refine and abstract situated knowledge and practice of methods, tools, or concepts into refined theory and defined tools and methods." Bubbling up knowledge through practice-led research has the potential to not only inform HCI theoretical

development, but also facilitate the professionalization of HCI-related occupations such as UX. Better knowledge exchange between the realities of industry practice and the distinct goals of academic research may facilitate the specification and alignment of occupation and disciplinary boundaries. While we do not propose a direct mapping from industry to academia, there is potential value in more greatly aligning curricula with the current and projected future realities of practice.

The Role of Online Communities in Professionalization

The online community served as a catalyst for practitioners to collectively identify the status of their occupation and reach consensus regarding its possible future. This case indicates the importance of understanding the organizing and knowledge-sharing potential embedded in information communication technologies, particularly as they relate to organizing and professionalization.

General-purpose social media tools such as Reddit allow practitioners to form and sustain community interactions. We have shown that this subreddit supported communication among practitioners from diverse backgrounds, providing opportunities for practitioners with differing levels of expertise and lived experience to share knowledge in ways that would be difficult or impossible in an offline setting. This egalitarian approach to knowledge and consensus building does not operate without expertise, but values expertise in a more diffuse way. While a traditional CoP model relies upon a relatively stable body of knowledge and practices which is passed from senior to junior members, knowledge and practices in this community resulted from a confluence of inexperienced and experienced practitioners alike.

Newcomers and experienced practitioners have different roles to play in these discursive activities. Although the subreddit is a largely anonymous space open to UX practitioners at different levels, existing work shows that in the community newcomers and experienced practitioners have different ways of presenting themselves and participating in discussions [37]. Newcomers are more likely to ask questions regarding occupational knowledge that focus on entering the occupation (e.g., how to get a UX job; the relevance of particular skills). Self-claimed experienced practitioners tended to engage in deep discussions about the challenges to and future directions of UX, drawing on their rich industry experiences. Therefore, newcomers and experienced designers' engagement in professionalization discourses differed dramatically. Newcomers often recognized the emerging nature of UX and shared their stories about difficulties they were facing; however, we observed little to no engagement of newcomers in topics such as specifying UX knowledge and enhancing societal recognition, possibly because they were inexperienced in providing valuable insights in these topics.

Based on this case, we consider a *community of emerging occupation* as a type of community of practice where members' online activities revolve around negotiating, defining, and defending occupational boundaries. The CoP lens is powerful in structuring a synchronic description of what activities are happening in a community at a particular moment. However, the perspective of professionalization is more concerned with the diachronic dimension of the community, seeking to locate these activities within the practice's history of evolution and desire for a bounded and specific future. This perspective is vital in understanding communities that are focused on a rapidly changing practice or topic, and represents an important area for future study.

Implications for CSCW

While much CSCW work concerns how technology supports collaboration and social learning between multiple occupations in organizational settings [5,6,15], little attention has been paid to these interactions as they relate to professionalization and evolution of occupations. Professionalization will become an increasingly significant factor as occupational groups in these emerging spaces demand more power and recognition from organizations. It is important for CSCW researchers to leverage the perspective of professionalization and attend to the liminal tensions between emerging and existing occupations.

In attending to professionalization in the development of information and communication technologies, this work also highlights opportunities for CSCW researchers to study the relation of online community interactions (and the knowledge generation and learning practices these interactions represent) to practitioner interactions in formal organizational contexts. Our case study shows that UX practitioners who were distributed across various organizations gathered in the same online community to discuss issues of importance to their shared occupational identity. Such a phenomenon echoes the open call from the Facebook co-founder Mark Zuckerberg to build global communities that "strengthen traditional institutions in a world where membership in these institutions is declining" [60]. These bottom-up movements organized by practitioners depend on a robust social infrastructure that enables effective communication, organization, and collective action, and may inform organizational policy and the education of future practitioners in profound ways.

Implications for Policymaking

Emerging occupations at the edge of the digital economy create the potential of an ever-enlarging talent gap. Unless the occupation is properly professionalized to the extent that a definite career path can be created, the future of emergent disciplines that captures the original character and distinctive occupational features could be in jeopardy. For professionalization to occur, there needs to be a general recognition that such work—if it is to be sustained and made consistent—requires a specialized body of knowledge that can be obtained only through formalized procedures such as training, education, or licensure. These formal means of standardization are what UX and other emergent

disciplines still lack, resulting in volatility in relation to the skills of job seekers and the expectations of companies. While universities are beginning to create relevant programs to address this gap, these programs often reside in traditional disciplinary spaces including library science and computer science, thus taking on different (and sometimes contradictory) areas of focus. While such a decentralized approach partially corresponds to the interdisciplinary nature of HCI and UX and allows a growing diversity of topics and interests, it also hinders the professionalization of UX and other related disciplines.

The professionalization of emerging occupations may be difficult or impossible to achieve if disciplinary discourses are highly decentralized. This set of factors may render the occupation sufficiently underdeveloped to consistently meet projected talent needs, introducing chaos into the process of professional preparation and licensure. There are opportunities for policymaking to play an important role in shaping these professionalization processes. For example, the U.S. government has previously defined STEM majors and passed numerous corporate, educational, and immigration bills to facilitate the training and education of more science, technology, engineering, and mathematics professionals [24]. In a similar vein, policymakers might identify and define emerging occupations of high job demand and provide benefits at the policy level. However, it is critical that these definitions—regardless of the source—remain flexible, able to adapt to changing industry needs and the creation of still other emergent occupations.

CONCLUSION

We reported how a group of professionals set occupational boundaries and moved towards professionalization. The online community supported practitioners to collectively identify the immaturity and rapid growth of their occupation, engage in deep conversations about disciplinary knowledge, and brainstorm actionable strategies to further develop this occupation. While this occupation lacks a centralized governing body—perhaps a trend as new inter- and trans-disciplines begin to emerge—these grassroots interactions among practitioners appear to be essential to the maturing process of occupations in the digital age.

More research is needed to understand the role of digital technologies in the definition, negotiation, and professionalization of emerging occupations. This research will not only enrich existing theories of professionalization, but also carry practical value for educational systems, industry partners, and society as a whole to better prepare for the opportunity of emerging occupations enabled by advances in information and communication technologies.

ACKNOWLEDGEMENTS

We are grateful to the anonymous reviewers for their constructive and insightful comments, which helped strengthen the paper in important ways.

REFERENCES

1. Andrew Delano Abbott. 2014. *The system of professions : an essay on the division of expert labor.* University of Chicago Press.

2. Alexa. 2017. How popular is reddit.com? *Alexa.* Retrieved from http://www.alexa.com/siteinfo/reddit.com

3. Neil Allison. 2014. UX activity in UK Higher Ed web teams. *usability ed.* Retrieved from http://usability-ed.blogspot.co.uk/2014/07/ux-activity-in-uk-higher-ed-web-teams.html

4. Ash Amin and Joanne Roberts. 2008. Knowing in action: Beyond communities of practice. *Research Policy* 37, 2: 353–369. http://doi.org/10.1016/j.respol.2007.11.003

5. Lynda M. Applegate, Benn R. Konsynski, and J. F. Nunamaker. 1986. A group decision support system for idea generation and issue analysis in organization planning. *Proceedings of the 1986 ACM conference on Computer-supported cooperative work - CSCW '86*, ACM Press, 16–34. http://doi.org/10.1145/637069.637073

6. Jakob Bardram. 1998. Designing for the dynamics of cooperative work activities. *Proceedings of the 1998 ACM conference on Computer supported cooperative work - CSCW '98*, ACM Press, 89–98. http://doi.org/10.1145/289444.289483

7. Eli Blevis, Kenny Chow, Ilpo Koskinen, Sharon Poggenpohl, and Christine Tsin. 2014. Billions of interaction designers. *interactions* 21, 6: 34–41. http://doi.org/10.1145/2674931

8. David Brain. 1991. Practical Knowledge and Occupational Control: The Professionalization of Architecture in the United States. *Sociological Forum* 6, 2: 239–268.

9. Virginia Braun and Victoria Clarke. 2006. Using thematic analysis in psychology. *Qualitative Research in Psychology* 3, 2: 77–101. http://doi.org/10.1191/1478088706qp063oa

10. Bureau of Labor Statistics. 1996. *Occupational employment statistics, 1994.* U.S. Dept. of Labor, Bureau of Labor Statistics.

11. Colin Campbell. 2005. *The romantic ethic and the spirit of modern consumerism.* Alcuin Academics.

12. Peter Conrad and Joseph W. Schneider. 2011. Professionalization, monopoly, and the structure of medical practices. In *The Sociology of Health and Illness.* 156–162.

13. Juliet Corbin and Anselm Strauss. 2007. *Basics of Qualitative Research: Techniques and Procedures for Developing Grounded Theory.* SAGE Publications.

14. Jennifer Duncan-Howell. 2010. Teachers making connections: Online communities as a source of professional learning. *British Journal of Educational Technology* 41, 2: 324–340. http://doi.org/10.1111/j.1467-8535.2009.00953.x

15. Kate Ehrlich and Marcelo Cataldo. 2012. All-for-one and one-for-all?: a multi-level analysis of communication patterns and individual performance in geographically distributed software development. *Proceedings of the ACM 2012 conference on Computer Supported Cooperative Work - CSCW '12*, ACM Press, 945–954. http://doi.org/10.1145/2145204.2145345

16. Eliot Freidson. 1974. *Professional Dominance: The Social Structure of Medical Care.* Transaction Publishers.

17. Michael. Eraut. 1994. *Developing professional knowledge and competence.* Falmer Press.

18. Jillian Eugenios, Emily J. Fox, Steve Hargreaves, and Kathryn Vasel. 2015. Best Jobs in America: CNNMoney/PayScale's top 100 careers with big growth, great pay and satisfying work. *CNN Money.* Retrieved from http://money.cnn.com/gallery/pf/2015/01/27/best-jobs-2015/index.html

19. Sarah Evans, Katie Davis, Abigail Evans, et al. 2017. More Than Peer Production: Fanfiction Communities as Sites of Distributed Mentoring. *Proceedings of the 2017 ACM Conference on Computer Supported Cooperative Work and Social Computing - CSCW '17*, ACM Press, 259–272. http://doi.org/10.1145/2998181.2998342

20. Robert Fabricant. 2013. Scaling Your UX Strategy. *Harvard Business Review.* Retrieved from https://hbr.org/2013/01/scaling-your-ux-strategy

21. Umer Farooq, Patricia Schank, Alexandra Harris, Judith Fusco, and Mark Schlager. 2007. Sustaining a Community Computing Infrastructure for Online Teacher Professional Development: A Case Study of Designing Tapped In. *Computer Supported Cooperative Work (CSCW)* 16, 4–5: 397–429. http://doi.org/10.1007/s10606-007-9049-0

22. Jodi Forlizzi and Katja Battarbee. 2004. Understanding experience in interactive systems. *Proceedings of the 2004 conference on Designing interactive systems processes, practices, methods, and techniques - DIS '04*, ACM Press, 261–268. http://doi.org/10.1145/1013115.1013152

23. Eliot Freidson. 1994. *Professionalism reborn : theory, prophecy, and policy.* University of Chicago Press.

24. Heather B. Gonzalez and Jeffrey J. Kuenzi. 2012. *Science, Technology, Engineering, and Mathematics (STEM) Education: A Primer.*

25. Colin M. Gray, Erik Stolterman, and Martin A. Siegel. 2014. Reprioritizing the relationship between HCI research and practice: bubble-up and trickle-down. *Proceedings of the 2014 conference on Designing interactive systems - DIS '14*, ACM Press, 725–734. http://doi.org/10.1145/2598510.2598595

26. Colin M. Gray, Austin L. Toombs, and Shad Gross. 2015. Flow of Competence in UX Design Practice. *Proceedings of the 33rd Annual ACM Conference on Human Factors in Computing Systems - CHI '15*, ACM Press, 3285–3294. http://doi.org/10.1145/2702123.2702579

27. Rebecca E. Grinter. Supporting articulation work using software configuration management systems. *Computer Supported Cooperative Work (CSCW)* 5, 4: 447–465. http://doi.org/10.1007/bf00136714

28. Ole Hanseth, Kari Thoresen, and Langdon Winner. The politics of networking technology in health care. *Computer Supported Cooperative Work* 2, 1–2: 109–130. http://doi.org/10.1007/bf00749286

29. David Harvey. 2005. *A brief history of neoliberalism.* Oxford University Press.

30. Marc Hassenzahl and Noam Tractinsky. 2006. User experience - a research agenda. *Behaviour & Information Technology* 25, 2: 91–97. http://doi.org/10.1080/01449290500330331

31. Eric Hoyle. 1982. The professionalization of teachers: A paradox. *British Journal of Educational Studies* 30, 2: 161–171. http://doi.org/10.1080/00071005.1982.9973622

32. Leslie Jensen-Inman. 2013. Why is there an increase in demand for UX designers? *Center Centre.*

33. Jonathan G. Silin. 1985. Authority as Knowledge: A Problem of Professionalization. *Young Children* 40, 3: 41–46.

34. Yiasemina Karagiorgi and Chrystalla Lymbouridou. 2009. The story of an online teacher community in Cyprus. *Professional Development in Education* 35, 1: 119–138. http://doi.org/10.1080/13674580802269059

35. Julie T. Klein. 1990. *Interdisciplinarity : history, theory, and practice.* Wayne State University Press.

36. Yubo Kou and Colin Gray. 2017. Supporting Distributed Critique through Interpretation and Sensemaking in an Online Creative Community. *PACMHCI* 1, 2: 60.

37. Yubo Kou, Colin Gray, Austin Toombs, and Robin Adams. 2018. Knowledge Production and Social Roles in an Online Community of Emerging Occupation: A Study of User Experience Practitioners on Reddit. *HICSS'2018.*

38. Carine Lallemand, Guillaume Gronier, and Vincent Koenig. 2015. User experience: A concept without consensus? Exploring practitioners' perspectives through an international survey. *Computers in Human Behavior* 43: 35–48.

39. Magali Sarfatti Larson. 1979. *The rise of professionalism : a sociological analysis.* University of California Press.

40. Lisa R. Lattuca. 2001. *Creating Interdisciplinarity: Interdisciplinary Research and Teaching among College and University Faculty.* Vanderbilt University Press.

41. Jean Lave and Etienne Wenger. 1991. *Situated Learning: Legitimate Peripheral Participation.* Cambridge University Press.

42. Effie Lai-Chong Law, Virpi Roto, Marc Hassenzahl, Arnold P.O.S. Vermeeren, and Joke Kort. 2009. Understanding, scoping and defining user experience: a survey approach. *Proceedings of the 27th international conference on Human factors in computing systems - CHI 09*, ACM Press, 719–728. http://doi.org/10.1145/1518701.1518813

43. Zeno C.S. Leung, C.W. Lam, T.Y. Yau, and William C.K. Chu. 2010. Re-empowering social workers through the online community: The experience of SWForum in Hong Kong. *Critical Social Policy* 30, 1: 48–73. http://doi.org/10.1177/0261018309350808

44. Jennifer Marlow and Laura Dabbish. 2014. From rookie to all-star: professional development in a graphic design social networking site. *Proceedings of the 17th ACM conference on Computer supported cooperative work & social computing - CSCW '14*, ACM Press, 922–933. http://doi.org/10.1145/2531602.2531651

45. Jennifer Marlow, Laura Dabbish, and Jim Herbsleb. 2013. Impression formation in online peer production: activity traces and personal profiles in github. *Proceedings of the 2013 conference on Computer supported cooperative work - CSCW '13*, ACM Press, 117–128. http://doi.org/10.1145/2441776.2441792

46. Michael J. Muller and Kenneth Carey. 2002. Design as a minority discipline in a software company: toward requirements for a community of practice. *Proceedings of the SIGCHI conference on Human factors in computing systems Changing our world, changing ourselves - CHI '02*, ACM Press, 383–390. http://doi.org/10.1145/503376.503445

47. Elizabeth D. Mynatt, Annette Adler, Mizuko Ito, and Vicki L. O'Day. 1997. Design for Network Communities. *Proceedings of the ACM SIGCHI Conference on Human factors in computing systems*, ACM, 210–217. http://doi.org/10.1145/258549.258707

48. Reddit. 2017. New subreddits by date. *redditmetrics.* Retrieved from http://redditmetrics.com/history

49. Michael Reed and Peter Anthony. 1992. Professionalizing Management and Managing Professionalization: British Management in the 1980s. *Journal of Management Studies* 29, 5: 591–613. http://doi.org/10.1111/j.1467-6486.1992.tb00680.x

50. Yvonne Rogers. 2005. New theoretical approaches for human-computer interaction. *Annual Review of Information Science and Technology* 38, 1: 87–143. http://doi.org/10.1002/aris.1440380103

51. Fred Stevens, Frans van der Horst, Frans Nijhuis, and Silvia Bours. 2000. The division of labour in vision care: professional competence in a system of professions. *Sociology of Health and Illness* 22, 4: 431–452. http://doi.org/10.1111/1467-9566.00213

52. Erik Stolterman. 2008. The Nature of Design Practice and Implications for Interaction Design Research. *International Journal of Design* 2, 1: 55–65.

53. Erik Stolterman and James Pierce. 2012. Design tools in practice: studying the designer-tool relationship in interaction design. *Proceedings of the Designing Interactive Systems Conference on - DIS '12*, ACM Press, 25–28. http://doi.org/10.1145/2317956.2317961

54. Randall H. Trigg and Susanne Bødker. 1994. From implementation to design: tailoring and the emergence of systematization in CSCW. *Proceedings of the 1994 ACM conference on Computer supported cooperative work - CSCW '94*, ACM Press, 45–54. http://doi.org/10.1145/192844.192869

55. Adnan Türegün. 2013. Immigrant Settlement Work in Canada: Limits and Possibilities for Professionalization. *Canadian Review of Sociology/Revue canadienne de sociologie* 50, 4: 387–411. http://doi.org/10.1111/cars.12025

56. Lynn Uyen Tran and Heather King. 2007. The Professionalization of Museum Educators: The Case in Science Museums. *Museum Management and Curatorship* 22, 2: 131–149. http://doi.org/10.1080/09647770701470328

57. Harold L. Wilensky. 1964. The Professionalization of Everyone? *American Journal of Sociology* 70, 2: 137–158.

58. Volker Wulf, Markus Rohde, Volkmar Pipek, and Gunnar Stevens. 2011. Engaging with practices: design case studies as a research framework in CSCW. *Proceedings of the ACM 2011 conference on Computer supported cooperative work - CSCW '11*, ACM Press, 505–512. http://doi.org/10.1145/1958824.1958902

59. Robert K. Yin. *Case study research : design and methods*. SAGE Publications.

60. Mark Zuckerberg. 2017. Building Global Community. *Facebook page*. Retrieved from https://www.facebook.com/notes/mark-zuckerberg/building-global-community/10154544292806634/

Working toward Empowering a Community: How Immigrant-Focused Nonprofit Organizations Use Twitter during Political Conflicts

Hanlin Li[*†], Lynn Dombrowski[*], Erin Brady[*]

[*] IUPUI, Indianapolis, USA, [†] Northwestern University, Evanston, USA

lihanlin@u.northwestern.edu, lsdombro@iupui.edu, brady@iupui.edu

ABSTRACT

In the digital age, social media has become a popular venue for nonprofit organizations to advocate for causes and promote social change. The 2016 United States Presidential Election occurred amidst divisive public opinions and political uncertainties for immigrants and immigration policies were a frequently-contested debate focus. Thus, this election provided an opportunity to examine nonprofit organizations' social media usage during political conflicts. We analyzed social media posts by immigrant-focused nonprofit organizations and conducted interviews probing into how they managed their online presence and social relations. This study finds that these nonprofit organizations adopted three key strategies to support their target community: *1) disseminating content about immigration-related issues and policies; 2) calling for participation in collective endeavors to influence the political climate; 3) engaging in conversations with outside stakeholders including political actors, media, and other organizations.* We use empowerment theory, which has been used widely to study marginalized populations, as a theoretical lens to discuss how NPOs' social media usage on Twitter reflects their endeavors to bring information and calls to action to immigrant communities. We, then, present design opportunities to amplify the advantages of social media to help nonprofit organizations better serve their communities in times of political upheavals.

Author Keywords

Social media; nonprofit organizations; politics; empowerment theory.

ACM Classification Keywords

H.5.m. Information interfaces and presentation (e.g., HCI): Miscellaneous.

INTRODUCTION

Social media is a popular resource used by nonprofit

organizations (NPOs) to communicate with various stakeholders and advance social causes [20]. However, such social media use largely depends on the causes that NPOs focus on and the related political climate [13]. Knowledge about how NPOs use social media during political conflicts can advance our understanding of NPOs' computer-mediated communication. How do these NPOs respond to political news in online spaces? What calls-to-action do they propose to affect political uncertainties? How do NPOs use social media to benefit their communities?

The 2016 presidential election in the United States provided an ideal opportunity to address our inquiries. In the past years, presidential elections in the United States and overseas have prompted researchers to analyze and understand the ever-changing dynamics on social media, focusing on specific social issues [11,18,24,46]. Immigration became one focal point of discussion during the 2016 election year in the United States [38]. The polarized opinions on immigration across presidential candidates led to divisive voices among the general public, organizations, government agencies, and immigrant communities. Seeing a series of election-related political events and the prevalence of social media-mediated debates online, our study chose to focus on immigrant-focused NPOs to understand how such NPOs' social media use reflects their public engagement and support for immigrant communities.

Our mixed-method study combined social media data analysis with a qualitative interview study, focusing on how immigrant-focused NPOs used Twitter during the 2016 presidential election and the transition between two presidential administrations. We examined 36 NPOs' tweets and interviewed eight participants who managed their organizations' social media accounts to analyze how such NPOs use Twitter in a politically polarized context.

The results show a variety of strategies adopted by NPOs on social media to support the immigrant population in the United States while they were exposed to amplified political conflicts during the 2016 presidential election. Strategies included *1) disseminating content about immigration-related issues and policies; 2) calling for participation in collective endeavors to influence the political climate; and 3) engaging in conversations with outside stakeholders including political actors, media, and other organizations.* These findings are further examined through the lens of community empowerment theory, which shows that nonprofits' social media use reflects their effort to empower the communities they serve through three approaches: *asking why and problem analysis, calls for participation, and reaching out to outside agents* [30].

The contribution of this work is two-fold. First, we empirically situate community empowerment theory in a social computing ecosystem. We provide evidence that NPOs applied a variety of methods in an effort to empower their communities through social media. The second fold of our contribution is practical. By investigating NPOs' social media use, we explore the advantages and limitations of current information technology for advocacy in the nonprofit sector. Our study provides design implications for existing socio-technical systems to better facilitate NPOs' efforts in promoting social and political changes. This study extends prior research on computer-mediated communication, NPOs, and studies of civic participation around social issues and debates on social media.

STUDY BACKGROUND

We chose our data collection period (from Oct 1st, 2016 to Jan 31st, 2017) to include important events that are related to the presidential election, including all presidential debates, election day, and the transition of two presidential administrations. As a historically important social cause in the United States, immigration became a focal point of discussion over this timespan.

The United States is the largest recipient of immigrants worldwide, attracting 20 percent of the world's migrants, with one percent (41.3 million) of the U.S. population as of 2013 being immigrants [54]. People emigrate from their homes due to a variety of economic and political factors, religious persecution or natural disasters. The migration exposes immigrants to an unfamiliar cultural context, which can be a disruptive event for many families [8]. Prior work has examined barriers that immigrants face from different perspectives, including culture differences, communication, health, employment, and education [27]. Although immigrants are legally eligible for many state-level and nationwide human service and health programs, barriers to accessing these resources still exist due to a variety of factors, including how the programs are administered, each immigrant's legal status[1], and the general climate toward immigrant communities [37].

A growing body of HCI work focuses on various aspects of immigrant communities and has provided implications on how technology could be designed and implemented to support this population [8,9,23,43]. Such work has shed light on the role and opportunities of technology in

---

[1] See the Immigration and Nationality Act (INA) for definition of "immigrant" in the United States.

immigrant lives, particularly as they adapt to new education systems, seek healthcare, and communicate with others. However, to our best knowledge, there has not been a study conducted to explore immigrant-focused NPOs' technology-mediated role in supporting the immigrant population. Our study explored this domain by focusing on how such NPOs use Twitter in times of critical political conflicts.

Legal Restrictions for NPOs

NPOs play an integral role in civic society through the provision of services to consumers [5]. However, their political engagement remains restricted [4]. There are two main types of NPOs in the United States – *501c(3)* and *501c(4)* – based on their tax exempt status [33]. The Internal Revenue Code 501c(3) means an organization "may not attempt to influence legislation as a substantial part of its activities and it may not participate in any campaign activity for or against political candidates" [55]. 501c(4) means the organization is allowed to seeking legislative changes as a method of attaining their social welfare goals [56]. 501c(3) organizations account for the majority of the nonprofit sector financially, contributing to over three-quarters of the whole sector's revenue and expenses ($1.73 trillion and $1.62 trillion, respectively) and more than three-fifths of nonprofit assets ($3.22 trillion) in 2013 [33].

RELATED WORK

There has been a large body of HCI work in understanding how the nonprofit sector adopts social technologies in their work, from collaborative data system [51] to e-governing portals connecting with communities [50]. As social media becomes a prominent communication channel, studying the use of these platforms during political conflicts reveals how stakeholders cope with and react to debatable issues [4].

Our work builds on prior literature by investigating how social media content can illustrate the online behaviors' of NPOs during a series of political uncertainties and upheavals. Existing research in this area mostly focused on the generic use of social media (*e.g.*, [32] proposed an information, community, and action model as a framework using the most representative NPO social media accounts; [35] examined the internal factors that affect NPOs' social media presence). However, to our best knowledge, the NPO literature in HCI has not examined how they respond to political conflicts in the general environment through social media. Our study focused on a period of time that spanned the 2016 presidential election in the United States and the transition between two presidential administrations when political debates on certain social causes became heated. Understanding NPOs' social media use under such circumstances provides implications for technological design researchers, as social media could potentially be improved to better facilitate NPOs' work in a time when their causes may lead to divisive public opinions and create uncertainties or even crises for their communities.

Although not directly studying NPOs, recent research on social media use has demonstrated its usefulness in revealing public opinions on social causes. Studies focused how other populations (including LGBT, racial equality activists, and Native American advocates) practice advocacy work through social media have been conducted [6,17,49]. There has also been ample work using social media data to understand, model, and predict people's opinions on political discourse (*e.g.,* [24,46]). These studies revealed various stakeholders' efforts toward making a difference in a community and policymaking. We contribute to this body of work by providing knowledge about how NPOs use social media to get involved with communities and policymaking process.

Another line of research relevant to our study is crisis informatics, which shows how the general public use social media to deal with crisis-introduced uncertainties through engaging with government organizations, emergency responders, and media/news companies [40,48]. Such case studies around natural and manmade disasters supported social media's important role in emergent communication. In our study, a critical consequence of political conflicts is policy change that may cause crises for certain populations in society. Building on prior crisis informatics literature, we study what stakeholders that NPOs intend to engage with to address potential crisis under a political climate that may affect their communities negatively.

Combining existing work across HCI and communication fields regarding NPOs and social media provides us an opportunity to study how NPOs' behaviors on social media relate to the prolonged political conflicts and the possible approaches to manifest NPOs' work online.

METHODS AND DATA

We collected social media data to examine how immigrant-focused NPOs used social media during the 2016 U.S. presidential election to discuss immigration-focused issues. This data included their Twitter posts and metadata, followers, interactions, linguistic attributes, and temporal changes to better understand how such NPOs use Twitter. To deepen our understanding of how the sampled NPOs managed their online presence and social relations, we conducted eight interviews with staff in charge of social media channels. These interviews focused on the changes in their social media use during the election and their reasons, strategies, and decision-making processes, while using social media to discuss immigration issues and politics.

Data Collection

We manually searched Twitter for accounts using immigration-related hashtags, such as #immigrant and #immigration. We screened for accounts that were affiliated with or represented an immigrant-focused nonprofit organization. Through this approach, 36 Twitter accounts were identified. We collected the accounts' tweets,

retweets, and replies from Oct 1st, 2016 to Jan 31st, 2017 with the Twitter Streaming API.

The interview participants were recruited from these 36 NPOs. We contacted all NPOs through social media and email and received eight responses. All eight participants were affiliated with one or more NPOs and in charge of managing their organizations' social media accounts at the time of interviewing. Their job titles included communication manager, outreach director, and social media specialist. The interview questions started with how they used their NPOs' social media accounts in the election year. Then, we asked questions focusing on the particular content they favor or tend to avoid in times when the public opinions on immigration become divisive.

Data Analysis

Our data analysis consists of three components: inductive coding of interview transcripts, content analysis of a subset of social media data, and quantitative analysis of the whole social media dataset. As we analyzed our collected structured and unstructured data, our qualitative and quantitative methods helped to cross-test, verify and support each other. Below we provide details about our data analysis approach.

Coding interview transcripts: We approached our interview transcripts through an inductive coding process, where the first author used memoing and mapping techniques to identify emergent themes and patterns and discussed the codes with the rest of the research team [41]. The codes were iteratively revised.

Content analysis of sample tweets: We randomly extracted a subset of social media data, consisting of 7932 tweets, to collect evidence supporting our interview findings. This subset of data was analyzed through deductive coding, using the three-phase model – *information, action, community* [4,32] – as our major categories. We then approached each major category through inductive coding, finding themes that arose in each phase. The final codes we used can be seen in Table 1.

Linguistic attributes: Linguistic Inquiry and Word Count (LIWC) was applied to our social media dataset to investigate whether there were significant differences in organizations' linguistic styles. LIWC is a dictionary-based algorithm that can reveal emotionality, thinking style, and social relationships in text samples [44].

Descriptive statistical analysis: Our descriptive statistical analysis focused on the sampled accounts' followers, number of tweets, codes, and linguistic attributes to examine the differences in social media activity.

Data Overview

The automated data collection resulted in 28,526 tweets from 36 immigrant-focused NPOs. The 36 NPOs' followers and frequencies of use varied to a large extent. Follower counts ranged from 161 to 49597 (Mean=8903, SD=2035),

Phase	Codes	Example Tweet
Information provision	Policy report	"UPDATE: Executive orders have been signed so far. Nothing on #immigration yet."
	Clarification about misconceptions	"Every year undocumented #immigrants in Kentucky pay over $38 million in state and local taxes. "
	Educating about immigrant rights	"Know your rights available in Chinese! Print & post in your neighborhood to help your community!"
Action announcing	Call for volunteers & employees	"TAKE ACTION NOW: 11AM, JFK TERMINAL 4. Protest sponsored by @thenyic + @MaketheRoadNY. More info: [link] #nobannowall"
	Lobbying and advocacy	"We denounce all hate against all communities who have suffered because of hate!"
Community building	Announcement of events	"Our community call Jan 23rd @ 8pm EST"
	Giving recognition and thanks	"Thank you Senator @ChrisVanHollen for standing with immigrants and refugees and joining us today in DC! We are all #HereToStay!"

Table 1: Codes adopted from Lovejoy & Saxton's models [25]

and the frequency of use ranged from 21.17 tweets/day to 0.04 tweet/day (Mean=3.05, SD=1.14). The frequency of use is strongly correlated with the number of followers (r=0.63, p<0.001). NPOs' numbers of daily tweets in total peaked when important political events occurred, including the three presidential debates, the election day, and Women's March on DC.

All interviews were conducted over the phone from December 12th, 2016 to February 11th, 2017. Interviews lasted 40 minutes on average and were later transcribed for further analysis in this study. Among all eight participants, seven belong to 501c(3) NPOs, with the remaining one (P4) coming from a 501c(4) NPOs. The significant fewer portion of 501c(4) NPOs identified on Twitter (3 out of 36) skewed our interview participants; however, we believe our open-ended interview questions about organizational types in all interviews were able to generate representative insights that allow us to understand the differences between 501c(3)s and 501c(4)s.

RESULTS

Through our study, we observed how NPOs use social media during a series of political events including presidential debates, policy changes, and rallies that affect immigrant communities. We investigated how social media content is managed and what external factors affect NPOs' social media use under this hostile political climate. We focus on three key aspects of our findings: how NPOs *1) disseminate content about immigration-related issues and policies; 2) call for participation in collective endeavors to influence the political climate; 3) engage in conversations with outside stakeholders including political actors, media, and other organizations.*

Disseminating Content

According to our interviews and sampled tweets, NPOs use social media to disseminate critical information to both the general public and their community members. In particular, immigrant-focused NPOs use social media to provide informational support on immigration policies for their community members (*e.g.*, *"Join our workshop for*

DACA [2] *", "Know your rights"*) and dispel immigrant-related misconceptions, especially when the political climate began to grow hostile towards immigrants.

Using Social Media

Consistent with previous studies [13,32], our participants from immigrant-focused NPOs described social media as a powerful broadcast communication channel. During our study period, because of political uncertainty during the election year, this communication channel is especially essential for NPOs to convey timely messages to their community members.

Our participants further described the value of social media to cope with political uncertainties in the general environment. First, it allows them to publish credible news to address any rumors or concerns that their communities may have under the unstable political climate. This is critical for those NPOs whose clients are sparsely located in rural areas and cannot make in-person visits very often.

P1: "If you live in the middle of nowhere, it takes hours for you to get somewhere if you need help... They hear a rumor; they are not sure if it is true or what they can do. So social media might be the only way to connect with organizations and find out more."

Second, timeliness is of utmost importance to address any possible crises that may arise from policy conflicts and affect immigrants. Many participants described their efforts to post up-to-date information on social media to ensure their audiences knew what was going on. These efforts help their audiences know what actions to take and may prevent them from getting hurt by immigration policies.

P3: "We have to be timely. We want to make sure the information is the most up-to-date. It could potentially hurt somebody. Especially for immigration policy."

Immigrant community members are not the only target audiences of the social media content. Participants also

---

[2] DACA: Deferred Action for Childhood Arrivals

recognize non-immigrants who are interested in immigration-related discourse as an important portion of their audiences. For this population, NPOs use social media as a way to further their readers' understanding of the immigrant population and clarify issues existing in current policies, summarized by one participant as *"broadcast, educate, and advocate" (P4)*:

> P6:*"It is all about the issues at hand and the policy that has been proposed... We try to clarify who people[immigrants] are and why we need to change things, and why certain policies don't work for people."*

Our content analysis of NPOs' sampled tweets further reflect the above-mentioned practices. Using the three-phase model from prior studies [4,32], we found the content published by such NPOs reflected their efforts in *disseminating information, provoking actions*, and *building communities* [32]. For tweets falling into these three major categories, we applied inductive coding and identified themes which arose in each category (see examples in Table 1). When disseminating information, NPOs focused on describing policies, dispelling immigrant-related misconceptions, and educating readers about immigrant rights. NPOs also are dedicated to announcing actions to further engage their audiences or show their standing. To build or reinforce communities, local events were announced on Twitter and recognitions were given to related stakeholders.

Reservations about Social Media
Our interviews further probed into how NPO staff members manage their social media content. Participants described the factors that affect their decisions about what to post due to amplified political conflicts during the 2016 presidential election.

The most important factor that is considered by all the interviewed participants is their organizations' tax exempt status. As mentioned in the background section, 501c(3) NPOs face harsher restrictions than their 501c(4) counterparts in terms of political engagement. Our 501c(3) participants described the external limits on their ability to show political engagement on social media, while 501c(4) status provides more leeway to take on political viewpoints and show public support for a particular candidate in elections. One participant from a 501c(3) organization expressed his workaround to address their legal restrictions. Because of its tax-exempt status, his NPO could not show direct support to a political candidate, but once the election result became public, they posted a tweet to support the elected candidate:

> P5 [501c(3)]: *"For example, once she [a former senator candidate] won the election, I used our Twitter account to say congratulations!"*

501c(3) organizations also expressed other ways to show their political engagement while complying with the legal regulations. To try to engage with policymaking, NPOs get involved with discussions on specific social issues, policies, and facts instead of directly taking sides of politicians.

> P7[501c(3)]: *"We tell them [followers] where they can take action, we give them information. Make sure it is relevant. Some politicians said something, and we want people to know."*

P4, from a 501c(4) organization, expressed how the less restrictive regulations for their organization allowed them to be involved in political discourse. While many 501c(3) avoid directly criticizing a particular politician or candidate, this organization decided to take a specific side by voicing objection to a presidential candidate. The organization used Twitter as a way to direct their audiences to their website, where they analyzed this candidate's proposed immigration policy in detail.

Another key factor that influences NPOs' social media use is the balance of sentiment and objectivity. Most participants expressed their preferences to post positive content on social media, such as celebrating community achievements and acknowledging contributions made to immigrant communities. However, the furious discourse on immigration and disruptive policies occurred during the political upheaval require NPOs to remain objective and realistic. While most participants expressed the need to keep their social media content positive, the gap between this idea and the actual political environment is noted.

> P4: *"We know that people respond more to positive content, so we want to keep our posts positive, but we have to be realistic at the same time."*

The 36 NPOs' follower counts had a weak negative correlation with the amount of expressed emotions (using LIWC's linguistic attribute, *affective processing*) in their social media content (r=-0.23, p<0.05). This finding suggests that NPOs with fewer followers tend to express emotions more often. One possible explanation for this is that NPOs who have greater perceived audiences may feel obliged to remain objective. Because social media is public and often chaotic, different opinions can spark backlash, and thus lead to damage of NPOs' online reputations and images [21]. Participants from NPOs with a large number of followers on Twitter emphasized the importance of keeping the content objective and informative, instead of directly confronting people who have different views on immigration.

> P5: *"We try to avoid arguments, especially with [political] leaders. We try to post news as we see them, but not respond to any explanatory, or exploratory information. Just what is happening at a state and local level. People are allowed to have their own opinion. We just want to inform them."*

Overall, we studied how NPOs used Twitter to deal with the political uncertainties caused by the 2016 presidential election and related political conflicts. Our work shows that NPOs' content largely depends on their tax-exempt status, and they use a balance of personal narratives and objective facts and statistics.

Calling for Participation

Participants note that merely focusing on providing information on Twitter is not enough. To make real changes in political conflicts, actions are the ultimate goal of their engagement in social media.

> *P2: "Social media is a tool. It should never be the only way to act. We are an organization that firmly believe that in order to make actual changes, it is wonderful if you do it online, but you have to be physically present. 'Oh I don't like this person', but if you don't vote, you are not taking the advantage to be involved."*

During our interviews, participants provided a variety of examples of call-to-actions, including making phone calls to lawmakers, signing e-petitions, going to town hall meetings, and joining offline protests. Using these examples, we further approached the collected tweets and identified call-to-action ones. 15 phrases (*e.g.,* "register to vote", "call your [senator/congressional representative]", "join us/our") were identified, with the majority of phrases relating to the 2016 presidential election in the United States. Using such phrases as keywords, 1256 tweets were extracted from the dataset and screened as call-to-action tweets.

From the call-to-action tweets, we identified NPOs' various goals. Some actions are attributed to influence policymaking directly. Before the election day, many NPOs encouraged communities to vote.

> *Tweet: "Your participation is critical. Deadline 2 register to vote is Mon. 10/24. Your vote has power."*

Other promoted actions that were not directly related to the election include making phone calls, writing emails, and joining town hall meetings to influence local lawmaking. During the time when Muslim immigrant communities were affected by a presidential executive order signed on Jan 27[th], 2017, NPOs focused on coordinating actions to form rallies and protests.

> *Tweet: "NYIC will be at #JFK all afternoon. 6pm join us for #JFK Immigration Detention Ral[l]y/Vigil #nobannowall #MuslimBan"*

Other actions were common-good oriented and aimed to support community members.

> *Tweet: "Print & post in your neighborhood to help your community!"*

During our interviews with participants, we discovered NPOs have different focuses on call-to-actions. Smaller NPOs who focus on local communities expressed an emphasis on community call-to-actions. National NPOs or NPOs that focused on online advocacy tend to use social media to advocate for political changes and raising awareness of existing issues that affect immigrant populations in general.

Another distinct difference among the sampled NPOs is the portion of call-to-action tweets in their general use. Through interviewing NPOs with various influences online, we speculated that NPOs with a smaller reach will also have a smaller focus on actions. By counting the portion of call-to-action tweets in each NPO, we confirmed that NPOs' number of followers was strongly correlated with call-to-action use ($r=0.81$, $p<0.05$).

One possible explanation for this phenomenon is smaller NPOs' lack of legislative resources. P1, a member of a local NPO, expressed concerns with provoking actions as it could mean political engagement. However, another NPO with the same tax exempt status, 501c(3), has a team of staff with legal expertise to decide whether a tweet is to be posted or not. Future work is needed to validate this explanation.

Whether the various call-to-actions on social media were effective among NPOs' followers remains unclear. Participants have yet succeeded to conceptualize how many actions were taken when deploying a campaign on social media.

> *P5: "We don't know how many people called, but we have an idea of how many thought about calling as they reacted on Twitter."*

Engaging with Outside Stakeholders

Social media not only enables NPOs to initiate communication with their community members and the public but also provides a platform for participating in conversations with various stakeholders. Through investigating how NPOs leverage the networking functionality on social media, we gain an overview of how they engage broader stakeholders online.

Hashtag Use

Hashtags are a feature on Twitter that allows Twitter users to tag their tweets to be searched by broader audiences. It is an approach to engage with communities who are interested in the same topics; in existing studies about collective actions on social media, hashtags are identified as important in building and facilitating online communities [17,39]. Through examining NPOs' hashtag use, we found specific causes and communities that NPOs are focusing on social media during the study period.

In our dataset, 4263 hashtags were used. Several topics emerged from the most commonly used hashtags in the dataset. Through inductive coding of hashtags used more than 20 times (121 hashtags), we found four hashtag themes: 1) *general immigration issues (e.g., #immigration,*

#immigrants), 2) *collective actions* (*e.g.* #nobannowall, #stopsessions); 3) *presidential campaign* (*e.g.* #trump, #debate), 4) *miscellaneous* (*e.g.* #blacklivesmatter, #womensmarch). In Table 2, we provide the most frequently used hashtags along with the corresponding lengths of circulation. NPOs use several common hashtags when posting content, but may have more detailed focuses over time on specific events (*e.g.,* #daca). Especially around critical events such as the release of immigration-focused presidential executive order, NPOs' use of hashtags suggest collective action emerging in a short period of time (*e.g.,* #nobannowall).

Hashtag	Count	Circulation (days)	Users
#heretostay	3297 *	56	17
#immigration	848	104	27
#daca	670	10	7
#savedaca	461	4	3
#nobannowall	459	7	9
#immigrants	282	87	20
#stopsessions	263	5	7
#not1more	243	21	8
#debatenight	209	4	7
#womensmarch	194	6	7
#immigrantny	189	4	4

Table 2: The most frequently used hashtags
(* One NPO contributed to 55% of tweets that use #heretostay)

Leveraging the Networking Functionality
The hashtag feature on Twitter enables NPOs to engage with broader audiences, yet one-to-one communication is also prominent among NPOs' social media content. Because of the prevalence of Twitter, NPOs recognize it as a platform to connect and communicate with different roles.

　　P1: "Twitter connects us with other organizations and advocates that work on this issue, also journalists and other media outlets. Twitter has been great to do these things."

On Twitter, at-mentioning allows NPOs to mention or reach out to specific Twitter users. Table 3 shows the eight most frequently at-mentioned users. From this list, it is clear that NPOs are mentioning primarily presidential candidates, politicians, and government agencies.

While at-mentioning activities reveal NPOs' intention to call for attention from policy-related stakeholders, their replying and retweeting activities are much more complex. Such activities are generally intertwined with diverse roles

including individual advocates, fellow organizations, and mainstream media. While at-mentioned social media users tend to be unified across the sampled NPOs (see Figure 1 (a)), their retweeting and replying activities indicate varied focuses. In our Figure 1 (b) and (c), we can see that a few NPOs are located in the center of their retweeting and replying networks, indicating that they are the only ones had retweeted from or replied to the social media users around them. This finding suggests that these NPOs tend to have their own retweet sources and reply targets on Twitter, which may not be overlapped with other NPOs' choices. Through gaining an overview of the stakeholders that are involved in the dataset, it became clear that NPOs try to attract attention from or respond to a series of politics- and policy-related stakeholders through at-mentioning, retweeting, and replying. Meantime, NPOs use features like retweeting and replying to engage broader and more diverse audiences with their own specific focuses.

Users	Description	Count
realDonaldTrump	45th President of the United States of America	389
POTUS	45th President of the United States	287
marcorubio	US Senator for Florida.	195
SenatorDurbin	Senate Democratic Whip.	165
HillaryClinton	2016 presidential candidate, women+kids advocate, FLOTUS, Senator, SecState	130
DHSgov	Department of Homeland Security	103
RepGutierrez	Congressman representing the 4th District of IL.	102
USCIS	US Citizenship and Immigration Services	72

Table 3: The most frequently at-mentioned social media users

DISCUSSION
We demonstrated that immigrant-focused NPOs use social media to further their mission by disseminating content, scaffolding action, and reaching broader stakeholders in response to amplified political conflicts during the 2016 presidential election. Our interview data highlighted how such social media content was managed and how content and activities were generated in response to the general political climate. To comply with the law, frequently NPOs cannot criticize politicians or take political positions. Instead, these NPOs find alternative ways to use social media to respond to pressing social issues and legislative policies.

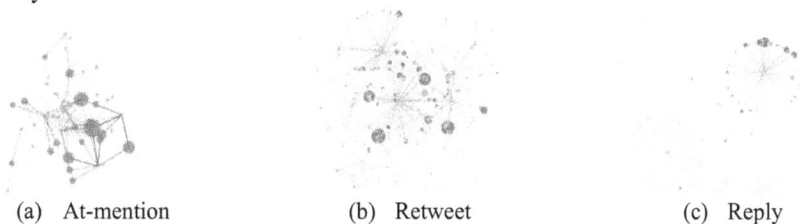

(a)　At-mention　　　　(b)　Retweet　　　　(c)　Reply

Figure 1: How NPOs leverage networking features on Twitter
(Orange dots represent NPOs; blue dots represent social media accounts that NPOs reached out to)

In this section, using empowerment theory as a theoretical lens [53], we discuss how NPOs' social media usage in times of political uncertainties mirror their efforts to advance positive changes by empowering communities. Then, we provide design implications focusing on how social media could be improved for NPOs' communication with stakeholders.

Immigrant Empowerment during Political Uncertainties
Empowerment theory describes the process in which individuals gain control over existing resources, political forces or personal capabilities [52]. It has been widely used to study marginalized populations, including women [10,16], parents of children with special needs [3], low-income neighborhoods [36], makers with disabilities [34], and larger populations (*e.g.*, [28,29,31]). In the United States, immigrants are frequently considered marginalized because they typically lack resources, social capital, and influence on policymaking [27]. Thus, we found empowerment theory applicable in our study.

Zimmerman proposed that different types of empowerment theory, depending on the process, can be self-motivated, led by hierarchical leaders, or community-driven [53]. In our study, we draw from community empowerment, focusing on NPOs' role in community development on social media.

Community empowerment relies on community members working collectively to gain access to resources and to participate in community development and decision making [53]. Laverack's literature review of existing literature described how community empowerment is achieved through nine factors: "*participation; community-based organizations; local resource mobilization; asking 'why'; assessment of problems; links with other people and organizations; role of outside agents; and programme*" [30]. Considering the variety of work NPOs perform on social media platforms, social media use could be used to situate and test this framework.

In our study, we found: 1) NPOs' information dissemination regarding policy issues reveal their efforts in "*asking why*" and "*assessment of problems*" [30]; 2) their call-to-action tweets promote community members' participation in collective endeavors; and 3) the variety of networking features leveraged by NPOs emphasized outside agents' role in community development. Below, we enrich the literature by expanding the role of social media in community empowerment more in depth.

First, for communities to be able to self-direct, they first must be able to form group goals. Communities being able to ask why something happened and assess problems are critical initial steps towards forming group goals [26]. Through content analysis, our study shows that NPOs use social media to express their analysis of policies and issues, including causes of problems and corresponding solutions. By providing such information, NPOs keep their audiences well-informed of the latest news stories, policy changes,

and correspondent coping mechanisms. For immigrant communities, this is especially crucial for a variety of reasons, including lack of literacy of basic rights, language barriers, lack of social support, and financial limitations. Social media enables NPOs to deliver timely information to their communities timely, especially during disruptive events.

Second, community participation is another integral part of community empowerment, as community members take civic actions to improve community's power and resources [30]. Our analysis shows immigrant-focused NPOs encourage their audiences to take specific civic actions to influence the on-going political conflicts. Unlike previous studies investigating how NPOs use social media broadly, this study reveals that such NPOs encourage specific call-to-actions during political contentious times. As key stakeholders in public relations and social work, such NPOs provide general suggestions and guidance for the public to initiate certain actions through social media under particular political climates that may affect their communities negatively.

Third, addressing social issues like immigration require engagement from a variety of stakeholders, including the general public, fellow organizations, government agencies, lawmakers, and media outlets. Connecting with more stakeholders facilitates community empowerment by raising awareness of a problem's existence and negotiating common goal. This is especially critical for immigrant populations who are often left out in the policymaking process [27]. In our study, NPOs, acting as proxies for immigrants, leverage the at-mentioning, replying and retweeting features on Twitter to initiate interactions and develop connections with fellow organizations and outside agents. Such use of social media allows NPOs to call for recognition of the issues, and attract potential social resources for the benefit of their communities, as efforts dedicated to increasing community's power and voices in related discourses.

However, the aforementioned approaches to empower communities do not only lead to benefits. As our participants noted, because of the openness of social media, their published content may lead to confrontations with people who hold different opinions on immigration. Further, it may even cause backlash to immigrant communities and the NPOs, especially in times of polarized political debates. Another potential risk NPOs considered is the imposing legal restrictions for being over-involved with political activities as 501c(3) NPOs. Because of a large amount of news and debates in the election year, NPOs have to cautiously balance their involvement and goals to maintain sustainable informational services for immigrant communities. Overall, immigrant-focused NPOs demonstrated their endeavors to influence policymaking and empower communities through social media. Next, building on our findings, we identify opportunities for technology to facilitate NPOs' work.

Design Implications

In this section, we first highlight how NPOs manage and engage diverse stakeholders on social media. We, then, reveal key social media challenges for NPOs: the inability to signal impact made by NPOs and the risks of over-involving NPOs in political discourse. For each challenge, we provide design recommendations.

Managing Stakeholder Complexity

Our study shows that NPOs use Twitter to engage diverse stakeholders, including community members, public advocates, media outlets, and political actors. The mixed stakeholders may make some of NPOs' social media content irrelevant to other audiences, causing information overload. As Twitter users commonly follow content that is appealing to them [42], targeting multiple stakeholders via the same account may damage an NPO's potential online impact, and cause them to lose some of their existing or potential audiences. Having stakeholders choose which roles they play in the immigration debate (*i.e., community member, volunteer, reporter, fellow NPOs, or policymakers*), or which kind of content they are interested in, would give NPOs a better understanding of who and how to interact with their stakeholders. Furthermore, customizing content based on stakeholder type gives NPOs an opportunity to disseminate more tailored content. For example, NPOs could choose to post community event information only to local community members. On current platforms, NPOs could develop unique hashtags which demarcate content meant for different audiences to help users choose to hide or engage with certain types of content.

Signaling Community Engagement

NPOs use Twitter to scaffold civic participation from immigrant communities and try to influence policymaking. However, it remains unanswered when and under what conditions social media is an effective venue for social change or not. This finding echoes prior work questioning the legitimacy of online advocacy and activism [14].

To signal NPOs' success in engaging relevant communities, Twitter could allow community members to respond to call-to-action posts, informing NPOs of whether an action is taken or not. As giving real-time progress reports is crucial to sustaining civic actions (by making them tangible, durable, and effective) [47], having community members confirm the actions they have taken could also make the collective efforts visible to more people, thus attracting broader and more sustainable participation. NPOs could use this intuitive data to help evaluate if their calls to actions were successfully directed. This may be especially helpful when NPOs deploy campaigns on different scales (*e.g.* statewide or nationwide). NPOs could combine this data with people's self-disclosed locations to understand how their online campaigns have unfolded spatially. From the

perspective of data practices among NPOs, this dataset would provide a clear and coherent measurement for NPOs' impact, and ultimately improve their data management to facilitate their organizational missions [7]. Designing for signaling engagement could help NPOs to better understand their impact on social media and thus better manage their staff's efforts in future work.

Connecting Policymakers with Communities

Prior work studying NPOs' social media use shows that NPOs work and interact with mainstream media, fellow organizations, and interested parties [25]. Our study further demonstrates how NPOs reach out to political actors and government agencies at the same time, who are the most frequently mentioned social media users in their tweets. The political environment during our study period led to divisive public opinions on immigration and, consequently, the creation of specific draft policies and political stances affecting immigrant communities. NPOs may find reaching out, by calling attention to policymakers, to be necessary to serve immigrant communities. However, according to our participants, NPOs' tax exempt statuses limit their capabilities to confront political actors when public policies affect their communities.

These in-depth discussions about issues and politics among NPOs, political stakeholders, community members, and other interested parties may serve as a form of *crowdsourced policymaking* [1]. In prior work, crowdsourcing policymaking is shown to enable governments to access people's needs efficiently [12,45] and encourage exchange of deliberative arguments and reasoning [2]. To support such crowdsourced policymaking process on social media, an engaging, trustworthy environment must be provided [15]. NPOs' must be able to reinforce their role in addressing social issues, without endangering their tax-exempt status, on the social media platforms they use. One solution may be to highlight NPOs' role as moderators in policymaker-community interaction. When pressing issues arise, NPOs could provide a venue integrated within social media (*e.g., in forms of webinar, polling, or focus groups*) for policymakers and community members to communicate and voice opinions. By harnessing NPOs' existing networks on social media for crowdsourced policymaking, they would be able to direct community's voices to policymakers, without over-engaging with political issues.

While we see the opportunities to improve communication effectiveness for NPOs on social media, we caution that there could be unexpected consequences of such mechanism. Displaying NPO's impact on civic engagement and policymaking may be seen by NPOs as surveillance over their political engagement, and causes concerns about using social media in general. Thus, designing for NPOs requires designers and technological practitioners to consider how to ensure data privacy, and the possibility to remove historical data once it becomes outdated.

Study Limitations

Because our sampled NPOs' frequency of use varies to a large extent, the majority of our dataset come from ones that are very active online. Our results may aggregate such types of NPOs and not reveal the true use of social media of smaller ones.

We leveraged existing algorithms, LIWC, as tools to help us understand the nature of the dataset. Although such tools have been used in a variety of studies [17,22], we acknowledged that there might be biases in the design of algorithms, which could essentially affect the validity of our study [19].

Using the dataset, we studied the correlations between NPOs followers and other social media usage attributes, *e.g.* portion of call-to-actions. However, the small sample size (36 NPOs) may limit the study's statistical power.

CONCLUSION

In this study, immigrant-focused NPOs' social media use was examined through quantitative analysis, linguistic analysis, and open coding. Combined with interviews of participants who manage such social media accounts, this study shows how immigrant-focused NPOs use social media in a political climate what is hostile to their communities, through three key strategies: *1) disseminating content about immigration-related issues and policies; 2) calling for participation in collective endeavors to influence the political climate; 3) engaging in conversations with outside stakeholders including political actors, media, and other organizations.* Using community empowerment theory as a theoretical framework, we show that social media becomes a venue where NPOs work toward empowering their communities through disseminating information, calling for civic participation, and drawing attention from outside agents. We, then, provide design recommendations for social media to help NPOs manage stakeholder complexity, understand community engagement, and connect policymakers with community members on this type of platform.

ACKNOWLEDGMENTS

We thank our reviewers for comments that improved this paper. We would also like to thank Andrew Miller for helpful early feedback on this work.

REFERENCES

1. Tanja Aitamurto. 2012. *Crowdsourcing for Democracy: A New Era in Policy-Making*. Social Science Research Network, Rochester, NY.

2. Tanja Aitamurto and Hélène Landemore. 2016. Crowdsourced Deliberation: The Case of the Law on Off-Road Traffic in Finland. *Policy & Internet* 8, 2: 174–196. https://doi.org/10.1002/poi3.115

3. Tawfiq Ammari and Sarita Schoenebeck. 2015. Networked Empowerment on Facebook Groups for Parents of Children with Special Needs. In *Proceedings of the 33rd Annual ACM Conference on Human Factors*

in Computing Systems (CHI '15), 2805–2814. https://doi.org/10.1145/2702123.2702324

4. Giselle A. Auger. 2013. Fostering democracy through social media: Evaluating diametrically opposed nonprofit advocacy organizations' use of Facebook, Twitter, and YouTube. *Public Relations Review* 39, 4: 369–376. https://doi.org/10.1016/j.pubrev.2013.07.013

5. Michael J. Austin. 2003. The Changing Relationship Between Nonprofit Organizations and Public Social Service Agencies in the Era of Welfare Reform. *Nonprofit and Voluntary Sector Quarterly* 32, 1: 97–114. https://doi.org/10.1177/0899764002250008

6. Lindsay Blackwell, Jean Hardy, Tawfiq Ammari, Tiffany Veinot, Cliff Lampe, and Sarita Schoenebeck. 2016. LGBT Parents and Social Media: Advocacy, Privacy, and Disclosure During Shifting Social Movements. In *Proceedings of the 2016 CHI Conference on Human Factors in Computing Systems* (CHI '16), 610–622. https://doi.org/10.1145/2858036.2858342

7. Chris Bopp, Ellie Harmon, and Amy Voida. 2017. Disempowered by Data: Nonprofits, Social Enterprises, and the Consequences of Data-Driven Work. In *Proceedings of the 2017 CHI Conference on Human Factors in Computing Systems* (CHI '17), 3608–3619. https://doi.org/10.1145/3025453.3025694

8. Deana Brown. 2015. *Designing technologies to support migrants and refugees*. Ph.D. Dissertation. Georgia Institute of Technology, Atlanta, GA.

9. Deana Brown, Victoria Ayo, and Rebecca E. Grinter. 2014. Reflection Through Design: Immigrant Women's Self-reflection on Managing Health and Wellness. In *Proceedings of the SIGCHI Conference on Human Factors in Computing Systems* (CHI '14), 1605–1614. https://doi.org/10.1145/2556288.2557119

10. T. Cai, H. E. Chew, and M. R. Levy. 2015. Mobile value-added services and the economic empowerment of women: The case of Usaha Wanita in Indonesia. *Mobile Media & Communication* 3, 2: 267–285. https://doi.org/10.1177/2050157914564236

11. Mario Cataldi, Luigi Di Caro, and Claudio Schifanella. 2010. Emerging topic detection on twitter based on temporal and social terms evaluation. In *Proceedings of the Tenth International Workshop on Multimedia Data Mining*, 4. https://dl.acm.org/citation.cfm?id=1814249

12. Yannis Charalabidis, Anna Triantafillou, Vangelis Karkaletsis, and Euripidis Loukis. 2012. Public Policy Formulation through Non Moderated Crowdsourcing in Social Media. In *Electronic Participation* (Lecture Notes in Computer Science), 156–169. https://doi.org/10.1007/978-3-642-33250-0_14

13. Curtis D. Child and Kirsten A. Grønbjerg. 2007. Nonprofit Advocacy Organizations: Their Characteristics and Activities. *Social Science Quarterly* 88, 1: 259–281.

14. Henrik Serup Christensen. 2011. Political activities on the Internet: Slacktivism or political participation by

other means? *First Monday* 16, 2. Retrieved September 26, 2016 from http://firstmonday.org/ojs/index.php/fm/article/view/3336

15. Henrik Serup Christensen, Maija Karjalainen, and Laura Nurminen. 2015. Does Crowdsourcing Legislation Increase Political Legitimacy? The Case of Avoin Ministeriö in Finland. *Policy & Internet* 7, 1: 25–45. https://doi.org/10.1002/poi3.80

16. Meghan Corroon, Ilene S. Speizer, Jean-Christophe Fotso, Akinsewa Akiode, Abdulmumin Saad, Lisa Calhoun, and Laili Irani. 2014. The Role of Gender Empowerment on Reproductive Health Outcomes in Urban Nigeria. *Maternal and child health journal* 18, 1: 307–315. https://doi.org/10.1007/s10995-013-1266-1

17. Munmun De Choudhury, Shagun Jhaver, Benjamin Sugar, and Ingmar Weber. 2016. Social Media Participation in an Activist Movement for Racial Equality. In *Tenth International AAAI Conference on Web and Social Media*.

18. Nicholas A. Diakopoulos and David A. Shamma. 2010. Characterizing debate performance via aggregated twitter sentiment. In *Proceedings of the SIGCHI Conference on Human Factors in Computing Systems*, 1195–1198. https://dl.acm.org/citation.cfm?id=1753504

19. Paul Dourish. 2016. Algorithms and their others: Algorithmic culture in context. *Big Data & Society* 3, 2: 2053951716665128. https://doi.org/10.1177/2053951716665128

20. Chao Guo and Gregory D. Saxton. 2013. Tweeting social change: How social media are changing nonprofit advocacy. *Nonprofit and Voluntary Sector Quarterly*: 899764012471585.

21. Oliver L. Haimson, Jed R. Brubaker, Lynn Dombrowski, and Gillian R. Hayes. 2016. Digital Footprints and Changing Networks During Online Identity Transitions. In *Proceedings of the 2016 CHI Conference on Human Factors in Computing Systems* (CHI '16), 2895–2907. https://doi.org/10.1145/2858036.2858136

22. Oliver L. Haimson and Gillian R. Hayes. 2017. Changes in Social Media Affect, Disclosure, and Sociality for a Sample of Transgender Americans in 2016's Political Climate. In *ICWSM*, 72–81.

23. Tad Hirsch and Jeremy Liu. 2004. Speakeasy: overcoming barriers and promoting community development in an immigrant neighborhood. In *Proceedings of the 5th conference on Designing interactive systems: processes, practices, methods, and techniques*, 345–348. https://dl.acm.org/citation.cfm?id=1013176

24. Sounman Hong and Daniel Nadler. 2012. Which candidates do the public discuss online in an election campaign?: The use of social media by 2012 presidential candidates and its impact on candidate salience. *Government Information Quarterly* 29, 4: 455–461. https://doi.org/10.1016/j.giq.2012.06.004

25. Youyang Hou and Cliff Lampe. 2015. Social Media Effectiveness for Public Engagement: Example of Small Nonprofits. In *Proceedings of the 33rd Annual ACM Conference on Human Factors in Computing Systems* (CHI '15), 3107–3116. https://doi.org/10.1145/2702123.2702557

26. Barbara A. Israel, Barry Checkoway, Amy Schulz, and Marc Zimmerman. 1994. Health education and community empowerment: conceptualizing and measuring perceptions of individual, organizational, and community control. *Health education quarterly* 21, 2: 149–170.

27. Fernando Chang-Muy JD and Elaine P. Congress DSW. 2015. *Social Work with Immigrants and Refugees, Second Edition: Legal Issues, Clinical Skills, and Advocacy*. Springer Publishing Company.

28. Weiling Ke and Ping Zhang. 2011. Effects of Empowerment on Performance in Open-Source Software Projects. *IEEE Transactions on Engineering Management* 58, 2: 334–346. https://doi.org/10.1109/TEM.2010.2096510

29. N. Kumar. 2014. Facebook for self-empowerment? A study of Facebook adoption in urban India. *New Media & Society* 16, 7: 1122–1137. https://doi.org/10.1177/1461444814543999

30. Glenn Laverack. 2006. Improving Health Outcomes through Community Empowerment: A Review of the Literature. *Journal of Health, Population and Nutrition* 24, 1: 113–120.

31. Manning Li, Jie Hou, Henry Zhang, and others. 2014. A Tale of two Virtual Advisors: an Empirical Study Investigating the Empowerment effect of Mobile Mental-Health Advisory Systems on Emergency rescuers. In *PACIS*, 227. http://aisel.aisnet.org/cgi/viewcontent.cgi?article=1162&context=pacis2014

32. Kristen Lovejoy and Gregory D. Saxton. 2012. Information, Community, and Action: How Nonprofit Organizations Use Social Media*. *Journal of Computer-Mediated Communication* 17, 3: 337–353. https://doi.org/10.1111/j.1083-6101.2012.01576.x

33. Brice McKeever. 2016. The Nonprofit Sector in Brief 2015: Public Charities, Giving, and Volunteering. *Urban Institute*. http://www.urban.org/research/publication/nonprofit-sector-brief-2015-public-charities-giving-and-volunteering

34. Janis Meissner, John Vines, Janice McLaughlin, Thomas Nappey, Jekaterina Maksimova, and Peter Wright. 2017. Do-It-Yourself Empowerment as Experienced by Novice Makers with Disabilities. In *Proceedings of DIS 2017*. http://dis2017.org/conference-program-3/

35. Seungahn Nah and Gregory D. Saxton. 2012. Modeling the adoption and use of social media by nonprofit organizations. *New Media & Society*: 1461444812452411.

36. Andrea Parker, Vasudhara Kantroo, Hee Rin Lee, Miguel Osornio, Mansi Sharma, and Rebecca Grinter. 2012. Health promotion as activism: building community capacity to effect social change. In *Proceedings of the SIGCHI Conference on Human Factors in Computing Systems*, 99–108. https://dl.acm.org/citation.cfm?id=2207692

37. Krista M. Perreira, Robert Crosnoe, Karina Fortuny, Juan Pedroza, Kjersti Ulvestad, Christina Weiland, Hirokazu Yoshikawa, and Ajay Chaudry. 2012. Barriers to immigrants' access to health and human services programs. *ASPE Issue Brief. Washington, DC: Office of the Assistant Secretary for Planning and Evaluation.* http://webarchive.urban.org/UploadedPDF/413260-Barriers-to-Immigrants-Access-to-Health-and-Human-Services-Programs.pdf

38. POLITICO Staff. Full transcript: Third 2016 presidential debate. *POLITICO.* Retrieved March 6, 2017 from http://politi.co/2eHYqDM

39. Kate Starbird, Jim Maddock, Mania Orand, Peg Achterman, and Robert M. Mason. 2014. Rumors, false flags, and digital vigilantes: Misinformation on twitter after the 2013 boston marathon bombing. *iConference 2014 Proceedings.* https://www.ideals.illinois.edu/handle/2142/47257

40. Kate Starbird and Leysia Palen. 2013. Working and sustaining the virtual Disaster Desk. In *Proceedings of the 2013 conference on Computer supported cooperative work*, 491–502. http://dl.acm.org/citation.cfm?id=2441832

41. Anselm L. Strauss and Juliet M. Corbin. 1990. *Basics of qualitative research: grounded theory procedures and techniques.* Sage Publications.

42. Hikaru Takemura, Atsushi Tanaka, and Keishi Tajima. 2015. Classification of Twitter Follow Links Based on the Followers' Intention. In *Proceedings of the 30th Annual ACM Symposium on Applied Computing* (SAC '15), 1174–1180. https://doi.org/10.1145/2695664.2695940

43. Reem Talhouk, Sandra Mesmar, Anja Thieme, Madeline Balaam, Patrick Olivier, Chaza Akik, and Hala Ghattas. 2016. Syrian Refugees and Digital Health in Lebanon: Opportunities for Improving Antenatal Health. In *Proceedings of the 2016 CHI Conference on Human Factors in Computing Systems* (CHI '16), 331–342. https://doi.org/10.1145/2858036.2858331

44. Y. R. Tausczik and J. W. Pennebaker. 2010. The Psychological Meaning of Words: LIWC and Computerized Text Analysis Methods. *Journal of Language and Social Psychology* 29, 1: 24–54. https://doi.org/10.1177/0261927X09351676

45. Ioannis Tsampoulatidis, Dimitrios Ververidis, Panagiotis Tsarchopoulos, Spiros Nikolopoulos, Ioannis Kompatsiaris, and Nicos Komninos. 2013. ImproveMyCity: an open source platform for direct citizen-government communication. 839–842. https://doi.org/10.1145/2502081.2502225

46. Andranik Tumasjan, Timm Oliver Sprenger, Philipp G. Sandner, and Isabell M. Welpe. 2010. Predicting Elections with Twitter: What 140 Characters Reveal about Political Sentiment. *ICWSM* 10: 178–185.

47. Ion Bogdan Vasi and Michael Macy. 2002. The Mobilizer's Dilemma: Crisis, Empowerment, and Collective Action. *Social Forces* 81: 979–998.

48. Sarah Vieweg, Amanda L. Hughes, Kate Starbird, and Leysia Palen. 2010. Microblogging during two natural hazards events: what twitter may contribute to situational awareness. In *Proceedings of the SIGCHI conference on human factors in computing systems*, 1079–1088. https://dl.acm.org/citation.cfm?id=1753486

49. Morgan Vigil-Hayes, Marisa Duarte, Nicholet Deschine Parkhurst, and Elizabeth Belding. 2017. #Indigenous: Tracking the Connective Actions of Native American Advocates on Twitter. In *Proceedings of the 2017 ACM Conference on Computer Supported Cooperative Work and Social Computing* (CSCW '17), 1387–1399. https://doi.org/10.1145/2998181.2998194

50. Amy Voida, Lynn Dombrowski, Gillian R. Hayes, and Melissa Mazmanian. 2014. Shared Values/Conflicting Logics: Working Around e-Government Systems. In *Proceedings of the SIGCHI Conference on Human Factors in Computing Systems* (CHI '14), 3583–3592. https://doi.org/10.1145/2556288.2556971

51. Amy Voida, Ellie Harmon, and Ban Al-Ani. 2011. Homebrew databases: Complexities of everyday information management in nonprofit organizations. In *Proceedings of the SIGCHI Conference on Human Factors in Computing Systems*, 915–924. https://dl.acm.org/citation.cfm?id=1979078

52. Marc A. Zimmerman. 1995. Psychological empowerment: Issues and illustrations. *American journal of community psychology* 23, 5: 581–599.

53. Marc A. Zimmerman. 2000. Empowerment Theory. In *Handbook of Community Psychology*, Julian Rappaport and Edward Seidman (eds.). Springer US, Boston, MA, 43–63. https://link.springer.com/10.1007/978-1-4615-4193-6_2

54. 2017. Frequently Requested Statistics on Immigrants and Immigration in the United States. *migrationpolicy.org.* Retrieved March 15, 2017 from http://www.migrationpolicy.org/article/frequently-requested-statistics-immigrants-and-immigration-united-states

55. Exemption Requirements - 501(c)(3) Organizations. Retrieved April 11, 2017 from https://www.irs.gov/charities-non-profits/charitable-organizations/exemption-requirements-section-501-c-3-organizations

56. Social Welfare Organizations. Retrieved April 11, 2017 from https://www.irs.gov/charities-non-profits/other-non-profits/social-welfare-organizations

Effects of Comment Curation and Opposition on Coherence in Online Policy Discussion

Brian McInnis[1]**, Dan Cosley**[1]**, Eric Baumer**[2]**, Gilly Leshed**[1]

[1]Information Science, Cornell University
[2]Computer Science & Engineering, Lehigh University
[1]{bjm277, drc44, gl87}@cornell.edu, [2]ericpsb@lehigh.edu

ABSTRACT

Public concern related to a policy may span a range of topics. As a result, policy discussions struggle to deeply examine any one topic before moving to the next. In policy deliberation research, this is referred to as a problem of topical *coherence*. In an experiment, we curated the comments in a policy discussion to prioritize arguments *for* or *against* a policy proposal, and examined how this curation and participants' initial positions of *support* or *opposition* to the policy affected the coherence of their contributions to existing topics. We found an asymmetric interaction between participants' initial positions and comment curation: participants with different initial positions had unequal reactions to curation that foregrounded comments with which they disagreed. This asymmetry implies that the factors underlying coherence are more nuanced than prioritizing participants' agreement or disagreement. We discuss how this finding relates to curating for coherent disagreement, and for curation more generally in deliberative processes.

ACM Classification Keywords

H.5.m. Information Interfaces and Presentation (e.g. HCI): Miscellaneous.

Author Keywords

deliberation; curation; preferences; coherence; agreement; openness

INTRODUCTION

Coherence in online policy discussion refers to the *consistency of the topics within a thread of comments* [67]. When discussion participants are regularly off-topic, or move away from topics too quickly, the behavior leads to an incoherent discussion that cannot deeply consider a policy issue. Too much attention on a single topic is also limiting, although in practice online policy discussions often result in far more than one topic being deeply considered [12, 14, 28, 31, 43, 71].

GROUP '18, January 7–10, 2018, Sanibel Island, FL, USA

© 2018 ACM. ISBN 978-1-4503-5562-9/18/01...15.00

DOI: https://doi.org/10.1145/3148330.3148348

Low coherence in online discussions about political issues has been observed across various forms of digital media: newspaper comment threads [14, 43], political [12] and non-political discussion forums [28], social platforms [31, 44], and field trials of advanced policy deliberation systems [29]. Although there are many recommendations [3, 11, 13, 70, 73] and prototype designs to encourage people using an online discussion system to build on the existing discussion [35, 38, 75], this empirical research indicates that *supporting coherence remains an unresolved design challenge*.

Here we examine the relationship between coherence and a commonly referenced design lever to affect the ways that people contribute to an online discussion: *content curation* [1]. Curating a comment thread means choosing which comments to include [14, 73], how to order those comments [40], and when to present them [49]. Such curation is useful when the chronological order of a comment is less relevant than its content (e.g., demoting profanity [14, 40] or highlighting political opinions [52, 53]).

Much of the work on comment curation has focused on how a reader's agreement or disagreement with the content presented affects their willingness to read or engage with it [55, 59, 74]. This is a tough sell, as most people prefer agreeable content most of the time [42, 53]. When people encounter content that challenges their own position, people may downvote it [10, 40], request fact-checks [36], or actively avoid it [20, 23]. This tendency to avoid disagreeable content raises questions about whether, when people do participate in discussions that feature positions contrary to their own, they are more likely to go off topic or introduce new topics, i.e., be less coherent.

In this paper, we extend this line of work to explore how curating comments around particular positions on a policy issue might affect new posters' willingness not just to reply but to reply coherently, increasing the chance that their comment furthers the discussion. We present results from an experiment that asked Amazon Mechanical Turk (AMT) crowd workers ("Turkers") to consider a proposed policy amendment to the AMT participation agreement to offer *partial payment* for rejected work. This proposal was presented in the context of an online discussion where comments were curated to prioritize arguments *for* or *against* the policy. We collected participants' initial positions of *support* or *opposition* to the policy as well as their comments and examined how agreement with the position in the curated comments correlated with their own comments' coherence with existing topics.

Overall, participants were less likely to add comments that cohere with existing discussion topics when the thread curation disagreed with their initial perspective. However, this was largely driven by people who disagreed with the proposed partial payment policy, who were especially unlikely to contribute comments that cohere with existing topics when seeing a thread that prioritized support for partial payment. By contrast, people who agreed with the proposed partial payment policy were more likely to add topic-coherent comments regardless of whether the curated comments were for or against partial payment. This *asymmetric* relationship between comment curation and coherence with opposition in a policy discussion suggests that designers of both discussions and discussion forums need to consider factors beyond whether a person agrees with a particular position when considering how to support effective participation.

COHERENCE AND CURATION IN POLICY DISCUSSIONS
In a discussion, topics advance as participants reply and respond to each other along a common thread of subjects [4, 27, 67]. In this context of analysis, coherence is a function of how recent comments remain on the same topics introduced by the existing comments, which "seed" the discussion [67]. Without a coherent discussion of the pros and cons of a policy topic, it is impossible for a deliberating group to carefully weigh a policy issue [6, 26, 66].

Policy deliberation scholars have developed a few research methods for studying how groups of people talk with each other during a discussion about policy or civic issues [4]. For example, the Discourse Quality Index (DQI) is a communication coding scheme that is used to understand a policy discussion in terms of the *speeches* that people make during a discussion and how others might respond (e.g., with interruptions, counter-argument, or incivility) [65]. While the DQI is useful for studying the range of positions and level of respect during a policy discussion, a single speech may incorporate multiple topics to present a cohesive argument.

As an alternative, policy deliberation scholar Stromer-Galley [66, pg. 9] has developed a communication coding scheme to study policy discourse at the *thought* level of analysis: *A thought is defined as an utterance (from a single sentence to multiple sentences) that expresses an idea on a topic. A change in topic signaled a change in thought.* Stromer-Galley and Martinson [67] expand on the definition of topic, to characterize thoughts that add new topics to the discussion, versus thoughts that address the materials that establish the policy issue discussion (called "structuring topics") or thoughts that address topics that emerge through the ongoing exchange (called "interactional topics"). Stromer-Galley and Martinson [67, pg. 201-205] apply what they refer to as a *dynamic topic analysis* to measure *coherence* with the interactional topics, by tracking whether new thoughts add to or divert from topics already seeded in the discussion.

We chose these methods of characterizing and measuring coherence for multiple reasons. First, Stromer-Galley [66] has been applied in research revealing a lack of coherence in online discussion forums [28, 31]. Second, we found that the analytic granularity of distinguishing between coherence with the structural versus interactional topics was useful in our experimental design, which controls both the structuring and available interaction topics in the seeded discussion thread. Third, when people do post their thoughts to an online discussion forum, they are often in the form of comment(s), which felt closer to Stromer-Galley's definition of a thought than the DQI's notion of delivering a speech.

Coherence is one of a much broader set of concerns around deliberative discussion [4]. In this paper, we zoom in on coherence with the interactional topics because *talking-with*, and not *-past*, others in discussion is a fundamental precursor to deliberation [6, 26, 33] that is rare in online discussions [12, 64, 72], even more so when people disagree [42].

Curation and Disagreement
Disagreement is useful for small group and public decision-making. To quote John Stuart Mill's argument for why groups should not ignore opposition, *"If the opinion is right, they are deprived of the opportunity of exchanging error for truth; if wrong, they lose what is almost as great a benefit, the clearer perception and livelier impression of truth produced by its collision with error"* [50]. However, the individual experience of disagreement in a group can lead to feelings of threat [22, 42, 63], and people's reactions to these feelings can negatively affect the group [51, 41, 69]. This tension between value to group and threat to individual arises in a number of computer supported cooperative work (CSCW) contexts where people conflict with each other [19].

One potential lever designers have to manage disagreement and encourage engagement is comment curation: they can choose which comments are displayed, when, and in what order. Common strategies include showing the most recent comments, the most popular comments, and recommending personalized comments people would prefer to read [1, 53]. Many of these strategies, notably the popularity-based and personalized algorithms, tend to give people more of what they already like [57].

In this article we examine how coherence in an online policy discussion is affected by curating the discussion to promote either pro or con statements about a policy [40, 53]. Thread curation is particularly important when there are many [40] (and redundant [35]) comments in the discussion. In a policy context, thread curation can also be applied as a civic engagement lever to expose people to different views of an issue [42, 37, 52, 70, 64].

However, there is a tension in just how much opposition to present [53] and how its presentation affects a person's willingness to express their view [55, 59, 74]. This is especially risky for curation strategies that favor one side of a position over another, as might happen when trying to choose comments based on agreement or disagreement with a given participant's position, or to ensure that a particular view is heard. Further, even position-neutral strategies such as chronological order might naturally lead to situations where the discussion appears to be tilted toward one side or another, simply because the most recent subset of comments tend to agree [40].

Curation and Cognitive Dissonance

Managing the amount of disagreement present in a curated comment thread is important because it is easy for people to avoid disagreement online [42]. While online discussion can provide people with an opportunity to form community around shared values [15, 30], properties of digital environments also enable people to stay silent among the "invisible audience" of a policy discussion [5, 25, 60].

There are various reasons why people remain silent in the face of opposition. When a person's views are challenged they can experience *cognitive dissonance*, which can be unsettling and elicit an avoidance response [20, 23, 54], as people generally prefer not to be challenged [53]. Many people also feel unable to argue their positions, either due to a lack of training in argumentation, lack of leisure to study a particular policy matter [33, 63], or social risks of stating a position publicly [56, 64, 69].

These factors can discourage engagement with discussion topics when people see opposition in the thread, but might also encourage alternate forms of engagement that actively avoid or reduce the dissonance, such as by up/down voting comments [10, 40] or issuing fact-check requests [36]. Coe et al. discuss how people use such lightweight discussion system features in place of explicit disagreement: *"[...] users often used this thumbs up/down metric in place of expressing explicit agreement/disagreement within the text of a comment."* [10, pg. 676]

This leaves open the question of when people do add a comment to a discussion thread that prioritizes views counter to their own, whether their tendency toward avoidance translates to responses that are less coherent with the existing discussion. Drawing on cognitive dissonance theory, we argue that participating in a comment thread prioritizing "agreeable" content [53] will be more pleasant [20, 23] than one that presents disagreement, and that people will be more willing and able to coherently engage an existing discussion that is on comfortable, familiar ground. Further, we would expect people who disagree to tend to change the topic in order to reduce conflict between the expressed positions and their own.

Hypothesis: *Contributions to a policy discussion are more likely to cohere when participants are exposed to a thread that prioritizes comments that match their initial position.*

METHOD

We examine the relationship between comment curation, level of agreement, and coherence in an online policy discussion via an experiment with Turkers participating in a policy discussion about the AMT participation agreement.

Interface Design

We used a discussion forum interface modeled after RegulationRoom, a platform for civic engagement in public policy-making [61]. The interface included two panels: a summary of the AMT Participation Agreement and proposals to amend

it on the left, and the comment discussion thread with a comment box on the right (Figure 1). Like RegulationRoom, the interface did not include *up/down* voting or other lightweight mechanisms for engaging with the content as our focus was specifically on topical coherence of comments rather than other behaviors.

To set basic interface design elements we first prototyped the interface. We varied the placement of the comment text box (above or below the discussion thread) and the length of the discussion thread (short, with 3 seeded comments, or long, with 20 seeded comments that required scrolling) and tested these design variations in a pilot HIT.

A total of 408 Turkers accepted the pilot HIT, of whom 292 completed it (72%). Participants averaged 35 years old and about half identified as female; about 80% were U.S.-based. Participants were randomly assigned to one of the four conditions varying the comment box position and the discussion thread length. Participants were more likely to enter a comment when exposed to the longer discussion thread (OR 9.914, $p < 0.001$). We found no effect of the comment box position on the likelihood to enter a comment. We decided to place the comment text box below the thread (as in Figure 1) based on eye-tracking research about how people read and skim articles online [18] with the hope that it would increase the likelihood of reading and engaging with other comments.

Materials

We developed the policy information presented in the discussion interface based on a summary of the AMT Participation Agreement around rejected "Human Intelligence Tasks" (HITs) posted by Requesters. A key concern for Turkers is whether a Requester accepts their work on a HIT [47], as the AMT Participation Agreement grants this power to Requesters with no recourse for workers.

We chose this specific policy topic because it has a direct impact on Turkers' everyday lives [46, 32, 34, 47] and therefore increases the ecological validity of the study. Based on suggestions by Turkers in a prior study [47], we proposed two changes to the policy. In the first, *partial payment*, Turkers would be paid for parts of the work that were considered acceptable by the Requester. In the second, *second chance*, Turkers would have the opportunity to fix their errors in a rejected HIT.

We constructed the experiment so that the policy summary material (left pane of Figure 1) presented both partial payment and second chance; however, the comments that were seeded into the discussion thread (right pane) were exclusively about partial payment. We did this because there was more disagreement about the partial payment proposal, and because by focusing the discussion topics on partial payment, we were able to easily identify when new topics or structuring topics, like second chance, were introduced to the discussion.

To populate the discussion thread, we selected 20 comments contributed in the prior study [49], half in favor of and half opposed to partial payment. We then chose three comments pro- and three anti-partial payment as the focus comments that would be initially visible, according to the experimental

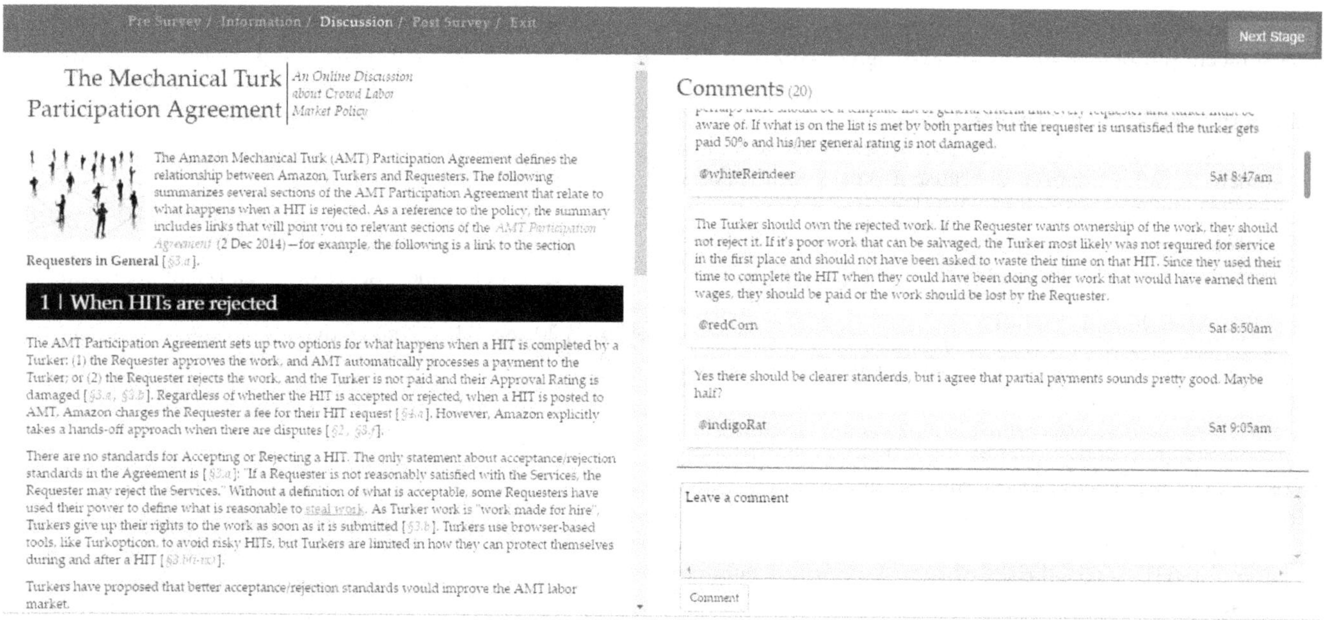

Figure 1. The experiment interface, showing the policy summary on the left and the discussion thread on the right. The three comments that are initially visible and closest to the textbox are controlled to be either pro- or anti- the partial payment proposal.

condition. We added timestamps to make the discussion look recent and assigned pseudonyms (a concatenated color and animal, e.g., @blueMonkey) to each seed comment.

Participants and Recruitment

The HIT description recruited Turkers to test the user interface of a new online discussion forum platform. To attract viewpoints from a broad audience of Turkers, we did not restrict access to the HIT (e.g., to Turkers from specific countries or with specific levels of experience).

A total of 201 Turkers accepted the HIT, with 147 completing it (73%). On average, participants were 36 years old, about half identified as female, and 77% were U.S.-based. Turkers were paid $3 for their participation; the average time to completion was 17 minutes, resulting in a pay rate of about $10 per hour, a bit above the local state minimum wage. This payment structure adheres to the *WeAreDynamo* guidelines for Fair Payment in Academic Research[1].

Procedure

Upon accepting the HIT, participants were presented with a pre-survey that asked about their Turking experience, variables we used as controls in our quantitative analyses. They were also directed to select a pseudonym similar to those in the seed comments, using a random name generator that concatenated colors with animal names, e.g., *@blueMonkey*.

Prior to entering the discussion interface, participants were informed that the discussion would be "about what happens when a HIT is rejected" and that as part of the experience they will "have an opportunity to take part in the discussion." We informed participants that the intent is to help resolve a lack

[1] http://wiki.wearedynamo.org/index.php/Guidelines_for_Academic_Requesters

of consensus among Turkers around the proposals that was observed in prior research [47]. They were asked to rate their initial position toward the two policy proposals on separate 5-item scales, from strongly disagree to strongly agree.

Participants were then placed in the discussion forum. They were able (but not required) to read a summary presentation of the relevant part of the AMT Participation Agreement and a description of the policy options, read a set of comments seeded in the simulated discussion, and add comments of their own. Participants were required to spend a minimum of one minute in the experiment interface; the average dwell time was 4.9 minutes (SD 3.6).

Curation Conditions

Each participant was randomly assigned to one of the following two conditions, each presenting the same twenty seeded comments, but sorted so that the first three comments emphasized different views toward *partial payment* (PP).

- *Pro-PP*: Three seed comments ordered closest to the comment text box presented support for partial payment.

- *Anti-PP*: Three seed comments ordered closest to the comment text box presented opposition to partial payment.

The specific comments for each condition are presented in Table 1. We randomized the order of the three comments to control for order effects and separately randomized the order of the other seventeen comments. We realize that binary categorizations as pro and anti (or agreement and disagreement) are simplifications, and that real policy discussion and positions are often more complicated. However, most prior research and many real discussion contexts do have this binary flavor, so we adopt it as well; we will return to it in the discussion.

The curated comments for each condition were selected because they share not only a similar position (Pro- or Anti-PP), but to the extent possible, similar topics in the discussion. The Pro-PP comments relate to the Partial Payment Amount (Topic 4 in our analysis; see *Coding for Topic Coherence*). The Anti-PP comments relate to the Hands-Off Labor Market (Topic 5).

While the comments are different in their position on partial payment and topic, we did not control for other characteristics of the comments (e.g., character length, expressiveness). Without an *a priori* argument about how positions on questions about the AMT participation agreement would affect Turker responses, we chose to expose Turker participants to these positions in the unaltered words of other Turkers.

Ethical considerations

Tasking AMT Turkers to discuss topics related to the AMT Participation Agreement is a familiar research context for studying systems that support policy engagement and deliberation [37, 38, 49, 62]. While this context is convenient, it requires Turkers to respond to their unequal economic position in the AMT labor market [32, 34, 47]. Unlike traditional labor markets, it is not clear how to address crowd work labor disputes through existing regulatory authorities [22], and unlike other social platforms (e.g., Reddit [8]), Turkers are not well positioned to effect change in AMT [62]. Performing research in this experimental context therefore has special ethical circumstances that need to be considered.

We received IRB-approved informed consent from all participants and compensated their time based on Turker approved standards for academic research [62]. We also implemented several Turker-supported best practices for HIT design [48], as it is important to remember that Turkers participate as part of a *task* they perform for a *reward*. In addition to taking these measures to treat participants *fairly*, we also worked with the community manager at *TurkerNation* [46] to develop the specific policy language for the study to make the content of the policy proposals relevant and engaging to the participating Turkers. Finally, we indicated that our research group is not associated with Amazon and that the purpose of the experiment was purely for research.

DATA ANALYSIS

Coding for Topic Coherence

The twenty seed comments were chosen to cover six topics identified based on 1092 Turker comments from a prior study [47] using an affinity diagramming analysis process:

1. *HIT Design*: Unclear instructions or acceptance standards and technical errors should result in partial payment

2. *Requester Communication*: Lack of Requester-to-Turker communication

3. *Turker Quality*: Low quality Turker work should not be paid (e.g., completed too quickly, robot accounts)

4. *Partial Payment Amount*: Proposes an amount or scheme for implementing partial payment (e.g., 10%, 25%, 50%)

5. *Hands-Off Labor Market*: Amazon's "hands-off" approach to the labor market (e.g., partial payment could lead to more rejections or low quality work)

6. *HIT Specific Policies*: Different protocols for different tasks (e.g., Turkers should own or receive a base payment for rejected creative work)

To identify when a comment made by a participant cohered with topics in the discussion, we used a coding scheme based on Stromer-Galley's definition of topic coherence [66, 67]. Two coders independently categorized each comment as either "new topic" or assigned a set of Topic ID numbers (1-6) identifying the topics referenced by a comment. The two coders trained initially with a set of 95 comments, resolving disagreements during the training period. Training continued until the Cohen's Kappa score for inter-rater reliability was above 0.8 and then the coding was tested on a holdout set of 95 comments. The final Cohen's Kappa score was 0.85.

The following is a sample participant comment from the current study that coheres with Topic 4 (Partial Payment Amount): "*I think partial payment should be more like 85% rather than 10%. If you only get 10% for partial payment, then I'd probably rather just redo the HIT.*" [P69][2]

As an example of a comment that *did not* cohere with the seeded comments: "*I liked the idea of a second chance better than partial payment. I would like the chance to fix my mistake (if I make one). I'm honest. When I answer surveys, I read every question. I don't randomly just choose answers.*" [P14] This comment does not address the seeded topics, as it raises the *second chance* proposal which was excluded from the discussion thread. The response is somewhat related to Topic 3 (Turker Quality), though it does not speak to the specific concern that offering partial payment encourages low quality work. Unlike the prior example, the response does not provide any contextual markers that connect it to any existing interaction topic, such as the brief comparison of *10%* vs. *85%* that indicates that the prior comment coheres with Topic 4.

Metrics

Response Variable

The response variable used the above coding scheme to examine if a comment coheres with topics in the discussion or not.

- *Coherence (relating to existing topics)*: A hand-coded binary variable at the comment level capturing whether the comment coheres to one of the six topics addressed by the existing seeded comments.

Independent Variables

Independent variables were based on the experimental conditions and initial survey responses to the partial payment proposal.

- *Curation Condition (Pro-PP, Anti-PP)*: Captures whether participants were exposed to a discussion prioritizing comments that were pro- or anti-partial payment.

---

[2]Comments are associated with a unique identifier of the participant ranging from P1 to P147.

Pro-Partial Payment Condition	Anti-Partial Payment Condition
#995: *"I mean, for work of creative nature, a base pay should be fixed. If the requester keeps and uses the work, he should pay more."*	#976: *"No. Turker won't get any partial payment. If he completes the hit with prescribed instructions ,then he will get full pay otherwise rejection."*
#1094: *"perhaps there should be a template list of general criteria that every requester and turker must be aware of. If what is on the list is met by both parties but the requester is unsatisfied the turker gets paid 50% and his/her general rating is not damaged."*	#1119: *"Allowing partial payment is a slippery slope, since some requesters would simply reject and give partial pay to almost everyone, citing the quality of their responses or whatever. What we need is real moderation from Amazon when there's real abuse of the system, instead of telling us it's between us and the requester and not their problem."*
#1136: *"I believe that Turkers should receive atleast 25% of the task (if less than $5.00) or 10% (if more than $5.00) if it is rejected. However, they would need to have atleast shown effort and not just sped through the task. I've spent quite some time on a few tasks only to be rejected for something that was not clearly stated in the rules or was completely false. I believe their should atleast be an appeal system."*	#1342: *"There should absolutely be clearer standards for rejecting hits and those standards should be put forth to the worker up front. Workers should be able to discuss why the hit was rejected and also able to make a case for any problem or mistake made. Unless the requester can prove that a worker was clearly just hurrying through I think a rejected work should be paid in full. If we start accepting partial payments for rejected work it will lead to requesters looking for anything to reject and then paying less than they had advertised. It could be a sticky downward spiral."*

Table 1. Comments selected to emphasize alternate views toward *partial payment* (PP) in the thread curation experimental conditions.

- *Initial Position (Support, Neutral, Oppose)*: Participants who rated their position toward partial payment as strongly agree or agree were coded as *support*; those who rated as strongly disagree or disagree were coded as *oppose*; others were coded as *neutral*.

For modeling "simple agreement" (see Table 4) we combine the Curation Condition with Initial Position into a single Matching Preference variable.

- *Matching Preference (True, False)*: Captures whether the participant's Initial Position matched the Curation Condition (i.e., Support x Pro-PP or Opposed x Anti-PP). For this analysis of simple agreement, we removed participants with a "Neutral" view.

Control Variables
At the participant level, we controlled for participants' self-efficacy, geographic location, and their past experience with rejections.

- *Self-efficacy*: Eight scale items of generalized self-efficacy and confidence in one's own abilities and skills [9] were averaged into a single measure (Cronbach's $\alpha = 0.93$). In prior research, newcomers to an online policy discussion with high assessments of their own self-efficacy contributed comments that were longer and more responsive to the policy topics [49].[3]

- *Country*: A binary variable coded as 1 for United States-based participants and 0 for others.

[3]We chose to use generalized self-efficacy as opposed to a context specific self-efficacy measure because research shows feelings of ability can translate across contexts [2]. Further, our task required multiple specific self-efficacy constructs (e.g., reading efficacy, writing efficacy, political efficacy); if we were to choose one, it is unclear which would be the most appropriate to measure, and measuring several would introduce extra burden on participants.

- *Rejected HITs*: In the pre-discussion survey, participants estimated the total number of HITs they have had rejected. We centered and standardized this variable, such that a one unit increase in Rejected HITs reflects a one standard deviation increase in the variable.

At the comment level, we controlled for comment length.

- *Total Words*: Total number of words in a comment, centered and standardized in the same way as Rejected HITs.

Statistical Models
As some participants made multiple comments, we treated *participant* as a mixed-effects nesting variable to account for non-independence. Mixed-effects logistic regressions were used to predict topic coherence at the comment level, as a binomial distribution was appropriate for the binary response variable. Model-level significance was evaluated using the log-likelihood ratio test, the Akaike Information Criterion (AIC), and the Bayesian Information Criterion (BIC).

The model coefficients are interpreted as the expected change that each independent variable contributes to the logits of the response variable. In the findings we exponentiate the logits to present the odds ratios. Odds ratios can be interpreted as the change in the response variable expected from a one-unit increase to an independent variable, holding others constant.

However, when evaluating the effect of an interaction, the coefficient estimated for the interaction is added to the main effect of the interacted variable. The combined effect of the interaction can then be exponentiated to present the effect as an odds ratio, i.e., exp(*main effect + interacted effect*). After a model is fit to the data, the model can be used to estimate the expected likelihood of the dependent variable at various levels and combinations of the coefficients—these expected values are in terms of predicted marginal means. We use a Tukey-based pairwise comparison of the expected marginal

Participation	Count
Accepted HITs	201
Completed HITs	147
Commented	139
Total Comments	155
Control Variables	
Self-Efficacy (*Mean, SD*)	2.7 (0.46)
Country: US-based (*Count, Percent*)	122 (82.9%)
Rejected HITs (*Mean, SD*)	84.54 (258.43)
Total Words (*Mean, SD*)	296.8 (239.41)
Initial Positions for Partial Payment	*# Participants*
Support	53 (33.1%)
Neutral	39 (28.1%)
Oppose	55 (38.6%)

Table 2. Descriptive statistics capturing participation in the experiment, control characteristics, and details about participant initial position for partial payment prior to the discussion stage of the experiment.

	Pro-PP	*Anti-PP*	*Total*
Participants	74	73	147
Total Comments	81	74	155
Coherent	38	34	72

Table 3. Descriptive statistics capturing the count of participants, comments, and coherent comments in each curation condition (Pro-PP, Anti-PP). Almost 95% of participants contributed a comment.

means to examine the interactions within the models (using a 95% confidence interval).

FINDINGS

Descriptive Overview

Table 2 presents the descriptive statistics for the study. As part of our question is whether initial position might influence behavior, we first confirm that the distribution of initial positions was not significantly different between the curation conditions: $\chi^2(2, 147) = 3.013$, $p = 0.2217$.

Table 3 reports the number of participants, comments, and coherent comments by condition. Although the task instructions explicitly did not require participants to leave a comment, most participants did so, with just under half cohering with existing topics (46.4%). We found no significant difference in the likelihood to make a comment by condition: $\chi^2(1, 147) = 1.9e\text{-}29$, $p = 1$. Therefore, we focus on the likelihood to cohere with the existing topics within the discussion thread.

Agreeing with Curated Position Increased Coherence

The data support our hypothesis that presenting participants with content that matches their initial position increases the likelihood of contributions that cohere with the existing discussion topics. Comments made by participants whose initial position matched the curation condition were 2.970 times more likely to cohere with the existing discussion ($p < 0.05$, see Table 4). This mirrors HCI research about recommending content that is agreeable [53] and similar to what a user already likes [1, 57].

	Coherence	
	Est (SE)	*OR*
Curation Condition and Initial Positions		
(Intercept)	-2.691 (1.54)	0.067 .
Matching Preference	1.088 (0.44)	2.970 *
Control characteristics		
Self-Efficacy	0.691 (0.54)	1.995
Country: International	-0.338 (0.57)	0.713
Rejected HITs	-0.328 (0.71)	0.720
Total Words	0.408 (0.18)	1.503 *
Log likelihood	-70.02 (df=7)	

Table 4. Fixed-effects logistic regression predicting the likelihood that participants will engage specific seeded discussion topics when their expressed preference matches the curation condition (i.e., *Pro-PP x Support*, *Anti-PP x Opposed*).
p-value significance: *** 0.001; ** 0.01; * 0.05; . 0.1;

Opposed Positions were Overall Less Coherent

However, the significant *Intercept* in Table 4 and relatively weak significance of the *Matching Preference* covariate indicate that the model is missing a good deal of variance. Thus, we next examine a model that distinguishes between participants' initial positions (Table 5). This analysis shows that beyond agreement or disagreement, initial position matters. Participants *Opposed* to partial payment were significantly less likely to post responses that cohere with the discussion topics than those who *Support* it (OR = 0.173, $p < 0.01$). Further, *Opposed* participants in the Anti-PP condition, who see comments they agree with, were significantly more likely to cohere than in Pro-PP: exp(-1.753 + 2.224) = 1.600 OR ($p < 0.01$). This finding aligns with the primary argument, that agreement and coherence go hand in hand, although initial position also helps predict coherence.

Effects of Initial Position were Asymmetrical

Because interaction effects where there are multiple levels can be tricky to evaluate, we next applied a Tukey-based pairwise comparison of each of the variable levels (e.g., comparing coherence likelihood between initial Neutral and Support positions, while keeping the curation condition fixed at Anti-PP). Figure 2 graphically depicts the analysis as a predicted marginal means interaction plot between discussion curation (Pro-PP and Anti-PP) and initial position for partial payment (Support, Neutral, Oppose).

Two main points emerge out of this analysis. First, the Pro-PP curation condition generated significantly more *coherent* contributions from those with *Neutral* or *Support* initial positions compared to those *Opposed*, 7.054 times ($p < 0.01$) and 5.292 times, ($p < 0.05$) respectively, while the Anti-PP curation condition did not show this difference. Second, the main driver of this effect is those with an *Opposed* initial position, as their contributions were significantly less likely to cohere, by 0.228 times ($p < 0.01$) in the Pro-PP condition versus Anti-PP. This difference between the conditions does not occur in other cases.

DISCUSSION, IMPLICATIONS, AND LIMITATIONS

At a high level, the findings confirm our hypotheses that curating a discussion thread to match a participant's preferences

	Coherence	
	Est (SE)	OR
Curation Condition		
(Intercept)	-1.215 (1.26)	0.296
Anti-PP	-0.850 (0.60)	0.427
Initial Position for Partial Payment		
Neutral	0.208 (0.65)	1.232
Opposed	-1.753 (0.64)	0.173 **
Control characteristics		
Self-Efficacy	0.615 (0.42)	1.850
Country: International	-0.597 (0.53)	0.550
Rejected HITs	-0.568 (0.76)	0.566
Total Words	0.443 (0.17)	1.557 **
Interaction (Curation Condition x Initial Position)		
Anti-PP x Neutral	0.043 (0.92)	1.286
Anti-PP x Opposed	2.224 (0.85)	1.600 **
Log likelihood	-94.41 (df=10)	

Table 5. Fixed-effects logistic regression predicting the likelihood that participant responses will cohere with specific seeded discussion topics. Initial Position terms are by comparison to *Support* for partial payment and Curation features are by comparison to the *Pro-PP* condition, both of which are baselines in the Intercept. The odds ratios reflect the exponentiation of the estimates for each feature.
p-value significance: * 0.001; ** 0.01; * 0.05; . 0.1;**

increases the likelihood of contributions that cohere with the existing discussion. This observation extends existing research about how people prefer content that agrees with their preferences [42, 53, 57], by demonstrating how curation can affect whether new contributions cohere with or diverge from the existing discussion. However, the effect of comment curation and participant preference was asymmetrical: people who support partial payment were much more likely to engage coherently with the conversation when they saw comments curated to present the Anti-PP position, compared to people opposed to partial payment who saw the Pro-PP curation condition.

This observation implies that curating primarily for position consistency led us (and presumably, will lead others) to downplay other aspects of comments and contributors that might affect people's coherent engagement with diverse perspectives on a policy issue. For instance, Munson and Resnick found that reaction to individual items in a curated list of news articles depended not only on that single item but also on the others surrounding it [53]. Moving towards implementation, the discussion platform *ConsiderIt* [37] allows an individual user to adopt a variety of arguments both for and against any given policy decision.

This brings back to our choice of binarizing positions and comments on the policy into a pro versus anti framing, as such work shows how, in practice, reactions rarely occur in response to a single, isolated policy proposal. (Indeed, for that reason we originally planned to examine both second chance and partial payment rather than focusing on just one proposal. However, that plan was ultimately discarded, both due to the complexity of the analysis and the limited comparability to prior work.)

Taken together, these results and work suggest that research and design around engaging with disagreement would benefit

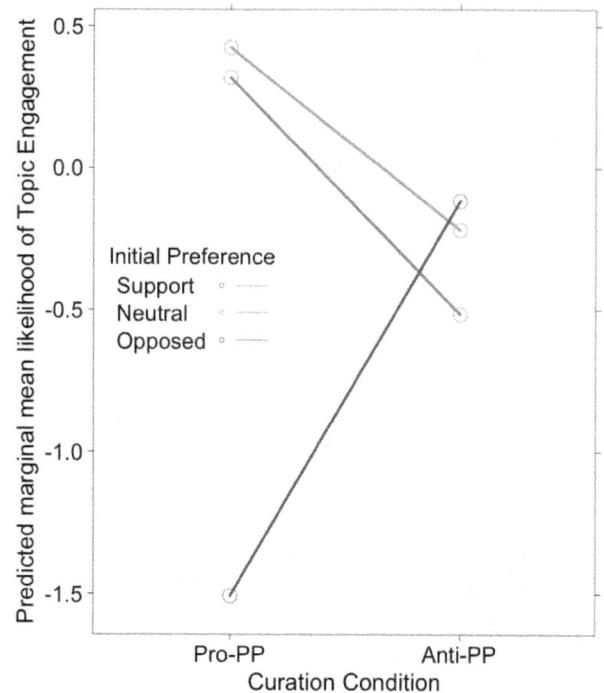

Figure 2. Predicted marginal means interaction plot between discussion curation (Pro-PP and Anti-PP) and initial position for partial payment (Support, Neutral, Oppose). Linear predictions are given on a log scale and reflect the estimated probability of a topic engagement.

from more nuanced views and analyses of how and why people agree or disagree with the positions proposed. Tools such as ConsiderIt, or argument analysis techniques from the area of natural language processing, could lead in fruitful directions for better supporting contentious policy discussions.

Curating for openness rather than agreement?
Our results also raise an important caveat around comment curation: curating comments risks systematically excluding viewpoints. The general versions of this are familiar: popularity tends to curate for and perpetuate majority opinion; personalization tends to curate for agreement, which may increase engagement but primarily with like-minded people [57]. In our case, although people in all conditions were equally likely to contribute a comment, people who were Opposed to partial payment were much less likely to cohere with the current discussion (especially when presented with Pro-PP arguments)—and contributions seen as off-topic are often ignored.

In this experiment, one possible driver of the asymmetry was a difference in the specificity of the featured Pro-PP and Anti-PP comments. Pro-PP was more specific around implementation decisions—i.e., setting the right level of partial payment—while Anti-PP comments were more general, describing how the partial payment proposal would have damaging effects on workers by giving HIT Requesters more room to reject requests.

We posit a parallel to how high fidelity interface prototypes tend to elicit comments about specific design elements, versus napkin sketches that give more room for considering the overall interaction [7]. Proposals that focus attention on specific implementation details will tend to concentrate attention on those details, arguably leaving less room for coherent discussion on topics where there is disagreement than more open discussions of the policy context. Opponents seeing Pro-PP curation may also have felt like they were joining the planning committee for a distasteful proposal—an unlikely scenario for effective, coherent contributions—while supporters seeing Anti-PP curation may have felt like their opinion on the issue still contributed to its deliberation.

In an attempt to integrate topic coherence [67] with common definitions of deliberation, such as careful weighing of diverse perspectives [6, 26, 66], we suggest that discussion and deliberation moderators might want to encourage (support) coherent disagreement: *a thread of comments that consistently contribute to a careful weighing of differing perspectives on a topic.* Designing to support coherent disagreement might imply highlighting content that leaves more room for debate (just as good interviewers, and bad lawyers, ask open-ended questions). How well this strategy for promoting coherent disagreement would work is an open question—choosing a controlled, one-shot experiment on one topic means we cannot make strong claims to generality or ecological validity—as is the question of what properties of a comment would invite openness.

Still, the idea has potential and is worth further study, both at the level of individual comments and of groups of them. Online discussion moderation means managing a stream of comments, often one at a time [14, 39, 40], or engaging specific comments to learn more about the experience of specific commenters [61, 21]. Supporting coherent disagreement might mean curating (or moderating) sets of comments based on characteristics of the group: expressing a range of positions, possessing topical coherence as a group, affording overall openness to discussion, representing a diversity of stakeholders, and so on.

Changing curation strategies and metrics over time
Another consideration is that the goals of a deliberation change over time—and another reading of the curated comments in this study is that the Pro-PP condition presented the deliberation as farther along than the Anti-PP condition. As the state of a deliberation transitions from investigating a common problem, to eliciting a range of potential ideas, to critiquing the ideas and refining them into a single proposal, each transition starts to impose constraints on the discussion topics. Thus, the discussion naturally tends to narrow through proposal development, making it harder to make coherent contributions, especially for those who disagree with the fundamental approach rather than with some implementation detail.

The shifting nature of policy discussion and deliberation group tasks over time suggest that curation strategies and metrics should likely change with them. We focused on coherence in this paper because it is understudied [24] and because *talking-with* the existing discussion is a common value in many policy

discussions [12]. However, our measure of coherence is only appropriate for some goals. In our definition, the opposite of being coherent was not "incoherent", but could include introducing novel topics and ideas; such divergent thinking has real value at many stages of many group processes [17, 16].

More generally, work around curation—including this paper—has tended to focus on the specific problem of curation to support engagement with disagreement. This is an important problem to be sure, but is a small part of a much wider range of deliberation desiderata [6, 26, 33]. One might curate (or moderate) for many of these values, including civility and quality [68], soliciting both objective and subjective descriptions [45], supporting both social and task processes [26], eliciting both logical arguments and situated experiences and stories [58, 61], and so on. Curating for disagreement might come at the expense of other goals such as civility, social affect, or solidarity; putting disagreement at the center leaves these other important concerns at the margin.

CONCLUSION
Online discussions about policy are shaped by the ways that contributors dynamically add to, expand on, or divert attention away from existing topics in the discussion. Here we operationalize this dynamic by measuring coherence with the interactional topics in an online discussion, and predict higher levels of coherence when participants are exposed to a comment thread that prioritizes positions of the policy that match their own preference. However, we observed an asymmetric relationship between preference and curation, which implies that curating primarily for or against consistency with a poster's current position may overlook other important aspects of comments, including their openness to coherent deliberation, that might affect people's willingness to engage coherently with diverse perspectives on a policy issue.

ACKNOWLEDGEMENT
We thank Daniel Wu for developing the infrastructure for this research and Sara Chau for her support through the analysis. Thanks also to Kristy Milland and the Cornell eRulemaking Initiative (CeRI) team for their support developing the policy context for the AMT Participation Agreement discussion. This work is supported by NSF HCC 1314778.

REFERENCES
1. Lars Backstrom, Jon Kleinberg, Lillian Lee, and Cristian Danescu-Niculescu-Mizil. 2013. Characterizing and curating conversation threads: Expansion, focus, volume, re-entry. In *Proceedings of the sixth ACM international conference on Web search and data mining*. ACM, New York, NY, 13–22. DOI: http://dx.doi.org/10.1145/2433396.2433401

2. Albert Bandura. 1997. *Self-efficacy: The exercise of control.* W. H. Freeman and Company, New York, NY.

3. Laura W. Black. 2012. Blog, chat, edit, text, or tweet? Using online tools to advance adult civic engagement. *New Directions for Adult and Continuing Education* 2012, 135 (2012), 71–79.

4. Laura W Black, Stephanie Burkhalter, John Gastil, and Jennifer Stromer-Galley. 2010. Methods for analyzing and measuring group deliberation. *Sourcebook of political communication research: Methods, measures, and analytical techniques* (2010), 323–345.

5. danah boyd. 2007. Why youth (heart) social network sites: The role of networked publics in teenage social life. *MacArthur foundation series on digital learning–Youth, identity, and digital media volume* (2007), 119–142.

6. Stephanie Burkhalter, John Gastil, and Todd Kelshaw. 2002. A conceptual definition and theoretical model of public deliberation in small face-to-face groups. *Communication Theory* 12, 4 (2002), 398–422.

7. Bill Buxton. 2010. *Sketching user experiences: getting the design right and the right design.* Morgan Kaufmann.

8. Alissa Centivany and Bobby Glushko. 2016. Popcorn astes good: Participatory policymaking and Reddit's amageddon. In *Proceedings of the SIGCHI Conference on Human Factors in Computing Systems (CHI16), San Jose, CA.*

9. Gilad Chen, Stanley M. Gully, and Dov Eden. 2001. Validation of a new general self-efficacy scale. *Organizational research* (2001). `http://journals.sagepub.com/doi/abs/10.1177/109442810141004`

10. Kevin Coe, Kate Kenski, and Stephen A. Rains. 2014. Online and uncivil? Patterns and determinants of incivility in newspaper website comments. *Journal of Communication* 64, 4 (8 2014), 658–679. DOI: `http://dx.doi.org/10.1111/jcom.12104`

11. Todd Davies and Reid Chandler. 2011. Online deilberation design: Choices, criteria, and evidence. *Democracy in motion: Evaluating the practice and impact of deliberative civic engagement* (2011), 103–131.

12. Richard Davis. 1999. *The web of politics: The Internet's impact on the American political system.* Oxford University Press.

13. Fiorella De Cindio and Cristian Peraboni. 2010. Design issues for building deliberative digital habitats. *Online Deliberation* (2010), 41.

14. Nicholas Diakopoulos and Mor Naaman. 2011. Topicality, time, and sentiment in online news comments. In *CHI'11 Extended Abstracts on Human Factors in Computing Systems.* 1405–1410.

15. Carl DiSalvo. 2009. Design and the construction of publics. *Design issues* 25, 1 (2009), 48–63.

16. Steven Dow, Julie Fortuna, Dan Schwartz, and Beth Altringer. 2011. Prototyping dynamics: sharing multiple designs improves exploration, group rapport, and results. In *Proceedings of the SIGCHI Conference on Human Factors in Computing Systems.* 2807–2816. `http://dl.acm.org/citation.cfm?id=1979359`

17. Steven Dow, Alana Glassco, Jonathan Kass, Melissa Schwarz, Daniel Schwartz, and Scott Klemmer. 2010.

Parallel prototyping leads to better design results, more divergence, and increased self-efficacy. *ACM Transactions on Computer-Human Interaction (TOCHI)* 17, 4 (2010). `http://dl.acm.org/citation.cfm?id=1879836`

18. Geoffrey B. Duggan and Stephen J. Payne. 2011. Skim reading by satisficing: Evidence from eye tracking. *Proceedings of the SIGCHI Conference on* (2011). `http://dl.acm.org/citation.cfm?id=1979114`

19. Steve M. Easterbrook, Eevi E. Beck, James S. Goodlet, Lydia Plowman, Mike Sharples, and Charles C. Wood. 1993. A survey of empirical studies of conflict. In *CSCW: Cooperation or Conflict?* Springer, 1–68.

20. Andrew J. Elliot and Patricia G. Devine. 1994. On the motivational nature of cognitive dissonance: Dissonance as psychological discomfort. *Journal of personality and social psychology* 67, 3 (1994), 382. `http://psycnet.apa.org/journals/psp/67/3/382/`

21. Dmitry Epstein and Gilly Leshed. 2016. The magic sauce: Practices of facilitation in online policy deliberation. *Journal of Public Deliberation* 12, 1 (2016). `http://www.publicdeliberation.net/jpdhttp://www.publicdeliberation.net/jpd/vol12/iss1/art4`

22. Alek Felstiner. 2011. Working the crowd: Employment and labor law in the crowdsourcing industry. *Berkeley Journal of Employment and Labor Law* (2011), 143–203.

23. Leon Festinger. 1962. *A theory of cognitive dissonance.* Vol. 2. Stanford University Press.

24. Dennis Friess and Christiane Eilders. 2015. A Systematic review of online deliberation research. *Policy & Internet* 7, 3 (9 2015), 319–339. DOI: `http://dx.doi.org/10.1002/poi3.95`

25. Susan R. Fussell and Leslie D. Setlock. 2014. Computer-mediated communication. *The Oxford Handbook of Language and Social Psychology* (2014), 471.

26. John Gastil and Laura Black. 2008. Public deliberation as the organizing principle of political communication research. *Journal of Public Deliberation* 4, 1 (2008).

27. Erving Goffman. 1976. Replies and responses. *Language in society* 5, 03 (1976), 257–313.

28. Todd Graham. 2012. Beyond "political" communicative spaces: Talking politics on the Wife Swap discussion forum. *Journal of Information Technology & Politics* 9, 1 (1 2012), 31–45. DOI: `http://dx.doi.org/10.1080/19331681.2012.635961`

29. Ali Gürkan, Luca Iandoli, Mark Klein, and Giuseppe Zollo. 2010. Mediating debate through on-line large-scale argumentation: Evidence from the field. *Information Sciences* 180, 19 (10 2010), 3686–3702. DOI: `http://dx.doi.org/10.1016/j.ins.2010.06.011`

30. Maarten Hajer. 2003. Policy without polity? Policy analysis and the institutional void. *Policy sciences* 36, 2 (2003), 175–195.

31. Daniel Halpern and Jennifer Gibbs. 2013. Social media as a catalyst for online deliberation? Exploring the affordances of Facebook and YouTube for political expression. *Computers in Human Behavior* 29, 3 (2013), 1159–1168. DOI: http://dx.doi.org/10.1016/j.chb.2012.10.008

32. Lilly C. Irani and M. Silberman. 2013. Turkopticon: Interrupting worker invisibility in Amazon Mechanical Turk. In *Proceedings of the SIGCHI Conference on Human Factors in Computing Systems*. ACM, 611–620. http://dl.acm.org/citation.cfm?id=2470742

33. Christopher F. Karpowitz and Chad Raphael. 2014. *Deliberation, democracy, and civic forums: Improving equality and publicity*. Cambridge University Press.

34. Aniket Kittur, Jeffrey V. Nickerson, Michael Bernstein, Elizabeth Gerber, Aaron Shaw, John Zimmerman, Matt Lease, and John Horton. 2013. The future of crowd work. In *Proceedings of the 2013 conference on Computer supported cooperative work*. 1301–1318.

35. Mark Klein. 2011. How to harvest collective wisdom on complex problems: An introduction to the MIT Deliberatorium. *Center for Collective Intelligence working paper* (2011).

36. Travis Kriplean, Caitlin Bonnar, Alan Borning, Bo Kinney, and Brian Gill. 2014. Integrating on-demand fact-checking with public dialogue. In *Proceedings of the 17th ACM conference on Computer supported cooperative work & social computing - CSCW '14*. ACM Press, New York, New York, USA, 1188–1199. DOI: http://dx.doi.org/10.1145/2531602.2531677

37. Travis Kriplean, Jonathan Morgan, Deen Freelon, Alan Borning, and Lance Bennett. 2012a. Supporting reflective public thought with ConsiderIt. In *Proceedings of the ACM 2012 conference on Computer Supported Cooperative Work*. 265–274.

38. Travis Kriplean, Michael Toomim, Jonathan Morgan, Alan Borning, and Andrew Ko. 2012b. Is this what you meant?: Promoting listening on the web with Reflect. In *Proceedings of the SIGCHI Conference on Human Factors in Computing Systems*. 1559–1568.

39. Cliff Lampe and Paul Resnick. 2004. Slash (dot) and burn: Distributed moderation in a large online conversation space. In *Proceedings of the SIGCHI conference on Human factors in computing systems*. 543–550.

40. Cliff Lampe, Paul Zube, Jusil Lee, Chul Hyun Park, and Erik Johnston. 2014. Crowdsourcing civility: A natural experiment examining the effects of distributed moderation in online forums. *Government Information Quarterly* 31, 2 (4 2014), 317–326. DOI: http://dx.doi.org/10.1016/j.giq.2013.11.005

41. Edward J Lawler. 2001. An affect theory of social exchange1. *Amer. J. Sociology* 107, 2 (2001), 321–352.

42. Azi Lev-On and Bernard Manin. 2009. Happy accidents: Deliberation and on-line exposure to opposing views.

Online deliberation: Design, research and practice (2009), 105–122.

43. Matthew T. Loveland and Delia Popescu. 2011. Democracy on the web. *Information, Communication & Society* 14, 5 (8 2011), 684–703. DOI: http://dx.doi.org/10.1080/1369118X.2010.521844

44. Rousiley C. M. Maia and Thaiane A. S. Rezende. 2016. Respect and disrespect in deliberation across the networked media environment: Examining multiple paths of political talk. *Journal of Computer-Mediated Communication* 21, 2 (3 2016), 121–139. DOI: http://dx.doi.org/10.1111/jcc4.12155

45. Meethu Malu, Nikunj Jethi, and Dan Cosley. 2012. Encouraging personal storytelling by example. *Proceedings of the 2012 iConference* (2012). http://dl.acm.org/citation.cfm?id=2132309

46. David Martin, Benjamin V. Hanrahan, Jacki O'Neill, and Neha Gupta. 2014. Being a Turker. In *Proceedings of the 17th ACM conference on Computer supported cooperative work & social computing*. 224–235.

47. Brian McInnis, Dan Cosley, Chaebong Nam, and Gilly Leshed. 2016a. Taking a HIT: Designing around rejection, mistrust, risk, and workers' experiences in Amazon Mechanical Turk. In *Proceedings of the 2016 CHI Conference on Human Factors in Computing Systems*. 2271–2282.

48. Brian McInnis and Gilly Leshed. 2016. Running user studies with crowd workers. *Interactions* XXIII, 5 (2016), 50. http://dl.acm.org/citation.cfm?id=2968077

49. Brian McInnis, Elizabeth Murnane, Dmitry Epstein, Dan Cosley, and Gilly Leshed. 2016b. One and done: Factors affecting one-time contributors to ad-hoc online communities. In *Proceedings of the 19th ACM Conference on Computer-Supported Cooperative Work & Social Computing*. 609–623.

50. John Stuart Mill. 1975. *On liberty (1859)*. Norton.

51. Richard L. Moreland and John M. Levine. 1982. Socialization in small groups: Temporal changes in individual-group relations. *Advances in experimental social psychology* 15 (1982), 137–192.

52. Sean A. Munson, Stephanie Y. Lee, and Paul Resnick. 2013. Encouraging reading of diverse political Viewpoints with a browser widget. In *ICWSM*. http://dub.uw.edu/djangosite/media/papers/balancer-icwsm-v4.pdf

53. Sean A. Munson and Paul Resnick. 2010. Presenting diverse political opinions: How and how much. In *Proceedings of the SIGCHI conference on human factors in computing systems*. 1457–1466.

54. Diana C. Mutz. 2008. Is deliberative democracy a falsifiable theory? *Annual Review of Political Science* 11, 1 (6 2008), 521–538. DOI: http://dx.doi.org/10.1146/annurev.polisci.11.081306.070308

55. Elmie Nekmat and William J. Gonzenbach. 2013. Multiple opinion climates in online forums: Role of website source reference and within-forum opinion congruency. *Journalism & Mass Communication Quarterly* 90, 4 (2013), 736–756. http://journals. sagepub.com/doi/abs/10.1177/1077699013503162

56. Elisabeth Noelle-Neumann. 1974. The spiral of silence: A theory of public opinion. *Journal of Communication* 24, 2 (1974), 43–51. http://onlinelibrary.wiley.com/ doi/10.1111/j.1460-2466.1974.tb00367.x/full

57. Eli Pariser. 2011. *The filter bubble: What the Internet is hiding from you.* Penguin, UK.

58. Francesca Polletta and John Lee. 2006. Is telling stories good for democracy? Rhetoric in public deliberation after 9/11. *American Sociological Review* 71, 5 (2006), 699–721.

59. Pablo Porten-Cheé and Christiane Eilders. 2015. Spiral of silence online: How online communication affects opinion climate perception and opinion expression regarding the climate change debate. *Studies in Communication Sciences* 15, 1 (2015), 143–150. http://www.sciencedirect.com/science/article/pii/ S1424489615000211

60. Jenny Preece, Blair Nonnecke, and Dorine Andrews. 2004. The top five reasons for lurking: Improving community experiences for everyone. *Computers in human behavior* 20, 2 (2004), 201–223. http://www.sciencedirect.com/science/article/pii/ S0747563203000876

61. Cynthia R. Farina, Dmitry Epstein, Josiah B. Heidt, and Mary J. Newhart. 2013. Regulation Room: Getting "more, better" civic participation in complex government policymaking. *Transforming Government: People, Process and Policy* 7, 4 (2013), 501–516.

62. Niloufar Salehi, Lilly C. Irani, Michael S. Bernstein, Ali Alkhatib, Eva Ogbe, Kristy Milland, and Clickhappier. 2015. We Are Dynamo. In *Proceedings of the 33rd Annual ACM Conference on Human Factors in Computing Systems - CHI '15*. ACM Press, New York, New York, USA, 1621–1630. DOI: http://dx.doi.org/10.1145/2702123.2702508

63. Lynn M. Sanders. 1997. Against deliberation. *Political theory* (1997).

64. Bryan C. Semaan, Scott P. Robertson, Sara Douglas, and Misa Maruyama. 2014. Social media supporting political deliberation across multiple public spheres: Towards depolarization. *Proceedings of the 17th* (2014), 1409–1421. http://dl.acm.org/citation.cfm?id=2531605

65. Marco R. Steenbergen, André Bächtiger, Markus Spörndli, and Jürg Steiner. 2003. Measuring political deliberation: A discourse quality index. *Comparative European Politics* 1, 1 (3 2003), 21–48. DOI: http://dx.doi.org/10.1057/palgrave.cep.6110002

66. Jennifer Stromer-Galley. 2007. Measuring deliberation's content: A coding scheme. *Journal of public deliberation* 3, 1 (2007).

67. Jennifer Stromer-Galley and Anna M. Martinson. 2009. Coherence in political computer-mediated communication: Analyzing topic relevance and drift in chat. *Discourse & Communication* 3, 2 (5 2009), 195–216. DOI: http://dx.doi.org/10.1177/1750481309102452

68. Abhay Sukumaran, Stephanie Vezich, Melanie McHugh, and Clifford Nass. 2011. Normative influences on thoughtful online participation. In *Proceedings of the 2011 annual conference on Human factors in computing systems - CHI '11*. ACM Press, New York, New York, USA, 3401. DOI: http://dx.doi.org/10.1145/1978942.1979450

69. Cass R Sunstein. 2006. Deliberating groups versus prediction markets (or Hayek's challenge to Habermas). *Episteme* 3, 03 (2006), 192–213.

70. W. Ben Towne and James D. Herbsleb. 2012. Design considerations for online deliberation systems. *Journal of Information Technology & Politics* 9, 1 (2012), 97–115.

71. Jing Wang, Clement T. Yu, Philip S. Yu, Bing Liu, and Weiyi Meng. 2012. Diversionary comments under political blog posts. In *Proceedings of the 21st ACM international conference on Information and knowledge management - CIKM '12*. ACM Press, New York, New York, USA, 1789. DOI: http://dx.doi.org/10.1145/2396761.2398518

72. Scott Wright, Todd Graham, and Daniel Jackson. 2016. Third space, social media and everyday political talk. *The Routledge companion to social media and politics. New York: Taylor & Francis* (2016), 74–88.

73. Scott Wright and John Street. 2007. Democracy, deliberation and design: The case of online discussion forums. *New media & society* 9, 5 (2007), 849–869.

74. Thomas Zerback and Nayla Fawzi. 2016. Can online exemplars trigger a spiral of silence? Examining the effects of exemplar opinions on perceptions of public opinion and speaking out. *New Media & Society* (2016). http://nms.sagepub.com/content/early/2016/01/22/ 1461444815625942.abstract

75. Amy X. Zhang, Lea Verou, and David Karger. 2017. Wikum: Bridging discussion forums and wikis using recursive summarization. In *Proceedings of the 2017 ACM Conference on Computer Supported Cooperative Work and Social Computing*. ACM, 2082–2096.

Workshop: Work in the Age of Intelligent Machines

Ingrid Erickson
Syracuse University
Syracuse, NY 13244
imericks@syr.edu

Lionel P. Robert Jr.
University of Michigan
Ann Arbor, MI 48109
lprobert@umich.edu

Kevin Crowston
Syracuse University
Syracuse, NY 13244
crowston@syr.edu

Jeffrey V. Nickerson
Stevens Institute of
Technology
Hoboken, NJ 07030
jnickerson@stevens.edu

ABSTRACT

This all-day workshop aims to promote convergence among its participants on research related to working with intelligent machines. We define intelligent machines as both material (e.g., robots) and immaterial (e.g., algorithms) computing technologies that can be characterized by autonomy, the ability to learn, and the ability to interact with other systems and with humans. The workshop has three goals: identifying specific research problems around work and intelligent machines, developing a common language base that can facilitate interdisciplinary collaboration among researchers, and identifying information and cyber-infrastructure needs to support convergent research. Workshop activities will facilitate interdisciplinary dialogue and strive to generate high-impact research ideas to advance each of these goals.

Author Keywords

work; intelligent machines; research convergence; workshop

ACM Classification Keywords

K.4.2 Social Issues: General; K.4.3 Organizational Impacts: Automation; K.4.1 Public Policy Issues: General

DESCRIPTION OF WORKSHOP THEME

This all-day workshop aims to promote disciplinary convergence among participants on research related to working with intelligent machines. The workshop is sponsored by the newly NSF-funded Research Coordination Network on Work in the Age of Intelligent Machines (NSF 17-45463, https://waim.network/).

This workshop has two foci—one topical and one methodological. The first centers on how the coming age of intelligent machines will impact work, especially how we design interactions and collaborations between humans and machines.

The second focus aims to encourage participants from diverse research disciplines and/or perspectives to apprehend, challenge, critique, and, hopefully, converge on a set of common research-related outcomes.

We use the phrase "intelligent machines" to describe both material (e.g., robots) and immaterial (e.g., algorithms) computing technologies that can be characterized by autonomy, the ability to learn, and the ability to interact with other systems and with humans. Intelligent machines, though incapable of the generalized intelligence of humans, nevertheless are increasingly capable of and increasingly utilized to perform tasks that traditionally have been the sole purview of humans.

Given these capabilities, the design and development of these systems is attracting enormous attention from industry, and their deployment in multiple contexts is rapidly unfolding. For example, machines are now being used to recognize images or speech with an ability that in particular domains is more accurate than humans, with greater speed and at less cost. By contrast, the human side of this relationship—the people, organizations, legal frameworks, social values, etc., affected by this influx of intelligent machines—is evolving more slowly. The result is an impedance mismatch between intelligent technologies and the organizational and individual contexts of their design and use. This mismatch risks unexpected or undesired consequences (e.g., deskilling, overly fragile systems, or automation surprises). This situation is leading to growing public concern and calls for researchers to attend to both sides of this divide.

Much of the current rhetoric around work and intelligent machines focuses on people being put out of work by automation. But this view is too simplistic. Taking a macro-level view, it is clear that the tasks that can be automated do not stand in isolation [2]; all are defined by important issues of context, e.g., when work is done in a group [5]. Take an automated system to diagnose skin cancer [3], for example. To be practicable, such a system needs to fit with the complex work of a medical practice. Someone must order the imaging, image the correct area of the body using the right lighting, explain the diagnosis to the patient, family members, or other doctors (in varied and appropriate ways), bill insurance companies, monitor ongoing performance, defend malpractice suits, and so on. All this surrounding work needs to adapt to an automated dermatologist (and vice versa). Discussion is only now beginning to turn to the question of the appropriate nature of the relationship between humans and intelligent machines.

Taking a micro-level view, it is clear that most people spend the majority of their time working, an act that provides them not only with material rewards, but, for many, personal identity, social status and psychological well-being. Designing work in the age of intelligent machines thus implicates a worker on variety of levels, including attitudinal outcomes such as satisfaction or motivation, behavioral outcomes such as performance or turnover, cognitive outcomes such as learning, or identify and well-being outcomes, such as anxiety, stress or burnout—much more than the black and white of employment or unemployment. But at present, we lack much understanding of possible futures for work, much less critical principles for designing organizational structures or individual jobs to accommodate potentially juxtaposed needs.

The challenge of understanding and designing work in the age of the intelligent machine requires renewed focus on work as a *socio-technological* problem, requiring the joint design of social and technological systems and attention to the implications of their interdependencies. To achieve this focus when facing a protean technology that can interact with workers and work at multiple levels, researchers will have to collaborate across traditional disciplinary boundaries. This workshop will begin to advance this agenda.

AIM AND GOALS
Our aim in this workshop is to bring together researchers from diverse disciplines with a shared interest in work and intelligent machines. More ambitiously, we intend for the workshop to provide an impetus and venue for disciplinary convergence: "the deep integration of knowledge, techniques, and expertise from multiple fields to form new and expanded frameworks" [4]. To address the challenges of work and intelligent machines requires integrating perspectives and knowledge related to labor, incentives, motivation, cognition, machine learning, human learning and systems design, among others, in coherent ways. Convergent research can build the deep and systematic knowledge required to engage the complex questions that need to be addressed when considering a future in tandem with intelligent machines; even more pressing, convergent ideas are **required** to design work that both leverages expanding technological capabilities and technologies and also serves workers at the same time.

The workshop is designed to advance three specific goals that create the conditions for convergence research. First, a key distinguishing feature of convergence research is that it is centered around a challenging real-world problem. Therefore, an initial goal of the workshop is to discuss and come to some consensus about specific important and challenging transdisciplinary research problems. For example, in past technological revolutions, people were able to acquire new skills that were in demand. In contrast, horses replaced by cars did not find new jobs [1]. What kinds of skills will be in demand in an age of increased automation? Taking a design perspective: What kinds of jobs can we create around those skills? How can we

structure relationships across the evolving human-technology frontier that benefits all parties?

Second, we want to start to create a common, integrated language among interdisciplinary researchers about the problems, phenomena, and issues surrounding work with intelligent machines. This language base can act as a boundary object to connect researchers and research done in disparate disciplines. NSF notes that "as disciplines interact, the knowledge, theories, methods, data, research communities and languages are increasingly intermingled or integrated" [4]. Roco et al. [6] (early proponents of convergence) advocate for the development of "higher-level convergence languages based on new concepts, relationships, and methods" [6, §4.1.2], stating that "by convergence language we mean the common concepts, network relationships, methods, and nomenclature used in a multi-domain of science, technology, and society" [6, §4.3.2].

Third, we want to define resource and technology needs to facilitate convergence research within the GROUP community and beyond. Roco et al. [6] note that "emerging technologies have developed both independently and jointly to a level that now more readily enables structured convergence" [6, §4.2]. For example, they call out the increased use of technologies to support virtual collaborations and note that "an example of a process to establish a convergent language is using shared databases" [6, §4.3.2]. They particularly mention the ways that open science can facilitate productive interactions [6, §4.3.9], as well as the benefits of citizen science. Accordingly, a final goal for the workshop will be to define needs and use cases for technology and cyber-infrastructure that support convergence research.

ACTIVITIES
The workshop activities will address the aims and goals outlined above. We take inspiration, again, from [6] who advocate problem setting—e.g., "using forecasting, early signs of change, scenario setting"—"... to establish a credible vision for what is desired in the longer term for a knowledge and technology field" [6, §4.3.8]. They also promote approaches such as "develop[ing] knowledge mapping and network visualization techniques for identifying large patterns in the knowledge, technology, and societal systems" [6, §4.3.1] in support of interdisciplinary dialogue.

The workshop will include:

1. an ice-breaker activity;

2. short presentations that will either ground participants' understanding of expert projections of the capabilities of intelligent technologies or instances of work with intelligent machines in bellwether settings, or present examples of research on these topics with an emphasis on methods; and

3. small-group activities to create deliverables for each of the three goals.

POTENTIAL OUTCOMES
The workshop's potential outcomes map to the three goals described above. In specific, we envision that the goal and vision setting involved in our day-long agenda will help us to better

describe the complex issues around AI and work as a socio-technical "grand challenge". Our discussions of terminology and language will yield a clearer understanding of the range of knowledge, theories, methods, and data in use by those in the GROUP community; these insights should also help lay the groundwork for establishing how tangential disciplinary groups might best connect with one another. We also expect that this workshop will produce actionable information about requirements for developing a collaborative infrastructure to support convergent forms of research, as well as commitments from attendees to provide shared resources. Finally, in addition to the intellectual products mentioned above, we hope that individual attendees may find new research directions and potential collaborators by identifying other disciplines that might inform their own studies.

ORGANIZERS

- Ingrid Erickson is an Assistant Professor at the School of Information Studies at Syracuse University. She received her PhD from the Center for Work, Technology, and Organization in the Department of Management Science and Engineering at Stanford University. Her research centers on the way that mobile devices and ubiquitous digital infrastructures are influencing how we work and communicate with one another, navigate and inhabit spaces, and engage in new types of sociotechnical practices.

- Lionel P. Robert Jr., is an Associate Professor at the University of Michigan School of Information. His research focuses on collaboration through and with technology. Dr. Robert research includes virtual teams, crowdwork, teamwork with robots, autonomous vehicles and the sharing economy. Dr. Robert was a BAT Doctoral Fellow and KPMG Scholar at Indiana University, where he completed his Ph.D. in Information Systems and minored in Social Informatics through the Center for Social Informatics.

- Kevin Crowston is a Distinguished Professor of Information Science and Associate Dean for Research in the Syracuse University School of Information Studies. He received his Ph.D. (1991) in Information Technologies from the Sloan School of Management, Massachusetts Institute of Technology (MIT). His research examines new ways of organizing made possible by the extensive use of information and communications technology. Specific research topics include

the development practices of Free/Libre Open Source Software teams and work practices and technology support for citizen science research projects, both with NSF support.

- Jeffery V. Nickerson is Professor and Associate Dean of Research in the School of Business at Stevens Institute of Technology. His research and teaching interests include collective intelligence, crowd work, decision making, and information systems design. Prior to joining Stevens he was a partner at PricewaterhouseCoopers and advised companies on issues related to the application of emerging technologies to business. Earlier in his career he developed decision support systems and trading systems for Bear Stearns and Salomon Inc. He holds a Ph.D. in Computer Science from New York University.

REFERENCES

1. Erik Brynjolfsson and Andrew McAfee. 2015. Will humans go the way of horses. *Foreign Affairs* 94 (2015), 8.

2. Michael Chui, James Manyika, and Mehdi Miremadi. 2015. Four fundamentals of workplace automation. *McKinsey Quarterly* (November 2015), 1–9.

3. Andre Esteva, Brett Kuprel, Roberto A. Novoa, Justin Ko, Susan M. Swetter, Helen M. Blau, and Sebastian Thrun. 2017. Dermatologist-level classification of skin cancer with deep neural networks. *Nature* 542, 7639 (2017), 115–118.

4. National Science Foundation. 2017. Convergence Research at NSF. (2017). https://www.nsf.gov/od/oia/convergence/index.jsp

5. Lionel P. Robert and Sangseok You. 2014. Human-robot interaction in groups: Theory, method and design for robots in groups. In *Proceedings of the 18th International Conference on Supporting Group Work*. ACM, 310–312.

6. Mihail C. Roco, William S. Bainbridge, Bruce Tonn, and George Whitesides. 2013. *Convergence of Knowledge, Technology, and Society: Beyond Convergence of Nano-Bio-Info-Cognitive Technologies*. World Technology Evaluation Center, Inc. http://www.wtec.org/NBIC2-Report/

Refugees & Technology: Determining the Role of HCI Research

Konstantin Aal
University of Siegen
Siegen, Germany
konstantin.aal@uni-siegen.de

Vasilis Vlachokyriakos
Open Lab
Newcastle upon Tyne, UK
Vasilis.Vlachokyriakos1@ncl.a
c.uk

Anne Weibert
University of Siegen
Siegen, Germany
Anne.weibert@uni-siegen.de

Karen Fisher
University of Washington
Seattle, USA
fisher@uw.edu

Reem Talhouk
Open Lab
Newcastle upon Tyne, UK
R.R.Talhouk2@ncl.ac.uk

Volker Wulf
University of Siegen
Siegen, Germany
Volker.wulf@uni-siegen.de

ABSTRACT

Currently, over 22 million people are considered to be refugees. Many of them are looking for shelter in the surrounding countries of their home country. Technology can be a helpful tool in addressing the challenges of the so-called "refugee crisis", facilitating initial orientation, information, as well as communication and networking support. This one-day workshop aims to (1) finalize the elaborated guidelines of the previous workshop and SIG meeting and to (2) formulate a manifesto for researchers who work with the vulnerable target group of refugees.

Author Keywords

Refugees; Research Agenda; Guidelines; Manifest; Ethics; Methods

ACM Classification Keywords

H.m MISCELLANEOUS;

BACKGROUND

Based on estimation of the United Nations High Commissioner for Refugees (UNHCR) there are around 22.5 million refugees [7]. In recent times, more and more researchers from the HCI community and related disciplines have focused on the "migration crisis" from various perspectives. Prominent among them is the focus on technology use among settled or settling refugees [2,3,8]. Another capacity building activity was conducted in Palestine [1,9], while other research focuses on improving access to antenatal care [6].

PREVIOUS WORK

This workshop had preceded a Special Interest Group (SIG) meeting in 2016 and a workshop in 2017.

In the first SIG meeting at the Computer Human Interaction conference 2016 [5], the organizers broadly approached the topic of refugees and the role of HCI for this vulnerable population with the wider HCI community. The majority of the participants highlighted the important role of researchers in identifying and addressing the needs of refugees. There was consensus that this can only be achieved by engaging deeper with the refugee communities themselves.

Building up on this initial approach of the topic, a workshop proposal was accepted at the Communities & Technologies conference 2017 in France [4]. In a one-day workshop over 20 participants discussed the methodological challenges that researchers encountered when engaging with refugees. Based on a speculative design case study about a future crisis, a first set of guidelines was elaborated, specifying the sensitive aspects of research work with refugees. A publication about these results in the interactions magazine[1] should complete the workshop.

WORKSHOP GOALS

This workshop now builds upon the work of the previous SIG meeting and workshop. Participants, who are working with vulnerable groups such as refugees and migrants, will discuss and critically reflect on these previous results. The exchange of experiences during the workshop aims to (1) finalize a set of guidelines for young and inexperienced researchers and to (2) define cornerstones for a manifesto, which guides current and evolving HCI research with refugees.

ORGANIZERS

Konstantin Aal (main contact) is a PhD student and a research assistant at the Institute for Information Systems

---

[1] http://interactions.acm.org/

and New Media, University of Siegen. He is part of come_IN[2], a research project which founded several computer clubs for children and their relatives including refugees. Currently he is one of the project leader of the Nett.Werkzeug[3] (which translates to "a tool to be nice"), a platform to provide orientation and information for newcomers in Germany especially refugees.

Anne Weibert is a PhD student and a research assistant at the Institute for Information Systems and New Media, University of Siegen. She is part of come_IN[2], and one of the project leaders of Nett.Werkzeug[3]. Her interest is in computer-based collaborative project work and inherent processes of technology appropriation, intercultural learning and community-building.

Reem Talhouk (main contact) is a doctoral trainee in Digital Civics at Open Lab, Newcastle University. Her research encompasses the use of technology to build refugee community resilience. One of her fields of application is Lebanon, where her research focus lies on health access and health issues for refugees.

Karen Fisher is a Professor of human information behavior, social innovation and design at the Information School, University of Washington. Karen works with Arab refugees to understand their information behavior, and building capacity through education, livelihoods, and social engagement.

Vasilis Vlachokyriakos is a research associate at Open Lab, Newcastle University and lead of OL:Athens. The OL:Athens initiative engages with local solidarity groups in Greece exploring the design of technology for the Solidarity Economy while exemplifying an alternative model of conducting Action Research.

Volker Wulf is a computer scientist with an interest in the area of IT system design in real-world contexts, This includes the development of innovative applications from the areas of cooperation systems, knowledge management and community support. One special focus lies on flexible software architecture which can be adapted by end-users. Further research focuses on methods of user-oriented software development and introduction processes. He is head of the Institute for Information Systems and New Media at the University of Siegen.

PRE-WORKSHOP PLANS

The workshop will be promoted through the already existing website (https://openlab.ncl.ac.uk/refugeesandhci/) and the new website (http://displaced-hci.info), that will present the results of the previous workshop and communicate the aims and structure of the upcoming workshop. The maximum number of participants is 15 persons, which will be selected based on extended abstracts

---

[2] http://come-in.cc/

[3] http://www.nett-werkzeug.de/

in which they relate their current/previous work to refugee contexts and needs. The position papers of the previous workshops are available and will be extended with the new accepted position papers.

CURRENT TECHNOLOGIES

Nett.Werkzeug is a platform for refugees, migrants and everybody who is new in a city. It aides with the resettlement process by providing initial orientation, overview on language courses, information on cultural aspects, work, housing, and the structure of everyday life in general.

Refugee.Info aids refugees overcome language barriers that hinder them in navigating in their new environments in Europe

Arriving in Berlin is a OpenStreetMap, which shows activities and places that are important or might be interesting for refugees.

Konfetti is an app designed to support local community-building among refugees and local residents.

Kiron University is a digital platform aiding refugee students and researchers to pursue their academic education and career.

WORKSHOP STRUCTURE

The workshop aims to be an interactive activity for the participants. The attending participants will work in small groups, based on the position papers, and utilize several interaction design methods. Their results will be presented to the other groups. A group discussion with all participants at the end of the workshop will ensure, that every opinion will be heard and included in the manifesto.

Timetable

09:00-09:15	Welcome
09:15-10:00	Icebreaker and short presentation of participants
10:00-10:30	Coffee break
10:30-12:00	Identifying and discussing methodological challenges
12:00-13:30	Lunch
13:30-15:00	Discussion of guidelines
15:00-15:30	Coffee break
15:30-17:00	Manifest cornerstones
17:00-17.15	Closing of the day and future plans

POST-WORKSHOP PLANS

After the workshop, the notes and documentation materials that were created during the discussion will be shared among the workshop participants. A poster with the main results (such as the finalized guidelines and cornerstones of the manifesto) will be presented during the poster session of the main conference. Together with other groups, who address the topic of refugees and migration, a special journal issue will be prepared, which will include the manifesto, best practices and guidelines.

CALL FOR PARTICIPATION
The different challenges faced by refugee communities and the humanitarian system in their support has instigated a call for technical innovation. This one-day workshop aims to provide a forum for researchers to discuss and extend the guidelines, which were elaborated in the previous workshop. More details regarding the previous workshop are available at our website.

We invite researchers interested in participating to submit a four pages' position paper (ACM Extended Abstract format). Papers should critically reflect on how the researchers' research/interest addresses issues faced by refugee communities. Experience reflected upon does not have to be specifically concerned with working with refugees, however those interested should discuss how lessons learnt and methods used in their works can be adapted and applied to refugee contexts.

Submissions should be sent to konstantin.aal@uni-siegen.de and/or anne.weibert@uni-siegen.de in .pdf format. Position papers will be reviewed based on relevance to the workshop. At least one co-author of each accepted paper should attend the workshop.

Important Dates:
Final Submission Deadline: November 21st, 2017

Final Notification: December 1st, 2017

Workshop Day: January 7th, 2018

REFERENCES
1. Konstantin Aal, George Yerousis, Kai Schubert, Dominik Hornung, Oliver Stickel, and Volker Wulf. 2014. Come_in@palestine: adapting a german computer club concept to a palestinian refugee camp. 111–120. https://doi.org/10.1145/2631488.2631498

2. Ruth Aylett, Michael Kriegel, Mei Yii Lim, Joao Dias, Karin Leichtenstern, Wan Ching Ho, and Paola Rizzo. 2009. ORIENT: interactive agents for stage-based role-play. In *Proceedings of The 8th International Conference on Autonomous Agents and Multiagent Systems-Volume 2*, 1371–1372.

3. Jennifer Baranoff, R. Israel Gonzales, Jay Liu, Heidi Yang, and Jimin Zheng. 2015. Lantern: Empowering Refugees Through Community-Generated Guidance Using Near Field Communication. 7–12. https://doi.org/10.1145/2702613.2726950

4. R. Talhouk, V. Vlachokyriakos, K. Aal, A. Weibert, S. Ahmed, K. Fisher, and V. Wulf. 2017. Refugees & HCI Workshop: The Role of HCI in Responding to the Refugee Crisis: Workshop. 312–314. https://doi.org/10.1145/3083671.3083719

5. Reem Talhouk, Syed Ishtiaque Ahmed, Volker Wulf, Clara Crivellaro, Vasilis Vlachokyriakos, and Patrick Olivier. 2016. Refugees and HCI SIG: The Role of HCI in Responding to the Refugee Crisis. 1073–1076. https://doi.org/10.1145/2851581.2886427

6. Reem Talhouk, Sandra Mesmar, Anja Thieme, Madeline Balaam, Patrick Olivier, Chaza Akik, and Hala Ghattas. 2016. Syrian Refugees and Digital Health in Lebanon: Opportunities for Improving Antenatal Health. 331–342. https://doi.org/10.1145/2858036.2858331

7. United Nations High Commissioner for Refugees. 2017. Refugees. *UNHCR*. Retrieved July 11, 2017 from http://www.unhcr.org/figures-at-a-glance.html

8. Ying Xu, Carleen Maitland, and Brian Tomaszewski. 2015. Promoting participatory community building in refugee camps with mapping technology. 1–4. https://doi.org/10.1145/2737856.2737883

9. George Yerousis, Konstantin Aal, Thomas von Rekowski, David W. Randall, Markus Rohde, and Volker Wulf. 2015. Computer-Enabled Project Spaces: Connecting with Palestinian Refugees across Camp Boundaries. https://doi.org/10.1145/2702123.2702283

Technology on the Trail

D. Scott McCrickard[1], Michael A. Horning[1], Steve Harrison[1], Ellie Harmon[2],
Alan Dix[3], Norman Makato Su[4], Timothy Stelter[1]

[1]Center for HCI
Virginia Tech
mccricks, mhorning, srh,
tstelter@vt.edu

[2]encountering.tech
ellieharmon@gmail.com

[3]Talis, LTD
alan@hcibook.com

[4]School of Informatics
and Computing
Indiana University
normsu@indiana.edu

ABSTRACT

The Technology on the Trail workshop will examine the encroachment of technology into hiking and outdoor adventures, with a focus on identifying and developing ways for technology to support positive and mutually beneficial connections among people. These connections include both intentional ones helpful in collecting scientific data, supporting the environment, maintaining safety, and sharing via social media. We will also explore more opportunistic connections, such as those that are leveraged when tracking and sharing biometric or geotemporal data. With the inclusion of technology in places where it is not used and sometimes not welcome, there will be mismatches of ethics and values that must be considered in the design and use of technology. The workshop will examine existing and emerging challenges of bringing technology onto the trail and reflect on ways to understand, design, and deploy appropriate technological solutions moving forward.

Author Keywords
hiking, communities, design, reflection

ACM Classification Keywords
H.5.m. Information interfaces and presentation (e.g., HCI): Miscellaneous.

DESCRIPTION OF WORKSHOP THEME
The Technology on the Trail workshop examines ways that technology is (and often intentionally isn't) used in hiking and other outdoor adventures, with a focus on supporting communication and connection between people. Technologies such as mobile phones, GPS systems, online maps, biometric devices, wearables, and augmented reality provide possibilities for collecting and sharing information during outdoor activities, and hikers have written about their experiences with technology in extended hiking settings [3,4,8]. These technologies often are not designed for

extended outdoor trail use, and indeed there are difficulties and tensions for outdoor settings that do not exist in urban areas [2]. The workshop will reflect on ways that technology has influenced trail experiences, and it will look ahead to how emerging technologies can be selected, designed, and deployed to appropriately meet extended outdoor needs.

The workshop will focus on connections that are both intentional and more opportunistic. Intentional ones are helpful when collecting scientific data, supporting the environment, and sharing via social media. Certainly scientific domains like plant pathology, weed science, weather and climate change, education, and health and fitness all have demonstrated benefit from technology use, particularly in outdoor settings away from urban areas [1,10,14,16]. However, technology use adds challenges and technology adoption can be difficult to encourage. And the communication and social media tools that people rely on in urban environments are difficult to abandon when on the trail, yet technological and social issues arise when these technologies are used in an outdoor environment for extended times.

We will also consider more unintentional, non-interruptive technology use, such as tracking and sharing biometric or geotemporal data. Just as technology tailored for drivers like Waze and Google Maps leverage information collected from mobile devices [14], the devices that are (or could be) carried by hikers can collect and share information that inform others about challenging trail conditions. This type of scenario represents both opportunities that may arise in carrying tracking and recording devices as well as ethical issues related to sharing data from sparsely-populated trails. We will consider the balance between opportunities and responsibilities during the workshop.

Important in the consideration of technology on the trail is the role of tech-generated notifications, particularly the ways in which attention can be diverted in ways that are interruptive and unwanted. Prior work suggests a need to understand the balance between attention allocation and task utility, most recently and relevantly in domains related to walking and hiking [5,6,9,11,12]. The workshop explores the balance between costs and benefits of tech-based notifications, and how designers, builders, and users can assess them based on their own values and scenarios.

The workshop examines existing and emerging challenges of bringing technology onto the trail and reflect on ways to understand, design, and deploy appropriate technological solutions moving forward. In addition, this workshop will also examine tensions in how technologies represent particular values and beliefs, with a focus on what constitutes legitimate activities in hiking and outdoor cultures [8,13]. We view the workshop as a time for reflection on the many technologies that already exist in extended trail-related situations, and a time to consider the future that we want for technology on the trail.

This workshop builds on an initial workshop held at Virginia Tech in March 2017. The initial workshop allowed us to identify key themes, innovative research methods appropriate for this area, and some prior research and researchers—with the plan to develop follow-up workshops on specific relevant themes. The workshop at GROUP seeks to examine group and community issues that arise on the trail with relation to technology, seeking to understand the differing goals and motivations of people who spend time on trails.

AIM AND GOALS

The Technology on the Trail workshops seek to allow people interested in the technology on the trail theme and the GROUP community to connect, share, and further ideas and projects. The following goals help focus the workshops:

- Connect people interested in the topic area, facilitate idea exchange, and identify collaborators and collaboration opportunities.
- Craft and advance projects based on the idea exchange that occurs at the workshop.
- Further a growing repository of information related to the workshop topic area.
- Produce a special issue of a journal to serve as scholarly output for dissemination of results related to the workshop theme.

ACTIVITIES

The Technology on the Trail workshops seek to live up to the "work" portion of the name, establishing relationships between workshop participants early on but focusing primarily on accumulating collective knowledge toward the workshop goals. Sample activity themes are described in this section.

Identifying roles

An initial activity will engage all participants toward identifying roles of trail-goers. Examples may include scientists who work outdoors, people who hike for fun or exercise, scouts who hike to learn, mushroom foragers who hike to find food, and many more. We will group them in multiple ways, evolve some into simple personas, and consider the relationships between pairs and groups of the personas. This activity seeks to encourage people to think about the many reasons that people may choose to bring technology on the trail.

Channeling conflicts

While people generally envision technology as an invention to solve a problem or make an activity easier, many trail walkers are specifically looking for the natural challenge that hiking through wilderness poses. As one would expect, conflicts between the technologists and the purists arise. This activity will explore how these cultural norms around technology develop, and how technology has evolved in ways not intended to make hiking easier. While supportive technologies might seem helpful, such as precise GPS locating, they have the potential to create divisions in the community between people who use them and people who spurn them. Communities can also develop rifts between the "old-timers" and the "newcomers" to an activity, and because many people hike far from their homes, an "outsiders" vs "locals" dynamic can also come into play. This work session digs into the cultural significance of technology both within and between communities of people.

Brainstorming beginnings

When it comes to technology on the trail, many people have preconceptions about how hikers feel about both their own usage and the usage of others. Activities like reading a book are experienced very differently depending on whether one is reading a paperback or reading on a Kindle. Both direct and indirect social interactions on the trail are affected by technology, and the very presence of technology outdoors can change the experience. Those taking part in this activity will bring to the discussion a broad range of experiences with hikers, trails, and other outdoor communities. Together, we can compare and contrast our own understandings of those who do and don't use technology on trails by delving into the mindsets of hikers through a series of cultural probe activities.

Lunchtime hike

The lunch break (and the fortuitous conference location) affords the opportunity to put into action our morning findings. Workshop participants will be invited to try out (physically or imagined) a technology that could be brought onto a hike while taking an out-and-back walk starting from the conference venue. Technology possibilities that many workshop participants have in their possession may include still/video cameras, step counters, smart watches, heath and wellness sensors, audio recorders, mobile phones, and more. But participants can also undertake their hike using an imagined technology, perhaps imagining a different activity or role. The conference location is known for hiking, bird watching, and shell collecting along its beaches. A few minutes at the end of the lunch break will be dedicated to sharing pictures, videos, and other artifacts--reflecting on thoughts and findings. This tends to be a fun and popular activity that helps drive discussion during future sessions.

Science and education on the trail

Smartphones and Internet-connected devices are changing the ways that data are collected in outdoor trail settings, and the widespread ownership of these devices make possible a role for the crowdsourcing of data collection on trails.

However, it is important for trained scientists, technologists, and educators to craft experiences that will be useful and enlightening to those who undertake them as well as productive and valid in terms of the data that are produced. This session will explore the kinds of data and experiences can be collected and crafted, toward understanding the types of experiences that are best suited for technology on the trail. The session will consider both formal science education and informal science education across a range of ages. The session will provide hands-on opportunities to explore tools and data that are in use in the field, and to speculate about the types of tools that could be developed with emerging technologies.

Prototyping with paper (and more)
Building on the roles identified in the opening session, and integrating findings from other sessions, this session seeks to generate focused, creative prototypes. This activity starts with simple sketches but includes crafting materials that enable more complex prototyping of mobile and wearable technologies that may be feasible in the near future. This session encourages participants to focus their creative efforts within realistic boundaries toward prototypes that address opportunities for which technology can play a role.

Reflecting on data
Hiking and other trail activities have the potential to generate large amounts of data, particularly with recent and emerging technologies that can meld temporal, biometric, location, and other data with minimal inconvenience to the hiker. While models for visualizing and understanding data are common, this session explores ways to reflect on trail data, both by exploring the uses and limitations of existing tools and by speculating on possibilities of novel, emerging technologies.

Paths toward progress
The closing workshop activity draws together all workshop attendees toward identifying future directions. Session leaders put forth promising directions from each of the prior sessions, and participants will present ways that they can further develop the ideas identified during the activities. By attaching names to ideas, there can be follow-up with the participants to identify progress.

EXPECTED OUTCOMES
The primary outcome of the workshop is to connect people interested in the topic area, facilitating idea exchange and identifying collaborators. It is expected that projects will be crafted or furthered based on the idea exchange, course initiatives and projects will be identified, and relevant data repositories created and extended.

Blog posts and pages on the Technology on the Trail site provide both immediate and enduring feedback to those interested in the workshop. They include personal narratives crafted prior to the start of the workshop, allowing attendees to become familiar with each others' ideas and directions. Relevant reading reflections will be encouraged prior to the workshop as well. Activity findings will be posted at or shortly after the workshop. The site will remain as a growing repository of information related to the workshop topic area.

Workshop outcomes will be published in a special issue of a journal, with preparations and journal selection under way. The target submission deadline is May 2018, seeking to allow sufficient time to develop and evolve themes from the workshop into publishable journal papers.

WORKSHOP DETAILS
The workshop is centered on the initiative blog site at technologyonthetrail.wordpress.com, which will serve as an enduring reminder of the workshop themes and findings. The site reflects the contributions of the core participants from our initial workshop, and to the many related topics identified through the initiative.

Candidate participants will generate a brief project statement to appear on the workshop blog, with links to other relevant papers, projects, and writings. Workshop participant selection is based on relevance to the theme and coverage of important aims and goals.

Workshop outcomes, and future outcomes of the Technology on the Trail initiative, will be available on the initiative blog site. We expect follow-up workshops to emerge from these efforts, as well as through a journal special issue and a book.

NAMES AND BACKGROUNDS OF THE ORGANIZERS
Scott McCrickard is an Associate Professor of Computer Science and a member of the Center for HCI at Virginia Tech. He is the director of the Technology on the Trail initiative, running an initial workshop at Virginia Tech and maintaining a blog of reading reflections, stories, projects, and other information related to the theme. His research focuses on awareness and notifications, with applications generally developed for mobile devices for areas in which appropriate notifications have great potential value like health and wellness, assistive technologies, educational situations, and technology on the trail.

Michael Horning is an Assistant Professor of Communication and co-director of the Social Informatics area of the Center for HCI at Virginia Tech. His research focuses on the social and psychological effect of communication technologies. He designs, develops, and evaluates web and mobile software solutions for support of communities.

Steve Harrison is an Associate Professor of Practice in Computer Science, director of the Human-Centered Design Program of the Graduate School, and co-director of the Social Informatics area of the Center for HCI at Virginia Tech. Among his varied research interests is the way in which ICT is re-shaping the idea of being on the trail.

Ellie Harmon is an ethnographer, researcher, writer, bicyclist, and hiker. She hiked the Pacific Crest Trail in 2013 and the Appalachian Trail in 2008, writing about her experiences as part of her dissertation and professional papers. She researches and writes about people and technologies as a freelance consultant through her company, encountering.tech.

Alan Dix is a computing professor at Birmingham University and researcher at Talis Ltd., working on most things that connect people and computers. He is first author of a widely-used human computer interaction textbook. From mid-April to July 2013 he walked the complete periphery of Wales, over a thousand miles. The walk was a personal journey, but also a technological and community one, exploring the needs of the walker and the people along the way. He is continuing to work on writing and collating data from his journey.

Norman Makoto Su an Assistant Professor in the School of Informatics and Computing at Indiana University Bloomington. Academically, his interests lie in HCI, CSCW, ubiquitous computing, organizational/management science, and science & technology studies (STS). He studies people's relationship with technology and how this relationship has and can be changed. He has studied a wide range of "users"; most relevantly he examined the dialectics of fair chase practices of hunters through interviews and observations of hunters in the American Midwest.

Timothy Stelter is a Ph.D. Candidate at Virginia Tech. His research interests lie in human-computer interaction, particularly in how technology can be used in extended outdoor situations. He serves as a graduate research assistant in the Social Informatics area within the Center for Human Computer Interaction at Virginia Tech.

ACKNOWLEDGEMENTS

Thanks to the Institute for Creativity, Arts, and Technology at Virginia Tech for funding the development of relevant background work through a SEAD grant, and to the Center for HCI and Department of Computer Science at Virginia Tech for their support of the initial workshop and initiative.

REFERENCES

1. E. Bonsignore, A. Quinn, A. Druin, and B. Bederson. 2013. Sharing Stories "in the Wild": A Mobile Storytelling Case Study Using StoryKit. *TOCHI 20* (3).

2. D. Cuff, M. Hansen, and J. Kang. 2008. Urban sensing: out of the woods. *Commun. ACM 51* (3). 24-33.

3. A. Dix. 2013. Mental Geography, Wonky Maps, and a Long Way Ahead. 2013. In *Proc. GeoHCI Workshop*.

4. A. Dix and G. Ellis. 2015. The Alan Walks Wales Dataset: Quantified Self and Open Data. *Journal of Open Data as Open Educational Resources*.

5. A. Esakia, S. M. Harden, D. S. McCrickard, and M. Horning. 2017. FitAware: Channeling Group Dynamics Strategies with Smartwatches in a Physical Activity Intervention. In *Proc CHI Extended Abstracts*.

6. A. Esakia, D. S. McCrickard, S. M. Harden, and M. Horning. 2018. FitAware: Promoting Group Fitness Awareness Through Glanceable Smartwatches. In *Proc GROUP*.

7. E. Harmon. 2015. *Computing as Context: Experiences of Dis/Connection Beyond the Moment of Non/Use*. Ph.D. Dissertation, University of California, Irvine.

8. E. Harmon and M. Mazmanian. 2013. Stories of the smartphone in everyday discourse: Conflict, tension, and instability. In *Proc. CHI*.

9. D. S. McCrickard, C. M. Chewar, J. P. Somervell, and A. Ndiwalana. 2003. A model for notification systems evaluation--Assessing user goals for multitasking activity. *TOCHI 10* (4).

10. N. Polys, J. Hotter, M. Lanier, L. Purcell, J. Wolf, W. C. Hession, P. Sforza, and J. D. Ivory. 2017. Finding frogs: Using game-based learning to increase environmental awareness. In *Proc. Web3D)*.

11. M. Posti, J. Schöning, and J. Häkkilä. 2014. Unexpected journeys with the HOBBIT: The design and evaluation of an asocial hiking app. In *Proc. DIS*.

12. Y. Rogers, S. Price, C. Randell, D. S. Fraser, M. Weal, and G. Fitzpatrick. 2005. Ubi-learning integrates indoor and outdoor experiences. *Commun. ACM 48*, 1.

13. N. M. Su and E. Cheon. 2017. Reconsidering Nature: The Dialectics of Fair Chase in the Practices of American Midwest Hunters. In *Proc. CHI*.

14. G. Wang, B. Wang, T. Wang, A. Nika, H. Zheng, B. Y. Zhao. 2016. Defending against Sybil Devices in Crowdsourced Mapping Services. In *Proc. MobiSys*.

15. H. Wang, X. Chen, N. Polys, and P. Sforza. 2017. A Web3D forest geo-visualization and user interface evaluation. In *Proc. Web3D*.

16. R. Yeh, C. Liao, S. Klemmer, F. Guimbretière, B. Lee, B. Kakaradov, J. Stamberger, and A. Paepcke. 2006. ButterflyNet: A mobile capture and access system for field biology research. In *Proc. CHI*.

Strengthening the Role of Female Young Professionals in IT-Organizations by Using a PAR Approach in Gender Studies

Michael Ahmadi
University of Siegen
Siegen, 57072, Germany
michael.ahmadi@uni-siegen.de

Abstract

Women interested in STEM fields (science, technology, engineering and mathematics), especially information technology (IT), are still facing several problems considering equality and career chances. Companies realize the opportunities of diversity and yet for several reasons they are struggling to hire or integrate female young professionals. Although gender study research provides promising frameworks there are still issues of making those usable in practical environments. Thus, there does exist a gap between science and practice – A gap which our project aims to close by promoting the transfer of knowledge between gender studies and IT practice. Therefore, we collaborate with IT-organizations over a timespan of three years using a Participatory Action Research (PAR) approach. This approach offers opportunities to reveal new, relevant insights and create social change in a collaborative way. Thus, my PhD thesis deals on the one hand with the results considering specific gender-related topics we gained in the organizations as well as, on the other hand, with an evaluation of our methodology in this specific context.

GROUP '18, January 7–10, 2018, Sanibel Island, FL, USA
© 2018 Copyright is held by the owner/author(s).
ACM ISBN 978-1-4503-5562-9/18/01.
https://doi.org/10.1145/3148330.3152696

Author Keywords

Gender, Feminism, HCI, Feminist HCI, Gender and IT, Methodology, Qualitative Research, PAR

ACM Classification Keywords

• Social and professional topics → Gender

Introduction

In the IT sector gender roles are still unequally distributed and female programmers are a minority [3]. However, a gender view can lead to competitive advantages for companies [4], which is also true for IT-related sectors like software development [5]. While there already exists excellent scientific expertise considering gender and IT topics [e.g. 2,5,8,9] practitioners in IT are still wondering about the requirements to design software equitable in the light of gender topics, which internal structures are necessary so that their company is an attractive workplace for women and how to establish a feminine friendly IT culture etc. That leads to the question how companies can include scientific gender knowledge into practice. The goal of our project is to make insights from gender studies usable in practice to support female young professionals in IT organizations.

Therefore, we collaborate with organizations who have a concrete practical research question considering gender topics. Such a close collaboration approach in the field offers opportunities to reveal new, relevant insights and create social change by making use of Participatory Action Research (PAR) [10].

Thus, my PhD thesis deals on the one hand with the results considering gender-related topics as each organization has its own research question rooted in practice. On the other hand, there is also the need to evaluate our methodology and the impact we as researchers have on this specific field.

Women in IT

There has been an extensive discussion about women facing entry barriers, prejudices as well as problems with organizational structures and cultures in computing. These problems hinder female young professionals, despite their qualification, to fulfil their potential and career opportunities [3,8]. Literature offers a range of guidelines on how to support gender sensitive approaches, e.g. ways to integrate feminism into HCI [1], (de-)gendering of IT artefacts respectively developing IT software in a gender sensitive way [2,9] or utilizing Scrum processes to create a better work environment for women [5]. Such discussions in academia are important and offer valuable suggestions for practice. This means however that existing corporate structures must be reconsidered and willingness for change has to be existent. Ideally, change happens directly in organizational context. To make research on gender and IT science usable in the abovementioned context, we utilize a PAR approach.

The PAR approach in gender studies

Participatory Action Research (PAR) can be understood as an extended form of Action Research (AR), emphasizing the collaborative aspects [10] of the AR process. Members of the organization that are studied are actively taking part in the research and change process. PAR paradigms have been used in Feminism and Gender Studies [7] before.

First steps of research practice

We acquired organizations interested in collaborating with us. Each organization has its own unique research question derived from the respective work context. Topics are diverse and deal with all types of themes in the context of gender and IT. The range of topics encompasses the development of models for organizational IT processes, gender-sensitive IT-design, aspects of gender in recruiting and talent development in IT-companies. To date there are five organizations, all located in Germany, who have expressed concrete interest in a research collaboration. The following figure presents a short description of the organizations as well as the already confirmed research questions.

Organization	Sector	Research question
A	Gaming	Talent development
B	Nano optic and sensor technology	Gender as a factor considering the development of IT-artefacts
C1	IT services for local government	Creation of a gender sensitive organizational environment
C2	Manifacturing of vehicle registration marks	Creation of a gender sensitive organizational environment
D	Digital fabrication in a scientific context	Gender sensitive development of community innovation/fabrication hubs

Figure 1: Organizations and research questions

The figure states two "C-companies", C1 and C2. These are two different companies which are however dealing with the same research question and are also quite comparable in terms of company size etc. Thus, with these two companies we hope to find additional interesting insights via comparative analysis. Overall we have a diverse mix of small and big organizations with a wide range of interesting topics and industry sectors. We furthermore strive to "broad" our view by including the organizations into a "Living Lab." In such a Living Lab [6] we try to understand the daily routines

of real life environments and involve several stakeholders in participatory processes to create a network of excellence. The establishment of such a network can be seen as a base for discussions on the topic among all stakeholders. I am confident that our project offers a lot of relevant insights and great potential for a PhD thesis.

Possible research questions

At GROUP's Doctorial Colloquium, I would like to focus on the discussion about possible research questions of my PhD thesis. There are two obvious areas of interest: Firstly, each organization has its own research question and offers insights to all kinds of gender related topics. This is part of "everyday project work." Secondly, I am also interested in methodological aspects of our work. To evaluate our methodological framework there has to be an identification of reasons for conflicts and failures but also for successful interventions. In the following I will present possible research questions that could be used to frame my PhD-thesis:

- Which effects did our interventions create and how well did our research approach worked? Are the introduced changes sustainable in practice?

- How well can the approach be adapted to the gender and IT context overall? What are the limitations and challenges of using this approach in gender studies context? What are the reasons?

- Which role does the intervention by the researchers play? Do practices in the organizations change because of or only when researchers are present?

By discussing my PhD project at the doctoral consortium I hope to offer new, interesting insights for other PhD students as well as earning input for my own work. At the moment I am still facing challenges with framing an overall topic and the problem statement for my thesis as well as finding appropriate research questions. Since many of the research questions are not yet fixed, this is open for discussion. Surely, the Doctoral Colloquium at GROUP will offer a lot of benefit.

Short Bio

Michael Ahmadi is a PhD student at the Institute for Information Systems and New Media, University of Siegen. He is working in a research project aimed at strengthening the role of female young professionals in IT.

Acknowledgements

This work was funded by the German Federal Ministry of Education and Research (Grant Numbers: 01FP1603, 01FP1604, 01FP1605).

References

1. Shaowen Bardzell. 2010. Feminist HCI: Taking Stock and Outlining an Agenda for Design. *Proceedings of the SIGCHI Conference on Human Factors in Computing Systems*, ACM, 1301–1310.

2. Corinna Bath. 2009. Searching for Methodology: Feminist Technology Design in Computer Science. In W. Ernst and I. Horwath, eds., *Gender in Science and Technology*. transcript, Bielefeld, 57–78.

3. Sapna Cheryan, Allison Master, and Andrew N. Meltzoff. 2015. Cultural Stereotypes as Gatekeepers: Increasing Girls' Interest in Computer Science and Engineering by Diversifying Stereotypes. *Frontiers in Psychology* 6.

4. Anna Fogelberg Eriksson. 2014. A Gender Perspective as Trigger and Facilitator of Innovation. *International Journal of Gender and Entrepreneurship* 6, 2: 163–180.

5. Ken Judy. 2012. Agile Values, Innovation and the Shortage of Women Software Developers. *45th Hawaii International Conference on System Sciences*, 5279–5288.

6. Benedikt Ley, Corinna Ogonowski, Mu Mu, et al. 2015. At Home with Users: A Comparative View of Living Labs. *Interacting with Computers* 27, 1: 21–35.

7. Patricia Maguire. 1987. *Doing Participatory Research: A Feminist Approach*. Center for International Education, School of Education, University of Massachusetts, Amherst.

8. Jane Margolis and Allan Fisher. 2003. *Unlocking the Clubhouse: Women in Computing*. MIT Press, Cambridge.

9. Els Rommes. 2009. Feminist Interventions in the Design Process. In W. Ernst and I. Horwath, eds., *Gender in Science and Technology*. transcript, Bielefeld, 41–55.

10. William F. Whyte. 1991. *Participatory Action Research*. SAGE, Newbury Park.

AAPI Identity Work on Reddit: Toward Social Support and Collective Action

Bryan Dosono
Syracuse University
Syracuse, NY 13210, USA
bdosono@syr.edu

Abstract

Asian Americans and Pacific Islanders (AAPIs) are perceived as the "model minority" with a monolithic identity, in contrast to other marginalized racial groups in the United States. In reality, they are composed of different ethnicities, socio-economic backgrounds, and political ideologies. My research employs social network analysis with qualitative research methods to explore, interpret, and visualize large collections of social media data. I seek to understand how Asian Americans and Pacific Islanders (AAPIs) construct and express their identity in online communities and my dissertation research uncovers the ways in which AAPIs negotiate collective action in the context of online identity work.

Author Keywords

Online identity; impression management; social network sites; Reddit; AAPI.

ACM Classification Keywords

H.5.3. Information interfaces and presentation (e.g., HCI).

Introduction

AAPIs: An Understudied Population in Social Computing Research

Recent scholarship in CHI and CSCW explores identity work—the process through which people make sense of

Study 1: Online Identity Construction

RQ1. How are AAPIs constructing and expressing their identity in online communities?

RQ2. What factors affect AAPI participation in online identity work?

Study 2: Social Support in Online Communities

RQ3. How do AAPIs navigate through privacy issues of censorship and anonymity when seeking support online?

RQ4. How do AAPI forum moderators respond/intervene in managing controversial or stigmatized discourse?

Study 3: Collective Identity Formation

RQ5. What ecology of technologies are AAPIs using as a means to form and sustain a collective identity?

RQ6. How do AAPIs form a collective identity online in relation to other intersectional social movements?

or re-construct their identities—by a number of groups on social media, including those undergoing gender transitions [8], and underprivileged college students [13]. Asian American and Pacific Islander (AAPI) youth lead all other racial groups in technology use and proficiency [15], but only a couple of studies illustrate how AAPIs use technology for identity work [5,16]. A review of intersectional identity in HCI literature demonstrated that only 1% of CHI conference proceedings from 1981-2016 archived in the ACM Digital Library used keyword classifiers that centered around identities of gender, ethnicity, race, sexuality, or class [18], and no proceeding used keywords of Asian American or Pacific Islander, signifying a gap in identity work within published social computing research. Ethnically similar yet culturally distinct from their transnational origins on the Asian continent, AAPIs are the fastest growing immigrant group in the United States. And yet despite their staggering growth, AAPIs are still one of the most understudied racial groups in the nation [21].

Impression Management in Online Spaces

According to Goffman [7], identity is constructed in relation to rules and norms in a social setting. Scholars have extended Goffman's dramaturgical work to the arena of social media. Hargittai's study on young adult Facebook users showed that most users care about managing their privacy settings to control how content was shared to their audience [9]. Marwick's study of content producers on Twitter found that users are strategically concealing information and targeting tweets to different audiences in an effort to maintain an interesting persona [12]. boyd explored how youth use social media in their everyday lives and the nuanced practices that teenagers arrange to hang out with their

friends in both online and offline settings [2]. Members of the AAPI community who engage in online identity work may be doing so to redefine their public facing identity and challenge existing stereotypes. For example, exclusionary rhetoric that cast AAPIs as perpetual foreigners continues to persist as subtle slights of racism in the form of microaggressions [20] in everyday conversation.

Technology Use for Social Support in Collectivist Cultures

Clinical research conducted on new AAPI immigrants has looked at how culture-of-origin values affect support seeking for college enrollment [4], family conflict resolution [11], and access to psychological services [10]. However, understanding how AAPIs seek support in online contexts, particularly for stigmatized topics, have yet to be fully explored. Identity work in collectivist cultures can get increasingly complex with respect to AAPI, as their identities have formed, over time, in a highly politicized and ever-evolving socio-historical context. For example, AAPIs are collectively perceived as high-income and well-educated, but in reality, AAPIs are scattered across the spectrum on socioeconomic attainment and civic participation [21].

Research Design

Site of Research

To disentangle monolithic perceptions of collectivity, I will analyze emergent identity work amongst AAPIs on the social networking site, Reddit—one of the largest and most frequented visited online community platforms. Any user (redditor) can is able to create a community (subreddit) on nearly any topic, where they can share content in the form of text, links, and images. Content can be either upvoted or downvoted

Count	Subreddits
16,349	r/asianamerican
15,963	r/asianparentstories
14,605	r/asianeats
10,399	r/asianmasculinity
9,419	r/abcdesis
8,409	r/aznidentity
6,606	r/hapas
6,199	r/asiantwox
4,916	r/gaysian
2,513	r/asiandrama
1,664	r/asianfeminism
1,376	r/asianamericanissues
1,236	r/easternsunrising
1,188	r/asianbros

Table 1. Subscriber count of popular AAPI subreddits. Updated 25 October 2017.

by any redditor. Participation in identity work occurs in the form of comments on each subreddit thread. Each community is moderated independently by volunteer users. Given AAPI's longstanding history of invisibility, silence, and exclusion [14], this work expands the ongoing work on impression management and support-seeking behavior within social media. Because AAPI identity work is not monolithic in nature, I am interested in understanding differences, if any, among identity work in comparable online communities.

Data Collection

I am currently storing collections of Reddit JSON files in MongoDB, scraping public comments (as well as metadata to changes and deletions from such posts) and changes to comments (such as edits and deletions) every 10 minutes on relevant public AAPI subreddits with over 1,000 subscribers (see Table 1). The Reddit API allows me to identify which comments have been deleted/modified and which users have been banned/deleted their accounts. I use R for all statistical and visual data analysis.

Research Methods

I will employ a three-pronged, mixed-methods approach to understand how AAPIs engage in identity work online.

Content Analysis

To answer RQ1 and RQ2, I employed a grounded theory approach to label variables and their relationships within the corpus [3]. The first round of comment rating involved an open coding process that established tentative labels for representing emerging themes from the data. The second round of comment rating proceeded into an axial coding process for

identifying relationships among the open codes [17]. I recruited a team of 2 advanced undergraduate students to help me with the coding process. I trained my research team to meet an acceptable threshold of inter-coder agreement as we code in parallel.

Interviews

To answer RQ3 and RQ4, in addition to collecting trace data and Reddit comments online, I will also contact and establish interviews with moderators of relevant Reddit. I will begin each semi-structured interview by asking Reddit moderators a series of probing questions to obtain an overall understanding of their community and how they moderate it. I will code interviews for inductive content analysis to find emerging patterns and trends using the qualitative data analysis software.

Field Observations

To answer RQ5 and RQ6, I will identify and attend Reddit meetups, which are in-person gatherings of redditors from a specific subreddit that are regularly organized by the community. At Reddit meetups, I will document first-hand observations of their collective organizing. Multiple methods of data collection from participant observation, field notes, and interviews facilitate analysis that allows for both bird's-eye view and a more in-depth portrait of the informants and their community. To observe the phenomena at hand and impose a minimal amount of personal bias in the data, I aim to maintain reflexivity to distance myself from participants in the study.

Completed Work

Exploratory Study

I retrieved over 72,000 Reddit comments posted between January to July 2016 in my initial pilot work for a mixed-methods study of AAPI identity work, analyzing discursive patterns of user-deleted and banned comments [6]. In looking at political ideology as a factor affecting identity work, I found that political orientation plays a significant role in determining how different groups suppresses non-conforming identities. While conservative AAPIs tend to comment anonymously more frequently, progressive AAPIs are significantly less likely to ban comments that did not fit the behavior and norms of their community.

Study 1: Identity Work as Deliberation

Using the 2016 US Presidential Election as a case study, I retrieved 4,406 Reddit comments posted between October 2016 to December 2016. I examined how users engage in an online community through a deliberation lens to understand the extent to which Reddit supports identity work as a deliberative process. Under the collective AAPI umbrella, I find that ethnic identifications complicate the types of discussion possible within r/asianamerica. I discuss how the expression of identity, and thereby solidarity, in a politicized online setting may lead to a social movement.

Forthcoming Work

Study 2: Identity Work as Social Support

Social support brings positive benefits for those who seek it, as it decreases stress, helps develop coping skills, improves mental health, and increases overall quality of life. However, in collectivist cultures, seeking support in public settings is frowned upon because it reflects poorly on the collective identity of the family and community [19]. I will be (1) analyzing the sociotechnical configurations of the r/asianparentstories subreddit—where redditors can apply tags to topical posts and seek support in nuanced ways—and (2)

conducting semi-structured interviews with moderators to answer RQ3 and RQ4. As no prior empirical study has yet to investigate how AAPIs self-disclose and seek social support in online communities for stigmatized topics such as mental health and sexuality, I am interested in unpacking additional dimensions of complexity to AAPI identity work emerging online.

Study 3: Identity Work as Performance

I will draw upon prior scholarship in feminist HCI [1] as a lens to analyze collective identity construction in two highly gendered subreddits: r/asianmasculinity and r/asianfeminism. In addition to close readings of those subreddits, I will take an ethnographic approach (documented through field notes and participant observation) to attending Reddit meetups, immersing myself in both online and offline interactions with AAPI redditors and the collective community to answer RQ5 and RQ6.

Expected Contributions

My dissertation work aims to expand the current literature on identity work embedded in social computing systems from the nuanced perspectives of a historically understudied population. Given AAPI's longstanding history of silence, exclusion, and immigration, my work has significant potential to inform how their involvement in contemporary social movements affect other groups who face similar oppressive challenges. My work also has the potential to inform how other marginalized or niche AAPI subgroups come together on online platforms to collaboratively make sense of their intersectional identities and develop a sense of community with others that share an identity with them.

References

1. Shaowen Bardzell. 2010. Feminist HCI: Taking stock and outlining an agenda for design. *Proceedings of the SIGCHI Conference on Human Factors in Computing Systems*, 1301–1310. http://doi.org/10.1145/1753326.1753521

2. danah boyd. 2014. *It's complicated: The social lives of networked teens*. Yale University Press.

3. Juliet Corbin and Anselm Strauss. 2014. *Basics of qualitative research: Techniques and procedures for developing grounded theory*. Sage publications.

4. Jessica M Dennis, Jean S Phinney, and Lizette Ivy Chuateco. 2005. The role of motivation, parental support, and peer support in the academic success of ethnic minority first-generation college students. *Journal of college student development* 46, 3: 223–236. http://doi.org/10.1353/csd.2005.0023

5. Linh Dich. 2012. Technologies of racial formation: Asian-American online identities. Retrieved from https://search.proquest.com/docview/1240653859?accountid=14214

6. Bryan Dosono, Bryan Semaan, and Jeff Hemsley. 2017. Exploring AAPI identity online: Political ideology as a factor affecting identity work on Reddit. *Proceedings of the 2017 CHI Conference Extended Abstracts on Human Factors in Computing Systems*, 2528–2535. http://doi.org/10.1145/3027063.3053185

7. Erving Goffman. 1959. The Presentation of Self in Everyday Life.

8. Oliver L Haimson, Jed R Brubaker, Lynn Dombrowski, and Gillian R Hayes. 2015. Disclosure, stress, and support during gender transition on Facebook. *Proceedings of the 18th ACM Conference on Computer Supported Cooperative Work & Social Computing*, 1176–1190. http://doi.org/10.1145/2675133.2675152

9. Eszter Hargittai and others. 2010. Facebook privacy settings: Who cares? *First Monday* 15, 8. http://doi.org/10.5210/fm.v15i8.3086

10. Bryan S K Kim, Donald R Atkinson, and Peggy H Yang. 1999. The Asian Values Scale: Development, factor analysis, validation, and reliability. *Journal of counseling Psychology* 46, 3: 342. http://doi.org/10.1037/0022-0167.46.3.342

11. Richard M Lee and Hsin-Tine Tina Liu. 2001. Coping with intergenerational family conflict: Comparison of Asian American, Hispanic, and European American college students. *Journal of Counseling Psychology* 48, 4: 410. http://doi.org/10.1037/0022-0167.48.4.410

12. Alice E Marwick and others. 2011. I tweet honestly, I tweet passionately: Twitter users, context collapse, and the imagined audience. *New Media & Society* 13, 1: 114–133. http://doi.org/10.1177%2F1461444810365313

13. Tsubasa Morioka, Nicole B Ellison, and Michael Brown. 2016. Identity work on social media sites: Disadvantaged students' college transition processes. *Proceedings of the 19th ACM Conference on Computer-Supported Cooperative Work & Social Computing*, 848–859. http://doi.org/10.1145/2818048.2819959

14. Keith Osajima. 1995. Racial politics and the invisibility of Asian Americans in higher education.

The Journal of Educational Foundations 9, 1: 35. Retrieved from https://search.proquest.com/docview/1468386182?accountid=14214

15. Andrew Perrin. 2016. English-speaking Asian Americans stand out for their technology use. *Pew Research Center*. Retrieved September 1, 2016 from http://www.pewresearch.org/fact-tank/2016/02/18/english-speaking-asian-americans-stand-out-for-their-technology-use/

16. Xi Rao and Libby Hemphill. 2016. Asian American Chicago Network: A case study of Facebook group use by immigrant groups. *Proceedings of the 19th ACM Conference on Computer Supported Cooperative Work and Social Computing Companion*, 381–384. http://doi.org/10.1145/2818052.2869077

17. Johnny Saldaña. 2015. *The coding manual for qualitative researchers*. Sage.

18. Ari Schlesinger, W Keith Edwards, and Rebecca E Grinter. 2017. Intersectional HCI: Engaging

Identity through Gender, Race, and Class. *Proceedings of the 2017 CHI Conference on Human Factors in Computing Systems*: 5412–5427. http://doi.org/10.1145/3025453.3025766

19. Bryan Semaan, Bryan Dosono, and Lauren M Britton. 2017. Impression management in high context societies: "Saving face" with ICTs. *Proceedings of the 2017 ACM Conference on Computer Supported Cooperative Work and Social Computing*, 712–725. http://doi.org/10.1145/2998181.2998222

20. Derald Wing Sue, Christina M Capodilupo, Gina C Torino, et al. 2007. Racial microaggressions in everyday life: implications for clinical practice. *American Psychologist* 62, 4: 271. http://doi.org/10.1037/0003-066X.62.4.271

21. White House Initiative on Asian Americans and Pacific Islanders. 2016. Issues and Facts. Retrieved September 1, 2017 from https://obamawhitehouse.archives.gov/administration/eop/aapi/data/data

Dynamics of Peer Production of Knowledge in Online Social Q&A Communities: A Life-Cycle Perspective of Successful and Failed Cases

Hengyi Fu
School of Information
Florida State University
146 Collegiate Loop, Tallahassee,
FL,32304
hf13c@my.fsu.edu

GROUP '18, January 7–10, 2018, Sanibel Island, FL, USA
© 2018 Copyright is held by the owner/author(s).
ACM ISBN 978-1-4503-5562-9/18/01.
https://doi.org/10.1145/3148330.3152698

Abstract

Online peer production communities, such as Wikipedia, Yahoo Answers, and Stack Overflow, not only generate knowledge resources with low cost access, but also have tremendous potential to complement both online and offline movement of societies. As peer production communities flourished, merely describing successful cases has become less useful. Instead, scholars must identify the dynamics, structures, and conditions that contribute to or impede that success, including how communities change, what makes some communities succeed while others fail, and how and when to intervene successfully. In this dissertation project I combine Activity Theory, computational techniques, and qualitative and quantitative methods to understand the differences of dynamics, structures, and conditions of two social Q&A communities that produced contrasting results within the same context, based on the community life cycle.

Author Keywords

Peer Production; Computer-Supported Collaborative Work; Social Q&A Site; Community Lifecycle.

development process and maximum success. Research regarding peer production community development based on community's life cycle is also necessary but very rare [6]. Implementation guidelines based on community's life cycle could help designers decide the exact point in time when certain design components are most relevant as opposed to others.

To fill this research gap, the purpose of this study is to *understand the difference in successful and unsuccessful online peer production communities and identify success factors in each stage of community evolution*: how they define their community purpose and scope; how they recruit, select, and keep their community members; how they motivate members' contribution, decide the community structures, and maintain the quality of community outputs. To be specific, this study will employ a mixed-method, comparative case study approach to examine different strategies and processes for community building of two Q&A communities that produced contrasting results within the same context.

Research Questions

RQ1: What are some of the activities in social Q&A communities at the different stages of their life cycles? This set of research questions will investigate the actions, division of labor, user roles, tools, norms and rules, and skills related to community building activities, with the guidance of Activity Theory [2].

RQ2: How does Stack Exchange define the success of a Q&A community at each stage?
This set of research questions will examine what criteria are used by Stack Exchange to evaluate if a Q&A community has succeeded through each stage; whether and how those criteria shape community dynamics;

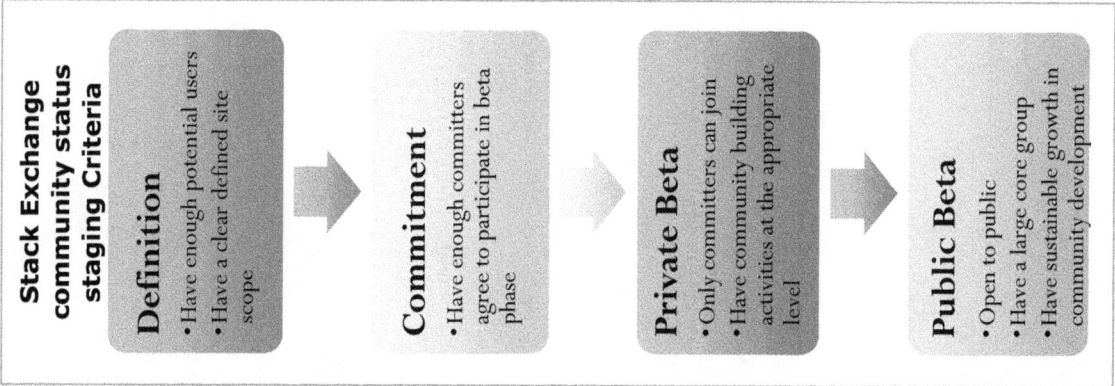

ACM Classification Keywords

H.5.3. Group and Organization Interfaces: Computer-supported cooperative work

Problem Statement and Significance

Online peer production communities have been seen as one of the most significant and visible examples of collective intelligence that emerged from Internet-mediated social practice. Successful peer production communities such as Wikipedia and Stack Overflow have created some of the most powerful publicly maintained resources and services, and enabled new forms of communities to thrive around them. However, not all new peer production communities get off the ground and thrive, as numerous wikis, open source projects, and online discussion forums languish in a perpetual state of inactivity due to the lack of participation [1,6,8]. Other communities, although are able to elicit user participation, still suffer from excessive spamming, in-fighting, low-quality contributions, and other unwanted and non-constructive forms of participation.

The current volume of online peer production communities research is vast but findings related to comparison between community success and failure are isolated [4,7]. Empirical studies about how new communities failed, especially comparing to those successful ones, can facilitate development and maximize success of online peer production communities. The differences in community design process and building strategies between successful and unsuccessful communities and how sociability-support and technological components are selected and incorporated in both could shed light on how the community building process to ensure an optimal

Stack Exchange community status staging Criteria

Definition
- Have enough potential users
- Have a clear defined site scope

Commitment
- Have enough committers agree to participate in beta phase

Private Beta
- Only committers can join
- Have community building activities at the appropriate level

Public Beta
- Open to public
- Have a large core group
- Have sustainable growth in community development

what do community members consider as criteria to measure the community success.

RQ3: What are some of the factors that may affect Q&A communities' success or failure?

Research Setting: Stack Exchange

Stack Exchange is a network of more than 170 Q&A communities including Stack Overflow. Area 51(http://area51.stackexchange.com/) is the Stack Exchange network staging zone where groups of experts come together to build new Q&A sites. Anyone can propose a new Q&A site (called a proposal), but reaching out to other experts and defining the type of wanted questions is a community-driven process.

A proposed Q&A site need to go through four phases before it becomes a full member of the Stack Exchange network: *Definition, Commitment, Private Beta,* and *Public Beta*. In every phase a proposed Q&A site should feature activities addressing different perspectives in community building, and criteria and measures used to evaluate if the site is qualified to move to the next stage also vary among phases.

To address the research questions, this study will examine two social Q&A sites from Area 51 – one *successful* and one *unsuccessful*. Data dumps for each site, including both the main site data (real question-answering threads) and the meta site data (site managing discussion threads), have been published by Stack Exchange. The *unsuccessful* site, called *Economics*, successfully passed the definition, commitment, and private beta phases, but failed to be launched and was closed by Stack Exchange after staying in the public beta phase for 206 days. The *successful* site, called *Mathematics* passed through

all four phases and was launched (considered as graduated from Area 51) in October 2010. These two sites were chosen for comparison based on the following criteria (1) they were proposed on the same day (6/3/2010); (2) the potential user groups/community sizes for both Economics and Mathematics are at the same order of magnitude (the researchers use the numbers of degrees conferred by postsecondary institutions each year to estimate the size of each science community). Two sites are compared from the proposed date (beginning) to the end of public beta phase (closed or graduated).

Research Design

The guiding theories used are Activity Theory and The Collective Effort Model [3]. This dissertation project consists of three parts: 1) Content analysis of the question-answering threads on the main sites (for community activities) and site management discussion threads on the meta sites (for community building discussion) in Math Stack Exchange and Economics Stack Exchange. Descriptive time series statistics based on four phases for community activity categories and site managing discussion categories for both sites have also been generated. 2) Social network analysis of user interactions on each site; 3) Semi-structured interviews with members of these two sites. I plan to interview at least 25 informants from both sites. The selection of informants is based on the accessibility and active level of potential informants.

Current Status and Preliminary Results

Currently I have finished content analysis and social network analysis. I have recruited 15 interview participants, ten from the successful Math Q&A site and five from the failed Economics Q&A site. 37 codes of community activities of two main sites and 14 categories with 47 subcategories of community management discussion of two meta sites have been generated from open coding. The results show the successful Q&A site devoted more efforts to (1) content creation and revision (questions and answers posted, question and answer body editing), (2) meta-content work (tag changed or rollbacked), (3) voting. Instead, the failed site members only focused on the first type of activities.

Regarding community building discussion, the failed Economics site struggled with whether to restrict the scope of the site to high levels, graduate questions (to recruit and retain experts) or whether to allow lay, normative, and homework type questions as well. The successful Mathematics site has more systematical discussion of the community objectives, as well as clearer social role assignments and more interactions between moderators/high-reputation users and other community members, compared to those in the Economics meta. The community governance related discussions in Mathematics meta were more diverse-- the community members tried to develop a more extensive policy system to govern areas ranging from the process of becoming a moderator to what constitutes plagiarism, to methods for managing conflict and consensus building. Some topics that didn't show in the Economics site included: (1) community structure, including what leadership roles are available to community members, how are people selected for those roles, and what privileges and responsibilities do people in these roles have; (2) behavioral expectations, including what types of user behaviors are acceptable or unacceptable and how the rules are enforced, (3) dispute resolution, including how violations of policy can be punished. They also devoted more efforts to

user education and abnormal behavior regulations, and highlighted the role of "old-timers" who are instrumental in conveying social norms to "newcomers". Such informal mentoring was not obvious in the Economics meta.

Expected Contributions

The contributions of my dissertation are twofold. For researchers, my dissertation advances the theoretical understanding of the underlying mechanisms of successful peer production systems, and provide insights to theoretical claims [5] regarding early stage community ecology and developing strategies (define and enforce scope, recruit, select, and retain early members, etc.) that haven't been tested by empirical studies yet. For practitioners, my dissertation offers practical advice to build more effective peer production communities and platforms. Findings of this study may guide community creators on how to effectively start new communities, policy designers on how to design community supporting systems (reputation system reward system, voting system, etc.) and tool designers on how to motivate contributions and control quality.

References

1. Ofer Arazy and Arie Croitoru. 2010. The sustainability of corporate wikis: A time-series analysis of activity patterns. *ACM Transactions on Management Information Systems* 1, 1: 6.
2. Yrjö Engeström. 1987. *Learning by expanding: An activity-theoretical approach to developmental research.* Orienta-Konsultit Oy, Helsinki, Finland.
3. Steven J. Karau and Kipling D. Williams. 2001. Understanding individual motivation in groups: The collective effort model. In *Groups at work: Theory and research.* 113–141.

4. Aniket Kittur and Robert Kraut. 2010. Beyond Wikipedia: Coordination and conflict in online production groups. *Proceedings of the 2010 ACM Conference on Computer Supported Cooperative Work*, ACM, 215–224.

5. Paul Resnick, Joseph Konstan, Yan Chen, and Robert E. Kraut. 2012. Starting New Online Communities. In *Evidence-based social design: Mining the social sciences to build online communities*. MIT Press.

6. Charles Schweik and Robert English. 2012. *Internet Success: A Study of Open-Source Software Commons*. The MIT Press, Cambridge, Mass.

7. Aaron Shaw and Benjamin Hill. 2014. Laboratories of oligarchy? how the iron law extends to peer production. *Journal of Communication* 64, 2: 215–238.

8. Andrea Wiggins and Kevin Crowston. 2010. Reclassifying Success and Tragedy in FLOSS Projects. *Proceedings of Open Source Software: New Horizons*, 294–307.

Investigating Collaboration Within Online Communities: Software Development Vs. Artistic Creation

Giuseppe Iaffaldano
University of Bari
Bari, BA, Italy
Giuseppe.iaffaldano@uniba.it

Abstract

Online creative communities have been able to develop large, open source software (OSS) projects like Linux and Firefox throughout the successful collaborations carried out over the Internet. These communities have also expanded to creative arts domains such as animation, video games, and music. Despite their growing popularity, the factors that lead to successful collaborations in these communities are not entirely understood. In the following, I describe my PhD research project aimed at improving communication, collaboration, and retention in creative arts communities, starting from the experience gained from the literature about OSS communities.

Author Keywords

Online communities; creative collaboration; music composition; overdub; remix; SNA.

ACM Classification Keywords

H.5.3. Information interfaces and presentation (e.g., HCI): Group and Organizational Interfaces – *collaborative computing, computer-supported cooperative work*.

Introduction

Online creative communities are virtual groups whose members volunteer to collaborate over the Internet to produce software, music, movies, games, and other cultural products. Despite the growing popularity of online communities, the factors that lead to success are not entirely understood [9]. For instance, we ignore whether success factors are domain dependent [6]. Previous research has established that open-source software (OSS) development is a form of creative peer-production [7] and that successful collaborations between developers in OSS communities depend on both social and technical factors [11]. Likewise, Luther et al. [6] found that participants' social reputation is key to the successful completion of collaborative animation efforts in online arts communities. Other studies suggest that active feedback actions, such as commenting, are fundamental to the success of creative communities [8]. More recent studies found that users who collaborate online are motivated by their will to learn, socialize, improve their reputation, and gain new opportunities for personal success [4,10]. Thus, research shows that success factors in online creative collaborations are closely related to the social and personal domain [11].

As part of my PhD research on online creative communities, I am currently investigating Songtree, a community for collaborative music creation [2,3]. The goal is to further the understanding of the factors influencing user activities, participation, and collaboration in such creative communities and whether these factors transfer across domains. I expect to advance the state of the art in the fields of CSCW and HCI by empirically identify the success factors of creative online communities, both specific to the artistic domain and in common with OSS communities; define new guidelines and tools to support collaboration in online communities, specifically with synchronous

creative activities (e.g. brainstorming, real time creative collaborations); define guidelines and tools to foster creativity in collaboration within software development communities, where newcomers typically encounter barriers that prevent them from participating.

Research Questions

RQ1: What are the success factors of collaboration in online creative communities?

First, I aim to identify the several success factors that determine the success of the interactions in different types of online creative communities. These factors will be retrieved through the review of the existing literature on collaboration in online communities and tested through empirical studies.

RQ2: Which of the identified success factors depend on the domain of collaboration?

Besides, I intend to determine which of the findings from previous research on OSS communities would carry over to the domain of creative arts communities.

Work and Findings to Date

Songtree is an online creative music community where artists collaborate to the creation of musical tracks. Several social-networking features are available, and users can grow in popularity through their songwriting activity within the community (see **Figure 1**). Songtree allows any user to derive (namely, *overdub*) any song shared in the community leveraging the metaphor of a growing tree (see **Figure 2**). Songtree's overdubbing feature shares many similarities with the Pull Request-based software development model supported by

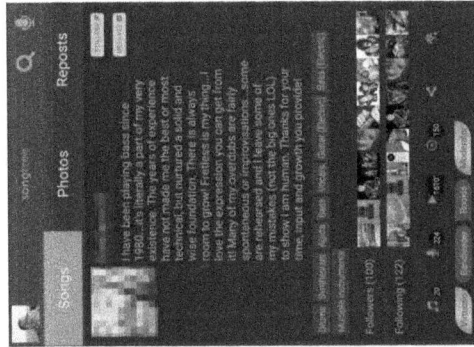

Figure 1: The stats available in the profile page of an artist in Songtree.

for the roles in the feedback network, we sought differences between the commenting behavior of authors and non-authors. Results showed that a higher percentage of authors do not provide comments, indicating that non-authors are more inclined to giving feedback. Finally, we analyzed the relationship between the commenting and songwriting activities by running a correlation analysis restricted to authors only. Results showed a weak rank correlation between the number of comments sent by a Songtree authors and the number of songs they recorded.

Antecedents of Overdubs: An Analysis of Success Factors

Tsay et al. [11] have studied collaboration success factors of in OSS communities. Specifically, they built a logistic regression model and showed that social factors (e.g., developer's status in the project) are more influent than the technical ones (e.g., presence of test cases in a pull request) in taking the decision of accepting or not a pull request in GitHub.

Similarly, I have investigated in [2] which song- and author-related factors can influence the probability of a song to be overdubbed. The results showed that the overdub likelihood of a song is strongly and positively associated with the amount of reactions (e.g., likes, bookmarks) that it generates. Some song-related variables, instead, were found to be negatively associated with the likelihood of a song to be overdubbed (e.g., time since the upload). As for the author-related predictors, author ranking in Songtree and the presence of the author profile picture were found to be positively associated with the overdub likelihood.

modern code-hosting platforms [2,5]. Considering the existing analogies between the two platforms, my work so far has focused on seeking confirmation that existing findings from prior work in OSS communities would also transfer to artistic communities. More specifically, I have focused on *mining roles and communication* in the Songtree community and *determining the success factors* of the collaborations carried out therein.

Roles and Communication: A Social Network Analysis

Bird et al. [1] built the social network of the Apache software foundation developers based on their communication through the mailing list. Their goal was to understand the properties of the social network, the differences in role between developers and non-developers, if development and communication activities are correlated, and the effect of developers' status in the project.

In [3], I reported on a study that mapped the research questions of Bird et al. [1] to Songtree in order to identify the main roles, activities, and key members in the community, thus uncovering the underlying communication network. I built a *feedback network*, a directed graph where nodes represent authors and links are comments on songs. Users commenting activity shows a power-law distribution, typical of online communities, where a small group of users is very active in commenting songs whereas the majority of members only sends a few comments. This evidence suggests authors of popular songs receive more comments. A moderate positive relation was also found between the number of comments sent by authors and their related in-degree (i.e., how many commented on an author's songs), suggesting that the commenting activity may contribute to increasing their visibility. As

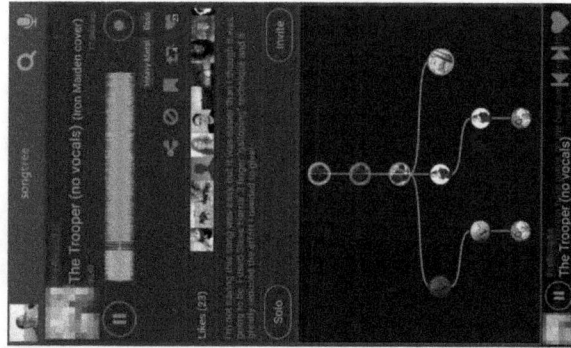

Figure 2: The tree of a song (topmost node) with branches generated by the overdubs received.

Next Steps

Future work on Social Network Analysis

I intend to analyze: (i) collaborations in song trees to uncover cliques of users forming distributed virtual bands and their motivations; (ii) the differences in role and behavior between core and peripheral community members.

Future Work on Success Factors

I intend to improve the statistical model by: (i) including new predictors of successful collaboration using SNA measures; (ii) conducting a longitudinal study to study retention and loyalty of community members over time using a survival analysis approach.

References

1. Christian Bird, Alex Gourley, Prem Devanbu, Michael Gertz, and Anand Swaminathan. 2006. Mining Email Social Networks. In *Proceedings of the 2006 International Workshop on Mining Software Repositories*, ACM, 137–143.

2. Fabio Calefato, Giuseppe Iaffaldano, and Filippo Lanubile. Collaboration Success Factors in an Online Music Community. In *International Conference on Supporting Group Work* (GROUP'18), ACM.

3. Fabio Calefato, Giuseppe Iaffaldano, Filippo Lanubile, Antonio Lategano, and Nicole Novielli. 2017. Mining Communication Data in a Music Community: A Preliminary Analysis. In *3rd International Workshop on Mining the Social Web* (SoWeMine'17).

4. Giorgos Cheliotis, Nan Hu, Jude Yew, and Jianhui Huang. 2014. The Antecedents of Remix. In *Proceedings of the 17th ACM Conference on Computer Supported Cooperative Work & Social Computing* (CSCW'14), ACM, 1011–1022. http://doi.acm.org/10.1145/2531602.2531730

5. Georgios Gousios, Martin Pinzger, and Arie van Deursen. 2014. An exploratory study of the pull-based software development model. In *Proceedings of the 36th International Conference on Software Engineering* (ICSE'14), ACM, 345–355. http://doi.acm.org/10.1145/2568225.2568260

6. Kurt Luther, Kelly Caine, Kevin Ziegler, and Amy Bruckman. 2010. Why It Works (When It Works): Success Factors in Online Creative Collaboration. *Association for Computing Machinery* 10: 1–10. http://doi.acm.org/10.1145/1880071.1880073

7. Sanna Malinen. 2015. Understanding user participation in online communities: A systematic literature review of empirical studies. *Computers in Human Behavior* 46: 228–238. http://dx.doi.org/10.1016/j.chb.2015.01.004

8. Daniel Schultheiss, Anja Blieske, Anja Solf, and Saskia Staeudtner. 2013. How to Encourage the Crowd? A Study about User Typologies and Motivations on Crowdsourcing Platforms. In *6th International Conference on Utility and Cloud Computing*, IEEE/ACM, 506–509. http://dx.doi.org/10.1109/UCC.2013.98

9. Burr Settles and Steven Dow. 2013. Let's Get Together: The Formation and Success of Online Creative Collaborations. In *Proceedings of the SIGCHI Conference on Human Factors in Computing Systems* (CHI '13), ACM, 2009–2018. http://doi.acm.org/10.1145/2470654.2466266

10. Michael A Stanko. 2016. Toward a Theory of Remixing in Online Innovation Communities. *Information Systems Research* 27: 773–791. http://dx.doi.org/10.1287/isre.2016.0650

11. Jason Tsay, Laura Dabbish, and James Herbsleb. 2014. Influence of social and technical factors for evaluating contribution in GitHub. In *36th International Conference on Software Engineering* (ICSE'14), 356–366. http://doi.acm.org/10.1145/2568225.2568315

Designing an ICT-based Training System for People with Dementia and their Caregivers

David Unbehaun
University of Siegen
Kohlbettstraße 15; 57072 Siegen, Germany
David.unbehaun@uni-siegen.de

Abstract

Demographic change is a challenge for every individual, families, society, science, the economy and the labor market, for social security systems and for policy as a whole. The challenge will increase with every year and the risk of suffering from dementia and therefore, being in need of care is increasing. To Care for those who are in need is a responsibility for the whole society. The use of ICT-based technologies combined with a holistic approach may support and promote a self-sustaining life-style for people with dementia and their caregivers. In this context, ICT-based solutions are a promising approach for patients suffering from early stage dementia and their caregivers. The objective of the PhD study is in the initial stage (pre-study), to analyze empirically the given practices in the specific field of dementia care in form of a requirement analysis. The next stage comes up with a design for an ICT artifact related to the findings of the first phase, and in the third stage, the author investigates the appropriation of the technical artifact over a longer period of time in different settings. The doctoral colloquium will serve as a platform to discuss and share current research activities, methodology, future publications and experiences in the field of qualitative work with respect to technology design for people with dementia.

Introduction

Increased expectation of life and constantly low birth rates are parts of a changing society, which lead to an increase of older adults, more people in need of care and therefore to a higher rate in care dependency and connected diseases such as dementia. An innovative opportunity for an autonomous and gracefully aging could be the integration of assistive technology into older adults' life. Information and Communication Technology (ICT) is key for developing age and disease appropriate assistance systems in terms of supporting health, safety, care and communication. A major challenge for developing an appropriate ICT-based solution for dementia patients is to identify relevant stakeholders in the environment of the patient and include their individual needs into the participatory design process. This field of design and research, concerning the highly sensitive setting with demented people and their social surrounding, represents a special challenge for researchers. Studies show that physical training improves mental health [1], cognitive performance (e.g. information processing, coordination) [2] and physical performance [3] and thereby daily competence of people with dementia may enhance [1], [4]. Therefore, embracing such programs may burden patients and their caregivers or relatives. Video game-based prevention and intervention programs like exergames, which are video games that involve different exercises, may ease the access for patients, improve their physical and mental capabilities and relieve related stakeholders. What seems to be a promising approach here, are ICT-based technologies with multi-level interventions that increase physical activity, cognitive resources and social participation in people with dementia and their caregivers. The integration of technology-based interventions into the

daily lives of older adults with dementia can be a key element for developing appropriate assistance systems in terms of supporting health, social participation, safety and communication, with the overall aim to enable older adults a self-determined life [5][6]. However, there are only few studies, which applied exergames as training measures in this context. In their study, Keogh et al. (2014) provided evidence that the use of exergames improved physical reliability and physiological well-being in older adults [7]. Schoene et al. (2013) illustrate that videogame-based exercises help to improve physical and cognitive aspects of the participants in the field of fall prevention. Nonetheless, these results refer to older adults not afflicted with dementia disease. What remains challenged, are long-term empirical studies, which examines the use of ICT-based interventions, like exergames, with people with dementia and their caregivers. Particularly how innovative technologies and long-term adherence to video game-based interventions and their integration into daily life as well as how it is used over a longer period of time by people with dementia and their relatives needs to be examined [8][9].

Organizational and practical Framework

The PhD study is part of the national research project "MobiAssist" in Siegen (Germany), with the goal to design, develop and evaluate an ICT-based assistant for people with dementia. Key aspects of MobiAssist address motivational aspects to increase physical activities of older adults with dementia and their caregivers in order to enhance mental and physical capabilities and relief caregivers. Hence, an ICT-based mobility-assistant is being developed for this target group and will be evaluated in different care settings like day care, home care and stationary care. The ICT-based system will consider biographical backgrounds of people with dementia like language, music, games, fun and emotions. Further, the system will address the needs of professional caregivers and family members. A multidisciplinary team consisting of partners for software development, care service providers as well as institutes of sport science and care science are involved in the development and evaluation of the system.

Research field, interests and related challenges

The PhD study-design follows a participatory design approach during the whole time from the elicitation of requirements to system evaluation in different practice settings in Siegen, Germany. Methods and tools from the field of Human Computer Interaction (HCI) (such as different levels of prototyping) and qualitative research, as well as a living lab network and evaluation will support the design of a system that addresses the needs of all stakeholders. Conducting qualitative research and involving people with dementia and their caregivers into research processes poses a variety of challenges. With regard to the overstrained situation and the burden of caring, getting access to people with dementia and their caregivers can be difficult. Not only the recruitment of participants rises some issues, also interview situations are challenging in a sense that people with dementia are only in a limited way (cognitively and emotionally) able to give appropriate feedback. Therefore, using and integrating caregivers of people with dementia, integrated as a spokesperson into the research and interview process may ease and improve the research process [10]. Having in mind, that people with dementia are limited in their verbal communication, memories, decision-making capacity and emotional instable, a successful integration of people with dementia into a research process demands

researchers to build trust and engagement to get an access to the complex situation. Furthermore, research should consider thoughts, emotions, and desires of this target group [11]. In order to learn and understand the different situations, needs and interests of people with dementia and their caregivers, both should be part of the research activity [12][13]. Researchers need more knowledge about the integration of people with dementia and their caregivers into research work, the design of technologies with regard to the respective social contexts, their daily life and their practices and attitudes. Therefore, the research focus of the PhD study will be about the whole process of exploring the different levels of needs and demands of all relevant stakeholders, the design of an appropriate system for older adults with dementia, and the technology evaluation in form of the appropriation process and usage evaluation in different contexts and settings in the field of HCI and dementia. Special research interests are the exploration of (1) long-term impacts on activities of daily living, (2) social and emotional benefits for caregivers, and (3) sustainable effects of exergames on physical and cognitive activities, quality of life and usage behavior of older adults with dementia.

Colloquium goals

After one year of working in the research setting, the colloquium will be used to present:

- current status of the Ph.D.
- early results
- first publications
- future project stages and
- publication ideas.

Furthermore, the colloquium can serve to discuss the results, project, and publication ideas, as well as the research questions and underlying methodological framework on a theoretical and practical perspective. The following question will serve as an orientation for discussion:

- How to include people with dementia in different stages of research?

- How to develop user or stakeholder-centered technology with regard to the special needs of this sensitive target group?

- How can professional and informal caregivers be relieved by integrating the system into the different settings?

- How to collect and analyze data in different settings?

- How to conduct interview with people with dementia with respect to the complex situation and challenging communication patterns?

- How to deal with the emotional challenging situations with this special target group with respect the mood-instability, anxiety, repressed memories, and emotional reactions like sensitive setting and deterioration of physical and cognitive capabilities, from researcher perspective?

- How to handle situations in which participants are not able anymore to interact with their social environment and the technology, as they did at the beginning of the project?

- How far can researchers take responsibility for the participants regarding long-term evaluations of technology with regard to the declining mental capabilities of the disease?

- What are the social consequences when the research project ends and the support of the researcher's is not possible anymore?

References

[1] P. Heyn, B. C. Abreu, and K. J. Ottenbacher, "The effects of exercise training on elderly persons with cognitive impairment and dementia: A meta-analysis," *Arch. Phys. Med. Rehabil.*, vol. 85, no. 10, pp. 1694–1704, 2004.

[2] S. Colcombe and A. F. Kramer, "Fitness effects on the cognitive function of older adults: A meta-analytic study," *Psychol. Sci.*, vol. 14, no. 2, pp. 125–130, 2003.

[3] K. Hauer, M. Schwenk, T. Zieschang, M. Essig, C. Becker, and P. Oster, "Physical training improves motor performance in people with dementia: a randomized controlled trial," *J. Am. Geriatr. Soc.*, vol. 60, no. 1, pp. 8–15, 2012.

[4] L. D. Baker *et al.*, "Aerobic exercise improves cognition for older adults with glucose intolerance, a risk factor for Alzheimer's disease," *J. Alzheimers Dis.*, vol. 22, no. 2, pp. 569–579, 2010.

[5] L. Wan, C. Müller, V. Wulf, and D. Randall, "Addressing the Subtleties in Dementia Care: Pre-study & Evaluation of a GPS Monitoring System," in *CHI 2014*, New York, NY, 2014, pp. 3987–3996.

[6] P. Robert *et al.*, "Recommendations for the use of Serious Games in people with Alzheimer's Disease, related disorders and frailty," *Front. Aging Neurosci.*, vol. 6, p. 54, 2014.

[7] J. W. L. Keogh, N. Power, L. Wooller, P. Lucas, and C. Whatman, "Physical and Psychosocial Function in Residential Aged-Care Elders: Effect of Nintendo Wii Sports Games," *J. Aging Phys. Act.*, vol. 22, no. 2, pp. 235–244, Apr. 2014.

[8] C. I. Martínez-Alcalá, P. Pliego-Pastrana, A. Rosales-Lagarde, J. Lopez-Noguerola, and E. M.

Molina-Trinidad, "Information and Communication Technologies in the Care of the Elderly: Systematic Review of Applications Aimed at Patients With Dementia and Caregivers," *JMIR Rehabil. Assist. Technol.*, vol. 3, no. 1, p. e6, May 2016.

[9] C. G. u.a. Blankevoort, "Review of Effects of Physical Activity on Strength, Balance, Mobility and ADL Performance in Elderly Subjects with Dementia," *Dement. Geriatr. Cogn. Disord.*, vol. 30, no. 5, pp. 392–402, 2010.

[10] R. G. A. Brankaert, "Design for dementia : a design-driven living lab approach to involve people with dementia and their context Eindhoven," no. Technische Universiteit Eindhoven, 2016.

[11] T. M. Kitwood, *Dementia reconsidered: the person comes first*. Buckingham [England] ; Philadelphia: Open University Press, 1997.

[12] H. Sanoff, *Participatory design theory and techniche: theory & techniques*. Raleigh, N.C.): The Author (405, West Park Drive, Raleigh, North Carolina 27605-1743, U.S.A., 1990.

[13] S. King, M. Conley, B. Latimer, and D. Ferrari, *Co-design: a process of design participation*. New York: Van Nostrand Reinhold, 1989.